THE ART OF PUBLICATION FROM THE NINTH TO THE SIXTEENTH CENTURY

INSTRVMENTA PATRISTICA ET MEDIAEVALIA

Research on the Inheritance of Early and Medieval Christianity

93

THE ART OF PUBLICATION
FROM THE NINTH
TO THE SIXTEENTH CENTURY

Edited by

Samu NISKANEN

with the assistance of

Valentina ROVERE

BREPOLS

2023

INSTRVMENTA PATRISTICA ET MEDIAEVALIA

Research on the Inheritance of Early and Medieval Christianity

Founded by Dom Eligius Dekkers († 1998)

Gert Partoens   Alexander Andrée   Rita Beyers   Emanuela Colombi
Georges Declercq   Jeroen Deploige   Paul-Augustin Deproost
Greti Dinkova-Bruun   Anthony Dupont   Jacques Elfassi   Guy Guldentops
Hugh Houghton   Mathijs Lamberigts   Johan Leemans   Paul Mattei
Marco Petoletti   Dominique Poirel   Kees Schepers   Paul Tombeur
Toon Van Hal   Marc Van Uytfanghe   Wim Verbaal

This project has received funding from the European Union's Horizon 2020
research and innovation programme under grant agreement No 716538
(MedPub, Medieval Publishing from c.1000 to 1500) and from the
Academy of Finland under grant agreement No 324246
(APEME, Authorial Publishing in Early Medieval Europe from c.400 to 1000).

D/2023/0095/39
ISBN 978-2-503-60296-7
E-ISBN 978-2-503-60297-4
DOI 10.1484/M.IPM-EB.5.131849
ISSN 1379-9878
E-ISSN 2294-8457

Printed in the EU on acid-free paper.

Table of Contents

Preface

Nearly all the chapters in this volume began as papers presented at the 2020 colloquium, *Authorial Publishing from the Carolingian Period to the Renaissance*. The two exceptions are the contributions of Jakub Kujawiński and James Willoughby, which were subsequently solicited. The colloquium, which was held remotely due to restrictions on travel during the Covid-19 pandemic, was held on 29–30 October 2020 under the auspices of the University of Helsinki and two research projects, *Medieval Publishing from c.1000 to 1500* and *Authorial Publishing in Early Medieval Europe*, funded by the European Research Council and the Academy of Finland respectively.

Dr Valentina Rovere has established the indices and assisted me in various ways in the process of editing the papers. Dr James Willoughby revised the essays for English and, in doing so, made observations on details of subject matter, for which several authors expressed their gratitude. I am very grateful to them both.

I was inducted into the territory of medieval authorial publication by Professor Richard Sharpe, who supervised my postdoctoral research at Oxford. He was planning a monograph on the subject, to be titled *Editio*. His untimely death in March 2020 robbed us of that, as it did the keynote he would have read at the colloquium, which should have joined the other essays here. Richard was a brilliant scholar, *doctissimus et acutissimus*, and this volume is dedicated to his memory.

Samu NISKANEN

Abbreviations

AA SS	*Acta Sanctorum*, ed. by J. Bolland et al., 1st edn., Antwerp and Brussels, 1643 and 3rd edn., Paris, 1863–1867
BAV	Biblioteca Apostolica Vaticana
BHL	A. Poncelet et al., *Bibliotheca Hagiographica Latina*, 2 vols, Brussels, 1898–1901); supplemented by H. Fros, *Bibliotheca Hagiographica Latina. Novum supplementum*, Brussels, 1986
BL	British Library, London
BM	Bibliothèque Municipale
BML	Biblioteca Medicea Laurenziana, Florence
BNCF	Biblioteca Nazionale Centrale di Firenze
BnF	Bibliothèque nationale de France, Paris
BNM	Biblioteca Nazionale Marciana, Venice
CCCM	*Corpus Christianorum. Continuatio Mediaevalis*
CCSL	*Corpus Christianorum. Series Latina*
CSEL	*Corpus Scriptorum Ecclesiasticorum Latinorum*
DBI	*Dizionario Biografico degli Italiani*
Ep.	*Epistola(e)*
GW	*Gesamtkatalog der Wiegendrucke*, vols 1–7, Leipzig, 1925–1940, vols 8–, Stuttgart, Berlin, and New York, 1972–
ISTC	Incunabula Short Title Catalogue
JL	*Regesta pontificum Romanorum ab condita ecclesia ad annum post Christum natum MCXCVIII*, ed. by P. Jaffé, W. Wattenbach, S. Loewenfeld, F. Kaltenbrunner, P. Ewald, 2nd edn., rev. by W. Wattenbach, 2 vols, Leipzig, 1885–1888
MGH	Monumenta Germaniae Historica
PL	*Patrologiae Cursus Completus. Series Latina*, ed. by J.-P. Migne, 217 vols, Paris, 1844–1855
SBB-PK	Staatsbibliothek zu Berlin-Preußischer Kulturbesitz
SS	*Scriptores*

Introduction

Samu Niskanen
(*Helsinki*)

To publish is to inaugurate reception. Transmission, without which the communication of literature from ancient and medieval times will fail, is predicated upon a text's first issue and primary circulation. It is a momentous consideration, that texts which may seem to us canonical depended for their survival on an initial act of release and often propagation by their authors or other interested parties. It is, therefore, a surprise to discover that scholarly efforts to appreciate that crucial step from writer to reader during the Middle Ages, when texts were circulated in manuscript and not in print, have been so few in number. The first considered comment on medieval publication was made in isolation more than a hundred years ago; sustained debate on the subject is a much more recent phenomenon.[1] Objectives,

---

[1] R. K. Root, "Publication before printing", *Publications of the Modern Language Association of America*, 28 (1913), pp. 417–31; K. Sisam, "The Publication of Alfred's *Pastoral Care*", in his *Studies of the History of Old English Literature*, Oxford, 1953, pp. 140–47, reprinted in *Anglo Saxon Manuscripts: Basic Readings*, ed. by M. Richards, New York, NY, 1994, pp. 373–81; S. J. Williams, "An Author's Role in Fourteenth-Century Book Production: Guillaume de Machaut's 'Livre ou je met toutes mes choses'", *Romania*, 90 (1969), pp. 433–54; P. J. Lucas, "John Capgrave, O. S. A. (1393–1464), Scribe and 'Publisher'", *Transactions of the Cambridge Bibliographical Society*, 5 (1969), pp. 1–35; *From Author to Audience: John Capgrave and Medieval Publication*, Dublin, 1997; A. I. Doyle, "Publication by Members of the Religious Orders", in *Book Production and Publishing in Britain 1375–1475*, ed. by J. Griffiths, D. Pearsall, Cambridge, 1989, pp. 109–23; K. Kerby-Fulton, "Langland and the Bibliographic Ego", in *Written Work. Langland, Labor, and Authorship*, ed. by S. Justice, K. Kerby-Fulton, Philadelphia, PA, 1997, pp. 67–143; R. and M. Rouse, "Publishing Watriquet's *Dits*", *Viator*, 32 (2001), pp. 127–75; P. Meyvaert, "Medieval Notions of Publication: The 'Unpublished'

The Art of Publication from the Ninth to the Sixteenth Century, ed. by Samu Niskanen with the assistance of Valentina Rovere, IPM, 93 (Turnhout, 2023), pp. 11–21.
© BREPOLS ॐ PUBLISHERS   DOI 10.1484/M.IPM-EB.5.133079

approaches, and other paradigms are still taking shape, a process towards which the chapters in this volume and its coming
companion seek to contribute.

The fact that medievalists do not generally recognize publication as a primary focus of research is doubtless due to an unfa-
miliarity with the subject. Conscious rejection of the concept of
manuscript publication has been rare.[2] Instead, one draws the
conclusion that because the idea of publication is so thoroughly
associated with the rapid multiplication of copies by the printing
press, it is perceived as foreign to the realities of the circulation
of books in manuscript. As such, publication would be one more of

Opus Caroli regis contra synodum and the Council of Frankfort (794)", *Journal of Medieval Latin*, 12 (2002), pp. 78–89; G. Ouy, "Le Célestin Jean Gerson: copiste et éditeur de son frère", in *La collaboration dans la production
de l'écrit médiéval. Actes du XIIIe colloque du Comité international de paléographie latine (Weingarten, 22–25 septembre 2000)*, ed. by. H. Spilling, Paris,
2003, pp. 281–313; O. Delsaux, "La publication d'auteur en moyen français:
enjeux d'une définition à partir du cas de Christine de Pizan. Une recherche
en chantier", *Le moyen français*, 63 (2008), pp. 9–44; R. Sharpe, "Anselm as
Author: Publishing in the Late Eleventh Century", *Journal of Medieval Latin*,
19 (2009), pp. 1–87; D. Hobbins, *Authorship and Publicity Before Print: Jean
Gerson and the Transformation of Late Medieval Learning*, Philadelphia, PA,
2009; L. Tether, "Revisiting the Manuscripts of Perceval and the Continua-
tions: Publishing Practices and Authorial Transition", *Journal of the International Arthurian Society*, 2 (2015), pp. 20–45; *Publishing the Grail in Medieval
and Renaissance France*, Woodbridge, 2017; J. Tahkokallio, *The Anglo-Norman Historical Canon: Publishing and Manuscript Culture*, Cambridge, 2019;
S. Niskanen, "Anselm's Predicament: The *Proslogion* and Anti-intellectual
Rhetoric in the Aftermath of the Berengarian Controversy", *Journal of the
History of Ideas*, 82 (2021), pp. 547–68; "The Emergence of a Literary Culture: Authorial Publication in Denmark in the Long Twelfth Century", in
The Meaning of Media: Texts and Materiality in Medieval Scandinavia, ed. by
A. C. Horn, K. G. Johansson, Berlin, 2021, pp. 71–91; *Publication and the
Papacy in Late Antiquity and the Middle Ages*, Cambridge, 2021; "From author
to authority: Anselm's public reputation and the council of Bari (1098)", *Jour-
nal of Medieval History*, 49 (2023), 1–22.

    [2] S. G. Nichols, "Introduction: Philology in a Manuscript Culture", *Spe-
culum*, 65 (1990), 1–10, at 6; E. L. Eisenstein, *The Printing Press as an Agent
of Change: Communications and Cultural Transformations in Early Modern
Europe*, 2 vols, Cambridge, 1979, vol. 1, p. 11. See the important corrective
to Eisenstein's work by Paul Needham's review of it in *Fine Print*, 6 (1980),
pp. 23–25 and 32–35. Her work is contested and has sparked a wide debate;
see e.g. F. A. Janssen, "The Battle of Perspectives in Book History, 1960–
2000", *La Bibliofilia*, 115 (2013), pp. 383–90.

the phenomena that are taken to distinguish the "modern" from the "medieval". Students of manuscript cultures have grounds for disagreement at least on two counts. First, the terminology related to publication in print is too flawed a construct when applied to manuscripts to command any compelling force. The central word here is "manuscript". The *Oxford Dictionary of English* defines it in the context of publishing as follows: "an author's handwritten or typed text that has not yet been published". The Italian *manoscritto* and the French *manuscrit* bear the same denotation, and so does the non-Latinate Finnish word *käsikirjoitus* for that matter. A typewritten manuscript is an oxymoron. More importantly, in the Middle Ages publication was conceived as an emphatic act belonging to the authorial process. That point has been made in previous scholarship and evidence is plentiful.[3] The dedicatory address by Bernard of Cluny to Abbot Peter the Venerable († 1156), taken from the preface to his *De contemptu mundi*, is a representative example. A work, of which a fine copy has been produced, is sent to a patron for assessment. Once endorsed, it will be released to readerships. The latter process constitutes publication.

> Vestrae igitur correctioni, doctissime pater et domine, committendum opusculum *de contemptu mundi* excogitavi. Scripsi, distinxi, nondum omnino absolutum edidi.[4]

Authorial efforts to secure readerships did not necessarily end with the first issue of a new writing. Probably more often than not, publication in manuscript was a process which consisted of various "publishing moments", a term coined by Daniel Hobbins.[5] In this construct, the first issue was one of several climaxes,

---

[3]   See HOBBINS, *Authorship and Publicity*, p. 153, citing instances from Jean Gerson's work with expressions such as *prodire in publicum* and *publicatio*. For a survey of Latin terms used for publication, see P. BOURGAIN, "La naissance officielle de l'œuvre: l'expression métaphorique de la mise au jour", in *Vocabulaire du livre et de l'écriture au Moyen Âge*, ed. by O. WEIJERS, Turnhout, 1989, pp. 195–205.

[4]   Bernard of Cluny, *De contemptu mundi*, i. Prologus, ed. by R. E. PEPIN, East Lansing, MI, 1991, p. 4. "I purposed this work to be submitted to your correction, most erudite father and lord. I have written and punctuated it, but I have in no way published it as yet."

[5]   HOBBINS, *Authorship and Publicity Before Print*, p. 154.

and to exclude posterior issues and other related acts would be
a mistake: many of the practices by which texts made their way
from writer to reader would then go unobserved. It is this wider
conceptualization of publishing that is adopted practically unanimously in modern scholarship, including in the present volume.[6]
Accordingly, Marco Petoletti demonstrates how Petrarch was concerned with the expression of his *De vita solitaria* years after his
first issue of it (chapter 8). Considering Boccaccio's testament as
an authorial instrument for posthumous publication, Valentina
Rovere goes further (chapter 9): to assess the impact of the testament, she identifies copies made from Boccaccio's originals in
the hands of his executors. Some works were written with a view
that they would be continued later, by the original author and/or
other parties. The *vita* and *miracula* of St Symeon of Trier, studied
by Tuomas Heikkilä, are a case in point (chapter 4). A virtuous
saint, Symeon healed believers and effected other miracles down
the generations, reports of which were incorporated in the existing accounts of his saintly deeds. As the authorial intention at the
onset was that the process of composition would be resumed after
the work's first release, publication in this case must be seen as a
long-term, intermittent, and iterative procedure.

   Equipped with these conceptual parameters, we may now look
at approaches to the subject in brief. Some of these are applied in
this book, while others form suggestions for subsequent research.
The discussion is divided into two sections, corresponding to the
two main types of evidence on which the study of publication in
manuscript builds.

Prefatory Texts

Medieval works regularly open with some sort of preamble, making remarks pertinent to the release and intended reception of the
work being introduced. These are of consequence to the study of
publishing. A category of prefatory text that practically always
benefits us in one way or another is the dedicatory letter. A literary device with a long history, dedicatory *exordia* carry much

---

[6] For an analytical discussion of conceptualizing publishing in manuscript, see TAHKOKALLIO, *Anglo-Norman Historical Canon*, pp. 3–9.

rhetorical gesturing.[7] But cliché is not devoid of practical value.[8] Provided that the dedicatee was a living person rather than a literary construct or a deceased authority, some real connexion is normally apparent. Actual manifestations of the dedicatory gesture were various. One was the common practice that dedicatees were gifted a presentation copy, physical proof of actual communication. Even the common request that the dedicatee amend the work, as in the passage given above from Bernard of Cluny's *De contemptu mundi*, were sometimes genuine requests and not mere politesse. A well-known case is that of St Anselm's *Monologion*, written in the late 1070s. Anselm sent the work to Archbishop Lanfranc, his former teacher, requesting that he revise it where needed and decide whether it should be published or perish. Disapproving of Anselm's exclusively rationalistic method of inquiry, Lanfranc's response was critical.[9] Such reactions must have been exceptional; the norm was endorsement, silent or articulated. It has recently been demonstrated that active commendation by an influential dedicatee could be a very effective operation for obtaining audiences for a new work.[10] Such prospects were certainly a factor for any number of medieval authors reflecting on the choice of dedicatee for their works. Construing the dedication of *Historia Normannorum* of Dudo of St-Quentin († 1027 or earlier) as an act of publication, Lauri Leinonen uses this axiom as a hermeneutical key (chapter 3).

The fundamental lesson here is that publishing was a social act, which involved third parties in addition to those two core agents, an author and his or her intended audience. When prefatory texts, or other sources, identify such third parties by their name, office, or status, then the networks that might have been deployed in publication come into view. The Venerable Bede († 735) might be held as an example. A number of individuals were enga-

---

[7]   E. R. Curtius, *European Literature and the Latin Middle Ages*, English translation W. R. Trask, Bollingen Series, 36, Princeton, NJ, 1953, reprint 1983, pp. 8–87.

[8]   K. L. Holzknecht, *Literary Patronage in the Middle Ages*, Philadelphia, PA, 1923, pp. 124–55.

[9]   Anselm, *Epistolae*, i. 63, 65, and 68, ed. by S. Niskanen, Oxford, 2019, pp. 186–87, 192–93, and 198–201 respectively.

[10]   Niskanen, *Publication and the Papacy*, esp. chapter 3.

ged in the publication of his works. They included Bishop Acca of Hexham (dedicatee and commissioner),[11] an anonymous nun (commissioner),[12] Abbot Hwætberht of Monkwearmouth–Jarrow (commissioner and critic),[13] Cuthbert the monk (commissioner),[14] King Ceolwulf of Northumbria (dedicatee),[15] Abbot Albinus of Canterbury (commisioner),[16] Nothhelm, archpriest of London, subsequently archbishop of Canterbury (commissioner),[17] and many others. These individuals were members of Bede's "publishing circle", a modern conceptualization to describe the social conduits by which writers sought and found readerships in the Middle Ages.[18] An author who could rely on a widespread and influential publishing circle could reach a variety of readerships within months of publication. Jakub Kujawiński introduces an impressive array of patrons and other connexions, some representing the very highest echelons of medieval society, who contributed to Nicholas Trevet's († after 1334) emergence as one of the most successful literary critics of his generation (chapter 6). Third-party input

---

[11]   Bede, Commentary on Genesis, ed. by C. W. JONES, CCSL, 118A, Turnhout, 1967; Commentary on 1 Samuel, ed. by D. HURST, CCSL, 119, Turnhout, 1962, pp. 5–272; Commentary on Ezra and Nehemiah, ibid., pp. 237–392; Commentary on Mark, ed. by D. HURST, CCSL, 120, Turnhout, 1960, pp. 427–648; Commentary on Luke, ibid, pp. 1–425; Commentary on Acts of the Apostles, ed. by M. L. W. LAISTNER, CCSL, 121, Turnhout, 1983, pp. 1–99 and 103–63; De eo quod ait Isaias, "Et claudentur", PL, 94, cols 702–10; De templo Salomonis, ed. by D. HURST, CCSL, 119A, Turnhout, 1969, pp. 143–234; Versus de die iudicii, ed. by J. FRAIPONT, CCSL, 122, Turnhout, 1955, pp. 439–44; and De mansionibus filiorum Israel, PL, 94, cols 699–702.

[12]   Bede, Commentary on the Prayer of Habakkuk, ed. by J. E. HUDSON, CCSL, 119B, Turnhout, 1983, pp. 381–409.

[13]   Bede, Commentary on Revelation, ed. by R. GRYSON, CCSL, 121A, Turnhout, 2001; and De temporum ratione, ed. by C. W. JONES, CCSL, 123B, Turnhout, 1975, pp. 268–544.

[14]   Bede, De arte metrica ed. by C. B. KENDALL, CCSL, 123A, Turnhout, 1975, pp. 81–141.

[15]   Bede, Historia ecclesiastica gentis Anglorum, ed. by B. COLGRAVE, R. A. B. MYNORS, Oxford, 1969.

[16]   Bede, Epistola ad Albinum, ed. by C. PLUMMER, in Venerabilis Baedae opera historica, 2 vols, Oxford, 1896, vol. 1, pp. 405–23.

[17]   Bede, In libros Regum quaestiones XXX, ed. by D. HURST, CCSL, 119, Turnhout, 1962, pp. 293–322.

[18]   TAHKOKALLIO, Anglo-Norman Historical Canon, pp. 2, 8–9.

was sometimes absolutely crucial; several texts were never released for public circulation by their authors but by associates. As
authors (re-)emerged from among the ranks of the laity towards
the end of our period, blood relations became increasingly involved in these affairs. Luca Azzetta, Outi Merisalo, and Giovanna
Murano expound three cases here, all from renaissance Italy (chapters 7, 10, and 11): one of these authors is Dante, and as Azzetta
demonstrates, our failure to appreciate how his works were first
made available risks masking his genuine, authorial voice.

The social status of third parties to publication ranged from
mediocre to grand, of which Bede's unidentifiable nun and Pope
John XXII, a patron of Nicholas Trevet's, are respective manifestations. Over the period from late Antiquity to the close of the
Middle Ages, the composition and operation of publishing networks
changed utterly. Members of the Roman civic administration were
replaced by ecclesiastics; monks gave way to secular priests; university teachers were outshone by humanistic lay scholars; scribes
were overtaken by printers. None of those parties had an absolutely
identical effect on the practice of publishing. Publishing, then, reacted
to profound large-scale trends in the wider world. The corollary
is that through publishing we can observe long-term societal
and cultural continuity and change in the Middle Ages. Jaakko
Tahkokallio's proposition (chapter 12) is apposite: that historians,
particularly scholars of intellectual, cultural, and political history,
should study publication in connexion to major phenomena, such
as the Crusades and the emergence of the universities.

In the history of manuscript publication, long-term transitions
are much in evidence. For instance, Nicholas Trevet's feat in
securing socially varied contemporary readerships from England
to Italy contrasts with the narrow prospects available, say, to
a seventh-century writer, but resonates with those available to
patristic authors. The latter could still rely on Roman channels of
communication upon publishing. Writing in north Africa, Augustine († 430) obtained audiences for his writings with ease around
the Mediterranean.[19] His contemporary readers included literary luminaries such as Jerome in Palestine, Paulinus of Nola in

---

[19] See, for example, Augustine, *Epistulae*, ccxxxi. 7, ed. by A. GOLD-
BACHER, *CSEL*, 57, Vienna, 1911, p. 510.

Italy, and Paulus Orosius in Spain, as well as a multitude of less renowned individuals. He dedicated his writings to high-ranking persons from a variety of backgrounds, including civil servants such as Marcellinus.[20] A tribune and notary with connections to the imperial court, Marcellinus represented the upper echelons of the Roman civil administration. Relying on transregional Roman apparatuses for publishing, Augustine successfully sought socially heterogeneous readerships far and wide.[21] The gradual demise of the imperial order diminished such horizons considerably. The last Latin author to benefit from conduits of publishing comparable with Augustine's was presumably Gregory the Great († 604).

The first investigation in the present volume relates to an age of revitalization, the Carolingian period. As regards publishing in Frankish kingdoms, contrast with the Merovingian past seems especially clear in the context of association between royal courts and authorial composition. Works were dedicated and sent to Carolingian kings and queens; authors were also commissioned by royalty. The cultural and political project of the Carolingian reforms is undoubtedly the key factor here.[22] While prospects for gaining wider readerships increased (although they were narrow in comparison to those of late antiquity), the need to control what should be published seems to have intensified at the same time. Jesse Keskiaho demonstrates how mid-ninth-century authors discussing the nature of the soul sought to contain the circulation of their commentaries (chapter 2).

These observations suggest that information on third-party participation in publication might have the potential to alleviate one of the biggest problems in the historical study of the Middle Ages: the dearth of statistical evidence of a uniform kind from all regions, running throughout the period. Because their sources

[20] Augustine, *De peccatorum meritis et remissione et baptismo parvulorum*, i.1, ed. by C. F. URBA, J. ZYCHA, *CSEL*, 60, Vienna, 1913, pp. 3–151, at 3; *De spiritu et littera*, i.1, *ibid.*, pp. 155–229, at 155; *De civitate Dei*, i. Praef. and ii.1, ed. by B. DOMBART, A. KALB, *CCSL*, 47–48, Turnhout, 1955, pp. 1 and 35.

[21] M. CALTABIANO, "*Libri iam in multorum manus exierunt*. Agostinio testimone della diffusione delle sue opere", in *Tra IV e V secolo, Studi sulla cultura latina tardoantica*, ed. by I. GUALANDRI, Milan, 2002, pp. 141–57.

[22] See, for example, G. BROWN, "Introduction: The Carolingian Renaissance", in *Carolingian Culture: Emulation and Innovation*, ed. by R. McKITTERICK, Cambridge, 1994, pp. 1–51.

are limited and unbalanced, medievalists are bound to arrive at scholarly judgements on the grounds of isolated testimonies rather than statistical observation. When working on long-term trends or wide geographical areas, the evidential basis often poses insurmountable obstacles. However, data on publishing networks do constitute a genus of evidence on societal interaction between identifiable agents across the whole medieval period and beyond. What is more, because prefatory statements about third parties tend to be short and relatively uniform, they can be processed in large quantities. *A Database for Medieval Publishing Networks*, an open-access repository accessible online at dmpn.helsinki.fi, brings together this information from Britain, Ireland, Scandinavia and the Baltic at an encompassing scale. Thousands of individuals, Latin authors and their associates who partook in publication, are introduced by the region and period of their activity, and their social status so far as is possible. One can, for instance, discover how monastic publishing networks were transformed in a given region in the course of a defined period. The results can be compared, say, with those from a survey focused on non-regular clergy. Another line of inquiry would be to measure how many works were dedicated to, or commissioned by, holders of given offices such as abbots, bishops, and kings. In short, the database will allow a gauging of the interaction between various regions, institutions, offices, orders, and social classes over the *longue durée*.

Manuscripts

Material testimonies to medieval publishing, manuscripts are an invaluable source of information for us. That much is self-evident, needing only a brief introduction here. While the whole tradition of a literary work hinges on publication and therefore must emit some sort of signals of it, autographs, presentation or dedication copies, and primary copies are of especial significance. Autographs and presentation copies, two categories that often overlap, represent authorial efforts to seek readers. Naturally, the important proviso for autographs is that the work in question did not remain on the author's desk but was published.

Primary copies testify to the impact of publication. While this class of manuscript by definition embraces copies contemporaneous with a given author, or nearly so, the rule *recentiores non deterio-*

res applies here. Brussels, Bibliothèque des Bollandistes, 445, one of the latest witnesses of St Symeon's *vita* and *mircula* should be classified as a primary copy at least in textual terms (chapter 4). According to a colophon found in it, the text was copied directly from the original. By virtue of their proximity to the starting point of a manuscript tradition, primary copies may preserve some distinct features of transmission as established and shaped by the author. These would have been liable to fade out in later circulation.[23] As such, primary copies provide invaluable evidence for us and for text-critical investigations in general. The latter are obligatory if one is to distinguish the authorial voice, heard clearly at publication but less so at subsequent stages of transmission. Needless to say, various methods of textual criticism, traditional and computational, find application in this volume. Kujawiński's examinations of the apparatuses of illustrations in Trevet's commentaries and of their text's *mise-en-page* represent a related but distinct approach (chapter 6); the focus is on variance or a lack of it from one primary copy to other. Finally, primary copies can take us unexpectedly close to communication between author and audience. Vat. lat. 3357, discussed by Petoletti, offers first-hand insights into how an anonymous reader conversed with Petrarch (chapter 8). The volume is a reminder of the reciprocality inherent in a publication culture which operated through several successive releases, or "publishing moments".

It is often difficult, or impossible, to recognize autographs and presentation copies with confidence. This pertains also to primary copies to a somewhat lesser degree, but even in their case the date and place of origin cannot necessarily be determined from palaeographical evidence with the requisite precision for the task. Meticulous analyses do bear fruit, however, as in James Willoughby's examination of the several layers of composition in BL, Cotton Vespasian D. x (chapter 5). Securely identified as a partial autograph, the volume betrays how an ageing author, Ralph of Coggeshall, felt the need to censor his own text. Colophons can, of course, provide indicators that resolve the question of a manuscript's status, as is demonstrated in several chapters below. But

---

[23]   A well-known case is the initial transmission of several of St Anselm's treatises as booklets; SHARPE, "Anselm as Author", *passim*.

such colophons are relatively rare, and holistic approaches are needed.

The chronological termini of this volume embrace the first hundred years of book printing in Europe. A new era of written communication began, but scribal publication did not end abruptly.[24] Both modes could be applied in tandem. Jacopo di Poggio Bracciolini († 1478), who rendered his father's *Historiae Florentini populi* into the vernacular, supervised the production of a *de luxe* manuscript copy of it and was in contact with a party who had the work published in print (chapter 10). The speed with which the press could multiply copies, with newly hungry markets springing up across wide distribution networks, meant that the choice of print for publication was natural and inevitable. Murano's study of Fiammetta Frescobaldi († 1586) reflects how, a century later, manuscripts were the inferior medium, albeit one that could provide an outlet to publication for disempowered communities, in this case a convent of nuns (chapter 11). Frescobaldi's target audience consisted of her *sorores*, and when she released her works, this must have been an entirely domestic operation. But her autograph manuscripts emulate the layout of printed books: publication was now firmly associated with print.

---

[24] See e.g. H. Love, *Scribal Publication in Seventeenth-Century England*, Oxford, 1993.

Publications and Confidential Exchanges

Carolingian Treatises on the Soul[*]

Jesse Keskiaho
(Helsinki)

What did publishing theological texts mean in the Carolingian period? In this chapter, I probe this question by focusing on treatises on the nature of the soul and their authors. The six ninth-century texts in question were written for different audiences and purposes, as educational treatises and as controversial pamphlets. As texts written by elite Carolingian scholars, the fact of their publication is easily taken as self-evident, and the privileged status of the authors probably means that publishing was relatively easy for them. Certainly the nature of the available sources makes the publication of these texts hard to perceive. Precisely for this reason, it is crucial to try to discern these processes. I will discuss all the treatises in rough chronological order, paying special attention to three mid-ninth-century treatises discussing related issues and apparently taking part in the same debates. While the subject-matter of these texts did not necessarily limit the size of their prospective audiences, many of them were nevertheless written for limited readerships. It is particularly in this regard that the question about whether they were published, and in what sense, serves to delineate the differences between publication and more confidential communication, and is crucial in trying to discern the

[*] I wish to thank my colleagues in the projects *Medieval Publishing* and *Authorial Publishing in the Early Middle Ages* for their comments on earlier versions of this article, especially Jaakko Tahkokallio, as well as Warren Pezé for his perceptive comments and suggestions. All remaining errors are my own responsibility.

The Art of Publication from the Ninth to the Sixteenth Century, ed. by Samu Niskanen with the assistance of Valentina Rovere, IPM, 93 (Turnhout, 2023), pp. 23–45.
© BREPOLS ❧ PUBLISHERS   DOI 10.1484/M.IPM-EB.5.133080

contours of these audiences. Since written communication within a small circle of acquaintances hardly required publishing,[1] it is interesting to see what kind of theological discourse was likely to be published, when, and in what way. Before embarking on this investigation, I will survey the general nature of theological authorship and the publics for theological texts in the Carolingian period.

Publics and Publishing

Writing on the reign of Louis the Pious († 840), Mayke de Jong observed that a "not uncommon" Carolingian model of publishing consisted of circulating a text first within one's peer network, then in having it read by an important member of the royal court, and dedicating it finally to the king.[2] This observation highlights the role of the royal court as an important public, and how it was accessed through patrons and gatekeepers. It serves as a useful starting point to a discussion of publishing and publics in the Carolingian period in general, and about theological publishing in particular.

In order to communicate in writing, it does not appear to have been strictly necessary to publish, and theological publishing in particular was nothing to be rushed into. Texts could evidently be circulated confidentially, within a restricted circle. Sita Steckel remarked that a monastic teacher might write freely for the use of his students, and that monks, although they were not supposed to, corresponded with parties outside of their communities.[3] Theological authorship in particular appears to have been controlled: religious knowledge aspired to treat of divine truth, but was at risk of merely representing human falsity or outright heresy. It was thus mostly the domain of spiritual professionals, monks,

---

[1]   S. STECKEL, *Kulturen des Lehrens im Früh- und Hochmittelalter. Autorität, Wissenskonzepte und Netzwerke von Gelehrten*, Köln–Weimar–Wien, 2011, pp. 563–64.

[2]   M. DE JONG, *The Penitential State. Authority and Atonement in the Age of Louis the Pious, 814–40*, Cambridge, 2009, p. 69 and n. 43; and "The empire as *ecclesia*. Hrabanus Maurus and biblical *historia* for rulers", in *The Uses of the Past in the Early Middle Ages*, ed. by Y. HEN, M. INNES, Cambridge, 2000, pp. 191–226, at 204.

[3]   STECKEL, *Kulturen des Lehrens*, pp. 563–64.

priests and bishops, whose ability to publish and publicize their texts was defined by their position in the ecclesiastical hierarchy. Authorship or publication was perhaps not to be taken lightly, but publishing on the *artes* or in historiography was subject to less control, if not by the authors then at least by their superiors, since such texts did not aim directly to discuss religious truths.[4]

Publishing became necessary when one wished to reach beyond one's confidential circle. The means of book production, what Jaakko Tahkokallio has called the "publishing framework", were in the Carolingian period controlled by abbots and bishops.[5] If an author did not, through his office, command access to book production, then patrons and friends — Tahkokallio's "publication circle" — could facilitate access. To gain the approval and support of the authorities, an author would often observe appropriate conventions and exercise self-censorship.[6] These conventions, exhibited in letters of dedication and other paratexts, were displays of humility and obedience, such as confessing one's own unworthiness for the task and requesting God's mercy, referring to a commission, and requesting that the recipient would judge the text and correct anything that required correcting.[7] However, not all authors observed such conventions,[8] suggesting that publication was ultimately less a matter of rhetoric and more to do with connections, networks, and status.

---

[4] *Ibid.*, pp. 536–37; for the Carolingian morality of writing and reluctance to publish, see also I. van RENSWOUDE, "'The Word once sent forth can never come back': Trust in writing and the dangers of publication", in *Strategies of Writing. Studies on Text and Trust in the Middle Ages*, ed. by P. SCHULTE, M. MOSTERT, I. VAN RENSWOUDE, Turnhout, 2008, pp. 393–413, esp. 405–06 and 411–12.

[5] J. TAHKOKALLIO, *The Anglo-Norman Historical Canon. Publishing and Manuscript Culture*, Cambridge, 2019, pp. 2, 8–9; STECKEL, *Kulturen des Lehrens*, pp. 566–67. On Carolingian book production, see e.g. D. GANZ, "Book production in the Carolingian empire and the spread of Caroline minuscule", in *The New Cambridge Medieval History, Volume II: c. 700 to c. 900*, ed. by R. McKITTERICK, Cambridge, 1995, pp. 786–808.

[6] STECKEL, *Kulturen des Lehrens*, pp. 569–71.

[7] *Ibid.*, pp. 544–48, 551–53, 573–78; I. VAN RENSWOUDE, *The Rhetoric of Free Speech in Late Antiquity and the Early Middle Ages*, Cambridge, 2019, pp. 209–10.

[8] See STECKEL, *Kulturen des Lehrens*, pp. 557, 616–17, for examples of what she regards as exceptions to the rule.

The Carolingian realms are perhaps best conceived of as a network of partly nested publics. The Church in the abstract sense was the main public, but it was instantiated only in part in a council or a synod, in the king's consensus with his lay magnates and bishops. Also, in a very concrete sense, councils were places of publication: they gathered the literate elite and afforded opportunities for turning up texts one might not otherwise have had ready access to, whether old and rare texts or new texts heard of only by report.[9] The Court, defined as the network of elites connected to and regularly attending the king at his court, was in practice often the most important public.[10] Bringing a text to the attention of the court and the king could be a way of ensuring its wide distribution.[11] Finally, by the time of the reigns of Louis the Pious and his sons, Carolingian educational reforms had borne fruit in an increased number of literate clerics, who read and formed opinions on their readings, even if they were not supposed to.[12] The way in which Florus of Lyon († c. 860) successfully waged a publicity campaign against his unwanted bishop Amalarius, and the controversy over predestination in which Archbishop Hincmar of Reims († 882) had to address the *simplices* of his diocese in a vain attempt to control the discourse, shows that such clerics could make even individual cathedral cities important local publics.[13]

---

[9]   K. Zechiel-Eckes, *Florus von Lyon als Kirchenpolitiker und Publizist*, Stuttgart, 1999, p. 222 and n. 31; Steckel, *Kulturen des Lehrens*, pp. 527–28; Hincmar of Rheims seems to have acquired a copy of *De tribus epistolis* by Florus of Lyon at the Council of Savonnières in 859: W. Pezé, *Le virus de l'erreur. La controverse carolingienne sur la double predestination. Essai d'histoire sociale*, Turnhout, 2017, p. 90 and nn. 284–85.

[10]   See generally on the court of Louis the Pious, and as a public especially for historiography, De Jong, *Pentitential State*, pp. 60–62.

[11]   For Charlemagne's court as a centre for dissemination: Alcuin, *Ep.* 149, ed. by E. Dümmler, Berlin, 1895 (MGH, *Epistolae*, 4), pp. 243–44; Nelson, *King and Emperor*, 341.

[12]   See M. De Jong, "From *scolastici* to *scioli*. Alcuin and the formation of an intellectual élite", in *Alcuin of York. Scholar at the Carolingian Court*, ed. by L. A. J. R. Houwen, A. A. MacDonald, Groningen, 1998, pp. 45–57.

[13]   Zechiel-Eckes, *Florus*, p. 223; Pezé, *Le virus*, pp. 325–31, 489–90; W. Pezé, "Doctrinal debate and social control in the Carolingian age: the predestination controversy (840–60s)", *Early Medieval Europe*, 25 (2017), pp. 85–101.

Treatises on the soul were in the ninth century written by learned monks, abbots, and bishops, centrally networked members of Carolingian elites. Discerning how they published is in part hampered by the apparent ease with which it happened, and in part by the patchy nature of the evidence. In some cases we have only the text, perhaps transmitted only in a late copy. The texts can of course be used to establish what their author wished to do. Texts demonstrating conventional professions of humility, referencing commissions and requesting correction, suggest that their authors intended to publish them, just as the way they address readers indicates the audiences they wished to reach. Whether such intentions, readable from the extant texts, could or even probably did lead to the intended ends, needs to be assessed in the case of each individual text.[14] Manuscript copies are a crucial part of this assessment, since the textual traditions of these works, and their presentation in individual copies, may provide insights into not only the circulation of these works, but also into how the authors intended to circulate them. Even later copies can provide indications of successful publication, if they can be shown to derive from a scriptorium connected with the dedicatee or a patron. Looking at how these texts, written for different audiences and in different situations, were published can show the kinds of audiences they reached, the discussions they were parts of, and the differences between confidential and published written discourse.

The Publication Success of Alcuin's *De ratione animae*

The earliest of the ninth-century treatises on the soul, and the one whose successful publication is the most apparent, is *De ratione animae* by Alcuin († 804). He was one of the more influential of the scholars Charlemagne († 814) recruited to design and implement his reform efforts. His centrality to these efforts is reflected in the popularity of his works; as David Ganz has noted, Alcuin was "the Carolingian best-seller".[15] The publication of his

---

[14]   ZECHIEL-ECKES, *Florus*, pp. 221–22.

[15]   D. GANZ, "[Review of] *Alcuini Eboracensis De fide Sanctae Trinitate et de incarnatione Christi. Quaestiones de Trinitate*", *Early Medieval Europe*, 22 (2014), pp. 233–34, at 233.

De ratione animae is a good example of how a leading Carolingian scholar, supported by imperial elite networks, published. Written between 801 and his death in 804, it was dedicated to Charlemagne's cousin Gundrada, half-sister of Adalhard of Corbie († 827) and Wala († 836) who eventually succeeded his half-brother as abbot of Corbie. Alcuin, who had retired from the court to the abbacy of St Martins in Tours, indicates in the preface that Gundrada had requested the treatise following discussions on the soul at court. The treatise is in epistolary form and addresses only Gundrada throughout, here called Eulalia by Alcuin.[16] Yet it was clearly intended for the court public: both the acknowledgement of Gundrada's commission and Alcuin's expression of doubt about his abilities are customary ways of authorizing public writing,[17] and he refers to *scholastici* at court who will have known that the work was commissioned.[18]

However, the text as we have it does not seem to descend directly from the copy Alcuin sent to Gundrada in Aachen, but from a subsequent compilation. Twenty-one out of the twenty-seven ninth-century copies of the work, and all of the earliest copies, are transmitted in a compilation with Alcuin's *De fide S. Trinitatis* and *Quaestiones de Trinitate*.[19] All the extant copies of *De fide* descend from this collection.[20] In his edition of *De ratione animae*, James Curry was able to establish the relationships of only a han-

---

[16]   For Eulalia's identity as Gundrada see Alcuin, *Ep.* 241, ed. by E. Dümmler, Berlin, 1895 (MGH, *Epistolae*, 4), p. 386. For the treatise as a letter: Alcuin, *De ratione animae*, ix; ed. by J. J. M. Curry, "Alcuin, *De ratione animae*: A text with introduction, critical apparatus, and translation", unpublished PhD diss., Cornell University, 1966, p. 62, ll. 19–21: "De cuius ratione et natura sicut flagitasti haec pauca perstrinximus prout epistolaris angustia concessit". See also I. Tolomio, *L'anima dell'uomo. Trattati sull'anima dal V al IX secolo*, Milan, 1979, pp. 62–71, with an Italian translation of the text at pp. 205–28.

[17]   Curry, "Alcuin", pp. 1–2; Steckel, *Kulturen des Lehrens*, pp. 544–48, 551–53, 573–78.

[18]   *Scholastici*: Alcuin, *De ratione*, ix; ed. by Curry, "Alcuin", p. 62, l. 21.

[19]   Curry, "Alcuin", p. 3.

[20]   See editors' introduction in *Alcuini Eboracensis De fide sanctae Trinitatis et de incarnatione Christi, Quaestiones de sancta Trinitate*, ed. by E. Knibbs, E. A. Matter, Turnhout, 2012 (*CCCM*, 249), pp. xlvii–xlix.

dful of witnesses.[21] However, his findings match the relationships Eric Knibbs and Ann Matter have established for corresponding copies of *De fide*, strongly suggesting that their conclusions apply to relationships between the witnesses of *De ratione* as well.[22] The compilation of these three texts may have been a creation of the Tours scriptorium, which was at this time already turning out high-quality Bibles.[23] But while *De ratione* was addressed to the court, *De fide* was presented *c.* 802 to Charlemagne himself.[24] Knibbs and Matter argue that Alcuin added *De ratione* to the two Trinitarian works in order to create a catechetical manual after an Augustinian model, and that the resulting collection was officially promoted by the court.[25]

The compilation, and *De ratione animae* with it, appears to have been centrally distributed through Carolingian elite networks, although there is no direct evidence of its promotion by the court. The editors of *De fide* identify six hyparchetypes for the surviving witnesses, five of which seem to have been virtually identical and the sixth deemed "a centrally promoted revision".[26] The compilation spread quickly and widely, and it is not surprising to find many copies from central Carolingian libraries, many with connections to Alcuin or Gundrada. There are twenty-seven extant manuscripts already from before the tenth century, eleven of them from the first quarter of the ninth.[27] The earliest dated copy may

---

[21] CURRY, "Alcuin", pp. 32–35.

[22] E.g. *ibid.*, p. 33: witnesses *Am* and the common exemplar of *Ag* and *At* descend from the same exemplar. KNIBBS, MATTER, *Alcuini Eboracensis De fide*, pp. xxix, lxiv–lxvi, determine that their M_2 (in the same manuscript as Curry's *Am*) belongs in family ζ_4, and that their Wo_2 (corresponding to *Ag*) and T_1 share (via intermediaries) exemplar ζ_{4a}. Similarly, Curry's (p. 34) *Rt* and *Rv* share an exemplar, and Knibbs & Matter's (p. lxi) corresponding T_2 and V both descend from ζ_1.

[23] So already D. A. BULLOUGH, "Alcuin's cultural influence. The evidence of manuscripts", in *Alcuin of York*, ed. by HOUWEN, MACDONALD, pp. 1–26, at 12–13.

[24] KNIBBS, MATTER, *Alcuini Eboracensis De fide*, pp. xlvi–xlviii.

[25] *Ibid.*, pp. xii–xiii. See also GANZ, "[Review]", p. 233.

[26] KNIBBS, MATTER, *Alcuini Eboracensis De fide*, p. xlix.

[27] For the manuscripts, see P. E. SZARMACH, "A preface, mainly textual, to Alcuin's *De ratione animae*", in *The Man of Many Devices, Who Wandered Full Many Ways. Festschrift in Honor of János M. Bak*, ed. by B. NAGY, M. SEBÖK,

have been produced in or before 806.[28] At least two of the early
copies originated in or near Tours.[29] The rest came from all over
the Frankish empire, and outside it: one of the earliest copies was
possibly produced in a Southern English centre.[30] Two copies came
from the core areas of the Frankish empire, from Flavigny, and
Orléans during the episcopacy of Theodulf, who, like Alcuin, was
a scholar connected with the court.[31] Two copies were written in
Italy, one in Verona, and another, accompanied by *De fide* in what
its editors call a revised edition, at Monte Cassino, between 811
and 812.[32] Both were important intellectual centres connected
with the Carolingian elites — among others, Adalhard, Gundrada's half-brother, had spent time at Monte Cassino, and was one of

---

Budapest, 1999, pp. 397–408, at 404–06. On early dissemination, see also R. J.
Lawton, *Knowing Rome from Home. Reassessing Early Manuscript Witnesses of
Papal Letters, Pilgrim Itineraries and Syllogae in England and Francia, c. 600–
900 CE*, unpublished PhD diss., University of Leicester, 2019, pp. 23–27.

[28]   St Gallen, Stiftsbibliothek, 272 + Zürich, Zentralbibliothek, C 78,
fols 1–6, at pp. 214–43 (St Gall). B. Bischoff, *Katalog der festländischen
Handschriften des neunten Jahrhunderts (mit Ausnahme der wisigotischen)*,
4 vols, ed. by B. Ebersberger, Wiesbaden, 1998–2017, no. 7577 (hereafter
cited as B + arabic numeral), dated the manuscript as *s.* ix 1/4 and *s.* ix 1/
(2)/4, and considered it a (West?) Swiss product. However, Knibbs, Matter,
Alcuini Eboracensis De fide, p. xxii, point to a note by the last scribe on p. 245
as dating evidence for the manuscript: "Anno dcccui ab incarnatione domini
indictione xiii anno xxxuiii regnante karolo imperatore uiii id(us) fe(brua-
rii) die ueneris diuisum est regnum illius inter filiis suis quantum unusquis
post illum habet, et ego alia die hoc opus [scripsi]"; see also F. Schnoor at
<https://www.e-codices.unifr.ch/en/csg/0272/>, suggesting Tours for the origin
of the manuscript.

[29]   Verdun, BM, 67 (B 7024: *s.* ix in., Tours (prov. S. Wito, Verdun)),
fols 88ʳ–104ᵛ; BL, Harley 4980, fols 76–143 (B 2485: *s.* ix 1/4, Tours area
(prov. Carcassonne, *s.* xiii)), at fols 131ᵛ–143ᵛ.

[30]   Valenciennes, BM, 195 (B 6366a: *s.* ix in., South England (prov. St
Amand, *s.* ix/x)), fols 76ʳ–89ᵛ. For a detailed examination of this manuscript,
suggesting it was copied in a Continental house, probably St. Amand, see
Lawton, *Knowing Rome*, pp. 38–64.

[31]   Montpellier, Bibliothèque interuniversitaire. Section Médecine, H 141,
fols 1–80 and 95–135 (B 2835: *s.* ix in., Flavigny), fols 25ᵛ–41ᵛ; Troyes, BM,
1528 (B 6275: *s.* ix in., Orléans), fols 81ʳ–96ᵛ.

[32]   Verona, Biblioteca Capitolare, LXVII (LXIV) (B 7051: *s.* viii/ix,
Verona), fols 19ᵛ–31ᵛ; Rome, Biblioteca Casanatense, 641 pt. 1 (B 5313:
AD 811–12, Monte Cassino), fols 37ᵛ–44ᵛ.

the men who advised Pippin, king of Italy, during his minority.[33] Two manuscripts come from South German centres, and one was copied at St Amand and soon after taken to Salzburg, during the tenure of Alcuin's friend Arn, abbot of St Amand and archbishop of Salzburg.[34] Arn may indeed have been the recipient of the common exemplar of the St Amand copy and of two others, a partial West Frankish copy possibly from Angers and a South German copy, both from the second quarter of the century.[35]

Three Treatises, One Discussion?

The next three ninth-century texts on the soul were written in the first half of the 850s and they have usually been regarded as taking part in the same conversation on the soul in West Francia. Studying their publication is beset by a number of problems. One of the three treatises is lost and known only by fragments, and two survive only as much later copies. Moreover, the authorship of one text and the addressees of the other two are not clear. Nevertheless, looking at how they might have been published is necessary in order to understand the discourses in which they took part, and serves as an example of theological publishing — or the lack of it — in a controversy.

The fragmentary text is a set of questions and answers by Gottschalk of Orbais († in the late 860s). Under house arrest at the mona-

---

[33] On Adalhard see J. Nelson, *King and Emperor. A New Life of Charlemagne*, London, 2019, pp. 409, 443 and 475. For Monte Cassino, see Paschasius Radbertus, *Vita Adalhardi*, *PL*, 120, cc. 11–12, col. 1514A–1515B. See also S. Meeder, "Monte Cassino's network of knowledge. The earliest manuscript evidence", in *Writing the Early Medieval West. Studies in Honour of Rosamond McKitterick*, ed. by E. Screen, C. West, Cambridge, 2018, pp. 131–45, at 143 for Casanatense 641.

[34] Munich, Bayerische Staatsbibliothek, clm 14510 (South Bavaria (prov. St Emmeram, Regensburg, *s.* ix)), fols 168ʳ–186ᵛ; Wolfenbüttel, Herzog August Bibliothek, 93 Weiss (B 7428: *s.* ix 1/4, South Germany), fols 58ʳ–71ʳ; Munich, Bayerische Staatsbibliothek, clm 15813, fols 37–102 (B 3282: St. Amand, *s.* ix 1/4), fols 90ᵛ–102ʳ.

[35] Angers, BM, 276 (270) (B 65: *s.* ix 2/4, West France (Angers?) (prov. St Aubin)), *De fide*, the *Quaestiones*, and, at fols 44ʳ–45ʳ, only the verse prayers *Te homo laudet* and *Miserere*, usually appended to *De ratione*, without that text; St Gallen, Stiftsbibliothek, 276, pp. 150–279 (B 5717: *s.* ix 2/4, South Germany?), pp. 123–47.

stery of Hautvilliers since 849, following the indictment of his teaching of so-called double predestination, namely that God not only
predestined the just to eternal happiness but also predestined the
reprobate to eternal torment, he was forbidden to teach or to write.
Nevertheless, Gottschalk appears to have been able to exchange letters with contacts outside the monastery.[36] Most of what survives of
his writings is found in a single manuscript copied in Reims in the
later ninth century. The collection is disordered and gives the impression of being the sole copy of personal, at least in part unpublished,
texts.[37] Among these is a collection of questions and answers that its
editor, Cyrille Lambot, descriptively titled *Reponsa de diuersis*. Here,
questions on the soul occupy items ten through thirteen and fifteen.[38]
However, due to missing folia, the answers to questions eight through
fifteen are all lost, meaning that we do not know the substance of
what Gottschalk wrote about the soul.[39]

   The *Responsa de diuersis* consists of booklets and letters that
Gottschalk had circulated previously: some address a single recipient, once referred to as *adolescentulus frater*, but other responses
address a group.[40] Although we no longer have the text on the
topics about the soul, the questions about it and the nature of
extant parts of the compilation are enough to suggest that these

---

[36]   See Pezé, *Le virus*, pp. 60–68, on Gottschalk's activities following his
condemnation at Quierzy in 849.

[37]   The manuscript is Bern, Burgerbibliothek, 584 (B 605: *s.* ix 4/4, Reims).
W. Pezé, "Débat doctrinal et genre littéraire à l'époque carolingienne: les
opuscules théologiques de Gottschalk d'Orbais", *Revue de l'histoire des reli-
gions*, 234 (2017), pp. 25–72.

[38]   Gottschalk, *Responsa de diuersis*, ed. by C. Lambot, *Oeuvres théologiques et grammaticales de Godescalc d'Orbais. Textes en majeure partie inédits*,
Louvain, 1945 (Spicilegium sacrum Lovaniense, Études et documents, 20),
pp. 130–79, at 131.

[39]   Gottschalk did write also on the origin of the soul: this treatise likewise survives in Bern 584, and appears to have been sent confidentially to
recipients who were asked by Gottschalk to keep it secret so long as he was
imprisoned; see Gottschalk, *Quaestiones de anima*, ed. by Lambot, *Oeuvres*,
pp. 283–91, at 290; Pezé, "Débat doctrinal", pp. 38, 68. For an Italian translation of this and the thematically related but distinct treatise, *De seminibus
animatis*, as a single text, see Tolomio, *L'anima*, pp. 342–56.

[40]   Pezé, "Débat doctrinal", pp. 31–35. On Gottschalk, see also M. B.
Gillis, *Heresy and Dissent in the Carolingian Empire. The Case of Gottschalk
of Orbais*, Oxford, 2017.

issues exercised monks and clerics. This may indeed be one reason why Gottschalk eventually gathered these materials and added a list of chapters and a short collective preface.[41] In that preface he uses the polite plural and asks the recipient to correct anything they deem necessary, and then to return the text.[42] Submitting the work to censorship by an authority not identified, Gottschalk may have intended to publish it to an audience beyond his confidential circle. On the other hand, the collection seems to be at an initial phase of drafting, with its nature as a compilation of pre-existing materials discernible, and if eventual publication was Gottschalk's aim, what we have appears to belong to a preparatory stage. It is also possible that for the time being, imprisoned, he was primarily attempting to make or solidify contacts with potential supporters, by showing off his learning.[43] In any case, there is no sign that the text was ever published.

The second text was printed by Jacques Sirmond in 1645 in his *Opera omnia* of Hincmar of Reims, from a subsequently lost manuscript from the abbey of Saint-Remi in Reims.[44] There it bore the title *Collectio cujusdam sapientis ex libris sancti Augustini de diuersa et multiplici animae ratione.*[45] However, we would expect that a manuscript from such a place would not have missed the opportunity to signal Archbishop Hincmar's authorship of a text. As, moreover, Flodoard of Reims († 966) does not mention the treatise in his catalogue of Hincmar's works, it is unclear as to whether Hincmar

---

[41]   J.-P. Bouhot, *Ratramne de Corbie. Histoire litteraire et controversies doctrinales*, Paris, 1976, pp. 43–45; Pezé, "Débat doctrinal", pp. 31–32.

[42]   Gottschalk, *Responsa*, p. 132: "Non mihi modo subueniunt in memoriam omnia quae proposui a uobis quaerenda".

[43]   For Gottschalk's attempts at currying favor with elites, see Pezé, *Le virus*, esp. pp. 65–68. I am grateful to Warren Pezé for his comments on this issue.

[44]   The manuscript may have been lost in the fire at the abbey of St-Remi in 1774; M. Carey, "The scriptorium of Reims during the archbishopric of Hincmar (AD 845–82)", in *Classical and Medieval Studies in Honor of Edward Kennard Rand*, ed. by L. W. Jones, New York, NY, 1938, pp. 41–60, at 47; M. Stratmann, "Briefe an Hinkmar von Reims", *Deutsches Archiv*, 48 (1992), pp. 37–81, at 39. My thanks to Matthias Schrör for these references.

[45]   For manuscripts of Hincmar's works, see J. Devisse, *Hincmar. Archevêque de Reims, 845–82*, 3 vols, Geneva, 1976, vol. 3, pp. 1152–60.

wrote it.[46] Jean Devisse added several arguments from the style of the text and the methods it reflects that suggest it is unlikely to be Hincmar's authentic work.[47] The text is a letter treatise addressed to a king who rules *res publica nostra*.[48] The author begins by explaining at length how happy he is that the king has taken an interest in true philosophy, and how this makes him like his eponymous grandfather, defender of the doctrine and faith of the church, and his father, who was exemplary in piety. Evidently a West Frankish scholar was here addressing his text to Charles the Bald († 877).

The author ends the preface with reference to having attentively studied "a page of chapters brought to us" and promising to respond to each topic using the writings of the Fathers.[49] This suggests he is reacting to a set of questions sent to him by the king. The author concludes the treatise by noting that more authors could have been cited, but no more have been introduced because the recipient is burdened by many cares and several questions needed answering. The author offers the text as a stimulant to minds eager for learning.[50] He thus anticipated critical readers besides the explicit addressee.

Ratramnus († after 868), learned monk of Corbie, was requested by Charles the Bald to comment on double predestination in

---

[46]   As already pointed out by H. Schrörs, *Hinkmar Erzbischof von Reims. Sein Leben und seine Schriften*, Hildesheim, 1967 [1884], p. 164 n. 72. Followed by M. Manitius, *Geschichte der lateinischen Literatur des Mittelalters, 1, Von Justinian bis zur mitte des zehnten Jahrhunderts*, Munich, 1911, p. 351; A. Wilmart, "L'opuscule inédit de Ratramne sur la nature de l'ame", *Revue Bénédictine*, 43 (1931), pp. 207–23, at 208; more recently, for example, C. Trottmann, *La vision béatifique des disputes scolastiques à sa définition par Benoît XII*, Rome, 1995, p. 75.

[47]   Devisse, *Hincmar*, vol. 1, pp. 20–21. Cf. G. Mathon, *L'anthropologie chrétienne en Occident de Saint Augustin à Jean Scot Erigène. Recherches sur le sort des theses de l'anthropologie augustinienne durant le haut moyen-age*, unpublished PhD diss., Université Catholique de Lille, 1964, pp. 247–51.

[48]   *De diuersa et multiplici animae ratione*, ed. by J. Sirmond, *PL*, 125, col. 929–48, at 947D: "huic capitulo sufficere credidimus tanti ac talis viri auctoritatem, caventes epistolaris schedulae prolixitatem". See also Tolomio, *L'anima*, pp. 82–88, with an Italian translation of the text (as Hincmar's) at pp. 301–36.

[49]   *De diuersa*, Praefatio, col. 931D: "schedulam ergo capitulorum nobis allatam".

[50]   *De diuersa*, viii, col. 948A: "ut animum discendi avidum provocemus ad majora".

849 or early 850, following Gottschalk's trial and incarceration.[51] Perhaps a few years after that he wrote also the third of the apparently related treatises on the soul. His *De anima* is also a letter treatise, and survives in two late copies, the early-twelfth-century Cambridge, Corpus Christi College, MS 332, and the thirteenth-century Cambridge, Sidney Sussex College, MS 71.[52] The text lacks a proper preface, which would have included a salutation, and goes directly into the matters at hand, so we cannot be sure to whom it is addressed. While *De diuersa* addresses the king very directly in the familiar second person, Ratramnus in *De anima* observes conventions making it clear that he is writing to his superior, concluding with a request that the recipient correct anything deemed to require it.[53]

Ratramnus could be addressing an abbot or a bishop, but the subject-matter and its resemblance to the questions *De diuersa* answered for King Charles has usually been interpreted to mean that he was also addressing the king. He is certainly responding to questions put to him by his addressee: "As far as I remember, you requested an explanation by the authority of ecclesiastical writers to two questions: whether the soul is circumscribed and whether it has a place".[54] He also seems to have anticipated discussion, because he finds it necessary to defend some of his choices.[55]

As publishing events, both Ratramnus's work and the *De diuersa* were commissioned expert opinions. Gottschalk's unpubli-

[51] Bouhot, *Ratramne*, pp. 35–41; Pezé, *Le Virus*, pp. 70–71.

[52] Ratramnus, *De anima*, ed. by Wilmart, "L'opuscule inédit", pp. 210–23; on the manuscripts see p. 207; Bouhot, *Ratramne*, pp. 27–28. Cambridge, Corpus Christi College, 332 (*s.* xii 1/4, Rochester), p. 41: "Incipit liber rathramni de eo quod christus ex uirgine natus est"; p. 70: "Incipit liber eiusdem Rathramni de anima. Duo quantum memini proposuistis ecclesiasticorum uobis auctoritate". See also Tolomio, *L'anima*, pp. 77–82, with an Italian translation of the text at pp. 225–93. On the copyist of CCCC 332, see S. Niskanen, "William of Malmesbury as librarian: the evidence of his autographs", *Discovering William of Malmesbury*, ed. by R. M. Thomson, E. Dolmans, E. A. Winkler, Woodbridge, 2017, pp. 117–27, at 119–20.

[53] On these conventions, see Steckel, *Kulturen des Lehrens*, pp. 544–48, 551–53, 573–78.

[54] Ratramnus, *De anima*, p. 210, ll. 1–2: "Duo, quantum memini, proposuistis ecclesiasticorum uobis auctoritate soluenda, sitne anima circumscripta siue localis".

[55] *Ibid.*, p. 223, ll. 557–58: "nonnulli, forte non contemnendae scientiae uiri, qui et corporalem et localem docuerunt eam fore".

shed work here points to the fact that these questions could be and probably were discussed in writing in confidential communication. Publishing on a controversial question could be an attempt to control the discussion, although while both envision a wider discussion, only *De diuersa* is openly polemical.

The themes of the three texts are closely related, but their relationship is a matter of conjecture, which depends partly on who one regards as the probable author of *De diuersa*. It is unlikely that, as an unrepentant heretic confined to a monastery, Gottschalk would have been consulted by a king or a bishop. Thus, his confidential letter or letters on these topics have been taken to be the beginning of the discussion. Jean-Paul Bouhot conjectured that Hincmar had intercepted such a letter by the end of 852 and wrote *De diuersa* to oppose it, sending it to Charles to initiate a new process against Gottschalk. In the meantime, Gottschalk, learning of developments, would have gathered his texts for publication. Finally, a supporter of Gottschalk, such as Abbot Lupus of Ferrières († after 860), would have learned of Hincmar's accusations at the Council of Soissons or the synod at Quierzy immediately following in the spring of 853, and enlisted Ratramnus to write in his defence.[56] *De diuersa* does sharply criticize those who hold that the soul is not contained by the body, and demands that they should be excommunicated. It also affirms that the soul is circumscribed by place. On the contrary, Ratramnus argues extensively that the soul is not local and not circumscribed.[57] The problem with Bouhot's ingenious reconstruction is that it does not do justice to the text of *De diuersa*: everything suggests that the latter is in fact a response to questions sent by the king and not simply intercepted by the author. Why else would the author

---

[56]   BOUHOT, *Ratramne*, pp. 41–48, esp. 47–48; cf. WILMART, "L'opuscule", p. 208; M. CAPPUYNS, *Jean Scot Érigène, sa vie, sa oeuvre, sa pensée*, Brussels, 1964, pp. 91–93. cf. E. A. MATTER, "The soul of the dog-man: Ratramnus of Corbie between theology and philosophy", *Rivista di storia della filosofia*, 61 (2006), pp. 43–53, at 50, suggesting in passing that the thematic proximity of Gottschalk's *Responsa* to *De diuersa* might indicate that Gottschalk was the author of the latter.

[57]   *De diuersa*, ii, cols 933C, 936B; iii, col. 937A; Ratramnus, *De anima*, i, pp. 210–11.

not tell more about what the questionnaire was while at the same time underlining the care he has taken in answering it? Moreover, the outburst demanding excommunication is the only sign that the *De diuersa* is aimed at refuting the views of a specific individual, although the text nowhere names Gottschalk, unlike Hincmar when indicting Gottschalk's views on double predestination.[58]

Taking a different view, Gérard Mathon suggested that the controversy began at court, catalysed in part by John Scottus Eriugena's († 870) controversial *De praedestinatione*. On the other hand, he pointed out that the wording of the questions that *De diuersa* responds to suggests that some of them were occasioned by texts like the fifth-century *De ecclesiasticis dogmatibus*, attributed variously in manuscripts to Gennadius of Marseilles, Augustine, or the Council of Nicaea of 325, that expounded materialist interpretations of the soul. Charles the Bald would have consulted both Ratramnus and Hincmar, and meanwhile Gottschalk's contacts would have requested his views.[59] One problem here is that it is far from certain that Ratramnus was answering the king. Moreover, the court does not appear to be the most likely locus of a controversy over Eriugena's teachings, as he was clearly under the king's special protection and taught at the court school.[60] Finally,

---

[58]   See e.g. Hincmar, *De praedestinatione prior*, PL, 125, col. 56A; Hincmar, *De praedestinatione posterior*, PL, 125, col. 84B–86B. Note, however, that Hincmar does not name Ratramnus in a letter to Odo of Beauvais critiquing a text by the monk of Corbie; see C. LAMBOT, "L'homélie du Pseudo-Jérôme sur l'assomption & l'évangile de la nativité de Marie d'après une letter inédite d'Hincmar', *Revue Bénédictine*, 46 (1934), pp. 265–82, at 269–70; I owe notice of this letter to RENSWOUDE, *The Rhetoric*, p. 209.

[59]   MATHON, *L'anthropologie chrétienne*, pp. 268–69, 271–84, 290–93; TOLOMIO, *L'anima*, 33–38. See also D. GANZ, "Theology and the organisation of thought", in *The New Cambridge Medieval History, II*, ed. by McKITTERICK, pp. 758–85, at 780–81. On *De ecclesiasticis dogmatibus* see now E. COLOMBI, "La trasmissione delle opere teologiche tra V e VIII secolo, con una riflessione sulla Definitio ecclesiasticorum dogmatum (CPL 958) attribuita a Gennadio di Marsiglia", in *La teologia dal V all'VIII secolo fra sviluppo e crisi. XLI Incontro di Studiosi dell'Antichità Cristiana (Roma, 9–11 maggio 2013)*, Rome, 2014, pp. 9–56.

[60]   PEZÉ, *Le virus*, pp. 188–93; see also J. MARENBON, "John Scottus and Carolingian theology: from the *De praedestinatione*, its background and its critics, to the *Periphyseon*", in *Charles the Bald: Court and Kingdom*, ed. by M. T. GIBSON, J. L. NELSON, 2nd edn, Aldershot, 1990, pp. 303–25.

neither of these two scenarios can be entirely correct if, as seems probable, Hincmar is not the author of *De diuersa*.

However, the conditions of survival of these three works suggests that all three were intended for different audiences. Ratramnus's *De anima* seems to survive through a copy made at his monastery after his death. Bernhard Bischoff first recognised that in *c.* 875 Corbie produced posthumous editions of the works of its main mid-ninth-century authors, Paschasius Radbertus († *c.* 860), Ratramnus, and Bishop Engelmodus of Sens († 865).[61] Bouhot concluded that Ratramnus's whole oeuvre, including his *De anima*, survives primarily thanks to this publishing effort. Ratramnus's *De corpore et sanguine Domini*, *De praedestinatione*, and *Contra Graecorum opposita* survive in manuscripts produced in Corbie *c.* 875. However, as noted above, *De anima* survives, together with his *De natiuitate Christi*, only in two later English manuscripts. Wilmart suggested that Sidney Sussex 71 was a copy of the earlier CCCC 332,[62] and the editor of *De natiuitate* asserted that all copies of that text depend on that one manuscript.[63] However, Bouhot disagreed, referring to the list of variants the editor had established and noting that the two Cambridge copies likely descend from the same lost exemplar. He also pointed out that the two manuscripts have different overall contents: Sidney Sussex 71 adds Cassiodorus' *De anima*, while in CCCC 332 Ratramnus's *De anima* is the odd one out in an otherwise Mariological collection. Ratramnus wrote these two texts for different dedicatees, on different subjects, but one after the other, so they may have been found together in his files. Bouhot thus concluded that both copies of *De anima* and *De natiuitate* derive from a lost volume of the Corbie edition of Ratramnus's works.[64] If so, it is perhaps less likely that Ratramnus addressed the work to the king; at least, the textual tradition of *De corpore et sanguine domini*, which certainly was addressed

---

[61]   B. Bischoff, "Hadoard und die Klassikerhandschriften aus Corbie", in B. Bischoff, *Mittelalterliche Studien*, 1, Stuttgart, 1966, pp. 49–63, at 56–57.

[62]   Wilmart, "L'opuscule inédit", p. 207.

[63]   J. M. Canal Sanchez, "La virginidad de Maria segun Ratramno y Radberto monjes de Corbie. Nueva edicion de los textos", *Marianum*, 30 (1968), pp. 53–100, at 63.

[64]   Bouhot, *Ratramne*, pp. 27–28 and n. 8.

to Charles, survives in copies that descend independently from a copy kept at Corbie and from the text sent to the court.[65]

If Hincmar or any member of his clergy did not write De diuersa, the fact that it survived in a Reims manuscript with authentic texts by the archbishop suggests that it nevertheless derived from his archives. This is to be expected, for it was, after all, addressed to the king and his court, and Hincmar was certainly a well connected member of the court network; for instance, he seems to have participated in drawing up or in preserving fifty-three of Charles the Bald's fifty-eight surviving capitularies.[66] Gottschalk's text, finally, survives in a single Reims copy of his files, perhaps an archival copy of the works of the heretic kept in custody by Hincmar. We do not know to whom Gottschalk sent his Responsa, which makes it difficult to assess what he aimed to do with the collection. He had few friends, and he may have misjudged the friendliness of the recipient of the Responsa. We know he had reached out to Archbishop Amolo of Lyon after his condemnation, only to be disappointed: Amolo did not share the Augustinianism of Florus, who did write against Gottschalk's critics.[67] If Gottschalk was intent on publishing, it is far from clear if any genuinely friendly authority in Charles' kingdom would have disseminated the work. Of his friends, Lupus at least would probably not have risked angering the king by disseminating the writings of a man condemned at Quierzy, as he wanted the king to restore confiscated lands to his abbey.[68]

This examination suggests that the controversy about the nature of the soul, such as it was, may have had multiple origins in the kind of confidential exchanges suggested by Gottschalk's De diuersa. The fact that he is not named by either the author of De diuersa or Ratramnus suggests that they did not regard him as the originator or main transmitter of this questioning. Certainly, as Mathon argued, older texts challenging Augustinian notions of

---

[65] On the witnesses of De corpore et sanguine domini see Bouhot, Ratramne, 107–11. I thank Warren Pezé for his comments on this issue.

[66] See J. L. Nelson, "Legislation and consensus in the reign of Charles the Bald", in Politics and Ritual in Early Medieval Europe, ed. by J. L. Nelson, London, 1986, pp. 91–116, at 97. I thank Warren Pezé for the reference.

[67] See e.g. Zechiel-Eckes, Florus, 135–36.

[68] On Lupus, see Pezé, Le virus, pp. 227–29.

the soul's immateriality were widely used and well known by the Carolingians, and may have catalysed at least a part of the discussion.[69] While it is not possible to determine the relative dates of *De diuersa* and Ratramnus's work, it seems that they may have been responses at different levels of the discussion, one perhaps conducted at an episcopal household, another at the royal court. The author of *De diuersa*, a prominent West Frankish scholar or ecclesiastical authority, such as Lupus of Ferrières or Prudentius of Troyes, answered a royal questionnaire, and it may have survived as a copy Hincmar, one among its intended court audience, made for himself. Ratramnus, instead, may have answered a bishop or an abbot, and certainly discussed a limited section of the set of questions; the fact that his work only survives through the Corbie edition nevertheless suggests it was never distributed as widely as a text intended for the court would have been. Although the main conclusion tends to rather underline what we do not know, these three works suggest that the related discussions about the soul were more diffuse, and thus perhaps had a wider reach, than has previously been supposed.

An Ageing Archbishop's Gift to a Young King

A few years after the nature of the soul was discussed in the western kingdom, probably in the first half of the 850s, the archbishop of Mainz, Hrabanus Maurus, published his *De anima*.[70] Interestingly, it bears no sign of connection to the debates in Charles the Bald's kingdom. Hrabanus's treatise is dedicated to Lothar II, who was crowned king of the middle kingdom on 29 September 855 at the age of eighteen. The treatise thus seems to mark the coronation; certainly, Hrabanus had written it before his death in February 856. Perhaps because he was old and tired — already in 850 Hrabanus had referred to his age and illness and sent an older treatise to Hincmar who had requested his insights into Gottschalk and double predestination[71] — Hrabanus produced the text by abbreviating Cassiodorus' *De anima* and augmenting it with pas-

---

    [69]   MATHON, *L'anthropologie*, pp. 284–85.

    [70]   Hrabanus Maurus, *De anima*; *PL*, 110, col. 1109–20. See TOLOMIO, *L'anima*, pp. 71–77, with an Italian translation of the text at pp. 235–58.

    [71]   CAPPUYNS, *Jean Scot*, p. 108; ZECHIEL-ECKES, *Florus*, p. 127.

sages from Julianus Pomerius's *De uita contemplatiua* and a collection of excerpts from Vegetius's *De re militari*. This last underlines the text's character less as a treatise on the soul and more as a gift suitable to a young king, Hrabanus himself explaining that he added it not only "since it is becoming to your excellence to know many things" but especially "due to frequent barbarian incursions". The treatise is best understood as a mirror for princes, and as a reminder of the expertise Hrabanus was offering. Its discussion of the soul is, like that of Hrabanus's teacher Alcuin, slanted towards the psychology of virtues and vices.[72] Beyond its royal recipient, Hrabanus gives no explicit indication of a wider audience. He concludes with a customary justification for writing publicly, asking that the recipient attribute anything good they find in the text to God and any errors to human frailty.[73]

There are no extant manuscript copies of the work; the collection of excerpts from Vegetius survives only in an eleventh-century manuscript from Trier, with a preface that allows it to be identified as the last part of Hrabanus's treatise.[74] As this selection evidently also circulated independently, this tells us little of the fortunes of the whole treatise. It was not controversial or very original, neither did it fill a gap in the available literature on the subject. There is thus little reason to expect that it would have been widely distributed or read.

Ratramnus's Other *De anima* and the Difference between Private and Published Discourse

Finally, Ratramnus of Corbie published another treatise *De anima*, probably in 863.[75] An example of publishing in order to halt a discussion, it serves to show, in addition to the discussions implied

---

[72] MATHON, *L'anthropologie*, pp. 225, 236–39.

[73] Hrabanus Maurus, *De anima*, xii; col. 1120C.

[74] Trier, Bistumsarchiv, Abt. 95 Nr. 133c, fols 25ᵛ–29ʳ; ed. by D. E. DÜMMLER, *Zeitschrift für deutsches Altertum* 15 (1872), pp. 443–50. See also R. KOTTJE (ed.) with T. A. ZIEGLER, *Verzeichnis der Handschriften mit den Werken des Hrabanus Maurus*, Hanover, 2012 (MGH, *Hilfsmittel*, 27), pp. 188, 235.

[75] Ratramnus, *De anima ad Odonem Bellovacensem episcopum*, ed. by C. LAMBOT, Namur–Lille, 1952 (Analecta mediaevalia Namurcensia, 2). See also Ph. DELHAYE, *Une controverse sur l'âme universelle au IXe siècle*, Namur–Lille, 1950.

by Gottschalk's *Responsa*, the ease of confidential discourse on the soul. It also shows the threshold between it and published discourse.

Ratramnus dedicated the work to Bishop Odo of Beauvais († 881), writing against the ideas of a monk of Saint-Germer-de-Fly about the existence of a world soul. Ratramnus tells us that the monk had assumed the idea from an Irish scholar called Macarius. Hearing about the matter, Odo had asked Ratramnus to look into it. Ratramnus had written to Odo and refuted the monk's ideas. But then the monk had bypassed the chain of command and written directly to Ratramnus, who wrote directly back, also without involving Odo. The monk seems to have written back again, but now Ratramnus *published* an extensive rebuttal, dedicating it to Odo, and this is the surviving text. Ratramnus not only disagreed with the monk but was disappointed with his lack of learning and his insolence: he should have accepted advice from a senior monk without talking back. Clearly Ratramnus had initially thought it self-evident to teach the monk in a confidential exchange. When it did not work, he concluded that the monk was guilty of heresy and demanded that Odo prevent him from writing or disputing. Steckel notes that Ratramnus enjoyed considerable latitude: he was consulted by the bishop, he granted the monk a confidential hearing, and it was finally he who demanded disciplinary action.[76] However, as a fragmentary letter shows, Odo did also exercise his oversight over the monk of Corbie, sending another of the latter's works to be checked by his metropolitan and Ratramnus's sometime adversary, Hincmar.[77] Thus, although in the case of the monk of Saint-Germer-de-Fly we can see Ratramnus adjudicating in a case of potential heresy, on another occasion he is subject to exactly the kind of episcopal oversight we would expect in the case of a monk, however learned.

Ratramnus's second treatise on the soul survives only in an eighteenth-century copy made from a now lost manuscript from the abbey of St Eligius of Noyon. While it could have come from the episcopal archives of Beauvais, and thus have been the copy Ratramnus presented to Odo, Bouhot preferred to consider it a

---

[76] STECKEL, *Kulturen des Lehrens*, pp. 604–07.
[77] LAMBOT, "L'homelie", pp. 269–70.

volume of the Corbie edition of Ratramnus's works, since it contained nothing but Ratramnus's text without any other documents related to the affair.[78] A note in the surviving copy suggests that another copy (also in St Eligius?) may also have existed.[79]

Publishing Theological Treatises in the Carolingian Period

What we can discern about the publication of these texts points to different kinds of publics and confirms the importance of the author's status and networks in successful publishing. The publics addressed at least by Alcuin, the author of *De diuersa* and Hrabanus Maurus were various Carolingian courts. Charles the Bald, for instance, like his father and grandfather, had a network of scholars connected with his court that interpreted texts for him and gave him literary advice. This was a formidable audience: it could and was expected to judge quality, and, as we saw in Ratramnus's case, a scholar valued as an expert could even press charges of heresy.[80] *De diuersa* and Ratramnus's first treatise were solicited expert opinions, but both show an expectation of scrutiny and discussion.

If it was not Charles the Bald whom Ratramnus was addressing in his first treatise on the soul, it was probably a bishop, as in his second treatise. A text such as the treatise to Odo of Beauvais, or at any rate its message, was primarily intended to be disseminated within the diocese, in this case to alert those responsible for silencing the monk and all who might have been exposed to his ideas. Gottschalk may have planned but probably failed to reach a diocesan or monastic public with the *Responsa de diuersis*. Such a public was in many cases the first step towards wider dissemination, but that required approval and networks. Of course, most of these are letter treatises: producing them may not have required such resources as turning out presentation copies of larger works. Moreover, Alcuin and Hrabanus at least controlled "publishing frameworks" through their abbatial and episcopal offices, allowing

[78] BnF, lat. 11687, fols 93[r]–146[v]. LAMBOT in Ratramnus, *De anima ad Odonem*, pp. 11–15; BOUHOT, *Ratramne*, pp. 26–27.

[79] Cited by LAMBOT in Ratramnus, *De anima ad Odonem*, p. 14, "Ut facilius codicem nostrum cum uestro comparetis, eaque opera continuo reperiatis".

[80] PEZÉ, *Le virus*, 201–04; STECKEL, *Kulturen des Lehrens*, p. 607.

them to produce high-quality presentation copies. Ratramnus also, though a mere monk, was an established scholar and author advising the royal court. Gottschalk the convicted heretic was at a clear disadvantage.

Aside from Alcuin's *De ratione*, most of these works survive in single copies, a few only in early-modern ones. Is this an accurate reflection of the extent of their circulation? It is possible that it is, not least because only a few of these can be shown to survive in copies deriving from the recipient of the work or a patron of the author. Such is probable for Alcuin's *De ratione*, and perhaps also for the anonymous *De diuersa*. At the same time, while the soul was far from being a marginal subject, issues such as whether or not it was circumscribed were fairly learned concerns. However, Gottschalk's *Responsa* suggest that even such ostensibly recondite issues were of interest to a wider literate audience. Even so, both Ratramnus and the author of *De diuersa* kept to official channels, as it were, addressing their texts only to those who had commissioned them and not seeking a wider public, unlike Florus and a few other scholars when writing on double predestination.[81] If the controversy over the soul involved a wider literate audience, and it is not clear if it did or, if so, how wide an interest it did command, Ratramnus and the author of *De diuersa* did not want to involve those that were not supposed to be interested in it.

Alcuin's and Hrabanus's works were slanted towards more practical questions, and as such had a wider appeal, and Alcuin's work certainly was distributed widely enough to reach a large audience. Extensive networks aided successful dissemination. The swift empire-wide dissemination of Alcuin's *De ratione animae* is testament to the extensive reach of Carolingian elite networks under Charlemagne; such distribution may have been harder to replicate for Hrabanus during the reigns of the sons of Louis the Pious. Hrabanus's treatise would also have been competing for attention against Alcuin's rather similar text, which was already widely disseminated.

It is apparent that the survival of a Carolingian text is no guarantee that its author had published it. In addition to texts such as Gottschalk's *Responsa*, which may only have been intended

---

[81]   ZECHIEL-ECKES, *Florus*, p. 224; PEZÉ, *Le virus*, pp. 350–61.

to be published, if even that, a couple of texts in this selection draw attention to the role of posthumous editions and collections of texts in their survival. Ratramnus's work, although probably published, only survives because his monastery (re-)published it posthumously. Gottschalk's largely unpublished work only survives because it was collected, whether by his enemy, Hincmar, or by his supporters. All of this should be taken into account when interpreting these texts as part of the intellectual history of the period.

Contextualizing the Publication
of Dudo of Saint-Quentin's *Historia Normannorum*

Lauri Leinonen
(*Helsinki*)

This paper asks how Dudo of Saint-Quentin published his *Historia Normannorum* (hereafter *HN*) and to what effect.[1] Identifying his pertinent social network, I seek to assess contributions not only by Dudo but also other parties involved in the process. The subtext of the following inquiry is the interplay between *HN*, the setting of its publication, and Dudo's intended audiences. The principal evidence consists of *HN*'s paratexts, particularly the explanatory rubrics that accompany many of the verses embedded in the text.

---

[1]   Previously the work was usually known by the editorial title *De moribus et actis primorum Normanniae ducum*, given to it by André Duchesne for the *editio princeps*, in *Historiae Normannorum scriptores antiqui, res ab illis per Galliam, Angliam, Apuliam, Capuae principatum, Siciliam, et Orientem gestas explicantes, ab anno Christi DCCCXXXVIII ad annum MCCXX*, Paris, 1619, pp. 49–160. Jules Lair preserved that title in his edition, *De moribus et actis primorum Normanniae ducum*, Caen, 1865 (Mémoires de la Société des Antiquaires de Normandie, 23) [henceforth *HN*, ed. Lair]. The title by Duchesne derives from a passage in which Duke Richard I commissions the work; *HN*, ed. Lair, p. 119. Even so, the title, not known from sources before Duchesne's edition, is hardly authorial. The most common medieval titles appear to have been "Gesta Normannorum" and "Historia Normannorum"; see, for example, "Incipit Historia Normannorum", BL, Cotton Nero D. viii, fol. 72^r (*s.* xii), and "Hec sunt Gesta Normannorum", Bern, Burgerbibliothek, Bongars Cod. 390, fol. 103^r (in an eleventh-century hand). In recent scholarship, and here, the work is called *Historia Normannorum*; B. Pohl, *Dudo of St Quentin's* Historia Normannorum: *Tradition, Innovation and Memory. Writing History in the Middle Ages*, York, 2015, p. 38; E. Christiansen, *Dudo of St Quentin: History of the Normans. Translation with Introduction and Notes*, Woodbridge, 1998, p. xiii.

The Art of Publication from the Ninth to the Sixteenth Century, ed. by Samu Niskanen with the assistance of Valentina Rovere, IPM, 93 (Turnhout, 2023), pp. 47–82.
© BREPOLS ❧ PUBLISHERS   DOI 10.1484/M.IPM-EB.5.133081

Dudo of Saint-Quentin was a Frank from the county of Vermandois.[2] In his youth he received a fine literary education. At some
point he was made a canon of the collegiate church at Saint-Quentin. In 987 he was sent on a diplomatic mission to Normandy,
during which he obtained preferment in Rouen. He was, in other
words, one of the many foreign *literati* whom the Normans recruited
in the eleventh century. This trend was connected to local efforts
to reform the practices and administration of the church and ducal
government that has since been dubbed a "renaissance" by some
scholars.[3] Dudo served in the court of the Norman dukes in administrative roles from the early 990s. At some point he was promoted
to the office of a ducal *cancellarius*, which represented the pinnacle of his secular career.[4] Dudo was rewarded for his administrative and literary work with benefices, which Duke Richard II later
donated, at his request, to the collegiate church of Saint-Quentin in
1015, most likely in preparation for Dudo's return there.[5] Some time

---

[2] The most comprehensive recent work on *HN*, including an extensive
biography of its author, is POHL, *Dudo of St Quentin's* Historia Normannorum.
The most recent translation, accompanied by scholarly notes, is CHRISTIAN-
SEN, *History of the Normans*. The most recent critical edition is Jules Lair's
from 1865 (*HN*, ed. LAIR). See also the *codex optimus* transcript, with translation, by F. LIFSHITZ, *Dudo of St. Quentin (c. 965–died before 1043): Gesta Normannorum, written btw. 996–1015* [Translation], originally published as part
of the ORB website in 1998 and republished as part of the Internet Medieval
Sourcebook in 2019. Accessed January 30, 2020: <https://sourcebooks.ford-
ham.edu/source/dudo-stquentin-gesta-trans-lifshitz.asp>, transcript: <https://
sourcebooks.fordham.edu/source/dudu-stquentin-gesta-transcription-lifshitz.
asp>. Lifshitz's work is based on one manuscript, SBB-PK, Phill. 1854, and
offers a very valuable control to Lair and Christiansen.

[3] POHL, *Dudo of St Quentin's* Historia Normannorum, pp. 161–62; J. M.
ZIOLKOWSKI, *Jezebel: A Norman Latin Poem of the Early Eleventh Century*, New
York, NY, 1989, p. 39.

[4] Dudo apparently attested a ducal confirmation of a gift of lands to
Saint-Quentin on 8 September 1015; BnF, Collection de Picardie, 352, no.
1, printed in *Gallia Christiana*, 11, Appendix, n. 2, cols 284–85. While the
attestation reads "Odo cancellarius scripsit et subscripsit", the name has been
taken as Dudo's: D. DOUGLAS, "The ancestors of William Fitz Osbern", *The
English Historical Review*, 59 (1944), pp. 62–79, at 73–74; and M. FAUROUX,
"Deux autographes de Dudon de Saint-Quentin (1011, 1015)", *Bibliothèque de
l'école des chartes*, 111 (1953), pp. 229–34, at 230.

[5] The 1015 charter records the donations of two benefices Dudo had
received from Duke Richard I to the church of Saint-Quentin; for the charter,

thereafter, Dudo, already at an advanced age, was elected dean of Saint-Quentin's.[6] He published *HN* shortly after his relocation to Vermandois.[7] He died in 1027 at the latest.[8]

The *Historia Normannorum*, Dudo's only known work, was written between *c.* 996 and 1015 × 1020.[9] Until recently there was a

see the previous footnote. The document provides a *terminus post quem*, as Dudo was still chancellor at the time. He is also styled as "pretiosi martyris Christi Quintini canonicus" and "fidelis idoneus" of Richard II, suggesting that he was still in the duke's service and not yet a deacon; cf. F. LIFSCHITZ, *Dudo of St. Quentin*, Introduction. M. H. GELTING, "The courtly viking: education and *mores* in Dudo of Saint-Quentin's Chronicle", in *Beretning fra toog-tredivte tvaefaglige vikingesymposium*, ed. by L. BISGAARD, M. BRUUS, P. GAMMELTOFT, Højbjerg, 2013, pp. 7–36, at 9, n. 8.

[6] Dudo styled himself deacon in the prefatory letter: "Dudo, super congregationem Sancti Quintini decanus"; *HN*, ed. LAIR, p. 115.

[7] The first possible publication date of *c.* 1015 is based on the approximate year Dudo became dean of Saint-Quentin (see above, nn. 4 and 5); see POHL, *Dudo of St Quentin's* Historia Normannorum, pp. 106–08). It cannot be known whether Dudo published *HN* immediately after becoming dean. It has been noted that of the persons mentioned in the prefaces, only Count Rolf is presumed to have died before 1020, for which reason *c.* 1020 has been taken as a *terminus ad quem*; CHRISTIANSEN, *History of the Normans*, pp. xii–xiii; *HN*, ed. LAIR, p. 125. So, a safe dating for the publication would be 1015 × 1020.

[8] A dean of Saint-Quentin by the name of Vivian is known to have occupied the stall in February 1015, and another dean, Rothard, is known either from 1021 or 1027. No records have survived of the deans of the collegiate church from the time in between; POHL, *Dudo of St Quentin's* Historia Normannorum, p. 111. CHRISTIANSEN, *History of the Normans*, p. xii.

[9] The first terminus, *c.* 996, derives from Dudo's remark that he had hardly started writing the work when Richard I died: "Stylus nostrae imperitiae nedum primas partes operis attigerat"; *HN*, ed. LAIR, p. 119. Dudo dated this event to 996; *ibid.*, p. 299. In two manuscripts the year is, however, given as 1002; *ibid.*, p. 299, n. 3, cf. LIFSCHITZ, *Dudo of St. Quentin*, Introduction. Dudo refers to a two-year period before Richard I's death as a time when he frequently visited the duke, and the commission happened "quadam die" during these two years; *HN*, ed. LAIR, p. 119. The commission could, then, have been given already in 994, as proposed, for example, by G. C. HUISMAN, "Notes on the manuscript tradition of Dudo of St Quentin's *Gesta Normannorum*", *Anglo-Norman Studies*, 6 (1984), pp. 122–35, at 122; and N. WEBBER, *The Evolution of Norman Identity, 911–1154*, Woodbridge, 2005, p. 13. The impression from Dudo's words is that he did not start writing immediately and could dedicate more time to the project only after Richard I's death; therefore, *c.* 996 seems more appropriate than *c.* 994–96 or *c.* 994–*c.* 1002 for the starting date. For the year of completion, see n. 7 above.

consensus that *HN* was published in two authorial recensions, an earlier "prose redaction" and a later "verse redaction" complemented by a dedicatory letter and poems.[10] However, Benjamin Pohl has persuasively argued that the manuscripts carrying the "prose redaction" must ultimately descend from exemplars which did include the poems as well. The surviving evidence suggests that the redaction with the poems and the dedicatory letter, datable to 1015 × 1020, is the first and only version published by our author. The copies without the poems result from scribal activity at various stages of transmission.[11]

HN was a commission, an aspect of crucial importance if one wishes to understand the work in its context. A providential history, it furnished the new *gens* of the Normans with an heroic past, an etiological myth of equal worth to that of their Frankish neighbours.[12] *HN* recounts the arrival in Normandy of the Northmen in the early tenth century and their subsequent rise to dominion there, with special emphasis on the process of Christianization. The work concludes with the death of Duke Richard I in 996.[13] *HN* was the first comprehensive history of the Northmen's

[10]   HUISMAN, "Notes", p. 135. Huisman dated the two redactions to *c.* 996 and *c.* 1015 respectively.

[11]   POHL, *Dudo of St Quentin's* Historia Normannorum, pp. 84–108, 136–42. Cf. L. SHOPKOW, *History and Community: Norman Historical Writing in the Eleventh and Twelfth Centuries*, Washington, DC, 1997, p. 184, n. 29.

[12]   WEBBER, *Evolution of Norman Identity*, pp. 18–52. R. H. C. DAVIS, *The Normans and their Myth*, London, 1976, pp. 51–57. Dudo extended the genealogy of the Normans back to Troy through the mythical forefather Antenor: "Igitur Daci nuncupantur a suis Danai, vel Dani, glorianturque se ex Antenore progenitos; qui, quondam Trojae finibus depopulatis, mediis elapsus Achivis, Illyricos fines penetravit cum suis"; *HN*, ed. LAIR, p. 130. Tracing a nation's lineage to Troy was commonplace, already done in Frankish contexts with reference to the same Antenor. Recourse to Antenor, then, was to demonstrate that the Normans and the Franks shared in the same cultural heritage and were equals. For Dudo's employment of the concept *translatio imperii*, see POHL, *Dudo of St Quentin's* Historia Normannorum, pp. 124–36, 197–223. For structural resonances with Bede's *Historia ecclesiastica*, see L. SHOPKOW, "The Carolingian world of Dudo of Saint-Quentin", *Journal of Medieval History*, 15 (1989), pp. 19–37, at 29.

[13]   Dudo styles Richard I as "dux Northmannorum", e.g. *HN*, ed. LAIR, p. 267. He uses the title of duke as well for Rollo and William I Longsword: "vade nunc ad Robertum ducem", "gloriosissimus dux praepotensque comes Willelmus"; *ibid.*, pp. 172 and 179 respectively. It is unlikely that the Norman

settlement in what became Normandy.[14] It made an impact, at least in the long run. It served as a key source for later Anglo-Norman historians, such as William of Jumièges and William of Malmesbury. *HN* survives today in fourteen manuscripts. Their chronological distribution suggests a moderate but sustained interest from the eleventh to the thirteenth century.[15] Neither autographs nor primary copies survive. The oldest extant manuscripts, Bern, Bürgerbibliothek, Bongars Cod. 390 and Rouen, BM, 1173/Y11, date roughly from 1050–1075.[16]

HN is prosimetric, that is, prose is interspersed by verse: the work includes ninety-one poems.[17] The testimony they offer as to

---

rulers were officially dukes before the time of Richard II. Dudo may well have used the word "dux" as a general term for a military leader. While I follow Dudo's practice of using the terms "duke" and "ducal court", since they adequately describe the position and powers of Richard II's predecessors, I acknowledge that as a technical term "duke" is inaccurate before his time. Cf. WEBBER, *The Evolution of Norman Identity*, pp. 29–30.

[14]   POHL, *Dudo of St Quentin's* Historia Normannorum, pp. 34–35. Dudo's sources are a much debated topic. The present consensus is that he utilized written works, such as Flodoard of Reims' *Annals*, and relied on oral tradition. Dudo credits Count Rolf of Ivry as his main source in poem 5, as demonstrated by its rubric "Versus ad Comitem Rodulfum, hujus operis relatorem"; *HN*, ed. LAIR, pp. 125–26. On Count Rolf, see further below, n. 37.

[15]   POHL, *Dudo of St Quentin's* Historia Normannorum, pp. 18–33, Appendices 1 and 2.

[16]   Bern, Bongars Cod. 390 was copied in Normandy, *c.* 1050–1075, and Rouen, BM, 1173/Y11 in Jumièges, Normandy, *c.* 1050–1075; POHL, *Dudo of St Quentin's* Historia Normannorum, p. 263, Appendix 1.

[17]   The total number of poems is in some respects open to discussion. Lair does not number the poems in his edition, and there is some disagreement about which poems are individual pieces. For instance, while Christiansen numbered eighty-nine poems in his translation, Pohl suggests that Christiansen's poem li is composed of two discrete items since a rubric "Hic loquitur ad librum" follows line 16 in three manuscripts: CCCC 276 (fol. 95ʳ), BL, Royal 13 B. xiv (fol. 42ʳ), and Antwerp, Museum Plantin-Moretus/Prentenkabinet, 17.2 (fol. 43ᵛ); POHL, *Dudo of St Quentin's* Historia Normannorum, p. 268. Another case is Christiansen's poem xiii, interrupted by the rubric "Oratio eleaico carmine decursa" after line 74 in the above-mentioned three manuscripts (fols 64ᵛ, 8ʳ and 11ᵛ respectively); see CHRISTIANSEN, *History of the Normans*, pp. 23–25, and *HN*, ed. LAIR, pp. 138–40. The total would then be ninety-one; POHL, *Dudo of St Quentin's* Historia Normannorum, p. 68, n. 69 arrives at the same figure. I have included Christiansen's numbering in Table 1 for reference.

whom Dudo intended his piece to be received — the subject of the
third section of this essay — are central to my main argument.
The work is divided into four books, each attending to the life
and times of a different Norman leader. As a result, *HN* reads as
a serial biography of "Hasting" (*Alstignus*), Rollo, William I Longsword, and Richard I.[18] The books grow in length as the text
progresses. The crux of the whole work stands out clearly: the
fourth book on Richard I is longer than the three preceding ones
put together.[19] The fourth book is also characterized by a higher
literary ambition. It carries a large proportion of the poems,
fifty-two out of ninety-one, as itemized in Table 3. Their metrical
variation is likewise wider; in Book IV the reader encounters the
bewildering variety of thirty-three different metres whereas in the
preceding three books there are only eight. Table 4 summarizes
the distribution of metres.[20]

HN boasts a wealth of paratextual elements. Each book is preceded by prefatory texts, both in verse and prose, and each book
ends with an epilogue. The first book — and thus the whole work
— goes with ten prefatory texts, the second book with two, the

[18]   Serial biographies had roots in antique and subsequent Christian literature, such as Suetonius' *De vita Caesarum*, the *De viris illustribus* tradition
and episcopal *gesta* as well as Bede's *Historia ecclesiastica*; SHOPKOW, "The
Carolingian world", pp. 27–29. The leaders personified *Normannitas* and their
whole new *gens*; WEBBER, *The Evolution of Norman Identity*, p. 33.

[19]   The first three books and the prefatory matter together amount to
roughly nine tenths of the length of Book IV; CHRISTIANSEN, *History of the
Normans*, p. xiii. The prefatory matter of the fourth book, comprising fifteen poems and a prose preface — more than the prefatory matter of all
the previous books put together — likewise accentuates the pre-eminence of
Book IV and its protagonist, Richard I; *HN*, ed. LAIR, pp. 210–18. Dudo
himself draws a distinction between the last book and the preceding ones
in poem 54: previously he has written only about the deeds of the Danes,
but now a "daunting mass rises before him", more important than the previous ones; "Dacorum olim, themata vili,/Ardua currenti mihi gesta/Consurgit
moles modo torva"; *HN*, ed. LAIR, p. 215, translation CHRISTIANSEN, *History
of the Normans*, p. 91.

[20]   These figures are based on Christiansen's division of poetic metres;
CHRISTIANSEN, *History of the Normans*, pp. 236–37, with the corrections
noted above in n. 17.

third with three, and the fourth with sixteen.[21] Several poems
within the text carry passages of paratextual nature, such as
direct addresses to readers or dedicatory verses to patrons. The
poems and paratexts are of significance here as they provide insights into Dudo's authorial process, ending with publication. It is
on their evidence that this essay seeks to contextualize publishing
in a social framework. The obvious starting point for this inquiry
is the dedicatory letter preceding the work. Identifying one dedicatee and three commissioners by name, the letter furnishes the
fundamental parameters for this essay.

The Dedication and Commissions

The addressee of Dudo's dedicatory letter is Bishop Adalbero of
Laon.[22] Adalbero was one of the greatest sources of ecclesiastical
power in the Frankish kingdom and close to King Robert II. He
was a famously learned man and a poet.[23] The cathedral school
was especially famous during his incumbency. The choice of Adalbero as the dedicatee seems likely to have been connected to
Dudo's relocation to Saint-Quentin, although his exact motives are
not clear. Several previous attempts to account for Dudo's choice

---

[21]   The prefaces to the first book are, in the order of appearance, the dedicatory letter, verse "Allocutio ad librum", poem to Richard II, verse "Trepidatio et dissuasio", poem to Archbishop Robert of Rouen, poem to Count
Rolf, three more poems to Archbishop Robert of Rouen, and a prayer; *HN*,
ed. LAIR, pp. 120–28. These pieces act as a preface to the whole work. The
other books have prefatory materials of varying length and number, which
concern the book in question and its protagonist rather than the whole
work. The second book, on Rollo, has a verse preface and a prayer; *ibid.*,
pp. 138–40. The third book, on William, has a verse preface, a prefatory
prayer, and a prose preface; *ibid.*, pp. 176–79. The fourth book, on Richard I,
is prefaced by eleven poems on the Muses and their praises to Richard I, a
verse preface addressed to Archbishop Robert, a verse preface on Richard I,
a prayer, another verse preface to Archbishop Robert, and a prose preface;
ibid., pp. 210–18.

[22]   "Inclyto et pie venerando, quem genus ornat, sapientia decorat, Adal-
beroni episcopo sanctae Dei Laudunensis ecclesiae cathedra residenti, sibi
commissarum ovium ducamen ante divinae majestatis conspectum, Dudo,
super congregationem Sancti Quintini decanus"; *ibid.*, p. 115.

[23]   One poem by Adalbero has been preserved, the *Carmen ad Rotbertum
regem*, a satirical piece dedicated to king Robert II written *c.* 1026 when the
king was still in his adolescence; *PL*, 141, cols 771–86.

of dedicatee have been made.[24] One approach has been to situate the dedication in a larger framework, to explain it from the perspective of major fluctuations in political and cultural currents. For instance, it has been proposed that *HN* was used as a tool for political rapprochement between the Franks and the Normans — either a recognition of an alliance between the parties or an attempt to establish one.[25] However, there is no evidence to connect *HN* to any specific political *entente*. The fact that the work was published only after Dudo had left Normandy likewise undermines arguments to the same effect. Alternatively, it has been suggested that the dedication to Adalbero stemmed from Dudo's anti-Cluniac sentiments. Yet, Adalbero became widely known as a champion of the anti-Cluniac cause only after Dudo had dedicated *HN* to him.[26] The dedicatory letter and *HN* do not betray any hint of sentiments that could be held as somehow anti-Cluniac. If there were immediate political motivations at play in *HN* in addition to the evident efforts to validate the Normans as a *gens*, they are not obvious to modern readers. Attempts have also been made to explain the dedication in the framework of a personal connection between Adalbero and Dudo.[27] No evidence of such a relationship

[24] CHRISTIANSEN, *History of the Normans*, pp. xxvii–xxix provides an overview of four most common interpretations. According to him "none of these four explanations [...] is wholly satisfactory".

[25] SHOPKOW, "Carolingian world", p. 33.

[26] As per Volpelius-Holzendorff, according to CHRISTIANSEN, *History of the Normans*, pp. xi–xii, xxviii. Volpelius-Holzendorff's dissertation is unpublished, and I have not had the opportunity of consulting it.

[27] A close relationship between Adalbero and Dudo has been argued for on the basis of an earlier, false supposition that a prose redaction of *HN* was written in the 990s. The same scholar has also proposed that an early copy of Flodoard's *Annals* was made by Dudo himself in Laon, the main evidence for which is a copy possibly having the title *Gesta Normannorum*. This is a distant possibility at best. It cannot be known who was responsible for the copy of *Annals* and where this was made; and the said title may have been a later addition. S. LECOUTEUX, "Une reconstitution hypothétique du cheminement des Annales de Flodoard, depuis Reims jusqu'à Fécamp", *Tabularia*, Guillaume de Volpiano: Fécamp et l'histoire normande, published online 15 January 2004 (accessed 19 April 2019): <http://journals.openedition.org/tabularia/1923>, DOI: 10.4000/tabularia.1923, pp. 7–10, 32–36. SHOPKOW, "The Carolingian world", pp. 22–27, puts forth Liège as the probable place of Dudo's earlier education on the grounds of her stylistical analysis of *HN* and

prior to *HN* exists, however.[28] Nor was Adalbero Dudo's direct superior. The deans of Saint-Quentin were directly subject to the counts of Vermandois, and Saint-Quentin belonged to the diocese of Noyon.[29] The primary reason for Dudo's having dedicated his work to Adalbero could hardly have been political or on the basis of a personal friendship. A fourth approach to account for the dedication is that Dudo was seeking to benefit from his new position as dean of Saint-Quentin and gain literary recognition outside Normandy.[30] Subscribing to that argument, this essay considers the dedicatory letter in terms of what such letters tended to be: a tool for publication.

To appreciate the dedication to Adalbero in context, the roles of all parties involved in publication and the target audiences must

its allusions and quotations. Her reasoning is plausible and, at the very least, shows that Dudo is unlikely to have received his education with Adalbero at Reims under Gerbert of Aurillac.

[28] Dudo recounts having only heard of Adalbero's fame and refers to his desire to visit him: "Quocirca, memorande Pater, postquam inclyta fama ex tuis miris actibus expressa aures meas irrupit, animis meis indesinenter stimulos ad te divertendi ministravit"; *HN*, ed. LAIR, p. 118. Therefore, Dudo could hardly have had an active or very deep relationship with Adalbero, even though some form of prior acquaintanceship is possible. The dedicatory letter does not convey references to any existant personal relationship.

[29] The collegiate church of Saint-Quentin was established in the tenth century when the counts of Vermandois, especially Albert I († 987) replaced the monks of the former monastery with secular canons. The counts retained the titular abbacy and appointed a dean to preside over the canons. The deans acted directly under the counts' direction and reported to them, not to the bishops of Noyon or the archbishops of Reims; POHL, *Dudo of St Quentin's* Historia Normannorum, pp. 110–11; CHRISTIANSEN, *History of the Normans*, p. xxvii; C. C. BRINKMANN, "Dudos Dedikationen: Formen und Funktionen der Widmung in der *Historia Normannorum* des Dudo von St. Quentin", in *Literarische Widmungen im Mittelalter und in der Renaissance: Konzepte – Praktiken – Hintergründe*, ed. by C.-F. BIERITZ, C. C. BRINKMANN, T. HAYE, Stuttgart, 2019 (Quellen und Untersuchungen zur Lateinischen Philologie des Mittelalters, Band 21), pp. 75–100, at 95.

[30] CHRISTIANSEN, *History of the Normans*, pp. xxvii–xxviii; SHOPKOW, *History and Community*, pp. 187–88. POHL, *Dudo of St Quentin's* Historia Normannorum, pp. 107–08, regards the reasons for the dedication to be two-fold: Adalbero was a famous literary figure, and Dudo earnestly sought "peer-review" and proof-reading from him. BRINKMANN, "Dudos Dedikationen", pp. 96, 100, considers Adalbero the central figure in the publication and thinks that *HN* was aimed primarily at the Capetian court.

be identified. Dudo's initial incentive to write is presented in the dedicatory letter. The project began as a commission from Duke Richard I (932–996), in whose court Dudo was employed in an administrative role. By Dudo's own account, Richard requested that he write about the deeds and habits of the Normans and the laws the duke had established in the lands conquered by Rollo, his ancestor.[31] Duke Richard did not live to see the work's completion; he died soon after the commission.[32] His son and successor, Richard II (996–1026) and his half-brother, Count Rolf of Ivry († after 1015/17) encouraged, or ordered, Dudo to continue writing the text, which he had merely started by that time.[33] By ensuring that the commission still stood, Richard II and Rolf of Ivry essentially recommissioned Dudo. Dudo belittled his own volition

---

[31] "Certum te reddere volo, ut non rearis me huic operi haesisse voluntarie, nec illud spontanea voluntate coepisse. Ante biennum mortis ejus ut more frequentativo fui apud eximium ducem Richardum, Willelmi marchionis filium, volens ei reddere meae servitutis officium, propter innumera beneficia quae absque meo merito mihi dignatus erat impartiri. Qui quadam die adgrediens coepit brachiis piissimi amoris me amplecti, suisque dulcissimis sermonibus trahere, atque precibus jocundis mulcere, quia etiam detestari et jurare in charitate, ut, si qua possem ratione, animis suis diu desideratis moderer: scilicet ut mores actusque telluris Normannicae, quid etiam proavi sui Rollonis quae posuit in regno jura describerem"; *HN*, ed. LAIR, p. 119. Dudo also refers later to the commission by Richard, in a poem to Archbishop Robert in which he urges the archbishop to look upon his composition, which "Richard the famous in this fleeting world, and/Claimant by right of the country eternal,/Made me write, albeit with brevity" ("Ricardi celebris orbi labanti,/Aeterna patria, jure potentis,/Quanquam sat breviter scribere fecit"); *ibid.*, p. 126, translation CHRISTIANSEN, *History of the Normans*, p. 12.

[32] "Stylus nostrae imperitiae nedum primas partes operis attigerat, heu pro dolor! quum lacrumabilis fama Ricardum, toto orbe principem, obiisse nuntiavit"; *HN*, ed. LAIR, p. 119.

[33] "Omnia haec in dolore hujus principis postposuissem, propter nimium fletum intolerabilemque planctum, qui non solum cor meum, verum etiam totius corporis membra quassans torquebat, nisi per praecellentissimum filium ejus, patricium Ricardum, adhuc superstitem, et praecipuum comitem Rodulfum res eadem repraesentaretur. Instistunt ambo praecibus, ut quod memorabilis vitae dux Ricardus precando praeceperat exsequerer; et ne propositum, quod illi spoponderam, in bilinguitatis vitium versum, videretur ullo mendacii inquinamento pollui, sed pollere totius modullis intellectus intimis, contestantur. Acquiescens ergo praeceptis precibusque eorum, opus exsecutus sum quod, licet dialecticis syllogismis, nec rhetoricis argumentis non glorietur"; *ibid.*, pp. 119–20.

to write according to the common medieval *topos* of authorial modesty.[34] The way he communicated the terms of his commission, namely that it had been renewed, also has parallels in earlier literature.[35] Yet, there is no reason to think that compliance with cliché would have been the sole reason for Dudo to invoke the circumstances of his commission.[36] The affair was more than a literary gesture. As a dynastic history, *HN* served the interests of the Norman court at large. Support by the court was also practical and influenced Dudo's work; Count Rolf's oral accounts were among his main sources.[37]

---

[34] This model in which the author laments his unworthiness to write and does so only by command of a superior was prevalent in Latin prefaces throughout the Middle Ages. It derived from classical authors and was common in saints' lives of the Antonian model. T. JANSON, "Latin prose prefaces, studies in literary conventions", *Acta Universitatis Stockholmiensis, Studia Latina Stockholmiensia*, 13 (1964), pp. 116–40; B. COLGRAVE, *Two Lives of Saint Cuthbert: A Life by an Anonymous Monk of Lindisfarne and Bede's Prose Life*, Cambridge, 1985, p. 310.

[35] One parallel is Heiric of Auxerre's prologue, which likewise presents a setting of commission and recommission after the first commissioner had passed away; MGH, *Poetae*, 3, pp. 428–32; CHRISTIANSEN, *History of the Normans*, p. xxiii.

[36] BRINKMANN, "Dudos Dedikationen", p. 84.

[37] Count Rolf is styled the "narrator" or even one type of "author" of the work in the rubric and the text of the verse eulogy: "Versus ad comitem Rodulfum, hujus operis relatorem", "Cujus quae constant libro hoc conscripta relatu,/Digessi attonitus, tremulus, hebes, anxius, anceps"; *HN*, ed. LAIR, pp. 125 and 126 respectively. The rubric could also refer to the recommissioning of the work, as noted by CHRISTIANSEN, *History of the Normans*, p. 180, n. 49. However, the text seems to prove Rolf was one of Dudo's main sources; this reading of the evidence seems to be the more usual one. William of Jumièges also attributes to Count Rolf the role of eyewitness and main source: "Principium namque narrationis usque ad Ricardum secundum a Dudonis, periti uiri, hystoria collegi, qui quod posteris propagandum karte commendauit a Rodulfo comite, primi Ricardi fratre, diligenter exquisuit"; *The Gesta Normannorum Ducum of William of Jumièges, Orderic Vitalis, and Robert of Torigni*, ed. E. M. C. VAN HOUTS, 2 vols, Oxford, 1992–1995, vol. 1, p. 4. What is more, Dudo was the scribe of the charter documenting Rolf's 1101 donation to St Ouen; DOUGLAS, "The ancestors of William Fitz Osbern", pp. 69–73. Rolf also acted as a mediator when Dudo transferred his benefices to the church of Saint-Quentin in 1015; *Gallia Christiana*, 11, Appendix, n. 2, cols 284–85.

The dedicatory letter thus records that the Norman lords commissioned *HN* and that Dudo, somewhat surprisingly perhaps,
chose to dedicate it to Bishop Adalbero of Laon. However, if the
testimonies of *HN*'s other paratexts are accounted for, a more
varied picture emerges. As mentioned above, each of the four
books is prefaced by one or more dedicatory poems and some
poems within the text proper have a dedicatory function. In
these, another son of Duke Richard I rises to the fore, namely,
Robert II the Dane (989–1037), archbishop of Rouen and count
of Évreux. Archbishop Robert was an important man at Rouen
and in Normandy. A member of the ducal family, he was a powerful lay magnate; as archbishop of Rouen, he was at the apex of
ecclesiastical power in the duchy. Robert was a great benefactor
to his cathedral.[38] His contribution to the advancement of education was considerable.[39] While not mentioning Robert in the
dedicatory letter, Dudo addressed seven lengthy eulogies to him,
more than to any other person apart from the four protagonists.[40]
When we consider the way the poems to Robert are arranged
within *HN*, his centrality becomes even more evident. Robert was
the addressee of four poems prefacing Book I (and, as such, the

[38]   ZIOLKOWSKI, *Jezebel*, p. 40; B. S. BACHRACH, "Writing history for a
Latin audience *c.* 1000: Dudo of Saint Quentin at the Norman court", *Haskins
Society Journal*, 20 (2008), pp. 58–77, at 66. In the history of the archbishops
of Rouen, written in the time of Archbishop John II (1067–1079), Robert was
depicted as a great benefactor of the church, although his wordly style of
living was lamented; he was married with sons. He was strongly contrasted
with his predecessor, Hugh, as a way of highlighting the financial developments and ecclesiastical reforms achieved under Robert; Rouen, BM, Y 27,
pp. 32–33 (later pagination); printed in *PL*, 147, col. 277. The tone is repeated
in the verse catalogue of the archbishops following the prose history: "Successit hugo legis domini uiolator,/Clara stirpe satus. sed christi lumine cassus./
Insignis presul claris natalibus ortus, Rotbertus felix deuoto fine quieuit";
Rouen, Y 27, p. 39.

[39]   The first decades of the eleventh century saw an advancement of education in Normandy, a program which modern scholarship credits to Archbishop Robert; ZIOLKOWSKI, *Jezebel*, pp. 37–47; C. J. MCDONOUGH, "Warner
of Rouen, Moriuht: a Norman Latin poem from the early eleventh century",
Studies and Texts, 121 (1995), p. 9; CHRISTIANSEN, *History of the Normans*,
p. xi; BACHRACH, "Writing history", pp. 65–66.

[40]   The number depends on how individual poems are counted, for which
see n. 17 above.

whole work).[41] He is also the only dedicatee of poems prefatory to Book IV, which was, as has been mentioned, the most hefty and important.[42] In addition, Robert features, again alone, in a poem towards the conclusion of Book IV's main narrative. The poem is situated immediately before the end of the account of Richard I's life; only Richard's death and a few pious acts follow the poem.[43] Excluding the four protagonists, *HN* praises no other living person as prominently as Robert. For instance, Richard II and Count Rolf, the declared commissioners, are addressed only in one poem each.[44]

The passages on Robert betray how Dudo perceived him in relation to his work. Robert is referred to as the author's patron.[45] He was requested to correct the work, thereby emphasizing his contribution to the authorial process and, by implication, his learning.[46] However, such requests were a literary convention and should not be taken as evidencing that the addressee would have complied. Dudo also requested that Adalbero amend the work.[47]

---

[41]   Prefatory material of Book I: dedicatory letter, *Allocutio ad librum*, verse to Duke Richard II, *Trepidatio et dissuasio*, verse to Archbishop Robert, verse to Count Rolf, verse to Archbishop Robert, verse to Archbishop Robert, verse to Archbishop Robert, prayer; *HN*, ed. LAIR, pp. 120–28.

[42]   Prefatory material of Book IV: Exhortations by the Muses (eleven poems), preface to Archbishop Robert, verse preface, prayer, preface to Archbishop Robert, prose preface; *ibid.*, pp. 210–18.

[43]   *Ibid.*, p. 292.

[44]   *Ibid.*, pp. 122, 125–26.

[45]   "O venerande, pie, recolende, verende patrone,/Praesul Rotberte, o recolende pie"; *ibid.*, p. 125.

[46]   "Quod restat siquidem, quodque instat, conditor almus,/Respice propitius, quaeso, favens precibus./Praesentes operas miserans compone, precamur,/Et sensus cumules, oraque fructifices"; *ibid.*, p. 217, lines 79–82. Christiansen notes that Archbishop Robert is not directly named in the poem, and the lines could alternatively be read as directed to God; CHRISTIANSEN, *History of the Normans*, p. 209, n. 315. Yet, the poem carries the rubric "Praefatio ad presulem Rotbertum" with slight variation in all the six manuscripts that have the poems: CCCC 276, fol. 95^v; Royal 13 B. xiv, fol. 42^v ("Prefacio ad presulem"); Antwerp, 17.2, fol. 44^r; Rouen, 1173/Y11, fol. 30^r; SBB-PK, Phill. 1854, fol. 48^v; and Cotton Nero D. viii, fol. 104^r.

[47]   "ut quae in hoc codice suis tenebris obscura videntur, per te ad lucem referantur"; *HN*, ed. LAIR, p. 118; "ut omnis scrupulositas injustae ambiguitatis tuis acutissimis bipennibus, ex purissimo calibe totius sapientiae confectis, funditus atque radicitus amputetur. Pene dimidia pars hujus operis

It should be mentioned that Robert was a patron of other writers, even if only one is known by name: Warner of Rouen dedicated his two known satires to Robert.[48] Although not mentioned in the dedicatory letter, Archbishop Robert was among Dudo's most significant patrons.[49] Indeed, Robert features so prominently in *HN* that if the work did not include the dedicatory letter, he could certainly be taken to have been its primary dedicatee. The frequent addresses to Robert imply that he had been Dudo's principal literary patron in the course of composition. Adalbero of Laon, in contrast, makes no appearance in *HN* other than in the dedicatory letter.

minime videtur respicere ad negotium utilitatis, nisi, te messore, sarriatur carduis superfluitatis"; *ibid.*, p. 119. See BRINKMANN, "Dudos Dedikationen", p. 83.

[48] Warner was a grammarian, a poet, Dudo's contemporary, and the author of at least two satirical poems written for the Norman elite. Warner dedicated his first satire, known as *Moriuht* after its protagonist, to Archbishop Robert and Duchess Gunnor: "Rotberto domino subnixo presulis ostro,/Et matri domine illius eximiae, Vuarnerius dubia non spe confisus utrisque/Nunc et post obitum uiuere per Dominum"; BnF, lat. 8121A, fol. 2^r; ed. McDONOUGH, "Moriuht", p. 72. His second satire, often referred to as "Poem to the Monk of Saint-Michel", was dedicated to Archbishop Robert: "Rotberto doctis fulgenti semper alumnis,/Warnerius famulus quicquid amat dominus"; L. MUS-SET, "Le satiriste Garnier de Rouen et son milieu", *Revue du Moyen Âge Latin: Études, Textes, Chronique, Bibliographie*, 10/4 (1954), pp. 237–66, at 259, lines 1–2. Both of Warner's works were written *c.* 996–1026, roughly contemporarily with *HN*; *ibid.*, pp. 243–44. Other Norman poets contemporary with Dudo and Warner are elusive figures. Warner's *Moriuht* is an invective against this Irish grammarian, resident in Rouen, and quotes a line from a poem supposedly written by Moriuht. Furthermore, the two poems *Jezebel* and *Semiramis* were probably Norman products of about the same time; see, respectively, ZIOLKOWSKI, *Jezebel*, and P. DRONKE, *Poetic Individuality in the Middle Ages. New Departures in Poetry 1000–1150*, pp. 66–113. Both *Jezebel* and *Semiramis* are in style and substance connected with the literary circle in Rouen to which Robert's patronage was crucial. They survive in a single manuscript. As the book also carries Warner's satires, some scholars attribute them to him, while others consider them anonymous productions from the same circle; e.g. ZIOLKOWSKI, *Jezebel*, p. 37; DRONKE, *Poetic Individuality*, pp. 80–84. Furthermore, two grammarians, Hugh and Albert, are known from Rouen. Dudo mentions lively competition and vituperation among poets in Normandy (which manifested also in *Moriuht*); *HN*, ed. LAIR, p. 120, lines 13–16.

[49] BRINKMANN "Dudos Dedikationen", pp. 97–98 also notes Robert's centrality, although with some reservations.

Remembrance and Target Audiences

A recurring theme in the poems to Archbishop Robert is the exhortation to remember. In the beginning of the first poem to him, Dudo uses a repetitive mantra: "Remember, O remember his memorable concerns/How worthily he lived: now, remember O!"[50] It is of interest that most of these passages in *HN* are directed to Archbishop Robert.[51] Robert is also referred to directly as a reader in several addresses. "Look upon this composition of mine!/ With holy hand, touch what I bring you, beseeching,/— Things unattempted by masters of grammar:/And search for and read of the deeds of the past", Dudo beseeches Robert. "Accept what I have revealed/In the form of a treatise prosaic/[...] and,/As you read [...]/Ponder them long, and whatever/Good things you find there, remember." "Imitate now these/Deeds of your father/ Faithfully published/Clearly illumined/Memorable deeds/*As you will find them/Here in this volume* [emphasis mine]."[52] It is obvious that Dudo envisaged the archbishop reading his work. These exhortations should be understood as something more than merely a suggestion about preserving a personal memory of the deeds recounted. The import of Dudo's words is in fact an insistence that Norman history is remembered *as it is written in* HN. The exhortations are not the words of a man begging for attention or readership; rather, they bespeak his confidence in the importance of his

---

[50] "Suspice gesta tui proavi, praesul recolende,/Et locupletis avi suscipe gesta tui./Quin etiam meritis patris super aethera non,/Participis Christo quin etiam meritis./Illius atque bonis animum depasce benignis,/Instrue te exercens illius atque bonis./Mirificos recolens actus sermones retracta,/Affatusque suos mirificos recolens./Et memora, memora causas ejus memorandas,/Digne quae gessit nunc memora, memora"; *HN*, ed. LAIR, pp. 123–24, translation CHRISTIANSEN, *History of the Normans*, pp. 9–10.

[51] Six poems (4, 6, 7, 8, 51 and 88) addressed to Archbishop Robert refer to Duke Richard I, exhorting the archbishop to remember his father; *HN*, ed. LAIR, pp. 123–25, 126–27, 127–28, 214 and 292 respectively.

[52] "Quae digesta meo, suscipe, sensu./Sacra tange manu quae fero supplex,/ Intemptata sciis grammaticae artis:/Ac rimare legens quaeque peracta.", "Ingenio reserata meo/Thematis ordina prosaici/[...]/Gesta legens, replicando diu,/Quae bona repperies memora.", "Tunc imitare/Hos patris actus,/Numine claro,/Satque retracta/Quos memoralis/Inveniesque,/Quamvis inepto/Codice in isto"; *HN*, ed. LAIR, pp. 126, 126–27 and 128 respectively, translations CHRISTIANSEN, *History of the Normans*, pp. 12, 13 and 14 respectively.

work to Robert. Dudo considered Robert the primary receiver and
keeper of memory within the Norman elite. He exhorts the archbishop to ensure that memories of the Norman past will be kept
alive. *HN* was to be the prime instrument of that project. That
role as guardian of the past explains in part why Robert was so
central to publication efforts. It was probably also a factor that in
his capacity as archbishop of Rouen, Robert would have had the
means to stimulate dissemination.[53]

The concept of remembrance found application elsewhere in
HN. An address to Duke Richard II, which concludes a poem
dedicated to him, exhorts him to remember.[54] In contrast to the
exhortations to Robert, this one has a less commanding tone. The
address to Richard shows that Dudo also envisaged lay magnates
as recipients of his work. Most men of that class were illiterate or
only partly literate. In such a case, reception could have taken
place through the mediation of oral recitation, either in Latin or a
vernacular rendition.[55]

Dudo obviously considered poetry to be the optimal means of
ensuring that memory was transmitted through the generations.
He lamented, no doubt with rhetorical exaggeration, that he could
not write the whole thing in verse; "expressed in this [verse heroic],
'men's valiant deeds' [would] live on".[56] He also connected verse
to remembering elsewhere, as in the poem *Apostropha ad Urbem*,

[53]   BRINKMANN, "Dudos dedikationen", p. 98.

[54]   "Quae cernis memora libro modeste;/Hic despasce tuum cor, atque pec-
tus,/Innecti ut valeas quibus recensis"; *HN*, ed. LAIR, p. 122.

[55]   SHOPKOW, *History and Community*, pp. 184–87; SHOPKOW, "The Carolingian world", p. 31. Pohl has pointed out that several manuscripts bear *positurae*, punctuation apparently meant to ease recitation and rhyme bracing.
He argues that the *positurae*, together with illumination in some copies, prove
the "multimedia" nature of *HN*, that its message was transmitted through
aural and visual mediums, in addition to translations, to the non-Latinate
Norman courtly audience. B. POHL, "Poetry, punctuation and performance:
Was there an aural context for Dudo of Saint-Quentin's *Historia Normannorum*?", in *Tabularia. Autour de Serlon de Bayeux: la poésie normande aux XIe–
XIIe siècles* (2016), published online 28 September 2016 (accessed January
30, 2020): <http://journals.openedition.org/tabularia/2781>, DOI: 10.4000/
tabularia.2781, p. 194.

[56]   "Rusticus inscitiae quamquam nostrae stylus ornet/Diversi variis hene-
ris metris opus istud,/Praevacuum nimis, indiguumque opis, artis inops-
que,/Rhetoricique favi redolentis nectari exsors,/Heroico potius metro pol-

directed to the city of Rouen: "But as in days past I was not of your sojourners,/I cannot rightly recount what he endeavoured to do./If only you had possessed some warbling poets/By whom the good he pursued would have been matter for study!/The teachers are to blame, that you lack rhetoricians;/Educate now in the arts boys unacquainted with metre/That what the great father's posterity achieves/They may know how to contrive into verse polymetric."[57] Dudo attributed a dearth of evidence for the Norman past to the fact that there had not been poets to compose verses about it. It was his mission to make sure that the same thing would not happen again.

A School-Book for Teaching Poetry and Grammar

The poems in *HN* betray yet another intended audience, the schools. Manifesting Dudo's passion for versification, the poems are a central component in *HN*'s design. A great many metres, thirty-three in total, are employed, some rare and obscure.[58] The variety is such that it certainly reflects the writer's appreciation of the needs of his target audiences.[59] The poems are itemized in Table 1; their number per book and the variety of metres are summarized in Tables 3 and 4. I will refer to the poems by their numbering in Table 1.

lere deceret;/Hoc lucubrata vigent quia fortia facta virorum"; *HN*, ed. LAIR, p. 280, translation CHRISTIANSEN, *History of the Normans*, p. 154.

[57] "Sed, quod colonus non fui quondam tuus,/Nescio digerere quae studuit facere./Utinam poetas possideres garrulos,/Quis bona quae studuit elucubrata forent./Quod vatibus culpa est, cares rhetoribus./Instrue nunc pueros artibus innumeros,/Successio quidquid peraget magni patris,/Carmina multicano elucubrare sciant"; *HN*, ed. LAIR, p. 273, translation CHRISTIANSEN, *History of the Normans*, p. 147.

[58] For a full list, see CHRISTIANSEN, *History of the Normans*, pp. 236–37, Appendix. This has some minor errors, of which his footnotes are free: as for Dactylic hexameters, xliv should read liv, and lxxxvii should read lxxxiv and lxxxviii; as for Phaelecian Hendecasyllabic pentameter, lxiv should read lxv. Note that Christiansen's terminology sometimes differs from those in the rubrics.

[59] Poetry was the most important mode of literature aimed at members of the Norman court. Examples include Warner's two satires, *Jezebel*, *Semiramis*, and the anonymous *Encomium Emmae Reginae*. POHL, "Poetry, punctuation and performance", pp. 192–93.

In those six extant *HN* manuscripts that convey its poems,[60] as
many as fifty-one poems are accompanied by explanatory rubrics.[61] These identify the metre of the poem in question.[62] Explanations for well-known metres are usually brief.[63] More exotic metres
are introduced in detail so that the poetic feet are identified and
their order is given.[64] The explanatory rubrics help the reader con-
ceive of the syllabic structure and the prosody and rhythm for

[60]   SBB-PK, Phill. 1854; Rouen, 1173/Y11; CCCC 276; Royal 13 B. xiv;
Antwerp, 17.2; and Cotton Nero D. viii; for descriptions, see POHL, *Dudo of
St Quentin's* Historia Normannorum, pp. 18–33.

[61]   *Ibid.*, pp. 264–67, Appendix 3, lists forty-nine explanatory rubrics.
In addition to those, there are two more rubrics found in manuscripts:
"ΜΩΝΟΚΩΛΩ ΜΩΝΩϹΤΡΟΦΩ DECVRSA [/DVCVRSA]" precedes poem 1
in CCCC 276, fol. 57[r], Rouen, 1173/Y11, fol. 2[r], SBB-PK, Phill. 1854, fol. 4[r],
Royal 13 B. xiv, fol. 2[v], and Antwerp, 17.2, fol. 3[v]. The rubric "Heroicum"
precedes poem 84 in CCCC 276, fol. 123[v] ("Eloicum"), and Royal 13 B. xiv,
fol. 92[v] ("Heloicum").

[62]   The term "explanatory rubrics" was coined by POHL, *Dudo of St Quentin's* Historia Normannorum, pp. 146–51 and Appendix 3, pp. 264–67. I am
here indebted to his discussion as well as to Dr Pohl personally, who kindly
provided me with images of the Rouen, Royal, Anwerp, and Berlin manuscripts. The rubrics were largely overlooked in earlier research; Duchesne
omitted them altogether and Lair reported them in footnotes. The explanatory rubrics are sometimes accompanied by other rubrics, introducing the
addressee or the topic of the poem in question, e.g. "Metrum monocolon ascle-
piadum tetrastrophon constans pedibus quattuor spondeo duobus cori iambis
et pirrichio. Praefatio tercij libri", and "Apostropha ad Arnulfum. Metrum
gliconicum constans trocheo cori iambo et pirrichio"; CCCC 276, fols 78[v]
and 103[r] respectively. Often, especially in Book IV, poems are preceded by
explanatory rubrics alone; e.g. CCCC 276, fols 106[r], 107[v], 109[r].

[63]   For example, "Metrum heroicum cum elegiaco"; *HN*, ed. LAIR, p. 210,
n. 1.

[64]   For example, "Iambicum traicum fenarium metrum in quo et spondeus
et iambus et dactilus et anapestus in primo loco invenitur, in tercio semper
spondeus, in quinto saepissime spondeus"; *HN*, ed. LAIR, p. 212, n. 1. Some
explanatory rubrics run to forty words and take several lines in the manuscript. An extreme case is the explanatory rubric for poem 81, "Hoc genus
iambicum est yponatium"; *HN*, ed. LAIR, p. 270, n. 4. On CCCC 276, fol. 121[r]
the rubric fills eight lines, whereas the poem it serves is only seven lines long.
Most of the explanatory rubrics are five to ten words in length. On occasion
they betray difficulty in naming or describing the metre. Consider the rubric
for poem 78: "Metrum dactilicum alcmanium constans trimetro ypercatalec-
tus versus est cui una sillaba super est habet sibi subiectum feretrarium quod
constat spondeo dactilo item spondeo sed in loco primo spondeus est ubi ana-

recitation.[65] Equipped with explanatory rubrics, Dudo's poems exemplify a great variety of poetic metres, common and rare. By form and function, the poetic sections operate as a metrical text-book, such as Bede's *De arte metrica*.[66] In the latter, concise explanations of the syllabic structure and metre precede short specimen poems. The analogy between these portions of *HN* and textbooks on poetic metre is too clear to have been accidental. Dudo composed the explanatory rubrics, I argue, primarily for the benefit of the classroom.

Crucial to my argument is the question as to whether the explanatory rubrics were authorial or later insertions by an involved reader.[67] This problem arises from the fact that eight of the four-

pestum contra regulam in centi metro traditum inveniamus"; *ibid.*, p. 266, n. 1.

[65] In some manuscripts there are also diagrams, or braces to connect verses ending in rhyming syllables. These work as both didactic and recitative guides, making it possible to visualize the rhymes and the metre; POHL, "Poetry, punctuation and performance", *passim*, and his *Dudo of St Quentin's Historia Normannorum*, p. 151.

[66] For example, poem 42 is preceded by the explanatory rubric: "Metrum falleuticum, constans spondeo, dactilo et tribus trocheis"; *HN*, ed. LAIR, p. 211, n. 3. In his *De arte metrica*, Bede introduces this metre, the Phalaecian pentameter, with the words "Est igitur metrum dactylicum Falleucium pentametrum, quod constat ex spondeo et dactylo et tribus trocheis"; Bede, *De arte metrica*, ed. by B. KENDALL, Turnhout, 1975 (CCSL 123A), p. 132. The rubric for poem 44, in Sapphic pentameter, reads: "Metrum saphicum continuatum, constans trocheo spondeo et dactilo et duobus trocheis"; CCCC 276, fol. 93ᵛ (note that *HN*, ed. LAIR, p. 211, n. 6, erroneously wants the word "trocheo"). Cf. Bede, *De arte metrica*, ed. KENDALL, p. 132: "Metrum dactylicum Saphicum pentametrum constat ex trocheo, spondeo, dactylo, duobus trocheis, cui metro post tres uersus additur semis heroici uersus". CHRISTIANSEN, *History of the Normans*, p. 207, nn. 303, 305 notes that Dudo's explanatory rubrics give odd descriptions of the metres, disregarding, for example, choriamb as the second foot of the Phalaecian hendecasyllabic pentameter. This is, however, characteristic of Bede, as demonstrated in detail in S. HEIKKINEN, *The Christianisation of Latin Metre: A Study of Bede's De Arte Metrica*, Helsinki, 2012, pp. 141–52. Bede might well have been Dudo's source; at least, his rubrics testify to Bedan influence. Bede's *De arte metrica* was listed in the earliest booklist from Rouen, an inventory from the time of Archbishop Geoffrey (1111–1128); Rouen, Y 27, p. 128 (fol. lxiiʳ).

[67] For instance, Lair and Christiansen considered the explanatory rubrics a later addition: CHRISTIANSEN, *History of the Normans*, p. xxxvi, and pp. 206–08 nn. 301–07, 310; *HN*, ed. LAIR, p. 219, n. 6. Christiansen

teen extant manuscripts do not include the rubrics or the poems. No autograph, which would straightforwardly resolve the issue, survives. However, Benjamin Pohl has demonstrated that all the extant manuscripts ultimately descend from copies carrying the poems and that the latter's transmission from one generation to the next was a precarious affair. Importantly, some manuscripts make it evident that poems were deliberately omitted. For instance, BL, Cotton Claudius A. xii omits most of the poems and all the explanatory rubrics, although its direct exemplar, BL, Royal 13 B. xiv has them.[68] The tendency to exclude materials resulted in copies deprived not only of poems but also of the dedicatory letter to Adalbero.[69] This and certain other features in *HN*'s reception imply that its prosimetric nature met with a lukewarm reception in some readerships.[70] Copyists skipped the non-prose and/or non-narrative passages, deeming them superfluous. Explanatory rubrics naturally fell victim to elimination whenever poems they were connected to were omitted. The inclusion of the explanatory rubrics was not certain even if the pertinent poems were copied.[71]

attributed both the explanatory rubrics and the marginal glossae to a Canterbury scribe, whom he called the "C metrist".

[68]   POHL, *Dudo of St Quentin's* Historia Normannorum, pp. 27–28 and 30.

[69]   Bern, Bongars, Cod. 390 is a case in point. Written in Normandy *c.* 1050–1075, it is one of our oldest copies; POHL, *Dudo of St Quentin's* Historia Normannorum, pp. 22, 262. While the dedicatory letter and all poems bar four (10, 17–18 and 28; Bern, Bongars, Cod. 390, fols 2^v–3^r, 12^r–13^r and 32^r, respectively) are omitted, paraphs indicate from fol. 14^v onwards where missing poems ought to be. The manuscript obviously descends (ultimately) from an exemplar which had all the poems and, one assumes, also the dedicatory letter.

[70]   POHL, *Dudo of St Quentin's* Historia Normannorum, pp. 226–27. William of Jumièges, who frequently relied on *HN*, rejected Dudo's hermeunetic style completely and rarely quotes *HN* without thoroughly rephrasing the text. In the dedicatory letter to King William I he asserts that he avoids the "elegant and weighty style used by rhetoricians". Such statements were cliché but one is tempted to see a critical allusion to Dudo. VAN HOUTS, *The Gesta Normannorum Ducum*, I, pp. lv, 4–7. Robert of Torigni, however, reintroduced several chapters from Dudo into his recension of *Gesta Normannorum Ducum*; *ibid.*, pp. lxxx–lxxxi.

[71]   Explanatory rubrics were sometimes left out even when the exemplar supplied them. As shown in Table 1, Royal 13 B. xiv does not include three explanatory rubrics (poems 4, 80 and 87), which may be assumed to have been present in its exemplar.

Yet, all six manuscripts that convey the poems in a systematic manner have at least some explanatory rubrics, an obvious indication that the rubrics were part of *HN* at an early stage of transmission.[72]

The said six copies fall in two branches, something that suggests that the explanatory rubrics were not only very early, but also authorial. The first constellation includes the three copies that stand closest to the early dissemination. The two oldest manuscripts preserved, Rouen, BM, 1173/Y11 (Jumièges, *c.* 1050–1075) and SBB-PK, Phill. 1854 (Normandy, *c.* 1075–1100), only convey three explanatory rubrics, introducing poems 1, 2 and 13.[73] They must ultimately descend from a copy or copies which also carried the other rubrics, evidencing an early date for the rubrics' existence.[74] Importantly, the third manuscript in this group, Cotton Nero D. VIII (England *c.* 1175–1200), preserves five explanatory rubrics, those for poems 13, 86, 87, 88 and 89.[75] It has recently been argued that it is "extremely likely" that the Nero manuscript descends from the same early exemplar as the Rouen manuscript.[76] The odds are that the ultimate shared ancestor of the Rouen, Berlin, and Cotton Nero manuscripts had more explanatory rubrics than those three copies convey. In other words, explanatory rubrics were excluded in the course of transmission. What

[72]   According to HUISMAN, "Notes", p. 123, these six manuscripts represent the "verse redaction". There is some confusion in the argument, however: at p. 125, Leiden, Universiteitsbibliotheek, VLF 47 (France, *s.* xvi) is included in the group of manuscripts with the poems, but at p. 126 it is mentioned as one in which the poems are omitted. The Leiden manuscript omits all poems except for the final four lines of poem 10 (fol. 6ʳ), and poems 11, 17 and 18 (fols 9ᵛ–10ʳ and 15ᵛ–16ᵛ). It most likely descends directly from the Rouen manuscript; POHL, *Dudo of St Quentin's* Historia Normannorum, p. 27.

[73]   Rouen, 1173/Y11, fols 2ʳ, 2ᵛ and 7ʳ, and SBB-PK, Phill. 1854, fols 4ʳ, 5ʳ and 13ʳ.

[74]   POHL, *Dudo of St Quentin's* Historia Normannorum, pp. 32–33. The Rouen manuscript was to be a lavishly illuminated luxury copy. It was left unfinished for some reason. The absence of the explanatory rubrics was probably intentional, reflecting the purpose intended for the volume. As noted above, copyists whose main interest was *HN*'s historical value skipped the versifications and their rubrics. The Berlin manuscript might have been copied directly from the Rouen manuscript or a shared exemplar; *ibid.*, p. 23.

[75]   Cotton Nero D. VIII, fols 79ʳ, 127ʳ, 130ᵛ, 132ʳ, 133ᵛ.

[76]   POHL, *Dudo of St Quentin's* Historia Normannorum, p. 29.

is more, the rubrics of the first group match those in the second
group, to be introduced below. It is highly unlikely, then, that
explanatory rubrics would have been inserted at some later stage.
Such a scenario would mean either that several copyists made original contributions precisely to the same effect independently of
each other, or that transmission was strictly linear because textual variation between rubrics in different manuscripts is dimi-
nutive, mainly orthographic.[77] Neither scenario can carry weight.
To conclude, a single person must have been responsible for the
explanatory rubrics and they were present in the earliest phases
of dissemination observable to us.

The three manuscripts that constitute the second branch are
Cambridge, Corpus Christi College, 276 (St Augustine's abbey,
Canterbury, c. 1100–1125),78 BL, Royal 13 B. xiv (England,
c. 1150–1175),[79] and Antwerp, Museum Plantin-Moretus/Pren-
tenkabinet, 17.2 (England, c. 1175–1200).[80] The manuscripts are
closely related and probably shared an exemplar (or exemplars).[81]

[77] Christiansen notes one major difference in the rubrics in the endnotes
to his translation: the rubric of poem 42 differs in manuscripts CCCC 276 and
Royal 13 B. xiv (CHRISTIANSEN, *History of the Normans*, p. 207, n. 303). This
discrepancy, however, resulted from a scribal error: the copyist of Royal 13
B. xiv attached the explanatory rubric of poem 41 to poem 42 (fol. 40ʳ).

[78] CCCC 276 is a composite volume, incorporating two originally independent books, which were put together at St Augustine's abbey sometime in the
twelfth century; B. C. BARKER-BENFIELD, *St Augustine's Abbey, Canterbury*,
3 vols, London, 2008 (Corpus of British Medieval Library Catalogues, 13),
vol. 2, pp. 924–25. Datable to the late eleventh century, the first unit carries Paul the Deacon's redaction to Eutropius' *Breuiarium ab urbe condita*.
This study is concerned with the second unit, fols 55–134.

[79] POHL, *Dudo of St Quentin's* Historia Normannorum, p. 30.

[80] *Ibid.*, pp. 18–20.

[81] It has been suggested that CCCC 276 was the exemplar of the other two:
GELTING, "Courtly viking", p. 34. I will argue below why this seems unlikely.
CCCC 276 is a compilation. It has been proposed that it probably derived
HN from a Norman source, possibly from Mont Saint-Michel; POHL, *Dudo of
St Quentin's* Historia Normannorum, pp. 24–26, 70–72. Mont Saint-Michel,
as a ducal monastery, would presumably have acquired a copy not long after
the first publication. Pohl observes that this group of three manuscripts
reveals "considerable loyalty to the text's original form", and that they were
produced as part of the text's canonization in the Anglo-Norman collective
memory; *ibid.*, pp. 74–76, 241–42. CCCC 276 also includes some glosses in
the main hand, most of which are found in *HN*, ed. LAIR, pp. 210–13. They

In combination, these three volumes convey fifty-one explanatory rubrics. Their distribution is suggestive of a governing principle: their frequency of appearance corresponds to Dudo's emphases. Table 1 lays out the poems and their rubrics in all six manuscripts. The arrangement in the three English manuscripts is as follows. In the first three books the prefatory poems have explanatory rubrics, while the poems within the text proper and the epilogues lack them. Those poems in Books I–III that are unaccompanied by a rubric are in hexameter, apart from one in elegiac distich (no. 9); both metres would have been well known to those with any previous engagement with Latin poetry. Most of the explanatory rubrics are situated in the fourth book, where they accompany almost every poem. In Book IV only poems 51–58, 76, and 90–91 (the two final poems) are devoid of rubrics. The variety of metres in Book IV is also much greater, as presented in Table 4; its fifty-two poems are in thirty-three different metres, with only six in heroic verse. The application of rubrics in Book IV differs from that in Books I–III in that most of the poems within the text proper are also equipped with them. The same applies to about half of the poems in hexameter; those devoid of rubrics belong to the above-mentioned poems 51–58, 76 and 90–91. In Book IV their frequent application resonates with this section's importance and length over Books I–III.[82]

appear also in Royal 13 B. xiv, fol. 40. Additionally, CCCC 276, fol. 94^v has a marginal note marked with a trefoil, "Scilicet ypaton, meson, synemenon, diezeumenon, yperboleon" (quoting Boethius, *De musica* 1, 21.1), which is repeated on Royal 13 B. xiv, fol. 42^r. These glosses were copied into Royal 13 B. xiv either from CCCC 276 or its source. They cannot be attributed to Dudo or any other known party. See also HUISMAN, "Notes", pp. 130–31; POHL, *Dudo of St Quentin's* Historia Normannorum, pp. 148–49.

[82] One function of paratexts and rubrication lies in their definition of textual hierarchies through their visual distinctiveness. CCCC 276, visually impressive, has numerous explanatory rubrics in red ink, followed by the poems, each verse of which begins with a coloured initial. The poems are written in smaller script to separate them from the body of the prose text. The beginning of the fourth book is different from the first three books in terms of presentation. It is clear at a glance that this is the most important section. Those manuscripts in which the poems and the rubrics are absent, e.g. Cotton Claudius A. xii, do not communicate the said hierarchy by visual means. The pictorial scheme that was meant to be executed in Rouen, 1173/ Y11 also supports the textual hierarchy: the places left for illuminations are

The explanatory rubrics comprehend practically all the metres applied in *HN*, thirty of the thirty-four, as summarized in Table 2. The only four metres (Christiansen's metres 19, 23, 24 and 26) lacking explanatory rubrics are situated in the gap extending from poem 51 to 58. Some rubrics repeat explanations found in others: for instance, "Metrum dactilicum tetrametrum quod constat spondeo dactilo catalecto" appears no less than four times.[83] Most metres are introduced several times. It seems unlikely, then, that the primary governing principle was to introduce systematically each metre in use. As shown in Table 1, they were applied methodologically to the prefatory poems and throughout Book IV, an authorial design.

The said three gaps in Book IV that lack explanatory rubrics raise the question as to whether or not the poems in question had originally had them. CCCC 276, likely to represent an earlier stage in transmission than its two English companions, is helpful here. Three absences, those in poems 76 and 90–91, can be attributed with some confidence to scribal error or recourse to a defective exemplar. While the manuscript introduces poem 76 with the rubric "Apostropha ad Ricardum", this does not describe the metre, which would simply have been the *heroicum*. Scribal error or a lack of space on the page may explain the absence. Or the explanatory rubric might have been wanting already in the exemplar, as the Royal manuscript also lacks it. Another explanation would be that heroic metre, very common and known to all students of Latin poetry, had been judged in the first place not to need a gloss. As for poems 90–91, the text of CCCC 276 breaks off slightly before them in the middle of fol. 134[v].[84] A straightforward explanation would be that the source on which the copyist drew was defective at the end. Elsewhere the manu-

concentrated in the fourth book (twenty-one places for illumination were left on leaves 28[v]–48[v]), with only a fraction of that number in the three other books (seven spaces are left on fols 6[r]–9[v], mainly to accompany the early history of Rollo). On the programme of illumination of the Rouen manuscript, see POHL, *Dudo of St Quentin's* Historia Normannorum, pp. 165–97.

[83]   *HN*, ed. LAIR, pp. 126, 213, 264, and 296.

[84]   The text breaks off at the beginning of the second column on the verso of the final leaf of quire X (fol. 134). The missing text amounts to two pages in Cotton Nero D. VIII, and four and half pages in Royal 13 B. XIV.

script is executed with diligence and care, with one notable exception. Most of the aforementioned poems 51–58 that lack the rubrics are textually corrupt. The order of lines is confused, in stark contrast to the perfect presentation elsewhere.[85] With no indication of any break, narrative or otherwise, corruption ceases before poem 59. CCCC 276 possibly received poems 51–58 from a source other than its main source, which, then, would have been defective in this section. The putative secondary source would not only have been of an inferior textual quality but would also have lacked the said rubrics.

Poem 58 can be cited in demonstration that the source of CCCC 276 (or a lost intermediary) did not bear explanatory rubrics at this point and had a different layout. The poem is short, running to eighteen lines.[86] Longer and shorter verses alternate, the former consisting of a spondee, choriamb, and two dactyls, and the latter of a spondee, choriamb, and a short syllable.[87] Yet, the hand responsible for CCCC 276 copied first the long verses and only then the shorter. Such an uncharacteristic error would have been caused by reading two columns in the source manuscript as consecutive entities rather than a device to demonstrate the change of metre from verse to verse. That is, the copyist seems first to have copied the left-hand column with the longer verses and then the right-hand column with the shorter verses. It is hard to see how the scribe, whose work was otherwise of high quality, could have committed such a mistake if the layout of the exemplar had remained constant,

[85] The copyist frequently miscopied bicolumnar arrangements into one column, as explained below. Such an error occurs in poems 51, 52, 53, 57 and 58. See also POHL, *Dudo of St Quentin's* Historia Normannorum, pp. 240–51, Appendix 4–5. *HN*, ed. LAIR, p. 214, n. A, and p. 219, n. 7 also notices the confusion characterizing this section in CCCC 276. Note also that Cotton Nero D. viii confuses the line order in poems 51, 54 and 57 (fols 103ᵛ, 104ʳ and 105ʳ respectively).

[86] *HN*, ed. LAIR, p. 221; CCCC 276, fol. 97ᵛ.

[87] The metre is described by Christiansen as "slightly irregular Third or Lesser Asclepiadic tetrameters (the endings pyrrhic rather than trochaic) alternating with Pherecratean dimeters or trimeters (ending short rather than long)"; CHRISTIANSEN, *History of the Normans*, p. 210, n. 325. The other five manuscripts have the correct, alternating line structure.

or if his source had a rubric introducing the metre.[88] Several
poems that use alternating verses are correctly presented in
CCCC 276, and they also have explanatory rubrics.[89] The textual corruption that characterizes fols 94ᵛ–98ʳ hints at some
irregularity in transmission.

The Royal and Antwerp manuscripts avoid the errors found in
the corrupt section of CCCC 276. Poem 58, for example, is given
in the correct order in the Royal manuscript, which presents it
as continuous text.[90] In the Antwerp manuscript the poem is set
in two columns without errors.[91] Amending these corruptions in
CCCC 276 would have been impossible without recourse to another
source. The Royal manuscript also includes the conclusion of
Book IV, although it lacks the explanatory rubrics for the last two
poems.[92] The Royal and Antwerp manuscripts are, then, hardly
direct copies of CCCC 276, although the three manuscripts must
have been closely connected. Solid conclusions are not possible as
the requisite text-critical evidence from the manuscripts is not
reported in printed editions.[93] To conclude, several of the anoma-

[88]   The confusion betrays the fact that the copyist of CCCC 276 did not
scan the metre while writing. The confused order of verses in poem 58 and
elsewhere could hint at an imperfect command of Latin prosody. It seems
improbable that a copyist who committed such glaring errors could have
composed rubrics for the more exotic metres.

[89]   For example, poem 26, the prefatory "Oratio" of the third book, uti-
lizes four different alternating metres. Its explanatory rubric reads "Metrum
tetracolon tetrastrophon. id est quattuor metri generibus. a quarto facta rep-
licatione. Habet enim primum uersum adonium. secundum archilodium. ter-
cium feretacium. quartum gliconium." The lines are written in the correct
order; CCCC 276, fol. 79ʳ. The same observations, *mutatis mutandis*, apply, for
example, to poems 72 and 73, *ibid.*, fols 115ʳ and 115ᵛ.

[90]   Royal 13 B. xiv, fol. 45ʳ.

[91]   Antwerp, 17.2, fol. 46ʳ.

[92]   Royal 13 B. xiv, fol. 45ʳ, fol. 108ᵛ. MS Antwerp lacks several quires at
the end, containing the latter half of the fourth book; Pohl, *Dudo of St Quentin's* Historia Normannorum, pp. 18–19.

[93]   Pohl, *Dudo of St Quentin's* Historia Normannorum, pp. 38–40. Poem
51, a twenty-nine-line Anacreontic dimeter addressed to Archbishop Robert,
is an illustrative example of the confusion in the editions of *HN*. The poem's
authorial form is not easy to determine. Much confusion, medieval and modern, has ensued from the layout in manuscripts, lost and extant. The crux is
that two columns were used to convey how the poem divides into verses. In
the process of transmission, new layouts, also in one column, emerged, with

lies observable in poems lacking rubrics were clearly transmission noise. Explanatory rubrics were also omitted deliberately, such that their number reduced at various steps in the transmission. The most likely scenario is that Dudo's authorial text attached rubrics to all prefatory poems in the first three books and to all poems in the fourth.

A survey of Dudo's sources shows that on furnishing poems with explanatory rubrics he complied with previous models. One of his most important literary paragons was Heiric of Auxerre, whose metrical *Vita sancti Germani* has comparable rubrics.[94] This also applies to their placement. They accompany the prefatory poems of each book.[95] The first explanatory rubric in *HN* reads "Adlocutio ad Librum ΜΩΝΟΚΩΛΩ ΜΩΝΩϹΤΡΟΦΩ DECVRSA". It unmistakably echoes Heiric's "Allocutio ad Librum ΔΥΚΟΛΩ ΔΙϹΤΡΟΦΩ DECVRSA".[96] Dudo drew on Heiric.

The authorial status of explanatory rubrics means that *HN*'s didactic aspect was Dudo's deliberate design. He was seeking readers in the classroom — something he stated quite explicitly. The verse "Address to the Book" ("Allocutio ad Librum"), *HN*'s opening poem, which Dudo might have composed only when he was back in Saint-Quentin, posed the rhetorical question, What fate would fall on his work? Will it "proceed at full speed to the Norman academies/or still remain in confinement to our Frankish

---

the result that the order of verses became confused. Royal 13 B. xiv and Antwerp, 17.2 preserve the two-column layout. CCCC 276 and Cotton Nero D. viii derive their form from a two-column presentation but make errors in the layout of the verses. Rouen, 1173/Y11 and SBB-PK, Phill. 1854 confuse the order of the first twelve verses. None of the printed editions gives the poem in its correct form; Lair wants the third verse, "Rhetorico sapore", completely. Interestingly, he observed that his text is based on the Cotton Nero manuscript, although it appears closer to MSS Royal and Antwerp; *HN*, ed. LAIR, p. 214 and *ibid.*, n. A. DUCHESNE, *Historiae Normannorum scriptores antiqui*, p. 108, and LIFSHITZ, *Dudo (Latin)*, Capitulum 28, give the poem as in the Berlin manuscript. I will discuss this poem in a forthcoming paper.

[94] CHRISTIANSEN, *History of the Normans*, pp. xiii, xxi–xxiii.

[95] Heiric's explanatory rubrics accompany his "Invocatio", "Allocutio ad Librum", and the prefaces to Books II to VI; MGH, *Poetae*, 3, pp. 432, 436, 451, 461, 474, 488 and 499 respectively. All the others describe the metre in Greek except the first one, which is in Latin.

[96] Rouen, 1173/Y11, fol. 2ʳ and MGH, *Poetae*, 3, p. 436 respectively.

high-schools"?[97] He assumed that his readers would be schooled in the seven liberal arts. The "Apostrophe to the Reader" (*Apostropha ad lectorem*) of Book IV opens as follows: "Reader, with prayers profuse I supplicate thee,/Skilled in the sevenfold art, and competent".[98] Another feature that associates *HN* with schools is its vocabulary, massive and complex. As a late proponent of the "hermeunetic" style, Dudo had a penchant for rare words.[99] His clauses are laden with extraneous adjectives and exotic nouns; synonyms, antitheses and various forms of repetition abound.[100] Works written in hermeunetic style were used as textbooks for the study of complex vocabulary and grammar.[101] Dudo's textual style probably reflects his own education. On account of its various educational features, *HN* has been characterized as an "encyclopedia, a reference book

---

[97] "Aut pergas Northmannica nunc gymnasia praepes/Aut scholis clausus Franciscis jam moruleris"; *HN*, ed. LAIR, p. 120, translation CHRISTIANSEN, *History of the Normans*, p. 7. It should be noted that Dudo's choice of words "gymnasia" and "schola" here probably do not denote any difference in the status of the schools but were simply examples of his varied vocabulary. Dudo avoided repetition of the same words for stylistic reasons and was always keen to demonstrate his wide vocabulary, using a great variety of synonyms; CHRISTIANSEN, *History of the Normans*, p. xxxi. For a different reading, see BACHRACH, "Writing History", p. 66, n. 43.

[98] "Profusis precibus, lector, supplex tibi dico/Artis septifluae gnare, capaxque bene"; *HN*, ed. LAIR, p. 269, translation CHRISTIANSEN, *History of the Normans*, p. 144.

[99] M. LAPIDGE, "The hermeunetic style in tenth-century Anglo-Latin literature", in *Anglo-Saxon England*, 4 (1975), pp. 67–111, at 71. The style flourished in the ninth and tenth centuries. In Northern Francia, Fleury and Laon were the main centres. Martianus Capella, an important model for Dudo, was an important influence; *ibid.*, p. 69.

[100] L. B. MORTENSEN, "Stylistic choice in a reborn genre. The national histories of Widukind of Corvey and Dudo of St. Quentin", in *Dudone di San Quintino*, ed. by P. GATTI, A. DEGL'INNOCENTI, Trento, 1995, pp. 77–102, at 89; CHRISTIANSEN, *History of the Normans*, p. xxxi.

[101] LAPIDGE, "Hermeunetic style", pp. 72–76. A regular feature was the use of Greek words, as in *HN*. In some manuscripts, e.g. CCCC 276, fol. 95ᵛ, they are accompanied by interlinear translations or transliterations into the Latin alphabet, with probably a primarily didactic function. The treatment of Greek words is not uniform; sometimes the Latinized forms replace the Greek words; e.g. CCCC 276, fol. 89ᵛ as against Royal 13 B. xiv, fol. 34ᵛ, which preserves the Greek spelling.

of synonyms, of prosody, metres, rhetorical devices, geography, and even theology — a comprehensive school-book".[102]

Adalbero

Dudo's target audiences were twofold. His primary audience was an educated, scholarly elite. In Normandy, Archbishop Robert was a central figure in such networks and in an excellent position to promote *HN*. The didactic aspect of the work was directed to school use. The Norman lay elite was a secondary target audience. In most cases illiterate, they must have received the history through mediation, perhaps orally, in vernacular translation. As regards its long-term success, endorsement by learned elites was naturally crucial; circulation within lay audiences, illiterate or semi-literate, would have amounted to a minor issue at best. To ensure that his work would be received and circulated, Dudo did not confine its publication to the duchy. Bishop Adalbero of Laon was to be a central agent in this.

Dudo's relocation to Saint-Quentin was certainly a factor in his decision to dedicate *HN* to Adalbero. It should be added that while his aforementioned Norman patrons might have received presentation copies furnished with dedicatory letters addressed to them, none of our manuscripts evidence that.[103] There is no evidence that Adalbero rewarded Dudo in some way, although of course he may have done so. More importantly, in Saint-Quentin Dudo had the opportunity to publish *HN* in a new framework. He could reach audiences unavailable to him before his relocation from Normandy. *HN* was not meant for Norman audiences exclusively. It could fully achieve its goal in providing the Norman with

---

[102]   Mortensen, "Stylistic choice", p. 100. The didactic functions of *HN* have been recently attested by many scholars, such as Pohl, *Dudo of St Quentin's* Historia Normannorum, and Christiansen, *History of the Normans*. Gelting, "Courtly viking", p. 18 notes that "Dudo's work would be ideally suited to imbue the schoolboys with loyalty to the exalted lineage of their virtuous dukes".

[103]   The dedicatory letter to Adalbero is found in nine of the fourteen extant manuscripts, including two of the three oldest preserved copies, the Rouen and Berlin manuscripts. Each of the six manuscripts that carry the poems, (and in that respect, preserve Dudo's orginal more faithfully) also have the dedicatory letter to Adalbero; Huisman, "Notes", p. 123.

a glorious past and redefining his status as belonging to a noble nation only if that narrative came to be accepted elsewhere. This was Dudo's own opinion. In the preface to Book IV, he asserted that the work was intended also for readers from other nations. "Him [Richard I] the kindly, him the modest,/will the written page proclaim/[...]/Let the other kingdoms wonder/At his deeds and holy sayings:/In reflection, deed, and speaking/No one greater has shone forth."[104] Foreign patrons and publication outside Normandy were, then, a requisite.

Dudo's publication strategy in Normandy helps us understand better why he dedicated the work to Adalbero. The personal profile of Adalbero strikes all the same chords as that of Archbishop Robert. He was the most powerful ecclesiastical magnate in northern Francia and had the ear of the French king. Adalbero was a spectacular patron of the arts. Laon cathedral was home to a leading school. A poet himself, Adalbero could appreciate Dudo's complex verses.[105] In short, he was an ideal patron to help disseminate HN. According to Dudo, Adalbero's endorsement would confirm the veracity of HN.[106] The poetic aspect of the work would have appealed to Adalbero and, in general, to readers for whom the preservation of the memory of the Normans' ancestors was not of personal importance but who were involved, in one way or another, in teaching. Dudo's dedicatory letter to Adalbero should, indeed, be read from that perspective. It employs complicated mathematical and musical metaphors, to demonstrate that the

---

[104]   Poem 53, lines 35–36, "Hunc benignum, hunc modestum/Concrepabit pagina", and lines 45–48, "Regna, facta, sancta dicta,/quin stupent et caetera:/Cogitatu, facto, dicto/Nemo major splenduit"; HN, ed. LAIR, p. 215, translation CHRISTIANSEN, History of the Normans, p. 91. Between these two passages, in lines 37–44, Dudo names Normandy, Francia and Burgundy as the witnesses of Richard I's greatness: "Hunc pium, justumque sanctum,/Et probatum et maximum./Almitatis hujus actus/Testis est Northmannia,/Largitatis atque hujus/Testis est et Francia:/Fortitudinemque ejus/Comprobat Burgundia"; HN, ed. LAIR, p. 215. These were the regions in which the duke was most active during his reign, but the passage can also be read as an indication of where Dudo thought his work would primarily find its audiences.

[105]   Dudo seems to allude to this in the dedicatory letter: "te, qui versaris in sacrorum praeceptis eloquiorum"; ibid., p. 119.

[106]   Ibid., p. 120: "tuae majestati mittere disposui, ut falsa amputarentur, et si quid veritatis in illo haberetur, tua auctoritate confirmarentur".

dialogue between the author and his dedicatee was one between men of letters.[107] Dudo also sought to appeal to Adalbero more directly. He affirmed that the work would consolidate and spread Adalbero's fame.[108]

However, judging by the extant manuscripts, *HN* was not a success in Francia. There survives a single relatively early copy with a probable origin in Francia: Douai, Bibliothèque Marceline Desbordes-Valmore, 880. The volume is a compilation written in Anchin *c.* 1150. The copy of *HN*, on fols 89^r–114^v, remains incomplete. Breaking off abruptly in the middle of Book III, the text wants more than the final half. Most of the poems are likewise omitted.[109] The absence of evidence to the contrary implies that Adalbero's contribution to publication proved to be rather less than was desired. One implication is that Dudo is unlikely to have been connected to him and that he chose his dedicatee at the time of publication. By consigning the work to Adalbero, Dudo did not seek to replace his Norman patrons with a French one; nothing suggests that Dudo would somehow undermine his frequent address to them within the work. The dedication to Adalbero was simply to extend Dudo's publishing circle to reach audiences in Francia.[110]

---

[107] *Ibid.*, pp. 117–18. These metaphors are based on Boethius' *De institutione arithmetica* and Martianus Capella's *De nuptiis Philosophiae et Mercuriae*; CHRISTIANSEN, *History of the Normans*, p. 178 nn. 16, 18 and 19. Shopkow notes that Dudo's usage of these metaphors — which are based, according to her, on either Boethius' *De arithmetica* or *De musica* — is "so confusing [...] that he either did not understand the material well or was copying", and concludes that Dudo's education in these matters was superficial; SHOPKOW, "Carolingian world", p. 25.

[108] It may be added that Dudo uses the word "patronus" for Adalbero in the context of the request that he correct the text. Patronage as conceived here embraces a literary contribution by way of emendation and a share of fame that would follow. "Talem et hujuscemodi honorem corde revolvo, et mente delibero decere tantum patronum ut quae in hoc codice suis tenebris obscura videntur, per te ad lucem referantur, quia non penuriosi et ingloriosi nomen compositoris, sed egregii correctoris laus acquiretur"; *HN*, ed. LAIR, p. 118.

[109] POHL, *Dudo of St Quentin's* Historia Normannorum, pp. 26–27, 262.

[110] Cf. BRINKMANN, "Dudos dedikationen", pp. 96–100.

While his mission was to define the Norman past in written form and to make it public,[111] Dudo's intended audiences went beyond Norman courtly circles. His style of expression was calibrated to appeal to broader readerships, teachers and other churchmen not only in Normandy but also in Francia. To realize such aspirations, he approached the highest ecclesiastical figures close to him. The earliest dissemination bespeaks some success in Normandy. Religious institutions supported by local elites and under the influence of Archbishop Robert took to copying the work. Attempts to woo Adalbero in order to gain a foothold in Francia were less successful. Likewise, *HN* failed to make it to the classroom. The didactic and poetic matter of the work was regarded as superfluous at various steps in the transmission, to which the omission of the poems and explanatory rubrics is testimony.

---

[111] The prose preface of Book IV reflects on these themes. Dudo is very conscious of his responsibility in publishing ("propalare") on Richard I's life. "Quocirca benignissimi ducis Richardi vitam aggrediamur, hebete licet stylo [...] Donetur nobis etiam ejus meritis vitam illius reverenter propalare; qui summa reverentia, summumque decus Ecclesiae exstitit"; *HN*, ed. LAIR, p. 218.

Tables

Table 1: The poems and explanatory rubrics in *HN*

Poem no.	*HN*, ed Lair, starting page	Christiansen no.	Meter (Christiansen)	Explanatory rubric begins on fol.						Poem	Book
				CCCC MS 276	BL MS Royal 13 B xiv	Antwerp MPM MS 17.2	Rouen BM MS 1173/Y11	Berlin SB MS Phill. 1854	BL MS Cotton Nero D viii		
1	120	i	1	57r	2v	3v	2r	4r	-	*Allocutio ad Librum*	
2	122	ii	3	57r	3r	4r	2v	5r	-	To Richard II	
3	122	iii	1							*Trepidatio et dissuasio*	
4	123	iv	22	57v	-	4v	-	-	-	To Archbishop Robert	
5	125	v	1							To Count Rolf	
6	126	vi	11	58v	4r	5r	-	-	-	To Archbishop Robert	I
7	126	vii	7	58v	4r	5v	-	-	-	To Archbishop Robert	
8	127	viii	16	59r	4v	5v	-	-	-	To Archbishop Robert	
9	128	ix	22							*Oratio*	
10	130	x	1								
11	135	xi	1								
12	137	xii	1								
13	138	xiii	22	63v	7v	11r	7r	13r	79r	*Praefatio*	
14	140	xiii (cont.)		64v	8r	11v	-	-	-	*Oratio*	
15	144	xiv	1								
16	145	xv	1								
17	148	xvi	1			*					
18	149	xvii	1								II
19	151	xviii	1								
20	153	xix	1								
21	163	xx	1								
22	163	xxi	1								
23	169	xxii	1								
24	175	xxiii	1								

25	176	xxiv	9	78v	21v	27r	-	-	-	*Praefatio tertii libri*	
26	178	xxv	33	79r	22v	27v	-	-	-	*Oratio*	
27	180	xxvi	1								
28	182	xxvii	1								
29	184	xxviii	1								
30	186	xxix	1								
31	188	xxx	1								
32	190	xxxi	1								III
33	191	xxxii	1								
34	194	xxxiii	1								
35	199	xxxiv	1								
36	200	xxxv	1								
37	202	xxxvi	1								
38	206	xxxvii	1								
39	209	xxxviii	1								
40	210	xxxix	22	93v	40r	42r	-	-	-	Exhortation of the Muses	
41	210	xl	9	93v	40r	42v	-	-	-	Clio	
42	211	xli	3	93v	40r	42v	-	-	-	Euterpe	
43	211	xlii	9	93v	40v	42v	-	-	-	Melpomenes	
44	211	xliii	4	93v	40v	42v	-	-	-	Thalia	
45	212	xliv	2	94r	41r	42v	-	-	-	Polyhymnia	
46	212	xlv	7	94r	41r	43r	-	-	-	Erato	
47	212	xlvi	14	94r	41r	43r	-	-	-	Terpsichore	
48	213	xlvii	15	94r	41r	43r	-	-	-	Urania	
49	213	xlviii	5	94r	41v	43r	-	-	-	Calliope	
50	213	xlix	8	94v	41v	43v	-	-	-	Muses in unison	
51	214	l	19							To Archbishop Robert	
52	214	li	23							*Item praefatio*	
53	214	li (cont.)								*Hic loquitur ad librum*	IV
54	215	lii	24							*Oratio*	
55	215	liii	22							To Archbishop Robert	
56	219	liv	1								
57	219	lv	14								
58	221	lvi	26								
59	222	lvii	17	98v	46r	47r	-	-	-		
60	224	lviii	10	99r	47r	47v	-	-	-		
61	228	lix	12	101r	49v	49v	-	-	-		
62	229	lx	16	101v	50v	50r	-	-	-		
63	231	lxi	18	102v	52v	51r	-	-	-		
64	232	lxii	6	103r	53v	52r	-	-	-		
65	234	lxiii	9	104r	55r	52v	-	-	-		
66	238	lxiv	32	106r	59v		-	-	-		

67	242	lxv	3	107v	63v		-	-	**		
68	245	lxvi	34	109r	66v		-	-	-		
69	247	lxvii	11	110r	68r		-	-	-		
70	253	lxviii	14	113r	74v		-	-	-		
71	255	lxix	4	113v	75v		-	-	-		
72	258	lxx	28	115r	78r		-	-	-		
73	258	lxxi	25	115v	78r		-	-	-		
74	259	lxxii	17	115v	78v		-	-	-		
75	260	lxxiii	27	116r	79r		-	-	-		
76	263	lxxiv	1							*Apostropha ad Ricardum*	
77	264	lxxv	5	118r	83v		-	-	-		
78	266	lxxvi	21	119r	85r		-	-	-		
79	268	lxxvii	30	120r	86v		-	-	-		IV
80	269	lxxviii	22	120v	-		-	-	-	*Apostropha ad lectorem*	
81	270	lxxix	13	121r	89r		-	-	-		
82	272	lxxx	29	122r	90v		-	-	-		
83	274	lxxxi	31	122v	91r		-	-	-		
84	275	lxxxii	1	123v	92v		-	-	-		
85	276	lxxxiii	20	123v	92v		-	-	-		
86	280	lxxxiv	1	125v	95v		-	-	127r		
87	288	lxxxv	1	130r	-		-	-	130v		
88	292	lxxxvi	25	132r	103v		-	-	132r	To Archbishop Robert	
89	296	lxxxvii	11	133v	106r		-	-	133v		
90	299	lxxxviii	1								
91	300	lxxxix	22								

▨	Wants leaves / text
-	Wants explanatory rubrics present in other manuscripts, carries the poem
	Carries the poem, no explanatory rubrics in any manuscript

*	Wants one leaf
**	Skips over *c.* one page length of text, has only the seven last lines of the poem

Table 2: Poems and explanatory
rubrics per meter

Meter (Christiansen)	Poems	Explanatory rubrics
1	35	4
2	1	1
3	3	3
4	2	2
5	2	2
6	1	1
7	2	2
8	1	1
9	4	4
10	1	1
11	3	3
12	1	1
13	1	1
14	3	2
15	1	1
16	2	2
17	2	2
18	1	1
19	1	0
20	1	1
21	1	1
22	7	4
23	1	0
24	1	0
25	2	2
26	1	0
27	1	1
28	1	1
29	1	1
30	1	1
31	1	1
32	1	1
33	1	1
34	1	1

Table 3: Poems and explanatory
rubrics per book

Book	Poems	Explanatory rubrics
I	12	6
II	12	2
III	15	2
IV	52	41

Table 4: Variety of meters
per book

Book	Amount of meters
I	6
II	2
III	3
IV	33
I-III	8

Publishing a Saint

The Textual Tradition of the Life and Miracles of St Symeon of Trier

Tuomas Heikkilä

(Helsinki)

Preliminary Remarks: Studying Whole Textual Traditions

Our understanding of the past is based, in the main, on written sources. The majority of the narrative texts that a medieval historian uses have been edited following the norms of classical textual criticism. Although both historians and philologists are interested in texts, there has traditionally been a division between a historical approach to manuscript traditions and a critical-philological approach to the textual contents of the manuscripts.[1] In many cases, scholars preparing or using a critical edition of a medieval text, or scholarly publishing houses invoking their editorial principles, cling to the nineteenth-century ideal of reconstructing the *Urtext*, the supposed "original" version. Such attempts are common in spite of the fact that both the most proven traditional means of textual criticism and the most developed recent computer-assisted methods of stemmatology may yield uncertain results in reconstructing the "original".

The historical details of the dissemination of texts have often received less attention. In numerous critical editions especially of

[1] J. Irigoin, "La Critique des textes doit être historique", *La critica testuale Greco-latina oggi: metodi e problemi*, ed. by E. Flores, Rome, 1981, pp. 19–36. See also the excellent introduction to the topic: C. Macé, "The stemma as a historical tool", in *Handbook of Stemmatology: History, Methodology, Digital Approaches*, ed. by P. Roelli, Berlin, 2020, pp. 272–91.

The Art of Publication from the Ninth to the Sixteenth Century, ed. by Samu Niskanen with the assistance of Valentina Rovere, IPM, 93 (Turnhout, 2023), pp. 83–130.
© BREPOLS ❧ PUBLISHERS   DOI 10.1484/M.IPM-EB.5.133082

Latin literature, the cataloguing of all known manuscripts of the
work in question is an exercise conducted without much analysis
beyond the identification of shared errors; the main emphasis is on
a limited number of witnesses considered the best. Such an approach risks oversimplifying inferences about relationships between
the witnesses. Traditionally, these connections are presented in
the form of a stemma, a family tree, as it were, of textual witnesses. However, ever so often the stemma and the story it tells
about dissemination and reception are not elucidated systematically — or at all — with respect to their historical context. In my
opinion, Latin textual scholarship should in general pay somewhat
more attention to reception and so follow what has been a trend in
the study of medieval vernacular texts for decades. At the present
time, such an approach becomes ever more topical as new computational tools, some of which are applied in study, provide for
analysis of unprecedented scope and precision.

   One of the outcomes of the traditional emphasis on a single part
of a textual tradition is the often overly simplified reconstruction
of a hypothetical stemma, a directed graph representing the relationships between various exemplars and copies of the text edited. The great majority of stemmata proposed for medieval texts
— be they Latin or vernacular — by generations of scholars are
bifurcating. That is, manuscripts fall into two main branches, and
sub-branches tend to bifurcate in their turn.[2] A closer look at the
editorial methods applied in *recensio* as well as at what is known
of medieval copying practices suggests that more often than not
such a mechanical, bifurcating dissemination of a text cannot hold
true. The excessive frequency of bifurcation, then, has to do with
the methodological imperative to look for divergence rather than
unity in the process of the textual comparison of witnesses. The

---

   [2] See the *loci classici* of this revelation: J. BÉDIER, *Jean Renart: Le lai
de l'Ombre*, Paris, 1913 (Société des anciens textes français); J. BÉDIER,
"La tradition manuscrite du 'Lai de l'Ombre'. Réflexions sur l'art d'éditer
les anciens textes", *Romania*, 54 (1928), pp. 161–96; A. CASTELLANI, *Bédier
avait-il raison? La méthode de Lachmann dans les éditions de textes du moyen
age. Leçon inaugurale donnée à l'Université de Fribourg le 2 juin 1954*, Fribourg,
1957; O. E. HAUGEN, "The *silva portentosa* of stemmatology: bifurcation in
the recension of Old Norse manuscripts", *Digital Scholarship in the Humanities*, 31 (2016), pp. 594–610.

explanation for the oversimplification of stemmata is a methodological emphasis rather than a historical verity.

Even if understandable from the viewpoint of the work economy, the tendency to limit the study of the manuscripts and textual witnesses of a given work to the ones considered the most
relevant prevents us from conceiving of textual traditions in their
entirety. If the text under investigation was important to wide and
various medieval readerships, it will probably survive in a number
of copies. Tracing manuscripts in a great number of libraries and
archives, and comparing textual variation between dozens or hun-
dreds of textual witnesses is a time-consuming undertaking. Yet,
several holistic enterprises, testifying to the benefits of an approach taking the broad variety of witnesses into account, have been
made. A case in point is J. B. Hall's 1969 edition of Claudian's
De raptu Proserpinae, for which he collated 132 of the 134 known
extant manuscripts. However, his study (among others) brought to
light another caveat about the difficulties, in addition to the work
economy, of studying a whole tradition. After analysing such a
high number of textual witnesses, he reached the convincing conclusion that the tradition was thoroughly open, or contaminated.[3]
Other holistic enquiries into the transmission of widely disseminated works, such as the *Divina Commedia*, *Parzival*, and *The Canterbury Tales*, have concluded the same: contamination is rife and
difficult to surmount by means of available methodologies.[4]

While our conceptions of manuscript transmission may remain
imperfect, stemmata established in an inclusive manner can fur-

---

[3] J. B. HALL (ed.), *Claudian: De raptu Proserpinae*, Cambridge, 1969,
pp. 61–64.

[4] P. TROVATO, *Everything You Always Wanted to Know about Lachmann's
Method: A Non-Standard Handbook of Genealogical Textual Criticism in the Age
of Post-Structuralism, Cladistics, and Copy-Text*, revised edn, Padua, 2017,
p. 137; E. TONELLO, P. TROVATO, "Contaminazione di lezioni e contamina-
zione per giustapposizione di esemplari nella tradizione della 'Commedia'",
Filologia Italiana, 8 (2011), pp. 17–32; M. STOLZ, "New Philology and New
Phylogeny: aspects of a critical electronic edition of Wolfram's 'Parzival'",
Literary and Linguistic Computing, 18 (2003), pp. 139–50; P. ROBINSON (ed.),
*Geoffrey Chaucer: The Wife of Bath's Prologue on CD-ROM. The Canterbury Tales
Project*, Cambridge, 1996. On the problems posed by and remedies against
contamination, see, for example, T. HEIKKILÄ, "Dealing with open textual
traditions", in *Handbook of Stemmatology*, ed. by ROELLI, pp. 254–71.

nish some significant points of reference for studies on the authorial process, reception, and dissemination. As such, holistic approaches would certainly lead to fresh answers also to a number of questions relevant to the process of publishing such as, What were the stages in the writing and circulation of the text? What was the intended audience? And who actually read and copied the text? What follows seeks ways to show how the study of a textual tradition in its entirety may benefit the study of medieval publication. The focus is the eleventh-century hagiographic composite text on St Symeon of Trier († 1 June 1035), known as *Vita et miracula S. Symeonis Treverensis* (*BHL* 7963–7964).[5]

A Colourful Life and its Authors

The interesting and versatile components of Symeon's life contributed significantly to the wide dissemination of the *Vita et miracula S. Symeonis*. The main source of Symeon's *vita* was the protagonist himself, who recounted his experiences to his friend, Abbot Eberwinus († after 1036).[6] Soon after Symeon's death, Eberwinus set down the story in writing, thus creating the first version of the *vita* of the saint-to-be. In the prologue addressed to Archbishop Poppo of Trier, Eberwinus affirmed that he only describes what

---

[5]   The best edition of the text is still the Bollandist edition of 1695 by Daniel PAPEBROCH (van Papenbroek, 1628–1714): *Vita S. Symeonis*, *AA SS*, Jun. I, pp. 86–90 (henceforth: *Vita et miracula*). The texts have been published and edited several times since 1572, but never critically and based on a representative set of manuscripts. A new edition is urgently called for. The materials and some results of this article are based on the work I have done while preparing a new edition. As the division of the text is very arbitrary and corresponds neither to the practice applied in the manuscripts nor to the needs of a modern scholar, this article employs a new division, which is of importance especially when counting the miracles. See Appendix 3 for a concordance between the system used here and the previous editions.

[6]   The exact year of his death is not known, but in 1036 he was still alive. A. HAVERKAMP, "Der heilige Simeon (gest. 1035), Grieche im fatimidischen Orient und im lateinischen Okzident. Geschichten und Geschichte", *Historische Zeitschrift*, 290 (2010), pp. 1–51, at 2: "nach 1036"; M. C. FERRARI, "From pilgrim's guide to living relic: Symeon of Trier and his biographer Eberwin", *Latin Culture in the Eleventh Century. Proceedings of the Third International Conference on Medieval Latin Studies I*, ed. by M. W. HERREN, C. J. McDONOUGH, R. G. ARTHUR, Turnhout, 2002 (Publications of The Journal of Medieval Latin, 5/1), pp. 324–44, at 324: "ca. 1040".

he himself heard from Symeon and learned from other trustworthy witnesses. Accordingly, long passages of the text are given
as quotations from Symeon's own mouth, a feature that was not,
admittedly, uncommon in medieval hagiographical writing. In
addition, many parts and aspects of the story can be verified from
other sources.[7] Several eleventh-century sources used Eberwinus'
testimony on Symeon, suggesting that Eberwinus' account was
considered reliable.[8]

The *vita* provides a rough framework for the life of Symeon.
It tells us that he was born in Syracuse in Sicily. At the age of
seven, Symeon was sent to Constantinople for his studies. Later,
as an adult, he moved to the Holy Land. He spent some time
in Jerusalem, and then worked as a pilgrims' guide. After seven
years, he began to follow his religious calling, first as the ser-
vant of a hermit on the banks of the River Jordan for a few
years, and then as a monk in the monastery of St Mary in Beth-
lehem and on Mount Sinai, and then as a hermit on Mount Sinai
and by the Red Sea.

Symeon was subsequently sent to Rouen with the mission of
collecting a gift of money promised to the monastery on Mount

---

[7]   On the sources for St Symeon, see F.-J. HEYEN, *Das Stift St. Simeon in
Trier*, Berlin/New York, 2002 (Germania Sacra, Neue Folge, 41, Die Bistümer
der Kirchenprovinz Trier, Das Erzbistum Trier, 9), pp. 468–80; T. HEIKKILÄ,
*Vita et miracula S. Symeonis Treverensis. Ein hochmittelalterlicher Heiligenkult
im Kontext*, Helsinki, 2002 (Annales Academiae Scientiarum Fennicae, 326),
pp. 138–46; HAVERKAMP, "Der heilige Simeon".

[8]   For example, *Descriptio translationis reliquiarum sanctae Catharinae ac
miraculorum ipsius*: A. PONCELET, "Sanctae Catherinae Virginis et Martyris
translatio et miracula Rotomagensia saec. XI.", *Analecta Bollandiana*, 22
(1903), pp. 423–38, at 431–38; T. HEIKKILÄ, "Between East and West: the
many uses of the Life of St Symeon of Trier", *Travelling Through Time: Essays
in honour of Kaj Öhrnberg*, ed. by S. AKAR, J. HÄMEEN-ANTTILA, I. NOK-
SO-KOIVISTO, Helsinki, 2013 (Studia Orientalia, 114), pp. 121–34, at 129–31;
HEYEN, *Stift St. Simeon*, pp. 471–72; R. FAWTIER, "Les reliques rouennaises
de sainte Catherine d'Alexandrie", *Analecta Bollandiana*, 41 (1923), pp. 357–
68, at 358–60. In addition, the *vita* of St Richard of Saint-Vanne: *Vita Richardi abbatis S. Vitoni Virdunensis*, ed. by D. W. WATTENBACH, MGH *SS*, 11
(1854), pp. 280–90; H. DAUPHIN, *Le bienheureux Richard, abbé de Saint-Vanne
de Verdun*, Louvain, 1946 (Bibliothèque de la Revue d'histoire ecclésiastique,
24).

Sinai.[9] It was during this journey that Symeon made the acquaintance of Richard (c. 970–1046), abbot of Saint-Vanne, and Eberwinus, his future biographer.[10] After his mission to Rouen, which proved futile, the saint-to-be accompanied archbishop Poppo of Trier († 1047), a friend of Eberwinus, on his pilgrimage to Jerusalem.[11] For reasons unexplained in the *vita*, Symeon then decided to return to Western Europe with the archbishop, and he was enclosed in the Porta Nigra, the Roman city gate of Trier, by Archbishop Poppo to live there as an incluse.[12] Symeon passed away in his cell in Porta Nigra on Sunday, 1 June 1035.[13]

The *inclusus* of Porta Nigra was certainly a very well-known figure in Trier already during his lifetime. He was an important figure in ecclesiastical circles, a close friend of both Archbishop Poppo and Eberwinus, who was abbot of no fewer than three monasteries: St Martin in Trier, St Mauritius in Tholey, and St Paul in Verdun. After the death of Symeon, it was this duo who launched a project to have him canonized. The archbishop com-

---

[9]   Another contemporary source testifies how the dukes of Normandy financed the Sinai monastery. Cf. *Ex Radulfi Glabri historiarum libris V*, MGH *SS*, 7 (1846), pp. 48–72, at 58. Radulfus died probably in 1047, and it is quite possible that he received this piece of information from an early copy of the *Vita et miracula S. Symeonis*. On the travel route, see F. MICHEAU, "Les itinéraires maritimes et continentaux des pèlerins vers Jérusalem", in *Occident et Orient au Xe siècle, Actes du IXe Congrès de la Société des historiens médiévistes de l'enseignement supérieur public, Dijon, 2–4 juin 1978*, Dijon, 1979 (Université de Dijon. Publications, 57), pp. 79–112, at 90, 92–93.

[10]   See R. LANDES, *Relics, Apocalypse, and the Deceits of History. Ademar of Chabannes, 989–1034*, Cambridge, MA, 1995 (Harvard Historical Studies, 117), pp. 154–58; MICHEAU, "Itinéraires", pp. 88–93; DAUPHIN, *Le bienheureux Richard*, pp. 281–96, 306–08. The original sources mentioning the pilgrimage are *Ademari Historia*, pp. 145–47, Eberwinus's *Vita S. Symeonis*, *Vita Richardi*, pp. 288–89, and *Chronicon Hugonis* by Hugo of Flavigny, pp. 393–98. As Hugo's text contains direct quotations of, and passages modified from, Eberwinus, it is obvious that he knew *Vita S. Symeonis*.

[11]   Poppo's letter to the pope: *AA SS*, Jun. I, p. 96 (1867 edition, p. 93); HEYEN, *Stift St. Simeon*, pp. 474–75; HEIKKILÄ, *Vita et miracula*, pp. 127–30, with further source references.

[12]   *Vita et miracula*, v23 (c. 15). In the references to *Vita et miracula*, I will henceforth refer to the passage within the text (v = *vita*, m = *miracula*) as well as to the illogically divided chapters (c.) of the Bollandist edition.

[13]   *Vita et miracula*, v29 (c. 19). On Symeon's tomb, see HEYEN, *Stift St. Simeon*, pp. 484–90.

missioned the abbot to write a *vita* of the deceased. As Eberwinus also listed the miracles Symeon had accomplished during his
lifetime as well as those that now began to take place after his
death, a constantly growing set of *miracula* was attached to the
vita.

The aim of this literary effort was obviously to create a sound
basis for canonization.[14] The affair as designed by Poppo and
Eberwinus was an ambitious one: instead of the traditional local
proclamation by the local archbishop and synod, they preferred
to seek papal canonization. Such operations were very much a
novelty at the time; the only precedent known to us had taken
place in 993.[15] Poppo and Eberwinus were swift in their actions,
and the *vita* and *miracula* were sent to the pope probably already during the autumn.[16] The canonization probably took place
around Christmas 1035.[17] Within a few years, a collegiate church
of St Symeon was established in Porta Nigra itself. When Archbishop Poppo died in 1047, he was buried there.[18]

The *Vita et miracula* is a text issued in multiple recensions and
written by several authors. As long as Eberwinus lived — probably until c. 1040[19] — he was the obvious expert on Symeon and

[14]   On the canonization, see O. KRAFFT, *Papsturkunde und Heiligsprechung.
Die päpstlichen Kanonisationen vom Mittelalter bis zur Reformation: ein Hand-
buch*, Cologne, 2005 (Beihefte der Archiv für Diplomatik, 9), pp. 28–44;
HEYEN, *Stift St. Simeon*, pp. 468–71; HEIKKILÄ, *Vita et miracula*, pp. 138–46;
W. SCHMID, *Poppo von Babenberg († 1047). Erzbischof von Trier – Förderer des
hl. Simeon – Schutzpatron der Habsburger*, Trier, 1998, pp. 23–25.

[15]   See JL 3848; *AA SS*, Jul. II, p. 80; *PL*, 137, col. 845; KRAFFT, *Papsturkunde*, pp. 19–28.

[16]   *Gesta Treverorum, additamentum et continuatio prima*, ed. by G. WAITZ,
MGH *SS*, 8 (1848), p. 178: "Proinde accersivit nos tam clerus quam popu-
lus ecclesiae nostrae, obsecrantes, uti litteris nostris ad hanc apostolicam
sedem [...] cum illius viri sancti vita et miraculis missis peteremus [...] quatinus, si ita vobis cautum videatur, dato nobis vestri apostolatus decreto,
nomen eius liceat cum sanctorum nominibus conscribi ceteraque honoris sanc-
tis debiti ipsi impedi."On the dating, cf. HEYEN, *Stift St. Simeon*, pp. 468–69;
M. COENS,"Un document inédit sur le culte de S. Syméon moine d'Orient et
reclus à Trèves", *Analecta Bollandiana*, 68 (1950), pp. 181–96, at 185.

[17]   KRAFFT, *Papsturkunde*, pp. 28–44; HEYEN, *Stift St. Simeon*, pp. 468–
71; HEIKKILÄ, *Vita et miracula*, pp. 144–45 with further source references.

[18]   See HEYEN, *Stift St. Simeon*, pp. 110–16.

[19]   See n. 6 above.

was undoubtedly in charge of polishing the text of the *vita* and adding new contents to the *miracula*. His successor as author was only identified when Symeon manuscript *Ep*, Épinal, Bibliothèque multimédia intercommunale Épinal, 147 *(olim* 67), was discovered in 2002. The manuscript contains a previously unknown prologue to a number of miracles added after Eberwinus' text. What is more, the prologue identifies the author of these additions: Warnerus, schoolmaster of the collegiate church of St Symeon. Warnerus also informs his readers that he was writing on the order of Gerammus, provost of the church.[20]

Gerammus is mentioned in the extant sources as provost between at least 1048 and 1071; in 1075 there was already another man leading the community.[21] Warnerus, in turn, is mentioned in sources as *magister scholarum* in 1068.[22] He was apparently the successor of Udalricus, who was still active as schoolmaster in 1048.[23] Thus, we can narrow down the termini of Warnerus's writing the *nova miracula* to 1048 and 1075. In addition to Eberwinus's and Warnerus's contributions, there are some miracles in the text that have been added by anonymous authors, to which we shall shortly return.

Groups of Textual Witnesses

The *Vita et miracula S. Symeonis* was a popular text that met with a relatively broad medieval dissemination. As will be discussed below, it had various audiences, ranging from individual readers, interested in Benedictine and anchorite history or experiences in far-away, exotic places, especially in relation to pilgrimage, to communities whose members read and listened to the text as part of the annual liturgical cycle and/or perhaps in non-liturgical events of communal reading, occasions crucial to

---

[20] See HEIKKILÄ, *Vita et miracula*, pp. 179–80, with the transcript of Warnerus' prologue.

[21] HEYEN, *Stift St. Simeon*, pp. 736–37; HEIKKILÄ, *Vita et miracula*, pp. 181–82, with further source references.

[22] Trier, Stadtarchiv, Urk. F 11.

[23] *Urkundenbuch zur Geschichte der, jetzt die Preussischen Regierungsbezirke Coblenz und Trier bildenden mittelrheinischen Territorien, Erster Band, Von den ältesten Zeiten bis zum Jahre 1169*, ed. by H. BEYER, Koblenz, 1860, pp. 382–83 no. 328.

the making of communal identities. There survive almost sixty manuscripts containing the text in one version or another. The shelf-marks of the manuscripts as well as the sigla used in this study are given in Appendix 1.

Based on the dates of the extant manuscripts and taking into account the probably higher rate of manuscript losses during the earlier centuries, it seems that the *Vita et miracula* were copied most eagerly during the eleventh and twelfth centuries, and again towards the very end of the Middle Ages, as demonstrated in the figure below.

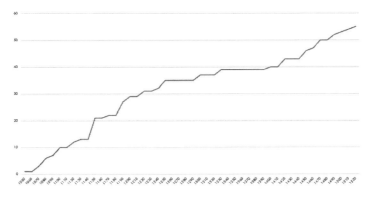

Fig. 1. A cumulative graph showing the extant manuscripts by date

My full collation of nearly sixty witnesses of *Vita et miracula* results in the identification of five *errores significativi*, or *Leitfehler*. The five significant variant readings allow us roughly to divide the material into seven groups, each representing a phase either of composition or subsequent transmission. The variants are given below.

1. Where did Symeon and his companion Hilarius act as pilgrim guides (c. 3 of the Bollandist edition)? According to some manuscripts this happened in Laodicea, but some give Lichaonia or *ibidem* (i.e. in Jerusalem) as the location. Furthermore, several manuscripts do not give the name of the location.

2. Does the text report that Symeon travelled via Rome on his way from Belgrade to Normandy (c. 14)?

3. Is Symeon's year of death given at the end of the *vita* (c. 20)?

4. Are miracles 6 and 7 in c. 27 given as two separate entities or as one (so that it consists of the beginning of miracle 6 and end of 7)?

5. Is miracle 21, found in c. 34, included?

We can use these five simple criteria to sketch seven large groups of textual witnesses.[24] (In the following the variants are given in the five places/criteria described above.)

Group	Where as pilgrims' guide?	Through Rome?	Year of death?	Miracles 6 and 7 as separate?	Miracle 21?
α	*Ibidem*	Yes	Yes	Yes	No
β	In Laodicea	Yes	No	Yes	Yes
γ	In Lichaonia	No	No	Yes	Yes
δ	In Laodicea	No	No	No	No
ε	Not mentioned	No	No	No	No
ζ	*Ibidem*	No	No	Yes	Yes
η	*Ibidem*	No	No	No	No

Table 1. Main groups of textual witnesses

The overall collation of the texts of the nearly sixty manuscripts and their vast number of variants confirms this hypothesis of the seven main groups. In addition to this result based on a traditional text-critical approach, the groups can also be sketched using computerized methods of stemmatology.[25] Let us use the three most successful and reliable computer-assisted approaches: RHM, PAUP* and the *Leitfehler*-based method.[26]

---

[24] Group α corresponds to "Mixed group" in T. HEIKKILÄ, "The possibilities and challenges of computer-assisted stemmatology. The example of *Vita et miracula S. Symeonis Treverensis*", *Analysis of Ancient and Medieval Texts and Manuscripts: Digital Approaches*, ed. by T. ANDREWS, C. MACÉ, Turnhout, 2014 (Lectio, Studies in the Transmission of Texts and Ideas, 1), pp. 19–42, at 32. Groups β and γ correspond to "Group 34" and Groups δ, ε and η correspond to "Group 33" in HEIKKILÄ, in *ibid.*, p. 32. *P* in group δ includes the year of death, but in a very different form to any other manuscript. Note that both *Ep* and *Me* are contaminated: *Ep* between groups α and η, *Me* between groups δ and η.

[25] See also the results of the preliminary work with a smaller group of manuscripts: HEIKKILÄ, "Possibilities and challenges", pp. 27–32.

[26] On the comparison of various computer-assisted methods, see T. ROOS, T. HEIKKILÄ, "Evaluating methods for computer-assisted stemmatology

The hypothesis of the RHM algorithm[27] developed for stemma-tology shows the version families and their relationships with one another very concretely:[28]

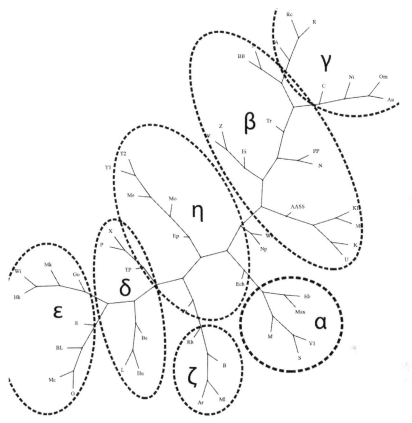

Fig. 2. Relationships between textual witnesses
as hypothesized by RHM algorithm

using artificial benchmark data sets", *Literary and Linguistic Computing*, 24 (2009), pp. 417–33.

[27] Compact description of the method: T. Roos, T. Heikkilä, P. Myl-lymäki, "A compression-based method for stemmatic analysis", *Proceedings of the 2006 conference on ECAI 2006: 17th European Conference on Artificial Intelligence*, Amsterdam, 2006, pp. 805–06.

[28] Here, we have omitted the very short or fragmentary witnesses *Ec*, *Mm* and *V2*. The graph is based on the analysis of the entire length of the textual witnesses. AASS is the Bollandist edition of 1695.

The PAUP* software,[29] originally developed to construct phylogenetic trees for the needs of evolutionary biology but often used
in computer-aided stemmatology, also finds the version families
clearly.[30]

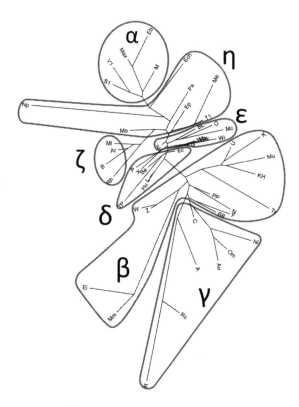

Fig. 3. Graph describing the relationships of the textual
witnesses according to PAUP* (Maximum parsimony on)

---

[29]   Description of the method: D. L. Swofford, *PAUP*: Phylogenetic Analysis using Parsimony (* and other methods), Version 4*, Sunderland, MA, 2003;
D. H. Huson, D. Bryant, "Application of phylogenetic networks in evolutionary studies", *Molecular Biology and Evolution*, 23 (2006), pp. 254–67.

[30]   Here, the algorithm applies the maximum parsimony method. PAUP*
and *Leitfehler*-based methods do not cope well with witnesses of varying
lengths. Therefore, their graphs are the result of analysing only the text of
the *vita*.

The *Leitfehler*-based method[31] yields the same result.[32] This method first identifies the *errores significativi* and then follows the traditional procedure of finding the best possible *stemma codicum*. Contrasting with the other computerized approaches, the method owes its central principles to classical textual criticism.[33]

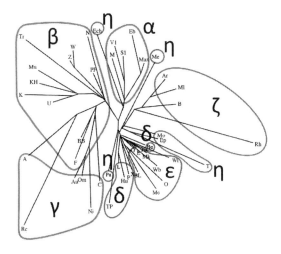

Fig. 4. Hypothesis of the *Leitfehler*-based approach

It must be emphasized that the stemmata of the three computational methods applied here are only hypotheses and share many of the shortcomings inherent in classical textual criticism. The identification of possible direct copies of the existing

[31]   Description of the method: P. ROELLI, D. BACHMANN, "Towards generating a stemma of complicated manuscript traditions: Petrus Alfonsi's Dialogus", *Revue d'histoire des textes*, 5 (2010), pp. 307–21.

[32]   At first glance, versions *Me* and *Pa* seem to lie outside their family, but on closer inspection it is merely a question of drawing technique. Unlike RHM, this method — and PAUP* too — also shows the relative distance between the text versions. Therefore *Ei*, *R*, *Mm* and *Np* are missing from this figure; in terms of content, they would appear so far from the other versions that the scale would be uninformative.

[33]   ROELLI, BACHMANN, "Generating a stemma"; P. ROELLI, "Petrus Alfonsi, or: On the mutual benefit of traditional and computerised stemmatology", *Analysis of Ancient and Medieval Texts and Manuscripts*, ed. by ANDREWS, MACÉ, pp. 43–64.

versions or contamination are beyond today's algorithm-based inquiries. Furthermore, their hypothesized stemmata are bifurcating. Be that as it may, the results from these inquiries are persuasive. For the three computerized methods applied build on different basic principles and, naturally, operate through diverse algorithms; even so, their hypothesized textual families almost entirely correlate with each other and those suggested by a classical text-critical analysis. In other words, relationships between the manuscripts and manuscript families emerge as nearly identical in each of our analyses.[34]

Our explorations, classical and computer-based, also suggest further divisions into subgroups. These results are given in Appendix 2. Another result of significance is that affinities between main groups emerge. On the one hand β and γ and on the other hand δ and ε share a large number of *errores coniunctivi*, i.e., readings unique to the said groups. These groups must, then, be closely related to each other. The variants show that γ descends from β and ε descends from δ. The group ζ, on the other hand, testifies to successive contamination:[35] its *vita* was taken from η and the collection of miracles from β.

The Early Versions of the *Vita*

When publication had taken place, the author and his or her institution could not control transmission in any effective way. Dissemination is a process that is difficult to describe and understand in detail since, more often than not, we only have a minority of the witnesses that once existed to provide evidence of the work's diffusion. Even so, the good quantity of evidence on which this present inquiry rests does allow many insights into the earliest intentional phases of distribution — that is, publishing.

---

[34] See also the similar results from P. A. MAAS, "Computer aided stemmatics — the case of fifty-two text versions of Carakasaṃhitā Vimānasthāna 8.67–157", *Wiener Zeitschrift für die Kunde Südasiens*, 52–53 (2009–2010), pp. 63–119, at 57, 97–98: the computer-aided methods give trustworthy insights into the structure of the stemma of a very complicated handwritten tradition. The tradition he studied has fifty-two textual witnesses, i.e., almost the same number as the present investigation.

[35] See HEIKKILÄ, "Dealing with open textual traditions", pp. 260–66.

The often bewildering combinations of textual variants testifies to contamination at primary stages of transmission. For instance, on the simplistic level of the five important traits discussed above, any other explanation would require a polygenesis of criteria 1 and 2 of Table 1 above, which is highly improbable. In spite of there being several authorial layers of the *Vita et miracula*, we can safely assume that the actual *vita* was written by Abbot Eberwinus. However, it is impossible to trace the textual tradition back to one "original" version by him. Rather, the "authorial original" is a complex textual whole, a result of copying and disseminating several slightly different versions under Eberwinus's oversight, or "editions", as it were. Such a genesis must explain the contaminated status of the tradition.

Differences in the *vita* between the main groups are not of crucial significance to the work's substance. For the whole biography of Symeon and its audience, it was of next-to-no importance whether Symeon acted as a pilgrims' guide in Laodicea, Lichaonia or *ibidem* (criterion 1), or whether Symeon visited Rome on his journey to France or not (2). At the same time, such additions and clarifications were just the kind of changes the author might have wanted and could have made when reviewing and improving his text.[36]

The earliest versions of the *vita* cannot be clearly traced back to a single original manuscript. Importantly, early on there were four versions of the text being transmitted more or less simultaneously. They are shown in Figure 5 below.

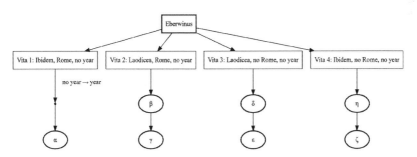

Fig. 5. The development of the *vita* text (main traits and text groups)

---

[36] Generally on this challenge, see TROVATO, *Lachmann's Method*, p. 161; M. L. WEST, *Textual Criticism and Editorial Technique Applicable to Greek and Latin Texts*, Stuttgart, 1973, pp. 15–16.

These four versions did not necessarily descend from four parallel authorial manuscripts. Such a mode of authorial preservation would have been impractical with regard to modifying the text. Textual layers are likely to derive from corrections and additions made to one or two authorial manuscripts, upon which four subsequent primary copies drew. As such, the tradition attests to contamination already in the course of authorial publication. In the passage that mentions Symeon as a pilgrims' guide, the first variant may have read *ibidem*, but, preferring accuracy, the author might later have elaborated the text by replacing the word with *Laodiciae* in the margins or between the lines. Perhaps *iter faciens per Romam* was added to the description of Symeon's journey to Western Europe in the same way. Or perhaps these two adjustments embody a reverse editorial policy, from scrupulousness to indistinctness. Copyists at subsequent stages of transmission could therefore encounter any of four "authorial recensions". But all of this remains speculation. Leaving speculation to one side, we have to suffice with the knowledge that there were several parallel versions very early on, to which the survivors are more or less distorted witnesses.

As it is obvious that some of the earliest manuscripts had several text layers resulting from modification, correction, and other alteration, the transmission was thoroughly contaminated from the beginning. The realities of publication and primary dissemination cannot be captured here as a neat stemma, an observation of significance in the context of this present volume.

The hypothesized primary transmission from several versions of the *vita* suggests swift dissemination already in the late 1030s and 1040s. This, in turn, resonates with the known facts about the swift making of Symeon's cult: an early version was sent to the pope in 1035; there was an altar (probably dedicated to Symeon) at Porta Nigra in autumn 1035; the collegiate church dedicated to St Symeon was established in Trier in 1041 at the very latest;[37] the cult spread quickly especially in the course of its first deca-

---

[37] HEYEN, *Stift St. Simeon*, pp. 103, 263; cf. Trier, Stadtarchiv, Urk. F 10; E. WISPLINGHOFF, "Untersuchungen zur ältesten Geschichte des Stiftes S. Simeon in Trier", *Archiv für mittelrheinische Kirchengeschichte*, 8 (1956), pp. 76–93, at 78–80, 87–90.

des.[38] All this would point towards a need for manuscripts containing the texts on Symeon at the very time the textual canon was still in the making.

Although the extant manuscripts only represent an unknown fraction of the whole medieval textual tradition of the *Vita et miracula*, they do testify to a very early spreading of the text. Of the textual groups shaped above, at least β, δ and η are indeed very old and can be securely dated to the eleventh century.[39] A look at the geographical provenances of the oldest manuscripts up to *c.* 1100 yields an interesting insight: the extant manuscripts of Group β and its derivative Group γ originate from the west of Trier, from France and Belgium, whereas the early representatives of Groups δ and its derivative Group ε are from the east of Trier. Group η, in turn, seems to have remained rather locally disseminated (see Figure 6).[40] This pattern strengthens our hypothesis of at least three roots of the family tree. It also suggests that the early dissemination of the text was a result of copying from three exemplars — or at least from three differing states of modified text.

---

[38]   There were relics of St Symeon in the monastery of St Arnulf in Metz as early as in 1049 (*Dedicationes ecclesiae S. Arnulfi*, ed. by G. WAITZ, MGH *SS*, 24 (1879), pp. 545–49, at 547). Interestingly, we know of an eleventh-century manuscript in the same monastery (Metz, BM, 398 (*s.* xi), destroyed in 1944). The relics and cult of St Symeon were present in the monastery of Tholey (the abbot of which was Eberwinus himself!) in the eleventh century (SCHMID, *Poppo*, p. 49; N. IRSCH, *Der Dom zu Trier*, Düsseldorf, 1931 (Die Kunstdenkmäler der Rheinprovinz, Dreizehnter Band, I. Abteilung: Die Kunstdenkmäler der Stadt Trier), pp. 323–24). In the East, the earliest mentions of Symeon's relics are in St Emmeram in Regensburg in 1052 (*Notae S. Emmerammi* (MGH *SS*, 15/2 (1887–8), pp. 1094–1098, and 17 (1861), pp. 572–76), 573, 1096).

[39]   β: *BB* (Toul?, *s.* xi^ex) and *F* (Fécamp, *s.* xi/xii); δ: *Ec* (Echternach, 1051–1081) and *Be* (Trier region?, *c.* 1100); η: *T1* & *T2* (Trier/Mosel region?, *s.* xi²) and *Ep* (Senones, *s.* xi/xii). Group α does not have this early *terminus post quem non*, *Max* (Trier, soon after 1235) being its oldest surviving manuscript.

[40]   In fact, the geographical dissemination of the groups follows the same pattern until the very end of the Middle Ages, with the popular group β as the only exception, as it was spread also in south-western Germany in the twelfth century (*Ei* (Einsiedeln, *s.* xii), *W* (Weissenau, *c.* 1170–1200), and *Z* (Zwiefalten, *c.* 1120–1225)).

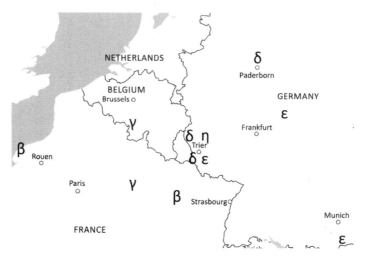

Fig. 6. The known manuscripts up to *c.* 1100.
The labels indicate the textual groups

Of the two parts of the Symeon text, *miracula* was by nature a
"living" text. As new miracles took place, these were added to the
whole. *Vita*, in turn, was not expected to be modified after it was
completed other than perhaps in small details. The addition of a
foreword to the text was often considered a sign that the work
had reached completion.[41] In this respect, the early groups differ fundamentally: all copies of βγ contain Eberwinus' prologue,
whereas none of the witnesses of δε has it.[42] Is this an indication
of pre-publication circulation? That is, did group δ originate from
a text that was circulated prior to Eberwinus's completion of the
work? As we shall see in the analysis of the *miracula*, it is also
probable that the texts were disseminated from two different geographical locations from very early on.

Whereas groups βγ and δε are interesting in terms of the early
circulation, even groups α and η may be traced back to the early

---

[41]   See A. WENZ-HAUBFLEISCH, *Miracula post mortem. Studien zum Quel-
lenwert hochmittelalterlicher Mirakelsammlungen vornehmlich des ostfränkisch-
deutschen Reiches*, Siegburg, 1998 (Siegburger Studien, XXVI), pp. 97–99,
with several examples.

[42]   *P* (group δ) contains the foreword, but only as a later addition from the
twelfth century.

publishing of *vita* and *miracula* from the collegiate church of St Symeon in Trier. Manuscript *Ep*, belonging to Group η, is the only one known to include St Symeon's schoolmaster Warnerus' foreword to the *nova miracula*. Since Warnerus wrote at St Symeon's sometime between 1048 and 1075, his prologue in a manuscript within group η (and only in this group) proves the existence of an early version, representing Group η, within the said chronological termini. Warnerus informs his readers that he wrote under commission from the provost of the church, Gerammus.[43] His work was, therefore, an integral part of propagating the sainthood of Symeon. Still, his prologue was by all appearances very seldom copied, since it is known from no other member of group η. Neither is it contained in the later manuscripts with known provenance from St Symeon's.

In group α, the relatively young fifteenth- and sixteenth-century composite manuscript *S* is of special interest. Its colophon states that it was copied directly and word for word from the original manuscript at St Symeon's.[44] Because *S*'s textual tradition repeatedly differs from our other manuscripts, it is obvious that there had been more than one copy of the *Vita et miracula* available in the church of St Symeon during the preceding centuries. All this variation between versions within the same small ecclesiastical community evidences an early and constant interest in modifying and developing the text.

Miracle Collection

Let us now turn our attention to the latter part of the *Vita et miracula S. Symeonis*, to the miracle collection. As mentioned above, it was in the very nature of a medieval *miracula* collection that its contents could and should be modified, extended and abbreviated according to local needs and as the saint's relics performed new miracles. After the first short collection of early

[43]   *Ep*, fol. 102[r].

[44]   *S*, fol. 31[v]: "Habetis omnia divi Symeonis miracula, charissime frater, et totam eius vitam, nihilque deest neque vitae neque miraculis, sed omnia de verbo ad verbum habetis, ut scriptum est et habetur in libro originali ecclesiae Sancti Symeonis." In the late sixteenth century, the first of the two parts of the manuscript belonged to Johann Kyllburg, a canon of the collegiate church of St Symeon in 1559–1592. See fol. 1[r]: "Johannes Kilburch".

miracles written down by Eberwinus and included in the version
of the text sent to the pope in 1035,[45] many more miracles were
added to the text canon in the course of the following decades.
In its longest form, the *miracula* contains thirty-two miracles.
The thorough study of the manuscripts and their text provides
insights into the writing and accumulating of the miracles, and
their publishing.

Many of Symeon's earliest miracles are either explicitly dated
in the text or are datable on the basis of internal evidence.
Interestingly, there are two miracles Symeon performed while
he was still alive (miracles 4 and 5, i.e. c. 25–26 of the Bollandist edition). The miracles performed by a living saint were
exceptional and highly respected, since they created an analogy
to Christ himself.[46] As it would have not made any sense to
hide such gems in the middle of more generic miracles, I propose that they constituted the grand finale of the *miracula* sent
to the pope.[47]

Analysis of high-medieval miracle collections has shown
that authors normally aimed at organizing the miracles primarily according to chronology and secondarily according to theme.[48] Symeon's *miracula* is obviously a mixture of both systems.
It consists of several sequences following different principles.
While preparing the "papal" version of the collection, Eberwinus followed chronology, with one exception: he placed the
miracle which Symeon performed before his death at the end of
the "papal" *miracula*. After this initial version had been fixed,
Eberwinus did not want to deconstruct the text but added the

---

[45]   The letter of Archbishop Poppo of Trier to Pope Benedict IX clearly
indicates that already the first text version included a collection of miracles.
See, for example, *Gesta Treverorum*, ed. WAITZ, p. 178: "litteris nostris ad
hanc apostolicam sedem […] cum illius viri sancti vita et miraculis missis".
See HEYEN, *Stift St. Simeon*, p. 468.

[46]   On such miracles, see, for example, WENZ-HAUBFLEISCH, *Miracula*,
p. 38; P.-A. SIGAL, *L'homme et le miracle dans la France médiévale (XIe–XIIe
siècle)*, Paris, 1985, pp. 32–34.

[47]   HEIKKILÄ, *Vita et miracula*, pp. 170–73. In earlier scholarship, the end
of this version has been located cautiously and loosely somewhere between
miracles 6 and 15. See WENZ-HAUBFLEISCH, *Miracula*, p. 101; COENS, "Un
document inédit", p. 185.

[48]   WENZ-HAUBFLEISCH, *Miracula*, pp. 121–24.

subsequent miracles following two principles: on the one hand, he grouped together miracles which shared some common aspect; on the other hand, he pulled together miracles that had occurred around the same time.

It is obvious that not all miracles belonging to the whole canon of the *miracula*, stretching from the 1030s to the 1080s, were written down by Eberwinus, who died probably in the early 1040s. In fact, a stylistic detail lets us estimate the full extent of his text. The *miracula* can be divided into two groups according to the terminology used when describing Symeon and his burial place in Porta Nigra. The first group employs the respectful, but not strictly saintly epithets of *vir Dei* and, more rarely, *famulus Dei* or *famulus Christi* (miracles 1–20, c. 22–33). Here, Porta Nigra is only referred to as the tomb of Symeon (e.g. *sepulchrum viri Dei*). In the second group, the terms *sanctus*, *beatus* and *confessor* are used for Symeon. Such epithets were used for established, venerated saints. Here, Porta Nigra is called an *ecclesia* (miracles 21–32, c. 34–43). As there is no culmination point or radical change in Symeon's status in the text between miracles 20 and 21, the difference is probably based on authorial conventions rather than Symeon's being actually canonized only after miracle 20. External evidence suggests that the canonization had taken place much earlier. Therefore, one may assume that the change in vocabulary between miracles 20 and 21 indicates a change of author. If so, Eberwinus would have been the author of miracles 1–20.

We have already discussed above the contribution to the *miracula* of Warnerus, schoolmaster at St Symeon's. He took over the task of adding new miracles to the text after the death of Eberwinus. In addition, Warnerus also composed a prologue to the *nova miracula*, which precedes miracle 22 (c. 35). Yet, the study of the manuscripts and the textual tradition shows that the canon of Symeon's miracles contains material that does not originate from Symeon or Warnerus. The contents of the surviving manuscripts suggest that Warnerus contributed nine new miracles (22–27, 29–31, i.e. c. 35–40, 41–43). The implication is that yet another author, an anonymous one, was responsible for miracles 21 (c. 34), 28 (missing in previous editions), and 32 (c. 43).

Interestingly, none of the manuscripts with Warnerus' *nova miracula* contains miracle 21.[49] As it must have been Warnerus' intention to include as many miracles as possible to honour the patron of his community, this absence is striking. The only plausible explanation is that the manuscript he chose to continue with his new miracles did not contain miracle 21. This solution is in line with the fact that the manuscripts that convey miracle 21 end with it; that is, they do not contain any later miracles.[50]

This is a key point in understanding the publishing of *Vita et miracula S. Symeonis.* As Eberwinus was the abbot of three monasteries — St Martin in Trier, St Paul in Verdun and St Mauritius in Tholey — he did not write at the collegiate church of St Symeon, to which he was never affiliated. Accordingly, his working copy must have been kept somewhere other than in St Symeon's. On the other hand, that community dedicated to St Symeon had need of their own manuscript(s) of the *vita* and *miracula* of their patron. A division must have taken place in the manuscript tradition around the time the church of St Symeon was established in the latter half of the 1030s. Subsequently, it is logical that the text was being continued and the miracles accumulated in two places: (1) in one of Eberwinus' monasteries[51] by Eberwinus, the "grand old man" of all things related to Symeon; and (2) in Symeon's own collegiate church in Porta Nigra, Trier. The collegiate church's base manuscript contained miracles 1–20, and Warnerus' work was based on that. To conclude, Eberwinus or another anonymous author, working in a church other than St Symeon's, added miracle 21, and Warnerus, who continued a manuscript produced for St Symeon's prior to the said addition, remained unaware of that insertion.

---

[49] *Ech, Ep, M* and *Mo.* The very young *S* is an exception, since it has been put together from two parts, of which at least the latter (*S2*) is thoroughly contaminated. It was apparently collected to contain as many miracles as possible centuries after Warnerus' time.

[50] *Ar, Au, B, BB, C, Ei, Ml, Ni, Om, Pa, Rc, Rh, S2, Tr, V2, W* and *Z.* These manuscripts belong to groups β, γ and ζ. The young and contaminated *S2* is an exception.

[51] Probably not in St Martin's at Trier, as the extant *M* originating from that very monastery belongs to another group (α, not β, γ or ζ that contained Eberwinus' version). The incipit of *M* actually mentions Eberwinus as the abbot of St Martin in Trier.

Consequently, both Eberwinus' own community and the church of St Symeon were obvious, authoritative centres for the dissemination of the text. The recognition that the text originated from two centres helps us understand the complicated publishing history and dissemination of the text. When Eberwinus died, the text of that branch of the tradition was no longer continued — with the exception of miracle 21, which may, or may not, have been authored by Eberwinus. At any rate, it was circulated only with his version of the *miracula*.[52] Consequently, groups β, γ and ζ transmit the text closest to the version authored by Eberwinus. At St Symeon's, in turn, it was logical to keep on adding new miracles as they took place. After all, it was at St Symeon's where most of the recorded miracles were performed and reported.

The two anonymous miracles 28 and 32 highlight the multilateral evolution of the miracle collection. Miracle 28 is probably a local addition made outside of Trier, perhaps in the monastery of Echternach. It has survived in a single manuscript, *Ech* (Echternach, s. xii), and it did not make its way into the *miracula* in other witnesses of the same group. Interestingly, miracle 28 has not been added to the end of the *miracula* in its manuscript, but in the middle of Warnerus' text, obviously according to the contextual principle of arrangement. The case manifests the diffusion of Symeon's cult to faraway places.[53]

The final miracle (32) of the text is clearly a later addition. According to the text, the miracle took place at the tomb of the saint in Porta Nigra on 14 May 1086.[54] Warnerus could hardly have authored his passage at so late a date. More probably, this widely transmitted miracle is revealing of the efforts of the members of the church of St Symeon in recording new miracles and thus cherishing the memory of their patron saint after Warnerus' time.[55] The foregoing conclusions about the authorship of various sections of the *Vita et miracula* are laid out in the following table.

---

[52] An epilogue was composed to mark this. It did not find a very broad dissemination, and has only survived in a single manuscript, *Ei*, pp. 455–56.

[53] *Ech*, fol. 192ᵛ; see *Vita et miracula*, m27 (c. 40).

[54] *Vita et miracula*, m32 (c. 43).

[55] This text passage is included only in manuscripts *Ech*, *M* and *S2*.

Author	Passage	Date
Eberwinus	*Prologus Eberwini, Vita, Miracula* 1–20 (c. 1–33)	Summer 1035 to c. 1040 (?)
Eberwinus/ Anonymous A	*Miraculum* 21 (c. 34), *Epilogus*	Late 1035 to late eleventh century
Warnerus	*Prologus Warneri, Miracula* 22–27, 29–31 (c. 35–40, 41–43	Between 1048 and 1075
Anonymous B	*Miraculum* 28	After 1086, not later than the twelfth-century date of the manuscript
Anonymous C	*Miraculum* 32 (c. 43)	1086 or soon after, before miracle 28

Table 2. Textual layers of the *Vita et miracula*

We may now complement the results from our discussion of the fifth criterion (that is, the inclusion or omission of miracle 21) with the fourth criterion, which concerns the text of miracles 6 and 7. Originally, they were quite obviously two separate miracles. Yet the manuscripts of groups δ, ε and η combined them as a result of a copyist's *saut du même au même*. Taking into account the two criteria related to the *miracula*, the text groups can be divided as demonstrated in Figure 7 below.

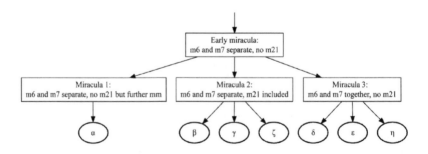

Fig. 7. Development of the *Miracula*

Publishing St Symeon

The publication of the texts on St Symeon, or their primary dissemination in a premediated fashion, was a long process, not a single act. The text canon was being modified and new materials were being added for more than half a century. Several parties were involved, the most important contributors being Eberwinus and, after his death, Warnerus. During his lifetime, Eberwinus, the original author of the *vita*, was apparently in charge of continuing the *miracula* in one of his monasteries. It was also logical for the newly established church of St Symeon to take care of this task in addition. Thus, the miracle collection was being worked on in two different locations, and the collection was continued in both places on the basis of manuscripts representing slightly different traditions. This explains in part the very complicated history of the text.

There was never only one "original" version of the text in circulation, but several texts, characterized by authorial revision. On account of the mixture of authorial and scribal variants, the tradition became very complicated. That sort of textual condition also implies that significant effort was put into editing and copying the text. The work was obviously of importance to copyists and audiences.

In general, there must be several factors at play behind the complex manuscript dissemination of a text. First would be the authorial intention.[56] The tradition of the *Vita et miracula S. Symeonis* implies that Eberwinus revised his text on several occasions. Should we consider his last version to be the final, "correct" authorial version? We must reply in the negative. One of the main propagators of the cult of St Symeon, Eberwinus

---

[56]   Unravelling the final authorial intention has been the governing principle of one editorial tradition. See D. VAN HULLE, "Genetic maps in modern philology", in *Handbook of Stemmatology*, ed. by ROELLI, pp. 524–33, at 525; G. T. TANSELLE, "The editorial problem of final authorial intention", *Studies in Bibliography*, 29 (1976), pp. 167–211, at 171–72; F. BOWERS, "Textual criticism", in *The Aims and Methods of Scholarship in Modern Languages and Literatures*, ed. by J. THORPE, New York, NY, 1970, pp. 23–42, at 30; W. W. GREG, *The Editorial Problem in Shakespeare: A Survey of the Foundations of the Text*, Oxford, 1951, pp. x–xii; R. B. McKERROW, *Prolegomena for the Oxford Shakespeare: A Study in Editorial Method*, Oxford, 1939.

must have hoped, and expected, that many more miracles would be added to the *miracula*, even after his own death. At any rate, the combination of evidence on Symeon's canonization and the study of the manuscripts makes it clear that the work was deliberately disseminated — and thus published — continually after 1035. Should one want to find an extant text as close to Eberwinus' version as possible, one should study the manuscripts of group β. If, on the other hand, one prefers to scrutinize the authorial version of *nova miracula* by Warnerus, the focus would be manuscripts in group α, and Warnerus' prologue in the contaminated *Ep*.

While authors were the principal operators of publication, the role of copyists was decisive for subsequent circulation. It was the latter, and their supervisors or clients, who decided which texts and which parts of texts were to be disseminated. The tradition of our text shows that it was the Life, rather than the miracles, of Symeon that was of primary interest to parties responsible for dissemination after publication. There are versions without *miracula* or with an abridged collection of miracles.[57] Although the authors of the *miracula* added local flavour by including names and places, the types of miracles performed by Symeon were rather generic. As was the case with most *vitae*, audiences apparently preferred to dwell on episodes from the saint's life by virtue of their exemplary value. In addition, the *vita* also contained a wealth of exotic stories, which would have been found fascinating, especially for their association with pilgrimage. Another example of such an interest in exotica is the *Navigatio S. Brendani*, which is conveyed together with the Symeon texts in a number of manuscripts (as discussed below).

The text on Symeon also circulated as a part of hagiographical collections, a prime instance of which is the *Magnum legendarium Austriacum*, a collection eagerly copied in Austrian monasteries (manuscripts *Hk*, *Mk*, *Wi*; see also the list of lost manuscripts in Appendix 1). In such cases, when the *Vita et miracula S. Symeonis* was copied as only one of several hundred texts in a collection,

---

[57]   Manuscripts containing only the *vita*: *F*, *Hu*, *Mm*, and *PP*. Interestingly, *F*, *Mm*, and *PP* belong to group β2 that is probably closest to Eberwinus' own text. The manuscripts containing a selection of miracles are *A*, *Be*, *K*, *KH*, *Mo*, *Mu*, *N*, *NP*, *U*, and *V*.

the copying naturally does not evidence any special interest in Symeon.

The minute comparison of variant readings of the whole textual tradition through classical methods of textual criticism, as well as through computer-assisted approaches, allows us to shape a hypothetical stemma of the whole textual tradition based on the known extant witnesses. The stemma is given below in Figure 8. It must be emphasized that hypothetical stemmata cannot do justice to the complexity and fluidity of a convoluted textual tradition such as ours. Under such circumstances stemmata should be taken as general overviews rather than precise depictions of transmission. Various forms of contamination were in evidence in the tradition of the *Vita et miracula S. Symeonis*: simultaneous and successive contamination of manuscripts as well as contamination of various versions of the text all played their part while the text was being disseminated.[58] For instance, the stemmatological study of the separate *vita* and *miracula* sections of group ζ reveals an interesting insight into its textual history. In the *vita*, this group's closest textual relatives can be found within the representatives of group η, whereas in *miracula* they are in group β. In other words, ζ is a result of a successive contamination, as the *vita* must have been copied from η and *miracula* from β. To conclude, a stemma describing the history of any medieval text always and inevitably remains a hypothesis, and as such ours should be treated as a practical tool to visualize the probable diffusion of the text.

[58] See HEIKKILÄ, "Dealing with open textual traditions", pp. 258–61, 263–65 (with *M* of this article as an example of successive contamination).

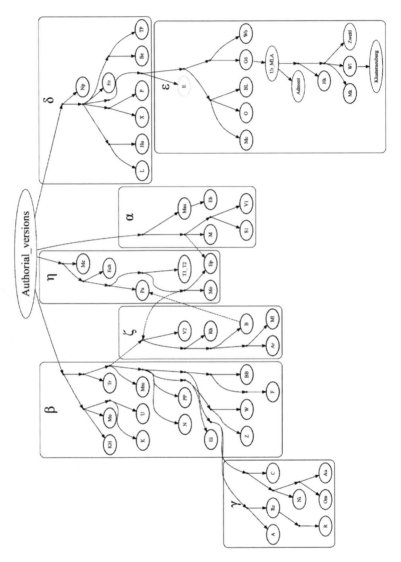

Fig. 8. The hypothesized stemma of the textual tradition.
with the seven main groups of witnesses

We have identified seven textual families, each of which descends ultimately from manuscripts held either at St Symeon's or in one of Eberwinus' monasteries. While it is impossible to capture the precise minutiae of transmission at each step, we can often follow the chain of copying through extant manuscripts, as displayed in Figure 8. In one case, an elementary step in manuscript transmission, an exemplar and its copy, *Max – Eb*, has been preserved. It would be too straightforward to consider the emergence of each of the seven families purely as representing deliberate authorial publishing. Rather, what is witnessed by the extant manuscripts pertains also to the non-authorial sphere of scribal dissemination, undertaken by copyists and occasionally shaped by the vagaries of manuscript transmission. On account of the complex nature of our text's transmission, it would be a futile exercise to seek to distinguish precisely between the authorial and the scribal. Even so, our results do suggest multiple "bursts of publishing" at the primary steps of the transmission. What is more, a survey of geographical diffusion of the witnesses of individual textual groups provides us with insights of interest into the mechanics of how the text was disseminated. (See Appendices 1 and 2 for the dates, provenances and groups of individual witnesses.) Figures 9 and 10 below chart the results.

It is striking how the seven groups shaped by the text-critical and stemmatological study of the whole tradition correlate with geographical distribution. Groups α, γ, η, and ζ are geographically very coherent: their witnesses are clearly concentrated on the map. Groups β, δ, and ε, in turn, show somewhat broader geographical variation. Interestingly, β and δ belong to the earliest phases of the textual mutation of *Vita et miracula*. In the larger picture (Figure 10), it may be seen that all groups spread in one geographical direction from Trier — with the exception of the early group β containing the final version of the text composed by the extremely well connected Eberwinus. A plausible scenario would be that his final version, the author's original, enjoyed a special authority and was copied several times directly from Eberwinus's own manuscript — and direct copies were disseminated to the east and west.

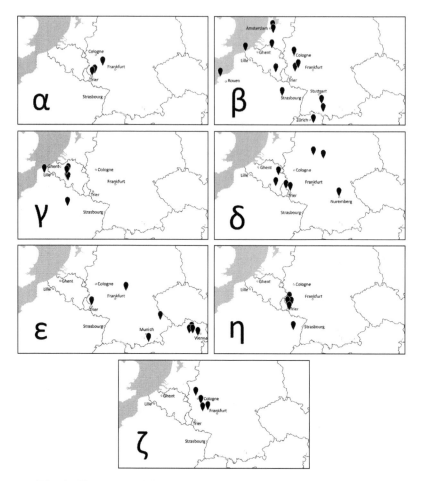

Fig. 9. The geographical dissemination of the seven groups. All
known manuscripts are included; the groups, dates and provenances
of individual manuscripts are given in Appendices 1–2

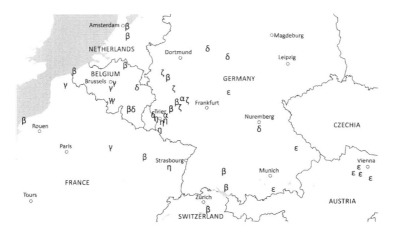

Fig. 10. The dissemination of all manuscripts.
The Greek letter indicates the textual groups

The Audiences and their Interests

Patterns and choices in copying were closely related to the expectations of the audience. Does the study of the whole textual tradition allow conclusions to be drawn about the readership of *Vita et
miracula?* The readership was drawn from ecclesiastical and religious circles. As might be expected, we do not know of any manuscript of the text with lay origins. The tradition reveals that the
texts were widespread in monasteries and collegiate churches and
among secular clerks. At the same time, however, it is clear that
it was the Benedictine monasteries that were the most important
nodes in the network of transmission. In addition, the manuscript
tradition shows that religious communities of women played only
a minor role in the dissemination.

We have early Benedictine manuscripts from Abdinghof,
Echternach, Einsiedeln, Fécamp, Göttweig, Saint-Hubert en
Ardenne, Saint-Laurent in Lüttich, Saint-Pierre-aux-Monts in
Châlons, Saint-Pierre in Senones, Tegernsee, and Zwiefalten.
Although Symeon was not, strictly speaking, himself a Benedic-
tine, the original author of our text was a Benedictine abbot. It
has even been suggested that Eberwinus particularly emphasi-

zed the "Benedictine" features of the life of Symeon.[59] Be that
as it may, it would seem that, at least initially, circulation was
strongly tied to the passing of exemplars between Benedictine
monasteries. The observable Benedictine prominence in the
manuscript evidence no doubt betrays where the text was mainly
read during the first flush of its circulation in the eleventh and
twelfth centuries.

The Premonstratensians and Cistercians should also be mentioned. In the surviving manuscripts from the communities of the
Premonstratensian order, founded in 1120, we have Symeon texts
from the second half of the twelfth and early thirteenth centuries: from Arnstein, Knechtsteden, Weissenau, and Windberg.
The first two of these witnesses are very similar: both are early
representatives of the so-called *Rheinisches Legendar*, which apparently circulated widely in Premonstratensian monasteries.[60] The
versions from the Cistercian order are somewhat younger, mainly
from the thirteenth century: from Aulne, Clairmarais, Heiligenkreuz (*s.* xii[ex]), Lilienfeld, St Thomas an der Kyll, Nizelles (*s.* xv),
and Zwettl.

The very centre of the cult — St Symeon in Porta Nigra, Trier
— was not a monastery but a collegiate church. Interestingly, it
was only towards the last centuries of the Middle Ages that other
collegiate churches and houses of Augustinian canons began to
play a more significant role in the transmission and thus the readership of *Vita et miracula*. There are some early examples (for
example, from the Augustinian house of Sankt Pölten, and the
collegiate church of Münstermaifeld), but the majority of the surviving manuscripts from Augustinian houses and collegiate churches date from the fourteenth and fifteenth centuries: from the
Augustinian houses of Böddeken, Eberhardsklausen, Corsendonk,
Herrenleichnam in Cologne, Rouge-Cloître, Springiersbach, and
Niederwerth, as well as from the collegiate churches of Münstermaifeld, St Lambert in Düsseldorf, and St Paulin in Trier. From
a geographical point of view, these relatively late copies of the

---

[59]   HEYEN, *Stift St. Simeon*, p. 480.

[60]   W. LEVISON, *Passiones Vitaeque sanctorum aevi Merovingici. Conspectus
codicum hagiographicorum. Conspectus codicum hagiographicorum*, Hannover/
Leipzig, 1919 (MGH *Scriptores rerum Merovingicarum*, 7), p. 538; F. HODDICK,
Das Münstermaifelder Legendar, Bonn, 1928, pp. 36–43.

Symeon texts do not mark the diffusion of the text into new areas but rather testify to new ecclesiastical foundations, mainly Augustinian houses, in need of books.

The historical Symeon was a man with several careers and roles. Judging from the titles and incipits in the copies, he was venerated more as a saintly monk than a holy hermit. The epithets most frequently applied to him are *monachus* and *confessor*, and in joint third place are *diaconus* and *inclusus*.[61] The same emphasis remained unchanged for centuries. The *tituli* were certainly often copied from one manuscript to another, but it suffices to have a look at the manuscripts of groups β, γ, ε, and η to see that this was not always the case. The varying epithets give us a glimpse on how the later copyists and readers of these texts conceived of Symeon, and which sides of the saint they emphasized.

It is obvious that the burst of copying of texts on St Symeon in the fifteenth century had to do with the *Devotio moderna*. A great number of the extant late manuscripts were copied in and for Augustinian canons of the Windesheim congregation.[62] Symeon exemplified a monk who lived in the world and set a high moral standard. This resonated perfectly with the *Devotio moderna*'s reform programme for the clergy, which was much inspired by monastic ideals.

With the intense support of the local archbishop backed up by the extraordinarily rapid canonization by the pope, one could have predicted a golden future for the cult of St Symeon. This turned out not to be the case, however. Hagiographical texts on a saint are a prerequisite for an effective cult. What kind of a role did the actual cult play in the dissemination and publishing of the texts on Symeon? Some of the manuscripts indicate that their Symeon texts — normally *vita*, not *miracula* — were used in a liturgical context.[63] For the others, we need to resort to a comparison: were

[61]   *monachus*: *Gö, F, Ml, Mm, Mo, N, P, R, Rc, Rh, Wb, X*; *monachus et diaconus*: *Ei, K, KH, Mu, Me, U*; *monachus et heremita*: *A*; *heremita*: *Au, C, Om, Ni*; *inclusus*: *BB, BL, Hk, Mk, Np, Wi*.

[62]   *Eb, K, KH, Rc*, and *V*. In addition, *Mu* was written for a community of lay sisters associated with the Windesheim congregation through their confessors.

[63]   For example, the text has been divided into *lectiones* in *BB, E, Ec, Ech, L, Mc*, and *Mo*.

the places where the saint was culted and the manuscripts containing texts on him similarly spread? In order to answer that question, one must sketch the geographical dimensions of the St Symeon's cult.

An examination of the liturgical commemoration of Symeon — the spread of his relics, the churches under his saintly patronage, and other common features of medieval saintly cults — is suggestive of a cult of secondary importance. Although the cult has not so far been studied thoroughly, the present state of knowledge yields a picture that is clear enough for the purposes of this discussion. The cult spread especially within the ecclesiastical province of Trier and its vicinity. Symeon never became a well-known or popular saint elsewhere.[64] The focus of his liturgical veneration can be seen in the diocese and especially in the city of Trier, and by the time of arrival of printed liturgical books in the late fifteenth century, the feast of St Symeon was only included in the diocesan kalendar of Trier. Outside of Trier, the cult spread mainly in the west, in Lorraine, but also in the Rhineland. Interestingly, most of the sources of liturgical veneration come from the west of Trier, while the evidence for Symeon's relics comes from the east, especially from southern Germany.

---

[64] On the cult and the liturgy, see T. BAUER, "Zur Liturgie des hl. Simeon", in HEYEN, *Das Stift St. Simeon in Trier*, pp. 513–27, at 516–27; E. A. OVERGAAUW, *Martyrologes manuscrits des anciens diocèses d'Utrecht et de Liège. Étude sur le développement et la diffusion du Martyrologe d'Usuard*, Hilversum, 1993 (Middeleeuwse Studies en Bronnen XXX: I–II), I, pp. 79–123, 317–421, II, p. 760 and *passim*; HEYEN, *Stift St. Simeon*, pp. 484–502; HEIKKILÄ, *Vita et miracula*, pp. 237–53; P. MIESGES, *Der Trierer Festkalender. Seine Entwicklung und seine Verwendung zu Urkundendatierungen. Ein Beitrag zur Heortologie und Chronologie des Mittelalters*, Trier, 1915 (Trierisches Archiv, Ergänzungsheft, 15), 1. Jun., *passim*. In Trier, the following churches: the cathedral, St Agnes, St Alban, St Eucharius/Matthias, St Irminen, St Marien ad martyres, St Maximin and St Symeon (cf. the calendar in BL, Harley MS 3062). In Trier diocese: Altenberg über der Lahn, Andernach, Arnstein, Dietkirchen, Echternach, Klausen, Laach, Marienberg, Pfalzel, Prüm and Schönau. In Cologne diocese: St Gereon, St Pantaleon, St Severin, Xanten. Strassburg diocese: the cathedral, Honau, Münster. Diocese of Verdun: Saint-Airy, Saint-Maur, Saint-Vanne. Belgium and the Netherlands: St Servatius in Maastricht, St Mary in Maastricht, SS Michael and Gudula in Brussels, Petit-Bigard/Brussels, Liège.

The comparison between the dissemination of the *Vita et miracula S. Symeonis* and the spread of the actual cult does not reveal any very dramatic results. Most of the extant manuscripts descend from areas where Symeon was also revered as a saint. The provenances of several manuscripts are precisely those religious communities in which the cult is attested: Trier, Echternach, Rouge-Cloître, Utrecht, and Muiden-Weesp.[65] Furthermore, a (now lost) manuscript and a relic are known from Metz; a similar combination is known from Benediktbeuern (relic) and Tegernsee (manuscript *Mc*), some thirty kilometres away. The Bavarian monastery of St Emmeram also had a relic of the saint in the time of Otloh of St Emmeram, who copied the Symeon text (manuscript *O*) in person in the 1060s. From Liège we have an early manuscript and much younger evidence of the liturgical cult.[66]

Some of the results of our comparison come as surprises. In Germany, with the exception of a few places in western Hesse, we find almost no evidence of the culting of Symeon east of the Rhine. What we have from there are some early mentions of his relics from Minden, Hirsau, Salem, Benediktbeuern, and St Emmeram — and a variety of copies and different versions of the Symeon texts from Paderborn, Bursfeld, Magdeburg, Fulda, Nuremberg, Windberg, Tegernsee, Zwiefalten, Weissenau, and Einsiedeln, as well as from Austria. This may suggest that the *Vita et miracula* was not disseminated together with Symeon's cult in these regions, but that some aspects of the text were considered interesting for other reasons. The copies of the *Magnum legendarium Austriacum* that contain a version of the Symeon texts are a case in point;[67] his cult is not known either in the communities in which the texts were copied or in Austria in general. However, Symeon texts were copied in the *Magnum legendarium Austriacum*

---

[65]   *Ec*, *Ech*, *Rc*, *U*, and *Mu*. On the cult, see Bauer, *Liturgie*, pp. 517, 524; Miesges, *Festkalender*, 1. Jun., *passim*; H. Quentin, *Les martyrologes historiques du moyen âge. Étude sur la formation du martyrologe romain*, Paris, 1908, p. 235.

[66]   *Notae s. Emmerammi*, pp. 573, 1096; Munich, Bayerische Staatsbibliothek, clm 4566.

[67]   *Hk*, *Mk*, *Wi*, and *Gö* (*Gö* representing an exemplar used to create an early version of the collection).

emphatically as part of a collection, not because of any special interest in Symeon, as noted above.

The same tendency can be seen elsewhere: the texts are attested further west than is known of the extent of the cult. Symeon manuscripts from Fécamp, St Omer, Vaucelles,[68] and Ter Duinen[69] are from an area with no other evidence for Symeon's veneration. Interestingly, manuscripts from Fécamp and St Omer represent an early burst of dissemination of the text, as has been pointed out already.

On the whole, it transpires that although the cult and the manuscripts spread in the same directions, the manuscripts and medieval knowledge of Symeon texts covered a wider area than did his cult. The conclusion is an expected one: to ignite a cult in another centre required more effort than merely providing it with a manuscript. It should be emphasized, however, that as the cult of St Symeon has never been thoroughly explored, new evidence may still emerge.

The maps in Figure 11 sum up the present state of knowledge of the spread of the cult and the *Vita et miracula S. Symeonis c.* 1100, *c.* 1200, and in the early sixteenth century.

Two caveats are in order. First, the surviving manuscripts of *Vita et miracula* are likely to constitute but a fraction of the original number. There may well have been copies in every place where his cult is in evidence. The same caveat applies to our evidence for the extent of his cult; Symeon may have been venerated, or his relics may have existed in locations from which no manuscripts are known to survive. In many cases, the spread of a cult was probably coterminous with the dissemination of hagiographical texts on the saint. But it cannot be known if this was certainly the case with St Symeon.

---

[68] A thirteenth-century *Legendarium Valcellense* from the Cistercian monastery of Vaucelles was bought by Jean Bolland and Godfrey Henschen for the library of the Bollandists in 1637. It was used in Daniel Papebroch's early edition of Symeon texts, but it was lost in the late eighteenth or early nineteenth century. Judging by the variants given by Papebroch, the lost manuscript belonged to group β.

[69] A fifteenth-century exemplar, now lost, from Ter Duinen monastery was used by Jean Gielemans for his copy (Rc) of the text.

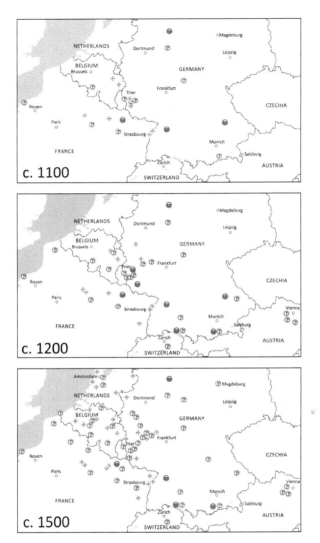

Fig. 11. Dissemination of the text and the cult in *c.* 1100, *c.* 1200, and *c.* 1500. Icons: book = attested manuscript; cross = Symeon in liturgy/kalendar; skull-and-crossbones = relics of Symeon

The dissemination of the *Vita et miracula S. Symeonis* was certainly not motivated exclusively by interests of a religious nature. Symeon's exciting life story could also captivate readers in other ways, something that may have been a factor in the making of copies. Symeon's *Vita et miracula* seems to have circulated with some texts more frequently than with others. One of these is the *Navigatio Sancti Brendani* (*BHL* 1436–1440b), which is conveyed together with the Symeon texts in a number of manuscripts.[70] Since the *Navigatio*, like the *Vita S. Symeonis*, is largely a travelogue in the context of a pilgrimage, the transmission of both texts in one manuscript may point to this aspect's being in play when the texts were chosen to be copied. On the other hand, secular journeys, often equated with human life and the journey towards the heavenly Jerusalem, were generally a popular topic in hagiography. It is interesting that Trier and St Maximin's monastery play an important role in the history of the circulation of the Brendan text; it has even been plausibly speculated that the text was written at St Maximin's.[71]

Another text transmitted even more frequently with the texts on Symeon was the *Vita S. Pachomii* (*BHL* 6410).[72] Both saints shared many traits: their connection to Eastern Christianity, anchoritism and cenobitism. Symeon's connection to the exotic East may have played a role here: for example, most of the texts contained in manuscripts *P*, *N* and *X* refer to Eastern Christianity.[73] Likewise, in manuscripts *A* and *F*, the proportion of Greek saints and Eastern Christianity is clearly evident.

Conclusion: Combining Traditional and Digital Approaches

Scrutiny of the whole textual tradition has revealed a number of fresh insights into the writing, dissemination, and influence of

---

[70]   *Mc, P, Ep*. They were all written already in the eleventh century. On the dissemination of *Navigatio S. Brendani*, see C. SELMER, *Navigatio Sancti Brendani Abbatis from Early Latin Manuscripts*, Notre Dame, IN, 1959 (Publications in Mediaeval Studies of the University of Notre Dame, 16).

[71]   R. REICHE, "Iren in Trier", *Rheinische Vierteljahrsblätter*, 40 (1976), pp. 1–16, at 12.

[72]   See *BB, Max, P, N* and *X*. Both texts also belong to the canon of texts of the *Magnum Legendarium Austriacum* (*Gö, Hk, Mk, Wi*). On the dissemination of the Pachomios-*vita*, see H. VAN CRANENBURGH, *La vie latine de saint Pachôme traduite du grec par Denys le Petit. Édition critique*, Brussels, 1969 (Subsidia hagiographica, 46), pp. 50–55.

[73]   In *P* almost half, in *X* over sixty per cent, and in ı more than three quarters of the texts concern Greek saints.

the *Vita et miracula S. Symeonis*. Through collation and holistic comparison of a large number of manuscripts and their textual contents, we have identified layers of authorial work, centres of publishing, and various recensions: seven branches with several sub-branches. In sum, it has been possible to judge the publishing and diffusion of the text as a whole. Furthermore, our textual analysis proves that the manuscript tradition had become seriously contaminated in the course of the authorial process. This, together with the fact that there were several manuscripts that were already being modified early on, is of interest to students of medieval publishing.

The most important outcome from the combined application of the traditional text-critical method, more modern computer-based approaches, and historical scholarship in the study of an unusually high number of textual witnesses and their manuscript carriers, is that we can now observe at close range how complex the tradition in question actually is. And if this should be the case with *Vita et miracula S. Symeonis*, a text that was not of the first importance or popularity, it is reasonable to wonder how complex the traditions of more important and more widely disseminated literary works may have been — and how poorly stemmata and the reconstructed textual contents proposed in their critical editions may reflect the medieval realities.

At the beginning of this essay, I propagated the study of the whole tradition as a means to gain an extensive understanding of how a given text was published, disseminated and received. It is questionable whether the traditional arboreal model of a stemma, seeking to capture the development of, and relationships between, the earliest authorial textual versions, is the best way to represent the multitude of authorial decisions taken in the course of repeated acts of publishing.[74] In this study, the hypothetical stemma of the tradition has not been taken as the basis of truth, but rather as a tool to visualize the relationships between different textual witnesses and various parts of the tradition. A plausible hypothesis as to how a very complex transmission emerged was proposed, but due to the frequency of authorial revision and subsequent scri-

[74] Interestingly, exactly the same question is being asked in the field of modern philology. See, for example, VAN HULLE, "Genetic maps", pp. 524–33.

bal interventions and errors, all the relationships between all textual witnesses cannot be demonstrated graphically. An accurate
and comprehensive chart would be a multi-dimensional design,
more fluid than the traditional stemmata hitherto employed. In
other words, while the study of the broad textual tradition certainly yields results of significance, the approach and related tools
do have their limitations.

One obvious caveat has to do with the material itself. Even if all
extant manuscripts of a text are studied, they may still constitute
only a minority of all the exemplars that were made during the
era of manuscript transmission. *Habent sua fata libelli.* The vagaries of survival, in which chance and coincidence play a significant
role, have shaped the transmission of medieval texts more often
than not. Even so, one has to make the most out of the sources
that one has. The thorough scrutiny of a multitude of textual witnesses, as Ludwig Traube maintained, is a *sine qua non* for understanding the text and its various aspects — its author, publishing,
copying, audience, sources, and impact. We may instance one of
the examples mentioned at the beginning of this article, *Parzival.*
Irrespective of generations of editorial work, it was only through
the application of digital approaches to the study of transmission
and a digital edition based on as high a number of witnesses as
possible that a comprehensive view of the transmission and textual history could be achieved.[75] Applying a combination of traditional virtues of historical scholarship and textual criticism
together with constantly developing digital approaches shall certainly enhance our understanding of the complex and fluid nature
of medieval literary works and their transmission, from publication to this day.

---

[75] G. Viehhauser, "Heuristics of witnesses", *Handbook of Stemmatology*,
ed. by Roelli, pp. 140–48, at 145.

Appendix 1

Medieval manuscripts containing *Vita et miracula S. Symeonis* (*BHL* 7963–7964)

In all, the text is known today in fifty-eight witnesses, as follows:

o   A = Brussels, Bibliothèque Royale de Belgique, MS II. 1050

o   Ar = BL, Harley MS 2800

o   Au = Brussels, Bibliothèque Royale de Belgique, MS II. 1146

o   B = Brussels, Bibliothèque Royale de Belgique, MS 207–08

o   BB = Bern, Burgerbibliothek, 24

o   Be = SBB-PK, MS theol. lat. quart. 169

o   BL = BL, Add. MS 18359

o   C = Châlons-en-Champagne, BM, 56

o   E = Trier, Stadtbibliothek, 118/06 4°

o   Eb = Trier, Stadtbibliothek, 1167/469 4°

o   Ec = Luxembourg, Bibliothèque nationale du Luxembourg, 264

o   Ech = BnF, lat. 9740

o   Ei = Einsiedeln, Stiftsbibliothek, Codex 247 (379)

o   Ep = Épinal, Bibliothèque multimédia intercommunale Épinal (*olim* BM), 147 (*olim* 67)

o   F = BnF, lat. 2628

o   Gö = Vienna, Österreichische Nationalbibliothek, Cod. 748

o   Hk = Heiligenkreuz, Stiftsbibliothek, 12

o   Hu = Namur, Musée des Arts Anciens, 53

o   K = Brussels, Bibliothèque Royale de Belgique, MS 858–61

o   KH = Cologne, Historisches Archiv der Stadt Köln, W164

o   L = Brussels, Bibliothèque Royale de Belgique, MS 9290

o   M = Trier, Stadtbibliothek, 1384/54 8°

o   Max = Trier, Stadtbibliothek, 1151/454 4°, Band II (*olim* 963)

o   Mc = Munich, Bayerische Staatsbibliothek, clm 18625

o   Me = Trier, Stadtbibliothek, 2002/92 4°

o   Mk = Melk, Stiftsbibliothek, 492 (*olim* 675, *olim* M5)

o   Ml = Bonn, Universitäts- und Landesbibliothek, S 369

TUOMAS HEIKKILÄ

o Mm = Koblenz, Landeshauptarchiv, Best. 701 Nr. 129

o Mo = Mons, Université de Mons-Hainaut, Bibliothèque centrale, Cod. 26/210 (vol. 2)

o Mu = Den Haag, Koninklijke Bibliotheek, 70 E 21 (*olim* L29)

o N = Namur, Musée des Arts Anciens, 12

o Ni = Brussels, Bibliothèque Royale de Belgique, MS 8272–8282

o Np = Nuremberg, Stadtbibliothek, Cent. III.69 (Teil II.)

o O = BL, Add. MS 22793

o Om = Brussels, Bibliothèque Royale de Belgique, MS II. 932

o P = BAV, Reg. lat. 481

o Pa = BnF, lat. 10875

o PP = BML, Ashburnham 58

o R = Rome, Biblioteca Vallicelliana, P. 196

o Rc = Brussels, Bibliothèque Royale de Belgique, MS 982

o Rh = Düsseldorf, Universitäts- und Landesbibliothek, C10b

o S (S1 and S2) = Brussels, Bibliothèque des Bollandistes, 445

o T (T and T2) = Einsiedeln, Stiftsbibliothek, Codex 323 (1065)

o TP = Trier, Bibliothek des Bischöflichen Priesterseminars, 33 (*olim* R. I. 8)

o Tr = Trier, Stadtbibliothek, 321/1993 4°

o U = SBB-PK, MS Theol. lat. fol. 707

o V (V1 and V2) = Trier, Stadtbibliothek, 1353/132 8°

o W = Cologny, Fondation Martin Bodmer, Bodmer 127

o Wb = Munich, Bayerische Staatsbibliothek, clm 22241

o Wi = Vienna, Österreichische Nationalbibliothek, Cod. 336

o X = Brussels, Bibliothèque des Bollandistes, 209

o Z = Stuttgart, Württembergische Landesbibliothek, Cod. Bibl. 2° 57

The following abridged versions are known:

o Vienna, Österreichische Nationalbibliothek, Cod. Ser. n. 12814, fol. 54[r-v][76]

[76] The Symeon text of this hagiographical collection by Johannes Gielemans of Rouge-Cloître was probably copied from *Collectaneum martyrologii*

o   SBB-PK, MS Magdeb. 26, fols 379ra–380^{vb77}

o   Trier, Stadtbibliothek, 1163/465

o   Trier, Stadtbibliothek, 927

o   Klosterneuburg, Stiftsbibliothek, 701, 708–10 (Symeon text in MS 708)[78]

o   Erpernburg, Schlossbibliothek, 7, one leaf with text on St Symeon[79]

Lost manuscripts with *Vita et miracula S. Symeonis*:

o   Metz, BM, 398 (lost in 1944)

o   Strassburg, *Bibliotheca Publica*, a manuscript with *vitae Lupi, Eucharii, Maximini, Simeonis*.[80] Lost between 1830 and 1870

o   St Omer, BM, 716 t. VII, fols 155^r–160^r. A legendary of *s*. xiii of Clairmarais monastery, lost during the Second World War.[81]

o   Other manuscripts of the *Magnum legendarium Austriacum (MLA)*: Admont, Stiftsbibliothek, MS 24–25 (*c*. 1200, Symeon in MS 24); Lilienfeld, Stiftsbibliothek, 60 (*s*. xiii^{in}); Zwettl, Stiftsbibliothek, MS 13–15, 24 (*s*. xiii^1, Symeon in MS 24).

sanctorum of Aegidius de Damnis († 1463). Aegidius, in turn, seems to have copied the text from an exemplar that belonged to text group γ.

[77]   The very abridged text is closely related to *Hu, L, Np, P, TP* and *X* (group δ).

[78]   The text about Symeon was probably copied directly from *Wi*.

[79]   The text is heavily modified viz-a-viz the contents of *Vita et miracula S. Symeonis*. Still, it is possible that there was a link to the tradition of that text through *Max*. See H. MORETUS, "De magno legendario Bodecensi", *Analecta Bollandiana*, 27 (1908), pp. 257–358, at 263.

[80]   G. HAENEL, *Catalogi librorum manuscriptorum qui in bibliothecis Galliae, Helvetiae, Belgii, Britanniae M., Hispaniae, Lusitaniae asservatur, nunc primum editi a D. Gustavo Haenel*, Liepzig, 1830, p. 451.

[81]   A. DOLBEAU,"La légendier de l'abbaye cistercienne de Clairmarais", *Analecta Bollandiana*, 91 (1973), pp. 273–86, at 273–74; *Manuscrits de la bibliothèque de Saint-Omer*, Paris, 1861 (Catalogue générale des manuscrits des bibliothèques publiques des départements, tom. III), pp. 1–386, at 317; "Catalogus codicum hagiographicorum latinorum bibliothecae publicae Audomaropolitanae", *Analecta Bollandiana*, 47 (1929) pp. 241–306, at 280.

Appendix 2

Manuscript groups according to the contents of *Vita et miracula S. Symeonis*

α		Eb	*s.* xv^{ex}
		M	*s.* xiii^{in}
		Max	soon after 1235
		S1	*s.* xv–xvi
		S2	*s.* xv–xvi
		V1	*s.* xv
β	β1	K	1490
		KH	1462–1463
		Mu	1461 and just before
		U	1506
	β2	BB	*s.* xi
		Ei	*s.* xii
		F	*s.* xi/xii
		Mm	*s.* xii^{ex}
		N	*s.* xii
		PP	*s.* xii^{in}
		Tr	*s.* xv
		W	*c.* 1170–1200
		Z	*c.* 1120–1125
γ	γ1	A	*s.* xi
		R	*s.* xviii^{in}
		Rc	*s.* xvi^{1}
	γ2	Au	*s.* xiii
		C	*s.* xi$^{3/3}$
		Om	*s.* xii
		Ni	*s.* xv

δ		Be	*c.* 1100
		Ec	1051–1081
		Hu	*s.* xii
		L	*s.* xii
		Np	*s.* xv^{in} (before 1441)
		TP	*s.* xv
		X	*s.* xiii/xiv
		P	*s.* xi^{ex}
ε	ε1	BL	*s.* xii
		E	*s.* xi^2
		O	1062–1066
		Mc	*s.* xi/xii
	ε2	Gö	*s.* xii^{med}
		Wb	1141–1191
	ε3	Hk	*s.* xii^{ex}
		Mk	*c.* 1470
		Wi	*c.* 1200
ζ		Ar	*c.* 1170–1180
		B	*s.* xiii^{in}
		Ml	*s.* xiv^1
		Rh	*c.* 1400
		V2	*s.* xv
η		Ech	*s.* xii
		Ep	*s.* xi/xii
		Me	*s.* xv^{in}
		Mo	*s.* xiii
		Pa	*s.* xv (xvi?)
		T1	*s.* xi^2
		T2	*s.* xi^2

Appendix 3

Concordance of the textual divisions cited in this article and in the Bollandist editions (of 1695 and 1867)

This article	Bollandist edition, 1695	Bollandist edition, 1867
1 Prologus Eberwini (v1)	c. 1, S. 89B	c.1, S. 86F
2	c. 2, S. 89C	c. 2, S. 86F–87A
3	c. 2, S. 89C	c. 2, S. 87A
4	c. 3, S. 89D	c. 3, S. 87A–B
5	c. 4, S. 89D–E	c. 4, S. 87B–C
6	c. 5, S. 89F	c. 5, S. 87C–D
7	c. 5, S. 89F–90A	c. 5, S. 87D
8	c. 6, S. 90A	c. 6, S. 87D–E
9	c. 6, S. 90A–B	c. 6, S. 87E
10	c. 7–8, S. 90B–C	c. 7–8, S. 87E–F
11	c. 8, S. 90C	c. 8, S. 87F–88A
12	c. 9, S. 90E–F	c. 9, S. 88C
13	c. 9, S. 90F	c. 9, S. 88C–D
14	c. 10, S. 91A	c. 10, S. 88D
15	c. 10, S. 91A–B	c. 10, S. 88E
16	c. 11, S. 91B–C	c. 11, S. 88E–F
17	c. 11, S. 91C	c. 11, S. 88F–89A
18	c. 12, S. 91C–D	c. 12, S. 89A
19	c. 13, S. 91D	c. 13, S. 89A–B
20	c. 13–14, S. 91E	c. 13–14, S. 89B
21	c. 14, S. 91E	c. 14, S. 89B–C
22	c. 14, S. 91E–F	c. 14, S. 89C
23	c. 15, S. 92C	c. 15, S. 89F

24	c. 15, S. 92C	c. 15, S. 89F–90A
25	c. 16, S. 92C–D	c. 16, S. 90A
26	c. 16, S. 92D–E	c. 16, S. 90A–B
27	c. 17, S. 92E	c. 17, S 90B–C
28	c. 18, S. 92F	c. 18, S. 90C
29	c. 19, S. 92F–93A	c. 19, S. 90C–E
30	c. 20, S. 93B–C	c. 20, S. 90E–F
31	c. 21–22, S. 93C–F	c. 21–22, S. 90F–91C
Miraculum 1 (m1)	c. 22, S. 93F	c. 22, S. 91C
m2	c. 23, S. 93F–94A	c. 23, S. 91C–D
m3	c. 24, S. 94A	c. 24, S. 91D
m4	c. 25, S. 94A–B	c. 25, S. 91E
m5	c. 26, S. 94C	c. 26, S. 91F
m6	c. 27, S. 94C	c. 27, S. 91F
m7	c. 27, S. 94C	c. 27, S. 91F
m8	c. 28, S. 94C–D	c. 28, S. 91F
m9	c. 28, S. 94D	c. 28, S. 91F–92A
m10	c. 28, S. 94D	c. 28, S. 92A
m11	c. 29, S. 94D	c. 29, S. 92A
m12	c. 29, S. 94D–E	c. 29, S. 92A–B
m13	c. 29, S. 94E	c. 29, S. 92B
m14	c. 29, S. 94E	c. 29, S. 92B
m15	c. 30, S. 94E	c. 30, S. 92B
m16	c. 31, S. 94F	c. 31, S. 92B–C
m17	c. 31, S. 94F	c. 31, S. 92C
m18	c. 32, S. 94F–95A	c. 32, S. 92C
m19	c. 32, S. 95A	c. 32, S. 92C–D
m20	c. 33, S. 95A–B	c. 33, S. 92D–E
m21	c. 34, S. 95B–C	c. 34, S. 92E–F
Epilogus	*missing*	*missing*
Prologus Warnheri	*missing*	*missing*

m22	c. 35, S. 100A–B	c. 35, S. 97C–D
m23	c. 36,[82] S. 100B–C	c. 36, S. 97D
m24	c. 37, S. 100C	c. 37, S. 97E
m25	c. 38, S. 100C–D	c. 38, S. 97E–F
m26	c. 39, S. 100D–E	c. 39, S. 97F
m27	c. 40, S. 100E–F	c. 40, S. 97F–98A
m28	*missing*	*missing*
m29	c. 41, S. 100F–101A	c. 41, S. 98B–C
m30	c. 42, S. 101A–B	c. 42, S. 98C–D
m31	c. 43, S. 101B–C	c. 43, S. 98D–E
m32	c. 43, S. 101C	c. 43, S. 98E

[82] In the edition of 1695 incorrectly designated as c. 33.

The Chronicle of Ralph of Coggeshall

Publication and Censorship in Angevin England[*]

James WILLOUGHBY
(*Oxford*)

In 1877, shortly before becoming Regius Professor of History at Oxford, Edward Augustus Freeman wrote, "to me a manuscript becomes practically useful only when it is changed into the more every-day shape of a printed book".[1] That Freeman's comment should occur in the preface to one of the great editions in the Rolls Series is a sign of the scholarly self-confidence of the age: the second half of the nineteenth century was a remarkable moment in Britain for the making of editions.[2] Those of the Rolls Series — administered on behalf of the government, its editors on

* This essay derives from a paper originally delivered in 2014 as the University of London's John Coffin Memorial Lecture in Palaeography. I remain very grateful to Elizabeth Danbury and Pam Robinson for their invitation to speak on that occasion. I am also pleased to record my gratitude to Nicholas Vincent for always enlightening discussion and to Samu Niskanen for his insightful comments that have improved this text.

1 From his preface to the seventh volume of *Giraldi Cambrensis opera*, ed. by J. F. DIMOCK, 8 vols, London, 1861–1891 (Rolls Series, 21), p. ciii. Freeman was completing the work of James Dimock, his late friend.

2 The Rolls Series (properly named *Rerum Britannicarum medii aevi scriptores, or Chronicles and Memorials of Great Britain and Ireland during the Middle Ages)*, whose editions occupy 259 physical volumes, began printing in 1858 and concluded in 1911. An entertaining account of the project's inception and history is given by D. KNOWLES, *Great Historical Enterprises. Problems in Monastic History,* London, 1963, pp. 99–134. As well as numerous county record series that began publishing at the same time, kindred contemporary enterprises that might be mentioned, still alive today, are the Early English Text Society (1864), for the publishing of medieval literary sources in English, the Pipe Roll Society (1883), for documents of medieval royal

The Art of Publication from the Ninth to the Sixteenth Century, ed. by Samu Niskanen with the assistance of Valentina Rovere, IPM, 93 (Turnhout, 2023), pp. 131–166.
© BREPOLS ❧ PUBLISHERS   DOI 10.1484/M.IPM-EB.5.133083

civil-list pensions — occupy a high position. The great proportion of these editions of medieval texts have been relied upon for more than a century and are still current. Historians have taken it on trust that the Victorian editor, in forming the everyday shape of his printed book, saw in the manuscript everything that he ought to have seen. But of course any edition — any fair copy — of an author's draft, as much one copied by hand as typeset in print, will flatten the uneven landscape of the exemplar, smoothing its corrections, additions, and second thoughts. Sometimes that will not matter very much, sometimes it will. To make any theoretical statement about medieval publication, and to understand reception, it is in fact necessary to see Freeman's process in reverse. One must begin by reifying the text as a manuscript book, imagining it in the hands of its medieval makers, and learn to see transmission as a concessionary process, from writer to reader.

The early thirteenth-century chronicle that is the principal object of discussion here is another of those edited in the Rolls Series, published in this case only two years before Freeman's. In this case, too, the edition is still current. What is unusual about this chronicle is that the author's copy happens to survive. In it may be tracked all manner of additions, corrections and second thoughts, the import of which have not been fully understood. The editor, Joseph Stevenson, recognizing the national interest of the chronicle, gave the work the title *Chronicon Anglicanum*.[3] The chronicler was Ralph, abbot of the Cistercian abbey of Coggeshall in north Essex, in the medieval diocese of London.[4] His work has an independent fame. It is one of only a handful of contemporary English chronicle sources for the reigns of Kings Richard I (1189–1199) and John (1199–1216), and is the unique contemporary source for some picturesque and famous events in English history, such as the circumstances of King Richard's capture in Austria and the disaster of John's loss of his baggage train in the Wash

---

government, the Henry Bradshaw Society (1890), for liturgical texts, and the Canterbury and York Society (1904), for medieval ecclesiastical records.

[3] *Radulphi de Coggeshall Chronicon Anglicanum*, ed. by J. STEVENSON, London, 1875 (Rolls Series, 66) [hereafter *CA*].

[4] An account of his life is given by D. CORNER in the *Oxford Dictionary of National Biography*.

off the East Anglian coast.[5] While not a self-conscious stylist or reflective about either his sources or his role, Ralph can be a vivid story-teller. He offers much on the Third and Fourth Crusades — some of it told to him by returning crusaders — and on the relations of Richard and John with each other, with the English barons, with King Philip II of France, and with the papacy. There are censorious accounts of heresies, such as that of the Publicani in the diocese of Reims, and credulous accounts of visions, a genre much enjoyed by Cistercians.[6] Ralph retells visions of purgatory, as well as the story of an angelic visitation at Coggeshall itself. There is also a strand of marvels.[7] In Ralph's account of two green children who had come from a land under the earth, found in a pit in the neighbouring county of Suffolk, folklorists identify England's first fairy story.[8]

As with any author attempting to chronicle his own times, Ralph's sources of information were various. His knowledge of the circumstances of King Richard's capture at Vienna in 1192 came from conversation with Anselm, the king's chaplain and mem-

---

[5] Summaries of the chronicle's contents are given by A. GRANSDEN, *Historical Writing in England c. 550–c. 1307*, 2 vols, London, 1974, vol. 1, pp. 322–31; and, with a particular interest in demonstrating how Ralph shaped his history to appeal to specifically Cistercian interests, E. FREEMAN, *Narratives of a New Order: Cistercian Historical Writing in England, 1150–1220*, Turnhout, 2002 (Medieval Church Studies, 2) pp. 179–213. Ralph's status as a historian is discussed by M. STAUNTON, *The Historians of Angevin England*, Oxford, 2017, esp. pp. 117–20.

[6] For the Cistercian interest in purgatory and vision literature, see B. McGUIRE, "Purgatory, the Communion of Saints and medieval change", *Viator*, 20 (1989), pp. 61–84, at 75–78; C. WATKINS, "Doctrine, politics and purgation: the Vision of Tnúthgal and the Vision of Owein at St Patrick's Purgatory", *Journal of Medieval History*, 22 (1996), pp. 225–36; FREEMAN, *Narratives of a New Order*, pp. 188–93.

[7] Summarized and discussed, in relation to a Cistercian orthodoxy, by FREEMAN, *Narratives of a New Order*, pp. 193–213; further discussed by STAUNTON, *Historians of Angevin England*, pp. 120–27.

[8] *CA*, pp. 118–20. The story was first popularized by T. KEIGHTLEY, *The Fairy Mythology: Illustrative of the Romance and Superstition of Various Countries*, rev. edn, London, 1878, pp. 281–83; see also K. BRIGGS, *The Fairies in Tradition and Literature*, London, 1967, pp. 7–8, and many other dictionaries of English folklore. The fullest consideration of the Green Children is by J. CLARK, "The Green Children of Woolpit" (2018), online at <https://www.academia.edu/10089626>.

ber of his tiny fugitive retinue.[9] Ralph's detailed description of Richard's death came from Milo († 1226), the king's almoner and Cistercian abbot of Le Pin in the Île-de-France, who had taken confession, administered extreme unction, and closed the dead king's eyes.[10] Hugh de Neville († 1234), royal forester, supplied a valuable eyewitness account of the Siege of Jaffa in 1192.[11] Most of Ralph's informants are unidentified, but it may be suspected that Cistercian networks as well as local ones provided him with significant assistance.[12] As he received information, Ralph also disbursed it. The evidence is inferential, but combines strongly to suggest that Ralph was ambitious for his work and cultivated publishing circles to receive and propagate it.[13] Before turning to an examination of his major work and what it can say to the mat-

[9]   *CA*, p. 54, illustrated in Plate 1 below.

[10]   *Ibid.*, pp. 94–98. See further J. GILLINGHAM, "The unromantic death of Richard I", *Speculum*, 54 (1979), pp. 18–41, at 27. Ralph had himself met King Richard and remembered him vividly: *CA*, pp. 92, 97.

[11]   *CA*, p. 45. Ralph replaced his earlier account with Hugh's: in Cotton MS Vespasian D. x, discussed below, it is written on an erasure and carried over on an inserted bifolium (*RC*, pp. 44–46; Vespasian, fols 60ᵛ, 62–63). Hugh de Neville had been chief justice of the forest since 1198. On 1 January 1204, Coggeshall abbey was granted licence to enclose its park, which would normally have brought the justice to the abbey, offering one occasion on which Hugh could have given Ralph his account: *Pipe Roll 6 John*, ed. D. M. Stenton, Publications of the Pipe Roll Society, n.s. 18 (1940), pp. 33–34.

[12]   Local networks will be discussed further below. Cistercian networks were tightly integrated through monasteries' own affiliations and through the requirement upon abbots to attend general chapters of the order. As abbot, Ralph is known to have been at Cîteaux in 1214 when he was called on to deliver the decision of the General Chapter on three separate lawsuits (*Statuta* 1214, §§ 10, 24, 40; ed. by J.-M. CANIVEZ, *Statuta capitulorum generalium ordinis Cisterciensis ab anno 1116 ad annum 1786*, 8 vols, Louvain, 1933–1941), 1. 420, 422, 425). On such an occasion he could have met Abbot Milo, from whom he had his vivid account of the death of King Richard mentioned above; also Adam of Perseigne, abbot of Le Mans, who gave Ralph the details of his interview in Rome with the visionary, Joachim of Fiore (*CA*, pp. 68–69). Both men were intimates of the king, respectively his almoner and confessor; see further H. SHAW, "Cistercian abbots in the service of British monarchs (1135–1335)", *Cîteaux: Commentarii Cistercienses*, 58 (2007), pp. 225–45, at 235, n. 46.

[13]   I use the notion of "publishing circle" as defined by J. TAHKOKALLIO, *The Anglo-Norman Historical Canon. Publishing and Manuscript Culture*, Cambridge, 2019.

ter of Ralph's strategies for composition and publication, it will be helpful to review other texts associated with his name for what they can reveal about his practices as a publishing author.

Ralph's Life and Works

Four facts about Ralph's life are supplied by two passages in the *Chronicon Anglicanum*: that he was the sixth abbot of Coggeshall, from 1207 to 1218; that he resigned through ill health, much against the wishes of the brethren; that he wrote vision stories; and that he composed a chronicle of the years 1187 to 1226 or 1227.[14] Earlier scholarship had it that Ralph had been in the Holy Land, present at the siege of Jerusalem where he took an arrow to the face, the tip of which remained embedded in his nose for the rest of his life.[15] The picture of the abbot as a spent crusader retiring to the cloister to take up the writing of history is an enjoyable vignette to conjure; but this aspect of Ralph's *pseudo*-biography rests on an accident of transmission. An account of the disasters suffered by the Christians in Palestine in 1186 and 1187, known editorially as the *Libellus de expugnatione Terrae Sanctae per Saladinum*, whose anonymous author it really was who took the arrow to the face, happens to have been transmitted with Ralph's chronicle.[16] It was therefore attributed to Ralph by the

[14] *CA*, pp. 162–63: "Anno mccvii, obiit domnus Thomas, abbas quintus de Cogeshal, cui successit domnus Radulfus, monachus eiusdem loci, qui hanc chronicam a captione Sancte Crucis usque ad annum undecimum Henrici regis III, filii regis Iohannis, descripsit, ac quasdam uisiones quas a uenerabilibus uiris audiuit, fideliter annotare ob multorum edificationem curauit." *Ibid.*, p. 187: "Eodem anno [*sc.* mccxviii] domnus Radulfus abbas sextus de Cogeshale, cum iam per annos xi. et mensibus duobus administrasset, circa festum sancti Ioannis Baptiste, contra uoluntatem conuentus sui, cure pastorali sponte sua renunciauit, frequenti egritudine laborans."

[15] As, for example, Edmond MARTÈNE and Ursin DURAND, *Veterum scriptorum et monumentorum historicorum, dogmaticorum, moralium; amplissima collectio*, 9 vols, Paris, 1724–1733, vol. 5, coll. 543–44.

[16] An edition was included by Stevenson with his printing of Ralph's chronicle: *CA*, pp. 209–62. It is newly edited, with full discussion, by K. BREWER, J. H. KANE, *The Conquest of the Holy Land by Ṣalāḥ al-Dīn: A Critical Edition and Translation of the Anonymous* Libellus de expugnatione Terrae Sanctae per Saladinum, Abingdon, 2019. Sensible reasons for preferring the title *Libellus de expugnatione Terrae Sanctae* over *Chronicon Terrae Sanctae*, which was John Bale's coinage and has had currency in the past, are given at p. 1, n. 1. The

Tudor antiquary, John Bale (1495–1563), and became empanelled as such in the bibliographical tradition.[17] In fact, as Bishop Stubbs first showed, the account of events in the Holy Land that can be found in Ralph's chronicle and the account given by the *Libellus de expugnatione Terrae Sanctae* bear no relation to each other either stylistically or in tone, and they tell much of the same story in very different ways and with reference to different, and sometimes inconsistent, details.[18] The author of the *Libellus* wrote a memoir in rhetorical and indeed exegetical mode; Ralph, using the impersonal voice of the annalist, produced a condensed account deriving his information at second hand from the *Libellus* as well as Roger of Howden's *Chronica*.

However, this is not to say that the monks at Coggeshall played no part in the transmission of the *Libellus*. Quite the contrary: in three of its four manuscripts, all copied at Coggeshall, the *Libellus*

wound mentioned by the author ("the one relating these things") is at p. 200: "Nam et facies hec referentis, sagitta per medium nasum infixa uulnerata est, atque extracto ligno ferrum usque hodie permansit"; discussed further by BREWER, KANE, *Conquest of the Holy Land*, pp. 11–12.

[17]   John BALE, *Index Britanniae scriptorum*, ed. by R. L. POOLE, M. BATESON, *John Bale's Index of British and Other Writers*, London, 1902, repr. Woodbridge, 1990, pp. 327–28; IDEM, *Scriptorium illustrium Maioris Britanniae catalogus*, 2 vols, Basel, 1557–1559, vol. 1, p. 275; John PITS, *Relationum historicarum de rebus Anglicis tomus I* (Paris, 1619), pp. 301–02; Thomas TANNER, *Bibliotheca Britannico-Hibernica; sive, De scriptoribus, qui in Anglia, Scotia, et Hibernia ad saeculi XVII initium floruerunt, commentarius*, ed. by D. WILKINS, London, 1748, p. 187; D. N. BELL, *An Index of Authors and Works in Cistercian Libraries in Great Britain*, Kalamazoo, MI, 1991, pp. 119–20; R. SHARPE, *A Handlist of the Latin Writers of Great Britain and Ireland before 1540*, Turnhout, 1997, pp. 445–46. In editions, Bale's attribution was followed in the *editio princeps* by MARTÈNE, DURAND, *Veterum scriptorum et monumentorum historicorum* [...] *collectio*, vol. 5, coll. 548–82; the nineteenth-century editors preferred to consider the work anonymous. But the attribution to Ralph continues, as in S. de SANDOLI (ed.), *Itinera Hierosolymitana Crucesignatorum*, vol. 3, pt 1, Jerusalem, 1983, pp. 109–19.

[18]   W. STUBBS, *Itinerarium peregrinorum et gesta regis Ricardi*, Rolls Series 38/1, London, 1864, pp. lv–lvi. The same conclusion was reached by Stevenson in his edition, *CA*, p. xviii, and, in a work published the following year, by H. PRUTZ, "Anonymi Chronicon Terrae Sanctae s. Libellus de expugnatione, 1186–1191", in his *Quellenbeiträge zur Geschichte der Kreuzzüge*, Danzig, 1876, pp. xix–xxv. The matter of Ralph's assumed authorship through the work's various editions is carefully set out by BREWER, KANE, *Conquest of the Holy Land*, pp. 12–14, 98–105.

is transmitted with Ralph's chronicle, and the fourth, the oldest copy, was written by a known scribe following normal Coggeshall scriptorium practices of ruling thirty-one long lines to a page in a written space of 155 × 100 mm.[19] This manuscript, BL, Cotton MS Cleopatra B. I, is a discrete component in a volume assembled by Sir Robert Cotton (1571–1631). Its original context is not known, but there is at least a possibility that Cotton had separated it from the other Coggeshall manuscript he had in his possession, Vespasian D. x. The Coggeshall texts in Vespasian D. x are all primary, as is the copy of the *Libellus* in Cleopatra B. I.[20]

Just as the monks of Coggeshall were central to the transmission of the *Libellus*, it seems that they can also be awarded a share of the authorship. For it is a curious fact that the narrative appears to be the work of two separate personalities. From the declamatory opening apostrophe to the grandiloquent narrative of events leading to the spoliation of the Holy Sepulchre, the authorial voice is coherent. At that point, however, the text breaks off and the remainder of the work, closing with the letter sent by the Emperor Frederick to Saladin in 1188 with Saladin's reply, is otherwise nothing but a recapitulation of the chapters of the first book of the *Itinerarium peregrinorum et gesta regis Ricardi* attributed to Richard de Templo, Augustinian canon of Holy Trinity, Aldgate, in London, to which the reader is then referred for fuller information: "si quis plenius nosse desideret, legat librum quem dominus prior sancte Trinitatis Londoniis ex gallica lingua in latinum, tam eleganti quam ueraci stilo, transferri fecit".[21] This

[19]   J. M. W. WILLOUGHBY, "A Templar chronicle of the Third Crusade: origin and transmission", *Medium Ævum*, 81 (2012), pp. 126–34. A further manuscript, Cambridge, Corpus Christi College, MS 343 (*s.* xv), descends directly from London, College of Arms, Arundel 11 and has no independent value. See further BREWER, KANE, *Conquest of the Holy Land*, pp. 69–72.

[20]   In two other early copies of the *Libellus* from Coggeshall, London, College of Arms, 11, and BnF, lat. 15076, the *Libellus* is the first item in the manuscript. As was argued by BREWER, KANE, *Conquest of the Holy Land*, p. 69, the creased and rubbed condition of the opening recto of the copy in Cleopatra B. I suggests that it too was at the front of its original manuscript. The possibility of a connection with Vespasian D. x "has much to recommend it".

[21]   "If anyone wishes to know more, let him read the book that the lord prior of Holy Trinity, London has translated from French into Latin, in a style as elegant as it is faithful."

highly unsatisfactory conclusion and abrupt change of tone and style makes it more convenient to assume that the continuation is the work of another hand, a suggestion given support by small orthographical differences between the two sections and also by the palaeography of Cleopatra B. i, in which this continuation is written in a browner ink and by a scribe who also worked on Ralph's chronicle.[22] The words recommending Richard de Templo's work are strongly reminiscent of words Ralph used in his chronicle to praise the work of Adam of Eynsham, who wrote "preclaro atque eleganti stilo", and to direct his reader into further research: "sed quisquis [...] plenius scire desiderat, legat libellum in quo predicte uisiones diligenter exarate sunt".[23] Weaving that sort of quotation into an independent narrative is entirely in keeping with Ralph's own habits of work as a collector and compiler of historical materials. It is plausible to believe that Ralph himself was the continuator of the *Libellus*. He considered the work to be incomplete and decided that it needed rounding off in some way before being brought into his dossier of historical materials. He then ensured its dissemination with his own chronicle.[24]

[22] WILLOUGHBY, "Templar chronicle", pp. 127–29; BREWER, KANE, *Conquest of the Holy Land*, pp. 26–29.

[23] Adam wrote "in a pellucid and elegant style"; "whoever wishes to know more, let him read the little book in which the foresaid visions have been carefully laid out"; Vespasian D. x, fols 70ᵛ–71ʳ (new foliation); *CA*, p. 72. Adam was praised again for his composition "eleganti stilo" in the *Visio Thurkilli*, a work which can be safely attributed to Ralph (discussed in what follows). To strengthen the case, a repeat of the same diction is found in the annal for 1204 (*CA*, p. 151): "Si quis autem plenius nosse desiderat qualiter urbs Constantinopolis semel et iterum ab exercitu Latinorum Hierusalem tendentium capta sit [...] legat epistolas quas idem imperator et H. comes de Sancto-Paulo direxerunt ad amicos suos in occiduas mundi partes commanentes." (As was pointed out by by BREWER, KANE, *Conquest of the Holy Land*, pp. 28–29).

[24] In a previous article ("A Templar chronicle", p. 131), I suggested that Cressing Temple, only a few miles away from Coggeshall, might have been the channel through which Ralph received his copy of the *Libellus*, believing the author to have been connected with the Knights Templar. BREWER, KANE, *Conquest of the Holy Land*, pp. 23–25, advance sound arguments against Templar authorship, making the connection to Cressing less interesting. They make a tentative suggestion that the author might have been a Cistercian (*ibid.*, pp. 47–50), which would open the possibility of a straightforward channel of transmission to Ralph through Cistercian networks.

Another work attributed to Ralph's pen is the *Visio Thurkilli*, a lengthy account of a dream-vision of Purgatory experienced by a peasant named Thurkill living in Stisted in Essex: "in partibus nostris" as the text says, and Stisted is not four miles from Coggeshall.[25] The authorial identification was first made by Henry Ward in 1875 and has not been challenged since.[26] Ralph certainly had an interest in such material.[27] His chronicle includes a vision of a monk of the Cistercian abbey of Strata Florida in Wales, and one of the first English accounts of the Italian visionary, Joachim of Fiore (1135–1202).[28] The latter is followed by Ralph's précis of the vision in 1191 of a monk of Eynsham abbey (Oxon), as written by Adam of Eynsham, mentioned above.[29] It is worth noting that Adam is also referred to in the *Visio Thurkilli* and praised for his

[25]   *Visio Thurkilli*, ed. by P. G. Schmidt, *Visio Thurkilli relatore, ut videtur, Radulpho de Coggeshall*, Leipzig, 1978.

[26]   H. L. D. Ward, "The vision of Thurkill, probably by Ralph of Coggeshall, printed from a manuscript in the British Museum with an Introduction", *Journal of the British Archaeological Association*, 31 (1875), pp. 420–59; and his *Catalogue of Romances in the Department of Manuscripts in the British Museum*, 3 vols, London, 1883–1910, vol. 2, pp. 506–07. The attribution has been affirmed by Schmidt, *Visio Thurkilli*, pp. v–vi. For discussion, see C. Watkins, "Sin, penance and purgatory in the Anglo-Norman realm: the evidence of visions and ghost stories", *Past & Present*, 175 (2002), pp. 3–33, at 18–22.

[27]   See further E. Freeman, "Wonders, prodigies and marvels: unusual bodies and the fear of heresy in Ralph of Coggeshall's *Chronicon Anglicanum*", *Journal of Medieval History*, 26 (2000), pp. 127–43; and C. M. Neufeld, "Hermeneutical perversion: Ralph of Coggeshall's 'Witch of Rheims'", *Philological Quarterly*, 85 (2006), pp. 1–23.

[28]   *CA*, pp. 141, 67–71. See further C. Egger, "A pope without a successor: Ralph of Coggeshall, Ralph Niger, Robert of Auxerre, and the early reception of Joachim of Fiore's ideas in England", in *Joachim of Fiore and the Influence of Inspiration: Essays in Memory of Marjorie E. Reeves (1905–2003)*, ed. by J. E. Wannenmacher, Farnham, 2013, pp. 145–79.

[29]   *CA*, pp. 71–72. Adam of Eynsham's *Visio Eadmundi monachi de Egnesham* (1197) is ed. by M. Huber, "Visio monachi de Eynsham", *Romanische Forschungen*, 16 (1904) 641–733; H. Thurston, "Visio monachi de Eynsham", *Analecta Bollandiana*, 22 (1903), pp. 225–319; H. E. Salter, *Cartulary of Eynsham*, 2 vols, Oxford, 1907–1908 (Oxford Historical Society, 49, 51), vol. 2, pp. 285–371; and R. B. Easting, *The Revelation of the Monk of Eynsham*, Early English Text Society, Original Series, 318 (2002), pp. 2–170. See also Ward, Herbert, *Catalogue of Romances*, vol. 2, pp. 493–506.

"elegant style" in exactly the same words as are used in the chronicle, as mentioned above.[30]

Ralph's autobiographical note in the *Chronicon Anglicanum s.a.* 1207 states that he had taken care to note down for general edification visions he had heard from trustworthy men.[31] It is unclear whether these *visiones* in the plural should be taken to refer to those included in the chronicle or to visions separately assembled in a dedicated manuscript and circulated independently, in the way that the *Visio Thurkilli* had its own circulation. A "book of visions" at the Cistercian houses at Coggeshall and nearby Sibton (Suffolk) was referred to in the mid-fourteenth century by the bibliographer Henry of Kirkestede, librarian and then prior of Bury St Edmunds abbey. He noted in his own miscellany of prophetic material that his excerpt on Joachim of Fiore could be found in that book.[32] The text he excerpted is included in Ralph's chronicle. If, instead, Henry was referring to an independent "book of visions", which is the more natural way to read his statement, then that collection is now lost.[33]

The *Visio Thurkilli* circulating on its own had a wider reach. A copy of the early thirteenth century, now BL, Royal 13 D. v,

[30]   *Visio Thurkilli*, ed. SCHMIDT, p. 3: "uisio [...] quam domnus Adam supprior eiusdem cenobii, uir ualde grauius ac religiosus, eleganti stilo conscripsit".

[31]   "domnus Radulfus [...] qui hanc chronicam [...] descripsit, quasdam uisiones quas a uenerabilibus uiris audiuit, fideliter annotare ob multorum edificationem curauit"; see n. 14 above.

[32]   Cambridge, Corpus Christi College, MS 404, fol. 66ᵛ: "Hec in libro uisionum apud Sibetone et apud Coggeshale". See further R. H. ROUSE and M. A. ROUSE, *Henry of Kirkestede, Catalogus de libris autenticis et apocrifis*, London, 2004 (Corpus of British Medieval Library Catalogues, 11), pp. lvii–lviii, also lxxvii–lxxxii. Nothing is known of the library at the Cistercian abbey of Sibton beyond one survivor, a fifteenth-century *Polychronicon*, Bodl. Laud. Misc. 545; see Medieval Libraries of Great Britain, online at <http://mlgb3.bodleian.ox.ac.uk>.

[33]   A contemporary effort in a similar direction was Peter of Cornwall's enormous *Liber reuelationum*, compiled at Holy Trinity, Aldgate in London, where Peter was prior (for which, see R. EASTING and R. SHARPE, *Peter of Cornwall's Book of Revelations*, Toronto, 2013). The monks of Coggeshall were in touch with the canons of Holy Trinity, to whom they paid an annual rent; see *The Cartulary of Holy Trinity Aldgate*, ed. G. A. J. HODGETT, London, 1971 (London Record Society, 7), p. 185, nos. 943 and 947.

reached the great Benedictine abbey of St Albans (Herts), where it was read by Roger of Wendover († 1236): he incorporated it *in extenso* in his *Flores historiarum*, under the year 1206; it was also used by Roger's confrere and successor as house historian, Matthew Paris († 1259), who included it in his famous *Chronica maiora*.[34] The Benedictine abbey at Peterborough (Northants) had two copies of the *Visio Thurkilli* in the late fourteenth century, now lost.[35] Other provenanced copies are Cambridge, University Library, Mm. 6. 4 (*s.* xiv), from the Cistercian abbey of Quarr (Hants), and a lost copy from the Augustinian priory at Thurgarton (Notts), reported in a fifteenth-century booklist ("Item visio turchildi in vno paruo quaterno").[36]

The near-contemporary production of at least four copies of the *Libellus de expugnatione Terrae Sanctae* at Coggeshall shows that these works were being copied for propagation. It is possible that the *Visio Thurkilli* was treated in a similar way for it had a wide, notably early, reception. In the spread of copies there are hints that Ralph had targeted particular publication channels for the dissemination of his work. It is a matter we shall return to below; but it is of significance at this point to note Roger of Wendover's role in the publication of *Visio Thurkilli*. The picture of what publishing meant at Coggeshall can be expanded by Ralph's authorial practices in his major work, the chronicle.[37]

[34]   Roger of Wendover, *Flores historiarum*: ed. by H. G. HEWLETT, 3 vols, London, 1886–1889 (Rolls Series, 84), vol. 2, pp. 16–35; Matthew Paris, *Chronica maiora*: ed. by H. R. LUARD, 7 vols, London, 1872–1884 (Rolls Series, 57), vol. 2, pp. 497–511. MS Royal 13 D. v is marked with a St Albans *ex libris* and contains the annotations of Matthew Paris, albeit he took his text verbatim from Wendover.

[35]   The lost Peterborough copies are reported in the late fourteenth-century *Matricularium* of the library; ed. by K. FRIIS-JENSEN, J. M. W. WILLOUGHBY, *Peterborough Abbey*, London, 2001 (Corpus of British Medieval Library Catalogues, 8), pp. 132, 166 (BP21. 212, 314).

[36]   T. WEBBER, A. G. WATSON, *The Libraries of the Augustinian Canons*, London, 1998 (Corpus of British Medieval Library Catalogues, 6), p. 425 (A36. 44b).

[37]   One other work, a collection of distinctions known as the *Distinctiones monasticae et morales*, composed around 1220, was attributed to Ralph without any strong foundation by G. MORIN, "Le cistercien Ralph de Coggeshall et l'auteur des *Distinctiones monasticae* utilisées par Dom Pitra", *Revue Bénédictine*, 47 (1935), pp. 348–55. R. W. HUNT, recognizing a regional interest

Chronicon Anglicanum

Where Ralph's authorship of the *Visio Thurkilli* and the evidence
of his intervention in the *Libellus* have to be inferred, the statement of authorship in the chronicle is definitive. It is internally
ascribed in an entry under 1207, the year of Ralph's election.
"Dom Thomas, fifth abbot of Coggeshall, died, and was succeeded
by Ralph, a monk of the same place, who wrote this chronicle
from the capture of the Holy Cross [i.e. 1187] to the eleventh year
of King Henry III, the son of King John [i.e. 28 October 1226–
1227 October 1227]".[38] That is the limit of the textual evidence for
Ralph's authorship, and it marks the inner limit of scholarly doubt,
for this statement has often been questioned since its description
of the chronicle does not match the text as it now stands. The
text begins in 1066 rather than in 1187, and ends not in Henry's
eleventh year but in 1224. Furthermore, the entries for the years
1206 to 1212 are bald annals and are barely "composed" at all.
Antonia Gransden judged that it is "not certain that the chronicle
is all the work of one man", and a modern trend has preferred
the circumlocution "the Coggeshall chronicle".[39] But there is no
need for such caution. The chronicle under the years 1066 to 1186
is purely annalistic and is largely derived from John of Worcester, Henry of Huntingdon, and the Margam Annals. In 1187 the
chronicle expands greatly and becomes original — "composed", as
the authorship ascription would have it, rather than merely "compiled". The other date, of the eleventh year of Henry III, may in
fact refer to Ralph's death, and I will return to that below. There
is no textual reason to doubt Ralph's authorship, and I will hope
to show that palaeography secures it.

It is, however, a textually complex work, particularly in its
later reaches. The expansive style employed from 1187 later came

in the text, argued instead for the author's having been a Cistercian of Louth
Park in Lincolnshire, but again on no strong grounds ("Notes on the *Distinc-
tiones monasticae et morales*", in *Liber Floridus. Mittellateinische Studien. Paul
Lehmann zum 65. Geburtstag*, Sankt Ottilien, 1950, pp. 355–62).

[38]   See above, n. 14.

[39]   GRANSDEN, *Historical Writing*, vol. 1, p. 323. Maurice POWICKE (as n. 42
below) had earlier commented that the entries for the years 1206–1213 show
that "Ralph was evidently unable to go on with his work" and that "it is difficult to estimate his responsibility for the rest" (p. 286, n. 1).

to be abandoned and the chronicle is baldly annalistic again for the years 1206 to 1212 and rather patchy thereafter. It is usually assumed that the burdens of abbacy had required Ralph to set his pen aside. This annalistic central portion of the work has always been a frustration to the historian since contemporary chronicle sources for the reign of King John are few. The matter has historiographical significance since John has been arraigned before the jury of Posterity like no other English monarch. "Bad King John" is a familiar figure in English legend and school history. William Stubbs's famous opinion of him, that he had "neither grace nor splendour, neither strength nor patriotism" took lineal descent from the so-called "Terrible Verdict" of the St Albans historians, Roger of Wendover and Matthew Paris, in which John's generalship grew ever more feeble, and the personal cruelties in which he indulged himself grew ever more vindictive and bizarre.[40]

In modern times, historians have sought to untangle John's reputation from the polemical distaste of those who were writing after John's time. In 1963 J. C. Holt assigned the chronicle sources for John's reign to three groups: those which were completed before or soon after John's accession; those which were completed by the time of his death; and those which were written after his death.[41] It was an important exercise, for it showed how the king's reputation progressively deteriorated; and it has demanded that the historian should tread carefully when dealing with the evidence. Chroniclers of the early group, the most important being Roger of Howden, were careful to present a judicious account of the reign. The chroniclers who were howling with outrage at the king's misdemeanours were those of the third group, who were writing after — sometimes decades after — John's death. The contemporaneity and content of Ralph's commentary on John therefore assumes some importance.

Maurice Powicke, who was the first to give serious attention to the chronicle's composition, argued that it was written up in

---

[40]   W. STUBBS, Preface to his edition of *Memoriale fratris Walteri de Coventria*, 2 vols, London, 1872–1873 (Rolls Series, 58), vol. 2, p. xi. On Roger of Wendover and the Terrible Verdict, see WARREN, *King John*, pp. 11–16.

[41]   J. C. HOLT, *King John*, London, 1963, reprinted in his *Magna Carta and Medieval Government*, London, 1985.

different stages in the 1190s and 1200s.[42] David Carpenter, in a
perceptive article on the earlier portion of the chronicle, demonstrated that the text for the period between 1195 and down to
nearly the end of 1200 was written up probably in 1201 with successive bursts of composition in the following years.[43] Holt judged
that Ralph did not begin his narrative of the period after 1207
"until 1221 or thereabouts".[44] Antonia Gransden argued that some
of the passages from the last years of Richard's reign were written
close in time to the events, but thought that in the main the chronicle was written "soon after John's death".[45] Passages from early
in the reign are rather complimentary about John, who initially
stood quite high in Ralph's estimation after the reign of Richard,
a king whom Ralph did not esteem. It remains the case that the
section from 1206 to 1224 is a complex one, and it is this section
which will be the principal focus here.

The field for speculation is offered by the primary manuscript,
BL, Cotton MS Vespasian D. x. It is the oldest copy of the work
and the exemplar on which all the others depend. As mentioned
above, it is remarkable for its numerous additions — marginal,
interlineated, *in rasura*, and interfoliated — all clearly work of
an authorial nature. There are numerous changes of hand in the
manuscript as well as of ink and nib, to show that work was being
kept up over a long period of time. It must be the working copy,
standing very close to the author's notes. Plate 1 illustrates how
new information was accommodated as it arrived. It shows the

[42]   F. M. POWICKE, "Roger of Wendover and the Coggeshall chronicle",
English Historical Review, 21 (1906), pp. 286–96. The essay was in unusual
territory for Powicke, who, like Freeman (see n. 1), preferred to base his
work on published sources; see M. T. CLANCHY, "Inventing thirteenth-century England: Stubbs, Tout, Powicke — now what?", in *Thirteenth Century
England* V, ed. by P. R. COSS, S. D. LLOYD, Woodbridge, 1995, pp. 1–20, esp.
4–5; also N. C. VINCENT, "Magna Carta and the *English Historical Review*: a
review article", *English Historical Review*, 130 (2015), pp. 646–84, at 658–61.

[43]   D. CARPENTER, "Abbot Ralph of Coggeshall's account of the last years
of King Richard and the first years of King John", *English Historical Review*,
113 (1998), pp. 1210–30.

[44]   HOLT, *King John*, p. 102.

[45]   GRANSDEN, *Historical Writing*, vol. 1, pp. 318, 324. Elizabeth FREE-
MAN, *Narratives of a New Order*, p. 179, likewise concluded that the chronicle
principally dates to "between 1200 and the 1220s".

passage mentioned above on the capture of King Richard I in Vienna which Ralph heard from Anselm, the king's chaplain and an eye-witness. The first account was erased and overwritten with the new information, continued in the margin at the foot and marked with a *signe-de-renvoie*.

The Vespasian manuscript naturally has priority, but there are two other principal witnesses: London, College of Arms, Arundel 11; and BnF, lat. 15076. These three are the witnesses used by Stevenson for his edition. There are also ten lesser witnesses which Stevenson did not notice.[46] The three chief manuscripts are all Coggeshall work of the early thirteenth century. While some of the marginal additions to Vespasian appear as continuous text in the Arundel manuscript, other additions are marginal to both, showing that the two copies were kept up side by side. Arundel 11, copied by one scribe, is therefore certain to be a Coggeshall production. The Paris manuscript, lat. 15076, shows the normal Coggeshall scriptorium layout of thirty-one or sometimes thirty-two long lines. It breaks off in 1216 at a point where the ink and hand can be seen to change in Vespasian.[47] It carries over into its text additions that are marginal to both Vespasian and Arundel.[48] Evidence that it was also made at Coggeshall and copied from Vespasian is communicated by a scribal blunder: on fol. 46ʳ (*s.a.* 1192) the scribe of Paris copied the passage on King Richard's capture of a desert train, ending 'ciuitatibus collocans', and passed directly to the passage beginning, 'Rege autem apud Ptolomaidem', over-

---

[46]   Cambridge, Corpus Christi College, 343 (*s.* xiv, *ex* Arundel 11); Dublin, Trinity College, 508 (*s.* xiii¹, a conflated text); 634 (*s.* xvi, excerpts copied by John Dee, probably *ex* Arundel 11); London, BL, Harley MS 545 (*s.* xvi, excerpts copied by John Stow); Royal 13 A. xii (*s.* xiii¹, a conflated text); Stowe MS 61 (*s.* xvii, excerpts copied by Sir Roger Twysden); London, College of Arms, Arundel 24 (*s.* xiii, excerpts); London, Lambeth Palace, 371 (*s.* xiiiᵉˣ, excerpts, *ex* BnF, lat. 15076, or family thereof); BnF, lat. 14359 (St Victor, Paris, *s.* xvii, *ex* lat. 15076); lat. 15077 (St Victor, Paris, *s.* xvii, *ex* lat. 15076).

[47]   Vespasian, fol. 119ᵛ (new foliation), Paris, fol. 29ᵛ (*RC*, p. 193 at n. 4).

[48]   For example, the passage "Hec pauperibus [...] et pace interrupta resarciri" which describes the life and miracles of St Alpais, a holy woman of Sens (*RC*, pp. 125–28), is interpolated on a separate half-leaf in Arundel (fol. 85*bis* new foliation, fol. 90 old foliation) and Vespasian (fol. 95), but is continuous text in Paris.

looking an intervening passage which is an interleaved addition to the Vespasian manuscript; he quickly spotted his mistake and cancelled the eight lines he had written with the comment *uacat* before proceeding with the transcription of the material contained in the interfoliation.[49]

The copy of the *Libellus de expugnatione Terrae Sanctae* in Cotton Cleopatra B. i, as has been seen, forms part of this tightly interconnected group. That the copy of the *Libellus* in Arundel 11 was taken directly from it is shown by an obscure error in Ralph's sentence about Prior Richard's elegant and veracious style. Cleopatra here shows 'ueraci sti | lo transferri fecit', where 'stilo' is split by a line-break; the scribe of Arundel wrote 'uerati\sci/stilo transferri fecit', adding 'sci' above the line as if confused by what he saw in his exemplar.[50] As suggested above, it is possible that Cleopatra was once part of Vespasian before being bound into its present volume by Sir Robert Cotton.

The fact that all the oldest manuscripts of both the *Libellus* and Ralph's chronicle can be shown to have been in production at Coggeshall at the same time suggests that they were being copied for propagation rather than for domestic consumption. Evidence internal to the chronicle is revealing about what publication meant for Ralph and about his practices in achieving it. Maurice Powicke showed long ago, in one of his first published articles, that it must have been Ralph's practice to send out his chronicle — to publish it — periodically during its composition, something that can be inferred from the verbatim use that was made of it at St Albans abbey by the historian Roger of Wendover, perhaps in the 1220s.[51] Ralph's chronicle was Wendover's principal source for his account of the years 1191 to 1195, after which no further use of it seems

[49] WILLOUGHBY, "Templar chronicle", pp. 128–29. A detailed discussion of the composition of the Paris copy has now been provided by BREWER, KANE, *Conquest of the Holy Land*, pp. 86–88, 89–90, 95, concluding that a Coggeshall origin "is beyond reasonable doubt".

[50] Cotton Cleopatra B. i, fol. 21ʳ (20ʳ old foliation); Arundel 11, fol. 14ʳ.

[51] POWICKE, "Roger of Wendover and the Coggeshall chronicle". Daniel HOBBINS makes a similar case that medieval publication could be an ongoing process of "publishing moments" from a study of the work of Jean Gerson: *Authorship and Publicity Before Print: Jean Gerson and the Transformation of Late Medieval Learning*, Philadelphia, PA, 2009, pp. 154, 178–82.

to have been made at St Albans.[52] Wendover's extracts from the Chronicle end at precisely the point in Ralph's narrative where in the Vespasian copy the ink and nib both change (fol. 68ᵛ), showing a break in Ralph's composition and explaining why the St Albans copy should have ended at that point: it marks the extent of one 'release' of material. It will be recalled that a separate Coggeshall publication, Ralph's *Visio Thurkilli*, which survives in a manuscript with St Albans provenance, was taken over into Wendover's History under the year 1206. St Albans was clearly a targeted publication channel for Ralph.

For his account of the years from 1191 to 1195, Wendover's pre-eminent source was Ralph's chronicle, quoted *in extenso*. He took very few liberties with the material and never departed from its burden, even if occasionally he chose to recast a shorter annal for the turning of a more felicitous phrase. Certain of Ralph's alterations to the Vespasian manuscript were made before this copy of it left Coggeshall for St Albans, because they are visible in Wendover's text, taken over verbatim. Other changes, however, were clearly brought into Ralph's text after this moment of publication, and Wendover in these cases preserves older readings than now survive. Some of them are of historical interest. For example, under the year 1193, in a section in Wendover that is otherwise a verbatim borrowing from Ralph, Wendover explains that while Richard I was away in the Holy Land, John plotted traitorously with Philip of France to usurp the crown, but was foiled by the laudable virtue of the English people:

> Rege autem Richardo, ut dictum est, ab imperatore detento, comes Iohannes frater eius, audito regis infortunio atque de eius regressu diffidens, foedus amicitie cum Philippo, Francorum rege, iniit, sinistroque usus consilio in Anglia pro fratre disposuit coronari, sed Anglorum uirtute laudabili fuit impeditus. Rex autem Philippus [...][53]

In Ralph's account there is an abrupt break at this point in the narrative and instead an inconsequential entry is intruded about the election of Savarinus as bishop of Bath (given here in italics):

---

[52] Roger of Wendover, *Flores historiarum*, ed. by HEWLETT, vol. 1, pp. 192–236.

[53] Wendover, *Flores historiarum*, 1, p. 229.

Rege autem Ricardo apud imperatorem detento, comes Iohannes frater eius, qui filiam comitis Gloecestrie duxerat in uxorem, audito fratris infortunio, atque de regressione regis diffidens, foedus amicitie iniit cum rege Philippo. *Sauarinus ad episcopatum Bathoniensem eligitur et consecratur.* Rex autem Philippus [...][54]

In the Vespasian manuscript, this revision is written *in rasura* in a distinctive style (Pl. 2). Although Ralph was no partisan for John, the criticism implied here, in the original version preserved by Wendover, is stronger and more outspoken than was usual with him. Two other significant differences between Wendover and Coggeshall concerning accusations against John were discussed by Powicke.[55] Their concealment suggests something in the nature of censorship.

That suggestion is supported by a far larger and far more important expurgation in the chronicle. For it is a peculiar fact, and a frustration for the historian, that for the years 1206 to 1212 Ralph abandoned the vivid and expansive narrative style of previous years and returned to writing bare, laconic annals.[56] His account of one third of King John's reign is therefore slim indeed. This sudden change of emphasis is the source of much of the subsequent insecurity over how much of the chronicle Ralph was personally responsible for. However, an inspection of the Vespasian manuscript shows that these annals occupy one leaf only, folio 112, an inserted leaf in a different hand (Pl. 3). Stevenson noted this discrepancy in the apparatus of his edition.[57] It was noted again by Antonia Gransden, who stated that four leaves had been excised and this singleton inserted in their place.[58] Subsequent scholarship has followed her, with the result that it is not suspected that any

[54] *CA*, p. 61.

[55] POWICKE, "Roger of Wendover and the Coggeshall chronicle", pp. 288–91. GRANSDEN, *Historical Writing*, vol. 1, p. 326, n. 51, pointed out that Wendover's two readings *s.a.* 1193 are too long to fit the erased spaces, but she did acknowledge that Wendover might have reworded Ralph's phrasing. I find her assertion that Powicke's "proposition cannot be proved" too defeatist.

[56] *CA*, pp. 162–65. For comparison, the annals for the single preceding year of 1205 cover twelve pages of the edition.

[57] *CA*, p. 162 n. 1: "The narrative of the Cotton MS is apparently defective, or incomplete, at this point; the contents of the leaf which is here inserted being an insertion by a different hand."

[58] GRANSDEN, *Historical Writing*, vol. 1, p. 323, n. 23.

great quantity of material has been lost. It is certainly true that for the most part the Cotton Manuscripts are notoriously tightly bound in their nineteenth-century boards; establishing the quiring in them can be difficult, and such is the case with Vespasian D. x. But I happen not to agree with Gransden's collation: it seems that only the first leaf of the original quire is intact, and the supplied singleton has been stuck to its stub. Four leaves therefore cannot have been excised — a quire of five not being possible — and one might in any case ask why only four leaves should be thought to have gone. Clearly, any number of discrete quires could have been removed following the excision of the first. There are, in fact, reasons for believing that a great deal of material in multiple quires has been plucked out here.

Palaeographically, the first significant thing to notice is that this hand is the same as the Censor's hand seen making the erasure about John's treachery, overwriting it with the note of Savarinus's election. Plate 4 shows the two specimens together. While at first glance they might seem to be rather different, they possess the same flat, squarish module as well as the left-leaning slant in the hand. There is a deliberateness in the formation of the *n* and *m*; they are carefully drawn, perhaps over-drawn, with a definite shoulder before the minim is traced. Most particularly, we might look at the very unusual *S*, which is formed by two overlapping but not intersecting curves: *Savarinus* may be compared with *Stephanus*. The similar construction of the word *consecratur*, appearing in the bottom line of each specimen, may be compared, as also the abbreviation mark for *-ur*.

The question then falls, who was the censor? There is a leading answer, since the principal feature of this hand is its ineptitude. One need only glance at the hand to be aware of its shortcomings.[59] No monastic scriptorium in the early thirteenth century could have been brought so low as to entrust book-work to such a scribe. Indeed, there were fine scribes available at Coggeshall, as is proved by the other manuscripts of the chronicle. Such a scribe as we see here must have stood in an important relation to the chronicle to have been permitted to write in it. It would be most

---

[59]   It is worth remarking that folio 112 is poorly prepared, rather greasy on the hair-side, which must contribute something to the writing's ragged appearance.

natural to assume that the hand is authorial. From that suggestion follows a larger one: that much of the Vespasian copy was
written by the same man. While it is true that multiple scribes
wrote in the manuscript, one hand predominates but at different
levels of achievement. It shows the same square aspect as the Censor's hand, the same firm treatment of shoulders and minims, the
same mode of construction of the abbreviation marks. The graphs
are always consistently shaped even when the aspect can differ.
It must be remembered that the Vespasian manuscript shows the
chronicle in a state of polygenesis, a text over whose composition
the author spent at least thirty years. That fact may be called
upon to explain changes in the writing. Its differences are no more
than the normal variations in a hand over time, writing neater
and closer at first, and looser and more irregularly towards the
close.

Palaeographers have been reluctant to discuss the longevity
of scribes, for the obvious reason that it is impossible to control for.[60] Few individual medieval hands have been tracked over
time. It is rare to encounter the sort of peculiarities that make
the so-called "Tremulous Hand" of Worcester so recognizable.
Presumed to have been a monk of the cathedral priory, he was
a thirteenth-century glossator of manuscripts in Old English: in
his case, the degree of tremor in the formation of his graphs,
worsening as his health deteriorated, allowed Christine Franzen
to assign specimens of his hand to a timeline.[61] John Grandisson, bishop of Exeter from 1327 to 1369, was a keen annotator of books for more than forty years.[62] An observable feature

---

[60] One exception being a thoughtful piece by A. S. G. EDWARDS, "What is
palaeography for?", *The Mediaeval Journal*, 8 (2018), pp. 21–40, esp. 31.

[61] *The Tremulous Hand of Worcester: A Study of Old English in the Thirteenth Century*, Oxford, 1991; an attempt at retrospective diagnosis, reported
at pp. 190–91, ends with the suggestion that the writer was afflicted with
"congenital tremor".

[62] The key discussion of the varieties of his handwriting is by M. W.
STEELE, "A study of the books owned or used by John Grandisson, bishop
of Exeter", unpublished DPhil diss., University of Oxford, 1994, pp. 15–21.
A. B. EMDEN, *A Biographical Register of the University of Oxford to A.D.
1500*, 3 vols, Oxford, 1957–1959, vol. 2, pp. 800–01, printed convenient lists
of Grandisson's identified books: those that passed to Exeter cathedral, those
that belonged to him, and those containing notes in his own hand.

of Grandisson's hand, rather like Ralph's later hand, is that the strokes are traced separately and do not flow; later specimens show less good consistency. Henry of Kirkestede, prior of Bury St Edmunds, who has been mentioned above, was another keen annotator of books. He acquired a noticeable tremor in his old age. Some years before he died another man was serving as prior, so, as was the case with Ralph, it would seem that infirmity had caused him to resign his office.[63]

The semi-automatic motor performance required for writing depends upon co-ordinated function by neuromuscular and visual systems. These systems deteriorate, to some extent, in every elderly writer, and even more so when neurological disease is present. A certain amount of forensic work has been done on age- and illness-related change in modern handwriting, partly to provide guidance in cases where a will has been contested because the elderly testator's signature looks like a forgery.[64] There is no reason to expect to see a tremor in an elderly hand, but one might plausibly expect a larger module and some inconsistency in duct. Angles instead of curves are understood to be a sign of arthritis. Square and flattened forms are typical of Parkinson's patients. Those aspects might be said to be present in Ralph's hand, but other indications are absent; his hand lacks, for instance, the typical micrographia of the Parkinson's sufferer; rather the reverse, in fact. Larger and more spread-out handwriting conforms to vision change. In ageing hands, the pen is lifted more often, because the hand is moving more slowly. Other aspects of an ageing hand may be seen in the performance on fol. 112: the leftwards lean, the greater size of the letters and the failure to join up strokes.

If some of what have usually been taken to be different scribes in the Vespasian manuscript are instead different stages of Ralph's own handwriting then it ought to be possible, and would be valuable, to assign specimens of his hand to a timeline. The increasingly larger module, the increasingly deliberate execution, and the more hesitant duct should allow one to venture the suggestion

---

[63]   ROUSE, ROUSE, *Henry of Kirkestede, Catalogus*, pp. lxxiv–lxxv.

[64]   See, for example, J. WALTON, "Handwriting changes due to aging and Parkinson's syndrome", *Forensic Science International*, 88 (1997), pp. 197–214.

that the state of the hand in the major expurgation is later than
the state seen in the Savarinus addition, and that both are later
than the state of the hand in the first part of the chronicle (as
illustrated in Pl. 1). It is clear that the expurgation must have
been made after John's death, because of the passage on the interfoliated leaf stating that Abbot Ralph kept up the chronicle until
the eleventh year of Henry III (Pl. 3). Although the regnal year in
question is an addition in the manuscript, the fact that it belonged
to the reign of Henry III is original, so the expurgation belongs
to this time. We do not have the final state of his hand, because
the back quire or quires of the Vespasian manuscript are missing,
and have been since at least the second quarter of the sixteenth
century, when John Bale supplied the missing material from Cambridge, Corpus Christi College 343.[65]

One of the four known facts about Ralph's life is that he resigned the abbacy in 1218 through ill health. The handwriting
of fol. 112 appears to be infirm — at least, it is a hand that
appears throughout the manuscript and which seems to suffer
a decline in its powers to the point where it was barely suited to its task. It accords with the state of the same hand in
a late stint of writing on fols 123^r–124^r, communicating a set
of short annals for 1223. That is the sort of date which might
be applied to the large expurgation. By 1223 the chronicle was
being kept up within one or two years of events. This understanding throws a sidelight on the chronicle's seemingly misleading assertion that Ralph wrote until late 1226 or 1227, or
the eleventh year of Henry III. The claim occurs on folio 112
in a space apparently left blank for the purpose. If the writing is autograph, as I think it is, then we must assume that
Ralph himself left the gap, expecting it to be completed after
his death. Although no annal survives for 1226 or 1227, the
scribe who added the regnal year was probably perfectly cor-

---

[65]   Bale's hand appears in the margin of Corpus Christi 343, fol. 28^r. In his
Index, ed. by POOLE, BATESON, p. 327, he reported taking his information on
Ralph of Coggeshall "ex magno libro Nicholai Brigan"; this was his friend,
the antiquary Nicholas Brigham († 1558), a collector of manuscripts. Albeit
Corpus Christi 343 is a large book of roughly folio size, the "great book"
referred to may have been Brigham's own *De venationibus rerum memorabil-
ium*, a collection on which Bale relied for information on other authors.

rect to record that Ralph was writing then, still working on his chronicle in what was the year of his death.

The question as to what purpose this major expurgation was intended to serve can be answered if we accept the palaeographical conclusions. (And the answer remains valid even if the palaeographical conclusions are not accepted.) The censorship affects annals hostile to John. That is unequivocally the case with the Savarinus addition; what the larger expurgation might therefore have concealed is a question of considerable interest. John Bale's work with the manuscripts mentioned above catches the attention since his play *King Johan* is the first occasion in English letters when King John is portrayed as a hero, a proto-Protestant with the courage to oppose the vicar of Rome even when the pall of interdict had been cast over the country.[66] Shakespeare's King John is a more nuanced character, drowned by events. But these are peaks in an otherwise deteriorating reputation that has left "Bad King John" as one of the villains of English history. Only in modern times have historians sought to rehabilitate the king, in so far as he can be. One very important plank in this rehabilitation has been a balanced consideration of the attitude of the chroniclers who were writing during his reign.[67] The annals of Margam and Waverley are neutral or only incidentally hostile — albeit the Waverley annalist takes a certain relish in listing John's misfortunes — while the so-called Barnwell Chronicle, now reassigned to Crowland, retains a judicious balance.[68] As has often been pointed out in this connection, Ralph's chronicle is merely annalistic for

---

[66]   John Bale, *King Johan*, ed. by B. B. ADAMS, San Marino, CA, 1969. Bale's thematic source was William Tyndale's *Obedience of a Christen Man*, first published in 1528; but for historical detail he drew also on the chronicle sources with which he was acquainted (*ibid.*, pp. 25–38).

[67]   See above, n. 41.

[68]   The Margam Annals are ed. by H. R. LUARD in *Annales Monastici*, 5 vols, London, 1864–1869 (Rolls Series, 36), vol. 1, pp. 3–40; and the Waverley annals, *ibid.*, vol. 2, pp. 129–411. The annals for 1202–1225 that have been known since the nineteenth century as the "Barnwell Chronicle" have now been assigned to Roger, a monk of Crowland: see C. ISPIR, "A critical edition of the *Crowland* Chronicle", unpublished PhD diss., King's College, London, 2015; also his "History writing in the cloister: the Crowland Chronicle", in *Guthlac: Crowland's Saint*, ed. by J. ROBERTS, A. THACKER, Donnington, 2020, pp. 426–77.

the central years of John's reign, so apparently unroused was the author by the king's alleged misdeeds.[69] The lack of material at this point in the chronicle is therefore found to be historiographically important, for these were the very years that a Cistercian writer ought to have felt most uncomfortable. The king had refused the pope's man as archbishop of Canterbury and brought a papal interdict on the country; he then retaliated against that by seizing the clergy's revenues, taxing the Cistercians particularly severely. The absence of comment by Ralph during these cruel years makes the revisionist point, that King John did not excite the outrage of his contemporaries but has been damned instead by the lurid imaginings of later historians.

We have seen that we do not in fact have Ralph's first thoughts for that crucial section of the chronicle. More than that, the inserted annals clearly stand across a lacuna. There is evidence to assert that this lacuna was substantial. It has escaped notice hitherto, but an epitome exists of the earlier, unexpurgated version of Ralph's chronicle. This epitome is really no more than a list of capitula, describing each annal, no matter its original length, in one or two sentences. But it amounts to a faithful summary of the entire chronicle. Such *chroniculae* are not unknown for medieval chronicles: they survive, for example, for Henry of Huntingdon, John of Worcester, and Matthew Paris. But rarely has one offered anything of such value to textual history. This epitome is transmitted by the Arundel manuscript and its dependent copy, Corpus Christi College 343. The last entry in the epitome is for 1225.[70] It does show what very severe changes Ralph

---

[69]   STUBBS, *Memoriale fratris Walteri de Coventria*, vol. 2, p. xii, notes that Ralph on John "ventures on no inferences from his acts to his character", and that Ralph, "although generally prone to run into descriptions of character, draws none of John; only an occasional adverb, 'dolose', 'crudeliter', or 'ignaviter', shows what he thought". Other historians writing about Ralph's chronicle of John's reign have noted the paucity of information: A. LLOYD, *King John*, Newton Abbot, 1973, p. 399: "the chronicle is sometimes illuminating but too often trivial and scrappy"; WARREN, *King John*, p. 8: "the weather and the crops, phenomena in the heavens, and strange happenings in East Anglia, have as big a place as King John".

[70]   It is worth mentioning that the start of Ralph's *Chronicon* follows the end of the epitome (fol. 51vb) without a break and in the same hand, establishing 1225 as the earliest date for the copying of Arundel 11.

imposed on his work. For the years before 1206 and after 1212, either side of the major expurgation, the contents of the chronicle and the epitome marry very exactly. The Savarinus insertion is not there, which confirms that the epitome was begun earlier than that act of censorship. For the years of the expurgation, however, epitome and chronicle differ wildly. The implication must be that the epitome was drawn up earlier and is the key to material that Ralph subsequently removed and replaced with the very blandest of his annals. These he selected from the epitome itself, for they are taken over verbatim.[71]

A fruitful comparison may be made between the two sources for just one year, 1211. The Vespasian manuscript and every other known copy of the chronicle transmit only three annals under that year; the epitome offers twenty-one. It is a similar picture for all the other years between 1206 and 1212. We are left to wonder what expanded hostility towards the king might have lain behind the laconic capitular descriptions of annals such as that on the "complaint of the king against the Cistercians"; or how much horror at one of the outrages of the year Ralph might have projected into his account of the death of William de Braose, the former royal favourite chased into exile, his wife and son murdered by John.

The possibility that the Terrible Verdict of the St Albans school might have come not from the imagination of a later generation but have its feet instead in the contemporary clay of Ralph's unexpurgated chronicle is a tantalizing proposition. After all, we know that Ralph shared an early state of his chronicle with St Albans — why not his later work too? But that would be a speculation too far: there seems to be little trace in the work of Roger of Wendover or Matthew Paris of the topics listed in the epitome: Ralph's account of those years appears in fact to have been very much richer. Instead, it is salutary merely to realize that we have inherited something very different from the full chronicle as it was once constituted for the years between 1206 and 1212. The state of the manuscript and Ralph's hand proves that the expur-

---

[71] The epitome, although it has escaped scholarly notice, was in fact partially printed, in parallel with the Vespasian text, for this expurgated section, in excerpts from the *Chronicon Anglicanum* edited by R. PAULI and F. LIEBERMANN, Hannover, 1885 (MGH SS [folio], 27), pp. 355–57.

gation was late, and that what was removed had been written as a contemporary witness to John's reign. It is worth remembering, when King John's reputation is discussed and decided, that one plank of his modern rehabilitation may not be as sound as has been assumed.

Publication and Dissemination

Ralph appears to have been ambitious for his work. An interim copy of his chronicle down to the return of Richard I from captivity in 1195 was sent to St Albans abbey, as we have seen. Another release, ending in 1216, the last year of John's reign, is represented by the Paris manuscript. As with the earlier release, this one breaks off at a point where in the Vespasian manuscript the ink and hand can be seen to change, showing another break in composition.[72] This version, however, is complicated: its text is jumbled and partial. But for the years between 1206 and 1212 it follows the expurgated Vespasian text, showing that it was copied only in the 1220s.[73] There was a copy at Reading abbey (Berks) deriving from the Paris family: it was excerpted there and worked into two accounts of the life and times of Richard I, composed towards the end of the thirteenth century.[74] There may also have been a copy at Glastonbury abbey (Soms), where a fifteenth-century library catalogue reported a chronicle extending from 1066 to the reign of King John.[75] As we have seen, two copies of Ralph's *Visio Thurkilli* were in the library at Peterborough abbey (Northants).[76] It could also be found at St Albans, whence it was taken over by

---

[72]   Other such breaks in composition are visible in Vespasian, such as at the end of the section from 1195 to 1200; see CARPENTER, "Abbot Ralph of Coggeshall's account", p. 1216.

[73]   WILLOUGHBY, "Templar chronicle", pp. 128–29; BREWER, KANE, *Conquest of the Holy Land*, pp. 85–90.

[74]   S. J. SPENCER, "Two unexamined witnesses to Ralph of Coggeshall's *Chronicon anglicanum* in London, Lambeth Palace Library, MS 371", *Manuscripta*, 62 (2018), pp. 279–86.

[75]   *English Benedictine Libraries: The Shorter Catalogues*, ed. by R. SHARPE, J. P. CARLEY, R. M. THOMSON, A. G. WATSON, London, 1996 (Corpus of British Medieval Library Catalogues, 4), p. 245 (B45. 68: "Chronica a Wilhelmo Normanno ad regem Iohannem").

[76]   See above, n. 35.

Roger of Wendover and Matthew Paris for their own chronicles. Henry of Kirkestede at Bury St Edmunds abbey knew of a book of visions from Coggeshall. All of these institutions were large, wealthy, regionally important Benedictine houses with strong historiographical traditions of their own. It is plausible to think that Ralph was cultivating a publishing circle.

The Paris manuscript of the *Chronicon Anglicanum* was owned by the famous Augustinian abbey of Saint-Victor in Paris, whose arms and fifteenth-century *ex libris* appear prominently at the foot of fol. 1ʳ and there is an earlier inscription in fourteenth-century Textura on the preceding flyleaf (fol. iᵛ) including an anathema. The most interesting inscription is a third one, over the top of the first page. It reads *Hic est liber Ecclesie beati Victoris Paris' quem qui ei abstulerit uel super eo fraude fecit, sit anathema maranatha*, where the words *Victoris Paris'* are written on an erasure. The original inscription is of the second half of the thirteenth century and the addition is of the fourteenth. The manuscript clearly had at least one intervening home between Coggeshall and Paris. (The form of the original *ex libris* inscription does not help identify it.) It would be plausible for St Victor to have acquired its copy through Augustinian networks. The Augustinian priory at Thurgarton — famous in a later age as the place where the mystical writer Walter Hilton († 1396) passed his final years — had a copy of the *Visio Thurkilli*.[77] That being the case, perhaps the Augustinian priory of St Osyth in Essex had been Ralph's conduit to wider Augustinian networks. A certain connexion existed between St Osyth's and Coggeshall, only seventeen miles distant from each other: Ralph was always scrupulous in observing the obits and elections of priors there, a practice he otherwise reserved only for his own community and the neighbouring Cistercian house of Tilty.[78] Accompanying the *Chronicon Anglicanum* in the Vespasian and Arundel manuscripts are annals from 1162 to 1178 which have been ascribed to a monk of Coggeshall, even to Ralph himself.[79] In fact, the two references in them to St Osyth's priory,

[77] See above, n. 36.

[78] *RC*, pp. 20, 162. Thurkill's closing vision was of SS Katharine, Margaret, and Osyth; *Visio Thurkilli*, ed. by Schmidt, p. 36, l. 15.

[79] The annals were ed. by R. Anstruther, *Radulphi Nigri Chronica. The Chronicles of Ralph Niger*, London, 1851 (Caxton Society) [hereafter *RN*],

one of them a long excursus, point rather to an origin there.[80] If Ralph received these annals from St Osyth's — and they are only transmitted in Coggeshall manuscripts — then nothing would have been more natural than a reciprocal exchange of information.

The St Osyth's Annals connect with a more substantial fellow traveller, the Shorter or 'English' Chronicle of Ralph Niger, which is likewise only transmitted alongside the *Chronicon Anglicanum* (save only in the Paris manuscript). It begins at the Incarnation and concludes around the year 1180: the death and burial of Louis VII of France in that year are mentioned.[81] Because of the way the St Osyth's Annals follow Niger's chronicle in the Vespasian manuscript — their oldest witness — they have been taken as a continuation of Niger's chronicle.[82] The surmise then follows

pp. 170–78. T. D. HARDY, *Descriptive Catalogue of Materials relating to the History of Great Britain and Ireland*, 3 vols in 4 pts, London, 1862–1871 (Rolls Series, 26), vol. 2, p. 415, states that this attribution is "on the authority of the Heralds' College MS" (i.e. London, College of Arms, MS Arundel 11). In fact, the manuscript does not ascribe the continuation to Ralph, although its former owner Lord William Howard of Naworth (1563–1640) has written a note to attribute to Ralph the *Additiones* (1114 to 1158) which follow, on the authority of John Bale (BALE, *Index*, ed. by Poole, Bateson, p. 327). For the collection context, see further R. OVENDEN, "The manuscript library of Lord William Howard of Naworth (1563–1640)", in *Books and Bookmen in Early Modern Britain. Essays Presented to James P. Carley*, ed. by J. WILLOUGHBY and J. CATTO, Toronto, 2018 (Papers in Mediaeval Studies, 30), pp. 278–318.

[80] *RN*, pp. 173, 177, for a long description of a fire-breathing dragon seen in the sky at St Osyth's in 1171 and mention of St Osyth's again in 1177 in relation to Henry II's foundation of another Augustinian house at Waltham. See further GRANSDEN, *Historical Writing*, vol. 1, p. 331, nn. 92–93. On the literary culture of St Osyth's at this time, see D. BETHELL, "The Lives of St Osyth of Essex and St Osyth of Aylesbury", *Analecta Bollandiana*, 88 (1970), pp. 75–127.

[81] *RN*, pp. 105–78. Ralph Niger wrote two chronicles, the first and probably the earlier is known as Chronicle I, or the "Universal Chronicle", ed. *RN*, pp. 1–104, covering the Creation to the 1190s (its final entries being variously dated by scholars between 1194 and 1199). It survives in BL, Cotton MS Cleopatra C. x, and Lincoln Cathedral, 15. The second chronicle is often called the "English Chronicle", which is something of a misnomer since there is no special concentration on English affairs.

[82] They are found on fols 35v–39v. The Annals were presented as a continuation by Anstruther in his edition of Niger's Chronicle, and, on the rare occasions they have attracted scholarly attention, they are so described. See, for example, HARDY, *Descriptive Catalogue*, vol. 2, p. 145; GRANSDEN, *His-*

that Coggeshall's copy of Niger's chronicle had likewise been received from St Osyth's.[83] Instead, the two items should be seen as
independent of each other. Albeit the St Osyth's Annals follow
Niger's chronicle on a verso in the same hand, to assume they
were likewise connected in the exemplar is to ignore the possibility that this is no more than the smoothing effect of the same
scribe's copying of two sources. It is in fact misleading to speak of
a "continuation" or "addition" since the St Osyth's Annals cover
years between 1162 and 1178 while Niger's chronicle ends around
1180. Both texts appear in a portion of the manuscript that conveys other, miscellaneous texts on historical subjects, including
the *Additiones* mentioned below. It would be better to see the St
Osyth's Annals and Niger's Chronicle as two discrete texts gathered into this dossier of historical materials.

The question of the route taken to Coggeshall by Niger's Shorter
Chronicle bears further reflection since the chronicle has no transmission outside of Coggeshall manuscripts. Ralph Niger († ?1199)
was a theologian and historian, the author of two chronicles.[84] He
was an Englishman, a Parisian master, sometime member of the
courts of Henry II and Henry the Young King, a friend to John
of Salisbury and companion in exile to Thomas Becket. Although
he clearly admired the Cistercians, there is no evidence that he
took any monastic vow. But there exists the smallest of hints that
he was known to Abbot Ralph in his friendship with the courtier
and historian Gervase of Tilbury († in or after 1222). Gervase,

---

torical Writing, vol. 1, p. 331; E. D. Kennedy, "Annals of St Osyth's", in
Encyclopedia of the Medieval Chronicle, ed. by G. Dunphy & C. Bratu, 2 vols,
Leiden, 2010, vol. 1, p. 88; the online edition is kept updated.

[83]   As I myself surmised in a previous article, "A Templar chronicle",
p. 131. I now think that this codicological connection lacks persuasive force.

[84]   The known details for his life are assembled by G. B. Flahiff, "Ralph
Niger. An introduction to his life and works", *Mediaeval Studies*, 2 (1940),
pp. 104–26, and see 122–23 for the Shorter Chronicle. Also A. Saltman,
"Supplementary notes on the works of Ralph *Niger*", *Bar-Ilan Studies in History*, 1 (1978), pp. 108–13; and see the article by A. J. Duggan in *ODNB*.
The account has been usefully enlarged by F. Lachaud, 'Ralph Niger and
the Books of Kings', *Anglo-Norman Studies*, 40 (2017), pp. 125–46, at 126–
28; there are also useful comments by H. Krause in his edition of Niger's
other chronicle, *Radulphus Niger—Chronica. Eine englische Weltchronik des 12.
Jahrhunderts*, Frankfurt, 1985, pp. 5*–22*.

in a complimentary passage about Ralph Niger's learning, tells that he and Ralph were fellows together in the court of Henry the Young King († 1183).[85] It is also the case that Gervase was acquainted with Abbot Ralph: it was Gervase who told Ralph about his meeting with a pretty girl in a vineyard near Reims who, it transpired, was a member of the heretical Publicani sect, a history that Ralph reported in the *Chronicon Anglicanum*.[86] The view is closed to us, but these connections triangulate the possibility that the two Ralphs also knew each other, perhaps through court or diocesan networks.

Ralph Niger's biblical glosses were finished by 1191, when they were submitted to the archbishops of Sens and Reims for their *nihil obstat*. This scrutiny was a papal commission at the author's request, and the archbishops duly reported to the pope a year later that they had found nothing in the works contrary to sound doctrine.[87] The postills survive uniquely as a set at Lincoln cathedral, where Ralph held a prebend.[88] His chronicles came afterwards, the work of the 1190s, since his first Chronicle contains a completed list of his theological writings.[89] It seems that he was then

---

[85]   *Otia imperialia*, ed. by S. E. BANKS & J. W. BINNS, *Otia imperialia: Recreation for an Emperor*, Oxford, 2002 (Oxford Medieval Texts), pp. 186–87: "Vnde litteratus ille nostri temporis uir, magister Radulfus Niger, domini mei regis iunioris concurialis, cum Topica Aristotilis et Elencos uersibus glosaret, ait".

[86]   *CA*, p. 122: "magister Gervasius Tilleberiensis, videns quandam puellam in vinea solam deambulantem, lubrice iuuentutis curiositate ductus, diuertit ad eam, sicut ab eius ore audiuimus postea, cum canonicus esset". The girl, using theological arguments to fend Gervase off, provoked a cross-examination by the archbishop and was eventually burned at the stake as a heretic. See further NEUFELD, "Hermeneutical perversion".

[87]   G. B. FLAHIFF, "Ecclesiastical censorship of books in the twelfth century", *Mediaeval Studies*, 4 (1942), pp. 1–22, at 1–2, 17–22.

[88]   Lincoln Cathedral Library, 15, 23, 24, 25, 26, 27. The set is reported in an addition to the twelfth-century catalogue of the chapter library in Lincoln Cathedral, MS 1, fol. 1r: "Septem volumina Magistri Radulfi Nigri" (J. M. W. WILLOUGHBY and N. RAMSAY, *The Libraries of the Secular Cathedrals of England and Wales*, London, 2023 (Corpus of British Medieval Library Catalogues, 17), SC62. 104). The missing volume, postills on Joshua and Judges, was last reported in the 1450s (SC72. 14). An eighth, on Genesis and Exodus, had been lent to the abbot of Thornton and was already lost *c.* 1200 (SC62. 105).

[89]   For the chronicles, see FLAHIFF, "Ralph Niger", pp. 122–23. He was also the composer of offices for the four great Marian feasts (Nativity, Annun-

living in a house in London, for in 1199 King John made a regrant of the house he had formerly granted to Master Ralph Niger.[90] This grant and its date may therefore relate to Niger's death.[91] Ralph Niger is an example of an author who took pains to obtain ecclesiastical sanction for his works but failed to find publication channels thereafter. Other than the surviving set at Lincoln, his postills are only known by a reference from Henry of Kirkestede at Bury St Edmunds in the mid-fourteenth century.[92] Ralph was fortunate that where his Shorter Chronicle was concerned, it came into the hands of a man who was more positively committed to publication: it is entirely thanks to the monks of Coggeshall that Ralph Niger's Shorter Chronicle has survived at all.

The authorial ascription for Niger's chronicle is given in two places in the Vespasian manuscript: in the opening rubric ("Incipit prefatio Magistri Radulfi Nigri", fol. 4^r) and in a non-authorial passage at the end, before the start of the St Osyth's Annals (fol. 35^v, beginning at line 4). The author of this paragraph states that Ralph Niger's chronicle ends at this point ("Hucusque protraxit hanc cronicam Magister Radulfus Niger") and he continues by seeking to excuse Niger his patent hostility to Henry II since it was Henry who had sent Niger into exile (with Thomas Becket); that would have naturally coloured Niger's feelings about "so great and serene a king".[93] This apologetic paragraph might already

ciation, Assumption, and Purification), prefaced by a short didactic treatise, which survives uniquely in Lincoln Cathedral, MS 15; see further A. HUGHES, "British rhymed offices: a catalogue and commentary", in *Music in the Medieval English Liturgy: Plainsong & Mediaeval Music Society Centennial Essays*, ed. S. RANKIN, D. HILEY, Oxford, 1993, pp. 239–84, at pp. 250–51.

[90]   *Rotuli chartarum in turri Londinensis asservati*, ed. by T. D. HARDY, London, 1837, p. 22; FLAHIFF, "Ralph Niger", p. 113.

[91]   But for a suggestion that he might have lived on until at least 1205, see WILLOUGHBY, RAMSAY, *Secular Cathedrals*, SC62. 104. It is possible that he had left London and retired to his Lincoln prebend.

[92]   ROUSE, ROUSE, *Henry of Kirkestede, Catalogus*, p. 422 (K495).

[93]   "Hucusque protraxit hanc cronicam Magister Radulfus Niger, qui accusatus apud predictum principem [*sc.* Henricum] et in exilium pulsus, ob expulsionis iniuriam atrociora quam decuit de tanto ac tam serenissimo rege mordaci stilo conscripsit, magnificos eius actus quibus insignis utique habebatur reticendo, atque praua eius opera absque alicuius excusationis palliatione replicando, cum pleraque de his que commemorauit in pluribus articulis aliquantulam admittant excusationem si gestorum eius intentio iusto libra-

have existed in the exemplar that arrived at Coggeshall; it would be impossible to prove since Vespasian is the oldest manuscript. But it is also a possibility that Abbot Ralph himself wrote this apology. His own comments on Henry II in his *Chronicon Anglicanum* are more irenic, and in his panegyric on the king's death he was concerned to list the king's deeds in full.[94] That exercise might be considered a careful riposte to Niger since the main complaint in this anonymous passage about Niger's treatment of Henry II is that Niger had allowed exile, his and Becket's, to obscure the king's many other notable deeds. Also, the comment that Niger wrote with a biting pen ("mordaci stilo conscripsit") may be considered a verbal reminiscence of Abbot Ralph's preference for referring to other authors' styles, as has been mentioned above. Although it remains not proven, the suggestion is made that Ralph Niger's Shorter Chronicle was received at Coggeshall, perhaps through personal contact between the author and Abbot Ralph, that the latter Ralph then rounded it out with his own postscript — something he did with the other texts that passed through his hands — and then saw to its being copied and compiled with the annals he had received from St Osyth's, covering a similar period of years as the latter part of Niger's chronicle. The two texts were then transmitted together from Coggeshall.

A yet grander intention for publication is detectable in two overlooked manuscripts, both dating from the first half of the thirteenth century. In these, the Coggeshall chronicle was merged and interwoven with Niger's chronicle and the St Osyth's Annals to produce one unified, continuous history from the Incarnation. The manuscripts are affiliated: BL, Royal 13 A. xii (*s.* xiii[1]), later owned by the London Carmelites, and Dublin, Trinity College, 508 (*s.* xiii[1]). It was an ambitious scheme, albeit imperfectly car-

---

mine ponderetur, si regie potestatis lubrica libertas penseur, que fere cunctis potentibus dat licere quod libet, quorum uiciis fauent inferiores, proni ad imitandum, prompti ad adulandum, cum et impunitas prestet audaciam, diuitie uero accuant et accendant culpam." Printed in *RN*, pp. 169–70; also printed by T. Wright, *Biographia Britannica literaria*, 2 vols, London, 1842–1846, vol. 2, p. 423 n.; Hardy, *Descriptive Catalogue*, vol. 2, p. 287 n.; and Gransden, *Historical Writing*, vol. 1, p. 331, n. 92. On Niger's view of kingship, or *moralia regum*, see further Lachaud, "Ralph Niger and the Books of Kings".

[94]   *CA*, pp. 25–26, *s.a.* 1189.

ried through. Both manuscripts break off incomplete, the Royal manuscript in 1213 and the Dublin manuscript in 1205, so it is not possible to know how far they once extended.[95] A scribal addition to the text on the River Pant, then in flood, could only have been made by a writer possessing local information.[96] The River Pant rises east of Saffron Walden and runs through Coggeshall, where it is known as the River Blackwater. However, the name of Pant was used more widely in the Middle Ages, even to its limits at Maldon, where it empties into the sea in what is now named the Blackwater Estuary. The eleventh-century Old English poem "The Battle of Maldon", for example, described the Anglo-Saxon warriors massed "alongside Pante's stream" with the Viking army "westward across the Pante".[97] It is enough to affirm a local context for this amalgamated chronicle. Otherwise, local details such as abbatial elections are suppressed, as if the intention were to create a national chronicle of wider scope than either chronicle on its own could supply. The composition of this conflated chronicle deserves further investigation. What is of particular interest is that for the years 1206 to 1212 it conveys the fuller annalistic entries of the epitome of the *Chronicon Anglicanum* rather than the

---

[95]   The matter is complicated in the Dublin manuscript by the fact that, while the text does certainly break off, the last leaf (fol. 221) is a singleton added to a quire of six, suggesting that the quire was in this way "finished". It may hint at a break in ongoing composition at Coggeshall. The familiar layout of thirty-one ruled lines to a page would reinforce the suggestion of Coggeshall, albeit the text is bi-columnar, as in Arundel 11, rather than the scriptorium's more usual long lines. Marvin COLKER, in his *Trinity College Library Dublin: Descriptive Catalogue of the Mediaeval and Renaissance Latin Manuscripts*, Aldershot, 1991, p. 942, states that the abbreviated copy of Ralph de Diceto's *Ymagines historiarum* that is also in the manuscript (fols 1^r–142^v) was written by the same scribe of our portion. The scribes, while similar, are distinct, and the codicology confirms that these components are separate booklets: the final quire of the Diceto portion, fols 133–42, was made up to a ten so as to accommodate the end of the text. There is nothing to argue that the two components were bound together before early-modern times.

[96]   It is in the Royal manuscript, fol. 26^r, but is not found in the Dublin copy, which seems in general to be a text with a tighter grip on a purely universal narrative.

[97]   "The Battle of Maldon", ll. 68 ("Hī þǣr Pantan strēam | mid prasse bestōdon") and 97 ("wīcinga werod, | west ofer Pantan"); ed. by D. SCRAGG, *The Battle of Maldon, AD 991*, Oxford, 1991, pp. 20, 22.

diminished version copied on to the supply leaf in the Vespasian manuscript. It does not preserve the original, fuller material that Ralph later chose to censor. It shows that the conflated chronicle was compiled after the expurgation of the chronicle had taken place and with recourse to the Arundel copy, which preserves a fuller set of annals for those years than does Vespasian. It would be plausible to assume that this conflated chronicle was compiled at Coggeshall.

The same process of compilation can be observed in some derivative annals from 1114 to 1158 which are transmitted in Vespasian, Arundel, and Corpus Christi 343.[98] An early-modern hand described them in Vespasian (fol. 40[r]) as "Additiones monachi de Cogeshale", although Bale had treated them as Ralph's own.[99] There is in fact nothing to associate the annals textually with Coggeshall, they being merely excerpts from William of Malmesbury, Ralph de Diceto, and Orderic Vitalis. But it is possible to show that they were at least copied at Coggeshall since in Vespasian, the oldest manuscript, the *mise-en-page* follows normal Coggeshall scriptorium practices and the text is continuous in the same quire with the start of Ralph's *Chronicon Anglicanum*. They represent further evidence of the monks' historiographical ambitions.

It is owing entirely to the monks of Coggeshall that Ralph Niger's Shorter Chronicle and the St Osyth's Annals owe their survival. The same is true of the *Libellus de expugnatione Terrae Sanctae*. This remarkable memoir of the disasters suffered by the Christians in Palestine before the Third Crusade concludes with the defining act of the removal of the golden cross from the pinnacle of the Dome of the Rock. As discussed above, Ralph saw fit to continue this account with the history of the Third Crusade, by subjoining extended reference to the monumental *Itinerarium peregrinorum et gesta regis Ricardi* attributed to Prior Richard of Holy Trinity. That work's enormous size required him to refer to it in précis, offering no more than a concatenation of excerpts of chapter headings and opening lines, melded to produce something like a coherent narrative, with onward reference to the *Itinerarium*

---

[98]   In the Vespasian manuscript, the primary copy, they occupy fols 40[r]–45[r]. They were edited by ANSTRUTHER, *RN*, pp. 178–91.

[99]   BALE, *Index*, ed. by Poole, Bateson, p. 327.

for the reader wanting to know more.[100] Making that sort of intervention was entirely in keeping with Ralph's own habits of work as a collector and compiler of historical materials. The fact that the *Libellus* deals with events in 1186–1187 and that Ralph's own chronicle becomes original in 1187 may be more than coincidental, showing that he was trying to incorporate the *Libellus* as part of an overarching narrative, as he also did with Niger's chronicle. He certainly used the information from the *Libellus* to rewrite his account of the year in the *Chronicon*: a new hand operates on fol. 52^r to the top of fol. 54^r in Vespasian, where the first two lines on fol. 54^r had to be erased and overwritten, the new text spilling out into the margin; it signals an intervention that was probably made when the copy of the *Libellus* arrived at Coggeshall.[101] The *Libellus* was then given its place in Ralph's dossier of historical materials and disseminated.

There is a self-consciousness, even a grandeur, to these activities. Given his lofty designs, and his patent desire to gather as many sources of historical information as he could, one is left wondering why Ralph should have come to make so extensive an expurgation of his own chronicle. I have tried to argue that the palaeography shows that it must have occurred late in his life, during the period of his infirmity. It is possible that he was anxious to make a good end and decided to retract some of the vitriol he had spilled over his pages. Matthew Paris intended to make a similar retraction of some of his more controversial passages at the end of his life, expurgating some and marking others for deletion.[102] William of Malmesbury removed an unusually outspoken passage hostile to William I from his *Gesta regum*, which must have been done in later life.[103] There exist numerous examples from literary history,

[100]   BREWER, KANE, *Conquest of the Holy Land*, p. 63.

[101]   As was pointed out by BREWER, KANE, *ibid.*, pp. 79–81. This interpolation covers short annals from halfway through 1181 to 1186 (doubtless repeating what existed on the original page) and then a very expanded account for 1187 to the end of 1188.

[102]   R. VAUGHAN, *Matthew Paris*, Cambridge, 1958, pp. 117–24.

[103]   Not having his autograph, the change is visible as a variant in the transmission; M. WINTERBOTTOM, 'The *Gesta regum* of William of Malmesbury', *Journal of Medieval Latin*, 5 (1995), pp. 158–75, at p. 162; repr. in his *Style and Scholarship: Latin Prose from Gildas to Raffaele Regio. Selected Papers*, ed. R. Gamberini, Florence, 2020, pp. 206–21.

from Vergil to Kafka, of febrile demands from the death-bed to destroy work. Gogol and Gerard Manley Hopkins destroyed their own work after religious conversion. Would that we still had Ralph's first, enlarged thoughts on those years between 1206 and 1212, some of the most bruising of John's reign and likely to have inspired some of Ralph's most entertaining polemic — extravagances he would later wish to retract. In other parts of his chronicle Ralph felt he could make surgical interventions, lifting out hostile notices about John and transplanting bland news about episcopal elections and so forth. It is almost as if he felt that the section of the work between 1206 and 1212 was beyond that sort of repair and that instead, like an angry spleen, it would have to come out entirely. Were it not for the accidentally surviving epitome, we should have no sense at all of the extent of this expurgation. What is not known and probably now unknowable is whether Ralph made any attempts to circulate a replacement version of his chronicle within the same distribution channels he had used long before.

The suggestion that Ralph's expurgated material has been plucked out of the historian's hands not by the usual accidents of fire or theft but by an act of nervous compunction is not, perhaps, an implausible one for a historian of the Middle Ages to accept. Freeman's challenging assertion, with which this chapter opened, was that manuscripts are useful when they serve the making of editions. The activities of Ralph of Coggeshall as publishing author and self-censor emerge only from the manuscripts, and provide excellent reasons for preferring the manuscript to the smoother texture of the printed book.

Nicholas Trevet OP (*c.* 1258–after 1334) as Publishing Friar

Part I. Commentaries on the Authors of Classical and Christian Antiquity[*]

Jakub KUJAWIŃSKI
(*Poznań/Helsinki*)

Nicholas Trevet, an English Dominican friar, affiliated to the Dominican *studium* at Oxford, was a prolific writer to whom no fewer than twenty works can be attributed with certainty.[1] His literary legacy is distinguished by its remarkable variety. The body of work comprises *quaestiones*, short treatises, chronicles, and commentaries. His activity as a commentator was not limited to a single genre or group of texts: he expounded individual books of the Bible, the works of the Church Fathers and the authors of classical Antiquity. The corpus also shows linguistic variety: although Latin was the language of first choice, he wrote one of

---

[*]   I was very fortunate to have had the opportunity to discuss the draft of this chapter with Ralph Hanna, Samu Niskanen, and James Willoughby. Any remaining errors are my own.

[1]   The most authoritative lists of Trevet's works and manuscript witnesses are provided by T. KAEPPELI O. P., *Scriptores Ordinis Praedicatorum Medii Aevi,* III, Rome, 1980, pp. 187–96 (the works are numbered, therefore when referring to textual items of Trevet or other Dominican authors, I shall limit the reference to "Kaeppeli", followed by the number; when referring to particular information, e.g. from the biographical introductions to individual authors, I shall refer to SOPMA); with additions in idem, E. PANELLA OP, SOPMA, IV, Rome, 1993, pp. 213–15; and by R. SHARPE, A *Handlist of the Latin Writers of Great Britain and Ireland before 1540 with Additions and Corrections,* Turnhout, 2001 (henceforth Sharpe), no. 1119, pp. 394–98. In the total of twenty works I include certainly attested but now lost pieces.

The Art of Publication from the Ninth to the Sixteenth Century, ed. by Samu Niskanen with the assistance of Valentina Rovere, IPM, 93 (Turnhout, 2023), pp. 167–268
© BREPOLS ❧ PUBLISHERS   DOI 10.1484/M.IPM-EB.5.133084

his chronicles in Anglo-Norman. Trevet addressed his works to a wide range of dedicatees, both within and without the order, mostly clergymen; but the vernacular chronicle was written for an English princess. Some of these individuals also acted as commissioners of the works dedicated to them.

Trevet was a self-aware author, frequently offering the reader metatextual information. Most of his writings are provided with dedicatory letters, prologues, or other types of authorial paratext. The individual success of his works naturally varied, to judge by the numbers of extant manuscripts: from over one hundred copies of his commentary on Boethius's *Consolation of Philosophy* to a single copy of his commentary on Leviticus. Indirect tradition and the evidence of medieval booklists suggest that certain of his works enjoyed wider circulation than the number of surviving copies would lead us to believe. There is evidence that sheds light on the circulation of several of Trevet's works in the period immediately following their release. All these characteristics make of Trevet an interesting case study for how a late medieval friar published his works so as to obtain a targeted readership.

Our perception of authorial publishing is, unavoidably, influenced by the invention of print. From the time of Gutenberg on, the authors whose works were judged promising in terms of profit and not likely to offend the local civic or religious authorities could rely on the services of professional publishers when setting forth new compositions. The typographer-publishers provided for the production of multiple copies and took care to advertise a new work in order to sell as many copies of it as possible. Publishing in

---

I have considered jointly the university questions, normally grouped under two headings in the bibliography: Quaestiones disputatae and Quaestiones quodlibetales (Kaeppeli, respectively, nos. 3138 and 3139). On selected cases of uncertain attribution and on the lost works, see below, on the corpus of texts under examination in the present study. All quotations from manuscripts follow their orthography, except for normalization of u/v, i/j, capitalization and punctuation, albeit those exceptions do not concern a handful of citations (mainly ownership notes), which I offer in diplomatic transcription, in which abbreviations are expanded in parentheses and missing portions are restored within angle brackets. In citations from Trevet's commentaries, lemmata are underlined, irrespective of the way in which they are or are not distinguished in a manuscript copy.

a manuscript culture was a more complex and contingent process. Besides the authors themselves, who may have been directly involved in producing handwritten copies of their works and spreading the word of their achievement, the process involved a number of actors. These were book artisans, individual readers interested in securing a copy for themselves, and a range of patrons, individual or institutional, who were in a position to further circulate the work. Speaking of "those individuals and institutions which were actively engaged in the authorial effort to spread the text", I shall employ the category of "publishing circle" introduced by Jaakko Tahkokallio.[2]

For Nicholas Trevet the Dominican order was the most proximate and potentially most important supporter of his publishing endeavours. The Order of Preachers was involved in literary activity in manifold ways. The complex system of schools — conventual, provincial, and the few *studia generalia*, one of which was located at Oxford — offered the settings where most of the friars' scholarly works, such as biblical commentaries, commentaries on the Sentences or *quaestiones*, were composed. Dominican authorities, superiors and collective bodies, could act as commissioners, dedicatees and promoters of friars' writings. Those roles went together with the order's ambitions to supervise its friars' writing. An amendment to chapter 14 (*De studentibus*) of the *Constitutiones*, proposed in 1254 and confirmed two years later, allowed no work by a friar to be published without examination by experts appointed by the superiors.[3] Trevet's apogee coincides with the order's efforts to exercise that control, especially with regard to theological works and works published for non-Dominican audien-

---

[2] J. TAHKOKALLIO, *The Anglo-Norman Historical Canon. Publishing and Manuscript Culture*, Cambridge, 2019, p. 8; on the state of the art on medieval publishing see *ibid.*, pp. 2–9, and J. KUJAWIŃSKI, *Nicholas Trevet's* Commentary on the Psalms *(1317–c. 1321): A Publishing History* (forthcoming).

[3] "In capitulo de studentibus. in fine addatur sic. nulla scripta facta vel compilata a nostris fratribus. aliquatenus publicentur. nisi prius per fratres peritos quibus magister. vel prior provincialis commiserit; diligenter fuerint examinata", *Acta capitulorum generalium Ordinis Praedicatorum*, I, *Ab anno 1220 ad annum 1303*, ed. by B. M. REICHERT (Monumenta Ordinis Praedicatorum Historica [henceforth MOPH], III), Rome, 1898, p. 78 (as confirmed at general chapter of 1256; the addition had been proposed at the chapter of 1254, see p. 69, and approved in 1255, see pp. 73–74).

ces, as expressed by the provisions of general chapters in 1313 and
1316.[4] The distinction, implicitly expressed by the chapter of 1313,
between publishing within the order and "extra ordinem" should
be kept in mind when studying the circulation of friars' works, as
should the Christendom-wide network of Dominican convents and
schools as being the most natural audience for Dominican works
and channels for their distribution. Trevet's case illustrates the
role that the order played, or may have played, in the publishing
of friars' writings. At the same time it offers rich evidence that
a friar's publishing circles could include and benefit from parties
that did not belong to the order, albeit they may have been indi-
rectly associated with it.[5]

The question of Trevet's role in circulating his works and the
constitution of his publishing circles will be addressed through
an analysis of two main types of evidence. The first consists
of authorial utterances concerning the circumstances of composition and intended readership. This kind of meta-discourse
is mostly transmitted in authorial paratexts. Secondly, I shall
consider the evidence of primary circulation and readership, viz.
extant or attested copies and, to a lesser extent, indirect tradition. My focus will be on primary copies, by which I mean the
manuscripts contemporaneous, or nearly so, with Trevet's lifetime, dated or datable to the first half of the fourteenth century.
A less systematic account will be given of later circulation, as
far as it can shed light on the earlier stages. Particular attention

---

[4] See *Acta capitulorum generalium Ordinis Praedicatorum*, II, *Ab anno
1304 usque ad annum 1378*, ed. by B. M. Reichert (MOPH, IV), Rome,
1899, pp. 65 (Metz 1313), 93–94 (Montpellier 1316). The same issue was also
addressed by the chapter of at least some provinces: see, for instance, the
acts of the chapter of the Roman province (Orvieto, 1322), *Acta capitulorum
provincialium provinciae Romanae (1243–1344)*, ed. by T. Kaeppeli (MOPH,
XX), Rome, 1941, p. 224. The preservation of the acts of provincial chapters
varies enormously between provinces and no such acts from the English province from Trevet's time have survived.

[5] The distinction between the two tiers, suggested by Dominican legislation, is not the total explanation. Suffice it to recall the ambiguous position
of friars promoted to bishoprics, see A. Rigon, "Vescovi frati o frati vescovi?", and C. D. Fonseca, "Dal pulpito alla cattedra. Riflessioni conclusive", both in *Dal pulpito alla cattedra. I vescovi degli ordini mendicanti nel'200
e nel primo'300. Atti del XXVII Convegno internazionale, Assisi, 14–16 ottobre
1999*, Spoleto, 2000, respectively, pp. 3–26 and 377–93.

will be paid to any evidence of early ownership and readership. It is within that group of early owners and readers that I shall look for the parties who contributed to the publication and/or promotion of the work, in other words, who were part of a publishing circle.[6]

The study of the extant manuscripts will also touch on certain textual and material features. These include the presence (or absence) of illustrations; and of the authorial paratexts, especially the dedicatory letters which under certain circumstances could be omitted in individual copies; and of the text commented on and its relation to Trevet's commentary.[7] The underlying question is whether, or to what extent, Trevet determined the way in which his work was presented on the manuscript page.[8] In order to answer this question reliably, philological data must be taken into account. Also the chronological, geographical and social distribution of early copies, as reconstructed from the codicological and historical evidence ought to benefit greatly from the confrontation with textual variance across the witnesses. Regrettably, stemmatical relationships have only been established between the early witnesses of Trevet's commentary on Seneca's *Tragedies*. The scarcity of systematic studies on the textual tradition and the lack of reliable critical editions of most Trevet's other works has been a serious obstacle to the goals of the present study.

---

[6] My study of the primary copies of Trevet's works and their early owners, well advanced by March 2020, has been hindered since then by restrictions caused by the Covid-19 pandemic. Although brief visits to manuscript collections between the subsequent waves in 2020 and 2021 were not sufficient to accomplish the original agenda, I am confident that the material gathered thus far allows me to reach preliminary conclusions on the publishing histories of select works by Trevet.

[7] As shown by Louis Holtz, from the eighth century onwards commentaries could be transmitted in two main forms, independently (this was the standard mode of circulation in Antiquity) and laid out together with the text that was the object of commentary, according to various patterns developed in the Carolingian period and later (L. HOLTZ, "Glosse e commenti", in *Lo spazio letterario del Medioevo* 1. *Il Medioevo latino*, III, *La ricezione del testo*, ed. by G. CAVALLO, C. LEONARDI, E. MENESTÒ, Rome, 1995, pp. 59–111, at 62–68, 89–104).

[8] Cf. *ibid.*, p. 90.

This fact should not, however, overshadow the achievements of previous scholarship. In the interwar period three scholars laid the foundations of modern Trevet studies: Franz Ehrle,[9] Ezio Franceschini,[10] and Ruth Dean.[11] Although each was motivated by interest in particular section of Trevet's literary output — respectively, scholastic questions, the commentary on Seneca's *Tragedies*, and the Anglo-Norman *Chronicle* — they all significantly contributed to our knowledge of Trevet's biography, networks, and the tradition of his works. Among those three scholars, Dean alone would further her studies on Trevet and from the 1940s onwards published a number of pivotal articles on selected works or aspects of the friar's life. In the meantime, other scholars of medieval thought and literature have shown their interest in Trevet's legacy. Many of them will be cited in these pages. The question of publishing is not entirely absent from previous studies, but it has rarely been explicated and even then only in relation to individual works. It is rather through the study of publishing-related phenomena that previous scholarship has contributed to our understanding of the ways by which Trevet's works reached the intended or interested audience in the author's own lifetime. The first pertinent aspect to have gained scholarly attention was the patronage that Trevet enjoyed from commissioners, dedicatees and certain high-ranking readers, and its consequences for the dissemination of his work.[12]

[9] F. EHRLE, "Nikolaus Trivet, sein Leben, seine *Quolibet* und *Quaestiones ordinariae*", in *Abhandlungen zur Geschichte der Philosophie des Mittelalters. Festgabe Clemens Baeumker zum 70. Geburstag*, Münster, 1923, pp. 1–63.

[10] E. FRANCESCHINI, "Glosse e commenti medievali a Seneca tragico", in ID., *Studi e note di filologia latina medievale*, Milan, 1938, pp. 1–105 (in the same volume an article on a spurious commentary on the *Aeneid* ascribed to Trevet, pp. 129–40), and *Il commento di Nicola Trevet al* Tieste *di Seneca*, ed. by E. FRANCESCHINI, Milan, 1938.

[11] R. J. DEAN, "The Life and Works of Nicholas Trevet with Special Reference to his Anglo-Norman Chronicle", unpublished DPhil diss., Oxford, 1938. Soon after, she published a review E. Franceschini's two publications in *Medium Ævum*, 10 (1941), pp. 161–68. I express my gratitude to Mrs Judy DuBois Osterholt, Ruth Dean's niece and literary executor, for having kindly authorized the purchase of a copy of Dean's unpublished thesis.

[12] See R. J. DEAN, "Cultural relations in the middle ages: Nicholas Trevet and Nicholas of Prato", *Studies in Philology*, 45 (1948), pp. 541–64; R. WEISS, "Notes on the popularity of the writings of Nicholas Trevet, O. P., in Italy during the first half of the fourteenth century", *Dominican Studies*, 1 (1948),

Early circulation and reception has only been studied to a limited extent.[13]

In the rich and multiform corpus of the texts that are certainly Trevet's, the publishing history of some cannot be retrieved. This is the case, in the first instance, for a handful of texts that are attested as being Trevet's in contemporary, or nearly contemporary, sources, but which no longer survive.[14] Then there are extant works, which offer little or no evidence for their publishing history because they have no dedication or else were only transmitted in late manuscripts. Such is the case for the commentary on the Rule of St Augustine[15] and for the short treatise *Canon coniunctionum*.[16] In previous scholarship a few other undedicated and mostly unascribed works have been attributed to Trevet with some confidence. It is very probable

pp. 261–65; and G. Crevatin, "Le dediche di Nicola Trevet. Il posto della storia", in *Pratiques latines de la dédicace. Permanence et mutations, de l'Antiquité à la Renaissance*, ed. by J.-C. Julhe, Paris, 2014, pp. 399–414.

[13]   Among the few works that have explicitly addressed the question, see H. Pagan, "Trevet's *Les Chronicles*: manuscripts, owners and readers", in *The Prose* Brut *and Other Late Medieval Chronicles. Books Have Their Histories. Essays in Honour of Lister M. Matheson*, ed. by J. Rajsic, E. Kooper, D. Hoche, York, 2016, pp. 149–64.

[14]   See the biblical commentaries on *Exodus, Numbers, Deuteronomy*, and *Chronicles* (only those on *Exodus* and *Chronicles* were included in Sharpe's list). Another lost work, a treatise concerned with the controversies about evangelical poverty is known from its confutation by two Franciscans contemporary with Trevet, Richard Conyngton and Walter Chatton (D. L. Douie, "Three treatises on evangelical poverty", *Archivum Franciscanum Historicum* 24 (1931), pp. 341–69, at 343, 345, 360, 365; *ibid.*, 25 (1932), pp. 210–40; and Walter Chatton, *Reportatio super Sententias. Libri III–IV*, ed. by J. C. Wey, G. J. Etzkorn, Toronto, 2005, l. III, d. 16, par. 79–122, pp. 160–68). It has been tentatively identified with the tract reported in the papal library in 1375 with the title of "Scutum veritatis", and perhaps with that attested for the London Carmelites at the time of the Dissolution, bearing the title "De perfectione iustitiae" (see Dean, "Life and Works", pp. 133–35, Kaeppeli, no. 3140, and Sharpe, p. 396; the latter two scholars use the title "De perfectione vitae spiritualis").

[15]   Kaeppeli, no. 3141. R. Creytens, "Les commentateurs dominicains de la Règle de S. Augustin du XIIIᵉ au XVIᵉ siècle, II. Les commentateurs du XIVᵉ siècle. A) Nicolas Trevet", *Archivum Fratrum Praedicatorum* (henceforth AFP), 34 (1964), pp. 107–53, who, by internal evidence, was able to date it between 1314 and 1318 and to suggest a non-Dominican target audience.

[16]   Kaeppeli, no. 3148. Cf. Dean, "Life and Works", pp. 118–20.

that the friar authored commentaries on Virgil's *Bucolics*,[17] and on the *Dissuasio Valerii*,[18] and a short treatise *De computo Hebraeorum*.[19] They all potentially shed an interesting light on Trevet's legacy and publishing, but will not be discussed here as cases in their own right. Two other commentaries have only tentatively been attributed to Trevet: one on the *Liber viginti quattuor philosophorum* by Françoise Hurdy,[20] one on the pseudo-Boethian *De disciplina scholarium* by Olga Weijers.[21] I shall also exclude from this study the *Declamationes Senecae moralizatae*, a florilegium of Seneca the Elder's *Controversiae* provided with an allegorical interpretation.[22] This relatively short text, devoid of dedication or prologue, is distinguished by an abundant manuscript tradition, in which it is often ascribed to

[17]   The attribution was first proposed by the editors: A. A. Nascimento, J. M. Diaz de Bustamente, Nicolas Trivet Anglico, *Commentario a las Bucolicas de Virgilio*, Santiago de Compostela 1984 (edition unavailable to me). It was considered possible but only hypothetical by R. Vianello, "Su un commento virigiliano attribuito a Nicola Trevet", *Studi medievali*, series 3, 32 (1991), pp. 345–67, and F. Stok, "Nicholas Trevet e Giovanni da Firenze", *Studi umanistici piceni*, 12 (1992), pp. 233–41; finally reproposed with new arguments by M. L. Lord, "Virgil's *Eclogues*, Nicholas Trevet and the harmony of the spheres", *Mediaeval Studies*, 54 (1992), pp. 186–273.

[18]   The most comprehensive discussion of this work and its manuscript tradition, together with an edition, is offered in *Jankyn's Book of Wikked Wyves*, 2, *Seven Commentaries on Walter Map's "Dissuasio Valerii"*, ed. by T. Lawler, R. Hanna, Athens–London, 2014, pp. 121–267. Cf. G. Hays, "The *Dissuasio Valerii* and its commentators: some supplementary notes", in: *Teaching and Learning in Medieval Europe. Essays in Honour of Gernot R. Wieland*, ed. by G. Dinkova-Bruun, T. Major, Turnhout, 2017, pp. 173–99, at 181–90.

[19]   In the only witness, it follows Trevet's commentary on Leviticus, see C. P. E. Nothaft, *Medieval Latin Christian Texts on the Jewish Calendar. A Study with Five Editions and Translations*, Leiden-Boston, 2014, pp. 336–77 (edition, pp. 351–77).

[20]   *Liber viginti quattuor philosophorum*, ed. by F. Hudry, Turnhout, 1997 (*CCCM* 143 A, Hermes Latinus III, 1), pp. xxxvii–l.

[21]   Pseudo-Boethius, *De disciplina scolarium*, ed. by O. Weijers, Leiden–Cologne, 1976, p. 20.

[22]   The most recent contribution on this text is from E. Babey, "Du côté de Trevet et de l'anecdote savante ('exemplum')", in: *"Exempla docent": les exemples des philosophes de l'Antiquité à la Renaissance. Actes du colloque international 23–25 octobre 2003, Université de Neuchâtel*, ed. by T. Ricklin, Paris, 2006, pp. 241–61 (on the question of attribution, see p. 242, n. 1).

Trevet but also to his near-contemporary confrere, Robert Holcot.[23] At the current state of research, I consider this work to be of uncertain attribution.

The works that may be scrutinized from the perspective of authorial publishing will be studied in two essays. In this first part of my study, I shall discuss Trevet's commentaries on the authors of classical and Christian Antiquity. These works were composed and published during the span of about twenty years, coinciding with the first two decades of the fourteenth century, and they include the friar's earliest work. They are also associated through a group of shared readers. In the forthcoming part of this study, which will be published in the second collective volume of the Medieval Publishing project, I shall discuss the remainder of Trevet's works. Those fall mainly into two groups: scriptural commentaries, datable to various periods of Trevet's activity as a scholar, and historical works, published towards the end of Trevet's life.

In the present account I shall generally respect the chronological order of composition of the individual works, so far as it can be established. However, the necessary consideration of the primary circulation and early reception of each work, considered as the immediate consequence of, and witness to, its publication, will necessarily extend each discussion to a period of time following the composition and publication(s) of each work. As a consequence, individual histories will overlap and my discussion cannot avoid moving forwards and backwards in time. The connections with patrons and institutions are another important key to Trevet's publishing, and at certain junctures I shall give priority to that criterion over the chronology. Within this necessarily somewhat

---

[23] For the Trevet attribution see e.g. the fourteenth-century copies: BNCF, Conv. soppr. H.IX.1523 (fols 117ra–131ra), and Rome, Biblioteca Angelica, MS 508 (fols 19ra–29vb). Is it, instead, ascribed to Holcot in SBB-PK, MS Theol. Lat. qu. 249 (fols 31^{v}–42^{r}), datable to the same century. Cf. KAEPPELI, no. 3504 (SOPMA, III, p. 319). The most complete list of witnesses is provided by N. F. PALMER, "Das 'Exempelwerk der englischen Bettelmönche': ein Gegenstück zu den 'Gesta Romanorum'", in *Exempel und Exempelsammlungen*, ed. by W. HAUG, B. WACHINGER, Tübingen, 1991, pp. 137–72, at 168–72. However, BML, Conv. soppr. 509 (included in the list with a query mark) transmits Trevet's commentary on the *Controversiae* (KAEPPELI, no. 3146), which will be discussed in this article.

diffuse arrangement of the evidence, certain lines of development should become recognizable. In the subtitles given to sections of this study, I shall highlight the individual works that are my focus at that point of the discussion.

I shall begin with the episode that appears to have marked an important caesura in Trevet's literary career. On 14 April of an unspecified year between 1307 and 1316, probably 1315,[24] a high-ranking member of his order, Cardinal Niccolò da Prato, bishop of Ostia and Velletri, staying at Valence on the Rhône, addressed a letter to Trevet that happens to be entirely dedicated to the friar's scholarly and literary activity. In the first section, the cardinal congratulates Trevet on his achievements. He claims that he has obtained and read with benefit the commentary on Boethius's *Consolatio philosophiae*, and praises its qualities. The cardinal also asks to be sent any commentary that Trevet might have written on any other work worth elucidation. At least one such commentary, on the *Declamationes* of Seneca the Elder, is known to the sender by hearsay.[25] These lines are witness to the early circulation of two of Trevet's works as also to the author's repute. Suspending, therefore, discussion of the remainder of the

---

[24]   The letter does not carry its year. On its dating see EHRLE, "Nikolaus Trivet", pp. 12, 14–15; FRANCESCHINI, "Glosse e commenti", pp. 31–32; S. MARCHITELLI, "Nicholas Trevet und die Renaissance der Seneca-Tragödien", I, *Museum Helveticum* 56 (1999), pp. 36–63, at 39–43; and P. BUSONERO, "La mise-en-page nei primi testimoni del commento trevetano a Seneca tragico", *Aevum*, 75 (2001), pp. 449–76, at 451–52. To this previous discussion I shall only add that of the two outer dates, the years 1312 and 1313 can be excluded due to the cardinal's sojourn in Italy (see A. CADILI, "La diplomazia e missioni legatizie", in *Niccolò da Prato e i frati predicatori tra Roma e Avignone*, ed. by M. BENEDETTI, L. CINELLI, *Memorie domenicane*, n.s., 44 (2013), pp. 85–139, at 113–22).

[25]   "Sic scriptum, quod super christianissimum philosophum Boetium de consolatione philosophie scripsistis, ad nos perveniens studiose ac attente perlectum inextimabilem nobis consolationem adduxit [...] Huius rei odore sumus allecti ut petamus a vobis communicari nobis si qua alia obscura per vigilantie vestre studium in lucem producta sunt et exhortemur vos ad investigandum que imbecillioribus videntur obscura. Eapropter cum intellexerimus vos iam scripsisse super declamationibus Senece, petimus et eiusmodi et cuiuscumque alterius vestri laboris et egregii, ut firmiter credimus, operis, velitis facere copiam et eius nobis exemplaria destinare" (ed. by FRANCESCHINI, in *Il commento di Nicola Trevet al Tieste di Seneca*, pp. 1–2).

letter, I shall turn first to the publication histories of the commentaries on Boethius and the elder Seneca.

The Commentary on Boethius's *Consolation of Philosophy*

The commentary on *De consolatione* is the earliest among Trevet's datable works.[26] It was written sometime before 1304, when the author referred to his exposition in a quodlibetal disputation.[27] Fortunately, we are informed about the circumstances that led to the composition and release of the work by its dedicatory letter. Although the commentary has survived in more than one hundred copies, the letter is known only from a single fourteenth-century Italian witness, where it was discovered,

[26]   The commentary still awaits a proper critical edition. A reading edition, based on eight witnesses, was prepared, but never published, by Edmund Taite Silk (1901–1981). The typescript, somewhat revised and developed after the editor's death (*Exposicio fratris Nicolai Trevethi Anglici Ordinis Predicatorum super Boecio de Consolatione*, ed. by E. T. SILK, s.a., Introduction, p. xxiv, n. 11) has been scanned and made available by Alastair Minnis, with the collaboration of Andrew Kraebel: <https://campuspress.yale.edu/trevet/minnisnote/> (last accessed 25/9/2021). I quote from that edition (henceforth SILK). Silk's edition of the exposition on Book 3, metres 9 and 11, together with explanatory notes and A. B. Scott's English translation, has been printed in an appendix to A. J. MINNIS, L. NAUTA, "*More Platonico loquitur*: what Nicolas Trevet really did to William of Conches", in *Chaucer's* Boece *and the Medieval Tradition of Boethius*, ed. by A. J. MINNIS, Cambridge, 1993, pp. 1–33 ("Extracts from Trevet's Commentary on Boethius: Texts and Translations", pp. 35–81). Besides that article, the positions assumed by Trevet in this commentary are extensively discussed by L. NAUTA, "The scholastic context of the Boethius Commentary by Nicholas Trevet", in *Boethius in the Middle Ages. Latin and Vernacular Traditions of the* Consolatio Philosophiae, ed. by M. J. F. M. HOENEN, L. NAUTA, Leiden, 1997, pp. 41–67; and B. FITZGERALD, *Inspiration and Authority in the Middle Ages. Prophets and their Critics from Scholasticism to Humanism*, Oxford, 2017, pp. 154–82. The most comprehensive bibliography, down to the start of the 2000s, is offered by O. WEIJERS, *Le travail intellectuel à la Faculté des arts de Paris: textes et maîtres (ca. 1200–1500)*, VI, *Répertoire des noms commençant par L–M-N-O*, Turnhout, 2005, pp. 200–02.

[27]   Quoted by EHRLE, "Nikolaus Trivet", p. 25, n. 3, as Quodlib. I, q. 25. The same quodlibet is II according to the order established by P. GLORIEUX, *La littérature quodlibétique de 1260 à 1320*, 2 vols, Kain, 1925–1935, vol. 1, pp. 246–54, at 248–49, and followed by R. L. FRIEDMAN, "Dominican quodlibetal literature, ca. 1260–1330", in *Theological Quodlibeta in the Middle Ages. The Fourteenth Century*, ed. by Ch. SCHABEL, Leiden–Boston, 2007, pp. 401–91, at 428, n. 77 (cf. p. 429 on the dating of Trevet's quodlibeta).

copied after the commentary, by Ruth Dean. The manuscript is now Milan, Biblioteca Ambrosiana, MS A. 58 inf. (fol. 95$^{\text{ra–va}}$).[28] The negligible transmission and very personal tone imply that the letter was not intended to be a part of Trevet's commentary, unlike dedicatory letters for certain of his later works. Rather, it must have been sent separately, as a *lettre d'envoy*, to accompany a copy of the commentary intended for the dedicatee. The latter is named Paulus and is addressed as "preceptor olim et nonc [*sic*] quippe amic*us* et maior" ("once a teacher and now certainly a friend and elder"). The sender recalls their farewell in Pisa when Trevet was leaving for Florence, and Paul's doubts as to whether Trevet would keep the promise to provide him with a commentary on Boethius's *Consolation*. Writing to a friend, Trevet did not need to make explicit all the details of that project, but one gains the impression that he had taken up the task of expounding Boethius before the meeting at Pisa and had then procrastinated.[29] The addressee has been persuasively identified

---

[28] R. DEAN, "The dedication of Nicholas Trevet's commentary on Boethius", *Studies in Philology*, 63 (1966), pp. 593–603, edition at pp. 600–03; a more detailed description of the manuscript and a new edition have been offered by G. BILLANOVICH, *La tradizione del testo di Livio e le origini dell'Umanesimo*, 1, *Tradizione e fortuna di Livio tra Medioevo e Umanesimo*, I, Padua, 1981, pp. 34–38 (unless otherwise specified, the reference is always to Giuseppe Billanovich). The letter was not included in Silk's typescript. Dean also provides black-and-white images of the two pages of the Ambrosiana manuscript transmitting the letter, while colour images of the opening bearing the end of the *Consolation* with Trevet's commentary, on fol. 94^{v}, and the part of the letter copied on fol. 95^{r}, as well as of fol. 95^{v}, are found in G. BRUNETTI, "Nicolas Trevet, Niccolò da Prato: per le tragedie di Seneca e i libri dei classici", in *Niccolò da Prato*, pp. 433–34, tab. 1–2 (on the letter, see pp. 352–55). In the most recent description, this manuscript is dated to the second half of the fourteenth century and localized to central Italy (M. BOLLATI, M. PETOLETTI, *Manoscritti miniati in Italia della Biblioteca Ambrosiana (fondo inferior)*, Rome, 2022, pp. 19–21 and fig. 1). On the manuscript tradition of the work see below, n. 52. Since not all of the extant witnesses of the commentary have been studied or provided with satisfactory descriptions, there is still a good chance that other witnesses of the letter have survived. Such a discovery, however, would not change the general impression that the commentary normally circulated without the letter.

[29] I quote from Billanovich's edition (*La tradizione del testo di Livio*, p. 36): "Recordor itaque hactenus cum personaliter a tua amicitia (amititia, *ms.*) Pisis diverti Florentiam, in capite scalarum te exemplariter verbis Ovidii me

with Friar Paolo dei Pilastri, who, among various offices in the Roman province of the Dominican order, served as prior of the convent of Saint Catherine in Pisa in 1297–1298. In November 1297 Trevet is attested at Oxford, but they could have met the following year, before Paolo's absolution from the office in September.[30] In the part of the letter more directly concerned with the work, Trevet apologizes for the long delay in fulfilling his promise and alludes to further obstacles which he had encountered having embarked on the project. He had to write a "comentum" to an unnamed person in order to obtain an "exemplar". Only then could Trevet finalize the commentary on Boethius. He claims to have worked relentlessly from Palm Sunday until Pentecost and produced 300 "carte" of writing, from which he took out two copies, one for the person who had provided him with the "exemplar", another for Paul.[31]

---

allocutum fuisse: 'Demofon, ventis vela et verba dedisti, Vela queror reditu, verba carere fide'; hexitans, ut comento sive lucido scripto super Boetio de Consolatione phylosophie meo studio atque labore fultus iusta promissionem a me pollicitam utique fores, non quidem mee sponsioni modicam exhibere fidem".

[30] The identification, which was first proposed by KAEPPELI (no. 3143), has been developed by E. PANNELLA OP, "Priori di Santa Maria Novella di Firenze 1221–1325", *Memorie domenicane*, n.s. 17 (1986), pp. 253–84, at 259–63, and accepted in subsequent scholarship, although not without reservations; see G. BILLANOVICH, "Il testo di Livio da Roma a Padova, a Avignone, a Oxford", *Italia Medioevale e Umanistica* (henceforth IMU), 32 (1989), pp. 53–99, at 87–89. Cf. B. DUFAL, "Nicholas Trevet: le théologien anglais qui parlait à l'oreille des Italiens", in *The Dominicans and the Making of Florentine Cultural Identity (13th–14th centuries)*, ed. by J. BARTUSCHAT, E. BRILLI, D. CARRON, Florence, 2020 (Reti Medievali E-Book 36), pp. 87–103, at 90, who dates the meeting to the beginning of 1297.

[31] Also I quote here from BILLANOVICH, *La tradizione del testo di Livio*, p. 37, only once modifying the punctuation: "Notificetur ergo amicabili tue discretioni [...] non quampluribus modis quibus expertus fui potui intentioni mancipare effectum, nisi prius exemplar prestanti mea manu (manus, *ms.*) comentum unum exemplarer et scriberem; sicque, omni pretio cessante multisque precibus rogitantibus, quasi gratis, postquam sibi prefatum librum scripsi, petitum exemplar optinui. Itaque, iactatis a tergo omnibus aliis meis vicibus, incipiens a sancto die dominico Olivarum usque ad Sacrum Pasca ac Floridum Pentecostes, quasi per continuas dietas scribens, quibus insudans, noctis crepusculum (-lus, *ms.*), vesperum et conticinium quoque addens, trecentarum consumavi scripturam cartarum. Ex quibus, vix interpolato labore [vix, interpolato l., *Billanovich*], volumina, ut predixi, elicui quippe duo:

The passage, surprisingly precise in certain details, is rather allusive in others and is therefore open to various interpretations, as has been shown by previous scholarship.[32] The first point requiring explanation is the meaning of "exemplar", without which Trevet could not accomplish his work. Ever since Ruth Dean introduced the letter into scholarly discussion, the opinion has prevailed that the "exemplar" was a copy of Boethius's work. B. S. Donaghey, however, has proposed an alternative interpretation, suggesting that the "exemplar" consisted in Trevet's notes, either in self-standing form, or in the form of annotations in a copy of Boethius. Donaghey's proposal was based on the premises that Trevet had begun preparing his commentary in England, before meeting Paul in Pisa, and that he finished it in the period following that episode, while residing in Florence, and therefore depended on the assistance of a person who would have brought his materials from England. In this way Donaghey was able to explain the carefully selected references to King Alfred's Old English translation of the *Consolation*, a text that would hardly have been available in Florence.[33]

---

unum videlicet <ei> qui michi comodavit exemplar, aliud autem tue prorsus morigerate nec non gratuite iuventuti".

[32] Beside the contributions already mentioned of DEAN, "The dedication"; PANNELLA, "Priori"; and BRUNETTI, "Nicolas Trevet", the letter is discussed by: B. S. DONAGHEY, "Nicholas Trevet's use of King Alfred's translation of Boethius, and the dating of his commentary", in *The Medieval Boethius. Studies in the Vernacular Translations of* De consolatione philosophiae, ed. by A. J. MINNIS, Cambridge, 1987, pp. 1–31, at 3–11; CREVATIN, "Le dediche", pp. 401–03, and A. PEGORETTI, "Lo 'studium' e la biblioteca di Santa Maria Novella nel Duecento e nei primi anni del Trecento (con una postilla sul Boezio di Trevet)", in *The Dominicans and the Making of Florentine Cultural Identity*, pp. 105–39, at 132–34.

[33] DONAGHEY ("Nicholas Trevet's use", pp. 6–11) develops an argument in favour of a two-stage composition of the commentary. In such a case, the first group of references to King Alfred (in the prologue and Book 1) would have belonged to the original materials included in the work finished and presented in Florence, while the second (in Books 4 and 5) would have been added during revision of the work on his return to Oxford. It should be added that there is another author used by Trevet, easily available in England but not in Tuscany. In the commentary on Book 4 metre 3, Trevet quotes, partly *verbatim*, an episode from the *Gesta regum Anglorum* of William of Malmesbury, II.171.1–2 (SILK, pp. 563–64, and William of Malmesbury, *Gesta regum Anglorum. The History of the English Kings*, ed. by R. A. B. MYNORS, com-

The medieval polyvalency of the term "exemplar", which was used to denote, among other things, a manuscript model for another copy, a reference copy, a copy authorized by a university, any manuscript copy, as well as a version of a work,[34] does not help to determine its meaning in Trevet's letter. The want of critical editions of most of the friar's works, including his commentaries, makes it impossible to reach conclusive observations on Trevet's use of the word. In the Boethius commentary it is apparently employed in philosophical contexts alone, in the sense of a model, cosmological, formal or moral.[35] More telling is its use in the exposition of the Psalms, written some twenty years later. In that commentary, Trevet meant by "exemplar" his reference copies of the *textus*, which is to say the Psalter, Latin and Hebrew alike, the readings of which he was comparing.[36] It is therefore unlikely that in the letter to Paul "exemplar" referred to a sheaf of notes. Trevet rather spoke of a reference copy of the *Consolation*, which might have also contained the commentary of William of Conches, Trevet's leading source, and set(s) of other glosses,[37] and might have also

pleted by R. M. THOMSON, M. WINTERBOTTOM, 2 vols, Oxford, 1998, vol. 1, p. 292).

[34] See L. J. BATAILLON, "Exemplar, pecia, quaternus", in *Vocabulaire du livre et de l'écriture au moyen âge. Actes de la table ronde, Paris 24–26 septembre 1987*, ed. by O. WEIJERS, Turnhout, 1989, pp. 206–19, at 211–19; cf. F. DOLBEAU, "Noms de livres", in *ibid.*, pp. 79–99, at 92–93.

[35] See Book 1 prose 4 (SILK, p. 91); Book 3 metre 9 (*ibid.*, pp. 391, 402); and Book 4 prose 6 (*ibid.*, p. 626).

[36] See, for example, Oxford, Bodleian Library, Bodley 738, fols: 95ra ("In pluribus tamen et in exemplari quod nos habemus scribebatur el cum tribus punctis", on Ps. 51:3; note that Trevet comments on the Latin Psalter *iuxta Hebraeos* but he follows the Psalm numbering of the Gallican version); 134rb ("Asaph psalmus in veris exemplaribus non habetur", on the title of Ps. 76); 207rb ("Et hic nota quod in priore versu in aliquibus exemplaribus ponitur bis salva", on Ps. 117:25). Instead, in the few instances when Trevet refers to textual variance in the *Consolation*, he speaks of "aliqui/quidam/omnes libri" (see, for example, Book 1 metre 4; Book 2 metre 1; and Book 3 metre 7; SILK, respectively, pp. 87, 190, 361). Cf. L. NAUTA, "Trevet's use of the Boethius commentary tradition", in *Chaucer's* Boece, pp. 192–96, at p. 196.

[37] The *Consolation* and William's commentary often circulated together, see MSS L, H, T, D, P, Q of the latter as described in Guillelmus de Conchis, *Glosae super Boethium*, ed. by L. NAUTA, Turnhout, 1999 (*CCCM* 158), pp. lxxxvi–cxi. On Trevet's relation to William and the previous commen-

hosted his preparatory annotations.[38] That latter characteristic would help to explain why obtaining that copy conditioned the progress of his work, why it was worth rewarding the supplier with a copy of the Boethius commentary, and would also help explain the speed with which the commentary was completed. As for the place where the commentary was finished, the letter does not compel us to localize it to Florence. On the contrary, the very fact of the existence of a cover letter and the emphasis on the distance between the sender and the addressee suggest that Trevet was writing from Oxford, as has already been maintained by Emilio Pannella and Anna Pegoretti.[39]

According to the reconstruction proposed by Ruth Dean, Trevet, after borrowing the "exemplar", i.e. a copy of the *Consolation*, made a copy of it for himself and then wrote the 300 "carte", which besides the two explicitly mentioned copies would have also included Trevet's personal copy. B. S. Donaghey found the making of three copies in eight weeks, especially if the commentary had been prepared from scratch, a hard task to achieve. Neither was he convinced about how reasonable it would be to have copied Boethius first. Instead, he proposed that "producing a draft commentary in proper continuous form" preceded the making of the two copies in the declared span of time. Speaking about the preparatory phase, before the *tour de force* beginning on Palm Sunday, both scholars were apparently referring to a work of copying performed by Trevet and twice mentioned in the

---

tary tradition see MINNIS, NAUTA, "*More Platonico loquitur*", and NAUTA, "Trevet's Use".

[38] Cf. L. HOLTZ, "Le rôle des commentaires d'auteurs classiques dans l'émergence d'une mise en page associant texte et commentaire (Moyen Âge occidentale)", in *Le commentaire entre tradition et innovation. Actes du colloque international de l'Institut des traditions textuelles (Paris et Villejuif, 22–25 septembre 1999)*, ed. by M.-O. GOULET-CAZÉ et al., Paris, 2000, pp. 101–17, at 104–5.

[39] DEAN, "The dedication", p. 596, left this question open. Cf. DUFAL, "Nicholas Trevet", p. 90, who maintains that Trevet visited Florence for the second time and wrote his commentary there in 1304–1305. However, the series of five quodlibets following Trevet's inception at Oxford, coinciding with his first regency and datable to the period between 1303 and 1307 (cf. FRIEDMAN, "Dominican quodlibetal literature", p. 429) leaves little room for another trip to Italy.

letter in direct relation to his efforts to secure the "exemplar".
However, the copy was made for a third party ("exemplar prestanti", later referred to by "sibi"), before (and as a condition)
obtaining the "exemplar" ("nisi prius exemplar prestanti mea
manu comentum unum exemplarer et scriberem [...] postquam
sibi prefatum librum scripsi, petitum exemplar optinui").[40] That
deal, of which the details remain unknown to us, has been correctly construed by Anna Pegoretti.[41] B. S. Donaghey's supposition of a full draft prior to the making of two copies is, however, worthy of consideration. In fact, Trevet seems to present
as distinct operations the writing, first, of 300 "carte" between
Palm Sunday and Pentecost, and, second, producing out of that
body the copies for Paul and for another person. The two jobs
would have followed one after another with hardly any inter-
ruption ("vix interpolato labore"). If such an understanding
is valid, the total of 300 "carte" would refer to an autograph
draft of the entire commentary, written in one pass which took
eight weeks, and was immediately followed by the production of
two fair copies.[42] Without the possibility of knowing the size of
"carte", or the size and density of Trevet's handwriting, and also
given the uncertain meaning of the word "carta",[43] every comparison with the capacity of the extant manuscript copies of the

[40] "[I could not fulfil my intention] before I wrote and made a copy by
my hand of a certain commentary for the person who provided me with the
exemplar [...] when I had copied the aforementioned book for him, I obtained
the requested exemplar". For the context see above, n. 31.

[41] DEAN, "The dedication", pp. 596–97; DONAGHEY, "Nicholas Trevet's
use", pp. 4–6; PEGORETTI, "Lo 'studium' e la biblioteca", p. 134.

[42] It would make sense, and could be suggested by the parenthetical "ut
predixi", which introduces mention of the two copies, that receipt of a copy
of the Boethius commentary was the very condition insisted on by the supplier of the exemplar. But, as has been mentioned, Trevet is quite explicit
about his having first written a certain book for that person and then having
received the exemplar.

[43] DONAGHEY ("Nicholas Trevet's use", p. 6) wondered whether Trevet
meant a sheet to be folded in half (i.e. bifolium) or a single leaf. If one takes
into account the English custom of numbering pages of manuscripts (see
P. SAENGER, "The British Isles and the origin of the modern mode of biblical
citation", Syntagma. Revista del Instituto de Historia del Libro y de la Lectura,
1 (2005), pp. 77–123, at 84–85), it is also plausible to think that Trevet gave
Paul a number of written pages.

commentary is of little significance. Trevet's "carte" were not necessarily arranged in quires to form a codex. One might think of them as independent sheets of parchment, such as those used for charters and indentures, or smaller slips of writing material, typically used for notetaking, such as those reported by Trevet's contemporary, William of Alnwick, as "cedule" among Robert Grosseteste's materials at Oxford Greyfriars. The total of 300 "schedulae" is more likely to have been filled in eight weeks.[44] The two fair copies would have been written under Trevet's supervision, rather than by his hand.

Despite certain ambiguities, the letter clearly witnesses the first instance of publication, in which the author, in person or assisted by professional scribes, released two copies of his work. It is worth noticing that the premeditated authorial circulation went beyond Trevet's personal relations with the commissioner-dedicatee and involved a third party, unfortunately anonymous, who had played an important role in the process of composition. Before we explore further, by recourse to external evidence, the significance of that testimony to the history of publishing, the work itself still has something to tell us about its making and destination. Although Paul as the principal intended reader is also addressed with the pronoun "tibi" in the commentary proper,[45] Trevet may still have had in mind a wider readership. In the opening clause of the prologue, he states that he had been induced to undertake the exposition of Boethius by the urging of certain friars and by pastoral

[44]   For the meanings of the terms under consideration here, see *Dictionary of Medieval Latin from British Sources*, ed. by R. E. LATHAM, D. R. HOWLETT, R. K. ASHDOWNE, Oxford, 1975–2013, s.v. "charta", and "schedula" (consulted via Brepolis platform). On the evidence of Grosseteste's "cedule", see A. PELZER, "Les versions latines des ouvrages de morale convervés sous le nom d'Aristote en usage au XIIIe siècle", in IDEM, *Études d'histoire littéraire sur la scolastique médiévale*, ed. by A. PATTIN, E. VAN DER VYVER, Louvain-Paris, 1964, p. 170, and R. W. HUNT, "The library of Robert Grosseteste", in *Robert Grosseteste, Scholar and Bishop. Essays in Commemoration of the Seventh Centenary of his Death*, ed. by D. A. CALLUS, Oxford, 1955, reprint 1969, pp. 120–45, at 127). I thank Ralph Hanna and James Willoughby for suggesting this interpretation to me and Ralph Hanna for bringing the analogy of Grosseteste to my attention.

[45]   DEAN, "The dedication", p. 594. This locution occurs in some of the phrasing introducing the illustrations (see below, n. 48).

responsibility towards both junior and senior confreres.[46] Whether the encouragement had come from Paul alone or was supported by others, Trevet gives Paul's request a more general value in bringing the work to the attention of a wider audience, at least within the order.

Trevet's participation in producing the first fair copies, which in the letter is summarized by the verb "elicio", may have manifested in a variety of forms, from scribal work, to dictation, to instructing scribes, and correcting finished copies. One aspect of those copies certainly requiring close authorial supervision was the diagrams. As shown by explicit references, in the first person, to "figura", it was Trevet's decision as to which natural and astronomical phenomena discussed in the commentary should be given visual representation. This apparatus has not been systematically scrutinized across the manuscript tradition. However, from a preliminary survey of the witnesses it is possible to distinguish two groups.[47] Seven diagrams, all announced in the com-

[46] "Explanacionem librorum Boecii de consolacione philosophica aggressurus uotis quorundam fratrum satisfacere cupiens, qui me censentes ex ordinis predicatorum professione tam maioribus quam minoribus apostolico debito obligatum ad hoc propter non nulla que in eis uidebantur obscura deuota supplicacione compulerunt, historiam Theodorici regis Gothorum ex diuersis cronicis collectam censui prelibandam" (SILK, p. 1). This clause introduces the first part of the prologue. It consists of the history of King Theodoric, which provides the context for the bio-bibliographical information about Boethius. The second opens with a biblical lemma (Ps. 93:19, according to the Gallican Psalter): "Consolaciones tue letificauerunt animam meam" (SILK, p. 7), providing discussion of the Aristotelian four causes of the work. In some studies the two parts are referred to as the first and second prologue (e.g. DEAN, "Life and Works", pp. 160, 169–70). There is more on the prologue in LORD, "Virgil's 'Eclogues'", pp. 203–05; C. H. KNEEPKENS, "Consolation for the soul. The personal prologues of late medieval commentators of Boethius's *De consolatione philosophiae*", in *Self-Fashioning. Personen(selbst)darstellung*, ed. by R. SUNTRUP, J. R. VEENSTRA, Frankfurt, 2003, pp. 211–33, at 214–17; FITZGERALD, *Inspiration and Authority*, pp. 156–61; and CREVATIN, "Le dediche", pp. 403–04.

[47] Among the manuscripts that I have had the opportunity to consult at first hand or from reproductions (the latter distinguished by an asterisk), I have chosen ten of various origin (England, Italy, France), dated or datable no later than the end of the fourteenth century: *Avignon Bibliothèques (Ville d'Avignon), MS 1085 (s. xiv^ex); Cambridge, Gonville and Caius College, 484/480 (England, s. xiv^2/2); Cambridge, Peterhouse, 275 (England, s. xiv^ex);

mentary, appear regularly or else blank space was reserved for them.[48] Although in the commentary all these figures are described

BML, Plut. 22 dex. 9 (III codicological unit, Tuscany, *s.* xiv[in], <http://mss. bmlonline.it/s.aspx?Id=AWOMrpZcI1A4r7GxMYbv#/oro/235>, last accessed 25/9/2021), Plut. 25 sin. 1 (Italy, *s.* xiv, <http://mss.bmlonline.it/s.aspx?Id=A-WOMq-9YI1A4r7GxMYG3#/book>, last accessed 25/9/2021), Plut. 33 sin. 7 (Italy, *s.* xiv, <http://mss.bmlonline.it/s.aspx?Id=AWOMrHsGI1A4r7Gx-MYLP#/book>, last accessed 25/9/2021); Oxford, Bodleian Library, Auct. F. 6. 4 (II codicological unit, England, *s.* xiv[in]); Oxford, Bodleian Library, Rawl. G. 187 (southern France, *s.* xiv[1/2]; the dating of this manuscript is discussed below, in the section dedicated to the commentary on the *Controversiae*; a selection of images, including the diagrams, is available at Digital Bodleian: <https://digital.bodleian.ox.ac.uk/objects/a709a245-d7c7-4a7a-a3ab-82381df-cfb82/>, last accessed 25/9/2021); *BAV, Vat. lat. 562 (Italy, *s.* xiv[ex], <https:// digi.vatlib.it/view/MSS_Vat.lat.562>; see *Codices Boethiani. A Conspectus of Manuscripts of the Works of Boethius*, III: *Italy and the Vatican City*, ed. by M. Passalacqua, L. Smith, London–Turin, 2001, pp. 529–30, no. 518); BNM, Lat. VI, 64 (= 2667) (northern Italy, *s.* xiv[med]).

[48]   The seven diagrams illustrate the commentary on: [no. 1] Book 1 metre 2 (Silk, pp. 44–47; "Ad intellectum eorum que hic dicuntur describam circulum [...] Hec omnia patent diligenter intuenti figuram subiectam"); [no. 2] Book 1 metre 3 (Silk, pp. 61–65; "Premissa de uentis, qui scilicet et quot sunt cardinales uenti, quis cui opponatur, et quid cuius sit collateralis, planius patere poterunt si describatur figura"); [no. 3] Book 1 metre 5 (Silk, pp. 124–25; "Ad huius euidenciam describam figuram cuius circulum exteriorem ymaginabor esse circulum solis"); [no. 4] Book 1, metre 5 (Silk, pp. 130–33; "Quod ut planius uideatur describam tibi figuram"); [no. 5] Book 1 metre 5 (Silk, pp. 138–41; "Ut tamen aliqualiter eciam sine spera possint ymaginari, describam ea in figura eo modo quo per planam figuram possint ymaginari"); [no. 6] Book 2 prose 7 (Silk, pp. 273–75; "Ad cuius euidenciam describam tibi circulum"); and [no. 7] Book 4 metre 5 (Silk, pp. 597–98; "Et ut ista magis pateant describam tibi figuram"). Among the ten manuscripts taken into consideration seven have all the diagrams: Gonville and Caius College, 484/480 (no. 1, fol. 5[ra]; no. 2, fol. 6[vb]; no. 3, fol. 12[rb]; no. 4, fol. 12[vb]; no. 5, fol. 13[vb]; no. 6, fol. 25[va]; no. 7, fol. 55[vb]); Peterhouse, 275 (no. 1, fol. 10[v]; no. 2, fol. 15[r]; no. 3, fol. 31[v]; no. 4, fol. 33[r]; no. 5, fol. 34[v]; no. 6, fol. 74[v], lower margin; no. 7, fol. 146[r]); Plut. 22 dex. 9 (all diagrams on fol. 126[r]); Plut. 33 sin. 7 (no. 1, fol. 5[v]; no. 2, fol. 7[v]; no. 3, fol. 13[ra]; no. 4, fol. 13[v]; no. 5; fol. 14[vb]; no. 6, fol. 26[va]; no. 7, fol. 56[va]); Bodleian Auct. F. 6. 4 (no. 1, fol. 72[r]; no. 2, fol. 76[r]; no. 3, fol. 91[v]; no. 4, fol. 95[r]; no. 5, fol. 97[r]; no. 6, fol. 130[v]; no. 7, fol. 217[v]); Bodleian Rawl. G. 187 (all diagrams on fol. 54[v]); and Vat. lat. 562 (no. 1, fol. 5[v]; no. 2, fol. 8[v]; no. 3, fol. 18[r]; no. 4, fol. 19[r]; no. 5, fol. 20[r]; no. 6, fol. 43[rb]; no. 7, fol. 96[rb]). In the remaining three, the apparatus is imperfect: Avignon, 1085 (no. 1, fol. 8[rb]; no. 2, fol. 11[ra]; no. 3, fol. 19[rb]; no. 4, fol. 21[r]; no. 5, fol. 22[va]; no. 6, blank space on fol. 37[vb]; wanting no. 7); Plut. 25 sin. 1

in detail, Trevet would have had every interest in not leaving their execution to the potentially liberal interpretation of book artisans. It is plausible that the personal copy of the author and the two mentioned in the dedicatory letter included the diagrams, either inserted in respective sections of the commentary, as they appear in many extant manuscripts, or gathered on one page and tie-marked to their respective *loci*. The latter solution is attested by two early copies: BML, Plut. 22 dex. 9, and Oxford, Bodleian Library, Rawl. G. 187.[49] That arrangement was less convenient for readers but sui-

(no. 1, blank space on fol. 3rb; no. 2, fol. 4rb; no. 3, fol. 7ra; no. 4, fol. 7rb; no. 5, fol. 8ra; no. 6, fol. 14vb; no. 7, fol. 30va), and BNM, Lat. VI, 64 (= 2667) (no. 1, fol. 5vb; no. 2, fol. 7vb; no. 3, fol. 15rb; no. 4, fol. 16ra; no. 5, fol. 16vb; no. 6, blank space on fol. 34ra; wanting no. 7). It is worth adding that diagrams 1–5 have also been transmitted in the apparatus of Italian glosses, based on Trevet, that is present in a part of the tradition of the Italian translation of the *Consolation* by Alberto della Piagentina. The glosses may be dated to the second half of the fourteenth century (V. NIERI, "Sui paratesti del *De conso- latione philosophiae* volgarizzato da Alberto della Piagentina: le chiose volgari e il commento di Trevet", in *"Agnoscisne me?" Diffusione e fortuna della* Conso- latio philosophiae *in età medievale*, ed. by A. M. BABBI, C. CONCINA, Verona, 2018, pp. 137–72; on the 'astronomic' glosses and respective illustrations, see pp. 158–72), on the *volgarizzamento* see below.

[49]   BML, Plut. 22 dex. 9, is a multi-block manuscript consisting of three units, the third of which (fols 113–31) transmits Boethius's *Consolation*, Book 1, with the respective commentary by Trevet. The calligraphic Italian *littera textualis* of the copy has been dated to the beginning of the fourteenth cen- tury in R. BLACK, G. POMARO, La Consolazione della Filosofia *nel Medioevo e nel Rinascimento italiano. Libri di scuola e glosse nei manoscritti fiorentini*, Florence, 2000, pp. 123–24; while A. LABRIOLA ("Firenze e Siena: miniature tra XIII e XIV secolo", in *Da Giotto a Botticelli. Pittura fiorentina tra Gotico e Rinascimento*. Atti del Convegno internazionale: Firenze, Università degli studi e Museo di San Marco 20–21 maggio 2005, ed. by F. PASUT, J. TRIPPS, Florence, 2008, pp. 19–39, at 30, and p. 31, fig. 12) has attributed the initial on fol. 115r with the representation of Boethius to the *Primo Maestro dei corali del Duomo di Siena* and dated it also to shortly after 1300. The three units were bound together by the fifteenth century when the table of contents and the ownership note of the Franciscan convent of Santa Croce in Florence were written on fol. iv. The diagrams have been gathered on the recto page of a leaf added after leaf 3 of what originally would have been intended as a quater- nion (fol. 126r: the verso page has the commentary and no textual lacuna has been identified between fols 125v and 127r). Diagrams nos. 1–6 are provided with didascalies indicating their relation to the text, e.g. on no. 1 "Ista fig- ura super secundo signatur metro libri primi". On additional diagrams, see below, n. 51. In Bodleian, Rawl. G. 187, a complete copy of the *Consolation*

ted better the makers of manuscripts, who did not need to trouble fitting each diagram into a manuscript page. Indeed, when in the surviving manuscripts the diagrams are inserted in the commentary, their exact position within the section they belong to often varies, due to the dimensions and layout of individual copies.[50] The status of three other diagrams is less certain. Although they can be

and Trevet's commentary, the diagrams have been executed on fol. 54ᵛ, the last of the final binion (the *textus* and the commentary end on the recto of the same folio). The diagrams are distinguished by letters A–H (on H see below, n. 51) and annotations have been provided by a contemporary reviser next to respective sections, see e.g. two notes added on the lower margin of fol. 3ᵛ, referring to A (no. 1): "hic debuit describi figura que describitur infra in tali signo. .A." (under col. a), and "hic debet esse figura et invenies figuram in fine libri cum tali signo .A." Apparently, the person responsible for the production of the copy had initially intended to have diagrams inserted into the commentary, as is suggested by blank space left for diagram no. 1, towards the end of fol. 3ʳ, col. b. A switch between the two solutions, but in the opposite direction, probably occurred in BML, Plut. 25 sin. 1, when the blank space reserved for diagram no. 1 (the only one not to have been executed) bears an annotation: "require hanc figuram retro in ultima carta" (fol. 3ʳᵇ). The current last leaf (40) presents the end of the commentary (40ᵛᵇ), so the reference must have been to an old flyleaf which, since the other six diagrams were inserted in the commentary, would have been considered superfluous.

[50] The variation concerns first the position of the diagram on the manuscript page, whether within the written space or in the margins, and — if the former is the case — its exact position in relation to the commentary. That variance has led a copyist to adjust the textual references to the figures. For instance, diagram no. 1 tends to be executed immediately after the reference to "figura subiecta", which closes its description (cf. above, n. 48). Such is the case for Cambridge, Gonville and Caius College, 484/480; Cambridge, Peterhouse, 275; BML, Plut. 33 sin. 7 (the reference occurs in the last but one ruled line of fol. 5ʳ, col. b, and reads "figuram presentem"; the diagram is executed on fol. 5ᵛ), and Bodleian, Auct. F. 6. 4. (here "hec omnia patent in figura subiecta" has apparently been added just below the bottom line on fol. 71ᵛ by a contemporary hand, perhaps the same that executed the diagram in the upper part of fol. 72ʳ); the two elements occur in the vicinity of one another in Avignon, 1085 (within the following column), Vat. lat. 562, and BML, Plut. 25 sin. 1 (blank space occupies part of the column, where the reference occurs). Instead, in BNM, Lat. VI, 64 (= 2667), diagram no. 1 is executed in the lower part of col. b, on fol. 5ᵛ, at the beginning of the respective section, following the introductory words: "Ad intellectum eorum que hic dicuntur describam circulum a b c d". The final reference to the same diagram occurs in col. a on fol. 6ʳ and reads "figura suprascripta" instead of "subiecta". On the same phenomenon as regards diagram no. 2 in the vernacular tradition of Trevet's glosses see NIERI, "Sui paratesti", pp. 160–61.

related to precise points in Trevet's commentary, they are not explicitly introduced by the author. Moreover, they are less regularly distributed in the extant manuscripts and present greater variation in form.[51] It is a task for future research to address the question of whether they belonged to the original project or to authorial revision, or should be attributed to the initiative of early readers.

The apparatus of illustration has already provided the opportunity to cite evidence other than the text of the commentary. The current state of research on the manuscript transmission of Trevet's work does not permit a satisfactory understanding of the earliest stage of the textual history: our knowledge of the textual variance is still too unformed. Preliminary conclusions can be reached from the history of individual witnesses, from the evidence of early attested copies, and from studies on the indirect tradition. Previous scholarship is in agreement that the Boethius commentary was the most successful of Trevet's works in terms of the number of extant and attested witnesses, and has drawn attention to the way the work circulated rapidly immediately after publication. Indeed, the commentary survives in some 115 complete or

---

[51] Diagram no. 8 refers to the discussion of the four elements, their qualities and relations, in the commentary on Book 3 metre 9 (SILK, pp. 408–11) and is found in Cambridge, Gonville and Caius College, 484/480 (fol. 38[rb], imperfect) and Cambridge, Peterhouse, 275 (fol. 103[r], lower margin). Diagram no. 9, referring to the discussion of Plato's *integumentum* about the creation of soul (Plato's World Soul), still in Book 3 metre 9 (SILK, pp. 413–14), has been executed in more copies, but presents essential formal variants: Avignon, 1085 (fol. 54[v], split between the outer and lower margins); Gonville and Caius College, 484/480 (fol. 38[vb]); Peterhouse, 275 (fol. 104[r], lower margin, identical with the Gonville and Caius copy); BML, Plut. 33 sin. 7 (fol. 40[r], lower margin); and it is also found among the diagrams gathered on fol. 126[r] in BML, Plut. 22 dex. 9. Despite the variance it always includes a lambda-shaped figure representing the progressions 1, 2, 4, 8, and 1, 3, 9, 27 (on the exegetic tradition of *Timaeus* 35, cf. LORD, "Virgil's 'Eclogues'", pp. 218–19, and on this passage of Trevet's commentary, p. 222). Diagram no. 10, illustrating the eclipse of the sun, which is discussed in the commentary on Book 4 metre 5 (SILK, pp. 600–01), is definitely the most frequent among those three and only presents decorative variation. It is found in the following manuscripts: Peterhouse, 275 (fol. 146[v], lower margin); BML, Plut. 25 sin. 1 (fol. 30[vb]); Plut. 33 sin. 7 (fol. 57[ra]); Vat. lat. 562 (fol. 96[vb]), as well as in the two copies where the diagrams have been gathered on one page: BML, Plut. 22 dex. 9, and Bodleian, Rawl. G. 187 (distinguished by the letter H). In another copy, Bodleian, Auct. F. 6. 4, blank space has been reserved for it on fol. 218[v].

fragmentary copies, without taking into account many others that transmit only extracts.[52] It has also a remarkably rich indirect tradition since many subsequent commentaries and vernacular translations used Trevet, from the early fourteenth century onwards.

---

[52] The most comprehensive list, including some manuscripts with extracts, is provided by KAEPPELI, no. 3143 (with corrections and additions in SOPMA, IV, p. 214). At least one item must be taken out of the list: the Bodleian Rawl. G. 186, which is a twin volume to the already mentioned Rawl. G. 187, has been included as a separate witness to this commentary. I give here the shelf-marks of the manuscripts which I have found in bibliographies and repertories but which are absent from Kaeppeli's checklist: Bologna, Biblioteca Universitaria, 732 (*Bibliographie annuelle du Moyen Âge tardif*, 18, Turnhout, 2008, no. 3190); Durham, University Library, Cosin V.ii.11 (*s.* xiv^ex, *Codices Boethiani*, I, *Great Britain and the Republic of Ireland*, ed. by M. T. GIBSON, L. SMITH, London, 1995, pp. 91–92, no. 62, and <http://reed.dur.ac.uk/xtf/view?docId=ark/32150_s241687h49b.xml>, last accessed 25/9/2021); Glasgow, University Library, MS Hunter 374 (V.1.11) (Italy, dated 1385, *Codices Boethiani*, I, pp. 101–02, no. 72, and <http://collections.gla.ac.uk/#/details/ecatalogue/296744>, last accessed 25/9/2021); Holkham Hall, Earl of Leicester, MS 402 (*s.* xiv^ex, *Codices Boethiani*, I, p. 105, no. 75); New Haven, Yale University, University Library 198 (France, *s.* xiv^ex; *Census of Medieval and Renaissance Manuscripts in the United States and Canada*, ed. by S. DE RICCI, with the assistance of W. J. WILSON, *Supplement*, originated by C. U. FAYE, continued and edited by W. H. BOND, New York, NY, 1962, p. 39); BnF, Coislin 84 (Italy, Padua? before 1478; <https://archivesetmanuscrits.bnf.fr/ark:/12148/cc25534g>, last accessed 25/9/2021); Salamanca, Biblioteca General Historica, 2666 (unit I, Spain 1409–1410; *Codices Boethiani*, IV, *Portugal and Spain*, ed. by M. PASSALACQUA, L. SMITH, London, 2009, pp. 94–95, no. 54). Finally, in 2005 another copy was sold at Sotheby's in London, 5 July or 6 December, lot 58, for the description, see: <https://www.sothebys.com/en/auctions/ecatalogue/2005/western-manuscripts-l.05240/lot.58.html?locale=en> (last accessed 25/9/2021). That copy is dated 6 April 1383 and signed by Honofrius Angeli. The scribe should be identified with Don Nofri di Angelo Coppi da S. Giminiano, a Benedictine monk who also served as public grammar master in Colle Valdelsa (1393–1395, 1402–1403) and communal grammar teacher in San Giminiano (1395–1396). On 14 June 1394 Don Nofri signed an apparatus of glosses deriving from Trevet's commentary, which accompany a copy of the *Consolation*, finished by himself on 18 May of the same year, now SBB-PK, Hamilton 101 (fols 1^r–49^v). Due to the derivative character of the glosses, the Hamilton manuscript has been excluded from the total number of witnesses cited here. On the manuscript see H. BOESE, *Die lateinischen Handschriften der Sammlung Hamilton zu Berlin*, Wiesbaden, 1966, pp. 54–55; on the copyist and his apparatus see R. BLACK, *Education and Society in Florentine Tuscany. Teachers, Pupils and Schools, c. 1250–1500*, vol. 1, Leiden–Boston, 2007, pp. 82, 102, 553.

Since most of those later works of Boethius-exegesis remain unedited, their character and scale and sometimes their dependence on Trevet are open to further clarifications.

No doubt, the status of the commented author and the *Consolation* contributed to the immediate success of Trevet's *Expositio*. Deliberate publishing initiatives by Trevet and his associates may have further stimulated both interest in the commentary and also its availability. One such initiative by Trevet targeted at two readers is witnessed by the dedicatory letter discussed above. Ruth Dean, when arguing for the contextual production of Trevet's personal copy wrote:

> He [*sc.* Trevet] did not mention making up a third copy of his commentary for himself, but the three hundred folios that he used in Florence must have included one, unless Paul or the Florentine lender became in effect the publisher of the work. After Trevet's return to Oxford his personal copy would have become available for local copying.[53]

The two channels are not mutually exclusive. Trevet, who probably kept a working copy of the commentary, could effectively shape the distribution of the work, first of all at Oxford, when, as has been said, he referred to this work in his quodlibetal discussion. The recipients of the first two copies may have also worked to that effect. We have no key to unlock who the third party may have been; but, contrary to Dean's supposition, he probably was not Florentine. However, if the dedicatee of the work was a Dominican friar, which is never stated explicitly in the letter but is suggested by the role of Trevet's former teacher, and if the declared target audience were Trevet's confreres, we should first consider the role that the order may have played in the early history of the commentary.

The evidence of Dominican ownership and readership is early and abundant. Since Niccolò da Prato's reading, declared in his letter to Trevet, cannot be dated with greater precision than sometime before 1316, the earliest witness is a booklist of Friar Hugolinus, a prominent Italian Dominican. A copy of Boethius's *Consolation* with Trevet's commentary was part of the collection of fourteen books that he bequeathed to the Bologna convent on 20 January 1312. That early date therefore offers a secure *terminus ante quem* for the production

---

[53]   DEAN, "The dedication", p. 598.

of that lost, or unidentified, copy. The donor was a not insignificant figure in the order. He had served as *socius* to several masters-general, most recently Aymeric of Piacenza (1304–1311), whom we shall meet in the publishing circle of Trevet's scriptural commentaries. At the time of his bequest, Hugolinus was guardian of the sepulchre of Saint Dominic in Bologna.[54] The beneficiary institution of Hugolinus' bequest was also a prestigious one: besides being the resting place of the founder, San Domenico also hosted one of the *studia generalia* of the order.[55] Trevet's commentary is not found among the extant manuscripts or in the medieval inventories of Santa Maria Novella in Florence, which apparently was the home convent of Paolo dei Pilastri and would therefore have been the most probable destination for his books at his death.[56] It is only in the first half of the fifteenth century that the commentary is certainly attested among the Dominican friars in Florence: a late-fourteenth-century copy belonged to Benedetto Dominici († 1453), friar at Santa Maria Novella, who towards the end of his life transferred to the reformed convent of San Marco, which also benefited from his book donations.[57]

----

[54] "Item liber Boetii De consolatione cum glosis fratris Nicolai Anglici" (L. GARGAN, "Biblioteche bolognesi al tempo di Dante. I libri di un frate converso domenicano (1312)", in *Studi per Gian Paolo Marchi*, ed. by R. BERTALOZZI *et al.*, Pisa, 2011, pp. 475–87, at 486, no. 12).

[55] It is not certain whether the copy bequeathed by Hugolinus is the same as appears in the late-fourteenth-century inventory of San Domenico and which apparently contains the commentary alone: "Item scriptum magistri Nicholai Traveth super Boetium de consolatione" (edited in M.-H. LAURENT, *Fabio Vigili et les bibliothèques de Bologne au début du XVIᵉ siècle d'après le Ms. Barb. Lat. 3185*, Vatican City, 1943 (Studi e Testi 105), p. 225, no. 316; the editor dated the inventory between 1371 and 1386, see *ibid.*, pp. xxviii–xxxii; but G. MURANO, "I libri di uno *Studium generale*: l'antica *libraria* del convento di San Domenico di Bologna", *Annali di storia delle università italiane*, 13 (2009), pp. 287–304, at 289, has argued for 1378 as *terminus ante quem*).

[56] Only partial lists survive from the fourteenth century, whereas a comprehensive inventory dates from 1489. For the edition of the documents and identification of extant manuscripts see the fundamental study of G. POMARO, "Censimento dei manoscritti della biblioteca di S. Maria Novella", parts 1–2, *Memorie Domenicane*, n.s. 11 (1980), pp. 325–470, and 13 (1982), pp. 203–353; cf. the recent contribution by PEGORETTI, "Lo 'studium' e la biblioteca", pp. 119–27, 134.

[57] BNCF, Conv. soppr. J.IV.3, fol. iᵛ, bears the fifteenth-century ownership mark of the convent of San Marco, which also gives the name of the donor: ".270. De xiiij [*number written on erasure, cancelled and replaced in darker ink*

If — the aforementioned absence notwithstanding — one accepts the identification of the dedicatee as Paolo dei Pilastri, he would also have been the most obvious person through whom Niccolò da Prato became acquainted with Trevet's commentary. Having served as prior at Pisa and Florence at the end of the thirteenth century, Paolo became a member of the household of the cardinal, whom he followed to France at the beginning of the fourteenth century, and to Avignon, where he died in 1314 as the newly appointed patriarch of Grado.[58] Instead, if the identification of the dedicatee is rejected, the cardinal may have come across the work in Italy, before moving to the curia in France, or during his Italian missions on behalf of Pope Clement V (1311–1313).[59] Niccolò, in his turn, was in a position to promote the work north of the Alps, especially at the papal

by 9°] banco ex parte occidentis. Nicolaus Traveth ordinis predicatorum Super Boetium de philosophica consolatione. Conventus S. Marci de Florentia ordinis eiusdem. Quem habuit a fratre Benedicto Dominici de Florentia eiusdem ordinis". On the evidence of the script (Southern *littera textualis* with many cursive elements) and watermarks, the copy of Trevet's commentary would have been produced in Italy during the second half of the fourteenth century. The paper is distinguished by watermarks of two types, each presenting two variants: 1. arbalest, 70 mm high, triangular or round; 2. Bow with arrow, ordinary (75 × 115 mm) or reflective (70 × 80 mm, cf. Piccard Online, no. 123571, Pisa 1386, and no. 123666, Bologna 1351). The book is no. 686 (bench no. 13, western row) in the late-fifteenth-century catalogue of San Marco, see B. L. ULLMAN, P. A. STADTER, *The Public Library of Renaissance Florence: Niccolò Niccoli, Cosimo De' Medici, and the Library of San Marco*, Padua, 1972, p. 202, on Benedetto Dominici and his books, see *ibid.*, p. 23.

58   On the career of Paolo dei Pilastri, see BILLANOVICH, "Il testo di Livio", pp. 89–92, who, however, was not entirely convinced of that identification and therefore of Paolo's mediation.

59   The personal acquaintance between Niccolò and Trevet remains only a hypothesis. They might have met during Trevet's visit to Italy, recalled in Trevet's letter to *Paulus*, which would have coincided with Niccolò's service as prior provincial of the Roman province (September 1297–September 1299). DEAN ("The dedication", p. 600), believed that Trevet visited Avignon between *c.* 1308 and 1312, but there is no evidence other than a gap in his Oxford quodlibets. Niccolò's visit to England in 1301, emphasized by B. SMALLEY (*English Friars and Antiquity in the Early Fourteenth Century*, Oxford, 1960, p. 61), is doubtful as well. On Niccolò's diplomatic missions see CADILI, "La diplomazia" (pp. 86–90, on the cardinal's mediation between Philip IV and Edward I, which in 1301 brought Niccolò to France but not as far as England).

court. The letter to Trevet is witness to his readership and appreciation.[60] His experience was shared by at least some of the scholarly minded members of his household, as is suggested by a copy owned by Simone d'Arezzo, the cardinal's *familiaris*. In Simone's will of 1338 he left it to the Dominicans of his native town.[61] Another copy belonged to Niccolò's close friend and fellow-cardinal, Guillaume de Pierre Godin († 1336), also a Dominican. Godin's connections with Niccolò and his owner-ship of Trevet's works will be discussed in more detail in rela-tion to the commentary on the *Controversiae* of Seneca. It might have been Niccolò who brought Trevet's work to the attention of Pope John XXII, elected in 1316 and known for his book acquisitions. Papal ownership of the Boethius commentary is only attested by the first systematic inventory of the Avignon palace, which was made under Urban V in 1369.[62] However, the ownership of still another copy by a lower-ranking administra-tor of Popes John XXII and Benedict XII, Arnaud de Verdale, hints that the pope's exemplar as reported in 1369 may have been acquired much earlier.[63] Another Avignon library, that of

[60]   It reasonable to think that Niccolò had a personal copy at his disposal, but none has been identified among the extant or attested copies. In his will of 1321 the only books to have been listed are those bequeathed or returned to recipients other than the main beneficiary, i.e. the Dominican convent in Prato. Very little is known about the medieval book collection of the latter (L. PELLEGRINI, "La biblioteca di Niccolò da Prato", in *Niccolò da Prato e i frati predicatori*, pp. 241–56).

[61]   "Item expositiones ad licteram Iob dicti sancti Thome, cum libello de missa composito per fratrem Nicolaum de Treveth Anglicum ordinis fratrum predicatorum, in uno volumine. [...] Item Boetium de consolatione, cum scripto dicti fratris Nicolay" (U. PASQUI, "La biblioteca d'un notaro aretino del secolo XIV", *Archivio Storico Iitaliano*, 5th Series, 4 (1889), pp. 250–55, at 253).

[62]   "Item liber fratris Nicolay super Boecium de consolacione, coopertus corio albo discolorato cum postibus papireis, qui incipit in secundo corundello primi folii: *captivitatis*, et finit in ultimo corundello penultimi folii: *per quam*" (ed. EHRLE, *Historia bibliothecae romanorum pontificum tum Bonifatianae tum Avenionensis*, vol. 1, Rome, 1890, p. 319, no. 416).

[63]   The *Consolation* with Trevet's commentary is one of the books that Arnaud donated in 1337 to a college he had founded in Toulouse: "Boetium De consolatione cum apparatu fratris Nicolai Anglici, || *fortuna*, valet decem libras" (*Bibliothèques ecclésiastiques au tempts de la papauté d'Avignon*, II, ed. by M.-H. JULLIEN DE POMMEROL, J. MONFRIN, Paris, 2001, 337.9, no. 127,

the Dominicans, was reportedly the former owner of the copy that is now Avignon Bibliothèques (Ville d'Avignon), MS 1085. The Avignon convent was among the most important in the province of Provence and benefited from the patronage of Niccolò da Prato and Godin. The manuscript, however, is datable to the end of the fourteenth century and therefore belongs to subsequent generations of Avignon copies.[64]

Last but not least, Dominican authors on both sides of the Alps and across the Channel are responsible for one part of the indirect tradition of Trevet's commentary. In Italy, it served as a source for the Latin commentary ascribed to Guglielmo di Cortemilia, friar of the province of Lombardy, which must have been prepared before 1342 (the year of his death), but perhaps before his appointment to the bishopric of Scala in the Kingdom of Naples in 1328.[65] In France,

---

p. 146). Arnaud is attested as pope's collector in the dioceses of the *Midi* from 1326, he performed various services for John XXII and Benedict XII, graduated as *doctor utriusque juris* in Toulouse in 1330, was elected bishop of Maguelonne in 1339, and died in 1352 (see *ibid.*, pp. 140–41; A. LE ROUX, "La fiscalité pontificale en Languedoc sous Jean XXII", in *Jean XXII et le Midi*, Toulouse, 2012 (Cahiers de Fanjeaux 45), pp. 237–54).

[64] For a summary description of the manuscript see <https://ccfr.bnf.fr/portailccfr/ark:/06871/004D32B12353> (last accessed 25/9/2021); an examination of the paper part would perhaps allow a more precise dating. On the Avignon convent, see A. RELTGEN-TALLON, "Nicolas da Prato et le milieu dominicain en Avignon au XIVe siècle", in *Niccolò da Prato e i frati predicatori*, pp. 155–67.

[65] This is implicitly suggested by G. BRUNETTI ("Nicolas Trevet, Niccolò da Prato", p. 354) who has observed that in the rubric in one of the earliest witnesses, BML, Plut. 76.56 (<http://mss.bmlonline.it/s.aspx?Id=AWOMMB-fyI1A4r7GxMQyy#/book>, last accessed 25/9/2021), the author is referred to without the title of bishop. In that copy, Boethius with Cortemilia's commentary is preceded by the prologue of Trevet's commentary and by some extracts to form an *accessus*. In some other witnesses, however, it is transmitted together with a dedication, in which the author presents himself as "frater" alone (the incipit provided by KAEPPELI, no. 1479). This is the case with BnF, lat. 6773 (quoted by P. COURCELLE, *La Consolation de Philosophie dans la tradition littéraire. Antécédents et Postérité de Boèce*, Paris, 1967, p. 327, cf. p. 417, who dated the commentary to the fifteenth century): "Reverendo in Christo patri fratrique ordinis fratrum Praedicatorum frater Guillermus de Cortumelia, ordinis eiusdem, reuerenciam debitam et deuotam". Cf. the early-modern transcript of a lost fifteenth-century copy: Rome, Biblioteca Casanatense, MS 998 (my knowledge of this witness is based on the description in Manus: <https://manus.iccu.sbn.it//opac_SchedaScheda.php?ID=15893>,

Renaut de Louhans composed *Le Roman de fortune et de felicité*, which is a vernacular verse adaptation of Boethius, also using Trevet's commentary. The work was completed in 1337 in the convent of Poligny in the Jura.[66] In England, Trevet's exposition was used by some of his younger confreres, who were active in the second quarter of the fourteenth century and were all connected with Oxford: William D'Eyncourt,[67] Robert Holcot,[68] and perhaps John Bromyard.[69]

---

last modified 19/9/2012, last accessed 25/9/2021), where the name of the dedicatee is abbreviated as "D". The wording suggests that the dedicatee was the author's senior confrere. Consultation of all the identified copies should enable the commentary to be better contextualized. Besides the eight witnesses listed by Kaeppeli two manuscripts transmitting the *Consolation* with the extracts have been identified, both of Florentine provenance and apparently also origin: BML, Ed. 163 (*s.* xiv/xv, the glosses were added by the main copyist as was an *accessus* derived from Trevet's commentary on fols 1[ra]–2[vb], see BLACK, POMARO, *La* Consolazione, pp. 102–03, and *Codices Boethiani*, III, p. 133, no. 109); and BML, Plut. 23 dex. 11 (*s.* xiv[med], a near contemporary hand added an *accessus* and glosses extracted from Trevet's commentary, and from fol. 6[r] excerpts from Cortemilia's commentary, as well as a partial *volgarizzamento*, see BLACK, POMARO, *La* Consolazione, pp. 124–26 for description, and pp. 234–47 for generous quotations from the apparatus; cf. *Codices Boethiani* III, pp. 102–03, no. 74).

[66]   KAEPPELI, no. 3425; G. M. CROPP, "Boethius in medieval France: translations of the *De consolatione Philosophiae* and literary influence", in *A Companion to Boethius in the Middle Ages*, ed. by N. H. KAYLOR, Jr. and P. E. PHILLIPS, Leiden–Boston, 2012, pp. 319–55, at 332–33. See also: L. BRUN, "Renaut de Louhans", in *ARLIMA. Archives de littérature du Moyen Âge*, <https://arlima.net/no/1937> (last modified 24/9/2021, last accessed 25/9/2021).

[67]   Many quotations from Trevet in D'Eyncourt's commentary on *Ecclesiastes* (KAEPPELI, no. 1484), about 1340, have been noticed by SMALLEY, *English Friars*, p. 206. On the author see H. GOODENOUGH GELBER, *It Could Have Been Otherwise. Contingency and Necessity in Dominican Theology at Oxford, 1300–1350*, Leiden–Boston, 2004, pp. 102–03.

[68]   J. B. ALLEN ("The library of a classicizer: the sources of Robert Holkot's mythographic learning", in *Arts libéraux et philosophie au Moyen Âge. Actes du Quatrième Congrès international de philosophie médiévale, Montréal 27 août–2 septembre 1967*, Montréal–Paris, 1969, pp. 721–29, at 727) has proposed Trevet's commentary as the source of individual information provided by Holcot in his commentary on the Twelve Prophets (KAEPPELI, no. 3498). On the author see GOODENOUGH GELBER, *It Could Have Been Otherwise*, pp. 92–98.

[69]   One instance of borrowing has been noticed in Bromyard's *Summa praedicantium* by MINNIS and NAUTA (*More Platonico loquitur*, p. 5, n. 17) and

Early Dominican owners help to explain how Trevet's work reached certain non-Dominican readers. However, the circulation and reception that the commentary enjoyed outside the order, among readers belonging to other mendicant or religious orders, secular clerks and, still more significantly, among laymen, was much wider and could sometimes be beneficial to the Dominicans themselves. That much is illustrated by the case of Galvano Fiamma OP († after 1344) who, when writing one of his chronicles, the *Chronica maius*, in 1337–1338, consulted a copy of Trevet's commentary belonging to archpresbyter of the cathedral of Milan, Roberto Visconti.[70] Apparently the work

concerns the circumstances of Aristotle's utterance: "Si uterentur homines linceis oculis" (Book 3 prose 8, SILK, pp. 367–68; and *Summa praedicantium* P XIIII, "Pulchritudo", consulted from the edition printed Nuremberg, Anton Koberger, 1485, from the copy Munich, Bayerische Staatsbibliothek, 2 Inc.c.a. 1562 c, fol. 340[ra], <https://www.digitale-sammlungen.de/en/view/bsb00043212?page = ,1>, last accessed 25/9/2021). At the beginning of the respective passage, Trevet refers to a "commentator", perhaps an interpolated version of the commentary of William of Conches or another apparatus of glosses, cf. NAUTA, "Trevet's use", pp. 194–95, and Guillelmus de Conchis, *Glosae super Boethium*, p. 140, apparatus ad v. 18; cf. *ibid.*, p. cxviii. A question as to whether Bromyard might have used the same source as Trevet should, therefore, be kept open. Bromyard's *Summa* (KAEPPELI, no. 2236) was written between *c.* 1330 and *c.* 1348. If he proceeded in alphabetical order, the entry on "Pulchritudo" would have been composed after "Paupertas", which is datable after 1346 (see L. E. BOYLE, "The date of the *Summa praedicantium* of John Bromyard", *Speculum*, 48 (1973), pp. 533–37, at 535). On the author, based at the Hereford priory, and his oeuvre, see P. BINKLEY, "John Bromyard and the Hereford Dominicans", in *Centres of Learning: Learning and Location in Pre-Modern Europe and the Near East*, ed. by J. W. DRIJVERS, A. A. MACDONALD, Leiden–New York–Cologne, 1995, pp. 255–64.

[70] It is included in the list of works consulted, provided at the beginning of the chronicle, as "Nicolaus super Boetium de Consolatione", and was among the books found "apud archipresbiterum ecclesie majoris". The list was edited by L. GRAZIOLI, "Di alcune fonti storiche citate ed usate da fra Galvano Fiamma", *Rivista di scienze storiche*, 4 (1907), pp. 3–14; 118–54; 261–69; 355–69; 450–63, at 120, no. 66, cf. p. 147, no. 66). On the chronicle and its dating, see S. A. CÉNGARLE PARISI, "Introduzione", in *La* Cronaca estravagante *di Galvano Fiamma*, ed. by S. A. CÉNGARLE PARISI, M. DAVID, Milan, 2013, pp. 40–43 and 158; on the owner, see *ibid.*, p. 629, n. 26, and A. CADILLI, "Visconti, Roberto", in *DBI*, 99 (2020), <https://www.treccani.it/enciclopedia/roberto-visconti_%28Dizionario-Biografico%29/> (last accessed 25/9/2021; the entry is dedicated to his homonymous nephew, but also offers discussion on the uncle).

was not available at Galvano's convent of Sant'Eustorgio in Milan.[71]

For the early stage, which is our focus here, two environments offer the most abundant documentation of non-Dominican readership: first, the communes of central and northern Italy, and second, the university of Oxford. In Italy the earliest witness to Trevet's reception is reportedly Tolomeo Asinari (Bartholomaeus de Asinariis), who in 1307 finished his own commentary on the *Consolation*. The author was a jurist and incumbent of various offices in his native commune of Asti in Piedmont. As a consequence of internal conflict in 1304 he lost his position and, judging from biographical references in the prologue, fled into exile.[72] The place of composition of the commentary is therefore uncertain. His knowledge of Trevet's recent exposition, notable for its early date as widely accepted by scholarship, is based on one reference to Trevet, brought to light by Pierre Courcelle. However, it occurs in a sort of *accessus*, which is found in one of the two known witnesses, where it is copied before the prologue proper and may therefore not necessarily have formed part of the subsequent commentary.[73]

[71] One item in the inventory of 1494 has been identified with Trevet's commentary: "Boecius cum commento, qui incipit *Explanationem* et finit *bona fide*" (Th. KAEPPELI, "La bibliothèque de Saint-Eustorge à Milan à la fin du XVe siècle", *AFP*, 25 (1995), pp. 5–74, at 35, no. 215). However, it must be observed that the explicit provided is not that of Trevet's *Expositio*, and therefore the entry may refer to a hybrid commentary that included Trevet's prologue.

[72] For the biographical background of the prologue see KNEEPKENS, "Consolation for the soul", pp. 230–32; on the author, see A. GORIA, "Asinari, Tolomeo", in *DBI*, 4 (1962), <https://www.treccani.it/enciclopedia/tolomeo-asinari_(Dizionario-Biografico)/> (last accessed 25/9/2021).

[73] BnF, lat. 6410, fol. 1ᵛ: "Et hec faciunt ad evidenciam materie huius libri, licet eciam glosator huius libri, scilicet Nicholaus Travet, prima glosa super ipsum nonnulla de premissis ponat non tamen sic clare" (cf. COURCELLE, *La Consolation*, pp. 318, n. 4, and 413). The prologue begins on fol. 2ʳᵃ. Judging by the script, the copy dates to the fifteenth century (reproduction of the microfilm is available at Gallica: <https://gallica.bnf.fr/ark:/12148/btv1b9076657z>, last accessed 25/9/2021). Another copy, Vienna, Österreichische Nationalbibliothek, Cod. 53, begins with the prologue (fol. 1ʳ). Both manuscripts transmit the colophon of the archetype: the latter was copied under Tolomeo's dictation and decorated by Philippus de Altavilla in 1307. I quote the most significant portion of that lengthy colophon in the Vienna manuscript, fol. 162ᵛ, compared to the Paris copy, fol. 172ʳᵃ: "Ego vero Phylippus de Alta Villa famu-

It is the task of future studies to revisit the question of Tolomeo's use of Trevet.[74] The extent to which Trevet's commentary was laid under contribution for the Italian (Tuscan) translation, probably the oldest one, of the *Consolation*, ascribed to Master Giandino da Carmignano, is likewise uncertain. The author, perhaps a Franciscan friar, is attested at the end of the thirteenth century.[75]

Instead, the familiarity with Trevet's commentary of another Italian author, the Florentine notary Alberto della Piagentina, has been well illustrated by previous studies. Alberto is responsible for the most successful Italian *volgarizzamento* of *De consolatione*, which he composed or completed in prison in Venice, between 1330 and his death in 1332. Alberto's prologue includes Trevet's two-fold prologue, rendered in the vernacular. Trevet's commentary was also the source of amplifications in Alberto's translations

lus ipsius fidelis transcripsi et illuminavi et prout ipse dictaverat cum labore non modico ordinavi et ad finem produxi [perduxi *in Paris*] M° CCC° VII° Indiccione V^a de mense septembris" ("V" in both copies would be the result of misreading of "II", since the year 1307 corresponded to Indiction 2). The Vienna copy is signed by Nicolaus de Ytro and is datable to the latter part of the fourteenth century (reproduction of the microfilm available at: <https://onb.digital/result/10000C9F>, last accessed 25/9/2021). For description see H. J. Hermann, *Die italienischen Handschriften des Dugento und Trecento*, Part 1, *Bis zur Mitte des 14. Jahrhunderts*, Leipzig, 1928 (Beschreibendes Verzeichnis der illuminierten Handschriften in Österreich, V, Die illuminierten Handschriften und Inkunabeln der Nationalbibliothek in Wien), pp. 23–24, and *Codices Boethiani*, II, *Austria, Belgium, Denmark, Luxembourg, The Netherlands, Sweden, Switzerland*, ed. by L. Smith, London–Turin, 2001, pp. 67–68, no. 51 (in both catalogues the manuscript is dated 1307).

74   The question has not been addressed by G. N. Drake, despite the inclusion of both commentators in the scholar's comparative examination of the commentary tradition on Book 1, metre and prose 1 ("The Muses in the Consolation. The late medieval mythographic tradition", in: *New Directions in Boethian Studies*, ed. by N. H. Kaylor, Jr. and Ph. E. Phillips, Kalamazoo, 2007, pp. 169–219).

75   This attribution is only given in one out of three witnesses: BML, Plut. 23 dex. 11 (already mentioned for the excerpts of the commentary of Guglielmo di Cortemilia, see above, n. 65). On Giandino's *volgarizzamento* see Black, Pomaro, *La* Consolazione, pp. 85–88; G. Brunetti, "Preliminari all'edizione del volgarizzamento della *Consolatio philosophiae* di Boezio attribuito al maestro Giandino da Carmignano", in *Studi su volgarizzamenti italiani due-trecenteschi*, ed. by P. Rinoldi, G. Ronchi, Rome, 2005, pp. 9–45, cf. eadem, "Le letture fiorentine: i classici e la retorica", in *Dante. Fra il Settecentocinquantenario della nascita (2015) e il settecentenario della morte (2021)*, ed. by E. Malato, A. Mazzucchi, vol. 1, Rome, 2016, pp. 225–53, at 245–46.

of Boethius's *metra*.[76] Trevet's *Expositio* itself had become a work worth translating. A handful of the fourteenth-century Italian *volgarizzamenti* have survived: two are anonymous,[77] one is attributed to a certain Master Giovanni di Beninato.[78] A Latin copy, lost or not yet identified, belonged to Alberico da Rosciate, a jurist from Bergamo, who bequeathed it in his will of 1345.[79]

A rather intense circulation of the commentary during the fourteenth century, on both sides of the Apennines and among lay and religious, is suggested by two extant copies and the chain of their ownership in the course of the latter part of that century and the beginning of the next. In 1356 a parchment manuscript bearing both

[76] Among many contributions to the study of this *volgarizzamento* see, on Alberto's use of Trevet: D. BRANCATO, "Readers and interpreters of the *Consolatio* in Italy, 1300–1550", in *A Companion to Boethius*, pp. 357–411, at 366–70; and V. NIERI, "Sui paratesti", pp. 149–54 (on the short series of glosses on the translation, also based on Trevet's prologue and ascribable to Alberto); on Alberto's biography and literary background, see L. AZZETTA, "Tra i più antichi lettori del *Convivio*: ser Alberto della Piagentina, notaio e cultore di Dante", *Rivista di studi danteschi*, 9 (2009), pp. 57–91, at 65–77.

[77] The distinction is due to O. LÖHMANN, "Boethius und sein Kommentator Nicolaus Trevet in der italienischen Literatur des 14. Jahrhunderts", in *Bibliothekswelt und Kulturgeschichte. Eine internationale Festgabe für Joachim Wieder zum 65. Geburtstag dargebracht von seinen Freunden*, ed. by P. SCHWEIGLER, Munich, 1977, pp. 28–48 (see also T. RICKLIN, "*Quello non conosciuto da molti libro di Boezio*. Hinweise zur *Consolatio Philosophiae* in Norditalien", in *Boethius in the Middle Ages*, pp. 267–86, at 271–74). The apparently oldest witness of the first one, Berlin, Preussische Staatsbiliothek, Ital. fol. 174, considered lost during the Second World War, has in fact been deposited in Cracow, Biblioteka Jagiellońska, where is kept under its former shelf-mark (for description and digital reproduction, see: <http://info.filg.uj.edu.pl/fibula/en/content/ital-fol-174>, last accessed 25/9/2021). On the only witness of the second translation, Florence, Biblioteca Riccardiana, 1540, see BLACK, POMARO, *La* Consolazione, p. 88.

[78] The translation, which in the extant form is limited to the commentary on Books 1 and 2, is transmitted in Florence, Biblioteca Riccardiana, 1523. See RICKLIN, "Quello non conosciuto", p. 273. According to G. Pavlica, the author was probably a clergyman, active around the middle of the century and the translation may have been prepared for a Sicilian audience. See G. PAVLICA, "Il commento di Giovanni di Beninato alla *Consolatio Philosophiae* di Boezio primo libro (Firenze, Biblioteca Riccardiana ms. 1523)", unpublished MA diss., Università di Bologna, 2002/2003, pp. 14–23. I owe to Giuseppina Brunetti the opportunity to consult these pages.

[79] G. CREMASCHI, "Contributo alla biografia di Alberico da Rosciate", *Bergomum. Bollettino della Civica Biblioteca*, 50 (1956), pp. 3–102, at 100, no. 73.

the *Consolation* and Trevet's commentary, written in elegant Italian *littera textualis* (BNM, Lat. VI, 64 (= 2667)) was sold by Bonincontro, probably from Mantua, to Bartolomeo de Placentinis from Parma, apparently both laymen.[80] In 1406 a bibliophile Franciscan friar, Tedaldo della Casa, passed a parchment copy of Trevet's *Expositio* to the convent of Santa Croce in Florence (BML, Plut. 33 sin. 7). Previously, the book had belonged to at least two other owners, both laymen.[81] Tedaldo's was one of the three copies owned by the Franciscan convent. The others are BML, Plut. 22 dex. 9,[82] and Plut. 25 sin. 1,[83] both from the fourteenth-century. Regrettably, nothing is known about their owners before the Santa Croce *ex libris* inscriptions were added in the fifteenth century. In a similar way, the early ownership of another fourteenth-century Italian copy, including the *Consolation* and the commentary (Padua, Biblioteca Universitaria, 1596), is not known. In the seventeenth century it belonged to the Austin friars at Padua.[84] Irrespective of the time it entered the library of the con-

[80]   Both inscribed their ownership notes on the parchment front flyleaf (fol. i^v, provided here in diplomatic transcription): (1) "Iste Boecius est [*the rest of the line is erased, but readable under UV light:*] Boni(n)(con)tri filij d(omi)ni Gra(n)dei de malancijs [?] de mantua [?]", followed immediately by (2) "e(m)ptus p(er) me Barth(olomeu)m de place(n)tinis de p(ar)ma p(ro) duc(atis) v au(r)i die | me(r)curij vij°. Sept(em)b(ris) Anno d(omi)ni Mille(simo) iij^c lvj quos sibi dedit Peregrin(us) [?] famulus meus". For a summary description, see *Codices Boethiani*, III, pp. 378–79, no. 365.

[81]   On fol. 78^v the well preserved note by Tedaldo ("Iste liber fuit ad usum fratris Thedaldi de Casa quem vivens assignavit armario fratrum minorum de Florencia. Anno domini 1406") is preceded by three other notes, partly erased or damaged, which are given here in diplomatic transcription, beginning from the top: (1) "Iste liber e(st) fra(n)cisci d(omi)ni Johannis [*the note continues till the end of line, unreadable*]"; (2) "franciscus d(omi)nj Joh(ann)is de [*material damage*]ris possidet me"; (3) "Iste liber e(st) mei angeli [*a faded word, partly damaged*] de bas[*material damage*]s | et chostitit lx [*numeral cancelled*] florenis".

[82]   On this manuscript see above, n. 49.

[83]   The front pastedown of this fourteenth-century copy, which has already been cited for its illustrations, bears a document dated 1355. At the top, a note in Humanistic cursive reads: "Iste liber est conventus sancte Crucis de Florentie ordinis minorum [*continues a linea*] Nicolai Travet [Treuhet *suprascr.*] super Boetio de consolatione philosophie".

[84]   The manuscript has the typical early-modern pressmarks of the convent of SS. Filippo e Giacomo and can be recognized in the entry in the oldest extant booklist, compiled by I. P. TOMASINI, *Bibliothecae Patavinae Manuscriptae publicae et privatae*, Udine, 1639, p. 77: "Boetius de Consolati-

vent, it had been used by a friar or clergyman as a preaching aid, apparently not long after the date of production. This may be deduced from a number of glosses written in Gothic cursive, highlighting certain moral themes or *exempla* in Books 1 and 3 and the respective commentary.[85] Early reception among Italian friars of other mendicant orders is also demonstrated by Guido da Pisa, Carmelite, who in the second quarter of the fourteenth century used Trevet's *Expositio* on Boethius in the commentary on Dante's *Inferno*.[86] Finally, two unidentified copies are attested around the middle of the fourteenth century as the property of high-ranking clergymen operating in southern Italy, Arnulphe Marcellin, vice-rector of the papal city of Benevento (1334–1345)[87] and Bishop Robert of Tropea (1322–1357).[88]

one Philosophica edita à Fr. Nicoleo Treueli Anglico Fratrum Ordinis Praedicatorum Theologiae professore fol. m." (the description reproduces a part of the rubric on fol. 1ra, with the peculiar misconstruction of the author's family name, which reads, in diplomatic transcription: "Incipit expositio q(ui)nq(ue) libror(um) boecij d(e) (con)solatio(n)e phy(losophi)ca edita a f(rat)re Nicolao treueli anglico f(rat)r(u)m ord(in)is p(re)dicator(um) theologie p(ro)fesso(r)e. p(re)facio"). On the library of the convent, cf. D. GUTIÉRREZ, "De antiquis Ordinis Eremitarum Sancti Augustini bibliothecis", *Analecta Augustiniana*, 23 (1953–1954), pp. 164–372, at 240–51.

[85]   See for instance (notes are offered in diplomatic transcription): "no(ta) p(ro) co(n)solatio(n)e alicui(us) (con)(tra) morte<m> fillij u(e)l uxoris u(e)l aliquis suor(um) pare(n)tum" (fol. 27[r], upper margin, Book 2 prose 2); "p(re)-dica de crudelitate" (fol. 38[v], outer margin, Book 2 metre 6); "cap(itu)lu(m) (con)(tra) luxuria<m>" (fol. 51[v], lower margin, Book 3 prose 7).

[86]   L. LOMBARDO, *Boezio in Dante. La* Consolatio philosophiae *nello scrittoio del poeta*, Venice, 2013, pp. 204–06, 254–56, 289, 615–16. On Guido and his *Expositiones et glose super Comediam Dantis*, see A. TERZI, "Guido da Pisa", in *DBI*, 61 (2004), <https://www.treccani.it/enciclopedia/guido-da-pisa_%28Dizionario-Biografico%29/> (last accessed 25/9/2021). Among the fourteenth-century exegetes of the *Commedia*, the anonymous *Ottimo commento* (Florence, 1334) would have used Trevet's commentary either in the original or a vernacular translation, whereas Francesco da Buti from Pisa (1396) explicitly referred to Trevet (LOMBARDO, *Boezio in Dante*, pp. 617–19, 636–39).

[87]   "Die XIII[a] marcii ejusdem indictionis Lombardus Laurencii, nepos dicti condam rectoris, restituit et assignavit eidem domino collectori [...] Item alium librum qui incipit in rubro 'Incipit prologus fratris Nicolai Trevensis', et in nigro 'Explanationem librorum', et finit 'sit cunctis annis custos Deus Johannis'" (*Bibliothèques ecclésiastiques au temps de la papauté d'Avignon*, II, 345.1 A, no. 28, p. 202).

[88]   Trevet is found among eight books belonging to Bishop Robert, which were collected for the papal nuncio in the kingdom of Naples: "Item liber

At Oxford, Trevet's publishing initiative may have benefited not only from the support of the English province of his order but also from the author's position as an Oxford master. Trevet's inception as doctor of theology and his first regency began shortly after, or even coincided with, the completion and publication of the commentary, which is referred to, as has been mentioned, in his *Quodlibet* II. Again, the indirect tradition provides the earliest evidence of the circulation and reception in the environment of the university. Previous scholarship has shown that Trevet's commentary was one of the sources used by another early-fourteenth-century English commentary on the *Consolation*.[89] Scholars also agree in attributing that commentary to William Wheteley (*fl.* 1305–1317), a secular clerk and schoolmaster at Stamford in Lincolnshire and then of the grammar school at Lincoln cathedral between 1309 and 1317. Wheteley is likely to have studied in Paris before 1305 and then at Oxford (in 1306 he was granted a bishop's licence to study there).[90] Irrespective of the attribution, the oldest

---

alius cum tabulis qui inc. 'Explanationem librorum Boetii De consolatione philosophica', et fin. 'saeculorum amen', vend. per me Neapoli et recepi pro ejus pretio in auro fl. 3" (*Bibliothèques ecclésiastiques au temps de la papauté d'Avignon*, I, ed. by D. WILLIMAN, Paris, 1980, 357.5, no. 4, p. 209).

[89] The relation between the two commentaries has been illustrated by KNEEPKENS, "Consolation for the soul", pp. 217–20, and IDEM, "The reception of Boethius' 'Consolatio' in the later middle ages: Trevet, Wheteley and the Question-commentary, Oxford, Exeter C., 28", in: *Nova de veteribus. Mittel- und Neulateinische Studien für Paul Gerhard Schmidt*, ed. by A. BIHRER, E. STEIN, Munich–Leipzig, 2004, pp. 679–712 (where selected fragments are discussed).

[90] The most comprehensive discussion of the previous attributions and the arguments for Wheteley's authorship is offered by A. LUCIA, "'Unde Boetius in tractatu de summo bono dicit'. Il 'De summo bono' di Boezio di Dacia nel commento di William Wheatley (XIV secolo) alla 'Consolatio Philosophiae' di Boezio", *Studi Medievali*, 53 (2012), pp. 93–115, at 93–102. On Wheteley, see N. ORME, "Wheatley, William (fl. 1305–1317)", in *Oxford Dictionary of National Biography* (published online 23/9/2004, this version: 23/9/2010, <https://doi-org.libproxy.helsinki.fi/10.1093/ref:odnb/29483>, last accessed 22/5/2021). According to Orme, the commentary was dedicated to Henry Mamesfeld, dean of Lincoln, and would therefore have been written when Wheteley served as master of Lincoln cathedral school (1316–1317). Beside a possible coincidence at Oxford (1306–7) there is one more indirect connection between Wheteley and Trevet. The former was presented to his first attested position, as rector of Sulham, Berkshire, in 1305, by John Droxford, at that

witnesses of this commentary accord with its dating to the first half of the fourteenth century.[91]

Several attested or extant copies augment the numbers of early Oxonian readers. A copy, lost or not yet identified, belonged to an Oxford artist (*magister* by 1296) and later rector of West Keal (Lincolnshire), John Cobbledik († 1337). It is registered, with the donor's name, in the fourteenth-century inventory of the books at Oriel College.[92] Shortly after the middle of the century, Trevet's commentary was included in a large miscellany of scholastic and classical texts commissioned by the Oxford friar Geoffrey de Wighton OFM: Cambridge, University Library, Mm.2.18.[93] Another English copy, datable to the early fourteenth century, Oxford, Bodleian Library, Auct. F. 6. 4, belonged at the time of Dissolution to an Augustinian canon from Osney abbey, just outside Oxford's city walls.[94] It is tempting to believe that the book came from the abbey's library.

time Keeper of the Wardrobe. In 1309 or later John, already bishop of Baths and Wells, became the dedicatee of Trevet's *De officio misse.*

[91] Both have belonged to Oxford colleges since the fourteenth century: Exeter College, 28, and New College, 264 (summary descriptions provided in *Codices Boethiani*, I, pp. 227–28, no. 215, and 237–38, no. 228).

[92] "Triuet super Boetium de consolatione per Cobildyk prec' d^i marc' 2° fo. *Ytali*" (R. THOMSON, *The University and College Libraries of Oxford*, 2 vols, London, 2015 (CBMLC, 16), U80. 28, vol. 2, p. 1221). On the inventory and the donor, see *ibid.*, pp. 1215–17.

[93] See the note on the old flyleaf (i^v): "Iste liber est fratris Galfridi de Wyghtone quem fecit scribi de elemosinis amicorum suorum". The friar is attested between 1358 and 1365. For the description of the manuscript see *Western Illuminated Manuscripts. A Catalogue of the Collection in Cambridge University Library*, ed. by P. BINSKI, P. ZUTSHI, Cambridge, 2011, no. 170, pp. 161–62.

[94] The manuscript consists of two codicological units, the first being a thirteenth-century copy of the *Consolation* (fols 1–61), the latter an early fourteenth-century copy of Trevet's commentary (fols 62–267, the status of parchment fols 268–75 is uncertain), beginning with the second part of the prologue, *inc.* "Consolaciones tue letificaverunt animam meam. Psalmo nonagesimo tercio. Inter letari et letificari". Fols. ii^r, 1^r (upper margin), and 274^v present complementary notes, according to which in 1543 the book belonged to Oxford priest, Thomas Corser, who had received it as a gift from Ralph Bloore, former canon at Osney. The two outer notes are offered by MLGB3 <http://mlgb3.bodleian.ox.ac.uk/mlgb/book/4193/> (last accessed 25/9/2021), the one on fol. 1^r (partly re-written?) reads: "Liber Thomae Corsaeri presbiteri oxoniensis". For a summary description, see *Codices Boethiani*, I, p. 182, no. 166.

More evidence of ownership or readership across the kingdom and across institutional and social affiliations comes from the latter part the century and the start of the following: we find, among others, a monk in East Anglia, Henry Kirkestede OSB (Bury St Edmunds),[95] two Cambridge scholars,[96] and, not least, vernacular poets, of whom Chaucer is the first.[97] Significant as witnesses to the long-lasting reception and success of Trevet's commentary, these late instances shed no further light on the ways in which the work was published by Trevet and his proxies.

It is not, indeed, necessary to look as far as the late fourteenth century to perceive the wide circulation, geographically and socially, of the commentary. Already in Trevet's lifetime, it seems to have reached as many readers from outside his order — religious, clerical, and, most significantly, lay — as his own confreres. Besides the author's initial publishing endeavour (illustrated by the dedicatory letter), possibly repeated for the benefit of select other readers now unknown, and besides the plausible contribution of some early readers (Niccolò da Prato), certain other factors may have contributed to that immediate success. The mul-

---

[95] In his catalogue of writers, compiled during the 1340s and 1350s, Henry of Kirkestede dedicated a separate entry to Trevet, and the commentary on the *Consolation* opens the list of the friar's works (Henry of Kirkestede, *Catalogus de libris autenticis et apocrifis*, ed. by R. H. ROUSE, M. A. ROUSE, London, 2004 (CBMLC, 11), p. 365, no. 398). Beside this, the commentary is also mentioned as the witness to the second part of Freculph's chronicle (*ibid.*, p. 218, no. 198: "Frethulfus [...] scripsit Historiam vel librum temporum a principio mundi usque ad Christum lib. 7 *Cum aliquem ... in me sunt*. Item a Christo usque ad obitum S. doctoris Gregorii papae secundum Trivet in commentario Boetii de consolatione philosophiae", cf. "Introduction", in *ibid.*, pp. xcix–c).

[96] The already mentioned copy, Cambridge, Peterhouse, 275, was bequeathed to Peterhouse by its former master (1382–1397), John Newton, in the codicil of 30 June 1414, and appears in the college's catalogue of 1418 (see P. D. CLARKE, *The University and College Libraries of Cambridge*, London, 2002 (CBMLC, 10), UC149. 10, p. 721, and UC48. 162, p. 485; on the donor, see *ibid.*, p. 720). Cf. description in R. M. THOMSON, *A Descriptive Catalogue of the Medieval Manuscripts in the Library of Peterhouse, Cambridge*, Cambridge, 2016, p. 172. A copy of Trevet's commentary, unidentified, is also found among the books given to the same college by Edmund de Kirketon, fellow between 1384 and 1404 (CLARKE, *University and College Libraries of Cambridge*, UC48. 141, p. 478, on the donor, see *ibid.*, p. 705).

[97] See for all A. J. MINNIS, "Chaucer's commentator: Nicholas Trevet and the *Boece*", in *Chaucer's* Boece, pp. 83–166.

tiple interactions between the Dominican friars and their social environments is a circumstance that to various degrees concerns the history of the publication of Trevet's other works as well. Doubtless, not every context in which a friar could engage with non-Dominicans was equally appropriate for the use or advertisement of works such as Trevet's commentary. But one definite match was conventual schools, which were also attended by secular clergy or even laymen.[98] Two other factors concern particularly this work of Trevet's. Building on its well established status and comprehensive contents, the *Consolation* became a popular school-text in late medieval grammar schools. This fact must have prepared a receptive audience for new commentaries. The phenomenon has been particularly well studied for Italy (with the focus on Tuscany) by Robert Black and Gabriella Pomaro. As they have shown, the commentaries on the *Consolation* were rarely used in full, but frequently excerpted. This is also the case with Trevet's exposition, whose influence in Italian grammar schools was manifested mainly through the glosses added to copies of Boethius's work, reaching a peak in the early fifteenth century.[99] Wheteley's

[98]   M. M. MULCHAHEY, "The rôle of the conventual *schola* in early Dominican education", in *Studio e* Studia*: le scuole degli ordini mendicanti tra XIII e XIV secolo. Atti del XXIX convegno della Società internazionale di studi francescani, Assisi, 11–13 ottobre 2001*, Spoleto, 2002, pp. 117–50, at 126–28; A. REEVES, "English secular clergy in the early Dominican schools: evidence from three manuscripts", *Church History and Religious Culture*, 92 (2012), pp. 35–55.

[99]   The examples of full copies of Trevet's commentary (with or without the *Consolation*) copied or used in the school context and known to Black and Pomaro are few and date from the turn of the fourteenth and fifteenth century: BML, Plut. 89 sup. 87 (the *Consolation* and the commentary, late fourteenth century, used by a student of a grammar school in Teano in Campania in the second quarter of the fifteenth century; BLACK, POMARO, *La* Consolazione, pp. 15, 66, 121–23, 230–34) and BML, Plut. 77.3 (commentary alone, copied in Pistoia in 1402 and owned by a grammar teacher, Mattia Lupi; *ibid.*, pp. 15, 106–08). Another copy of the commentary, written by Don Nofri di Angelo Coppi da S. Giminiano, should be added to this pair (now in private collection, see above n. 52). Instead, many are copies of the *Consolation* with the apparatus excerpted from Trevet's commentary. All the evidence is discussed in R. BLACK, "Boethius at school in medieval and renaissance Italy: manuscript glosses to the *Consolation of Philosophy*", in *Talking to the Text: Marginalia from Papyri to Print. Proceedings of a Conference held at Erice, 26 September–3 October 1998, as the 12th Course of International School for the Study of Written Records*, ed. by V. FERA, G. FERRAÙ, S. RIZZO, 2 vols, Messina,

initiative suggests that in England too the commentary tradition of the *Consolation* extended to grammar schools.

The second factor that may have played some role in the successful publication and circulation of Trevet's commentary has to do with its dimensions. The work provides a comprehensive discussion of the entire *Consolation* while at same time being of reasonable size. If copied without the *textus*, it could be contained in a few large-format quires, as is shown by BML, Plut. 25 sin. 1, consisting of four quinternions (the sum of the height and the width of the written space: 538 mm). In a smaller manuscript, Rome, Biblioteca Casanatense, MS 176 (319 mm), Trevet's commentary occupies nearly seven sexternions.[100] If the *textus* were included, such an edition could extend over five quinternions and a binion of large dimension (Oxford, Bodleian Library, Rawl. G. 187: *c.* 589 mm)[101] or fourteen smaller quaternions (Padua, Biblioteca Universitaria, 1596: 316 mm, last quire wanting the eighth leaf). The two manuscripts present two distinct patterns for the laying out of Boethius with Trevet's commentary. In the former, the *textus* is copied in larger script in the middle of the page, displayed in two columns, and surrounded by the commentary.[102] In the latter, the *textus* and the commentary alternate within a

2002, vol. 1, pp. 203–68, at 231–43; see also, IDEM, *Humanism and Education in Medieval and Renaissance Italy. Tradition and Innovation in Latin Schools from the Twelfth to the Fifteenth Century*, Cambridge, 2001, pp. 326–30; and, IDEM, *Education and Society*, pp. 101–02, 111. Cf. M. GIBSON, "Codices Boethiani", *Revue d'Histoire des Textes*, 14–15 (1984–1985), pp. 71–75, at 73–74. On the circulation of copies of the *Consolation* in Italy before the publication of Trevet's commentary, between the eleventh and thirteenth centuries, see also P. NASTI, "Storia materiale di un classico dantesco: la *Consolatio Philosophiae* fra XII e XIV secolo tradizione manoscritta e rielaborazioni esegetiche", *Dante Studies*, 134 (2016), pp. 142–68, at 144–56.

[100]   The manuscript is of French origin and may be dated to around the middle of the fourteenth century. The last quire wants leaf 12.

[101]   The dimensions of the written space present slight variations, the sums ranging from 594 mm on fol. 6ʳ to 583 on fol. 26ʳ.

[102]   This essentially corresponds to pattern 6 in the classification of G. Powitz, "Textus cum commento", *Codices manuscripti*, V (1979), pp. 80–89, at 82. In manuscripts of smaller dimensions the *textus* was copied in long lines, with the surrounding commentary in two columns, as is the case in BNM, Lat. VI, 64 (= 2667), of 446 mm (= Powitz's scheme 4).

column.[103] Alongside a mechanical gathering together of pre-existing copies of text and commentary,[104] these two patterns seem to be the prevailing ones as applied to manuscripts in which the *textus* and the commentary are combined; but systematic scrutiny is still waiting to be carried out. The wording of the cover letter, a group of early copies that transmit only the commentary, and the variation of layout in those that include both the *textus* and the commentary, lead to the conclusion that the commentary was originally published alone. It follows as a corollary that commissioners of individual copies, as early as the first half of the fourteenth century, would have been responsible for comprehensive editions.[105] The analysis of the textual identity of Trevet's exemplar, as reflected in the *lemmata* embedded in his commentary, and of the full copies transmitted together with the commentary, should shed more light on that aspect of the publishing history.

The Commentary on the *Controversiae* of Seneca the Elder

The commentary on the Elder Seneca's *Declamationes* is the second work by Trevet to be mentioned in Cardinal Niccolò da

---

[103]   Powitz's scheme 9. In the Paduan copy the layout is in two columns, which sometimes may be further subdivided in two, with or without the support of additional ruling, in order to condense Boethius's metres (see fol. 24[rb–va]), or to display metres alongside the commentary (see fol. 78[rb]), cf. fol. 70[r].

[104]   Such is the case with Oxford, Bodleian, Auct. F. 6. 4 (see above, n. 94), and Cambridge, Gonville and Caius College, 484/480. The latter manuscript consists of two units, copied in England during second half of the fourteenth century by two different scribes. The units may have circulated separately, as suggested by individual series of quire registers: a–j (quires I–IX, the last quire being a ternion, I–VII quaternions, VIII sexternion) and a–b (quires X and XI, quaternion and quinternion). The *Consolation* is transmitted by unit II. For a summary description, see *Codices Boethiani*, I, p. 67, no. 34.

[105]   Two already cited fourteenth-century manuscripts of Italian and English origin may suggest that the commentary and the *Consolation* circulated in blocks. In BML, Plut. 22 dex. 9, Book 1 with respective commentary, preceded by Trevet's prologue, occupies a separate unit of two quires (see above, n. 49). Cambridge, Peterhouse, 275, is a mono-block manuscript, but the *caesurae* after quires IX, XV, and XX (the first two irregular) suggest that the copy was produced from an exemplar split into four units consisting of: I, Bks 1–2; II, Bk 3; III, Bk 4; IV, Bk 5. They were copied by three different scribes, working partly in parallel, two of which, however, collaborated in copying units II and III.

Prato's letter. What the cardinal, and also Trevet, were referring to as "Declamationes" was in fact, as already observed by
Ruth Dean, a particular edition of Seneca's work, which is to
say the excerpted *Controversiae*.[106] In most witnesses known to
me the commentary proper, including a prologue, is preceded by
a dedicatory letter, in which Trevet addresses Friar John Lenham as confessor to the king of England.[107] This title allows the
completion of the work to be dated to 1307 at the earliest, the
year of the accession of Edward II, to whose household Lenham
had belonged when Edward was Prince of Wales. The work must
have been presented before 1315, when John was succeeded as

[106] DEAN, "Life and Works", p. 212. On the tradition of Seneca's *Declamationes* see the introductions to the two modern critical editions: The Elder
Seneca, *Declamations*, trans. by M. WINTERBOTTOM, Cambridge, MA–London,
1974 (The Loeb Classical Library), I, pp. xix–xx; and L. Annaeus Seneca
Maior, *Oratorum et rhetorum sententiae, divisiones, colores*, ed. by L. HÅKAN-
SON, Leipzig, 1989 (Bibliotheca Teubneriana), pp. v–xv (for the *textus* commented on by Trevet I shall henceforth refer to the latter as *Exc. Contr.*).

[107] The work remains unedited. The dedicatory letter has not been
included in the following, otherwise complete, witnesses (I distinguish with
an asterisk the manuscripts only known to me through reproductions):
Assisi, Biblioteca e Centro di documentazione francescana del Sacro Convento, Fondo Antico, ms. Assisi Com. 302 (the prologue has also been omitted); Oxford, Bodleian Library, Rawlinson G. 186; and *Toulouse, BM, 806.
Another copy, Cambridge, Peterhouse, 162, begins imperfectly (quire I wants
the first leaf), in the middle of the *Expositio prohemii*, which is the section
immediately following the prologue: "//pare id est ad plenum apprehendere"
(fol. 1ʳᵃ). The letter has been printed by DEAN ("Life and Works", pp. 444–
45), from *BnF, lat. 16229 (fol. 39ʳᵃ⁻ᵇ), with the variants of BL, Royal 15 C.
XII (fol. 2ʳᵃ⁻ᵇ). In the quotations offered here I shall attempt a provisional
reconstruction of the correct text, basing myself on those two and these following witnesses: SBB-PK, Diez. C fol. 4 (fol. 1ᵛᵃ⁻ᵇ), BAV, Arch. Cap. S. Pietro, C.121 (fol. 141ʳ); BML, Conv. soppr. 509 (fol. 1ʳᵃ⁻ᵇ); BML, Plut. 25 sin. 6
(fol. 1ʳ); Madrid, Biblioteca Nacional de España (henceforth BNE), MSS 8212
(fol. 1ʳᵃ⁻ᵇ); *BnF, lat. 7798 (fol. 1ʳᵃ⁻ᵇ); Pisa, Biblioteca Cathariniana, MS 155
(fol. 1ʳᵃ⁻ᵛᵃ); BNM, Lat. XI, 50 (= 3931) (fols iiiᵛ–ivʳ, the letter is copied without the *salutatio*), and Wolfenbüttel, Herzog August Bibliothek, Guelf. 171
Gud. lat. (fol. 1ʳᵃ⁻ᵇ). Only the most significant rejected readings will be registered. The letter opens with the following *salutatio*: "In Christo sibi dilecto
fratri Iohanni de Lenham illustris regis Anglie confessori [confessori domini
r.A.i. *Royal 15 C. XII*] frater Nicholaus Treveth fratrum [ordinis *pro* f. *Royal
15 C. XII*] predicatorum minimus primam veritatem [p. virtutem *Berlin, Diez.
C fol. 4; BNE 8212* prime veritatis claritatem *Royal 15 C. XII*] in eternitatis
gloria [gaudio *pro* gloria *Royal 15 C. XII*] contemplari".

confessor by his confrere John of Warefield.[108] The request for
this commentary, made in 1316 at the latest by Niccolò da Prato,
who was resident in the south of France, corroborates the dating
and proves that information about Trevet's new achievement was
already circulating by that time. Lenham must have been held
in high esteem by Edward II. After the death of his confrere
and compatriot, Cardinal Thomas Jorz, in December 1310, he
became the king's candidate for English cardinal. However, neither Lenham nor any other Englishman was created a cardinal
by Pope Clement V.[109]

The letter is once again personal in tone. Rather than a cele-
bration of the relationship with the dedicatee, a description of
the forty-nine-year-old author's illness[110] occupies the lion's share
of the epistle. It was during this infirmity that Trevet would
have undertaken the reading of Seneca's work and have appreciated its difficulties.[111] Lenham is said to have encouraged their
explanation and therefore, as "the first cause" ("primum motivum"), he is also the first to receive the fruits of Trevet's endeavours. Besides Lenham, however, there is also a collective protagonist: Trevet states that he has been supported by his confreres

---

[108]   On Lenham see S. PHILLIPS, *Edward II*, New Haven, CT, 2010,
p. 65; J. RÖHRKASTEN, "King Edward II of England and the Carmelites",
in *Historiography and Identity. Responses to Medieval Carmelite Culture*, ed. by
J. RÖHRKASTEN, C. ZERMATTEN, Zürich, 2017, pp. 39–62, at 46–48; IDEM,
"Dominicans in England and their relations with the Crown", in *A Companion
to the English Dominican Province From Its Beginnings to the Reformation*, ed.
by E. J. GIRAUD, J. C. LINDE, Leiden–Boston, 2021, pp. 33–68, at 52–54.
Surprisingly DEAN ("Cultural relations", p. 549) counted Lenham among Trevet's non-Dominican patrons.

[109]   J. R. WRIGHT, *The Church and the English Crown 1305–1334. A Study
based on the Register of Archbishop Walter Reynolds*, Toronto, 1980, p. 126, and
P. N. R. ZUTSHI, "Proctors acting for English petitioners in the Chancery of
the Avignon Popes (1305–1378)", *Journal of Ecclesiastical History*, 35 (1984),
pp. 15–29, at 28, n. 82.

[110]   "Exacto septennarii annorum natalium quadrato", begins the *narratio* of the letter. Trevet's date of birth being unknown, this reference has no
value for the work's dating. Vice-versa, the earliest year in which the work
could have been completed, 1307, would put his date of birth around 1258.
Cf. DEAN, "Life and Works", pp. 37–39.

[111]   Cf. CREVATIN, "Le dediche", pp. 404–05.

("fratrumque innixus meritis") and signals that their (spiritual) growth is his aim.[112]

Lenham, apparently, did not live long enough to have played any significant part in the publishing circle of Trevet's work: he died in August 1316. We may assume that the dedicatee, when he was presented with the work, was based at the English royal court and therefore located somewhere in the British Isles, except perhaps during Edward II's short visits to France in 1308 (22 January to 7 February) and 1313 (23 May to 16 July).[113] In contrast, it is far from certain where Trevet was based in those years. He is not attested at Oxford after 1307 and before December 1314, the period that coincides with the timespan during which the commentary was completed. A sojourn in Paris, recalled between 1320 and 1323 in the prologue to his *Annales*, should probably be dated to within that period. That circumstance would help to explain the existence of two relatively early copies, datable to the second quarter or middle of the fourteenth century, whose origin may be assigned to northern France, perhaps Paris. Both are kept at the BnF: lat. 7798 and lat. 16229. The latter was kept in the *magna libraria* of the Sorbonne, by 1435 at the latest, but before that had belonged to an unknown Dominican convent.[114] The former

---

[112] "Denique tamen cum vestri desiderii esse suggestum [subiectum *pro* suggestum *Berlin, Diez. C fol. 4; BAV, Arch.Cap.S.Pietro C.121*] mihi fuisset, ut latentes predictarum declamationum sensus absconditasque sentencias in lucem producerem, librum repetii animum resumpsi et in dei adiutorio confisus fratrumque innixus meritis, quorum incrementis labores meos subseruire affecto [-tum *BnF, lat. 7798; Guelf. 171 Gud. lat. 4o; the expansion of compounded word in Berlin, Diez. C fol. 4 is uncertain*; affectam *or* -ui *BnF, lat. 16229*; affectavi *Dean*], prefatum librum expositione illustrandum aggredi ausus fui. Quam pro viribus iam consummatam vestre dilectioni transmitto, ut primum laboris parcipiatis fructum, qui primum operis extitistis motivum".

[113] On both trips see PHILLIPS, *Edward II*, pp. 133–35, 209–14.

[114] The manuscript consists of copies of the *Excerpta Controversiarum* (fols 3ra–36vb) and Trevet's commentary (fols 39ra–150rb). The two copies seem to belong to distinct, but contemporary units of production, insofar as it can be deduced from the black-and-white reproduction of the microfilm, available online at Gallica <https://gallica.bnf.fr/ark:/12148/btv1b9067169g/f.1.item> (last accessed 25/9/2021) (It has not been possible to obtain colour reproductions of selected folios due to the poor conditions of the binding, as per a communication from the Département Images et prestations numériques of BnF, 17/06/2021). François Avril has attributed the pen-flourishes at fol. 39^r

was taken to northern Italy some time after its production: it is reported in the 1426 inventory of the library of the Visconti in Pavia.[115] Another transalpine copy, Madrid, Biblioteca Nacional de España, MSS 8212, is datable to the latter part of the fourteenth century or the beginning of the following, but cannot be localized with confidence ("Lowlands" according to Ruth Dean). In 1419 it is attested in Sicily.[116]

to Jaquet Maci, the renowned illuminator active in Avignon and Paris in the first half of the fourteenth century (F. AVRIL, *Fichier des manuscrits enluminés du département des Manuscrits*, BnF, n.a.l. 28635 (3): <https://gallica.bnf.fr/ark:/12148/btv1b100005067/f. 750>, last accessed 25/9/2021; on Maci see F. MANZARI, "Jaquet Maci", in *Enciclopedia dell'Arte Medievale*, 1996: <https://www.treccani.it/enciclopedia/jaquet-maci_%28Enciclopedia-dell%27Ar-te-Medievale%29/>, last accessed 25/9/2021). The tally of leaves occupied by both works and skins used, inscribed in the front pastedown in a mix of Latin and French (of the Île-de-France), shows that they were produced in the same professional workshop, probably in Paris, apparently to be sold or delivered together (here in diplomatic transcription from the reproduction, cf. DEAN, "Life and Works", p. 210; I thank Outi Merisalo for palaeographic and linguistic expertise): "xxxiiij[or] fol(ia) text(us) | (com)m(en)tu(m) cent dix fol(ia) | s(um)ma vij[xx] iiij[or] [*i.e. 144*] fol(ia) | [*an illegible sign* A *Dean*] iiij fueill(es) en la peau | seroie(n)t xxxvj peaulx". They were certainly bound together when, on 11 November 1435, Pierre de la Hazardière, master of arts and student of theology, borrowed them from the library of the Sorbonne: "Declamaciones Senece cum commento Nicolai Traveth in eodem volumine" (*Le Registre de prêt de la bibliothèque du collège de Sorbonne 1402–1536*, ed. by J. VIELLIARD, Paris, 2000, pp. 336, 664). There are traces of at least two inscriptions witnessing to prior ownership (given here in a diplomatic transcription). The first, of which only the beginning and the end are readable, occurs in the top of fol. 2[v]: "Iste lib(er) est frat(ru)m p(re)di [...] | co(n)ue(n)t(us) ab illo". The second was inscribed on fol. 150rb, just below the colophon: "Iste lib(er) est [*the name abrased*] | empt(us) de pecunijs eiusdem | p(re)cij .iiij. libr.". It may refer to the friar who would have left the book to the convent mentioned in the previous note.

[115] E. PELLEGRIN, *La Bibliothèque des Visconti et des Sforza ducs de Milan, au XVe siècle*, Paris, 1955, pp. 241–42 (A.765). The black-and-white microfilm of this manuscript has been digitized at Gallica: <https://gallica.bnf.fr/ark:/12148/btv1b90776541/f. 1.item.r = 7798> (last accessed 25/9/2021).

[116] Cf. DEAN, "Life and Works", p. 209, and *Inventario general de manuscritos de la Biblioteca Nacional*, XII, Madrid, 1988, pp. 271–72. The manuscript is written in Gothic cursive and provided with red-and-blue pen-flourished initials of not the highest quality. According to the note on fol. 109[v] (given below in a diplomatic transcription), in 1419 the book was given to the viceroy of Sicily by Roger de Berlione from Palermo. The receiver speaks

Irrespective of whether Trevet was based in Paris or had already returned to Oxford when he received the letter of Cardinal Niccolò da Prato, he must have provided the copy requested by the prelate. This may be deduced from the evidence of attested or extant copies that belonged to people connected to Niccolò. The first in chronological order is dated 1317. On 31 July that year Guillaume de Labroue was reimbursed for a copy of the Senecan *Declamationes* "cum expositione", purchased for Pope John XXII.[117] There can be no doubt that the "expositio" is that of Trevet. Franz Ehrle identified that copy with the one registered in the inventory of the papal library in Avignon made in 1375 by order of Pope Gregory XI.[118] Guillaume de Labroue, a Dominican friar and bishop of Cahors, was in charge of book provision for John XXII, both through purchase and supervision of copying, between 1316 and 1324.[119] It is known from the same accounts of

in the first person without giving his name. The date and the names of his colleagues, however, lead to the conclusion that it was Martino de Turribus: "hu(n)c libru(m) traueti s(upe)r [supra *Dean*] declamac(i)o(n)ib(us) Senece dedit m(ih)i [in *pro* mihi *Dean*] die xx° octobr(is) a(n)no M cccc° xix i(n) t(er)ra S(i)cil(i)e [Salernie *Dean*] Egregi(us) legu(m) doctor et magne Curie judex d(omi)n(us) Rogeri(us) de Berlione [Verlione *Dean*] Ciuis honorabilis felicis vrbis panormi eo t(em)p(o)re quo sim(u)l cu(m) magnificis [-co *Dean*] d(omi)nis antonio d(e) Cardona et ferra(n)do Velascis [s *faded* Velascii *Dean* Velasco *Inventario*] porrado officio viceregiis [*sic* viceregis *Inventario*] fungebar [fungebat *Dean, Inventario*] in Sicilie Regno". The manuscript has been digitized: <http://bdh-rd.bne.es/viewer.vm?id=0000056717&page=1> (last accessed 25/9/2021).

[117] "Die ultima iulii pro libro declamationum Senece cum expositione empto pro domino nostro solvi fratri Guillelmo de Broa: - XIX lib. turonensium parvorum" (F. EHRLE, *Historia Bibliothecae*, vol. 1, p. 147, cf. K. H. SCHÄFER, *Die Ausgaben der apostolischen Kammer unter Johan XXII. nebst das Jahresbilanzen von 1316–1375*, Paderborn, 1911 (Vatikanische Quellen zur Geschichte der päpstlichen Hof- und Finanzverwaltung 1316–1378, 2), p. 264).

[118] "Item declamaciones Senece cum glosis Nicolai Trevet; de littera Bolonnensi (!) in modica forma, cooperte de viridi" (EHRLE, *Historia Bibliothecae*, vol. 1, p. 541: Gr, no. 1343).

[119] *Ibid.*, p. 176; there is more on book acquisitions under Pope John XII and the role of Labroue in F. MANZARI, *La miniatura ad Avignone al tempo dei papi (1310–1410)*, Modena, 2006, pp. 30–72, and D. NEBBIAI, "I libri del papa e la biblioteca pontificia", in *Giovanni XXII. Cultura e politica di un papa avignonese. Atti del LVI Convegno storico internazionale, Todi, 13–15 ottobre 2019*, Spoleto, 2020, pp. 127–49, at 131–36.

the papal chamber that in November 1317 Guillaume bought four
books from the chamberlain of Cardinal Niccolò.[120] The source of
the July purchase is not mentioned, but if not directly supplied by
Niccolò, it is plausible that it was the cardinal who brought Trevet's new work to the attention of pope and/or Guillaume and that
he made his exemplar available to Avignon stationers.

Two other witnesses are later but not less significant. Both have
already been mentioned with regard to the commentary on the
Consolation. The commentary on the *Declamationes* appears among
the works of Trevet bequeathed in 1338 to the Dominicans of
Arezzo by Simone, a member of Niccolò's household.[121] The ownership of a copy of the same work by Cardinal Godin is worth closer
consideration.[122] Guillaume de Pierre Godin began his ecclesiastical and scholarly career in the Dominican province of Provence, of
which he was prior in 1301–1303, and after its division was elected
the first prior of the new province of Toulouse. After having
obtained a doctorate in theology in Paris in 1304, in 1306 he
was appointed *lector sacri Palatii*. He held that position until 1312,
when Pope Clement V created him a cardinal. From the time of
his service at the French court, 1308–1310, Godin had become
directly involved in the diplomatic and ecclesiastical affairs of
the papacy. On various occasions he acted jointly with Cardinal
Niccolò da Prato, whom he befriended. Niccolò must have thought highly of Guillaume, to judge by the gift of a pectoral cross,
mentioned in Godin's will, and from the fact that Godin was one
of the four executors of Niccolò's testament.[123] Godin also owned

---

[120] "solvi in summa fratri Guillelmo de Broa, qui de mandato domini
nostri dictos libros emerat de camerario domini Hostiensis, ut dixit —
LXXXXVI flor." (EHRLE, *Historia Bibliothecae*, I, p. 147; SCHÄFER, *Die Ausgaben der apostolischen Kammer*, p. 265).

[121] "Item scriptum dicti fratris super declamationes Senece" (PASQUI, "La
biblioteca d'un notaro aretino", p. 254).

[122] On Godin's biography see M. MORARD, "Le *studium* de la Curie pontificale et ses maîtres au temps de Jean XXII", in *Jean XXII et le Midi*,
pp. 511–13.

[123] On relations between the two prelates, see RELTGEN-TALLON, "Nicolas
de Prato", pp. 158–60, 166; M. BENEDETTI, "Promozione della santità e repres-
sione dell'eresia al tempo di Niccolò da Prato", in *Niccolò da Prato*, pp. 221–37,
at 230–31, 236; and L. CINELLI, "Il monastero di San Niccolò a Prato e i pri-
mordi della vita religiosa femminile", in *ibid.*, pp. 171–219, at 173–74.

a rich library, which he disposed of in his will of 1335 and in the codicil dated 26 April 1336, shortly before his death (4 June). In the latter, among the books given "ad usum" of Friar Peregrinus de Mercatore OP, but with a reversion to the convent of Bayonne, he included "librum declamationum Senece cum glossa magistri Nicolay Trevet ac glossam eiusdem super Boetium de consolatione" ("a book of *Declamations* of Seneca with the commentary of Master Nicholas Trevet and the commentary of the same on Boethius's *Consolation*").[124] The two works of Trevet are the same ones that were known to Niccolò da Prato, directly or by hearsay, at the time he was writing to Trevet. It is highly probable that Godin was introduced to the two commentaries by his friend and fellow, who may also have provided the exemplars from which Godin's copies were made.

Only two surviving manuscripts have been tentatively identified with items present in Godin's wills, both now kept at Toulouse, BM: MSS 365 (a collection of canons) and 370 (Henricus de Segusio, *Lectura* on the Decretals of Gregory IX).[125] I posit that two others, again hypothetically, may be added to that list: Oxford, Bodleian Library, Rawl. G. 186, transmitting *Excerpta Controversiarum* with Trevet's commentary, and G. 187 in the same collection, the above-mentioned copy of Boethius's *De conso-*

---

[124]   Here are the two items in their context: "Item legavit religioso viro fratri Peregrino de Mercatore, ordinis fratrum Predicatorum, oriundo de Baiona, magistro in theologia, quoad ipsius usum, infra proximum sequentes libros videlicet [...] ac rationes Augustini contra Pelagium cum quibusdam aliis in uno volumine et librum declamationum Senece cum glossa magistri Nicolay Trevet ac glossam eiusdem super Boetium de consolatione. Proprietatem vero ipsorum librorum omnium et singulorum ultra legata conventui fratrum Predicatorum Baionensi per eum in suo testamento eidem conventui Baionensi sub eidem conditionibus sub quibus ipse dedit plures alios libros et quedam ecclesiastica ornamenta legavit" (M.-H. LAURENT, O. P., "Le testament et la succession du cardinal dominicain Guillaume de Pierre Godin", *AFP* 2 (1932), pp. 84–231, doct. VI, pp. 147–48).

[125]   *Les Jacobins: 1385–1985. Sixième centenaire de la dédicace de l'église des Jacobins: Toulouse, exposition au réfectoire des Jacobins, du 19 septembre au 27 octobre 1985*, exhibition catalogue ed. by Y. CARBONELL-LAMOTHE, P. CAZALÈS-RICO, D. CAZES, C. ECZET *et al.*, Toulouse, 1985, p. 25, no. 11. On MS 365, cf. the detailed description based on Molinier's (1885) and revised by E. Nadal (2021): <https://ccfr.bnf.fr/portailccfr/ark:/06871/004D07A11389> (last accessed 25/9/2021).

latione with Trevet's exposition. As early as 1895 in the Bodleian's *Summary Catalogue*, they were rightly recognized as companion volumes, copied by the same scribe, but were mistakenly localized to Italy and dated to the second half of the fourteenth century.[126] That opinion has been widely accepted in subsequent scholarship (in which principal interest has focused on the Boethius volume).[127] Although the Southern *littera textualis* could belong to a scribe trained in Italy, the same style was also in use in southern France.[128] More importantly, the style of red-and-blue initials with red and violet pen-flourishes resonates with the pen-flourishing of manuscripts decorated in southern France, Avignon in particular, during the first half of the fourteenth century.[129] The origin of the

---

[126]   *A Summary Catalogue of Western Manuscripts in the Bodleian Library at Oxford which have not hitherto been Catalogued in the Quarto Series*, vol. 3, Oxford, 1895, nos. 14903–14904, pp. 375–76.

[127]   Dean, "Life and Works", pp. 165, 209; Silk, p. xxi; *Codices Boethiani*, I, p. 213, no. 199 (and pl. 10); Black, Pomaro, *La* Consolazione, pp. 15, 19–20; Black, "Boethius at School", p. 232; and Dufal, "Nicholas Trevet", pp. 97–98.

[128]   See A. Derolez, *The Palaeography of Gothic Manuscript Books. From the Twelfth to the Early Sixteenth Century*, Cambridge, 2003, pp. 116–17; P. Cherubini, A. Pratesi, *Paleografia latina. L'avventura grafica del mondo occidentale*, Vatican City, 2010, pp. 489–90. The colophon used by the scribe: "Explicit iste liber sit scriptor crimine liber" (G. 187, fol. 54rb), especially popular in the fourteenth century, is of little help in determining the place: it is most frequently found in Paris, northern and western France, seldom in Midi, and was not unknown in Italy (L. Reynhout, *Formules latines de colophons*, Turnhout, 2006, I, pp. 103–08, *formule* no. 8, A1, cf. vol. 2, p. 327, tab. III/1–4).

[129]   A selection of images of Rawl. G. 187 is available at Digital Bodleian: <https://digital.bodleian.ox.ac.uk/objects/a709a245-d7c7-4a7a-a3ab-82381df-cfb82/> (last accessed 25/9/2021). Their initials may be compared to those in the following manuscripts decorated at Avignon: BAV, Arch. Cap. S. Pietro, A.41ter (breviary commissioned by the Chapter of St Peter, *s.* xiv$^{2/4}$), see for instance fols 41^v, 414^v, 416^v (there are others ascribable to a Florentine pen-flourisher, see F. Manzari, "Manuscrits liturgiques réalisés à Avignon dans la première moitié du XIVe siècle. Nouvelles découvertes dans les collections du Vatican", in *Culture religieuse méridionale. Les manuscrits et leur context artistique*, ed. by M. Fournié, D. Le Blévec, A. Stones, Toulouse, 2016 (Cahiers de Fanjeaux 51), pp. 215–45, at 227–31; digital reproduction of the manuscript available at DigiVatLib: <https://digi.vatlib.it/view/MSS_Arch. Cap.S.Pietro.A.41.pt.ter>, last accessed 25/9/2021); Grasse, Bibliothèque Patrimonial, MS 3 (missal for the cathedral of Grasse, at that time part of

two manuscripts coincides with the historical setting of Godin's activities. The identification is only apparently hindered by slight discrepancies in the description of the contents. First, the booklist in the codicil makes no mention of the short pseudo-Senecan texts that accompany the *Excerpta Controversiarum* (referred to as "liber declamationum") and Trevet's commentary in G. 186. Secondly, it suggests that the copy of the commentary on the *Consolation* did not include the *textus*, which instead is present in G. 187. Neither of these differences, however, excludes the identification. Two short texts attributed to Seneca — *De moribus* (*inc.* "Omne pecatum actio voluntaria est", fols 32^(va)–33^(ra)) and *De paupertate* (*inc.* "Honesta inquit Epicurus res est leta paupertas", fols 33^(ra)–35^(va))[130] — by an unfortunate lack of coordination are copied in the middle of Trevet's commentary, interrupting the exposition of *Exc. Contr.* V, 2.[131] Perhaps the two short texts were copied in an appendix to the *Excerpta Controversiarum* in the exemplar of the *textus*, since the rubric of the title of the first is embedded in the explicit-rubric of *Exc. Contr.* on fol. 32^r (on the layout, see further below). As for G. 187, the rubric of Trevet's commentary is the first to be seen (fol. 1^(ra)), while the *Consolation* begins on the verso page (in contrast to the *Exc. Contr.*, which in G. 186 begins on the same page, fol. 1^r, as the commentary).

the county of Provence, ?1330, for which see: <https://ccfr.bnf.fr/portailccfr/ ark:/06871/004Ms_3>, last accessed 25/9/2021); Seville, Biblioteca Colombina, MS 56-I-28 (the Pontifical of Guillaume Durand, 1320s), together with the missing leaves scattered throughout various collections and virtually brought together by F. Avril, "Quelques éléments nouveaux relatifs à la production avignonnaise du temps du pape Jean XXII. À propos d'un pontifical de Guillaume Durand dépecé", in *Culture religieuse méridionale*, pp. 415–64, in part. ill. 3, 4, 8, 16). I am grateful to Francesca Manzari for precious consultation on the pen-flourishes of the two Rawlinson copies.

[130] Cf. E. Dekkers, *Clavis Patrum Latinorum*, 3rd edn, Steenbrugge, 1995, nos. 1090 and 1089.

[131] The commentary is interrupted in the last line of fol. 32^(rb): "sed tu nec tuum. scilicet filium diligis unde a parte tua est" (a tie-mark and a gloss by another hand in the margin: "quere hoc signum infra in .iiij°. folio in principio [?] .iiij^e. columpne"). It is resumed without lacuna on fol. 35^(vb): "causa inimicitie. Extra controversiam Rubrica. Senianus rem stultissimam" (in the upper margin the same tie-mark and an annotation: "Quer<e> hoc signum supra in proximo .iiij. folio in fine secunde columpne").

The order in which the Trevet titles appear in the codicil may imply that the respective copies were kept, or even bound, together. The wording, however, is inconclusive, in light of the fact that the document is explicit about certain other texts being contained "in uno volumine". If we look at the two Rawlinson manuscripts, the irregular final quires suggest that they were produced separately;[132] but they were products of the same workshop, as is proven by their common scribe, the style of pen-flourishing, and the similar dimensions of the written space.[133] The Boethius volume (G. 187), in the lower margin of fol. 54^r, below the final column of the commentary, has an annotation written in a less formal book-hand, a sort of *notularis*, witness to a campaign of revision. In diplomatic transcription it reads: "Correctu(m) e(st) ad ungue(m) totu(m) p(er) f(rat)rem b't. egidij qua [*sic*] a(n)i(m)a requiescat in pace" ("The entire copy was revised to perfection by Brother *b't.* of Egidius, may his soul rest in peace"). The identity of the reviser escapes our knowledge. The word left unexpanded has previously been deciphered as "beati",[134] but the form of abbreviation would rather suggest a name beginning with "Bart-" or "Bert-".[135] This hand made a number of annotations in the margins of G. 187, including the tie-annotations on the location of diagrams, discussed above, and some glosses of comment.[136] A

---

[132]   Collation of G. 186 (for both manuscripts I provide collation of the original parchment body, see below, n. 139): I^{5+5} (1–10), II^{5+5} (11–20), III^{5+5} (21–30), IV^{4+4} (31–38), V^{6+6} (39–50), VI^{4+4+1} (51–59). Fol. 59 has been added (a stub visible between fols 50 and 51) to accommodate the remainder of the *tituli* of the *Declamationes* (fols 58vb–59rb, 59^v blank). Collation of G. 187: I^{5+5} (1–10), II^{5+5} (11–20), III^{5+5} (21–30), IV^{5+5} (31–40), V^{5+5} (41–50), VI^{2+2} (51–54). The copy ends on fol. 54^r; the verso page, as already mentioned, presents the diagrams. Quires III–V have signatures a–c.

[133]   The particular features of the layout vary between the two manuscripts (on G. 186 see below, on G. 187 see above), but the number of written lines of the commentary is nearly the same: 87–88 in G. 186, and 85–88 in G. 187.

[134]   *Summary Catalogue*, p. 376, and *Codices Boethiani*, I, p. 213, no. 199.

[135]   A survey, thus far limited to BÉNÉDICTINS DU BOUVERET, *Colophons de manuscrits occidentaux des origines aux XVIe siècle*, 6 vols, Fribourg, 1965–1982, and to the catalogues of dated manuscripts from the French collections, has not produced any similar note. I am grateful to Outi Merisalo, Giovanna Murano, and Lucien Reynhout for their advice.

[136]   Beginning with a general one, written between the end of Trevet's *Expositio* and the declaration of the revision: "Nota quod in hoc scripto continetur

small number of marginalia in G. 186 can be attributed to the same hand.[137] Besides the hand of the near-contemporary corrector, a later glossing hand, using a careless, small, non-looped Gothic cursive, usually in brownish ink, is also found in both manuscripts.[138] This evidence of use allows us to conclude that the two manuscripts circulated together. In their present form they do not contain any ownership marks prior to those of Thomas Rawlinson (1720). It was not unusual for that collector to split the manuscripts in his possession.[139] Should Godin's identification as the owner of these manuscripts be disproved by future studies, Godin's codicil and the two Rawlinson manuscripts may be taken as independent witnesses to the early circulation of both of Trevet's commentaries in southern France.

Another early copy survives from the same region, though there is no evidence of direct connection with the milieu of the papal curia. According to the colophon in Toulouse, BM, MS 806, the manuscript was finished on the feast of Sts John and Paul (26 June) of 1333, "in ospitio fratrum predicatorum", after which another hand added: "in vico carcass.", i.e. in Carcassonne (fol. 112^r). The wording would suggest that a copy had been made by or for a non-Dominican commissioner, in which case the Blackfriars of Carcassonne would have provided the exemplar. The later notes on fol. 113^v state that at the beginning of the sixteenth century

---

declaratio multarum veritatum tam in philosophia quam in theologia breviter" (fol. 54^r, lower margin). Cf. fols 45^r (lower margin) and 47^v (lower margin).

[137] See monograms of "Nota" on fols 12^r (outer margin), 41^r (outer margin), and "Nota quid Olinchus" on fol. 22^r (inner margin, in relation to "victa Olincho", i.e. Olyntho, *Exc. Contr.* III, 8).

[138] In G. 186 see e.g. "vide si vacat usque ad declamacionem que incipit 'abdicavit'; omnino sed sequens est transportata" (fol. 6vb, in the intercolumnar space between the *textus* of *Exc. Contr.* II, 2, "Pauca nosti", and the commentary on *Exc. Contr.* I, 3, "Incesta de saxo"). Cf. in G. 187 the short glosses on fol. 45^r: "de Ulixe" (inner margin), "de Hercule", and "de centauris" (both in the outer margin).

[139] K. L. SMITH, "A fifteenth-century vernacular manuscript reconstructed", *The Bodleian Library Record*, 7 (1966), pp. 234–41, at 240–41. It should also be noted that in both manuscripts the medieval parchment body is followed by several paper quires, left blank, as if the early-modern owner was planning to provide a transcription: G. 186, fols 60–145, and G. 187, fols 55–122.

the book belonged to the Austin friars at Carcassonne.[140] A textual collation would be the only way to answer the question as to whether this copy is stemmatically related to Godin's presumed manuscript. It may be of significance that neither includes the dedicatory letter, a characteristic that may have derived from the copy sent by Trevet to Niccolò da Prato. At the same time they follow different patterns of laying out the commentary together with the *textus* (see below).

Both Avignonese and Dominican networks may have played an essential role in transmitting the work to Italy during the fourteenth century. In 1345, a copy was reported among the books of Alberico da Rosciate, the previously mentioned jurist from Bergamo, who in 1335, 1337–1338, and 1340–1341, went to Avignon on the behalf of the Visconti, as ambassador to the pope.[141] Regrettably, a dating of the beginning of the century for the Italian manuscript that was once kept at the Ohio Wesleyan University at Delaware cannot be ascertained since the manuscript is currently lost.[142] Another copy of the commentary (SBB-PK, Diez.

---

[140]   The manuscript has been digitized: <http://bvmm.irht.cnrs.fr//consult/consult.php?reproductionId=3185> (last accessed 25/9/2021). The colophon and the ownership notes are quoted in M. MORARD, "La bibliothèque évaporée. Livres et manuscrits des dominicains de Toulouse (1215–1840)", in *Entre stabilité et itinérance. Livres et culture des ordres mendiants*, ed. by N. BÉRIOU, M. MORARD, D. NEBBIAI, Turnhout, 2014, pp. 73–128, at 93, n. 81. The description, based on A. Molinier's (1885) but revised by E. Nadal (2021) is available in *Catalogue collectif de France*: <https://ccfr.bnf.fr/portailccfr/ark:/06871/004D07A13049> (last accessed 25/9/2021).

[141]   CREMASCHI, "Contributo", p. 99, no. 70. Cf. L. PROSDOCIMI, "Alberico da Rosate", *DBI*, 1 (1960), <https://www.treccani.it/enciclopedia/alberico-da-rosate_%28Dizionario-Biografico%29/> (last accessed 25/9/2021).

[142]   MS 6 in the list of the manuscripts kept at OWU in the *Census of Medieval and Renaissance Manuscripts*, vol. II, 1937, p. 1969. In the short description provided there, the manuscript is dated *c.* 1300, which, based on the work's date should be corrected to not earlier than 1307. It is localized in "northern Italy (Bologna?)". We are not told whether or not it included the *textus*, but, judging from its capacity (234 folios, 340 × 240 mm) it probably did. It was decorated with illuminated initials. The manuscript came to OWU in 1920 from O. A. Wright, but had belonged to Revd. Frank Wakeley Gunsaulus (1856–1921). The latter was portrayed by Arvid Nyholm (1866–1927) with his hand resting on an opening of this manuscript. Although far from an exact representation, the painting clearly shows a page with script laid out in two columns with three painted initials decorated with acanthus leaves.

C fol. 4) cannot be dated with more precision than to the fourteenth century. It was written in Southern *littera textualis* on reused parchment originally belonging to a late-thirteenth-century Italian accounts book, with blank space left for never completed initials. Apart from a coat-of-arms of an unidentified cardinal of the Visconti family, added in the early-modern period, nothing is known about its history until it appeared on the Venetian book market in 1747.[143]

The remainder of the known Italian evidence dates from the latter part of the century onwards, and will therefore be mentioned here only briefly. The earliest attested case of ownership concerns a lost or unidentified copy, which was reported in 1368 among the books of the late Guillelmus, abbot of San Paolo without the walls of Rome, destinated for the papal *camera*.[144] Another copy was reported in the above-mentioned inventory of the library of San Domenico at Bologna, datable before 1378.[145] Among the extant manuscripts, a copy transmitting Seneca's *Excerpta Controversiarum* with an apparatus of glosses based on Trevet's commentary (BML, Plut. 82.20) dates from about the middle of the fourteenth century.[146] A complete copy of the *Expositio* (BML, Plut. 25 sin.

The manuscript has been missing since 1988 or 1989. I am grateful to Stacy Chaney-Blankenship, Special Collections Librarian at OWU, for this information as well as for pictures of Gunsaulus's portrait (letter of 24/7/2020). I have not been able to trace the manuscript thus far.

[143]   U. WINTER, "Eine reskribierte Nicolaus Treveth-Handschrift in der Deutschen Staatsbibliothek Berlin", *Studien zum Buch- und Bibliothekswesen*, 6 (1988), pp. 29–33; EAD., *Die europäischen Handschriften der Bibliothek Diez*, Part 3, *Die Manuscripta Dieziana C.*, Wiesbaden, 1994, pp. 15–16.

[144]   "Item Expositiones fratris Nicolai Trevethe super libro De clamatione Lucii Arnei senatoris Corduensis, fuit ext. ad 1½ fl." (*Bibliothèques ecclésiastiques au tempts de la papauté d'Avignon*, I, 368.4, no 13, p. 239). Cf. D. INTERNULLO (*Ai margini dei giganti. La vita intellettuale dei romani nel Trecento (1305–1367 ca.)*, Rome, 2016, pp. 84–85), who argues that the list, beside the personal books of the abbot, also includes those that belonged to the abbey.

[145]   "Item declamationes Scenece cum glossis magistri Nicholai Traveth, ordinis Predicatorum et declamationes Quintiliani, in eodem volumine" (LAURENT, *Fabio Vigili*, p. 225, no. 315). None of the extant fourteenth-century copies of Trevet's commentary includes Quintilian. For dating of the inventory, see above, n. 55.

[146]   A. R. FANTONI, Entry no. 151, in *Seneca: una vicenda testuale*, ed. by T. DE ROBERTIS, G. RESTA, Florence, 2004 (exhibition catalogue, Biblioteca

6), written by six hands using Italian *littera textualis* and *cancelleresca*, should probably be dated to the second half of the fourteenth century and certainly before 1406. In that year it was given by the Franciscan friar, Tedaldo della Casa, whom we have already encountered among Trevet's later readers, to the convent of Santa Croce, Florence.[147] A paper copy, which is part of a multi-block manuscript, BNM, Lat. XI, 50 (= 3931), was purchased in 1443, in Venice, by Giovanni Marcanova († 1467), physician and professor of natural philosophy at the universities in Padua and Bologna.[148] The watermarks, however, allow its production to be antedated to the last quarter of the fourteenth century and to be localized in central or north-eastern Italy.[149]

Medicea Laurenziana), p. 407 (the scholar distinguishes three types of watermarks, attested in Lucca and Treviso, 1354–1357).

[147] See note on fol. 88ᵛ (seventh of the last quire): "Iste liber fuit ad usum fratris Thedaldi de Casa quem vivens assignavit armario fratrum minorum florentini conventus 1406." (cf. the ownership note of Santa Croce in the upper margin of fol. 1ʳ). The manuscript has been digitized: <http://mss.bmlonline.it/s.aspx?Id=AWOMq-0SI1A4r7GxMYGv&c=Nicolaus%20de%20Treveth%20super%20declamationes%20Senecae#/book> (last accessed 25/9/2021).

[148] The manuscript consists of three paper units: I (a binion consisting of outer parchment and inner paper bifolia, leaves unnumbered, referred here as ii–v, fols 1–171; Trevet's commentary); II (fols 172–210; quire of twenty bifolia, wanting the last leaf; the watermark, Briquet 6252, suggests Savoy, s. xiv²ᐟ⁴; *Excerpta Controvesiarum* of Seneca); III (fols 211–36; xiv³ᐟ⁴, dating based on the watermark, Briquet 3566; Cicero, *Tusculanae quaestiones*). The quire-register suggests two previous assemblages: (1) unit II (quire a) + unit I (quires b–n, s–z, without any lacuna); (2) unit II and I (at some point the order has been inverted) + unit III. Marcanova's ownership note, written in epigraphic capitals, dated 1443, is inscribed on fol. ivᵛ, belonging to unit I: "1443. Ioannes Marchanova artium et medicinae doctor p. s. pec. em. Venetiis" (followed by number "CXVII" in different ink). On fol. 236ᵛ, the last in unit III, another note, dated 1467, witnesses to the donation of "this book" to the canons regular of S. Giovanni in Verdara, outside the walls of Padua. On Marcanova's library, see L. Siɢʜɪɴᴏʟꜰɪ, "La biblioteca di Giovanni Marcanova", in *Collectanea variae doctrinae Leoni S. Olschki bibliopolae Florentino sexagenario obtulerunt Ludwig Bertalot [et al.]*, Munich, 1921, pp. 187–222; on the owner cf. D. Gɪᴏɴᴛᴀ, "Marcanova, Giovanni", *DBI*, 69 (2007), <https://www.treccani.it/enciclopedia/giovanni-marcanova_%28Dizionario-Biografico%29/> (last accessed 25/9/2021).

[149] The paper of unit I is distinguished by seven types of watermarks, of which I have been able to identify six: I (in two variants differing by width;

The other extant Italian manuscripts cannot be dated earlier than the end of the fourteenth century and more probably to the beginning of the fifteenth. That is the case with two parchment copies. The first (Pisa, Biblioteca Cathariniana, MS 155) includes Seneca's work with Trevet's commentary, and according to an early-modern ownership note it belonged to the library of the Dominican convent in Pisa.[150] The second (BAV, Arch. Cap. S. Pietro, C. 121) is a carefully decorated comprehensive miscellany of the works of Seneca the Younger (or believed to be his), which includes the *Excerpta Controversiarum* of Seneca the Elder, surrounded by Trevet's commentary (uncompleted, fols 141^r–150^v). In previous scholarship, the manuscript has tentatively been localized to Bologna and dated to the second half of the fourteenth century; yet it could have been decorated some time later, during the first decades of the fifteenth, just before it came into the possession of Cardinal Giordano Orsini († 1438).[151] The paper copy, part of a mul-

for the broader, see Briquet 8930); II (Briquet 7497, 7504); III (Briquet 788; Piccard-Online, no. 123463, 123520, 123531, 123552, 123537, 123651, cf. 123497); IV (fruit with two leaves, 90 mm high, the type is widely documented during the fourteenth century until the beginning of the fifteenth century, especially in northern Italy; none of examples provided by Briquet, 7345–79, presents the very same form and dimensions); V (cf. Briquet 13868 and Piccard-Online, no. 160219); VI (Briquet 7341). The attested dates of the quoted examples range between 1366 and 1410.

[150] The upper part of fol. 1^r has been badly damaged and later repaired. As a consequence the ownership note running in the upper margin is mostly lost, but it was still readable to the late-nineteenth-century cataloguer: "Hic liber est conventus S. Katherine de Pisis ex XIII banco ex parte meridionali" (C. VITELLI, "Index codicum latinorum qui Pisis in bybliotheca Conventus S. Catherinae et Universitatis adservantur", *Studi italiani di filologia classica*, 8 (1900), pp. 321–427, at 397). Today only the final three words can be partly read, the script could be dated to the sixteenth century. The copy is provided with Italian pen-flourished initials which are datable to the fifteenth century (I owe this dating to the expertise of Francesca Manzari).

[151] A detailed description is provided by E. PELLEGRIN, *Les manuscrits classiques latins de la Bibliothèque Vaticane*, vol. I, *Fonds Archivio San Pietro à Ottoboni*, Paris, 1975, pp. 30–35. Cf. C. BIANCA, "Dopo Costanza: classici e umanisti", in *Alle origini della nuova Roma. Martino V (1417–1431). Atti del convegno, Roma 2–5 marzo 1992*, Rome, 1992, pp. 85–100, at p. 99; C. RABEL, "Le Sénèque des ducs. Un cadeau lombard pour Jean de Berry", *Revue de l'art*, 135 (2002), pp. 7–22, at 12 and 20, n. 49. Digital reproduction is available in DigiVatLib: <https://digi.vatlib.it/view/MSS_Arch.Cap.S.Pietro.C.121> (last accessed 25/9/2021). The copy

ti-block manuscript (Assisi, Biblioteca e Centro di documentazione francescana del Sacro Convento, Fondo Antico, MS Assisi Com. 302), is also datable to the early fifteenth century.[152] As far as the gathered evidence permits us to go, the Italian circulation of this commentary within about a century of its composition and publication was concentrated in the central and north-eastern regions of Italy, with two transalpine copies imported to Lombardy and Sicily, the latter probably through the Aragon dominion.

In England, after the death of the dedicatee John Lenham, the source and provider of the text would have been Lenham's home convent — the most probable destination of the books of the departed friar — or Trevet himself. The earliest evidence, although it cannot be contextualized with confidence, hints that the English province of the Dominican order may have been involved in the publishing of the work. A manuscript kept today at the Biblioteca Medicea Laurenziana of Florence (Conv. soppr. 509), datable to the 1320s, is apparently the oldest among extant English copies.[153] It was probably through the mediation

could be identified with the entry in Orsini's will of 1434: "Item multa opera Senece" (C. S. CELENZA, "The will of Cardinal Giordano Orsini (ob. 1438)", *Traditio*, 51 (1996), pp. 257–86, at 281, section 31). Orsini may have not been the first owner of the manuscript. The dating of the decoration to the early fifteenth century has been suggested to me by Francesca Manzari.

[152]   The manuscript consists of three units, Trevet's commentary being transmitted in unit III (fols 239–73, three sexternions, the last wanting leaf 12). Although the unit has an in-folio format, I have not been able to identify the watermark occurring in most bifolia. Two bifolia of the last quire, however, are distinguished by two other types, one of which is close to Briquet 2641 (Reggio Emilia, 1427, 1432; Venice, 1430). Units I and II (fols 1–238) are made of the paper distinguished by a slightly smaller variant of the same type (close to Briquet 2640, Bologna, 1425). If the assembling of the two blocks took place in their area of origin, the copy would have been produced in north-eastern Italy (Emilia?), during the first half of the fifteenth century. A summary description is provided in Manus: <https://manus.iccu.sbn.it/opac_SchedaScheda.php?ID=235437> (based on Cenci's catalogue, published 25/11/2014, last accessed 25/9/2021); the manuscript has been digitized: < https://www.internetculturale.it/jmms/iccuviewer/iccu.jsp?id=oai%3Awww.internetculturale.sbn.it%2FTeca%3A20%3ANT0000%3APG0213_ms.302&mode=all&teca=MagTeca+-+ICCU> (last accessed 25/9/2021).

[153]   The non-Italian characteristics of the script, which indeed is a Northern *littera textualis*, have been noticed by G. POMARO ("Censimento", I, p. 453), while S. BIANCHI (entry no. 152 in *Seneca: una vicenda testuale*, pp. 408–09)

of English friars that the copy arrived at the convent of Santa Maria Novella in Florence, where it was reported in the inventory of 1489.[154] The origin of another early transalpine manuscript, Wolfenbüttel, Herzog August Bibliothek, Guelf. 171 Gud. lat., dated 4 August 1358 in a colophon, cannot be ascertained with confidence.[155] It confirms, however, the role that Dominican

was convinced of French influence in the style of painted initials. In fact, an oak leaf which incidentally appears in the vegetal decoration of the initial A (for *abdicato*) on fol. 77[vb], as well as ubiquitous red and green heart-shaped leaves growing directly from the initial's champ or at the tips of branches (see fols 1[r], 1[v], 20[v], 34[r], 40[v], 50[v], 67[r], 77[v], 88[v], 106[r], 116[r], 129[v]) are typically English. The latter form of vegetal decoration is close to that of BL, Harley 6563, datable to *c.* 1320–*c.* 1330, see L. FREEMAN SANDLER, *Gothic Manuscripts 1285–1385*, II, *Catalogue*, New York, NY, 1986 (A Survey of Manuscripts Illuminated in the British Isles, 5), no. 89, pp. 98–99 (description and digital reproduction also available at: <http://www.bl.uk/manuscripts/FullDisplay.aspx?ref=Harley_MS_6563>, last accessed 26/7/2021). I thank Lucy Freeman Sandler who has kindly inspected the images of the Florentine manuscript and confirmed my proposition.

[154]   "Declamationes Senece exposite secundum fratrem Nicholaum Trevet ordinis predicatorum; item M. T. C. de paradoxis, de senectute, de amicitia, de offitiis, et epithapia [*sic*] eiusdem" (POMARO, "Censimento", II, p. 331, no. 461). The part transmitting Cicero's works has been lost. The manuscript bears three ownership notes of the convent, on fol. II[v], followed by the table of contents (including Cicero's writings), attributed by POMARO ("Censimento", I, p. 454) to the librarian Dominicus Riccius († 1518), and two others, inscribed by the same hand in late rotunda, on fols 1[r] (upper margin) and 150[r]. Traces of another note above that of Riccius.

[155]   The manuscript was written by at least two book-hands using Northern *littera textualis* of varying quality of execution and including some cursive forms. Hand A (fols 1[ra]–8[rb], l. 10) is distinguished, among the other forms, by a two-compartment high *a* (used in the first lines, later replaced by one-compartment form) and *r* with detached shoulder connected by hair-line with the bottom of the minim (used alongside the regular *textualis* form). Hand B, which despite some variations seems to have been responsible for the rest of the copy (fols 8[rb], l. 10–75[vb]), is distinguished by an increasingly decomposed *ductus* and an *est*-abbreviation consisting of a 2-shaped sign with a comma underneath or similar forms displayed vertically (it alternates with the usual abbreviation consisting of *e* with the common mark of suspension). This kind of abbreviation is found in manuscripts from the Low Countries, see Utrecht, Universiteitsbibliotheek 375 (Utrecht, 1396, *Manuscrits datés conservés dans les Pays-Bas. Catalogue paléographique des manuscrits en écriture latine portant des indications de date*, II, *Les manuscrits d'origine néerlandaise (XIVe–XVIe siècles) et supplément au tome premier*, ed. by J. P. GUMBERT, Leiden, 1988,

channels played in the circulation of Trevet's work in northern
Europe some time after the author's death. In the said colophon,
an anonymous scribe described St Dominic as "our father".[156] It
has hitherto escaped the attention of scholarship that the manuscript only transmits a fragment of Trevet's work:[157] the dedicatory letter (fol. 1[ra-b]), the prologue (fol. 1[rb-vb]), the exposition of
Seneca's *Prohemium* (fols 1[vb]–9[ra]), and the very beginning of the
commentary on *Exc. Contr.* I, 1.[158] What follows is another commentary on the *Controversiae*, transmitted anonymously, with the
dedication to an unnamed addressee.[159] It certainly deserves closer

p. 205, no. 698, and pl. 627), cf. Den Haag, Koninklijke Bibliotheek 70 E
9 (1395, prov. Tongres; *ibid.*, p. 246, no. 918a, and pl. 963). Both hands use
(although not exclusively) as an abbreviation for *con-* and *cum-* an inverted *c*
in two strokes, the second developing alongside the baseline. This form was
more frequently used in German countries. On the two specific abbreviations
cf. DEROLEZ, *Palaeography of Gothic*, p. 97. The decoration is limited to initials in red ink with very simple pen-flourishing. I am grateful to Patrizia
Carmassi (Herzog August Bibliothek) for her help in verifying certain of
my observations made on seeing the original in September 2018 (letter of
7/6/2021).

[156] "Explicit exposicio declamacionum Senece completa anno domini M°
CCC° LVIII° in vigilia Dominici patris nostri. Amen." (fol. 75vb).

[157] See a short description provided in *Die Handschriften der Herzogli-
chen Bibliothek zu Wolfenbüttel*, 4, *Die Gudischen Handschriften*: *Die griechis-
chen Handschriften*, described by F. KÖHLER; *Die lateinischen Handschriften*,
described by G. MILCHSACK, Wolfenbüttel, 1913, p. 178; and the lists of the
witnesses of Trevet's commentary in DEAN, "Life and Works", p. 210, and
KAEPPELI, no. 3146.

[158] The last section reads: "Querere in istis declamacionibus artificiosam
divisionem videtur contra mentem auctoris qui supra in prologo se excusa-
vit de eo quod declamaciones non posuit secundum aliquem ordinem sed
sicut occurrebant. Unde quia memorie sue primo occurrebant declamaciones
Latronis ideo illas primo ponit in hoc primo libro et aliorum declamaciones in
sequentibus. Continet autem hic liber declamaciones VIII quarum prima est
de patruo nepotem abdicante quem prius adoptaverat" (fol. 9[ra-b], cf. Rawl. G.
186, fol. 5[rb-va]). On fols 1[v]–2[v], in addition to the exordial sections of Trevet's
commentary, the *textus* has been copied (*Contr.*, I Praef., 1–3). As a consequence the layout of those pages has been modified (*textus* in the middle of a
page in long lines, surrounded by the commentary in two columns).

[159] The dedication letter (fols 9[rb-va]), *inc.* "Appollinem circumsceptum [*pro*
circumseptum] musis admiratus", *des.* "vestro me subiciens examini eciam
correctioni aggredior opus mihi commendatum". Follows the commentary on
the Prohemium, *inc.* "Exigitis et cetera. Loquitur filiis suis Novato, Senece et

examination. Another partial witness, a very short excerpt, which is certainly English, but cannot be associated with the Dominican order, also belongs to the primary stage of reception. On the originally blank leaf following the previously discussed early-fourteenth-century copy of Trevet's commentary on the *Consolation*, a not much later hand added a passage from Trevet's commentary on the Preface to Seneca's *Controversiae*.[160]

The rest of the fourteenth-century English evidence is chronologically more distant from Trevet. BL, Royal 15 C. xii, is datable to the second half of the fourteenth century and belonged to a house of Austin canons, probably Bridlington priory.[161] The late fourteenth-century Peterhouse, 162 was bequeathed to the Cambridge college by its former master (1383–1397), John Newton, in 1414.[162] Since Newton held several dignities at York

Mele" (fol. 9[va]), and on the subsequent parts of the *Excerpta Controversiarum*, following the division in six books (contrary to that in ten, adopted by Trevet), ending: "Ita patet de toto opere declamacionum Senece quam potui clarius inserendo totum textum. Et quod vestre reverencie corrigendum videbitur corrigatis ad perfectum mee inperfectioni dictaminis inputantes" (fol. 75[vb]). After seven lines left blank follows the already cited colophon (n. 156).

160   Oxford, Bodleian Library, Auct. F. 6. 4, fol. 268[r]: "Cum multa ex me desideranda mihi [...] in quam prima senectus incurrit [= *lemma embedded in Trevet's commentary, cf. Seneca, Exc. Contr., Praef. 2, p. 1, ll. 9–13*] scilicet ut ipsam ledat [...] sunt subtilioris creacionis". For the corresponding passage of Trevet's commentary cf. Rawl. G. 186, fol. 2[rb], ll. 52–66. On the manuscript see above, n. 94.

161   According to the short description provided by the British Library online catalogue   <http://searcharchives.bl.uk/IAMS_VU2:LSCOP_BL:IAMS040-002107076> (last accessed 25/9/2021), the erased inscription that follows the colophon on fol. 147[vb] would have read: "Liber fratrum canonicorum sancti Augustini" (when consulting the original in August 2018 I could only read, with the help of an ultra-violet lamp, the ending "-tini"). The identification of its early owner with the priory at Bridlington is supported by the table of contents, partly erased, inscribed by an early-modern hand on fol. 1[v] (parchment flyleaf, not belonging to the first quire). At that time the copy of Seneca with Trevet's commentary was preceded by (1) Trevet's *Annales* and (2) "Appendix ad Cronico [*sic*] Trevetti incipiens a regno Edwardi de Carnarvan usque ad finem regni Edwardi 3[i] incerti sed videtur [*followed by one illegible word*] de Bredling [Bridlington *suggested by the catalogue*] innominati".

162   The manuscript bears the *ex-dono* note on fol. i[v] and has been identified with the entry in Newton's codicil of 30 June 1414: "Declamationes Senece cum glosa Nicholai Treuette super easdem in uno uolumine" (CLARKE,

minster from the 1390s onwards, his copy might have been made
from the lost or unidentified exemplar that had belonged to John
Erghome († after 1385), master regent and prior of the Austin
convent in York, and which was reported among the additions
to the catalogue of the Austins' library, begun in 1372.[163] Erghome's biography, so far as it is known,[164] opens room for speculation about further connections between his and other extant or
attested copies. The above-mentioned manuscript, Royal 15 C.
xii, of which the provenance was tentatively identified as Bridlington priory, could have been the parent of Erghome's copy.
The friar's family originated from and held lands in the East
Riding, in the near neighbourhood of the priory. Erghome authored a commentary on the so-called Bridlington Prophecy, which
originated at the house. The difficulty in establishing a close
dating for the Royal manuscript does not permit to say which
direction of transmission is more likely: whether the presumed
Bridlington copy would have been the model for Erghome's or
vice-versa. If Bridlington did not provide the exemplar, then a
strong candidate for the place where Erghome secured a copy
of Trevet's commentary is Bologna. By the time Erghome was
enrolled as a theology student there in 1380, Trevet's work had
already been reported in the oldest inventory of San Domenico
in the city. Oxford is a less forceful possibility, since the availability of Trevet's exposition there and, indeed, Erghome's edu-

---

The University and College Libraries of Cambridge, UC149. 9, p. 721; cf. above,
n. 96). For the description, see THOMSON, *Descriptive Catalogue*, p. 97.

[163] "Senece declamaciones cum exposicione Treueth" (K. W. HUMPHREYS,
The Friars' Libraries, London, 1990 (CBMLC, 1), p. 132, A8. 521; under the
heading "Libri magistri Johannis Erghom in Rethorica", *ibid.*, p. 131; a possible relation with Peterhouse, 162 is suggested by the editor). Humphreys was
convinced that "exposicio super declamaciones Senece", part of a Erghome's
miscellany reported in the same catalogue (pp. 70–71, A8. 293e), was also Trevet's, but this cannot be ascertained. The only other of Trevet's work reported
among Erghome's books is a set of "questiones" (p. 58, A8. 223k). Humphreys's
discussion of Erghome and his books (pp. xxix–xxx) is now superseded by
J. WILLOUGHBY, "John Erghome and the library of the Austin Friars of York",
in *Middle English Manuscripts and Their Legacies A Volume in Honour of Ian
Doyle*, ed. by C. Saunders, R. Lawrie, with L. Atkinson, Leiden–Boston, 2022
(Library of the Written Word, 102), pp. 96–117 (I am grateful to the author for
the opportunity of reading his contribution before publication).

[164] WILLOUGHBY, "John Erghome", pp. 98–100.

cation at the Oxford friary, are only logical assumptions, which are not corroborated by extant evidence. By way of contrast, another owner of an attested copy, William Reed, was certainly an Oxford man, fellow of Merton College in 1344 and still in 1357. In 1368 Reed was elevated to the bishopric of Chichester. In the indenture between him and two Merton fellows, probably of 1374, Reed bequeathed one hundred books to the college. The entry "tractatus T. Tryvet super declamaciones Senece et figuris deorum et ffabulis cum aliis 2° fo. *capta*", may be identified with our commentary, apparently accompanied by some other writings, which apparently were attributed to Trevet in that copy. The manuscript, if not lost, remains unidentified.[165]

At the current state of knowledge, it is not possible to give a conclusive answer to the question as to whether Trevet's commentary was originally published with or without the *textus*. Certain features of the early manuscript tradition would speak in favour of the latter proposition. First, five out of fourteen extant copies datable to within a century of the work's completion transmit the *Expositio* alone.[166] Two manuscripts in which the *textus* and the commentary belong to separate production units, mechanically united, should be considered jointly with the previous group.[167] Secondly, in seven remaining manuscripts, where the *textus* was part of the original design, the pattern according to which the two components were laid out varies remarkably. The most frequent layout has the *textus*, in larger script in the middle of the page, in one or two columns, surrounded by the commentary in smaller script.[168] This,

---

[165] THOMSON, *University and College Libraries of Oxford*, vol. 2, p. 858, UO49. 10. The editor tentatively identified the work following Trevet as Pierre Bersuire's *Ovidius moralizatus*. On the donor, see R. M. THOMSON, "William Reed, bishop of Chichester († 1385) — bibliophile?", in *The Study of Medieval Manuscripts of England: Festschrift in Honor of Richard W. Pfaff*, ed. by G. H. BROWN and L. E. VOIGTS, Tempe, AZ, 2010, pp. 281–93.

[166] Assisi 302; SBB-PK, Diez. C fol. 4; BML, Plut. 25 sin. 6; Madrid, BNE, 8212; and BnF, lat. 7798.

[167] BnF, lat. 16229 (see above, n. 114), and BNM, Lat. XI, 50 (3931) (see above, n. 148).

[168] The *textus* is copied in two columns (Powitz's scheme 6) in Oxford, Rawl. G. 186 (fols 1^r–32^r), in one column (Powitz's scheme 4) in BL, Royal 15 C. XII, and Toulouse, BM, MS 806.

together with the layout where the *textus* is copied in the middle of an opening and is surrounded by the commentary on three sides,[169] is also the least convenient for ensuring both components keep pace with one another. In fact, if the dimensions of the column(s) occupied by the *textus* were constant throughout the copy, the *textus* and the corresponding sections of the commentary could hardly keep together on the same page.[170] Peterhouse 162 inverts this pattern: the commentary is copied in two central columns while the large outer and bottom margins, sometimes also the inner, host the *textus*, copied in blocks in proximate to the respective expositions.[171] Pisa, Biblioteca Cathariniana, MS 155 has an unusual layout for a manuscript of moderate dimensions, the written space being 153 × 104 mm. The pages are ruled in four columns, measuring 20–21 mm. The *textus*, copied in slightly larger script, occupies columns a and c, and the commentary the parallel columns b and d. Since the *textus* is shorter, the commentary sometimes occupies all four columns. Two further layouts offer a better resolution between the two components. In BML, Conv. soppr. 509, the commentary is displayed in two columns. At the beginning of subsequent sections, the column of the commentary is indented to host the respective section of the *textus*, copied in larger script.[172] Finally, Bodleian, Rawl. G. 186, represents a case *sui*

---

[169] This is the case with BAV, Arch. Cap. S. Pietro, C.121. Powitz's scheme 2.

[170] In BL, Royal 15 C. xii, the dimensions of the *textus* column do not seem to change (100 × 73 mm, 16 written lines) until fol. 97^v where they begin to slightly decrease (89 × 58 mm, 14 written lines, on fol. 140^r, bearing the end of the *Exc. Contr.*). To illustrate the distance, the *Exc. Contr.* I, 1 begins on fol. 14^r, while the respective commentary runs on fols 11vb–13va; the *Exc. Contr.* X, 6 occupies fols 138^v–140^r, whereas the respective commentary is to be looked for on fols 146ra–147va.

[171] Apparently, both components were copied separately (the cursive script of the *textus* is more formal and in brighter ink), but, as suggested by the common pen-flourished decoration, they belong to the same project. The two hands responsible for the *textus* could be the same that copied the commentary.

[172] When necessary, the column is divided vertically by additional ruling to distinguish the space reserved to the *textus*. In case of longer partitions of the *textus*, the two components run in parallel sub-columns. The layout may be considered a variant of Powitz's scheme 8, see HOLTZ, "Glosse e commenti", p. 110 (scheme C2).

generis. As was observed by Ruth Dean, the *textus* has been copied twice: in the middle of the page but also intercalated, section by section, in the commentary.[173] All this variety speaks against there having been a pattern of laying out the commentary and *textus* in fixed form in the archetype or at the earliest stage of transmission.

However, the early dating of BML, Conv. soppr. 509, Rawl. G. 186 (where the *textus* alternating with the commentary must have derived from the exemplar), and Toulouse, BM, MS 806, shows that before about 1330 the commentary was already circulating together with the *textus*, either by authorial decision or by the initiative of a commissioner, or scribes, of individual copies. A careful collation of the early witnesses, which should cover the commentary, Senecan *lemmata* being part of it, and the *textus*, when copied in full, could perhaps supply an answer. Here I shall point out only one textual idiosyncrasy of Trevet's work: in Book Two the commentary first expounds *Exc. Contr.* II, 4 and then II, 3 (the inverted numbering is also reflected in the respective rubrics). As far as I have been able to check, this transposition is reflected in the *textus* in BML, Conv. soppr. 509 (fols 27vb–30ra);[174] Rawl. G. 186 (in the *textus* alternating with the commentary, fols 12vb–13rb, but not in that copied in the middle of the page, fol. 7$^{ra–b}$); Cathariniana 155 (fols 37ra–38^{rc}); and Toulouse 806 (fols 19^{v}–20^{r}). Three scenarios should be taken into consideration in future studies: either Trevet released the commentary together with the *textus* at his disposal, or the commissioners or scribes of certain early copies had access to the same tradition,[175] or they were careful enough to adjust the *textus*.

[173] DEAN, "Life and Works", p. 209.

[174] Already noticed by BIANCHI, entry no. 152, p. 409. The same variant has been brought to light by FANTONI (entry no. 151, p. 407) in BML, Plut. 82.20, transmitting an apparatus deriving from Trevet's commentary.

[175] The two most recent editions do not register this variance in the tradition of the *Controversiae*. However, the copy, which is transmitted in Unit II in BNM, Lat. XI, 50 (= 3931), fol. 178^{v}, certainly independent from the commentary (Unit I), confirms that it is found in the *recentiores*. The transposition is also present in BnF, lat. 16229 (fols 8vb–9ra), but since the two units transmitting Seneca's and Trevet's work share the origin, the *textus* may have been present in the exemplar.

Commentary on the *Tragedies* of Seneca the Younger

In the letter of Cardinal Niccolò da Prato, which has guided our discussion until now, the sender assumes multiple roles. Presenting himself first as a reader of Trevet's and therefore a witness to the friar's repute as a commentator of the authors of classical and Christian Antiquity, the cardinal also becomes the commissioner of a new work. In the final section of the letter, he requests that Trevet expound the *Tragedies* of Seneca, meaning the Younger. (At that time the works of father and son were still believed to have been composed by a single Seneca.) The cardinal's hope was that a commentary would be a help to him and to all those who were discouraged by the difficulties in Seneca's work.[176] Without much hesitation Trevet responded with a letter and a commentary. As early as the summer of 1317, a copy of his new work was purchased for the papal library. Guillaume de Labroue was reimbursed for a manuscript containing the *Tragedies* and an "expositio" on the same day, 31 July, that he was compensated for a copy of the commented *Declamationes*, as discussed above.[177] If we accept the dating of the letter of Niccolò da Prato as 1315 (14 April), the commission was fulfilled within about two years. Several extant manuscripts have transmitted the cardinal's letter and the friar's response at the head of the commentary.[178]

---

[176] "Tragediarum autem eiusdem memorandi viri [*i.e.* Senece *J. K.*] liber tantis est obscuritatibus plenus, tantis connexus latebris tantisque contextus et implexus fabellis, ut statim temptantem se legere obscuritate sua deterreat; quem, si facultas vobis suppetit, rogamus ut faciatis nobis domesticum et omnibus, qui tamquam teterrimum pelagus ipsum fugitant, natabilem perviumque reddatis" (FRANCESCHINI, *Il commento di Nicola Trevet*, p. 2).

[177] "Item pro libro tragediarum Senece cum exposicione empto pro domino nostro solvi eidem — XII lib. turonensium parvorum" (references as above, n. 117).

[178] The fullest account of the extant complete (or would-be complete) witnesses and their contents has been provided by M. PALMA, "Introduzione", in Nicola Trevet, *Commento alle* Troades *di Seneca*, ed. by M. PALMA, Rome, 1977, pp. xxv–xlv. Among thirty-six copies described by Palma, five include the two letters: Bologna, Biblioteca Universitaria, MS 1632 (lat. 851), fol. 1r; Burgo de Osma, Archivio-Biblioteca de la Santa Iglesia Catedral, 134, fol. 1r; BAV, Urb. lat. 355, fol. 3ra–va; BAV, Vat. lat. 7611, fol. 1ra–va; BnF, lat. 8034, fol. 1r. Cf. the following note.

Among thirty-six surviving witnesses of the commentary in its continuous form four can be dated with confidence to the first half of the fourteenth century.[179] They all transmit the text of the *Tragedies* together with Trevet's commentary. Two have been localized, with very good reasons, to Avignon, from a time not long after the work's composition. The sumptuous illumination in the first one, BAV, Urb. lat. 355, has been attributed in its entirety to the so-called *Liber Visionis Ezechielis* workshop, which operated in Avignon between 1315 and 1325. The same workshop was also responsible for the illumination of some parts of the second copy, BAV, Vat. lat. 1650.[180] This latter manuscript certainly belonged to the pope's library. It appears in the inventory compiled under Pope Urban V in 1369 (no. 358) and has been convincingly identified with the copy purchased on behalf of Pope John XXII in 1317.[181] Despite the common origin, the two copies present significant differences. In the textual tradition of Trevet's commentary, the editors have unanimously distinguished two families, usually referred to as α and β.[182] MS Urb. lat. 355 (V) transmits a generally correct

---

[179] There are many other copies of the *Tragedies* accompanied by *argumenta* and/or excerpts from Trevet's *Expositio*. These manuscripts may be found among the witnesses of the *Tragedies* listed in A. P. MacGregor, "The Manuscripts of Seneca's Tragedies: a handlist", in *Aufstieg und Niedergang der Römischen Welt. Geschichte und Kultur Roms im Spiegel der Neueren Forschung*, II, ed. by H. Temporini, W. Haase, Bd. 32, 2, *Principat. Sprache und Literatur*, ed. by W. Haase, Berlin, 1985, pp. 1134–1241. Many of those manuscripts in Italian collections have been described by Franceschini, "Glosse e commenti", pp. 56–105, and a selection, more recently (2004), in the catalogue *Seneca: una vicenda testuale*.

[180] Manzari, *La miniatura ad Avignone*, pp. 62–69 (on the workshop, see pp. 53–72). The digital reproductions of both manuscripts are available in the DigiVatLib repository: <https://digi.vatlib.it/view/MSS_Urb.lat.355>, <https://digi.vatlib.it/view/MSS_Vat.lat.1650> (last accessed 25/9/2021).

[181] M. Palma, "Note sulla storia di un codice di Seneca tragico col commento di Nicola Trevet (Vat. lat. 1650)", *IMU*, 16 (1973), pp. 317–22; cf. D. Williman, K. Corsano, *Early Provenances of Latin Manuscripts in the Vatican Library. Vaticani latini and Borghesiani*, Vatican City, 2002, p. 32.

[182] The expositions of individual *Tragedies* have been edited separately, beginning with the commentary on *Thyestes*, published by Franceschini in 1938 (see above, n. 10). The introduction to the most recent edition provides a helpful discussion of the achievements of the predecessors (Nicola Trevet, *Commento all'*Oedipus *di Seneca*, ed. by A. Lagioia, Bari, 2008, pp. xxiv–xxxii).

text of β and is the only witness of that family to have been commonly used by the editors for the reconstitution of Trevet's commentary.[183] It is also the oldest witness of the two letters, the presence or absence of which, however, is not a variant separating the two families. Last but not least, V transmits the most complete apparatus of illustrations as it was envisaged by the author, who at various points of his commentary referred to visual images.[184] The manuscript is known particularly for its full-page representation of a theatre, which is not announced by the commentary but corresponds with the description given at the beginning of the exposition of the first tragedy, *Hercules furens*.[185] MS Vat. lat. 1650 (P) combines the text of two families, first following α, then, from the commentary on *Troades* v. 703 (fol. 151ʳ) onwards, agreeing with β. Besides its complex stemmatical position it is also less careful in reprodu-

---

[183]   Besides Lagioia (see previous note) see PALMA, "Introduzione", p. lii.

[184]   On the illustrative programme and its variations across the tradition, see D. BLUME, M. HAFFNER, W. METZGER, *Sternbilder des Mittelalters und der Renaissance. Die Gemalte Himmel zwischen Wissenschaft und Phantasie*, vol. II: *1200–1500*, Part II.1. *Text und Katalog der Handschriften*, Berlin–Boston, 2016, pp. 107–08, and nos. 108–11 (pp. 709–24, the catalogue entries on Trevet manuscripts were prepared by W. Metzger, see *ibid.*, p. 10); and J. JIMÉNEZ LÓPEZ, *Materializar un manuscrito iluminado en la Italia del Trecento. El 'Comentario a las Tragedias de Séneca' de Nicholas Trevet (Salamanca, Biblioteca General Histórica, Ms. 2703)*, Salamanca, 2021, pp. 45–58.

[185]   The illustration occupies fol. 1ᵛ and is followed by another full-page illustration, showing the climate zones, on fol. 2ʳ (this one is referred to on fol. 52ʳᵃ). The two folios belong to a bifolium preceding another bifolium carrying the letters and then the quires transmitting the *Expositio* and the *Tragedies*, the first of which (quire III) has signature "a" (fol. 5ʳ). The description of the theatre is found on fol. 5ᵛᵇ (cf. the edition: *Nicolai Treveti Expositio Herculis furentis*, ed. by V. USSANI JR, Rome, 1959, p. 5, ll. 15–19). It seems to have escaped the attention of previous scholarship that in Vat. lat. 1650, the same definition of "theatre" (fol. 2ʳᵇ) is accompanied by a near-contemporary marginal annotation in red ink, which reads: "Theatrum describitur in principio huius quaterni". This rubric opens up two possibilities: either the manuscript originally opened with an illustration similar to that present in V, perhaps on an added support (currently the first quire is perfect), or the bifolium that is now found at the beginning of V was originally intended for Vat. lat. 1650. A sketch of a theatre is also found at the end of another early copy, London, Society of Antiquaries, MS 63 (family α), fol. 228ʳ, see BLUME, HAFFNER, METZGER, *Sternbilder des Mittelalters*, p. 722.

cing the text of the two families. P lacks the letters, although the commissioner is mentioned in the opening rubric on fol. 1ʳ. All the aforementioned qualities of V, together with the dedication scene representing a Dominican friar handing a book to a bishop in the historiated initial on fol. 5ʳᵃ, lead to the conclusion that the manuscript was made for the commissioner and dedicatee of the work, Cardinal Niccolò da Prato, as has been suggested by Francesca Manzari. In contrast, according to the same scholar, P would have been produced for sale.[186] However, the original supplier of the exemplar(s) to the artisans responsible for P may once again have been Niccolò da Prato.[187]

The two copies witness to very early publishing events. Yet, the textual evidence gathered by the editors of individual parts of the *Expositio* seems to necessitate that they were preceded by at least three lost copies, the hyperarchetypes of the two families, α and β, and the archetype of the entire tradition, conjectured on the basis of a small number of common errors. It has been observed that the text of the *Tragedies*, when copied together with the *Expositio*, differs from the Senecan *lemmata* in the commentary in a number of readings.[188] At the same

---

[186] Manzari, *La miniatura ad Avignone*, p. 64. Contrary to P, V presents numerous annotations by several medieval readers. One of them could have been the actual commissioner since was aware of the characteristics of the model, as is shown by an annotation in the outer margin of fol. 168ᵛ: "tale spacium fuit in exemplari constructio tamen perfecta et sensus plenus est". It refers to the lower part of col. a, left blank, after v. 173 of the *Octavia*, the *textus* continues on fol. 169ʳᵃ, while col. b hosts a part of the commentary corresponding to R. Junge, *Nicholas Trevet und die Octavia Praetexta. Editio princeps des mittelalterlichen Kommentars und Untersuchungen zum pseudosenecanischen Drama*, Padernborn–Munich–Vienna–Zürich, 1999, pp. 9, l. 24–10, l. 12. Cf. Busonero, "La mise-en-page", p. 462. Regrettably the handwriting of Niccolò da Prato has not been identified so far and therefore the gloss does not help to verify the hypothesis of da Prato's patronage and then ownership. On medieval users of V, see also C. M. Monti, entry no. 50, in *Vedere i Classici. L'illustrazione libraria dei testi antichi dall'età romana al tardo medioevo*, ed. by M. Buonocore, Rome, 1996 (exhibition catalogue, Biblioteca Apostolica Vaticana), p. 266.

[187] Cf. Palma, "Note", p. 318.

[188] In this paragraph I elaborate on the observations of Lagioia, "Introduzione", pp. xxxvi–xxxix, where references to previous scholarship may be found.

time, the Senecan text does not essentially differ across the
early manuscripts of the two families of the *Expositio*. Two
important conclusions have been drawn in previous scholarship.
First, the *Expositio* was released without the very text of the
Tragedies that had been commented on. Secondly, Seneca's text
was combined with the commentary for the first time in the
archetype of the extant tradition. This would explain the features of layout that are common to all the early manuscripts,
first among them the tendency not to differentiate the two textual components, which are usually copied in script of the same
style and size. Concurrently, the layout pattern applied in the
archetype did not exercise sufficient authority to stop scribes or
supervisors of the subsequent copies from introducing certain
variations. One might even suppose that in the archetype the
two components were copied one after the other and therefore
their further combination on the manuscript page was a scribal
decision. Generally, the *mise-en-page* in the extant early copies
oscillated between two main patterns: alternation of blocks of
textus and commentary within a column; and display of the two
in parallel columns.[189] Alessandro Lagioia has attributed to the
initiative of Cardinal Niccolò da Prato, or Simone d'Arezzo, a
learned member of the cardinal's household, the editorial operation of combining the commentary and the *Tragedies*, preceded
by the letters of commission and dedication, in the manuscript
that would have become the archetype of the entire tradition.[190]
It follows as a corollary that the author's copy and the copy of
the *Expositio* alone that was delivered to the commissioner (if
they were distinct copies) do not stand at the head of a separate transmission, or else that such a tradition was too weak to
leave any trace.

According to this reconstruction, Niccolò da Prato, relying on
his *familia* and the artisans available at Avignon, would have
been entirely responsible for the publication of the complete edi-

---

[189] For a detailed analysis of the layout in seven fourteenth-century copies, see BUSONERO, "La mise-en-page", esp. pp. 471–74.

[190] LAGIOIA, "Introduzione", pp. xxxviii–xxxix. A copy of the *Tragedies*
and Trevet's commentary appears in the previously cited will of Simone
d'Arezzo in 1338: "Item textus tragidiarum Senece cum scripto dicti fratris
Nicolay de Treveth" (PASQUI, "La biblioteca d'un notaro aretino", p. 254).

tion consisting of Trevet's *Expositio* with the *Tragedies* of Seneca. Such a scenario is plausible but not unproblematic. Most importantly, there is a possibility that the author's role did not end with the delivery of a copy of the *Expositio* to the dedicatee. In a very recent contribution, Jorge Jiménez López has proposed that the components of the illustrative apparatus that are only found in V must have been inserted by a person familiar with the work, most probably Trevet himself. The scholar goes so far as to ascribe to the author the original layout of the *Expositio* and the *Tragedies* and the supervision of V.[191] The authorial involvement in the production of V, posited by Jiménez López, does not take into full account the philological evidence turned up by previous scholarship. However, it does call for revisiting the textual variation as documented by the editors. Such a task is beyond the aims of the present study and therefore I shall point to only a few questions that I believe future research might profitably address.

The first concerns the variant readings that separate the two families. Are all of them necessarily scribal inventions or could at least some be due to authorial revision? The latter is likely to be the case with the variance in the commentary on the *Thyestes* v. 858, first documented in the apparatus of Ezio Franceschini's edition and recently brought to attention by Jorge Jiménez López, in regards to the constellations of Virgo and Libra.[192] For convenience, I shall offer the texts transmitted by the earliest witnesses of both families in a synoptic table, with the major differences highlighted in bold. The text of family α follows London, Society of Antiquaries, MS 63 (Soc), fols 45vb–46ra;[193] the variant readings of manuscripts Padua, Biblioteca Universitaria, 896 (T), fol. 58va, and P, fol. 57ra, are also provided. The text of family β follows V, fol. 52rb.

[191] Jiménez López, *Materializar un manuscrito*, pp. 33–58.

[192] *Il commento di Nicola Trevet al Tieste*, pp. 69, l. 27–70, l. 2; Jiménez López, *Materializar un manuscrito*, pp. 52–54, see also Blume, Haffner, Metzger, *Sternbilder des Mittelalters*, p. 722.

[193] I thank Jorge Jiménez López for sharing with me the pictures of selected pages of this manuscript.

α (Soc T P)	β (V)
Quinto de VII° signo quod est Libra **subdit dicens** et pondera iuste libre cadent. **Libra [libram** **TP] que** septimum signum est tenet hec Virgo astrea [astre *TP* astrea *T²*] merita hominum ponderans et Jovi [et J. *underlined* *TP*] presentans. **Hec duo signa lucent [*blank space of around* *eight characters, also in T, but* *not in P*] stellis [*s. om. P*] ut patet in subiecta figura.**	Quinto de VII° signo quod est Libra **dicit** et pondera iuste libre cadent. **Libra in qua** septimum signum est tenet hec Virgo astrea [hastrea *V¹*] merita hominum ponderans et Jovi presentans. **Tamen secundum descriptionem ymaginum quam faciunt astronomi moderni non Virgo tenet Libram sed alius quidam[194] ut in descriptione patet. Hec duo signa lucent XLIIII stellis ut patet in subiecta figura quarum XXV sunt in Virgine et XVIII in Libra.**

Beside the different ways of introducing the lemma and V's error "in qua" at the beginning, the main variation affects the latter part of the passage. By referring to the opinion of recent astronomers and giving exact numbers of stars belonging to each constellation, β offers a more comprehensive text. In α, not only is the position of "astronomi moderni" ignored, neither are the stars of the two constellations distinguished. In Soc and T, however, space has been reserved for the total number of stars. The scribe of the archetype of family α would have to have been extremely distracted to have omitted two such meaningful passages. No homoioteleuton or homoioarchon could ease this kind of error here. On the contrary, the α-text seems rather a self-sufficient version, subsequently developed into a more informative discourse which is transmitted in β. The textual variation finds a counterpart, though not a straightforward one, in the representation of the two zodiac signs. Among the copies of family α, T reserved blank space for the illustration, which was never executed; Soc offers a representation of Virgo as a female figure bearing fifteen golden discs, who holds Libra, a balance, distinguished by three stars, making eighteen stars in total. The iconography agrees with the α-text. P and V, instead, offer representations that reflect the opinions of "astronomi mod-

---

[194] Abbreviated as "qᵃdʳ", I adopt the reading provided by Franceschini.

erni", which, as has been mentioned, is only reported in V. In both manuscripts, Virgo is an independent, winged female figure, while Libra, in the form of a balance, is held by a distinct, male figure. The number of stars in P appears random (eighteen for Virgo and fourteen for Libra, the latter displayed on the holding figure alone). The numbers in V, twenty-five for Virgo and seventeen for Libra, come closer to those provided in the text.

This particular *locus* invites us to take into consideration a possibility that the families as distinguished by the editors may, in fact, be due only partly to scribal variation, but also reflect deliberate revision, made shortly after the release of the original version.[195] P helps us to catch sight of that moment. The work of copying would have begun from an exemplar transmitting the *Expositio* as originally delivered by Trevet and combined, probably under the supervision of the dedicatee, with the *Tragedies* (α). By the time production reached the commentary on the *Troades* (fol. 151ʳ), an exemplar of the revised text would have become available and copying was continued (by a new hand) from that new exemplar. The illustration would have been completed only when the texts had been copied to the end and, if so, the new textual model may have also become the iconographical one. This would explain the discrepancy between the description and the representation of Virgo and Libra in P.[196] The involvement of Trevet in the revision that resulted in the β-text is probable. There is no evidence that the author visited Avignon in that period to directly supervise the production of the archetype

---

[195] Similar to the *locus* discussed here is the case with an internal reference and a reference to an image in the commentary on *Hercules furens*: "De stellis Tauri habitum est carmine primo; Leo vero stellis XXXIIII lucet, ut in subiecta patet figura" (*Treveti Expositio Herculis furentis*, ed. by Ussani, p. 134, ll. 20–21). The passage is missing in the oldest witnesses of family α: Soc, T, and P (*ibid.*, apparatus). It is present in V (fol. 28ᵛᵃ), in which an image of Leo was also added in the lower margin below col. b (cf. Jiménez López, *Materializar un manuscrito*, p. 54). See also the variants separating the two families listed for the *Aganemnon* by P. Meloni, "Introduzione", in *Nicolai Treveti Expositio L. Annaei Senecae Agamemnonis*, ed. by P. Meloni, Palermo, 1961, p. xii; and the *Troades* by Palma, "Introduzione", pp. xlvi–xlviii (the same scholar, *ibid.*, p. liii, considers manuscripts Soc and T of the α family closer to the *usus scribendi* of Trevet).

[196] Cf. Blume, Haffner, Metzger, *Sternbilder des Mittelalters*, pp. 714–15.

of family β or its early descendant, V. It is possible, however, that the dedication letter was followed by a further epistolary exchange between the author and the dedicatee. Although Trevet's expectation, expressed in the letter of dedication, that his work be examined by Niccolò has the appearance of a commonplace,[197] the dedicatee may well have suggested some revision. The author, solicited or not, may also have communicated certain corrections and instructions, or allowed the cardinal to make editorial interventions.

Finally, the implications that the current views about the archetype have for the reconstruction of the geographical dissemination of the work, call for some brief consideration. If the entire tradition derived from the archetype established by Cardinal Niccolò da Prato at Avignon, it follows that the work was reintroduced to England from the Continent. The two early copies belonging to family α, Soc and T, have commonly been localized to England and dated to the first half of the fourteenth century. Of the two, I have only had the chance to examine T at first hand.[198]

In previous scholarship, the English origin of T has been deduced from the character of the Gothic script used by the two hands responsible for the text.[199] Wolfgang Metzker alone considered the English origin insufficiently proven. He vaguely pointed at French and Italian features and its Paduan provenance and suggested that the manuscript originated in southern France, in the milieu of the curia.[200] In fact, certain other features of T belong to English graphic and book culture more definitely than the Northern *littera textualis* used by the two scribes. First, a number of near contemporary marginalia are written in a tiny cursive,

---

[197] "Quam Dei adiutorio ad finem perductam vestre reverende discretionis examini presentandam transmitto" (*Il commento di Nicola Trevet al Tieste*, p. 4).

[198] The most comprehensive descriptions of the manuscript are provided (in chronological order) by PALMA, "Introduzione", pp. xxxiii–xxxiv; BUSONERO, "La mise-en-page", pp. 466–68; N. GIOVÈ MARCHIOLI, entry no. 31, in *Seneca: una vicenda testuale*, pp. 170–71; BLUME, HAFFNER, METZGER, *Sternbilder des Mittelalters*, no. 110 (pp. 718–20).

[199] PALMA, "Introduzione", pp. xxxiii–xxxiv, but GIOVÈ MARCHIOLI, entry no. 31, only considered the second hand to be of English origin.

[200] BLUME, HAFFNER, METZGER, *Sternbilder des Mittelalters*, pp. 718–19.

distinguished by bifurcated ascenders, frequent use of 6-shaped *s* at the beginning of words, as well as long *r* and high, two-compartment *a*, choices that characterize early Anglicana.[201] Secondly, within subsequent partitions of the work, columns are distinguished by letters.[202] Since they are subordinate to textual divisions and apparently written in the same ink, they were probably contextual with the copy. At this period column numbering is predominantly an English phenomenon.[203] Finally, the pen-flourished initials with infilling consisting of leaves on a hatched ground are also typically English.[204] We are relatively well informed about the later history of T. Based on the medieval but undated ownership inscriptions as well as the early-modern shelf-marks and a

---

[201]   See a rather high concentration of such annotations on fol. 70[r] (cited here in diplomatic transcription), beginning with "carm(en)" above col. a (this kind of running title is found across the manuscript), following with "n(ot)a difficile p(ro)blema" (inner margin), to which correspond a four-line diagram elaborating on "p(ro)blem(at)a" in the lower margin; and several individual words picked up from the main text and written in the margins, e.g. "tardus" and "loco" (inner margin). The latter sort of annotations, often consisting in expanding words that are abbreviated in the main text, is also found elsewhere in the manuscript. Another group of annotations in the Anglicana-like cursive provide tie-marks between the *textus* and the corresponding commentary, which due to varying patterns of display, sometimes are found on different pages, see e.g. fols 32[r] (inner margin), 65[r] (outer margin), 79[v] (inner margin), 109[v] (outer margin), and 142[v] (outer margin). On the variation of layout within T, see Busonero, "La mise-en-page", pp. 467–68, cf. 472–73. Despite some variation of ink and size all these annotations seem to be due to one hand.

[202]   For instance, the first twenty-two columns of the *Hercules furens* and the respective commentary, fols 1[vb]–7[ra], are signed "A–Y". Since in the middle of col. 7[ra] a new section begins, distinguished by rubric "Chorus. articulus 2. tragedie prime" (*inc.* "Turbine magno spes sollicite"), at col. 7[rb] the numbering restarts from "A". When a textual caesura occurs within a column the same column may be provided with two letters, see col. 32[ra], signed "S" in the upper margin, but the incipit of the commentary on carmen IX of the *Hercules furens* is distinguished by "A", written in the inner margin.

[203]   M. B. Parkes, "The provision of books", in *The History of the University of Oxford*, vol. 2, *Late Medieval Oxford*, ed. by J. I. Catto, T. A. R. Evans, Oxford, 1993, pp. 407–83, at 443–44, and P. Saenger, "The British Isles", pp. 84–85.

[204]   See e.g. T(ria), fol. 1[ra]; Q(uis), fol. 39[ra]; S(ecunda), fol. 39[rb]; T(ercia), fol. 65[rb]; Q(uarte), fol. 79[vb]; Q(uinta), fol. 109[va]; Q(uicumque), fol. 134[va]; S(exta), fol. 134[vb].

catalogue entry, previous scholarship has assigned the manuscript to the convent of Austin friars in Padua.[205] However, the inscription at the top of fol. 261v', which was once a pastedown and is therefore partly damaged, can be dated with some precision. It reads (in diplomatic transcription): "Iste liber e(st) magist(r)i Bonsem<blan>tis| de padua ord(in)is fr(atrum) her(emitarum) s(an)c(t)i aug<ustini>".[206] The owner can be identified with Bonsembiante, Austin friar, born into the renowned Paduan family of Badoer. The title of "magister" shows that the note was not made before Spring 1363, when Bonsembiante incepted as master of theology in Paris. The year of his death, 1369, provides the *terminus ante quem* of the acquisition of the book.[207] Considering the early dating of T and the age of the friar, born probably in or after 1328,[208] Bonsembiante could hardly be the first owner of this manuscript.

---

[205] The complementary accounts of the ownership evidence are offered by PALMA, "Introduzione", p. xxxiv; BILLANOVICH, "Il testo di Livio", pp. 97–98; and GIOVÈ MARCHIOLI, entry no. 31, p. 170.

[206] "This book belongs to Master Bonsemblans of Padua of the Order of Friars Hermits of Saint Augustine". BILLANOVICH, "Il testo di Livio", p. 97, has given portions of this inscription, without deciphering the name, and the two following notes in full: "p(r)ima bancha v(er)sus ortum", and "Conue(n)-t(us) pad(ue)" ("Padua" in Billanovich), and dated them all to the fourteenth century.

[207] On Bonsembiante see most recently R. MONETTI, "Il convento dei Santi Filippo e Giacomo all'Arena di Padova nel Trecento. *Studium*, comunità conventuale, circolazione di frati", in *Alberto da Padova e la cultura degli Agostiniani*, ed. by F. BOTTIN, Padua, 2014, pp. 19–73, at 40–41. Our manuscript may be added to the short list of books that belonged to Bonsembiante (which he often shared with his brother Bonaventura), which had first been established by the late Luciano GARGAN, "Libri di teologi Agostiniani a Padova nel Trecento", *Quaderni per la storia dell'Università di Padova*, 6 (1973), pp. 1–23, at 7–10.

[208] In March 1363 Bonsembiante, "bacchalarius Paris.", needed the pope's intervention to graduate early in theology in Paris. The supplication lists his lectureships held in the Order's *studia generalia* in Italy and states that he read the "Sentences" in Paris, he was therefore a "baccalaureus formatus". The document, however, is not clear about the reason he had to wait for inception ("tamen propter statuta sui Ord. et Universitatis Paris. oporteat eum adhuc amplius expectare facultatis theologice magistratum"). If it were his age that was the obstacle, Bonsembiante would have not reached thirty-five years by that time. The petition is printed in *Chartularium Universitatis Parisiensis*, ed. by H. DENIFLE, III, Paris, 1894, no. 1276, pp. 102–03; on the graduation of Austin friars, see E. YPMA, *La formation des professeurs*

He would have acquired it either in Paris (or on his way to or from Paris, for instance in Avignon),[209] or in the Veneto (as well as in Padua, he served as *lector* in Treviso and Venice).[210] The latter possibility could be supported by the fact that Trevet's commentary was known to the famous Paduan humanist, Albertino Mussato, before 1329. However, his short glosses in the margins of BAV, Vat. lat. 1769, do not provide sufficient proof that Mussato consulted T.[211] In any case, the rather short span of time that must have elapsed between the production of T and its acquisition by Badoer, together with the supposed continental and Avignonese origin of the archetype, lead to the conclusion that T was also produced on the Continent, perhaps by English scribes operating at Avignon.

The case of another early English witness of family α, Soc, is less clear. Its history remains unknown before its donation to the present keeper by George Allan in 1798.[212] However, a textually related copy, Philadelphia, University of Pennsylvania Library, MS Codex 77, is apparently also of English origin and

---

chez les Ermites de Saint-Augustin de 1256 à 1354. Un nouvel ordre à des débuts théologiques, Paris, 1956, pp. 81–123.

[209] Austin friars were granted allowances for books when sent to Paris (K. W. HUMPHREYS, *The Book Provisions of the Mediaeval Friars 1215–1400*, Amsterdam, 1964, pp. 68, 72).

[210] The price of "3 fior.", possibly followed by a name, perhaps "Jacobus", in the upper margin of fol. 35^r (the first of quire IV), may refer to the acquisition from the previous owner. The script is different from that of the ownership notes of "Jacobus quondam domini Zonis" in Padua, Biblioteca Universitaria, MS 1457, fol. 1^r, which later belonged to Bonsembiante and Bonaventura (see GARGAN, "Libri di teologi", p. 10; the book was worth six florins), and in MS 2175 from the same library (fol. 165^v).

[211] The glosses were first identified by Guido BILLANOVICH, who has also compared them with the editions of respective parts of the *Expositio* ("Abbozzi e postille del Mussato nel Vaticano lat. 1769", *IMU*, 28 (1985), pp. 7–35, at 16–18, 32), cf. Giuseppe BILLANOVICH, "Il testo di Livio", p. 98, and C. M. MONTI, "Il codice dei Girolamini e la tradizione medievale delle 'Tragedie' di Seneca", in Seneca, *Il teatro. Commentario*, ed. by M. CURSI, C. M. MONTI, A. PERRICCIOLI SAGGESE, Rome, 2018, pp. 39–57, at p. 46.

[212] BLUME, HAFFNER, METZGER, *Sternbilder des Mittelalters*, p. 724. As for origin, W. Metzker suggests a London workshop under French influence (*ibid.*, p. 722).

may be dated to the third quarter of the fourteenth century.[213] If
the Philadephia volume were to have been copied from Soc, the
latter would have been present in England by that time. If the
two manuscripts had a common ancestor, it might have been the
hyparchetype that is sometimes hypothesized as *codex interpositus*
between Soc and α.[214] That would open the possibility that Soc
was produced in England. The circulation of the work in the British Isles at that time is given support by the entry for Trevet
in Henry of Kirkestede's *Catalogus*, mentioned above, compiled at
Bury St Edmunds around the middle of the fourteenth century.
Kirkestede knew of three copies of the *Expositio*, kept in institutional libraries at Babwell (Suffolk, Franciscan friary), Brinkburn
(Northumberland, Augustinian priory), and Dunfermline (Fife,
Benedictine abbey).[215] It is impossible to ascertain whether they
also included the *Tragedies*. A careful examination of the extant
copies that transmit the *Expositio* alone should help in the assessment of yet another implication of the current views about the
archetype: that the authorial copy of the commentary alone did
not give rise to a separate line of tradition. All these questions
raised over the publication of Trevet's commentary on the *Tragedies* show that further work is needed to bring together the rich
and various results of previous scholarship.

Under the Patronage of the Cardinal and the Pope: Com-
mentaries on St Augustine's *City of God* and on Livy's *Ab urbe condita*

Irrespective of Trevet's involvement in the publication of the *Tragedies* commentary, his prompt answer to Niccolò da Prato's request

[213] For its textual characteristics, see PALMA, "Introduzione", p. lii
(cf. p. xxxvii, quoted under its former shelf-mark: Lat. 51). The description,
which expounds a summary one provided by the *Catalogue of Manuscripts in
the Libraries of the University of Pennsylvania to 1800*, ed. by N. P. ZACOUR
and R. HIRSCH, assisted by J. F. BENTON and W. E. MILLER, Philadelphia,
PA, 1965, p. 11 (s.v. Lat. 51), and reproduction are available online: <http://
hdl.library.upenn.edu/1017/d/medren/9915455993503681>   (last   accessed
25/9/2021).

[214] C. FOSSATI, "Introduzione", in Nicola Trevet, *Commento alla 'Phae-
dra' di Seneca*, ed. by C. FOSSATI, Florence, 2007, p. lxxix (*stemma codicum*);
LAGIOIA, "Introduzione", pp. xxviii–xxix.

[215] Henry of Kirkestede, *Catalogus*, no. 398.6, p. 365.

must have consolidated their relationship. The commission-dedication exchange between 1307 and 1317 is its best documented episode. In his letter, the cardinal refers to a long friendship with his confrere. However, it is not certain whether or how much such phrases as "memoria antiquate sodalitatis", "notitia experte probitatis", or "nexus sincere dilectionis" ("recollection of a long-standing companionship", "knowledge of proven uprightness", or "bond of sincere affection") denote a personal acquaintance.[216] Neither do we know enough about the chronology of Trevet's sojourns on the Continent or his itineraries to say whether their paths had ever crossed. After the delivery and publication of the commentary on the *Tragedies*, the cardinal had little time for further acts of patronage: he died on 27 April 1321. However — probably close in time to the Senecan project — Niccolò da Prato shared with Trevet his interest in yet another text of classical Antiquity. In the commentary on St Augustine's *De civitate Dei* (II 9), undated and devoid of dedication, Trevet states that he had searched in vain for Cicero's *De re publica*, referred to by Augustine, at the request of "dominus Hostiensis", that is Niccolò da Prato, cardinal bishop of Ostia.[217] The absence of "bone memorie", or similar expression, suggests that the cardinal was still alive when Trevet was writing

---

[216] "Licet quorumcumque studium, quos audimus ad opera virtuosa conari, ex caritatis officio nos delectet, potissime tamen fratrum, et eorum maxime, quorum in nobis perseverat sodalitatis iam antiquate memoria et probitatis experte notitia eos nobis nexu sincere dilectionis fecit adstrictos, mentem nostram in eiusmodi gaudio vehementiori letificat" (*Il commento di Nicola Trevet*, p. 1, ll. 4–11).

[217] The commentary is not yet available in a critical edition. I quote the passage from Oxford, Merton College, 256B, fol. 9[rb] (this and selected other witnesses are discussed in more detail in the following notes): "mencio fit de libris Ciceronis [*corr. from* -uonis] de re publica quos inveniri non potui licet eos aliquando diligenter quesierim ad rogatum domini Hostiensis". I have checked the passage in the following copies: Cambridge, Peterhouse, 75.2, fol. 2[ra–rb]; BAV, Arch. Cap. S. Pietro, D.203, fol. 42[v]; BAV, Ross. 34, fol. 7[va]; Oxford, Bodleian Library, Bodley 292, fol. 122[va]; Oxford, Merton College, 140, fol. 181[vb]; BnF, lat. 2075, fol. 118[rb] (this manuscript is only known to me through the reproduction, see below, n. 228); Rome, Archivum Generale Ordinis Praedicatorum (henceforth AGOP), XIV.3.28c (olim Ant. XIV.28c), fol. 76[va]; Toledo, Archivo y Biblioteca Capitulares, 13.1, fol. 3[vb]; Worcester, Cathedral Library, F. 154, fol. 171va. The most significant variant readings encountered in that sample are (1) the name of Cicero is omitted in Arch. Cap. S. Pietro, D.203, BnF, lat. 2075, Bodley 292; (2) BAV, Arch. Cap. S.

the commentary. At the same time, it is hard to believe that in his letter of commission (before 1316) Niccolò da Prato would not have mentioned that work of Trevet, had he known it existed or was in preparation.

So far no other connection between Trevet's exposition of the *City of God* and the cardinal's patronage has emerged. At the current state of research the context in which the commentary was composed escapes clear definition.[218] Apparently, it was prepared and published without the support of an individual patron who would have merited a dedication. In the prologue, Trevet refers to his confreres' insistence.[219] Also the way in which he recalls the work of Robert Kilwardby OP († 1279), who provided the *City of God* with some form of reading aid or aids, "dum in ordine nostro sacre doctrine intendebat", suggests that Dominican friars were the primary intended audience.[220] Being

---

Pietro, D.203, and Bodley 292 have "quandoque" instead of "aliquando"; (3) "ad rogatum d.h." has been omitted in Worcester F. 154.

[218] DEAN, "Life and Works", pp. 138–44, SMALLEY, *English Friars*, pp. 61–63; KAEPPELI, no. 3136; M. RINALDI, "'Tria genera theologiae': note sui commenti al 'De civitate Dei' di Agostino della prima metà del Trecento", in *Auctor et auctoritas in Latinis medii aevi litteris. Author and Authorship in Medieval Latin Literature. Proceedings of the VIth Congress of the International Medieval Latin Committee (Benevento–Naples, November 9–13, 2010)*, ed. by E. D'ANGELO, J. M. ZIOLKOWSKI, Florence, 2014, pp. 929–40.

[219] "Intencionis vero nostre est, fratrum meorum frequenti pulsatus instancia, hec impedimenta tollere et obscura huius lectoribus reddere clariora" (Merton 256B, fol. 2[ra]; "nostre" is also found in Peterhouse, 75.2; BL, Royal 14 C. XIII; Merton 140; BnF, lat. 2075, and AGOP, XIV.3.28c; but considering the singular "meorum", the reading "mee" is preferable, as transmitted in: BAV, Arch. Cap. S. Pietro, D. 203; BAV, Ross. 34; BL, Harley MS 4093; Bodley 292; and Toledo 13.1; the pronoun is omitted in Worcester F. 154; "lectionis" instead of "lectoribus" is found in Ross. 34 and Harley MS 4093).

[220] "When he directed efforts in the study of theology among our order". The entire passage is quoted by SMALLEY (*English Friars*, p. 62, n. 3) from Merton 256B, fol. 1[vb]. Whether the first-person plural pronoun should be intended as inclusive or as majestic plural depends on what we consider was Trevet's *usus scribendi* (cf. the manuscript variation in the passage quoted in the previous note). In any case, the readers' knowledge of the religious affiliation of both Kilwardby and Trevet was taken for granted. It could also be so because the author's Dominican affiliation was mentioned in what seems to be the original opening rubric of the work: "Incipit expositio hystoriarum

a selective commentary, focused on historical and mythological topics referred to by Augustine, the work is relatively short and, to the best of my knowledge, never copied with the *textus*.[221] It could therefore be distributed at relatively low cost among the friars or at the expense of interested external readers.

The earliest evidence for the work's circulation and reception leads first of all to Oxford-associated friars and secular clergy. Trevet's commentary was known by his two contemporary competitors in elucidating Augustine's work: Dominican Thomas Waleys, who commented on Books 1–10 (begun during his lectureship in Bologna, finished in 1332, in Avignon),[222] and Franciscan John

---

extranearum dictorumque poeticorum que tanguntur ab Augustino in libris de civitate dei facta per fratrem Nicolaum Treveth ordinis fratrum predicatorum". This rubric has been transmitted, with some variation, in the following manuscripts: Peterhouse 75.2, fol. 1[ra] ("ordinis predicatorum"); Ross. 34, fol. 1[r] (but omits "o.f.p."); Bodley 292, fol. 119[va] (but "ordinis minorum" sic!); Merton 256B, fol. 1[ra]; BnF, lat. 2075, fol. 113[ra] ("ordinis predicatorum"); and in Toledo 13.1, where it is copied at the end (fol. 30[va]), but only until "dei" (instead, no rubric is provided at the beginning, fol. 1[ra]).

[221] In the largest manuscripts known to me from my investigations, the work is contained in a number of leaves corresponding to a quinternion or in two sexternions. The first such is Cambridge, Peterhouse, 75.2, where Trevet's commentary occupies ten densely written leaves of the first sexternion (1[ra]–10[vb]). The sum of the height and the width of the written space on fol. 7[r] (the ruling being faint, the measurements are based on prickings) is 550 mm, with written lines ranging from 101 (col a) to 98 (col b), against eighty-eight prickings. The manuscript, of English origin, datable to the fourteenth century, was previously bound with what is MS 75.1. The latter has been tentatively identified with an entry in the 1418 catalogue of Peterhouse (CLARKE, *University and College Libraries of Cambridge*, UC48. 389, p. 530, on both cf. THOMSON, *Descriptive Catalogue Peterhouse*, p. 41). In Worcester Cathedral, F. 154 (514 mm, the number of written lines ranges from fifty-three to fifty-nine) the commentary occupies two sexternions (quires XV–XVI, the text ends on the recto of the last leaf). Cf. BL, Harley MS 4093 (223 mm), where eleven quaternions and one ternion were needed to host the commentary.

[222] DEAN, "Life and Works", pp. 145–52; SMALLEY, *English Friars*, pp. 88–100. The traditions of the two commentaries overlap. In certain manuscripts they were juxtaposed, as is the case with Merton 256B (see below n. 225). Numerous other manuscripts witness to an edition consisting of Waleys' commentary so far as X, 29 and part of Trevet's from X, 29 till the end, distinguished by rubrics (the meeting point presents some variation). This is, for instance, the case with BAV, Ross. 488 (<https://digi.vatlib.

Ridewall, who prepared his commentary in the 1330s.[223] The copies
that were used by the two friars have not been identified. The
extant English manuscripts that present early ownership marks
belonged to William Lynham († by July 1361), a fellow of Merton
College,[224] and to John de Grandisson († 1369), the Oxford-trai-
ned bishop of Exeter.[225] Another copy may have arrived at Wor-

---

it/view/MSS_Ross.488>, last accessed 25/9/2021), which by virtue of its decoration has been localized to Umbria and dated to the beginning of the fourteenth century (M. AMBROSETTI in *Catalogo dei codici miniati della Biblioteca
Vaticana*, vol. I. *I manoscritti Rossiani, 2. Ross. 416–1195*, ed. by di S. MADD-
ALO, with the collaboration of E. PONZI, Vatican City, 2014, pp. 794–96).
However, it must be dated after the completion of Waleys' commentary in
1332, or even after his release from the prison in Avignon, sometime between
1338 and 1342. DEAN ("Life and Works", pp. 150–51) attributes that edition to the Dominican authorities on the Continent and dates it after Waleys'
death, in the second half of the century. Among the earliest certainly dated
witnesses of that edition, BNCF, Conv. soppr. B. VII. 1277, was copied in Avignon, 23 January 1361, by Pelegrinus Spiker, a clerk from Utrecht, perhaps
for a Florentine friar Giovanni Camici OSM, who was its first owner (*Catalogo
di manoscritti filosofici nelle biblioteche italiane, 9, Firenze*, ed. by G. POMARO,
Florence, 1999, pp. 103–06). See also Rome, AGOP, XIV.3.28c, an elegant
manuscript of Italian (Tuscan?) origin datable to the turn of the fourteenth
and fifteenth centuries. It offers a part of the edition: Waleys' commentary
until X, 29 (fols 14[ra]–69[vb]) and Trevet's on X, 29–32 (fols 69[vb]–70[ra], the rest
of the leaf blank), together with the entirety of Trevet's work (fols 73[vb]–95[rb],
preceded by indexes, fols 71[ra]–73[vb]). Despite the fact that the caesura between
the two blocks of texts coincides with that between quires VI (quinternion)
and VII (sexternion wanting first leaf), and with apparent change in hand,
the homogeneity of the layout and decoration suggests common origin.

[223] SMALLEY, *English Friars*, pp. 109–10, and 121–32.

[224] Oxford, Merton College, 140 is a multi-block manuscript. Trevet's
commentary is transmitted as the only text of unit V, which consists of
two sexternions (fols 179–202). According to two near-contemporary medieval inscriptions on the front flyleaf, the book, apparently unbound ("hunc
librum [...] in quaternis"), was given by William Lynham to William Reed
(in exchange for other "libelli"), and finally left to Merton College. Their fel-
lowships overlapped between 1344 and 1349, the time when that exchange
would have taken place. It is not, however, totally certain that the flyleaf
originally belonged to this manuscript. See R. M. THOMSON, *A Descriptive
Catalogue of the Medieval Manuscripts of Merton College, Oxford*, Cambridge,
2009, pp. 110–11. On Reed, see above n. 165.

[225] Oxford, Merton College, 256B. The manuscripts contains commentaries on the *City of God* by Trevet (fols 1[ra]–72[vb]) and Waleys (fols 73[ra]–206[vb],
until VIII, 1). Despite an evident caesura (the sexternion which transmits

cester through the monks of the cathedral priory, many of whom had studied at Oxford.[226] Yet another early manuscript is found in East Anglia, among the books of Simon Bozoun, prior of Norwich

the end of Trevet has no catchword; Waleys begins on a quaternion, by a different hand, B, using a larger written space), the two textual units were produced by the same workshop. Indeed, the hand responsible for Trevet's commentary (hand A) also copied the larger part of Waleys', from fol. 87[va], l. 3, onwards. The intervention of hand A coincides with the use of sexternions (from fol. 89) and with a gradual reduction of the written space as if the scribe intended to harmonize Waleys' copy with Trevet's. The style of pen-flourished initials is also uniform in both sections. However, it is not certain whether they were bound together by Grandisson. On fol. v[v], which is a flyleaf, part of a parchment bifolium, the bishop wrote a short note only mentioning Trevet's commentary: "Exposicio fratris Nicholai Tryveth super Augustinum de civitate dei". What follows was added by another hand: "et postea fratris Thome Waleys eiusdem ordinis. [a capite] Iste liber quondam Johannis Episcopi Exon' assignatur alicui pauperi scolari Oxon' in theologia studenti in eius memoriam cuius erat. Et eo promoto vel decedente aliis sic studentibus relinquatur in aula de Merton' ad usum huius extunc perpetuo remansurus". That same hand, in the lower part of the same page, recorded the loan lent to John Gardener, Merton fellow c. 1382–1392 ("Traditur J. Gardener socio dicte aule illuc deferendus"). This allows the latter part of the previous note to be dated to the time after Grandisson's death, when the book arrived at Merton. On Grandisson and his books, see M. W. STEELE, 'A Study of the Books owned or used by John Grandisson, Bishop of Exeter (1327–1369)', unpublished DPhil diss., University of Oxford, 1994 (on our manuscript, see pp. 44–45). Contrary to THOMSON (Descriptive Catalogue of Merton College, pp. 197–98), who considered the script of the two hands to be French and the style of the initials to be Parisian, the decoration is English, whereas the two hands use rather undistinguished Northern littera textualis. According to N. R. KER (Medieval Manuscripts in British Libraries, III, Oxford, 1983, p. 659), the manuscript was written in England.

[226] Worcester Cathedral, F. 154 is a multi-text manuscript dated by the modern cataloguer to the end of the fourteenth century and bearing a near-contemporary ownership note for Worcester cathedral (R. M. THOMSON, A Descriptive Catalogue of the Medieval Manuscripts in Worcester Cathedral Library, Woodbridge, 2001, pp. 104–06, where there is also a detailed account of the contents). Frequent coincidence of structural, textual and graphical caesurae suggests that the manuscript was executed in instalments, though according to a similar pattern. This is also the case with Trevet's commentary, which occupies two quires (XV and XVI, fols 169–92, the text ends on fol. 192[rb], fol. 192[v] is blank) and is written by a hand that apparently does not appear elsewhere in the manuscript. However, the early assembly is confirmed by the medieval lists of contents in the front pastedown (Trevet is itemized as "extraccio quedam super Augustinum de Civitate dei 161 fo").

250 JAKUB KUJAWIŃSKI

cathedral (1344–1352).[227] By the middle of the century the commentary was also circulating across the Channel, in France and Italy, as witnessed by the extant or attested copies,[228] as well as

[227] BL, Royal 14 C. XIII (Bozoun's inscription in the upper margin of fol. 14[r], on fol. 13[va] a list of Bozoun's books, including ours, printed as B58 in R. Sharpe, J. P. Carley, R. M. Thomson, A. G. Watson, *English Benedictine Libraries. The Shorter Catalogues*, London, 1996 (CBMLC, 4), pp. 300–04, at p. 304, no. 29). Trevet's commentary is the last text of this miscellany of chronicles and travel descriptions, including the *Polychronicon* of Ranulf Higden OSB († 1364), in its short version, which ends at 1327 (cf. J. Taylor, *The Universal Chronicle of Ranulf Higden*, Oxford, 1966, pp. 96–97), and the recent Latin translation of Marco Polo by Francesco Pipino OP, made between 1302 and 1315 (see M. Zabbia, "Pipino, Francesco", *DBI*, 84 (2015), <https://www.treccani.it/enciclopedia/francesco-pipino_%28Dizionario-Biografico%29/>, last accessed 25/9/2021). The manuscript was apparently arranged in stages. That is suggested by several *caesurae*. The first sexternion (fols 3–13), which transmits the subject index to Higden, the prologue to same chronicle and the table of chapters of the *Expugnatio Hiberniae*, has not been included in medieval foliations or the numbering of quires. The two medieval foliations cover the current fols 14–195 (1–183) and 14–276 (1–263). One should also notice the tally of quires: "continet XIX quaternos de VIII fol." on fol. 165[v], coinciding with the end of Higden's chronicle, but in the middle of quire XIII (fols 158–68, the note is independent of the factual structure of thirteen sexternions, and should be intended as the sum of leaves: 19 × 8 = 152, fol. 165 was actually 152 according to the late medieval foliation) and the coincidence between the beginning of Trevet's commentary and the beginning of a new sexternion (fol. 276). However, the uniformity of script (perhaps due to one hand) and that of the layout (compare the written space on fol. 68[r], Higden's chronicle, of 278 × 150, fifty written lines, and fol. 281[v], Trevet's commentary, of 279 × 148, fifty written lines) reveals the different parts as belonging to the same evolving project, which by virtue of intrinsic and extrinsic features may be dated between 1327 and 1352. It would establish Bozoun's ownership of the copy of Trevet as well. The latter has been included in the table of contents written in an Anglicana hand on the former parchment flyleaf (fol. 1[v]): "Exposicio Trivet poemota [*sic*] et historie tracte in libro de Civitate dei .fo. [*the number added in different pen and ink but not much later*] .263.a.". Cf. M. B. Parkes, *English Cursive Book Hands 1250–1500*, Oxford, 1979, pl. 4 (ii), offering an image of part of fol. 236[r].

[228] The unit of BnF, lat. 2075, that transmits Trevet's commentary (fols 113[ra]–161[ra]), may be dated to around the middle or third quarter of the fourteenth century and localized to northern France, perhaps Paris, at least so far as the black-and-white reproduction allows us to go (<https://gallica.bnf.fr/ark:/12148/btv1b100366216/f. 229.item>, last accessed 25/9/2021). Toledo 13.1 was also produced about the same time in northern France or Flanders. The southern *littera textualis* of BAV, Ross. 34 suggests Italian

a supplement prepared by a Paris-trained Dominican friar of the Roman province, Jacopo Passavanti († 1357).[229]

Cardinal Niccolò's appreciation of Trevet's previous works and the commission of a new one, which was promptly satisfied, increased Trevet's visibility as an author, especially in the curial environment. The patronage of Pope John XXII can be seen as the most conspicuous consequence. In 1317 the pope became part of Trevet's publishing circle. As discussed above, in July of that year copies of the commentaries on the *Controversiae* and on the *Tragedies* were acquired for the papal library. Around the same time, on 18 January 1317 or 1318, the pope ordered his tax collector in England, Rigaud de Asserio, to provide for Trevet's expenses related to his ongoing work on the papal commission.[230] It is *communis opinio scolarium* that the papal allowance referred to the commentary on Books 1–10 and 20–30 of the *Ab urbe condita* of Livy,[231] one of the two of Trevet's works bearing a dedication to

---

origin, the decoration has not been executed (<https://digi.vatlib.it/view/MSS_Ross.34>, last accessed 25/9/2021). Finally, in 1347 an as yet unidentified copy was bequeathed by the Dominican friar and master at the *studium* in Bologna, Francesco de Belluno, to the convent of S. Niccolò in Treviso ("Item expositiones fratris nicolai trevec super augustinum de civitate dei", see C. Grimaldo, "Due inventari domenicani del sec. XIV", *Nuovo Archivio Veneto*, n.s. 36 (1918), pp. 129–80, at 151; the most recent contribution on his library is by S. Zanandrea, "Per Francesco de Belluno OP e la sua biblioteca", *AFP*, 71 (2001), pp. 301–10).

[229] The *Tractatus additionium in expositione quam fecit magister Nicolaus Treveth super librum Augustini De civitate Dei*, surviving in two manuscripts (the oldest being Rome, AGOP, XIV.3.28c, fols 1[ra]–9[ra]), has been convincingly attributed to Passavanti by T. Kaeppeli, "Opere latine attribuite a Jacopo Passavanti. Con un appendice sulle opere di Nicoluccio di Ascoli O.P.", *AFP*, 32 (1962), pp. 145–79, at 155–62.

[230] "Cum dilectus filius frater Nicolaus Trevetinus de ordine fratrum predicatorum, magister in theologia, de mandato nostro circa cuiusdam licteralis operis compositionem intendat, ecce nolentes opus ipsum, ad cuius perfectionem afficimur, ex defectu sumptuum intermicti quomodolibet vel differri, discretioni tue per apostolica scripta mandamus, quatinus eidem magistro presentes tibi licteras assignanti vel suo certo nuncio pro eodem, de pecunia camere nostre usque ad summam . . marcarum, necessarias tam factas quam faciendas pro opere memorato ministres expensas." (ed. in Ehrle, *Historia Bibliothecae*, p. 136).

[231] R. Dean, "The earliest known commentary on Livy is by Nicholas Trevet", *Medievalia and Humanistica*, 3 (1945), pp. 86–98, at 90–92; G. Cre-

Pope John XXII.[232] Indeed, the *explicit* formula transmitted in the most complete copy of the work (Lisbon, Biblioteca Nacional, IL 134 and 135) refers to the papal commission: "Et sic terminatur expositio viginti librorum Titi Livii quos biennali labore exposuit frater Nicholaus Treveth de ordine predicatorum, ex mandato et iussu sanctissimi patris et domini, domini Johannis pape XXII." (IL 135, fol. 223[rb]).[233] The acknowledgment of the papal order was a kind of dedication,[234] and the entire colophon should be considered as an authorial subscription. It also provides information about the time spent by the author on the task. Depending on the year of the letter, which was issued when the work was already in progress, the *Expositio* would have been completed in 1318 or 1319.

Expounding Livy was a novel idea — something that redounds to the credit of Pope John XXII and his entourage — and a pioneering endeavour, which required self-confidence in the commentator. Trevet's is the only commentary proper to have been written on the *Ab urbe condita* in the medieval period.[235] Such a

---

VATIN, "Dalle *fabulae* alle *historiae*: Nicola Trevet espone le Decadi liviane", in Reliquiarum servator: *il manoscritto Parigino latino 5690 e la storia di Roma nel Livio dei Colonna e di Francesco Petrarca*, ed. by M. CICCUTO, G. CREVATIN, E. FENZI, Pisa, 2012, pp. 59–116, at 83.

[232]   The other is the commentary on Genesis, which will be discussed in Part II.

[233]   "And so ends the commentary on twenty books of Titus Livius which at the commission and order of the most holy father and lord, lord Pope John XXII, Friar Nicholas Trevet, of the Order of Preachers, expounded in a two-year effort". The manuscript, of French origin, was illuminated by Maître de Jouvenel des Ursins, between 1462 and 1470. See *Inventário dos códices iluminados até 1500*, I, *Distrito de Lisboa*, ed. by I. VILARES CEPEDA, T. A. S. DUARTE FERREIRA, Lisbon, 1994, no. 435, p. 290, and the digital reproduction: <https://purl.pt/32215> (last accessed 25/9/2021). The copy was first introduced into Trevet-studies by R. Dean, in brief in the review of Franceschini's publications (see above, n. 11), p. 165, and by a more detailed discussion in "The earliest known commentary", pp. 87–90 (see above, n. 231). The scholar has observed, among other features, that the copy breaks at 30.44.6, and proposed two possible explanations, viz. that either Trevet's exemplar of Livy was incomplete or that the exemplar of the *Expositio* used by the scribe ended there.

[234]   CREVATIN, "Le dediche", p. 410.

[235]   See A. H. McDONALD, "Livius", in *Catalogus Translationum et Commentariorum. Mediaeval and Renaissance Latin Translations and Commentaries. Annotated Lists and Guides*, vol. 2, ed. by P. O. KRISTELLER, F. E. CRANZ,

work definitely had a more circumscribed audience than commentaries on the *Consolation* or the *City of God*. Moreover, the scholastic pattern of Trevet's *Expositio* and its extension, which covered the First and Third Decades alone (the Fourth, lost to general transmission, was to be recovered very soon), did not necessarily meet the expectations of every contemporary student of Livy, and especially later generations of students.[236] These circumstances, together with the dimensions of the work,[237] may explain the limited circulation — relative to the works of Trevet already discussed — of the Livy commentary.[238]

Washington, DC, 1971, pp. 331–48 (on Trevet, 340–42), "Addenda", in *ibid.*, vol. 3 (1976), pp. 445–49. The very idea of providing a historical work, which was not a school text, with an organic exposition was also far from usual, see J. KUJAWIŃSKI, "Commenting on historical writings in medieval Latin Europe: a reconnaissance", *Acta Poloniae Historica*, 112 (2015), pp. 159–200.

[236] On Trevet's approach see DEAN, "Earliest known commentary", pp. 94–98; L. VAN ACKER, "Nicolas Trevet et son interprétation de quelques passages de Tite-Live", *L'Antiquité Classique*, 31 (1962), pp. 252–57; and recent contributions of G. CREVATIN, among which the most comprehensive is "Dalle *fabulae* alle *historiae*". The commentary remains unprinted, except for a short fragment: Nikolaus Trevet, *Apparatus libri Titi Livi 'Ab urbe condita'* I.1–7.3, in C. WITTLIN, *Titus Livius, Ab Urbe condita I. 1–9. Ein mittellateinischer Kommentar und sechs romanische Übersetzungen und Kürzungen aus dem Mittelater*, Tübingen, 1970, pp. 2–27. For an updated and critical discussion of the circulation of individual decades of Livy in Trevet's times, see M. PETOLETTI, "Episodi per la fortuna di Livio nel Trecento", in *A primordio urbis: Un itinerario per studi liviani*, ed. by G. BALDO, L. BELTRAMINI, Turnhout, 2019, pp. 269–94.

[237] The two-volume copy at Lisbon consists of fols 1ra–280rb (IL. 134) and 1ra–223rb (IL. 135). The catalogue does not provide the collation or the measurements of the written space, but gives the number of lines in each of two columns as fifty-two and total dimensions 437 × 302 mm. Does the latter include the binding? Cf. the measurements that were provided to R. Dean by the Library ("Earliest known commentary", p. 88, n. 9): 380 × 260 mm (page) and 290 × 200 (written space).

[238] Besides the Lisbon two-volume set, the work has been transmitted in three copies, all partial or fragmentary. (1) SBB-PK, Lat. fol. 570 (Italy, probably Veneto, s. xv^{m}). Dating and localization is based on watermarks: of the two variants of three-mountains type, the second is similar to Piccard Online nos. 150305 and 150358 (Padua 1443–1444), more than Briquet 11728 (Verona 1443), as previously proposed. The commentary, misattributed to Paulus Spira de Colonia in the initial rubric, rewritten by a later hand on the erased original one, does not continue beyond Book 4 (fol. 144va, the cor-

The small number of extant or attested witnesses, some of which are of late date, does not mean a failed publication, however. The evidence at our disposal shows that the *Expositio* was delivered to its commissioner and that the pope's court acted as broker and promoter of the work. Three copies are attested in the inventories of the Avignon popes. The first, including Livy with Trevet's commentary, can be traced back to the first systematic inventory, made in 1369 under Urban V.[239] A distinct copy of Livy with Trevet's gloss and a copy of a part

responding locus in Lisbon, IL. 134, fol. 133[vb]). For a detailed discussion see McDONALD, "Addenda", pp. 446–47. This is the only witness out of the four that I have had the chance to study in the original. (2) Two folios, transmitting a fragment of the late-fourteenth-century copy of Book 3 of *Ab urbe condita* with Trevet's commentary, were used in the 1570s by an Oxford binder as pastedowns of the 1571 Cologne edition of Georgius Ederus, *Oeconomia Bibliorum*: London, Lambeth Palace Library, H890.E3 (olim 10.C.9). They have been identified and dated by N. R. KER, *Fragments of Medieval Manuscripts used as Pastedowns in Oxford Bindings with a Survey of Oxford Binding c. 1515–1620*, Oxford, 1954 (Oxford Bibliographical Society Publications, new ser., 5), p. 160, no. 1778, cf. p. 217. The script and pen-flourished initials suggest an English origin for the original book. (3) BnF, lat. 5745 (France, *s.* xiv; commentary on Books 1–10). T. KAEPPELI ("Une critique du commentaire de Nicolas Trevet sur le *De civitate Dei*", *AFP*, 29 (1959), pp. 200–05, at p. 200, n. 1), who first brought this witness to scholarly attention, believed the copy to be of Italian origin (perhaps meaning provenance), while VAN ACKER ("Nicolas Trevet", p. 253), attributed it to "une main italienne". Nevertheless, so far as we can go with the black-and-white reproduction available at Gallica (<https://gallica.bnf.fr/ark:/12148/btv1b9067771m>, last accessed 25/9/2021), it was copied by several hands using the Northern *littera textualis* with some cursive features. Regrettably, the decoration has not been completed. KAEPPELI (l. c.) has identified this manuscript with an entry in the inventory of the Visconti library of 1426 (A. 318).

[239] "Item liber Titi Livii glosatus, coopertus corio viridi, qui incipit in secundo folio in textu: *a deo*, et finit in textu penultimi folii: *ad trium*" (Ur 664, ed. by EHRLE, *Historia Bibliothecae*, p. 339). The comparison with the entries in the subsequent inventories of Gregory XI (1375) and in a fragmentary list of the books transported from Avignon to Peñiscola on behalf of Benedict XIII (undated, but probably from the end of 1409), all providing different but partly overlapping bibliological features, confirms that the unattributed gloss in Ur 664 would have been Trevet's. Cf. "Item in volumine signato per CCCXXXI Titus Livius ab Urbe condita cum glosa Nicolay Treveth" (Gr 832, ed. *ibid.*, p. 509), and "Titus Livius Ab urbe condita cum glosis N. Treveth in magno volumine copertus de viridi, et habet numerum CCCXXXI" (Bal 31, ed. by M.-H. JULLIEN DE POMMEROL, J. MONFRIN, *La*

of the commentary are attested at the beginning of the fifteenth century under Pope Benedict XIII.[240] The earliest witnesses
to the use or ownership of the *Expositio* concern persons
associated with Avignon during the pontificate of John XXII.
Landolfo Colonna († 1331) made extracts from Trevet's commentary in the margins of Book 1 and the beginning of Book
2 in his copy of Livy (BnF, lat. 5690).[241] Landolfo belonged
to a noble Roman family with many connections to the curia.
During the period when the *Expositio* was being composed, he
was domiciled mainly in Chartres, but in the 1320s he visited
Avignon often, for the last time in 1328–1329, before moving
to Rome later that year.[242] Giuseppe Billanovich posited that
Landolfo had access to the copy that belonged to Simone
d'Arezzo, frequently mentioned *familiaris* of Cardinal Niccolò
da Prato († 1321).[243] Simone's ownership is attested by his will
of 1338: "Item Titum Livium de ystoriis romanorum, cum

*Bibliothèque pontificale à Avignon et à Peñiscola pendant le Grand Schisme d'Oc-
cident et sa dispersion. Inventaires et concordances*, vol. I, Rome, 1991, p. 318).

[240] The first is listed in another lot of the books transported in 1409:
"Item Titus Livius et Trivet in pergameno cum postibus rubeis" (Bot 63,
ed. by JULLIEN DE POMMEROL, MONFRIN, *La Bibliothèque pontificale*, p. 312;
cf. Bup 418, *ibid.*, p. 223). The latter appears in the inventory of the personal
library and in the aforementioned undated list of transported books: "Item
Comentum Triveth super libros VI Tititi [*sic*] Livii, opertus de pargameno"
(Stu 60, ed. *ibid.*, p. 141), and "Item Commentum Triveth super libris VI Titi
Livii copertus de pergameno" (Bal 19, ed. *ibid.*, p. 317). The three copies
should probably be identified with the three entries in the inventory of the
"libraria maior" of the castle of Peñiscola, the residence of Benedict XIII:
"1007. Item Titus Livius de istoriis Romanorum glosatus, in magna forma.
1008. Item alius Titus Livius glosatus cum glosa N. Trevet. [...] 1010. Item
exposicio N. Travet super Titum Livium." (ed. by M. FAUCON, *La librairie des
papes d'Avignon. Sa formation, sa composition, ses catalogues (1316–1420)*, t. II,
Paris, 1887, p. 145; cf. JULLIEN DE POMMEROL, MONFRIN, *La Bibliothèque
pontificale*, pp. 339–40).

[241] See CREVATIN, "Dalle *fabulae* alle *historiae*", pp. 88–108, and the edition of the excerpts by EAD., "Expositio Titi Livi", in *Reliquiarum servator*,
pp. 117–73.

[242] M. MIGLIO, "Colonna, Landolfo", in *DBI*, 27 (1982), <https://www.trec-
cani.it/enciclopedia/landolfo-colonna_%28Dizionario-Biografico%29/> (last
accessed 25/9/2021).

[243] G. BILLANOVICH, "Dal Livio di Raterio (Laur. 63, 19) al Livio del
Petrarca (B.M., Harl. 2493)", *IMU*, 2 (1959), pp. 103–78, at 157.

expositione dicti fratris Nicolay".[244] His mediation is possible,
though not certain or necessary. After his patron's death in
1321, Simone left for Verona sometime between 1322 and 1326.
Landolfo, who dedicated his *Tractatus brevis de pontificali officio* to John XXII, might have been granted permission to consult the pope's copy.

The third protagonist, Pierre Bersuire, belongs to a younger
generation. First Franciscan friar, then Benedictine monk (Mail-
lezais), Bersuire was resident in Avignon from about 1320/25 to
c. 1350. He was a member of the household of Pierre des Prés
(Després), one of the cardinals created by John XXII. Bersuire
himself received his first benefice from that pope.[245] He composed his earliest works at Avignon. It was most probably during
the same period that he became acquainted with Trevet's commentary on Livy.[246] In his commented French translation of the
Ab urbe condita (including the Fourth Decade), made in Paris
during the 1350s at the command of King Jean le Bon, Bersuire used Trevet's commentary, more extensively than is suggested by an isolated reference to the "expositeur".[247]

The earliest evidence for the circulation and reception of Trevet's *Expositio* is concentrated clearly around the dedicatee, who
must have played an essential role in making the text available to
interested parties. Was he also responsible for laying out the commentary and Livy together in a complete edition, as has been sug-

---

[244]   Pasqui, "La biblioteca d'un notaro aretino", p. 253.

[245]   On the Avignon years of Bersuire, see C. Samaran, "Pierre Bersuire,
prieur de Saint-Éloi de Paris", in *Histoire littéraire de la France*, vol. 39, Paris,
1962, pp. 265–81.

[246]   C. Samaran ("Pierre Bersuire", p. 321) includes Trevet among the
sources of Bersuire's *Reductorium morale*, one of the works dating from the
Avignon period, without, however, providing the title.

[247]   J. Monfrin, "La traduction française de Tite-Live", section C in
Samaran, "Pierre Bersuire", pp. 358–414 (on the relation between Bersuire's
and Trevet's works see pp. 371–400, the reference to the "expositeur" quoted
on p. 371). Among various contributions by M.-H. Tesnière, see: "Les Déca-
des de Tite-Live traduites par Pierre Bersuire et la politique éditoriale de
Charles V", in *Quand la peinture était dans les livres. Mélanges en l'honneur de
François Avril à l'occasion de la remise du titre de docteur honoris causa de la
Freie Universität Berlin*, ed. by M. Hofmann, C. Zöhl, E. König, Turnhout–
Paris, 2007, pp. 345–51.

gested for Niccolò da Prato and the commentary on the *Tragedies*? The evidence concerning the Livy commentary provokes that question without allowing us to propose a satisfactory conclusion, at least at this stage. The copies attested around the papal curia, which is to say the item in late-fourteenth-century papal inventories, another from the times of Benedict XIII and the entry in Simone d'Arezzo's will, all refer to manuscripts including Livy's *Ab urbe condita* and Trevet's *apparatus*. Together with the dimensions of the commented work, this fact would suggest, as a logistically simpler solution, that Trevet delivered to the pope a copy of the commentary alone, which would have been teamed with Livy only in Avignon, laid out together in a manuscript destined for the pope's library. That edition would have been reproduced in a copy owned by Simone. The extant continental copies, two French and one Italian, which contain the commentary alone, would have either derived from the copy of the commentary as delivered to Avignon, or witnessed the decision of certain readers not to reproduce the *textus*.[248]

The late-fourteenth-century English fragment from Lambeth Palace Library, which uniquely among the extant witnesses transmits Livy with Trevet's commentary, none the less offers for consideration an alternative scenario. The two folios, which contain two consecutive textual portions, offer the unique possibility of comparing the *textus* and Trevet's *lemmata* for a fragment of Book 3.[249] Both agree in a number of more or less signi-

[248] G. Crevatin ("Dalle *fabulae* alle *historiae*", p. 119) has deduced from the separate tradition of the commentary on the First Decade, as witnessed in BnF, lat. 5745 and by Bersuire's use, also limited to the First Decade, that Trevet may have delivered his work to Avignon in two instalments. This hypothesis should be kept in consideration by future studies, but thus far it is supported by the Paris manuscript alone. Apparently, the scholarship on Bersuire used to refer to that copy of Trevet's commentary for comparison and therefore has only produced evidence for Bersuire's dependence on Trevet for the First Decade.

[249] For the basic information see above, n. 238. The *textus* and the commentary alternate in each of the two columns. The *textus* is copied by the same hand in a slightly larger script. Back pastedown, recto, *inc.* "<seda>ta alter enim consul" (commentary on Bk 3.1.4), *exp.* "quia is victor" (Bk 3.2.2). Back pastedown, verso, *inc.* "pacem Equis dederat" (Bk 3.2.2), *exp.* "ut prope violata" (commentary on Bk 3.2.6). Front pastedown, verso, *inc.* "id est violencia passi sint legati" (commentary on Bk 3.2.6), *exp.* "tamen non sustinu-

ficant errors,[250] such as: "ad eximplendum" for "ad explendum" (3.1.7);[251] "castra" (3.2.1);[252] "Quo" for "Q." (3.2.2);[253] "obesset" for "obsessus" (3.3.2); "proxime" for "proximi" (3.3.4; variant attested in the manuscript tradition); "timoris" for "timori" (3.3.5); and "in portis" for "portis" (3.3.5).[254] Instead, the *textus* and the commentary disagree in fewer and less significant readings.[255] As far as such a small sample may be indicative, it

ere Equi aciem romanam scilicet set cesserunt victi" (commentary on Bk 3.2.12). Front pastedown, recto, *inc.* "Pulsique cum in fines suos" (Bk 3.2.12), *exp.* "presidia id est auxilia militaria ad defencionem urbis" (commentary on Bk 3.3.5). I refer to the following edition: Titi Livii *Ab Vrbe Condita*, ed. by R. Seymour Conway, C. Flamstead Walters, vol. 1, Libri I–V, Oxford, 1914. Future studies could also try a comparison between the Livy-commentary and Trevet's *Historia ab orbe condito*, completed around 1327–1328, where Livy is often quoted: *verbatim*, paraphrased or abbreviated, probably not without the influence of the commentary.

[250] The readings of the *lemmata* in the commentary have been checked in the Paris (fols 68rb–69va), Berlin (fols 73rb–74va), and Lisbon (fols 64ra–65rb) manuscripts.

[251] Except for the Berlin copy, which has "ad implendum", reflecting the gloss following the lemma as transmitted by the Paris manuscript: "ad eximplendum id est p(er) implendum".

[252] "Castra" following "statiua habuit" is attested in certain manuscripts, but has been rejected by the editor. In the Lambeth fragment, the *textus* reads "statu uia habuit castra", where "statu uia" is evidently a scribal misreading.

[253] The initial of the name of Consul Quintus Fabius has been mistaken for a pronoun in both the *textus* and the commentary. The latter explains it as referring to the year: "quo, scilicet anno tercio post Ancium captum".

[254] When a respective passage from Livy is quoted in Trevet's *Historia*, the same variant readings are found: "castra", "timoris", "in portis" (AM 3486–3487, AUC 286–87, see BnF, lat. 16018, fol. 43v).

[255] More often the *textus* has errors where *lemmata* offer a correct or almost-correct reading. This is the case with omissions of individual words in the *textus*: "Fabio" ante "extra" (3.2.2); "die" post "crastino" (3.2.9); "reducitur" post "castra" (3.2.10); and of the variants: "utriusque" for "utrimque" (3.2.11; the Lisbon manuscripts reads "utrumque"), or "quidem" for "quod et" (3.2.11). In either of the last two cases abbreviation would have facilitated variance. Finally, in the commentary on Bk 3.2.2, the name of Consul Titus Quinctius (in Abl. "T. Quinctio", "T. Quincio" in the *textus* in the Lambeth fragment) has been misread as "T. Commucio" in the same witness. The error is also found in the Lisbon copy, but not in those from Paris and Berlin ("Quincio"), and it is also given as "Quincius" in the commentary on 3.2.7, in all four witnesses. The passages under consideration are not reflected in the *Historia*.

seems that the Livy transmitted by the Lambeth fragment corresponds to the version effectively commented on by Trevet. A
corollary, although not a necessary one, is that the copy of the
Expositio delivered to the pope may have also contained the *textus*. The costs of preparation involved in making such an edition
would also explain the allowance granted by the pope. Finally,
this scenario resonates with the proposition of Giuseppe Billanovich. Observing that Trevet's *lemmata* of the First Decade
reflect the Italian tradition, he suggested that the commentator
had been provided with an exemplar of Livy by one of the two
Italians at the papal court, Niccolò da Prato or Simone d'Arezzo.[256] It is tempting to think that the original book, from which
the Lambeth folios were taken and which apparently was present
at Oxford in the aftermath of the Dissolution, was a descendant
of an authorial copy.

Having presented the work to the dedicatee, Trevet did not
abandon Livy. He later used the work extensively in his Latin
universal chronicle. However, I am not aware of any witness to
his further involvement in the dissemination of the commentary.
The papal court, therefore, is the only documented environment
that was involved in the promotion of Trevet's *Expositio*. Since
all the attested readers and owners, except for the pope, eventually left Avignon — Landolfo Colonna and Simone for Italy,
Bersuire for Paris — the *Expositio* had a chance to become
known and circulate elsewhere. Landolfo is unlikely to have been
able to play any essential role. He died shortly after his depar-
ture from Avignon, in 1331. The fate of the Parisian Livy in the
years immediately following his death is unknown, but it was at
Avignon that Petrarch first consulted and eventually purchased
the book in 1351.[257] In any case, the manuscript only included
unattributed excerpts from Trevet's *apparatus* on the beginning

---

[256]   BILLANOVICH, "Il testo di Livio", p. 96.

[257]   On the history of the manuscript between the death of Landolfo Colonna and its acquisition by Petrarch, see G. BILLANOVICH, "Gli umanisti e
le cronache medioevali. Il 'Liber Pontificalis', le 'Decadi' di Tito Livio e il
primo umanesimo a Roma", *IMU*, 1 (1958), pp. 103–37, at 130–35 (the reading "1352" in Petrarch's note was later revised as "1351", see e.g. IDEM,
"La biblioteca papale salvò le storie di Livio", *Studi Petrarcheschi*, 3 (1986),
pp. 1–115, at 83).

of the First Decade. Simone d'Arezzo's copy was bequeathed to the Dominican convent in Arezzo in 1338.[258] Finally, the royal and courtly readers of Bersuire's translation in Paris, from 1358 onwards, benefited from the explanations borrowed from Trevet, referred to as "expositeur". It is beyond the scope of my study to follow the reception of the Livy commentary further. I shall restrict myself to discussing briefly the earliest datable episode that witnesses to the commentary's fortune outside the environment of the curia, albeit the context was perhaps one still under curial influence.

In 1373 Giovanni Boccaccio was hired by the commune of Florence to deliver public lectures on Dante's *Commedia*. He began on 18 October and continued, with interruptions, throughout the following year. In their written form, the *Esposizioni sopra la Comedia di Dante*, left unfinished in the author's draft, transmit sixty lectures, which would have been given by January 1374, and breaks at *Inferno* XVII 17. The allegorical exposition of *Canto* I bears an explicit reference to Trevet's commentary on Livy. Boccaccio, discussing the two meanings of the expression "in mezzo", says: "La seconda maniera del mezzo s'intende assai sovente ciò che si contiene intra due estremi, o infra la circunferenza del cerchio, sì come Niccolaio di Trevet, *Sopra'l Tito Livio*, dice che Arno è un fiume posto nel mezzo tra Fiesole e Arezzo".[259] Previous scholarship has rightly pointed to *Ab urbe condita* 22.2, where the river is mentioned in the context of Hannibal's

---

[258]   Little is known about the fate of the books of the Arezzo friary, see T. KAEPPELI, "Antiche biblioteche domenicane in Italia", *AFP*, 36 (1966), pp. 5–80, at 7.

[259]   Giovanni Boccaccio, *Esposizioni sopra la Comedia di Dante*, ed. by G. PADOAN, Verona, 1965 (Tutte le opere di Giovanni Boccaccio, 6), p. 67. "The second meaning of 'middle' is very commonly used to mean what is contained between two extremes or within the circumference of a circle, as when Nicholas Trevet says in his *On Titus Livius* that the Arno is a river located in the middle between Fiesole and Arezzo" (*Boccaccio's Expositions on Dante's* Comedy, translated, with introduction and notes, by M. PAPIO, Toronto–Buffalo–London, 2009, p. 90). On the chronology of the lectures and their written circulation, see L. AZZETTA, "Il culto di Dante", in *Boccaccio*, ed. by M. FIORILLA, I. IOCCA, Rome, 2021, pp. 313–33, at 324–31. I owe to Valentina Rovere the knowledge of these latter two contributions.

campaign during the Second Punic War.[260] Boccaccio's reference is puzzling, however. A comparison with the only copy transmitting the commentary on the Third Decade shows that it is not a quotation. Boccaccio seems to have mentally combined here the Livian references to Arno (22.2) and to the "campi Etrusci", localized by the Roman author between Arezzo and Fiesole (22.3). Both Livian passages have been included by Trevet in his commentary (with the usual modifications of word order), as we read in Lisbon, IL. 135 (the passages deriving from Livy are here underlined):

"Hanibal profectus ex hibernis, id est hyemalibus stationibus, quia iam fama erat Flaminum [*sic*] consulem prevenisse [*sic pro* pervenisse] Aretium, nomen urbis est, cum iter aliud longius onderetur [*sic pro* ostenderetur], scilicet Hanibali, ceterum, id est sed, commodius petit viam propiorem per paludem quam Sarnos fluvius inundaverat per eos dies magis solito. De hoc fluvio dicit poeta. Et qui [*sic pro* que] rigat equora Sarnos" (fol. 26[vb], on 22.2.1–2) [...] "Quarto, cum dicit regio, describit felicitatem [*sic pro* fertilitatem?] regionis ubi erat Hanibal dicens: regio campi Etrusci qui inter Fesulas Aretiumque iacet [*sic pro* iacent], ad quam iam venerat Hanibal" (fol. 27[rb], on 22.3.3).[261]

Boccaccio generously ascribes to Trevet wha t actually could have been deduced from Livy. The reference comes as even more of a surprise, since the friar was perpetuating the frequent confusion between the rivers of Arno, in Tuscany, and Sarno, in Campania, as shown by both the spelling and the quotation of Vergil's verse on Sarno. (Trevet will continue to use the spelling "Sar-

---

[260] Padoan's commentary at pp. 790–91, n. 62, with references to previous studies. The editor also refers to the copy from Lisbon, without providing the corresponding passage of the commentary or the folio reference.

[261] "Having left the winter quarters (that is, winter garrisons), Hannibal — for it was already known that Consul Flaminius had reached Arezzo, [which] is the name of a city — when another way was shown to be longer (that is, to Hannibal), yet (that is, but) more convenient, took a faster way through the marsh, which in those days the river Sarnos inundated to more than the usual degree. The Poet says about that river: 'and the plains which the Sarnos waters' [on Livy 22.2.1–2, cf. *Aeneis* VII, 738] [...] Fourthly, when he says region, he describes the good fortune [*in error, perhaps for* fertility] of the region where Hannibal was, saying: the region, the Etruscan plains, which are placed between Fiesole and Arezzo, where Hannibal had already arrived" [on Livy 22.2.3].

nus" when reproducing Livy's passage in the universal chronicle in the late 1320s.) Boccaccio, instead, was well aware of the
distinction.[262] (So too was a late-fourteenth-century anonymous
reader of Trevet's *Historia*, who called upon Boccaccio's authority to correct Trevet.[263]) Only a limited survey has been done so
far as to the use of Trevet's commentary on Livy in other compositions by Boccaccio, and the results remain unconclusive.[264]
Should future studies on Boccaccio's sources prove a more extensive and pointed use of Trevet's commentary, the question of the
supply of copies will need to be addressed. The extracts made
by Landolfo in a copy subsequently owned by Petrarch do not
reach Book 22. There are two possible sources for Boccaccio's
acquaintance with the commentary: Avignon once again, which
he visited twice as a Florentine ambassador in 1354 and 1365,[265]
or the Arezzo friary, the depositary of Simone's copy.[266]

*

I shall offer comprehensive conclusions on Trevet's publishing in
Part II of this study and will here limit myself to a few consid-

---

[262] See G. Brugnoli, "Sarno", in *Enciclopedia Dantesca*, Rome, 1970,
<https://www.treccani.it/enciclopedia/sarno%28Enciclopedia-Dantesca%29/>
(last accessed 25/9/2021), and V. Rovere, "Una copia del perduto autografo
del *De montibus* e la costituzione del testo critico", *Studi sul Boccaccio*, 49
(2021), pp. 101–43, at 137.

[263] "Nota quod fluvius iste Hanibali infestus non Sarnus sed Arnus dici-
tur et currit per medium Florencie usque in Pisas ut dicit Jo. Boctaci'"
(BL, Royal 13 B. xvi, fol. 193^v, lower margin; the abbreviation sign above
"Boctaci" is a long stroke, different from the ordinary 9-shaped abbreviation
for -*us*, used by the glossator; the annotation is not accompanied by any tie-
mark, but it must refer to: "Hannibal ex hibernis profectus audivit consulem
Flaminium Arecium prevenisse propioremque viam elegit per paludem quam
fluvius Sarnus magis solito inundabat" (the same folio, lines 25–27). The reference would be to the entry "Arnus" in Boccaccio's *De montibus* (V), where
both the episode of the Punic War and the course of the river are discussed,
rather than to *De casibus* V, 10. The manuscript of *Historia* is apparently of
southern French origin and datable during the second half of the fourteenth
century.

[264] L. Van Acker, "L'œuvre latin de Boccace et Nicolas Trevet", *L'Antiquité Classique*, 33 (1964), pp. 414–18.

[265] V. Branca, *Boccaccio. The Man and His Works*, trans. By R. Monges,
New York, NY, 1976, pp. 100–01, 150–53.

[266] Cf. Billanovich, "Dal Livio di Raterio", p. 157.

erations concerning the group of texts discussed in the first part. Among the five commentaries under examination, four were written at the request of, and dedicated to, individual readers, namely the commentaries on Boethius, the Senecas, and Livy. However, in two of those, Boethius and Seneca the Elder, and in the undedicated commentary on the *City of God*, Trevet more or less explicitly pointed to Dominican friars as his primary target audience. Did he intend the three works to be published within the order? Or was he induced to emphasize the Dominican audience in response to the order's efforts to control the works that could be circulated among non-Dominicans? It may be of some significance that Trevet did not consider it necessary to refer to a Dominican readership when introducing the commentaries on *Tragedies* and *Ab urbe condita*. Having been commissioned by, respectively, the dean of the college of cardinals and the pope, they did not need any further justification.[267] Whatever Trevet's original intentions and his ideas about the range of circulation, the five commentaries very quickly, in his own lifetime, reached the hands of several non-Dominican readers. Parties other than Trevet who were involved in the publishing of his works definitely contributed to that outreach.

In previous scholarship the role of the patronage of Cardinal Niccolò da Prato has been illustrated and emphasized many times in relation to Trevet's commentaries on classical authors. The cardinal has emerged from the present discussion as an even better documented member of the publishing circle for Trevet's commentaries on the texts of classical and Christian Antiquity. He assumed manifold roles: from reader of the Boethius commentary, to solicitor of a copy of the exposition of the *Controversiae*, to commissioner and probably also publisher of the commentary on the *Tragedies*. I have deduced from a passage in the commentary on the *City of God* that exchanges between Trevet and the prelate were more frequent and that the cardinal stimulated Trevet's studies on classical authors. There is sufficient evidence to assign to Niccolò da Prato an essential role in the promotion or even supply of those commentaries in the milieu of the curia.

---

[267] It was Niccolò da Prato who in the letter of commission alluded to a collective (but not Dominican) benefit of the requested commentary, see above, n. 176.

Certain witnesses have already been documented in previous studies: the copies of the Senecan commentaries acquired by Pope
John XXII in 1317 or the body of Trevet's commentaries present
among the books of the cardinal's *familiaris*, Simone d'Arezzo.
Giuseppe Billanovich deduced from the absence of Trevet's commentaries in Niccolò da Prato's will that the works by Trevet
that appear in the will of Simone had belonged to the cardinal.[268]
However, Niccolò's will, which Simone drafted (he is not named
as an executor), referred *en masse* to the cardinal's books that
were bequeathed to the Dominican convent in Prato ("omnes
libros nostros") and only listed the eleven that were destined to
go to other recipients.[269] It is plausible that Trevet's commentaries formerly owned by the cardinal ended up at the Prato friary,
while Simone had his own copies, some of them probably made
from his patron's exemplars. I posit that Cardinal Guillaume de
Pierre Godin should be added to that duo of early readers of
Trevet associated with Cardinal da Prato.

   Pope John XXII, who was apparently introduced to the early
Trevet commentaries by Niccolò da Prato, soon assumed the role
of commissioner (and perhaps editor) of the Livy commentary,
and therefore should also be considered part of Trevet's publishing circle. Within a short period of time that commentary had
become known to at least three Avignon residents or visitors:
Simone d'Arezzo, Landolfo Colonna, and Pierre Bersuire. The
pope and the papal library may have also contributed to the circulation of previously published commentaries, as suggested by
Arnaud de Verdale's ownership of the *Consolation* commentary.
Whatever the effective roles of Cardinal Niccolò da Prato and
Pope John XXII might have been, Avignon — that is, the papal
court, the cardinals' households, the Dominican friary and, not
least, stationers' workshops — was already an important centre
for the publication and dissemination of Trevet's works in the
author's own lifetime.

---

[268]   BILLANOVICH, "Dal Livio di Raterio" (1959), pp. 155–56; still maintained in 1986, ID., "La biblioteca papale", pp. 47–48.

[269]   PELLEGRINI, "La biblioteca di Niccolò da Prato", pp. 244–46, 255.
Niccolò's will has been edited by A. PARAVICINI BAGLIANI, *I testamenti dei
cardinali del Duecento*, Rome, 1980, pp. 427–37.

Two other centres are also well documented. The role of Oxford, the Dominican friary and the university, depended on Trevet's position as regent master, at least in part. The self-reference in a quodlibet demonstrates that his scholarly functions gave him an opportunity to use and promote his works in a teaching context. The contemporary (or near-contemporary) Oxford-related readers seem to have been mostly interested in the commentaries on the *Consolation* and the *City of God*. We find among them Trevet's confreres, William D'Eyncourt, Thomas Waleys, and perhaps Robert Holcot, and secular clerks, such as John Cobbledik and John de Grandisson, whose copies ended up at Oriel and Merton Colleges, respectively, and William Wheteley. Trevet may have relied on the support of the English province of the Dominican order to some extent. This is suggested by the early English copy of the commentary on the *Controversiae*, later found in the Dominican convent in Florence. Central and northern Italy is the third area for the early dissemination of the commentaries under examination. The evidence at our disposal does not allow us to identify a specific place or institution that would have played a role comparable with that of Avignon or Oxford. Dominican convents and *studia* in Bologna and Florence, with their connections to the surrounding religious and secular environments, are certainly good candidates. The discussion of the remainder of Trevet's legacy in Part II will add more details, and complexities, to this picture.

Alongside the circulation of copies and extension of readership, the history of the publishing of our commentaries has one more dimension. Beginning with Cardinal da Prato's letter, originally private, but published together with the commentary on the *Tragedies*, we observe the rise of Trevet's repute as the "Commentator" of the authors of classical and Christian Antiquity. Although seldom all together, those commentaries reappear in groups in a number of contemporary book collections. The pairing of Boethius and Seneca the Elder was owned by Cardinal Godin. The commentaries on Seneca the father and son were jointly acquired for Pope John XXII, who probably also secured a copy of the Boethius commentary, attested in the later Avignon inventory. Simone d'Arezzo had the entire set of the four commentaries, on Boethius, the two Senecas and Livy, plus *De officio misse*, dedicated to the bishop of Bath and Wells, which will be discussed in Part II. Alberico da Rosciate owned the commentaries on the *Consolation*, the *Controversiae*, and the *Tragedies*.[270]

The corpus of classical and patristic commentaries of Trevet seems to have developed into a sort of bibliographical canon by the middle of the fourteenth century. The author only timidly contributed to its formation himself by rare cross-references.[271] The credit should rather be given to his patrons and early readers. Two instances of medieval bibliography, datable respectively to around the middle and the second half of the fourteenth century, witness to the effects of that process. In Verona, Guglielmo de Pastrengo (*c.* 1290–1362), including Trevet in his *De viris illustribus*, applauded four out of our five commentaries, all except the exposition of the *City of God*, and only one of Trevet's other works, the commentary on the Psalms.[272] The second witness is more informal but not less significant. Manuscript IV.D.47 of the National Library in Naples transmits Seneca's *Tragedies* with abundant glosses, written by the same hand, declared to have been taken from Trevet's commentary: "Explicit apparatus editus et compositus super hoc libro Tragediarum Senece decem per virum eminentis et profundi ingenii, fratrem Nicolaum Altraveth

---

[270] CREMASCHI, "Contributo", pp. 99–100, nos 73, 70, and 77.

[271] A reference to the commentary on the *Consolation* in the exposition of *Troades* is well known to students of Trevet (*Commento alle* Troades *di Seneca*, ed. by PALMA, p. 5, l. 6: "sicut exposuimus plenius super quintum Boecii de Consolacione"). The commentary on Virgil's *Eclogues*, if Trevet's, offers five instances of references to the author's commentary on Boethius (see LORD, "Virgil's 'Eclogues'", pp. 206–39). It seems, however, that Trevet acted moderately and did not seize every occasion offered by intertextual references between the commented works to promote his own commentaries. See, for example, references to Seneca's *Declamaciones* in the commentary on Thyestes (*Il commento di Nicola Trevet al Tieste*, ed. By FRANCESCHINI, p. 64, l. 24) and in that on Livy (in the opening of the prologue, Lisbon, IL. 134, fol. 1ra), without any mention of his commentary.

[272] "Nicolaus de Trovech Anglicus, de ordine Predicatorum, sacre theologie doctor, Psalterium glosis utilibus illustravit; Boeti librum De consolatione philosophica, tragedias et declamationes Senece optime exposuit; in exposicione et declamatione Titi Livii grande volumen excudit" (Guglielmo da Pastrengo, *De viris illustribus et de originibus*, ed. by G. BOTTARI, Padua, 1991, p. 164, on the history of the text, see pp. xxiii–xxiv, xxxi–li, cf. KUJAWIŃSKI, *Nicholas Trevet's* Commentary on the Psalms).

de Anglia ordinis fratrum predicatorum" (fol. 167^v, outer margin).[273] According to the scribal colophon of the *Tragedies*, on the
same page, the copy was written at Lucca, in 1376, by Francesco
Petrucci da Camerino.[274] Following the colophon, the same scribe
added, in a few instalments, a long note concerned with Seneca's
authorship of the *Tragedies*. After having quoted Petrarch and
Boccaccio, in the last section (fol. 168^r), written with a different
pen and ink, apparently after an interval, Francesco also called
upon the authority of Trevet and his commentary on the *Consolation*:

¶ legi etiam in Comento quem fecit super Boetium <u>Nicholaus Tra-
vech</u> anglicus quod [*?corr. in* qui] in III°. libro Boetii in prosa que
incipit gloria in principio [?] volens de gloria hominum tractare
quam fallax sit, sic dicit <u>ad litteram</u>[275] ¶ gloria vero quam fallax
quam turpis est satis tibi patet ¶ quod autem sit fallax probatur
auctoritate <u>cuiusdam poete greci qui tragedias composuit et cet-
era</u>. Hec scrixi preter [*? pro* propter] tanti viri auctoritatem quid
sentiat. Qui Nicholaus supradictus tragedias Senece glosavit et
commentum fecit ut supra patet.[276]

---

[273] "So ends the commentary on this book of ten Tragedies of Seneca,
written and composed by a man of outstanding and profound abilities, Friar
Nicholas *Altraveth* from England, of the Order of Friars Preachers".

[274] "Petrutii" has been added in different ink between the lines. Both
explicits are quoted by FRANCESCHINI ("Glosse e commenti", pp. 88–90),
who has also provided a summary description of the manuscript. See also
A. PISCITELLI, entry no. 11, in *Seneca: una vicenda testuale*, pp. 142–43. The
scribe has been identified with physician and correspondent of Coluccio Salutati (MACGREGOR, "Manuscripts of Seneca's Tragedies", p. 1194, no. 226;
see a letter of 1405 addressed by Salutati "Magistro Francisco de Camerino
physico", *Epistolario di Coluccio Salutati*, ed. by F. NOVATI, 4 vols, Rome,
1891–1911, vol. 4, pp. 86–91; the editor tentatively identified the addressee
with Francesco di Marano da Camerino, professor of logic, astrology, natural philosophy, and medicine at Bologna, 1390–1397). The ours, however,
could have been a jurist of whom two *consilia* are known (see Progetto Irnerio
<http://irnerio.cirsfid.unibo.it/author/F/307/>, last accessed 25/9/2021).

[275] "Gloria vero — composuit" is a quotation of Trevet's commentary on
Book 3 prose 6 (SILK, p. 349).

[276] Underlining as in the manuscript. The entire note is offered, though
with several errors and omissions, by FRANCESCHINI, "Glosse e commenti",
pp. 89–90. Fol. 167^v is reproduced by PISTICELLI, entry no. 11, p. 143. "I
also read in the commentary which <u>Nicholas Trevet</u> the Englishman made
on Boethius that in Boethius's Book 3, in prose that starts 'gloria' at the

By the late fourteenth century, Trevet's commentaries on the authors of classical and Christian Antiquity had attained a position of canonical reference.

beginning, Boethius, intending to discuss how deceitful is human glory, says literally as follows: 'But how deceitful, how foul is glory' is certainly known to you. That it is deceitful is proven by the authority of a certain Greek poet who composed tragedies, etc. I wrote these things because of the authority of such a man, how he sees that. The abovementioned Nicholas glossed Seneca's tragedies and made a commentary as shown above."

Errors in Archetypes and Publication

Observations on the Tradition of Dante's Works

Luca Azzetta
(*Florence*)

After Dante's death during the night of 13–14 September 1321, those who were close to him, above all his sons Pietro and Iacopo, took possession of all his property, including his writings. It fell to them to take care of the dissemination of works that the poet, for various reasons, had not made public. In the absence of explicit evidence, the tracks that posthumous publication took have to be reconstructed by way of conjecture. There do exist some testimonials, albeit they are not entirely unambiguous, which are able to benefit the exercise.[1]

We owe to Giovanni Boccaccio an important note that sheds light on the dissemination of the final piece of the *Eclogues*, a bucolic correspondence between Dante and Giovanni del Virgilio. In a gloss that Boccaccio copied together with an eclogue that Giovanni del Virgilio had sent to Albertino Mussato, we read that the second eclogue, *Velleribus colchis*, which Dante wrote in the late spring of 1321, was delivered to Giovanni del Virgilio after the poet's death by one of his sons. The passage in question, commenting on verse 228 ("laxabas Tytiron ipsum"), reads as follows: "Nam postquam magister Iohannes misit Danti eglogam illam *Forte sub irriguos* etc. stetit Dantes per annum antequam faceret *Velleribus colchis* et mortuus est antequam eam micteret, et postea

---

[1] For the primary importance of Florence in the dissemination of some of Dante's works, see L. Azzetta, S. Chiodo, T. De Robertis (eds), *"Onorevole e antico cittadino di Firenze". Il Bargello per Dante*, Florence, 2021.

The Art of Publication from the Ninth to the Sixteenth Century, ed. by Samu Niskanen with the assistance of Valentina Rovere, IPM, 93 (Turnhout, 2023), pp. 269–292.
© BREPOLS ❧ PUBLISHERS   DOI 10.1484/M.IPM-EB.5.133085

filius ipsius Dantis misit illam predicto magistro Iohanni".[2] This note certifies that Dante's sons had a role in the publication of their father's works, even though in their own poems and commentaries on the *Commedia* they offer only a few (Pietro) or no (Iacopo) quotations to confirm specific knowledge of their father's other works.

As with the second eclogue, the last canticle of the *Commedia*, that is, the *Paradiso*, was published in its entirety only after Dante's death. Boccaccio's *Trattatello in laude di Dante* includes a well-known account of how Iacopo Alighieri discovered the *Paradiso*'s last thirteen cantos.[3] According to Boccaccio, they had been miraculously recovered some months after Dante's death and then put together and released for the first time in the spring of 1322. At that point they were joined to *Paradiso*'s other cantos and the *Commedia*'s first two canticles, *Inferno* and *Purgatorio*, which were already circulating. Boccaccio's note about the discovery, and his testimony as to the publication of *Paradiso* in various compilations of cantos, sent to Cangrande della Scala (1291–1329), lord of Verona, has stirred much debate.[4]

It is usually maintained today that although Dante did not publish the *Eclogues*, or *Commedia* (except for the said sections), or *Monarchia* — a work that enjoyed significant dissemination

---

[2] BML, 29.8, fol. 49ᵛ ("Indeed, after master Giovanni sent Dante the eclogue *Forte sub irriguos* etc., Dante waited for a year before composing *Velleribus colchis*, and he died before sending it, and later Dante's son sent it to the aforementioned master Giovanni"). See A. Mazzucchi, "Introduzione", in Dante Alighieri, *Egloge*, ed. by M. Petoletti, in Dante Alighieri, *Le Opere*, vol. V. *Epistole, Egloge, Questio de aqua et terra*, ed. by M. Baglio, L. Azzetta, M. Petoletti, M. Rinaldi, Rome, 2016, pp. 491–650, at 500 and 601.

[3] Giovanni Boccaccio, *Trattatello in laude di Dante*, ed. by M. Fiorilla, in *Le vite di Dante dal XIV al XVI secolo. Iconografia dantesca*, ed. by M. Berté, M. Fiorilla, S. Chiodo, I. Valente, Rome, 2017, pp. 11–154, at 102–03 (redaction 1, §§ 183–89).

[4] For instance, Quirini's sonnet *Segnor, ch'avete di pregio corona* can be cited in support of Boccaccio's account, even if the text is open to different interpretations; *Testi di compianto e altri testi poetici in volgare sulla figura e la fortuna di Dante*, ed. by F. Ruggiero, in D. Alighieri, *Le opere*, vol. VII, *Opere di dubbia attribuzione e altri documenti danteschi*, vol. 2, *Opere già attribuite a Dante e altri documenti danteschi*, ed. by P. Mastandrea with the collaboration of M. Rinaldi, F. Ruggiero, L. Spinazzè, Rome, 2021, pp. 262–66.

soon after his death — he had, however, finished them. His *De vulgari eloquentia*, *Convivio*, and *Epistola a Cangrande* were likewise released posthumously, but their cases are somewhat different: the first two were unfinished, and while the *Epistola* was completed, there was no fair copy. The transmission of these three works ultimately relied on originals not prepared to serve publication, resulting in *stemmata codicum* whose archetypes bore seriously deficient text.

The tradition of *De vulgari eloquentia* only embraces five witnesses: SBB-PK, lat. folio 437 (referred to here by the *siglum* B), discovered by Ludwig Bertalot in 1917; Grenoble, Bibliothèque Civique, 580 (*siglum* G), used by Jacopo Corbinelli for his *editio princeps* published at Paris in 1577; and Milan, Biblioteca Trivulziana, 1088 (*siglum* T), on which Giovan Giorgio Trissino's translation relied, printed by Tolomeo Ianiculo at Vicenza in 1529; and two *descripti* manuscripts (both descending from T), namely BAV, Reg. lat. 1370, made for Pietro Bembo in 1514 × 1517, and Vat. lat. 4817, which is Angelo Colocci's *zibaldone*, or commonplace book, and quotes *De vulgari eloquentia* II 9–10, 1–4. The stemma established by Bertalot and then by Mengaldo constitutes an "open recension". In other words, the tradition has two branches, both descending from the archetype X. B, by a northern Italian scribe, represents a family on its own. G and T, both from northern Italy (probably Padua), represent family *y*, derivative of X and collateral to B. A high number of errors, which become more frequent in the final chapters, characterizes the transmission. One gains an impression of what must have been an increasingly hasty process of composition and of the provisional state of the original, which was subject to several insertions.[5] Since B testifies to a tradition notably sounder than that witnessed by G and T, Pio Rajna proposed tentatively that B's text may reflect a campaign of emendation, undertaken at an unknown stage in the transmission and whose occurrence is difficult to measure. Long ignored, Rajna's proposition has recently been

---

[5]   Dante Alighieri, *De vulgari eloquentia*, ed. by P. V. MENGALDO, *I. Introduzione e testo*, Padua, 1968, pp. cvii–cix.

reconsidered and given credence by Enrico Fenzi, who regarded his observations on the manuscript tradition as plausible.[6]

*

The textual status of *Convivio* is even more compromised. The work is witnessed by forty-six manuscripts, all Florentine, two datable to the first half of the fourteenth century, three to its last decades, and the rest to the fifteenth century.[7] In the *Edizione Nazionale* undertaken by Franca Brambilla Ageno, the *Convivio*'s entire tradition is described as a corrupt affair, disfigured by roughly a thousand errors, including nineteen long gaps and eight mistaken transpositions of words entered in the course of transmission.[8] Ageno's edition has prompted considerations shedding light not only on the *Convivio*'s text, but also on the characteristics of the manuscript tradition. It is now maintained that, if evaluated through a different set of criteria than hers, some of the instances that Ageno considered to be errors do not represent actual corruption, and so some of her emendations are unnecessary. Furthermore, some readings that she regarded as non-authorial revision after Dante's death — she did not hypothesize where or by whom these were undertaken — may represent his authentic voice and be anterior to the archetype. So, because it has conclusively been confirmed that the archetype's seriously corrupt condition reflects the incompleteness of the original, one must ask whether all those errors that are attested by the entire tradition should be imputed to the archetype or whether some of them might derive from Dante's incomplete original. The question is difficult and must be answered case by case. Different solutions should prompt different outcomes: what can be attributed to the author should be retained whereas what can be confidently identified as not having preceded the archetype must be subject to emendation by conjecture.[9]

[6] Dante Alighieri, *De vulgari eloquentia*, ed. by E. Fenzi in collaboration with L. Formisano, F. Montuori, Rome, 2012, pp. xcvii–ccxxii.

[7] I. Ceccherini, "Il 'Convivio'", in *Dante fra il settecentocinquantenario della nascita (2015) e il settecentenario della morte (2021). Atti delle Celebrazioni in Senato, del Forum e del Convegno internazionale di Roma: maggio–ottobre 2015*, 3 vols, ed. by E. Malato, A. Mazzucchi, Rome, 2016, vol. 2, pp. 383–400.

[8] Dante Alighieri, *Convivio*, ed. by F. Brambilla Ageno, Florence, 1995.

[9] For considerations prompted by Ageno's edition, see G. Gorni, "Appunti sulla tradizione del 'Convivio' (a proposito dell'archetipo e dell'originale

The complexity of the picture briefly outlined above is confirmed by data from the *Convivio*'s indirect tradition. This shows that Florence was the centre in which this philosophical commentary began to be read in the course of the 1330s. All identifiable early readers were Florentines, who approached the work from different perspectives. They were: the notary and translator Alberto della Piagentina; the anonymous commentator of the *Commedia* whose work is known as *Ottimo Commento*; the anonymous referred to as Amico dell'*Ottimo*; Andrea Lancia; and perhaps Giovanni Villani.[10] The poet's son Pietro Alighieri may be added to this list of readers: the first draft of his *Comentum* on the *Commedia*, made in Verona by 1341 and thus constituting the only exception to otherwise Florentine diffusion, quotes the *Convivio* several times without explicit reference to author or title.[11] The textual quality of some of his quotations suggests recourse to a manuscript devoid of the errors that now affect the entire tradition and are, therefore, ascribed to the archetype. By way of illu-

---

dell'opera)", *Studi di Filologia italiana*, 55 (1997), pp. 5–22 (later published in ID., *Dante prima della "Commedia"*, Florence, 2001, pp. 239–51); A. MAZZUCCHI, "Per il testo del 'Convivio'. Considerazioni in margine all'edizione Ageno", in ID., *Tra "Convivio" e "Commedia". Sondaggi di filologia dantesca*, Rome, 2004, pp. 147–75 (relevant also for methodological remarks). For previous scholarship, see A. PÉZARD, *Le «Convivio» de Dante. Sa lettre, son esprit*, Paris, 1940, pp. 121–29.

[10]   For the *Convivio*'s indirect transmission, see L. AZZETTA, "La tradizione del 'Convivio' negli antichi commenti alla 'Commedia': Andrea Lancia, l'"Ottimo commento' e Pietro Alighieri", *Rivista di Studi Danteschi*, 5 (2005), pp. 3–34; ID., "Tra i più antichi lettori del 'Convivio': ser Alberto della Piagentina notaio e cultore di Dante", *Rivista di Studi Danteschi*, 9 (2009), pp. 57–91; ID., "Nota sulla tradizione del 'Convivio' nella Firenze di Coluccio Salutati", *Italia medioevale e umanistica*, 58 (2017), pp. 293–303. Also two late manuscripts of *Ottimo Commento* (BML, Pluteo 40.19, and Strozzi 160, datable to *s.* xv$^{1/4}$ and xv$^{4/4}$ respectively) with an obvious allusion to *Conv.*, II, 13 8–11 in a gloss to *Par.*, XXVIII, 70–78 refer to Florence. These two manuscripts came from a common ancestor *c1* and the gloss in question was interpolated by a scribe who had access to *Convivio*; see *Ottimo Commento alla 'Commedia'*, vol. 1, *Inferno*, ed. by G. BOCCARDO, vol. 2, *Purgatorio*, ed. by M. CORRADO, vol. 3, *Paradiso*, ed. by V. CELOTTO, Amico dell'*Ottimo*, *Chiose sopra la 'Comedia'*, ed. by C. PERNA, Rome, 2018, p. 1809.

[11]   Petri Allegherii *super Dantis ipsius genitoris Comoediam commentarium, nunc primum in lucem editum consilio et sumtibus G. J. Bar. Vernon*, ed. by V. NANNUCCI, Florence, 1845.

stration, I cite a remark on the providential character of the Roman empire, whose strength was an instrument in the hands of God.

Convivio IV 4 12 (74–77) critical text	*Convivio* IV 4 12 archetype X	PIETRO ALIGHIERI, *Purg.* VI (ed. by NANNUCCI, pp. 331–32)
La forza dunque non fu cagione movente, [...] ma fu cagione instrumentale, sì come sono li colpi del martello cagione <*instrumentale*> del coltello, e l'anima del fabro è cagione efficiente e movente	[...] om. *instrumentale* [...]	Nam vis non fuit belli causa movens et finalis, sed potius instrumentalis, ut sunt ictus martelli causa *instrumentalis* cultelli, et anima fabro motiva causa

In another case, Pietro does not react to what Ageno confidently regarded as a lacuna in the archetype, a much-discussed proposition.[12]

Convivio II 14 6 (34–35) critical text	PIETRO ALIGHIERI, *Paradiso* XIV (ed. by NANNUCCI, pp. 648–49)
Altri dissero, sì come fu Anassagora e Democrito, che [... che] ciò era lume di sole ripercusso in quella parte	Anaxagoras et Democritus dicunt quod est radius solis ibi repercussus

As for the aforementioned author of the *Ottimo Commento* and Andrea Lancia, whose glosses were written in Florence *c.* 1334 and 1341 × 1343 respectively, it should be noted at the outset that their perceptions of the *Commedia* are mutually reminiscent.[13] The two authors were associated by cultural proximity and, because they are often found in the same company, perhaps also by bonds of friendship. An expression of the former was their perusal of the same *auctores* and the same sources, including the *Convivio*, otherwise read only rarely at that time. Collaboration and exchange of ideas manifested in their works in various ways. Although formulated differently, their glosses often resonate with each other. On expounding

---

[12]   *Convivio*, vol. 1/*, pp. 51–52, elaborating on F. BRAMBILLA AGENO, "Nuove proposte per il 'Convivio'", *Studi Danteschi*, 48 (1971), pp. 121–36, at 125.

[13]   Andrea Lancia, *Chiose alla "Commedia"*, ed. by L. AZZETTA, 2 vols, Rome, 2012.

the *Commedia* and Dante's other works, they put forward analogous propositions, some accurate and some not, that are rare elsewhere. Their approaches, characterized by philological effort and a readiness to amend textual corruption, were similar. This is not to say that upon facing textual infelicities the two commentaries are never at variance. A case in point is their treatment of the *Convivio*'s discussion of the lapse of time for a complete revolution of the *primum mobile*, which includes an obvious error that now distorts the entire tradition and is taken to derive from the archetype X.

Convivio II 3 5 (29) critical text	archetype X + ANDREA LANCIA, gloss to *Paradiso* XXVII 97–99	*Ottimo Commento*, gloss to *Inferno* VII 76–81
quasi in ventiquattro ore, <cioè in ventitré ore> *e quattordici parti delle quindici d'un'altra*	quasi in ventiquattro ore *e quattordici parti d'un'altra delle quindici*	quasi in ventiquattro ore *e delle quindici parti le quattordici d'un'altra ora*

Lancia preferred to remain faithful to what he read in the manuscript, giving an impression of passive reception. In contrast, the *Ottimo*'s rendition, unattested elsewhere, betrays awareness of the said error. To amend the text, he put forward a conjecture.

It should be noted that in the passage in question the archetype reverses what must be the correct order of words. For Ageno, this represented one of the most significant traces of non-authorial revision imposed on X, for "in più luoghi parole integrate durante questa revisione sono state inserite fuori di posto nella successiva trascrizione".[14] However, to assume that someone other than the author revised the *Convivio* within a decade of his death amounts to a daring proposition. All the more so if this assumption is joined by one more that Ageno put forth: yet another judicious early corrector, working on family *b*, corrected numerous errors in the archetype without recourse to witnesses more authentic than those extant.[15] As noted by Pézard and later by Gorni, it is possible that the archetype was not the cradle of some of the errors,

---

[14] "In several cases words that were inserted in the course of this revision were placed incorrectly in subsequent transmission"; *Convivio*, VOL. I/*, p. 57.

[15] *Convivio*, VOL. I/*, pp. 235–58, and pp. 385–87; GORNI, *Appunti sulla tradizione*, pp. 12–15.

inversions in the word order, and lacunae. Rather, the odds are that the original of the *Convivio*, an unfinished work never published by Dante, was not a fair copy. This ultimate source may have included corrections, with words or phrases annotated in the margins or between lines and possibly executed in ways that could have led to misunderstandings. Gorni also advanced the hypothesis that two copies were made of that original. In other words, the manuscript tradition would go back to two archetypes rather than only one, X. This would explain the presence of better readings in the early indirect tradition, such as in the texts of Pietro Alighieri, *Ottimo Commento*, Andrea Lancia, as well as in witnesses of family *b* such as Pn, R², R³, Ott. The said texts would, then, have been independent of the archetype proposed by Ageno.[16]

*

As for the *Epistola a Cangrande*, the provisional condition of the original, implied by very many errors in the archetype, hints that Dante never sent the epistle to its recipient. That textual situation is of importance for the attribution of this letter to Dante, an attribution that has been questioned in the past and still continues to be questioned from time to time. It will be beneficial here to present the available evidence in some detail.

If taken at face value, the *Epistola a Cangrande*, a coherent but complex text, reads as a device by which Dante dedicated the *Paradiso* to Cangrande della Scala. It is a relatively recent notion that the reasons for and implications of the text, expressed in prose that reads at times as an apology in a moment of crisis and at times as an astounding commentary on poetry, can be appreciated only if placed in the proper historical context, namely in relation to political and personal events that characterized the last years of Dante's sojourn at the Scaligerian court, which ended late 1319 or early 1320.[17] The authenticity of the *Epistola* was questioned

---

[16]   Gorni, *Appunti sulla tradizione*, pp. 16–17.

[17]   Dante Alighieri, *Epistola XIII*, ed. by L. Azzetta, in *Le Opere*, pp. 271–487; for the *Epistola*'s political context, see C. Villa, "Cronologie dantesche: il canto xix dell''Inferno' e il memoriale per Cangrande (Ep. XIII)", *Studi danteschi*, 82 (2017), pp. 29–50; Ead., "Il Vicario imperiale, il poeta e la sapienza di Salomone: pubblicistica politica e poetica nell'Epistola a Cangrande (con una postilla per re Roberto e donna Berta)", *L'Alighieri*, n.s., 47

for the first time in 1819 by Filippo Scolari. The debate from the outset has focused on the contents of the letter.[18] More recently, it has been maintained that "i punti discriminanti sono la possibilità o meno di inviare l'intera cantica del *Paradiso* al signore di Verona in un periodo preciso della vita di Dante; l'originalità o meno della sezione di *accessus*; l'interpretazione dei primi versi del I canto".[19] It has also been questioned whether Dante, when he was still composing *Paradiso*, could have been responsible for the *Epistola*'s affirmation that the title of the whole work was *Commedia*, given "l'ipotesi interpretativa che, all'interno del poema, non viene assegnata a *comedia* valore di titolo".[20] Such a hermeneutic seems to hazard a degree of inherent subjectivity, all the more so as it invites us to impose our own sensitivities on medieval ones.[21] It is certainly problematic to maintain that, to be held as unquestionably authentic, a text must comply with modern hermeneutical requisites. Indeed, a philology that negates interpretation or

(2016), pp. 19–40; EAD., "L'Epistola a Cangrande, la scomunica dello Scaligero (6 aprile 1318) e la bozza 'Ne pretereat'", *Giornale storico della letteratura italiana*, 195 (2018), pp. 1–17; see also L. AZZETTA, "Visioni bibliche e investitura poetica. Spunti per una riflessione sulla poesia di Dante a partire dall''Epistola a Cangrande'", in *Theologus Dantes. Tematiche teologiche nelle opere e nei primi commenti*, Atti del Convegno Internazionale (Venezia, Università Ca' Foscari, 14–15 settembre 2017), ed. by L. LOMBARDO, D. PARISI, A. PEGORETTI, Venice, 2018, pp. 189–214.

[18]   F. SCOLARI, *Note ad alcuni luoghi delli primi cinque canti della "Divina Commedia"*, Venice, 1819, pp. 18–21.

[19]   "The relevant issues are the following: whether the entire canticle of the *Paradiso* could have been sent to the lord of Verona at a given period of Dante's life; whether the *accessus* found in the letter is authentic; how the first verses of the canto I should be construed". For reference, see the next footnote.

[20]   "[T]he unverifiable proposition that nowhere in the poem is the word *comedia* granted the status of title"; A. CASADEI, *Dante. Altri accertamenti e punti critici*, Milan, 2019, p. 14; see also his "'Canticam [...] offero' e altri problemi esegetici", in *Nuove inchieste sull'Epistola a Cangrande*, Atti della giornata di studi, Pisa, 18 dicembre 2018, ed. by A. CASADEI, Pisa, 2020, pp. 129–52, and *Dante oltre la "Commedia"*, Bologna, 2013, pp. 15–43.

[21]   It can be taken as proof of subjectivity that some of the issues mentioned here have been resolved in previous scholarship (for which see note 18). While many have found the arguments exhaustive, those who consider the *Epistola* a forgery would disagree. It may be added that scholarly discussion is not invariably immune to the human predicament that past contributions are sometimes ignored, considered partially, simplified, or misunderstood.

refuses to be a hermeneutical exercise is inconceivable; likewise, one cannot admit an interpretative process that fails to engage with, and seek substantiation by, material philology, that is, the study of the physical aspects of transmission.[22] For this reason it is appropriate to highlight some philological details that should be considered when expounding on the attribution of a work.

The manuscript tradition of the *Epistola a Cangrande* comprises ten witnesses, nine manuscripts and a print. Their relationships are summarized in the *stemma codicum* below, established by Enzo Cecchini in 1995.[23]

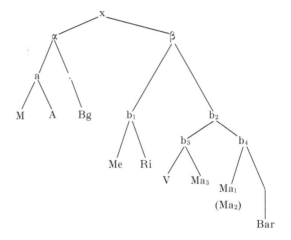

Fig. 1 The *stemma codicum* of the *Epistola a Cangrande* by Enzo Cecchini

[22] Commenting on A. Varvaro's rejection of a philology that abdicates from any aspect of interpretation, Mazzucchi noted that such a denunciation is valid not only "nel senso più ovvio in base al quale ogni processo filologico presuppone un impegno esegetico, ma anche che ogni interpretazione, ogni tentativo di valutazione storico-letteraria non potrà e non dovrà prescindere dai risultati conseguiti nell'accertamento puntuale della lettera e nella ricostruzione della storia della tradizione dei testi". A. MAZZUCCHI, "La critica del testo trent'anni dopo. La prospettiva dantesca", in *La critica del testo. Problemi di metodo ed esperienze di lavoro. Trent'anni dopo, in vista del Settecentenario della morte di Dante*, Atti del Convegno internazionale, Roma, 23–26 ottobre 2017, Rome, 2018, pp. 40–41.

[23] Dante Alighieri, *Epistola a Cangrande*, ed. by E. CECCHINI, Florence, 1995, p. xxxix.

The tradition is rather late. The three witnesses of family α come from the fifteenth century. They only retain the *nuncupatoria* section of the *Epistola*, so that the text breaks off at the end of paragraph 13. That paragraph, which concludes the third part of the *Epistola*, the *narratio*, resonates deeply with the preceding text as to rhetorical structure, anticipates a new rhetorical mode, and introduces the remaining part of the letter.[24] The manuscripts of family β, datable to the mid-sixteenth century and the first quarter of the seventeenth, convey the *Epistola* in its entirety. The *editio princeps*, Bar, printed in 1700, relied on a now lost exemplar. All the witnesses of direct tradition agree in explicitly attributing the epistle to Dante.[25]

The indirect tradition, which is considered here exclusively in relation to parties who knew the entire text of the *Epistola*, has its oldest witness in a gloss to *Commedia*, *Paradiso* I, 1, made by Andrea Lancia, the aforementioned Florentine notary.[26] His vernacular translation of the *Epistola*'s paragraph 43, part of the *expositio textus*, states that he is quoting a text written by Dante to Cangrande della Scala. That was something Andrea Lancia could have derived only from the *intitulatio* of the *Epistola*, the only place where the name of the Scaliger appears. Lancia's translation and the Latin original of the passage in questions are given below.

> Questa cantica si divide principalmente secondo che scrisse l'autore medesimo a messer Cane della Scala in II parti, cioè nel pro-

---

[24]   For *Epistola*'s structure, see Alighieri, *Epistola XIII*, pp. 275–82.

[25]   For the manuscript tradition, see Alighieri, *Epistola a Cangrande*, pp. xxv–li; Alighieri, *Epistola XIII*, pp. 298–318.

[26]   For the indirect tradition, see Alighieri, *Epistola XIII*, pp. 418–87. Among the *Commedia*'s earliest commentaries, of particular significance is the lengthy quotation from the *accessus* of *Epistola* in the first recension of Guido da Pisa's *Expositiones*, written before 1328. Unaware that the *accessus* was part of the *Epistola*, he must have received the text in its Florentine form, devoid of other sections; Alighieri, *Epistola XIII*, pp. 428–44; F. FRANCES-CHINI, "Guido da Pisa, l'"Epistola a Cangrande' e i primi 'accessus' a Dante", in *Da Dante a Berenson. Sette secoli tra parole e immagini. Omaggio a Lucia Battaglia Ricci*, ed. by A. PEGORETTI, C. BALBARINI, Ravenna, 2018, pp. 113–46; ID., "Ancora sull'"Epistola a Cangrande', Guido, Lana: il 'subiectum' della 'Commedia'", in *Nuove inchieste*, pp. 77–104. The composition of the *Expositiones* is antedated by a few years in L. JENARO-MACLENNAN, "Per la datazione fra il 1327–1328 e il 1332 delle 'Expositiones et glose' di Guido da Pisa", *Lettere italiane*, 71 (2019), pp. 354–68.

logo e nella parte executiva. La seconda parte comincia quivi, quasi in mezzo del primo canto: *Surge a' mortali per diverse foce*, la quale si divide in II parti [...].[27]

> Dividitur ergo ista pars, seu tertia cantica que *Paradisus* dicitur, principaliter in duas partes, scilicet in prologum et partem executivam. Pars secunda incipit ibi, quasi in medio primi: "Surgit mortalibus per diversas fauces" (*Epistola*, 43).

This is important evidence. Lancia is an authoritative source by virtue of his excellent knowledge of Dante's works, including pieces with minor circulation such as the *Convivio* and *Tenzone* with Forese Donati. Lancia's glosses are datable to 1341 × 1343, showing that, in agreement with the later direct tradition, the *Epistola* was considered to be Dante's and that it was accessible in its entirety in Florence some twenty years after his death. This significantly shortens the chronological gap between the *Epistola*'s composition and its earliest surviving copies, which are from the fifteenth century.

The later indirect tradition also provides relevant insights. Particularly significant is the witness of an anonymous sixteen-th-century treatise. Incorporating lengthy excerpts from the *Epistola*, the *Introduzione al poema di Dante per l'allegoria* makes the following remark:

> Ma in una epistola latina che egli scrisse a Can della Scala, signor grande in quelli tempi e gran benefattore di Dante, dichiarò diste-samente questa sua intenzione [*cioè la divisione del senso letterale e allegorico*] che ebbe in questo suo poema; e se bene detta epistola, che io ho veduta, è tanto scorretta che a pena si può leggere, non di meno riferirò l'istesse parole di essa come sono in latino [...] La quale epistola è in mano di molti e da alcuni antichi commentatori è messa nel principio del commento come una prefazione dell'ist-esso autore sopra la sua opera.[28]

---

[27] "This canticle is divided principally into two sections, according to what the author wrote to Messer Cane della Scala: the prologue and the exec-utive section. The second section begins there, almost in the middle of the first canto: *Surge a' mortali per diverse foce*, which divides into two parts", LANCIA, *Chiose alla "Commedia"*, II, p. 862; Alighieri, *Epistola XIII*, pp. 450–53.

[28] "But in a Latin letter he wrote to Can della Scala, a great lord in those times and a great benefactor of Dante's, he explicitly declared the intention [*that is, the division of the literal and allegorical sense*] which he had in this

The anonymous author's assessment of the *Epistola*'s textual quality testifies to serious corruption. The extract also evidences a
class of manuscripts, not attested among the survivors, which carried a commentary, perhaps the *Commedia* or at least a part of
it, and with the *Epistola* placed at its head.[29] A brief annotation
found at the beginning of the *Epistola* in all witnesses of family β
corroborates that arrangement. According to this note, which is
given below, the letter was copied into a manuscript of the *Paradiso* ("hanc canticam tertiam") — perhaps by an early commentator — as Dante's preface to it.

> Prefari aliqua in initio cuiusque operis sui antiquitas consuevit;
> que quanto pauciora fuerint, tanto ocius ad rem de qua agitur
> aditus fiet, presertim cui cure non erit exquisita et accurata locu-
> tio, que docentibus eloquentiam convenit. Expediam igitur ilico,
> ne, dum studeo devitare prolixitatem, in illam ipsam incurrerim.
> Satis ergo mihi hoc erit in loco vice prohemii fore consultum, si
> que Poeta rescribens domino Cani, cui hanc canticam tertiam
> dedicavit, pro ipsa prefatione indiderim, quo melius Poete intentio
> ab eiusdem observatoribus intelligatur. Que sub hac forma fuere.

This anonymous remark that the *Epistola* had come into "the
hands of many" is at variance with the relatively small number
of the survivors. Yet, it is obvious that several witnesses have not
been preserved. The *editio princeps* made by Baruffaldi relies on a
manuscript owned by Giuseppe Lanzoni, now lost. Furthermore,
none of those readers from the sixteenth century and the first half
of the seventeenth who explicitly cite the *Epistola* as Dante's —
Vincenzio Borghini, Giovan Battista Gelli, Lodovico Castelvetro,
Jacopo Mazzoni, Antonio degli Albizzi, and Benedetto Buonmat-
tei — seems to have consulted any of the extant manuscripts,

---

poem; and although this letter, which I have seen, is so full of errors that it
is hardly legible, I will, nonetheless, quote its words just as they are in Latin.
[...] This letter is in the hands of many and is placed by some early commentators at the beginning of the commentary as a preface of that author to his
work"; Alighieri, *Epistola XIII*, pp. 476–81.

[29] For early manuscripts in Florence in the sixteenth century, subsequently lost, and the first penetration of Dante's works there, see L. AZZETTA,
"Ancora sul 'Dante' di Giovanni Villani, Andrea Lancia e la prima circolazione fiorentina della 'Commedia'", *Rivista di Studi Danteschi*, 19 (2019),
pp. 148–67, with ample references to previous scholarship.

although their quotations may be connected to the textual families in the *stemma codicum* above.

The indirect tradition of the *Epistola* shows, indeed, that the manuscript families elucidated by Cecchini had already taken shape in the fourteenth century. A case in point is the *Expositio seu comentum super Comedia Dantis Allegherii*, a commentary made by Filippo Villani sometime between 1391 and 1405. He had been assigned by the *Studio fiorentino* to hold a *lectura Dantis*, a series of lectures on Dante, a commission previously held by Boccaccio. Villani knew the *Epistola* in its entirety. He learned from the *nuncupatoria* section about the dedication to Cangrande; he quoted extensively both the *accessus* and the *expositio*, at times word for word and at other times augmenting the text, an exercise known as *amplificatio*. The quotations are so accurate that Villani's copy of the *Epistola* can be precisely located in the *stemma codicum*. It falls under archetype β (*fatum* Villani, *factum* β, *subiectum* ed. *Epistola*, 18), then into sub-branch b2 (*in fine* Villani b3 b4, *et in fine* b1 ed. *Epistola*, 29), and finally with proximity to subgroup b4 (*scilicet* Villani b4, *om.* b3, *sicut* b1 ed. *Epistola*, 32).[30] What is more, two of Villani's quotations carry readings otherwise encountered only in Baruffaldi's *editio princeps*: *previatio* and *consuevere* in paragraphs 45 and 46 respectively. On the one hand, these agreements help to evaluate the status of Baruffaldi's text. Villani's *Expositio* confirms the antiquity and, indeed, the soundness of the two readings attested in the *princeps* and, hence, its source, the lost Lanzoni manuscript. In the absence of other evidence, it is only Villani's text that shows those two readings not to have been Baruffaldi's conjectures. On the other hand, it can be hypothesized that these sound readings entered the transmission through some casual collation with a lost manuscript unaccounted for by the archetype, from which the texts of Baruffaldi and Villani benefitted.[31]

A new collation of the witnesses of the *Epistola* verifies the quoted anonymous observations about textual corruption. The results offer us matter for reflection on how the *Epistola* has reached us, with significant implications for the question of authorship. It is

[30]   Alighieri, *Epistola XIII*, pp. 464–65.
[31]   *Ibid.*, pp. 311–12.

clear that infelicities and lacunae, around thirty of them, blemished the archetype. If the relatively short length of the *Epistola* is taken into account, the frequency of error is far greater than one would expect were it to have been published by its author by means of a fair copy.[32] A comparison with Dante's other works is illustrative. The tradition of the *Vita nova* attests to only three archetypal errors: more precisely, one certain mistake and, depending on how the evidence is construed, two potential ones. The *Monarchia*'s tradition has four errors. Both of the works are much longer than the *Epistola*.

The textual condition of the *Epistola*'s archetype resembles that of the *Convivio* in several respects: in both cases, the survivors document a text seriously compromised at the outset; all the surviving manuscripts are Florentine, and the direct tradition they represent is late; the earliest attested stages of indirect tradition anterior to our oldest manuscripts are likewise confined to Florence. Such analogies hint that the first issue of the *Epistola* was not unlike that of the *Convivio*, which Dante kept to himself and which was released only after his death, and of which neither a polished text nor a fair copy was prepared. In other words, the *Epistola* never left Dante's desk when he was alive, and, because not despatched to the Scaliger, its circulation was initiated only after his death. The large number of errors shared by all witnesses is best explained by reference to the archetype's reliance on an original whose condition was such that much confusion ensued.

[32]   These errors are of various evidential value. Some are significant, or indicative of stemmatical relationships, while some are worth noting mostly for their wide spread. As for the latter, it is unlikely that two scribes would commit the same error independently (D'A. S. AVALLE, *Principi di critica testuale*, Padua, 1978, p. 97). Therefore, when the number of such shared errors and those who committed them increase, the probability of random coincidence becomes lower. In other words, if taken into account *in toto*, all variant readings may bear evidential value to identify the text's original form. Some of the variants are analysed in *Nota al testo*, pp. 306–18 of the 2016 edition, others will be discussed in my forthcoming edition of the *Epistola*. A similar argument applies also to variants of equal persuasiveness widely attested in various branches of the stemma: they may reflect an archetype characterized by multiple readings for given words. For a pertinent discussion, see V. FERA, "Ecdotica dell'opera incompiuta: 'varianti attive' e 'varianti di lavoro' nell'Africa' del Petrarca", *Strumenti critici*, 25 (2010), pp. 211–24.

Many of the errors, which represent various types of corruption, become explicable if one thinks of an original with portions of text interlined or entered in the margins without obvious or precise indicators of the right placing. The outcome produced textual gaps, mainly short or very short, and the misplacing of words. Furthermore, there are clear misunderstandings, hinting at an original written cursively, not always easily legible and characterized by numerous abbreviations. We may consider two cases here, different from each other and useful for different reasons. Paragraph 12 of the *Epistola* reads in the archetype as follows.

> Illud quoque preterire silentio simpliciter inardescens non sinit affectus, quod in hac donatione plus dono quam domino et honoris et fame *conferri videri potest*.[33]

The manuscript tradition is substantially in agreement as to the *clausula*, and the arrangement of the words that I have italicized at the end: *conferri (ferri* β om. Ri) *videri* (om. Bg) *potest*. That reading was embraced by Pistelli in his edition prepared for the 1921 centenary, and then again by Cecchini in his 1995 critical edition.[34] The sequence is problematic, however, in that in the course of the first thirteen paragraphs, which are expected to comply with the rules of the *ars dictaminis*, this *clausula* is the only one failing to respect the *cursus*. As the use of *cursus* is systematic and intentional elsewhere in the *nuncupatoria* section, the fact that only a single *clausula* misses it is suggestive of error.[35] Already Toynbee proposed an emendation, that *potest* should be

---

[33] "That intense affection does not permit to pass over in silence the fact that in this donation it may seem that honour and fame are attributed more to the gift than to the lord".

[34] Dante Alighieri, *Epistole*, ed. by E. PISTELLI, in *Le Opere di Dante*, critical edition of the Società Dantesca Italiana, ed. by M. BARBI, *et al.*, Florence, 1921 (2nd edn, Florence, 1960), p. 437; Alighieri, *Epistola a Cangrande*, p. 6.

[35] For errors in *cursus*, see P. CHIESA, "L'impiego del '*cursus*' in sede di critica testuale: una prospettiva diagnostica", in *"Meminisse iuvat". Studi in memoria di Violetta de Angelis*, ed. by F. BOGNINI, preface by G. C. ALESSIO, Pisa, 2012, p. 289: "Le infrazioni al ritmo, quali quelle che si generano con una trasposizione indebita di parole, non sono dei veri e propri 'errori', non producono testi 'scorretti', e come tali difficilmente potevano essere riconosciute e sanate in seguito [...]. Il fatto che la trasposizione — in apparenza la più banale delle varianti —, e anche quella che è in genere in massimo grado adiafora — possa servire in sede critica è di per sé rimarchevole". On the use

advanced before *conferri videri*, a sequence of words that complies with the *cursus planus*.[36] Parodi agreed, observing: "pare ben difficile che Dante ammettesse qui un velox irregolarissimo *(con)férri vi | déri pótest*".[37] Cecchini was aware of the quandary but, cautious after the long history of previous editorial scholarship on Dante's works, he retained the reading. He remarked, however: "se appare giusto affermare che Dante avrebbe (probabilmente) evitato di chiudere in tal modo un periodo, la stessa considerazione sembra valere, e a maggior ragione, per un falsario non troppo ingenuo".[38] Cecchini's hypothesis about the genesis of the error requires that at least two interventions be made: the verb *potest*, which is unanimously attested, should be suppressed; and, as a result, the mood of *videri* should be changed (*conferri videri potest> conferri videri> conferri videtur*). It is instead more economical, and more faithful to the evidence, to assume that the original reading was *conferri potest videri*. This solution results in a period which concludes with a regular *cursus planus*. In comparison to Toynbee's conjecture (*potest conferri videri*), the reading proposed here has the advantage of only involving a single hyperbaton and being

of *cursus* in *Epistola*'s first thirteen paragraphs, see Alighieri, *Epistola XIII*, pp. 318–20.

[36] Dantis Alagherii *Epistolae. Letters of Dante*, emended text with introduction, translation and indices and Appendix on the *Cursus*, P. TOYNBEE, Oxford, 1920 (2nd edn, Oxford, 1966), p. 171.

[37] "[I]t seems very unlikely that Dante would have admitted here the most irregular *velox (con)fèrri vi | dèri pòtest*". E. G. PARODI, "Il testo critico delle opere di Dante", *Bullettino della Società Dantesca Italiana*, n.s., 28 (1921), pp. 7–46, at 34. See also ID., "Intorno al testo delle epistole di Dante e al 'cursus'", *Bullettino della Società Dantesca Italiana*, 19 (1912), pp. 249–75, at 274, then in ID., *Lingua e letteratura. Studi di teoria linguistica e di storia dell'italiano antico*, 2 vols, ed. by G. FOLENA, with an introductory essay by A. SCHIAFFINI, Venice, 1957, vol. 2, pp. 399–442, at 431.

[38] "[I]f it is fair to say that Dante would probably have avoided closing a sentence in this way, the same proposition could be valid, and even more so, for a not too injudicious forger"; Alighieri, *Epistola a Cangrande*, p. 38; E. CECCHINI, "Testo e interpretazione di passi dell'Epistola a Cangrande'", *Res Publica Litterarum*, 15 (1992), pp. 115–29, at 117–18; Cecchini suggests that "il testo originale fosse *conferri videtur*, e che la lezione *conferri videri potest* [...] ne sia discesa attraverso l'errata trascrizione *conferri videri*, frutto di meccanica ripetizione in *videri* della finale della parola precedente (onde la necessità di aggiungere *potest*)". For Cecchini's excessive caution, see CHIESA, *L'impiego del "cursus"*, pp. 300–01.

limited to the last two words; furthermore, the accumulation of two consecutive infinitives is avoided. The error could easily have been born of the original copy, with words inserted in the margins or between lines, resulting in later confusion.[39] Such a mistake, which did not affect the meaning, would have been rather difficult for copyists to observe and amend, provided that they were not experts alert to irregularities in the *cursus*.

Our second example comes from *Epistola*'s paragraph 56, *expositio* on *Paradiso*, I 3. The passage reads as follows:

> Et sic, mediate vel inmediate, omne quod habet esse habet esse ab eo; quia ex eo quod causa secunda recipit a prima, influit super causatum ad modum recipientis et *respicientis* radium, propter quod causa prima magis est causa.[40]

In this simile of a body receiving a ray and reflecting it in return, the manuscript tradition univocally reads *respicientis*. Since the nineteenth century, the said participle has been considered inadmissible and several emendations have been proposed, such as *respuentis*, *reiicientis*, and *repercutientis*. Furthermore, in his edition of 1882, Giuliani conjectured *reddentis*, accepted by subsequent editors. Yet he did not impose this emendation on his editorial text, which reads *reiicientis*, a previous conjecture by Torri and Witte. Giuliani only noted in his commentary that a little further, in paragraph 60, the *Epistola* reiterates the simile using the verbs *recipere* and *reddere*, or "recipient [...] et reddunt". The suggestion is that in the passage given above the verbs should correspond in the same way. However, because *respuentis* boasts a greater palaeographic proximity to the transmitted reading, it was preferred by Fraticelli, Moore, Boffito, and supported by

---

[39] An error of comparable genesis, although not concerning the *cursus*, is found at paragraph 50: "qui vidit retinere non potuit in primo celo". The locative ablative "in primo celo" was probably situated in the margin and then misplaced in a subsequent copy. Those words should be advanced between "vidit" and "retinere", as was clear to the scribe of the ancestor of b4, who observed and emended the error.

[40] "And so, mediately or immediately, everything that has existence, has existence from Him; for, because the secondary cause proceeds from the primary [cause], this exercises more influence on what is caused, like something that receives and *looks at* a ray, for which reason the first cause is the greater cause".

Parodi.[41] What is important here (but not necessarily relevant to how the word should be amended) is that the Amico dell'*Ottimo*'s vernacular commentary on the *Commedia*, written in 1337 × 1341, depends on the transmitted text. Incorporating a large section of the *expositio textus* of the *Epistola*, the gloss to *Paradiso*, I, 1 includes the following:

> Adunque tutte le cose, se non Esso, hanno l'essere da altri. E finalmente è di divenire ad uno, dal quale tutte l'altre cose hanno l'essere e questi è Dio, il quale, sì come prima cagione, getta sopra il causato, ad modo di ricevente e *di raguardante* il ragio.

The Amico dell'*Ottimo*'s *raguardante* is the direct translation of the Latin *respicientis*. The commentary, then, bears witness that the infelicitous *respicientis* had already emerged in the direct tradition and entered the indirect tradition by the turn of the 1330s.[42]

The details discussed and the long chain of mistakes characterizing the whole manuscript tradition imply the following. The transmission of the *Epistola* commenced with a copy which was complete, to which the coherent structure of the preserved text and its formulaic conclusion are proof, but which was untidy rather than a fair copy prepared by Dante or the addressee. In other words, the original was a manuscript with annotations in the margins and between the lines, and other such features. Difficult to read, Dante's manuscript occasioned a seriously corrupt archetype.

[41] Dante Alighieri, *Opere latine*, 2 vols, reintegrate nel testo con nuovi commenti da G. GIULIANI, Florence, 1878–1882, vol. 2, p. 222 (elaborating on his *Del metodo di commentare la "Divina commedia". Epistola di Dante a Cangrande della Scala*, Savona, 1856). For debate on this passage, see E. PISTELLI, "Dubbi e proposte sul testo delle 'Epistole'", *Studi danteschi*, 2 (1920) pp. 153–54; Alighieri, *Epistola a Cangrande*, p. 45.

[42] Alighieri, *Epistola XIII*, pp. 444–50; the use of the *Epistola* in this commentary is discussed in F. MAZZONI, "Per l'Epistola a Cangrande'", in *Studi in onore di Angelo Monteverdi*, 2 vols, Modena, 1959, vol. 2, pp. 498–516 (reprinted in ID., *Contributi di filologia dantesca. Prima serie*, Florence, 1966, pp. 7–37, and in ID., *Con Dante per Dante. Saggi di filologia ed ermeneutica dantesca*, IV. *Le opere minori*, ed. by G. C. GARFAGNINI, E. GHIDETTI, S. MAZZONI, with the collaboration of E. BENUCCI, Rome, 2016, pp. 301–31, and in AMICO DELL'OTTIMO, *Chiose sopra la 'Comedia'*, pp. xv–xviii.

The textual corruption that is rife in all the witnesses to the *Epistola* can, in fact, be adduced to invalidate the hypothesis that "la prima spinta a realizzare il falso fu quella di garantire a Cangrande e ai suoi eredi una prestigiosissima dedica".[43] Had the piece been a forgery, multiple parties would have been involved in the process of its making: Dante for the *nuncupatoria* (as some commentators admit his authorship only for this section while others consider it apocryphal); one or two commentators for the *accessus* and *expositio textus*; and a compiler, who joined these components together and edited them to make a coherent whole, and who was a forger, should the *nuncupatoria* be bogus, or else had access to the poet's personal writings should it be authentic. The objective of such a complex operation would have been to create a text homogeneous enough to pose plausibly as Dante's. Yet, a Scaligerian intention, hidden under that cumbersome project, would surely have manifested itself in a piece more ordinary in content than the *Epistola* is and in its subsequent dissemination from a

---

[43]   "[T]he main reason to make the forgery was to grant Cangrande and his heirs a very prestigious dedication"; CASADEI, *Dante. Altri accertamenti*, p. 59. As regards the date of the assumed forgery, it would have been made almost ten years after Cangrande's death, which took place in 1329: "all'altezza della seconda metà degli anni Trenta [...] nell'ambito dell'*entourage* scaligero, adatto per attestare una dedica del *Paradiso* a Cangrande, molto utile a fini propagandistici"; CASADEI, *Dante. Altri accertamenti*, p. 101. This hypothesis cannot be maintained for several reasons. Before 1328 Guido da Pisa had already quoted the *accessus* at length (for which see footnote 27) and the *expositio textus* was already circulating with errors in 1337. What is more, considering that the *Commedia* had been circulating throughout Italy for years, as attested by an abundance of copies, the forgery would have come rather late. As for the political context, the latter half of the 1330s was disastrous for the Scaligeri. Their expansionist ambitions, for which Cangrande was largely responsible, were made null by an anti-Scaligerian coalition of Venetian, Florentine, and Lombard forces in 1336–1339. In those years the Scaligeri would have needed something rather more effective than a forged dedication of the *Paradiso*, even provided that such a dedication would have been a useful propaganda tool in the first place. According to Casadei, another incentive to forge the *Epistola* was to give "valore a una serie di interpretazioni del poema (fine morale e non speculativo-teologico; allegoria e non profezia o visione ecc.), che comunque erano utili a contrastare le polemiche in atto sin dalla fine degli anni Venti, da parte di detrattori sia laici che ecclesiastici" (CASADEI, *Dante. Altri accertamenti*, 59); for this, see the pertinent references in footnotes 18 and 22 above.

fair copy across the Scaligerian regions. Our evidence yields a rather different narrative. There was an archetype, reliant on an unpolished and unpublished original and so corrupt that readers and copyists failed to apprehend several passages.

The absence of even the slightest suggestion that the *Epistola* was accessible or known in Verona and Scaligerian circles gives credit to the notion that it remained in Dante's drawer until his death, that he was the author (as our manuscripts assert in unison), and that it was never consigned to the lord of Verona. The lack of dissemination in Verona and Ravenna seriously undermines the proposition that the *Epistola* was a Scaligerian forgery. For corollaries of that argument would be the work's release in those regions and, one would presume, a wide subsequent dissemination. Furthermore, there is no attested circulation of news in the Scaligerian and Ravennese regions that Dante had dedicated the *Paradiso* to Cangrande. Such a silence is even more telling when one considers the quantity of contemporary literary tributes to Dante. Immediately after his death, epitaphs and poems were composed in his honour in the Veneto, Bologna, and Ravenna. Within Scaligerian circles, we find eulogies such Ferreto Ferreti's *Idibus atra dies augusti Cesaris ibat*; Bernardo Scannabecchi or Rinaldo Cavalchini's *Iura monarchie, superos Phlegetonta lacusque*; in Bologna, Giovanni del Virgilio's *Theologus Dantes nullius dogmatis expers*; and in Ravenna, Menghino Mezzani's *Inclita fama cuius universum penetrat orbem*.[44] Had the *Epistola* been issued by the Scaligers, it would certainly have made an impact on these texts; but no indication of that can be observed.

Our philological evidence is suggestive of how the direct and the earlier indirect tradition of the *Epistola*'s entire text was confined, so far as can now be seen, to Florence. The *Epistola* would have arrived in Florence after Dante's death, where it found only a few readers due to its controversial dedication. It would have been brought there by someone with access to Dante's personal library. A fine candidate would be Pietro Alighieri, his son, who quoted the *Epistola* in his *Comentum* on the *Commedia*, as mentio-

---

[44]   The only epitaph attributable to a Tuscan author is *Hic iacet excelsus poeta comicus Dantes*, two hexameters, which Guido da Pisa inserted in the final version of his *Expositiones*, dedicated to the Genovese Lucano di Giorgio Spinola.

ned above, without explicit reference to Dante, as was his practice also in the *Convivio*. Another candidate would be his brother Iacopo. Iacopo returned to Florence after his father's death, in 1325, and stayed there, but the *Commedia* was the only Dantean work he can be shown with absolute certainty to have known at first hand.

There is yet another textual aspect to be considered here, namely the status of the *Paradiso*'s verses quoted in the *Epistola* in Latin translation, *ad litteram* and in paraphrase. Already in the *Commedia*'s earliest manuscripts, closest to the archetype, contamination by transmission is endemic. In contrast, the *Epistola* invariably quotes the *Paradiso* accurately. As such, the quotations defy efforts to assign them with confidence to any of the stemmatical branches of *Commedia* manuscripts. Accuracy cannot, naturally, constitute a proof that Dante penned the *Epistola*. Even so, the fact that its Latin translations of the *Paradiso* reflect a tradition devoid of noise by transmission and scribal intervention is noteworthy. In demonstration, *Paradiso*, I 37, "Surge ai mortali per diverse foci", is translated *ad litteram* in *Epistola*, 43 as "Surgit mortalibus per diversas fauces". A plethora of *Commedia* manuscripts read "da diverse". While the reading *da* cannot alone evidence proximity in transmission, it should be noted that this variant is widespread in the *Commedia*'s primary circulation both in Florence and Bologna from the 1330s onwards. These earliest pertinent witnesses are Mart Triv Co Gv Lau Lo Pr Ricc Tz, Eg (*da diversa*), Laur (*con diverse*).[45] On copying the *Commedia*, Andrea Lancia opted for *da* in the text proper, writing, "Surge a' mortali da diversi foci". In contrast, his marginal gloss, relying explicitly on the *Epistola*, reads in vernacular translation, "Surge a' mortali per diverse foce". In addition, two correct readings in the *Epistola* distance its text from that of Ash and Ham, early witnesses from western Tuscany, strongly connected to each other. First, *Epistola*, 77 translates "si profonda" of *Paradiso*, I 8 as "profundat se", while Ash and Ham read "ci profonda", *ci* being a locative adverb. Secondly, "memoria" in *Epistola*, 77 equals "la memoria" in *Paradiso*, I 9, while Ash and Ham give the erroneous reading

---

[45] For the sigla, see Dante Alighieri, *La 'Commedia' secondo l'antica vulgata*, 4 vols, ed. by G. PETROCCHI, Milan, 1966–1967, 2nd edn, Florence, 1994.

"a la memoria", deriving from their ultimate common ancestor. A less significant disagreement concerns *Paradiso*, I 6 "chi", which reads "qual" in manuscripts Fi La Mart Parm Vat and To and in the printed editions until the nineteenth century, and which *Epistola* 77 translates as "qui", coming closer to the original pronoun. Finally, the reading "recipit" used in *Epistola*, 66 and 74 betrays no trace of "rende" transmitted by Urb, the main witness of the northern Italian tradition. Here the *Epistola* perfectly agrees with "prende" of *Paradiso*, I 4.

Our philological evidence, obtained by textual criticism and the study of the manuscript tradition, betrays the fact that the *Epistola* has the characteristics of a missive that its author never sent to the addressee. While this observation can neither remove nor resolve all the complexities of interpretation the piece poses, it does refute a scheme that has been considered a prerequisite for treating the letter as authentic, namely that Dante would have sent Cangrande the *Epistola* and the entire *Paradiso* — which he completed only in Ravenna towards the end of his life — in one consignment. It is one thing to ask when Dante wrote the *Epistola* and another thing to enquire whether or not he sent it to Cangrande. Going by the evidence assembled here, the apparent quandary that Dante should have published the *Epistola* and *Paradiso* together does not exist.

This conclusion provides for new lines of enquiry. For instance, one issue is related to the fact that *Epistola* can be dated only broadly to the last years of the poet's sojourn in Verona, a period whose length is debated. Should it prove to be datable to a point of time after the spring of 1318, this would be quite significant. The papal bull *Olim in nostra* of 6 April 1318 excommunicated Cangrande together with his advisers and allies, Matteo Visconti and Rinaldo (Passerino) Bonacolsi. The bone of contention was that Cangrande had defied the papal injunction, communicated by the apostolic nuncios Bertrand de la Tour and Bernardo Gui, that he abandon the title of imperial Vicar. Although the whole city was affected by the interdict, the Scaligerian administration did not renounce the contested designation. Two letters, of 30 March and 19 July 1319, referring to Cangrande as "dominus Vicarius" and "imperiali auctoritate Vicarius" respectively, and a letter by Pope John XXII signed on 27 June 1320, are proof of that.[46] If these dramatic events and the heated political circumstances surrounding the end of Dante's Veronese period are taken into account, it is relevant to ask whether the *Epistola*'s formulation "sacratissimi cesarei principatus [...] Vicario generali" was written before or after Cangrande's excommunication. We should also reassess the implications of the dedication, known only from a letter never sent and addressed to a party from whom Dante had swiftly to distance himself, as is clear from his move to Ravenna. It was perhaps not by chance that Cangrande, celebrated in *Paradiso* XVII and defended in a more allusive fashion in the following canto, is completely absent from the remaining fifteen cantos of the *Commedia*. These are significant aspects, which we must not fail to consider by dismissing the *Epistola* as bogus. Although an extraordinarily complex text, it helps us capture a dramatic juncture in Dante's authorial career.

[46] J. FIKER, *Urkunden zur Geschichte des Römerzuges Kaiser Ludwig des Baiern und italienischen Verhältnisse seiner Zeit*, Innsbruck, 1865, pp. 6–7; C. CIPOLLA, "Lettere di Giovanni XXII riguardanti Verona e gli Scaligeri (1316–1334)", *Atti e memorie dell'Accademia d'agricoltura scienze lettere arti e commercio di Verona*, s. 4, 8 (1909), pp. 180–84.

The Art of Publishing One's Own Work

Petrarch's *De vita solitaria*

Marco Petoletti
(*Milan*)

Several of Petrarch's famous works survive in autograph, manuscripts possessing preeminent cultural, philological, and palaeographical value. What is more, a number of volumes from his library have been identified: more than sixty books with Petrarch's marginal notes have been discovered. We also have direct copies of some now lost manuscripts from his library, and although their *marginalia* are not enriched with his handwriting, they mirror his passions and culture of learning. The combined evidence of his autographs and his other books provide first-hand insights into how he read and how he edited and published his masterpieces.[1]

An intriguing case study is offered by *De vita solitaria*, a huge treatise on the life of solitude, to the composition of which Petrarch devoted years of his life.[2] The study of Petrarch's letters, his manuscripts, embellished with his autograph marginalia, and the complicated manuscript tradition of the *De vita solitaria*, shed light on the strategies the author used to promote the circulation

---

[1] M. Feo, "Francesco Petrarca", in *Storia della letteratura italiana. X. La tradizione dei testi*, ed. by C. Ciociola, Rome, 2001, pp. 270–329.

[2] Francesco Petrarca, *De vita solitaria*, ed. by G. Martellotti, in Id., *Prose*, Milano–Napoli, 1955, pp. 286–591; *De vita solitaria. Buch I*, ed. by K. A. E. Enenkel, Leiden–New York–Copenhagen–Cologne, 1990; *De vita solitaria. La vie solitaire 1346–1366*, ed. by Ch. Carraud, Grenoble 1999. I am preparing a new critical edition of *De vita solitaria*, with Italian translation and commentary.

The Art of Publication from the Ninth to the Sixteenth Century, ed. by Samu Niskanen with the assistance of Valentina Rovere, IPM, 93 (Turnhout, 2023), pp. 293–310.
© BREPOLS ❧ PUBLISHERS   DOI 10.1484/M.IPM-EB.5.133086

of this work.[3] The way in which he built this text and initiated its transmission demonstrates a self-awareness as to the impact he had on other scholars of his age. In his letters, he often spoke of *De vita solitaria*, so that it is possible to follow the process of its composition and publication step by step. This treatise gained huge popularity in the fourteenth and fifteenth centuries: nearly 130 copies, most of which require further study to ascertain their origin, are known.[4] They contributed to the increase and spread of Petrarch's influence, not only in Italy but all over Europe, especially in Germany and France, where he became a celebrated master.

He began *De vita solitaria* in 1346 when he was living in Vaucluse, situated in the diocese overseen by his friend, Philippe de Cabassole (1305–1372), bishop of Cavaillon.[5] As Petrarch himself stated, in writing this treatise he was able to offer his tithe to the bishop.[6] He also disclosed that he finished the first draft in 1346, but went on working on the text for many years, enlarging some chapters whenever he found pertinent material. In 1366, twenty years after the first draft, Petrarch sent a refined version of *De vita solitaria* to Philippe de Cabassole, the work's dedicatee, now patriarch of Jerusalem, together with his letter *Sen.* VI 5, written in Venice on 6 June.[7] Philippe greatly praised him for this gift

---

[3] P. Rajna, "Il codice Vaticano 3357 del trattato 'De vita solitaria' di Francesco Petrarca", in *Miscellanea Ceriani. Raccolta di scritti originali per onorare la memoria di monsignor Antonio Maria Ceriani prefetto della Biblioteca Ambrosiana*, Milano, 1910, pp. 641–86; B. L. Ullman, "The composition of Petrarch's 'De vita solitaria' and the history of the Vatican manuscript" (1955), in his *Studies in the Italian Renaissance*, Rome, 1973² (Storia e letteratura, 51), pp. 135–75.

[4] Petrarca, *De vita solitaria*, ed. by Enenkel, pp. 42–51. Other copies have been pointed out by C. M. Monti, "Nella biblioteca di Philippe de Cabassole", in *Petrarca, Verona, l'Europa*, ed. by G. Billanovich, G. Frasso, Padova, 1997 (Studi sul Petrarca, 26), pp. 221–69, at 253.

[5] M. Hayez, "Cabassole (Cabassoles), Philippe", in *DBI*, 15 (1972), pp. 678–81; Monti, "Nella biblioteca di Philippe de Cabassole", pp. 221–69.

[6] *De vita solitaria*, proh. 6: "Accedit quod ex more institutoque meo veteri, nunc in rure tuo positus, ut frugum ceteri, sic ego tibi decimas otii debere videor primitiasque vigiliarum".

[7] Francesco Petrarca, *Res Seniles. Libri V–VIII*, ed. by S. Rizzo, Florence, 2009, pp. 126–35. See especially § 2: "Cum nempe olim solitarius et tui ruris in silentio otiosus ac tranquillus agerem prope felicem vitam, si diuturnior fuisset,

and promoted the transmission of the *De vita solitaria* in Avignonese literary circles, as *Sen.* VI 6, sent by Petrarch to Philippe
on 8 August 1366, witnesses: copies were made for Pope Urban V
and Gui of Boulogne, cardinal bishop of Porto, while Pierre d'A-
meil, archbishop of Embrun, and Pedro Gomez Barroso, bishop
of Lisbon, read the treatise.[8] The dedication copy addressed to
Philippe de Cabassole was prepared by a Paduan priest, who
has been identified as Giovanni da Bozzetta,[9] between 1365 and
1366.[10] I have recently discovered that very copy, which carries an
abundance of autograph *notabilia* (Madrid, Biblioteca Nacional de
España, 9633).[11] The discovery will shed light on the circulation
of the treatise in the Avignonese milieu.

While the presentation of a copy to Philippe de Cabassole constituted the act of publishing, neither the authorial work nor the

neve aut incomitata solitudo esset aut ines otium, quotidie novi aliquid medi-
tarer aut scriberem, contigit ut duo michi libelli totidem continuos per annos
in diebus quadragesime et sacro tempori et loco illi tuo et statui meo ex parte
convenientes occurrerent, *De solitaria* alter *vita*, alter *De otio religioso*".

[8]   Petrarca, *Res Seniles. Libri V–VIII*, pp. 200–01 (§ 3): "Illud miraculo
additum, quod et Pontificem Maximum et qui illi proximus gradu est, epyscopum Portuensem, de libello illo loqui atque eum dignanter expetere, insu-
per et Ebredunensem archiepyscopum et epyscopum Ulixbonensem, quorum
primus quanto sit ingenio iure me optimo testem facis — scio enim —, secundum vero nonnisi per famam et, quibus credo omnia, per literas tuas novi,
ambos doctrine uberrime altissimique iudicii viros, et legisse illum avidissime
et de eo multa certatim honorifice locutos scribis".

[9]   A. Foresti, *Aneddoti della vita di Francesco Petrarca*, Padua, 1977
(Studi sul Petrarca, 1), p. 483. Petrarch assigned his breviary to Giovanni
da Bozzetta in his last will. On this book, now BAV, Borgh. 364A, see
G. Goletti, "Il Breviario del Petrarca", in *Petrarca nel tempo. Tradizione
lettori e immagini delle opere*, ed. by M. Feo, Pontedera, 2003, pp. 513–15.

[10]   See *Sen.*, V 1, 26–29 to Boccaccio (Petrarca, *Res Seniles. Libri V–VIII*,
p. 28): "Nunc tandem post tot cassa primordia scribendum illud domo abiens
dimisi inter cuiusdam sacerdotis manus, que an ad scribendum sacre fuerint ut sacerdotis, an ad fallendum faciles ut scriptoris, nescio. Nuntiatum
tamen est michi amicorum literis iam factum esse quod iusseram. De qua-
litate, donec videam, mos horum certissimus me dubium facit; solent enim,
auditu mirum, non quod scribendum acceperint, sed nescio quid aliud scrip-
titare; tantum vel ignorantie est vel inertie vel contemptus. Hoc igitur, quod
in horas expecto, qualecunque erit, illi e vestigio transmittam. Scriptorem
quam me potius incuset".

[11]   M. Petoletti, "Il manoscritto di dedica del 'De vita solitaria' rivisto
e corretto da Petrarca", *Italia medioevale e umanistica*, 61 (2020), pp. 129–50.

publishing process had yet met with completion. On 1 May 1373, Petrarch wrote a letter (*Sen.* XVI 3) from Arquà to his friend Francesco Casini of Siena, the pope's doctor, who was one of the first readers of *De vita solitaria*, which he had probably obtained from Philippe de Cabassole.[12] In the letter Petrarch remarked that the year before, 1372, Giovanni degli Abbarbagliati of Borgo San Donnino, prior of Camaldoli, who corresponded with him and invited him in 1363 to his monastery in Tuscany,[13] read *De vita solitaria* in Venice thanks to an unidentifiable friend, who had opened to the prior the doors of Petrarch's library. The man was greatly surprised because the second book of this treatise, where Petrarch offers his readers a long list of solitary saints from Adam down to saints of his own age, lacked a biography of the founder of Camaldoli, St Romuald. Petrarch did not know the holy hermit at all. Giovanni sent Petrarch Romuald's Life written by Peter Damian so that a detailed portrait of the founder of Camaldoli could be included in *De vita solitaria*; it resulted in the so called *Supplementum romualdinum*.[14] In the same letter, Petrarch wrote that another friend was complaining about the absence of Giovanni Gualberto, the founder of Vallombrosa, and that he was waiting for the Life of Gualberto in order to complete his book.[15]

Petrarch was ready to modify his *De vita solitaria* by inserting new details or even an entirely new section; he was also ready to propagate his treatise, especially in literary circles and among the religious orders. It is also true that when writing biographies of contemporary saints, Petrarch showed the same philological care

---

[12]   Francesco Petrarca, *Res Seniles. Libri XIII–XVII*, ed. by S. RIZZO, Florence, 2017, pp. 334–55. See F.-C. UGINET, "Casini, Francesco", in *DBI*, 21 (1978), pp. 356–59.

[13]   *Sen.* II 8, 1 (Francesco Petrarca, *Res Seniles. Libri I–IV*, ed. by S. RIZZO, Florence, 2006, pp. 178–79): "At laborem veniendi ad me ut tuam me ad heremum ducas, quam tua sibi sumit humilitas, quia nec tibi conveniens nec debitus michi, acceptum habeo et perinde apud me est ac veneris".

[14]   *De vita solitaria*, II 8, 2–8.

[15]   *Sen.* XVI 3, 31–32: "Huius rei fama excitus amicus alter queri cepit quid Iohannem quendam, auctorem ordinis Vallis Umbrose, compatriotam meum, post terga relinquerem. Huic quoque respondi non id negligentia vel contemptu sed rei ignorantia contigisse et nunc maxime vitam eius expecto, in qua siquid erit ad solitudinem spectans et hunc inseram".

he had devoted to reconstructing those of the saints of ancient times. It is not by chance that he asked Giovanni Boccaccio to help him with the life of Peter Damian. Doubtful about the consistency of the biographical data he had collected on Peter Damian, Petrarch urged Boccaccio, via the intermediation of Donato Albanzani, who was in Ravenna, to send him the saint's life. Boccaccio told the whole story in a letter written in Ravenna in 1362 (letter XI). With this letter, he sent Petrarch a Life of Peter Damian. This text was Boccaccio's composition, rather than Giovanni da Lodi's, which he had discovered among dusty papers in the house of an old man, and which he judged to be stylistically horrible. It seems, however, probable that Petrarch never received Boccaccio's letter with his rewriting of the old Life of Peter Damian. Together with the *Vita sanctissimi Petri Damiani patris*, his letter has been preserved only in a late manuscript, now in Modena, Biblioteca Estense Universitaria, lat. 630 (α.R.6.7).[16]

In *Sen.* XVI 3, 27, Petrarch left a description of the first copy of his treatise that he had ordered to be prepared; this manuscript was full of his corrections and additions:

> Is penes amicum quendam meum fidelissimum librum illum repperit et erat forte quem primum scribi feceram atque ideo, ut fit, omnes undique margines additionibus pleni erant.[17]

The "very faithful friend of mine" was probably Donato Albanzani, who was allowed to use Petrarch's library in Venice.[18] In *Sen.* VIII 6, which Petrarch sent to Donato in 1367 from Pavia, he suggested some penitential texts as reading for his friend, which he affirmed could easily be found in his library.[19] Moreover, in *De sui ipsius et multorum ignorantia* Petrarch referred to Donato as his

---

[16]   P. PONTARI, "Boccaccio a Ravenna tra Dante e Petrarca: novità sulla Vita Petri Damiani", in *Boccaccio e la Romagna*, ed. by P. PONTARI, G. ALBANESE, Ravenna, 2015, pp. 119–47.

[17]   "He [the prior of Camaldoli] found that book in the hands of a very faithful friend of mine; it happened by chance to be the first one I arranged to be copied, so, as often happens, every margin was full of additions".

[18]   C. M. MONTI, "Il 'ravennate' Donato Albanzani amico di Boccaccio e Petrarca", in *Dante e la sua eredità a Ravenna nel Trecento*, ed. by M. Petoletti, Ravenna, 2015, pp. 115–60, with a careful portrait of Donato.

[19]   Petrarca, *Res Seniles. Libri V–VIII*, pp. 348–59. See M. PETOLETTI, "In nostro armariolo presto erunt: considerazioni sulla biblioteca patristica di

librarian: "Bibliotheca nostra, tuis in manibus relicta, non illit-
terata quidem illa, quamvis illiterati hominis, neque illis ignota
est" ("Our library, left in your hands, is not an unlearned affair
— even if an unlearned man owns it — and it is not unknown to
them").[20]

On 1 September 1366, just after Philippe de Cabassole had
received a copy of De vita solitaria, Petrarch wrote another letter
to Donato from Pavia (Sen. V 4), in which he referred to the fact
that Donato had been insistent in requesting the treatise.[21] At the
end Petrarch added (§§ 31–33):

> Ceterum Solitarie vite librum, quem pene iratus iure tuo postulas,
> sacerdoti meo paduano scripsi iam ut tibi transmitteret. Quem ut
> arbitrio tuo legas permitto; ne transcribas veto usque dum venero;
> adhuc enim verbum unum ibi addidi. Nosti morem: alter Protho-
> genes nescio e tabella manum tollere.[22]

This is a statement of paramount importance: Petrarch had
requested a Paduan priest, doubtless Giovanni da Bozzetta mentioned above, to send Donato the model that had served as the
exemplar for the dedication manuscript of De vita solitaria sent to
Philippe de Cabassole; but Petrarch forbade the further dissemination of this text because he was not yet satisfied with the work
and wanted to add some new material. Publication had taken
place, but the authorial process continued. To make the point, he
quoted a passage from Pliny the Elder (Historia naturalis, XXXV
80), comparing himself to the Greek painter Prothogenes, unable
to finish his works.[23] It is worthy of note that in his manuscript of

---

Petrarca", Atti e memorie dell'Accademia Galileiana di Scienze Lettere ed Arti in
Padova, 131 (2019), pp. 1–25.

[20]   Francesco Petrarca, De ignorantia. Della mia ignoranza e di quella di
molti altri, ed. by E. FENZI, Milan, 1999, p. 280.

[21]   Petrarca, Res Seniles. Libri V–VIII, pp. 76–83.

[22]   "As for De vita solitaria, which you are requesting almost in anger, jus-
tifiably so, I have already ordered my Paduan priest to send you a copy. I
agree to let you read it as you wish, but I forbid you to make a copy until I
come back, because I have to add some new passages to the extant text. You
know my custom; I am a second Prothogenes and I cannot pull my hand from
my painting".

[23]   "[Apelles Cous] dixit enim omnia sibi cum illo paria esse aut illi
meliora, sed uno se praestare, quod manum de tabula sciret tollere; memora-
bili praecepto nocere saepe nimiam diligentiam".

Pliny, now BnF, lat. 6802, at fol. 256ᵛ, Petrarch marked this passage with a *manicula* and a marginal note in which he addressed himself: "Attende, Francisce, dum scribis" ("Be careful, Francis, while writing").[24]

Already in 1361, while writing about *De vita solitaria* to his *Socrates* — the nickname of Louis of Beringen — Petrarch stated that he did not want to delay the dispatch of the text. But he required one condition (*Disp.* 45 = *Var.* 14):[25]

> Ego enim et illos sibi [Philippe de Cabassole] non negare nec subtrahere amplius institui [...] et te simul horum participem facere in animo est, sed ea lege ut vivo me nemo alius particeps per vos fiat.[26]

Petrarch's instruction may have been a rhetorical affectation; he is likely to have known that once he sent a copy of his writings to his friends they would spread them among their respective literary circles, his prohibition notwithstanding. That much had already happened with his famous lament for the dying Mago Barca, Hannibal's brother, the only passage of the *Africa* that was widely read during Petrarch's lifetime, because of his friends' disobedience.

---

[24] P. DE NOLHAC, *Pétrarque et l'Humanisme*, vol. 2, Paris, 1907², p. 74. On Par. lat. 6802: M. PETOLETTI, "Signa manus mee. Percorso tra postille e opere di Francesco Petrarca", in *L'antiche e le moderne carte. Studi in memoria di Giuseppe Billanovich*, ed. by A. MANFREDI, C. M. MONTI, Rome–Padua, 2007 (Medioevo e Umanesimo, 112), pp. 451–97, at 463–64, 468–71 and 475–79; ID., "L'opera, l'autore e la scrittura", *Quaderni petrarcheschi*, 15–16 (2005–2006), pp. 577–603, at 582–92 and 598–603; M. D. REEVE, "The editing of Pliny's Natural History", *Revue d'histoire des textes*, n.s., 2 (2007), pp. 107–79, at 132–39 and 152–55; G. PERUCCHI, "Le postille di Petrarca a Plinio nel ms. Leiden, BPL 6", *Atti e memorie dell'Accademia Toscana di scienze e lettere 'La Colombaria'*, n.s. 61, 75 (2010), pp. 65–116; EAD., "Boccaccio geografo lettore del Plinio petrarchesco", *Italia medioevale e umanistica*, 64 (2013), pp. 153–211.

[25] Francesco Petrarca, *Lettere disperse*, ed. by A. PANCHERI, Parma, 1994, pp. 336–39; Francesco Petrarca, *Lettere disperse*, ed. by E. NOTA, Turin, 2020, pp. 374–79 n. 38.

[26] "I decided to neither deny nor delay the dispatch to him [the dedicatee] any further [...] At the same time, it is my intention to share the treatise with you, but on the condition that neither of you [Philippe de Cabassole and Louis of Beringen] share it with anyone else, as long as I live".

In 1355 or shortly thereafter, Petrarch asked his friend Moggio Moggi to copy his works, and one request was perhaps for *De vita solitaria* (*Fam.* XIX 5).[27] This episode is recorded in two extant letters which were not included in the published collection of Petrarch's letters. The two letters survive as autographs, now BML, Plut. 53.35: *Disp.* 50 = *Var.* 12, and *Disp.* 53 = *Var.* 4, written respectively from Padua (10 June 1362) and Venice (17 November, with a brief addition made on 9 December).[28] In the first, Petrarch commends his little things ("*reculas*") to his friend and offers instruction on how to make changes both to the original manuscript Moggio has received and to the copy in progress so as to bring it up to date:

> Recommendo vobis reculas illas meas, quas dimisi vobis, nominatim *Solitariam vitam*. Libro II°, ubi agitur de Paula, ad finem capituli illius posueram signum additurus aliquid. Mutavi consilium. Amoveatis signum illud. Post illud, libro eodem, est capitulum magnum valde de Petro heremita, quod non memini quotum sit. Ibi non nimis a principio procul est ita: *tam nichil est animi nervorum*. Nolo usqueadeo famam Cesaris urgere, et ideo in utroque libro mutetis et ponatis sic: *quasi sub celo aliquid sit pulcrius*.[29]

In fact, except for a trivial difference (*tamquam* instead of *quasi*), the final draft of *De vita solitaria* (II 9, 5) shows the change Petrarch asked for from Moggio, thus mitigating the bitter invective against Emperor Charles IV and the other European sovereigns, who failed to pay due attention to the cause of the Holy Land.

---

[27] Francesco Petrarca, *Le Familiari*, ed. by V. Rossi, vol. 3, Florence 1937, pp. 320–22.

[28] Petrarca, *Lettere disperse*, ed. by Pancheri, pp. 368–71 and 378–81; Petrarca, *Lettere disperse*, ed. by Nota, pp. 386–91 n. 41, and 422–27 n. 46.

[29] "I commend to you those little things which I left to you, that is *De vita solitaria*. In the second book, where I speak about Paula, at the end of the chapter, I put a cross-reference mark because I wanted to add something. I have changed my mind. Delete that mark. Moreover, in the same book, there is quite a long chapter about Peter the Hermit, but I do not remember exactly where it is. There, not far from the start, it reads as follows: *tam nichil est animi nervorum*. I do not want to crush Caesar's renown up to this point, so you should change it in both books [the original manuscript and its copy] and insert the following: *quasi sub celo aliquid sit pulcrius*".

In the same *Disp.* 50 = *Var.* 12, Petrarch adds in a postscript another request to correct his text:

> Item eodem libro post tractatum de Benedicto est de quodam he-remita, Marsici montis accola et cetera. Debet esse Massici[30]

Here Petrarch suggests a correction. The above-mentioned hermit, whose name was Martin, lived on Mount Marsico. But the final draft shows no sign of this up-to-date refreshment: the extant man-uscripts read in this passage *Marsici*, not *Massici*.[31] Petrarch obvi-ously returned to his original choice. Be that as it may, Petrarch's source for this passage is Gregory the Great's *Dialogi* (III 16, 1–4), which presents Martin as a hermit living on the slopes of Mount Marsico, the medieval name of the ancient *Mons Massicus*, the moun-tain south of Sessa Aurunca, over the gulf of Gaeta, which was very famous for its wine (Petrarch knew that from Verg. *Aen.* VII 726, *Georg.* II 143 and from Hor. *Carm.* I 1, 19, *Sat.* II 4, 51).[32] When he checked Gregory's *Dialogi* again while revising his text, he decided to abandon this change. Because no other source spoke of this Mar-tin, Petrarch thought it safer not to use the old Latin name of the mountain.[33] The manuscript from Petrarch's library with Grego-ry's *Dialogues* has survived: it is now BnF, lat. 2540, fols 110ʳ–171ʳ, a collection of patristic and medieval texts, previously owned by Landolfo Colonna, a canon of Chartres of Roman origin. However,

---

[30] "Moreover, in the same book, after the portrait of Saint Benedict, there is another one about a hermit who dwells on the slopes of Mount Marsico. I think that the correct name of the mountain must be Massico". The following lines of this letter are almost illegible in Petrarch's autograph.

[31] *De vita solitaria* II 6, 6: "Occurret inde Martinus ille, Marsici montis accola; cui de rupe solida fluens perennis aque tenuis stilla dure rupis stillan-tis olim in deserto prodigium renovavit [cf. *Ex.* 17: 5–6]; quique cum serpente terrifico, sub cuius specie vetus serpens terribilior latebat, uno eodemque specu continue sine offensa toto triennio versatus, illo demum mira patientia procul pulso ipse victor solus substitit".

[32] Gregory the Great, *Storie di santi e di diavoli*, ed. by S. PRICOCO, M. SIMONETTI, vol. 2, Milan, 2006, pp. 72–75. The reference to the biblical episode of the water flowing from the rock hit by Moses' staff (*Ex.* 17: 5–6) was suggested to Petrarch by Gregory himself, who wrote (*Dial.* II 16, 2): "Qua in re ostendit omnipotens Deus quantam sui famuli curam gereret, cui vetusto miraculo potum in solitudine ex petrae duritia ministraret".

[33] ULLMAN, "The composition", p. 165, suggests that "apparently Petrarch forgot about this when he got his copy back".

this book shows very few marginal notes by Petrarch himself.[34] The passage of the *Dialogues* used in the second book of *De vita solitaria* is on fol. 141ʳ: here, the name of the mountain where the hermit Martin lived has been written in the form *Marsicus*.

A postscript added to *Disp.* 53 = *Var.* 4 is equally important. Here Petrarch recommends to Moggio his "little things" once again, in a passage that shows the care he took when commissioning copies of his works:

> Reliquum est ut rogem reculas illas meas vobis, frater carissime, cure esse, si vacat, saltem *Vitam solitariam*, que si transcursa erit, ut spero, minietur ligeturque solemniter per magistrum Benedictum[35] et mittatur ad me exemplum et exemplar, diligenter panno cereo obvoluta, inter ballas Iohannoli de Cumis, et quicquid opus fuerit ad hec solvet dominus Danisolus et Franciscolus meus diriget vos in his, qui predictos amicos meos bene novit.[36]

Among the extant copies of *De vita solitaria*, there are two manuscripts of paramount importance: the aforementioned dedication copy, now in Madrid, that I have recently identified, and Vat. lat. 3357, a paper codex of humble and unpretentious appearance.[37] In Pio Rajna's words the latter is a witness "più raro ancora che un autografo non sia" ("rarer than an autograph itself").[38] The importance of this book, which now preserves *De vita solitaria* followed by *Itinerarium*, was soon recognized: Bernard Bembo, the father of Cardinal Peter, who owned other famous autographs of Petrarch now in the Vatican Library, entered a short preface on

---

[34] DE NOLHAC, *Pétrarque et l'Humanisme*, vol. 2, pp. 206–07.

[35] M. M. DONATO, "'Minietur ligeturque [...] per magistrum Benedictum'. Un nome per il miniatore milanese del Petrarca", in *Opere e giorni. Studi su mille anni di arte europea dedicati a Max Seidel*, ed. by K. BERGDOLT, G. BONSANTI, Venice, 2001, pp. 189–200.

[36] "I have only to beg you to take care of those my little things, my dearest brother, if you can: of *De vita solitaria* at least. If it has been copied — as I hope — I want it to be illuminated and bound very carefully by master Benedict, and then to send me the original manuscript and its copy, wrapped with care in an oilskin with the luggage addressed to Giovannolo of Como. Every related charge must be paid by Danisolus: you will have instructions from my Franciscolus [his son-in-law], who knows well the friends I mentioned to you".

[37] M. VATTASSO, *I codici petrarcheschi della Biblioteca Vaticana*, Rome, 1908, pp. 28–30.

[38] RAJNA, "Il codice Vaticano 3357", p. 672.

the verso of the first folio in which he addressed the reader stating, incorrectly, that the book was written in Petrarch's own hand (albeit he noticed that the handwriting looked different from the more polished variety Petrarch usually employed). It preserves the *supplementum romualdinum* on a separate leaf (fol. 14) and many marginal notes. Some of them are quite extraordinary: they witness a dialogue between the book's owner or reader and Petrarch.[39] The following specimens instance the central aspects of their discussion. Emphases, in italics, in specimens 1–3 and 7 are mine and indicate the focus of the queries in question.

(1) fol. 3ʳ: "Neque enim magno studio incubui, neque id necesse ratus sum, *aut* defuturam veritus materiam de re uberrima scribenti" (*De vita solitaria*, I 1, 5); left margin: "pete an *haud*".

(2) fol. 3ᵛ: "Fumant ipsis *edentibus* stupenda fercula" (I 2, 12); left margin: "vel *e dentibus*. Pete".[40]

(3) fol. 4ʳ: "Iste *fragilitatis* sibi conscius omniumque quibus humanum corpus subiacet securus" (I 2, 18); left margin: "*frugalitais* [*sic*]. Pete./frugalitatis".

(4) fol. 4ᵛ: "Vix temperare michi potui, quominus unum satyrici dentis morsum huic loco valde, nisi fallor, congruentem interponerem" (I 3, 10); left margin: "Scito quis locus sit quem supprimit./ Dixit esse versus Iuvenalis: 'Et de virtute locuti' et cetera" (Iuv. 2, 20–21).

(5) fol. 5ʳ: "Quod illi olim molli et effeminato causidico sepe dixi, qui hec loca non quietis amore, quam non noverat, non appetitu otii quod oderat, sed nescio quonam imitandi studio frequentare ceperat, incertum an sibi molestior an michi" (I 3, 21); right margin: "Causidicus. Pete quis f[uerit]".

(6) fol. 8ʳ: "Sed hic ante alios occurrit, quem irrisor nobilis notum fecit" (I 7, 26); right margin: "Scito quis Servilii fit irrisor".

(7) fol. 13ʳ: "Que sequuntur attexere longum est et minime necessarium: finis est ut et [*om. ed.* Martellotti] se recordatione vite preterite torqueri acrius et in comparationem quiete viventium miserum fateatur, quorum plurimos in hac de qua loquimur vita

---

[39]   RAJNA, "Il codice Vaticano 3357", pp. 658–59.

[40]   The marginal note *Pete* has been written with an ink which is different from the one used for the proposed correction *vel 'e dentibus'*.

secretiore *placuisse* diffinit" (II 6, 2); right margin: "Scito an *Deo placuisse* vel aliter".

As for the first case, in his edition of *De vita solitaria*, Martellotti accepted the reading *aut* as belonging to the text proper of Vat. lat. 3357, whereas Enenkel preferred *haud*, a correction proposed in its margin. Having no effect on the meaning, the choice of word here is a stylistic one. Martellotti's choice (*aut*) is the right one; it has been confirmed by the reading preserved in the dedication copy. Moreover, the question *pete an "haud"* ("Ask him if *haud* must be written here") is left without a proper answer to solve the problem.

In the second example, Petrarch is discussing the dinner of the *occupatus* (the busy men). The question posed was whether the world *edentibus* ("There are smoking dishes which are the cause of amazement *while they are eating*") should be read as *e dentibus* ("There are smoking dishes *from their teeth*"). An ingenious conjecture, the query betrays meticulous scrutiny.

Let us consider the third example. The copyist of Vat. lat. 3357 wrote: "Iste *fragilitatis* sibi conscius omniumque quibus humanum corpus subiacet securus" ("That man, conscious of his weakness and feeling safe from the ills to which the human body is subject"). In the margin, we read the proposed correction *frugalitatis* (spelled incorrectly as *frugalitais*), "conscious of his soberness", perhaps a change made by Petrarch himself. The careful reader intends to ask Petrarch which of the two readings is the correct one, and writes in the margin "Pete", immediately after *frugalitatis*. Once he had Petrarch's answer, he deletes *fragilitatis* in the text and he rectifies *frugalitatis* with a marginal cross-reference mark, having struck out the erroneous *frugalitais*.

As regards the fourth specimen, in another passage Petrarch does not quote verbatim some lines of a classical satirical author, which were judged indecent (*De vita solitaria* I 3, 10): "Vix temperare michi potui, quominus unum satyrici dentis morsum huic loco valde, nisi fallor, congruentem interponerem. Sed cogitans ad quem sermo michi est, stilo potius aliquid quam verecundie subtrahendum credidi" ("I could barely refrain from inserting here the satirist's point, but I recalled to whom I was addressing myself and decided to sacrifice a vanity of style rather than be found wanting in respect"). The reader of Vat. lat. 3357 wants to investigate and to discover the source Petrarch has put aside: this is the meaning of the note *Scito*, which could be rendered as "Go and ask to know". In his response Petrarch pointed to the passage of Juvenal (2, 20–21): "et de virtute locuti, clunem agitant" ("While speaking of virtue, they are swaying their hips"). Petrarch could not use the coarse sentence *clunem agitant* in the lofty diction of *De vita solitaria*, so he preferred to make an allusive gesture towards Juvenal instead of quoting him.

The same niceness pertains to the fifth specimen. In *De vita solitaria* I 3, 21, Petrarch sketches an effeminate lawyer who withdrew to solitude not because he loved peace and quiet but because he wanted to imitate Petrarch. The reader would have liked to know the identity of this unnamed lawyer, but on this occasion his request was not satisfied: Petrarch gave no answer, because he did not wish to indulge in gossip.

The next extract, the sixth, relates to *De vita solitaria* I 7, 26, in which Petrarch describes as "ridiculous" Servilius Vatia's retirement to his villa near Cumae in Campania, drawing on a beautiful letter by Seneca (*Ep.* 55) in which the Latin author states (§ 4): "At ille latere sciebat, non vivere. Multum autem interest, utrum vita tua otiosa sit an ignava. Numquam aliter hanc villam Vatia vivo praeteribam, quam ut dicerem: 'Vatia hic situs est'" ("But this man knew how to hide, not how to live: there is a great difference if you live without worries or if you live like a slothful man. I never passed by this villa when Vatia was alive without saying: 'here Vatia is buried'"). Petrarch says: "Et quam multos esse credimus ubique Servilios? Sed hic ante alios occurrit, quem irrisor nobilis notum fecit" ("I suppose there are many people like Servilius everywhere, but he comes first to mind because a noble writer brought him to attention by his mockery"). The unnamed *irrisor nobilis* of Vatia in *De vita solitaria* is thus Seneca himself: here the reader, who had not understood Petrarch's hint as to to his classical source, intended to consult the author directly.

As for our last specimen, in the chapter dedicated to Gregory the Great (*De vita solitaria* II 6, 2) Petrarch quotes a passage of the *Dialogi* (I prol. 4) where the holy pontiff complains that, having enjoyed the peace of a retired life, his days are now "soiled with the dust of earthly activity" because of the duty of pastoral

care. Petrarch goes on: "It would be too much to add all that follows, and not at all necessary. The result is that he [Gregory the
Great] confesses that he is more painfully tortured now because of
the recollection of his past life, and wretched in comparison with
those who live quietly, most of whom he describes as finding pleasure in this more retired way of living which I am speaking of".
But in our reader's opinion the word *placuisse* without an indirect
object (in the dative case) was unclear, so he looked for an answer
addressed to the author. Petrarch alludes to Gregory's own words
in the preface to the *Dialogi* (§§ 4–6):[41]

De vita solitaria II 6, 2	Gregory the Great, Dialogi I prol. 4–6
Que sequuntur attexere longum est et minime necessarium: finis est ut et se recordatione vite pre-terite torqueri acrius et in compa-rationem quiete viventium mise-rum fateatur, quorum plurimos in hac de qua loquimur *vita secretiore placuisse* diffinit.	Perpendo itaque quid tolero, per-pendo quid amisi, dumque intueor quod perdidi, fit hoc gravius quod porto. [...] Et cum prioris vitae recolo, quasi postergum ductis oculis viso litore suspiro. [...] Nonnumquam vero ad augmen-tum mei doloris adiungitur quod quorumdam vita, qui praesens saeculum tota mente reliquerunt, mihi ad memoriam revocatur, quo-rum dum culmen aspicio, quantum ipse in infimis iaceam agnosco. Quorum *plurimi* conditori suo *in secretiori vita placuerunt* [...].

Gregory's sentence, paraphrased by Petrarch, "quorum *plurimi*
conditori suo *in secretiori vita placuerunt*" ("Most of them were
accepted to their Creator for their secluded lives"), corroborated
our reader's suspicion that something was missing. So the uncertainty of our reader, who would have added *Deo* to *placuisse* or
something to that effect (possibly Gregory's words *conditori suo*) is
not out of place.

Apparently, Petrarch left questions 5–7 above unanswered.
While he would not have replied to our fifth specimen because
he preferred discretion, there was no obvious reason to duck the

[41] This passage has been written on BnF, lat. 2540, fol. 110ᵛ.

remaining two. Perhaps Petrarch had no more time — cut short by his death — or there was simply not the opportunity.

Of course, the anonymous reader of Vat. lat. 3357 had every opportunity to question Petrarch in person and be enlightened: he has been identified, by Pio Rajna, as Donato Albanzani, a close friend of Petrarch's and Boccaccio's who translated into Italian, respectively, the *De viris illustribus* and *De mulieribus claris*.[42] He was also the scribe of a huge collection of Petrarch's letters preserved in Parma, Biblioteca Palatina, MS Pal. 79, as Agostino Sottili has shown on the basis of a comparison of the handwriting with Donato's holograph will (Venezia, Archivio di Stato, Archivio Notarile, Testamenti, Notaio Costantino da Cison, busta 915, nr. 14).[43]

Another potential autograph of Donato Albanzani survives as BAV, Vat. lat. 5223. However, the identification remains a hypothesis under discussion. This extraordinary collection of letters and speeches, closely connected with the Venetian area, was written in the first decade of the fifteenth century, possibly in Donato's hand: the handwriting of the Vatican collection is more elegant that that of the will, a disparity that raises uncertainties about the proposed identification of the collection.[44] A close palaeographical and philological comparison between the will and Donato's personal and official letters preserved in Vat. lat. 5223 would be valuable. There are yet more charters, invaluable in many ways, that can be added to this number: the Este chancery record, written in Niccolò III's times (Modena, Archivio di Stato, Nicolai II epistulae et decreta, 1401–1409), which, according to Agostino Sottili's suggestion, includes texts copied by Donato at

42   RAJNA, "Il codice Vaticano 3357", pp. 664–67.

43   A. SOTTILI, "Donato Albanzani e la tradizione delle lettere del Petrarca", *Italia medioevale e umanistica*, 6 (1963), pp. 185–201 (= ID., *Scritti petrarcheschi*, ed. by F. DELLA SCHIAVA, A. DE PATTO, C. M. MONTI, Rome–Padua, 2015, pp. 3–20).

44   T. CASINI, "Notizie e documenti per la storia della poesia italiana nei secoli XIII e XIV. I. Tre nuovi rimatori del Trecento", *Il Propugnatore*, n.s., 1/2 (1888), pp. 93–116, 313–66; F. NOVATI, "Donato Albanzani alla corte estense", *Archivio storico italiano*, s. V, 6 (1890), pp. 365–85, at 381–85; SOTTILI, "Donato Albanzani", p. 197 (= ID., *Scritti petrarcheschi*, p. 17); M. PETOLETTI, "Scrivere lettere dopo Petrarca: le epistole 'viscontee' di Giovanni Manzini", *Mélanges de l'École française de Rome – Moyen Âge*, 128/1 (2016), pp. 27–44, at 28.

fols 125^r–128^r.[45] Moreover, it should be taken into careful consideration that some of the marginal notes in Vat. lat. 3357 were written by Coluccio Salutati, whose handwriting much resembled Donato's, not only because they were contemporaries but also because they hailed from the same geographical area (Florence and Tuscany).[46] Palaeographical analysis within such parameters would not be a simple task, but it could contribute to our understanding of the early transmission of Petrarch's works. In my opinion, Pio Rajna's hypothesis about the identity of the mysterious reader — that is, Donato Albanzani — is correct.

Books surviving from Petrarch's library offer further evidence for how he processed *De vita solitaria* from its first draft undertaken in France in 1346 to its first publication twenty years later in 1366. New accessions to Petrarch's library and marginal notes in his hand communicate passionate reading.[47] The books he acquired also inspired Petrarch to make changes to his own works. Quintilian's *Institutio oratoria* is a case in point. Petrarch found a copy only in 1350, when travelling to Rome. Breaking his journey in Florence, Lapo da Castiglionchio the Elder gave him a copy of the *Institutio* as a gift, now BnF, lat. 7720.[48] It is a humble manuscript, a palimpsest, offering a bad text, *discerptus* and *lacer*

---

[45]   A. SOTTILI, *Donato Albanzani tra il Petrarca e Guarino*, unpublished diss., Università Cattolica del Sacro Cuore di Milano, 1961–1962, pp. 97–102.

[46]   ULLMAN, "The composition", pp. 136–45, denies this idea, but see S. GENTILE, "Un manoscritto forse appartenuto a Coluccio Salutati", in *Codici latini del Petrarca nelle biblioteche fiorentine. Mostra 19 maggio–30 giugno 1991*, ed. by M. FEO, Florence, 1991, pp. 205–10; T. DE ROBERTIS, "Nello scrittoio di Salutati: materiali per un'edizione di Cicerone?", I. CECCHERINI, "Cicerone, *De finibus bonorum et malorum*", and T. DE ROBERTIS, S. GENTILE, "Alcune lettere di Petrarca nel più antico autografo di Salutati", in *Coluccio Salutati e l'invenzione dell'umanesimo. Florence, Biblioteca Medicea Laurenziana, 2 novembre 2008–2030 gennaio 2009*, ed. by T. DE ROBERTIS, G. TANTURLI, S. ZAMPONI, Florence, 2008, pp. 308–12 n. 98, 312–13 n. 99, 314–16 n. 100, respectively.

[47]   PETOLETTI, "Signa manus mee".

[48]   M. PALMA, "Castiglionchio, Lapo da", in *DBI*, 22 (1979), pp. 40–44; *Antica possessione con belli costumi. Due giornate di studio su Lapo da Castiglionchio il Vecchio (Florence–Pontassieve, 3–4 ottobre 2003)*, ed. by F. SZNURA, Florence, 2005; G. MURANO, "Lapo da Castiglionchio il Vecchio († 1381)", in *Autographa. vol. 1.1. Giuristi, giudici e notai (sec. XII–XVI sec.)*, ed. by G. MURANO, Bologna, 2012, pp. 82–86.

in Petrarch's words. In his letter *Fam.* XXIV 7, Petrarch complained about the poor textual quality in which Quintilian's work was known at that time (a quandary that would be remedied by Poggio Bracciolini's famous discovery of the *Quintilianus integer* in the abbey of St Gall). He recognized and acknowledged, however, that the manuscript given to him was precious.[49] So, he left a huge number of marginal notes on those shabby pages, which betray his meticulous study of the text.[50]

By virtue of the abundant marginal notes in his hand, BnF lat. 7720 must be considered one of the most remarkable books from Petrarch's library. As evidence for how he read classical literature, it is on a par with the famous Vergil that is now Biblioteca Ambrosiana, A 79 inf., the Suetonius that is now Oxford, Exeter College, 186, and the *Historia Augusta* and the Pliny of BnF lat. 5816 and 6802 respectively.[51] In the first book of *De vita solitaria* (I 7, 3–4) Petrarch quotes a long passage of Quintilian's *Institutio oratoria* (X 3, 23) simply because the author was not widely known, as he writes in *De vita solitaria* I 4, 7: "Hec Quintilianus, que libentius inserui, quia secretior locus est" ("This was written by Quintilian, whom I willingly quoted because this passage is little known"). Quintilian's words created a certain problem for Petrarch's ideal of solitude: the antique orator was perplexed about the absolute need for *solitudo* to guarantee a good environment for writing ("Mihi certe iucundus hic magis quam studiorum hortator videtur esse secessus" "To me it definitely seems that to be secluded is a delight rather than an incentive to study"). To Quintilian's way of thinking, one must not always listen to those

[49]   C. M. MONTI, "Opto te incolumem videre. Petrarca e la scoperta del Quintiliano integro", *Studi petrarcheschi*, n.s., 20 (2007), pp. 105–23.

[50]   All Petrarch's marginal notes have been edited by M. ACCAME LANZILLOTTA, "Le postille del Petrarca a Quintiliano (Cod. Parigino lat. 7720)", *Quaderni petrarcheschi*, 5 (1988).

[51]   Francesco Petrarca, *Le postille del Virgilio Ambrosiano*, ed. by A. NEBULONI TESTA, M. BAGLIO, M. PETOLETTI, I–II, Padua–Rome, 2006 (Studi sul Petrarca, 33–34); M. BERTÉ, *Petrarca lettore di Svetonio*, Messina, 2011; J.-P. CALLU, "L'Histoire Auguste de Pétrarque", in *Bonner Historia Augusta-Colloquium 1984–1985*, Bonn, 1987, pp. 81–115; A. PIACENTINI, "*Se miscere cum magnis mira arte. L'*'Historia Augusta', *il* 'De remediis' *e le lettere* 'Senili'", *Studi petrarcheschi*, n.s., 21 (2008), pp. 1–80. On the Pliny that is BnF, lat. 6802, see n. 24.

who believe that woods and forests are the best setting for literary activity. Close to those sentences, in the margin of BnF lat. 7720, fol. 91ʳ, Petrarch, speaking to Quintilian himself, wrote: "Contra Silvanum" ("Against Silvanus", Petrarch's nickname), but immediately afterwards he wrote in the same margin another note, which unfortunately has been partially trimmed by the bookbinder: "Respondebis in tractatu *Vite solitarie*" ("You shall reply in the treatise *De vita solitaria*").[52] This note testifies to Petrarch's intention to discuss Quintilian's sentence in his *De vita solitaria*. In the end, having added to *De vita solitaria* Quintilian's adverse opinion, Petrarch wrote in the margin of his Quintilian manuscript "Feci ut potui" ("I did what I could"). This insertion has been dated on palaeographical grounds to between 1353 and 1361, when in Milan Petrarch was "hospes Ambrosii".[53] After having received a copy of the *Institutio oratoria* from his friend Lapo in 1350, he decided to include some of Quintilian's troublesome passages into his treatise, expressly to object to ideas that contradicted his own. Thanks to the notes in the margins of BnF lat. 7720, written at different times, it is possible to step inside Petrarch's private study.

Petrarch's books — those surviving and those recoverable through later copies — help us understand his authorial process and how he published; they are also helpful in emending mistakes and in conveying a better apprehension of his ideas; they are priceless tools to analyse the method and phases of Petrarch's literary work, thus allowing a more complete and detailed exegesis of his writings. And this is the true task of philology, which is the main avenue to unearthing the treasures that lie hidden in the different layers of transmission.

---

[52] ACCAME LANZILLOTTA, "Le postille del Petrarca", pp. 103–04.

[53] E. H. WILKINS, *Petrarch's Eight Years in Milan*, Cambridge, 1958.

To Publish *Post Mortem*

Boccaccio's Latin Works and Martino da Signa[*]

Valentina Rovere
(*Helsinki*)

Boccaccio's Testament as an Act of Authorial Publication

Little can be said for certain regarding Giovanni Boccaccio's use of authorial publication during his lifetime. Although some of his works, thanks to their significance for Italian and European literature, have received considerable scholarly attention, a comprehensive study on how his texts were first released is yet to be attempted. This applies to his writings both in Latin and in the vernacular. What is more, pertinent remarks in modern scholarship betray a certain amount of terminological confusion: release, publishing, dissemination, and circulation are often used as synonyms, which brings obscurity to a framework which is already unclear. While the history of how Boccaccio published during his lifetime remains largely obscure — a fact undoubtedly related to his lack of success in finding routes to publication — more solid observations can be made on the fate of his library after his death. He died in his hometown of Certaldo on 21 December 1375. About one and a half years before, on 28 August 1374, the notary ser Tinello di ser Bonasera drafted Boccaccio's last will and testament in Florence.[1] By this testament, Boccaccio left instructions

[*] I would like to thank Samu Niskanen and James Willoughby for their suggestions and insightful observations on this article. All remaining errors are naturally my own responsibility.

[1] Boccaccio's will is preserved as a contemporary notarial copy in Siena, Archivio di Stato, Diplomatico, Legato Bichi Borghesi, 28 agosto 1374. For

The Art of Publication from the Ninth to the Sixteenth Century, ed. by Samu Niskanen with the assistance of Valentina Rovere, IPM, 93 (Turnhout, 2023), pp. 311–330.
© BREPOLS ✥ PUBLISHERS   DOI 10.1484/M.IPM-EB.5.133087

as to where his books should be taken and how they were to be
treated after his death:

> Item reliquit venerabili fratri Martino de Signa, magistro in sacra
> theologia, conventus Sancti Spiritus ordinis Heremitarum Sancti
> Augustini omnes suos libros, excepto breviario dicti testatoris,
> cum ista condictione: quod dictus magister Martinus possit uti
> dictis libris et de eis exhibere copiam cui voluerit donec vixerit,
> ad hoc ut ipse teneatur rogare Deum pro anima dicti testatoris;
> et tempore sue mortis debeat consignare dictos libros conventui
> fratrum Sancti Spiritus, sine aliqua diminutione, et debeant micti
> in quodam armario dicti loci et ibidem debeant perpetuo remanere
> ad hoc ut quilibet de dicto conventu possit legere et studere super
> dictis libris, et ibi scribi facere modum et formam presentis testa-
> menti et facere inventarium de dictis libris.[2]

a transcript, see L. Regnicoli, "I testamenti di Giovanni Boccaccio", in
*Boccaccio autore e copista: Firenze, Biblioteca Medicea Laurenziana, 11 ottobre
2013–11 gennaio 2014*, ed. by T. De Robertis, C. M. Monti, M. Petoletti,
G. Tanturli, S. Zamponi, Florence, 2013, pp. 387–93; for a commentary, see
M. Papio, "An intimate self-portrait (*Testamentum*)", in *Boccaccio: A Critical
Guide to the Complete Works*, ed. by V. Kirkham, M. Sherberg, J. Smarr,
Chicago, IL, 2013, pp. 341–51. Two copies of *s*. xvii are preserved in BNCF,
Magl. IX, 123 and BAV, Barb. lat. 4000 (V. Branca, *Tradizione delle opere di
Giovanni Boccaccio*, vol. 1, Rome, 1958, pp. 117–18), but the current Covid-re-
lated impediments have prevented their consultation. Domenico Maria Manni
transcribed the will from the Florentine manuscript (D. M. Manni, *Istoria del
Decamerone di Giovanni Boccaccio*, Florence, 1742, p. 115). In general he is not
a trustworthy source, as shown by A. Maccarone, "Domenico Maria Manni
e l''Istoria del Decamerone'. Prime indagini", unpublished MA diss., Università Cattolica del Sacro Cuore di Milano, 2014.

[2]   "Item, he bequeaths to the venerable Brother Martino da Signa, master
in sacred theology, of the Convent of Santo Spirito of the Order of Hermits of
St Augustine, all his books with the exception of the said testator's breviary,
on the condition that the said Master Martino may have the use of the said
books and present cop[ies] to any who are interested as long as he shall live,
in exchange for this, that he is obliged to pray to God for the soul of the
said testator; and upon his death, he must consign the said books without
reduction in their number to the Convent of the Friars of Santo Spirito —
and they must be placed in a cabinet in the said place and remain there in
perpetuity, so that anyone of the said convent may read and study the said
books — and have the style and form of the present testament copied there
and make an inventory of the said books." The Latin text is quoted from
Regnicoli, "I testamenti", p. 392; for another English translation, see Papio,
"An intimate self-portrait", p. 345.

Boccaccio's friend Martino da Signa († 1387), an Augustinian friar of the Florentine convent of Santo Spirito who became its prior in 1385, was to receive all Boccaccio's books apart from his breviary.[3] While Martino could have free use of these books, he was to allow any interested party to make copies of them.[4] He was also to ensure that when he died all the books "without loss" should pass to the convent, where they should be placed in *armoires* and inventoried, and in that way be preserved for ever. Boccaccio's will should, I argue, be taken as an act of publishing for the benefit of posterity. For "anyone from the convent" had the right to study his works and, more importantly, to make new copies.[5]

Before assessing the effect of Boccaccio's will on the dissemination of his works, attention should be paid to its expression "all his books" (*omnes suos libros*). The words can be construed as referring to his own writings exclusively, or also to those books in his library that contained works by others. It is a virtual certainty that he was referring to his entire library. The evidence comes from the vernacular version of the testament, which was published

---

[3] For Martino da Signa see P. FALZONE, "da Signa, Martino", in *DBI*, 71 (2008), pp. 302–04. Not much is known about Martino's life. After participating in the General Chapter of his order in 1359 "per più di vent'anni, fino al 1384, si perde ogni traccia di lui; è impossibile pertanto stabilire quando abbia ottenuto la licenza di *magister sacrae theologiae*, titolo con il quale appare in un documento del 28 marzo di quell'anno". However, because he is referred to as *magister in sacra theologia* in Boccaccio's testament, Martino must have received that title much earlier, by 1374 at the latest.

[4] Boccaccio's decision to leave all his books to the Florentine convent was probably connected to Petrarch's unfulfilled plan to assign his *magnam et famosam bibliothecam ac parem veteribus* to the Venetian Republic. Petrarch made this decision in 1362, and probably discussed it with his friend Boccaccio during their meeting in Venice one year later and subsequently in several letters. Petrarch's project was abandoned when he left Venice for Padua, and his final will entrusted his library to a few private heirs (M. PASTORE STOCCHI, "La biblioteca del Petrarca", in *Storia della cultura veneta*. vol. 2: *Il Trecento*, ed. by A. GIROLAMO, Vicenza, 1976, pp. 537–65; A. MAGGI, "To write as another: the *Testamentum* (*Testamentum*)", in *Petrarch: A Critical Guide to the Complete Works*, ed. by V. KIRKHAM, A. MAGGI, Chicago, IL, 2009, pp. 333–46).

[5] A resonant argument was proposed in a recent conference paper, I. IOCCA, E. MORETTI, "Giovanni Boccaccio: quale volontà d'archivio?" (*Volontà d'archivio: l'autore, le carte, l'opera,* Padua, 26–28 Sept. 2022), to be published shortly.

in 1574 in a commentary on Boccaccio's *Decameron*.[6] At the end
of its *Proemio* we read that the copy on which the published text
relied was transcribed from a severely damaged autograph. A few
lines before the passage relevant here, Boccaccio set out in general
terms how his goods should be divided between his heirs and sold.
They were to take all his moveable, household goods but not his
books and his own texts: "ogni mio panno, masserizia, grano e
biada e vino e qualcunque altra cosa mobile, *exceptuati i libri et le
scripture mie* [emphasis mine]".[7] Because he distinguished between
his books and his own writings, the expression *omnes libros* used
in the Latin version of the will must have covered both.[8]

The next question one must ask is whether or not this entire
library included both Latin and vernacular titles. The odds are
that Boccaccio's vernacular manuscripts did not pass to the
ownership of the convent of Santo Spirito after Martino's death
in 1387, or at least there is no evidence that they did. The catalogues of its library holdings made in 1450–1451 itemize no vernacular text.[9] Furthermore, on account of their content Boccaccio's
vernacular works would easily have been considered inappropriate

---

[6] *Annotationi et discorsi sopra alcuni luoghi del 'Decameron' di m. Giovanni
Boccacci*, Florence, 1573 [*recte* 1574]. For the actual year of the printing and a
modern edition of the text, see *Le annotazioni e i discorsi sul 'Decameron' del
1573 dei deputati fiorentini*, ed. by G. CHIECCHI, Rome–Padua, 2001. The vernacular will is also published by REGNICOLI, "I testamenti", pp. 391–93. Boccaccio had prepared a will already in 1365, which is now lost but is referred
to in MANNI, *Istoria del "Decamerone"*, p. 109. By Manni's time, that will,
notarized on 21 August 1365 by ser Filippo di ser Piero Doni, was preserved
in the Gabella dei Contratti (Libro E, Duomo 1364). See also PAPIO, "An
intimate self-portrait", p. 478.

[7] "[A]ll my cloth, household goods, wheat and wine and all other moveable goods, except my books and my writings." The Latin version of this
passage reads simply "de masseritiis, rebus et bonis dicti testatoris, exceptis
libris dicti testatoris"; REGNICOLI, "I testamenti", p. 391.

[8] For a different reading, see G. FROSINI, "'Una imaginetta di Nostra
Donna'. Parole e cose nel testamento volgare di Giovanni Boccaccio", *Studi
sul Boccaccio*, 42 (2014), pp. 1–24. See also L. REGNICOLI, "La 'cura sepulcri'
di Giovanni Boccaccio", *Studi sul Boccaccio*, 42 (2014), pp. 25–79.

[9] D. GUTIÉRREZ, "La biblioteca di Santo Spirito in Firenze nella metà
del secolo XV", *Analecta Augustiniana*, 25 (1962), pp. 5–88; A. MAZZA, "L'inventario della 'Parva libraria' di Santo Spirito e la biblioteca del Boccaccio",
Italia medioevale e umanistica, 9 (1966), pp. 1–74.

for a religious literary diet in the fourteenth century. The questions is, however, open with regard to the period in which the friar was alive. Scholars have argued a great deal about whether or not Martino was also to receive Boccaccio's vernacular texts.[10] If he did, it would follow that the transmission of the vernacular works may have started from Martino's desk. In my reading of the evidence, it is possible to answer that question in the affirmative, although there remains a degree of uncertainty.

What has importance is the legal dispute between Martino da Signa and Boccaccio's brother, Iacopo. Their controversy revolved around the "24 quaderni e 14 quadernucci" containing Boccaccio's commentary on Dante's *Commedia*, the *Esposizioni sopra la "Comedia"*.[11] While the onset of this legal battle is not documented, it is known that the quires were soon entrusted to a neutral party, ser Francesco di Lapo Bonamichi, who kept hold of them until the dispute was solved. On 20 February 1377 Boccaccio's brother Iacopo submitted a petition to the leading members of the Consoli dell'Arte del Cambio, the Bankers' Guild, so as to acquire the said manuscript, presenting himself as the rightful heir.[12] Probably solicited by Iacopo himself, ser Francesco refused to give him the quires; as a document written in March testifies, he was waiting for a final resolution by the Consoli dell'Arte del Cambio.[13] The case was settled shortly afterwards. On 18 April, following a new petition again made by Iacopo, Barduccio di Cherichino and

---

[10]   MAZZA,"L'inventario" argues that Boccaccio left Martino only his Latin works. In contrast, Giorgio Padoan considered that the vernacular texts were also part of his legacy; G. PADOAN, "'Habent sua fata libelli': Dal Claricio al Manelli al Boccaccio", in ID., *Ultimi studi di filologia dantesca e boccacciana*, ed. by A. M. COSTANTINI, Ravenna, 2002, pp. 69–122.

[11]   For a general overview of this work, see L. AZZETTA, "Il culto di Dante", in *Boccaccio*, ed. by M. FIORILLA, I. IOCCA, Rome, 2021, pp. 313–33, at 324–31. The most recent edition is by G. PADOAN in *Tutte le opere di Giovanni Boccaccio*, ed. by V. BRANCA, vol. 6, Milan, 1965. A new edition and a new commentary on this work are currently in preparation by Marina Zanobi for her PhD dissertation, "Il commento alla 'Commedia' di Giovanni Boccaccio: edizione critica, commento, influenze culturali", Scuola Normale Superiore di Pisa, Classe di Lettere e Filosofia, Prof. C. Bologna.

[12]   L. REGNICOLI, "Elenco dei documenti", in *Boccaccio autore e copista*, pp. 394–402, item no. 187.

[13]   *Ibid.*, item 188.

Agnolo di Torino of the Consoli handed Boccaccio's *Esposizioni* to Iacopo.[14]

Two relevant observations may be made regarding this whole affair. When ser Francesco di Lapo Bonamichi stated that he was waiting for the Consoli's definitive decision, he added a precise request: he asked that whichever party ultimately obtained the contested quires, they would allow the other party and the other executors to make copies of them. That demand obviously echoes the instructions Boccaccio gave in his will as to making his books available for copying. This arrangement can be considered to have been effective, if the manuscript that is now BNCF, I.I.51 was made after 1377 and was transcribed directly from the autograph, as is argued by Zamponi.[15] Secondly, albeit Martino lost this legal controversy, the fact remains that he was involved in a disagreement over one of Boccaccio's vernacular texts, which would hardly have happened had he had nothing to do with Boccaccio's vernacular manuscripts from the outset.[16]

There is more circumstantial evidence to connect Martino to Boccacio's vernacular works, deriving from the celebrated manuscript BML, Pluteo 42.1. The volume carries Boccaccio's *Decameron* and *Corbaccio*, and was copied by Francesco di Amaretto Mannelli in 1384.[17] The book has received the meticulous attention of scholars because the text of the former work is very close to the extant autograph, SBB-PK, Hamilton 90.[18] It has likewise been

---

[14]   *Ibid.*, item 189.

[15]   S. ZAMPONI, "Le 'Esposizioni sopra la Commedia' in un codice trecentesco forse esemplato sul perduto autografo", in *Boccaccio autore e copista*, pp. 284–85.

[16]   The basis on which Martino lost this dispute remains unknown. It may be tentatively proposed that Boccaccio's *Esposizioni* was not considered part of his private estate because this *Lectura Dantis* had been delivered to the citizenry of Florence. The commentary would therefore have been regarded as something over which Florence could and should claim ownership.

[17]   For the relevance of this manuscript in the *Decameron* tradition, see M. FIORILLA, "Il capolavoro narrativo: il 'Decameron'", in *Boccaccio autore e copista*, pp. 95–140, at 102–03, with references to previous scholarship. For its description, see M. CURSI, "Il codice Ottimo del 'Decameron' di Francesco d'Amaretto Mannelli', in *Boccaccio autore e copista*, pp. 140–42.

[18]   The stemmatical role of this manuscript has been discussed at length, most recently by E. MORETTI, "Nuove indagini sulla tradizione del 'Deca-

hypothesized that the text of *Corbaccio* in the Pluteo manuscript also reports Boccaccio's original with great accuracy.[19] Martino da Signa and Francesco Mannelli were closely connected, a connection that has provided room for the argument that Mannelli copied the said volume at Santo Spirito at the time Boccaccio's books were in the hands of their first guardian, Martino.[20] To conclude, the odds are that Friar Martino da Signa obtained Boccaccio's whole library, embracing all the books Boccaccio had acquired and his own compositions, both in Latin and, so it seems, the vernacular. Not belonging to this inheritance, the *Esposizioni sopra la "Comedia"* and Boccaccio's breviary were exceptions.

An Effective Instrument for Publication: Martino da Signa and Boccaccio's Books

Irrespective of whether Boccaccio intended to entrust his library to his heirs in its entirety or only partially, we may ask how far Martino and the friars of Santo Spirito honoured Boccaccio's instructions. The requested *armaria* were financed at the beginning of the fifteenth century by Niccolò Niccoli (1365–1437), as is remarked in the biography of Niccoli written by Giannozzo Manetti.[21] The testament also stipulated an inventory be drawn up of the bequeathed books, and although we should not exclude the possibility that an early inventory, now lost, was indeed made, the earliest one known to survive was drawn up in 1450 and 1451, seventy-five years after the author's death. This was part of a larger project to review the collections stocked in Santo Spirito's *magna libraria* and *parva libraria*; as such it had nothing to do with the related stipulation in Boccaccio's testament.[22] As

meron': *varia lectio* e innovazioni di copisti", *Studi sul Boccaccio*, 48 (2020), pp. 5–19, with references to previous scholarship.

[19]   M. LA VITA, "Le postille al 'Corbaccio' nel codice Ottimo di Francesco D'Amaretto Mannelli", *Studi sul Boccaccio*, 48 (2020), pp. 21–75.

[20]   *Ibid.*, pp. 27–28.

[21]   A. SOLERTI, *Le vite di Dante, del Petrarca e del Boccaccio scritte fino al secolo decimosettimo*, Milan, 1904, p. 689. After Martino's death in 1387, this is the first piece of information we have about the convent's library, after a gap of almost two decades.

[22]   T. DE ROBERTIS, "L'inventario della 'parva libraria' di Santo Spirito", in *Boccaccio autore e copista*, pp. 403–09, which updates MAZZA, "L'inventa-

to the time Boccaccio's manuscripts were in Martino's possession (1376–1387) but already housed within Santo Spirito, his home community, the testament's stipulations as to the copying of his books proved to be effective. The evidence, which pertains to his Latin works, shows not only that the convent became a centre from where Boccaccio's scholarly texts were issued, but also that such transmission began even as Martino da Signa was alive. The friar was evidently scrupulous in complying with Boccaccio's instruction to provide access to his books and ensure that they could be copied. For many among the men of letters forming the so-called "circolo di Santo Spirito" went to the convent to make and obtain copies of Boccaccio's Latin works.[23] This phenomenon was a factor in Boccaccio's posthumous emergence as a successful author. Although already recognized as a great man of letters when alive, he had largely failed to realize his ambitions as an author (a subject I will elaborate on in a forthcoming study). His testament operated at a crucial juncture in his subsequent rise to eminence. By way of focusing on achieved effects, what follows assesses the testament as an instrument for posthumous publication.

Lorenzo di Antonio Ridolfi (1363–1443), a Florentine jurist,[24] emerged as a focus for modern students of Boccaccio when Garin

---

rio", with recent book identifications. These late inventories portrayed the library's extent in the mid-fifteenth century, attesting to acquisitions and losses by then. As pertains to Boccaccio's Latin works in 1451, the texts itemized in the *parva libraria* are *De casibus*, two manuscripts of the *Genealogia deorum gentilium* (one corresponding to BML, Plut. 52.9); two copies of the *De mulieribus claris* (neither corresponding to the autograph Plut. 90 sup. 98[1]); two copies of the *Buccolicum carmen* (one corresponding to the autograph Florence, Bibl. Riccardiana, 1232); no trace of Boccaccio's *De montibus*.

[23]   For the "circolo di Santo Spirito", see V. Branca, *Tradizione delle opere di Giovanni Boccaccio. Un secondo elenco di manoscritti e studi sul testo del 'Decameron'*, Rome, 1991, pp. 183–90.

[24]   F. Martino, "Umanisti, giuristi, uomini di stato a Firenze fra Trecento e Quattrocento. Lorenzo d'Antonio Ridolfi", in *Studi in memoria di Mario Condorelli*, vol. 3, Milan, 1988, pp. 183–200; G. Murano, "Lorenzo Ridolfi (1362/63–1443)", in *Autographa*, ed. by G. Murano, Bologna, 2012, pp. 136–44; G. G. Mellusi, "Ridolfi, Lorenzo", in *Dizionario biografico dei giuristi italiani (XII–XX secolo)*, vol. 2, Bologna, 2013, p. 1690; Id., "Ridolfi, Lorenzo", *DBI*, 87 (2016), pp. 455–57.

and Billanovich published one of his letters.[25] Together with other epistles (fols 11^r–19^v), this letter was preserved in Ridolfi's commonplace book, now BNCF, Panc. 147.[26] In 1380 or 1381, Ridolfi wrote a letter to Iacopo Sozzini Tolomei, bishop of Narni, who had requested Boccaccio's *De casibus virorum illustrium* but had not yet obtained it.[27]

> Petiisti an haberem librum *De casibus virorum illustrium* Iohannis Boccaccii, cui et quod verum censui respondere; denique, ut ne verbis insistam, accessi ad fratrem Benedictum ordinis beate Marie Sancti Sepulcri et ex parte mei patris ac preceptoris, vobis autem amicissimi, magistri Martini ordinis Heremitarum, cuius est, prefatum librum requisivi, unde respondit illico alteri his diebus prestitisse, demum bona fide promisit confestim procuraturum rehabere. Idcirco, cum habuero, non lento passu transmictam at celerrimo.[28] (fol. 16^r)

The letter also mentions Ridolfi's visit to Martino da Signa's library. There he accessed books once owned by Boccaccio, including some of his autographs:

> Volo scias, mi optime pater et domine, pridie, et non multum, cum forem in biblioteca clarissimi preceptoris mei ac patris spiritalis Magistri Martini ordinis heremitarum gloriosissimi Augustini, ubi tanta in morem silve librorum condensio, et, ut ritus est quam

---

[25]   E. GARIN, *La cultura filosofica del Rinascimento italiano*, Florence, 1961, pp. 29–32; G. BILLANOVICH, "Petrarca e i retori latini minori", *Italia medioevale e umanistica*, 5 (1962), pp. 103–64 (unless otherwise specified, the reference is to Giuseppe Billanovich).

[26]   *I codici panciatichiani della Biblioteca nazionale centrale di Firenze*, ed. by S. MORPURGO, P. PAPA, B. MARACCHI BIAGIARELLI, Rome, 1887, pp. 229–32.

[27]   The dating relies on the fact that the letter is preserved between pieces written in those years.

[28]   "You asked me if I had the book *De casibus virorum illustrium* of Giovanni Boccaccio, to which I decided to answer that so much was true; to be brief, I went to Brother Benedict of the Order of Santa Maria of Santo Sepolcro, and on behalf of my father and tutor, your dearest friend, Master Martino of the Order of the Hermits, the owner, I made a request for the book, to which he responded at once that he had lent it to someone else a few days before [and] promised in good faith that he would immediately ensure he got it back. Once I have it, I will send it to you not at a snail's pace but very quickly." In this letter Martino is not identified as prior of the convent but only as a friar, which confirms that the epistle was written before his promotion in 1385.

sepius, libros olim Iohannis Boccaccii circumvertendo viserem,
inter alios inveni quoddam volumen, in quo manu sua serenissime
ac ornatissime scriptus erat liber ille verborum et sententiarum
pondere facundus Pomponii Mele ac *Aulularia* Plauti.[29] Iterum et
quam plures alii libelli.[30] (fol. 16ᵛ)

The letter is testimony to the awareness, at the beginning of the
1380s, that Boccaccio's books were kept by Martino in Florence
and that they legally belonged to him. It also attests an early
instance of the loan of Boccaccio's books: the requested *De casibus*
was temporarily allocated to Benedetto, a friar affiliated to the
Florentine church of Santa Maria del Santo Sepolcro.[31] The bishop
of Narni seems to have requested precisely that book, rather than

---

[29]   From this passage, Billanovich could identify the volumes Ridolfi
referred to (BILLANOVICH, "Petrarca e i retori latini minori", p. 119): the first
one included Pomponio Mela's *De chorographia* and a Plautine play, acquired
by Boccaccio through Petrarch, while the other was a translation of the *pseudo*-Aristotelian *De mirabilibus auscultationibus* made by Leonzio Pilato. Both
these books are lost, but the quoted passage testifies that Ridolfi saw them in
Martino's library and that they were autographs. Another implication is that
Ridolfi was able to recognize Boccaccio's handwriting.

[30]   "I want you to know, my excellent father and lord, that earlier, not
long ago, when I was in the library of my very famous preceptor and spiritual father Master Martino of the Order of the Hermits of the most glorious
Augustine, where there was such a great, forest-like abundance of books, as I
wandered around, which I often did, I saw the books once owned by Giovanni
Boccaccio, I found one volume among others in which there was written in his
hand, in a very fair and elegant way, that book of Pomponio Mela eloquent
for the weight of words and sentences, and Plautus' *Aulularia*. And also many
other books." Ridolfi's words resonate with the description of Boccaccio's
library made by the Florentine humanist Giannozzo Manetti in his *Vitae Dantis et Petrarchae ac Boccaccii*, composed around 1440: "cum libros non haberet,
nec unde emere posset tenuitate patrimonii cogente, sibi suppeteret multa
non modo veterum poetarum, sed oratorum etiam, et historicorum volumina,
quicquid pene in latina lingua vetustum invenire potuit propriis manibus
ipse transcripsit, adeo ut copiam transcriptorum suorum intuentibus mirabile
quiddam videri soleat hominem [...] tanta librorum volumina propriis manibus exarasse" (SOLERTI, *Le vite*, p. 684).

[31]   This was the so-called monastery delle Campora near Florence, to
which Boccaccio bequeathed his private collection of holy relics: "Item re-
liquit et dari voluit et assignari per infrascriptos eius executores, et maiorem
partem ipsorum supervivent(ium) ex eis, monasterio fratrum Sancte Marie de
Sancto Sepulcro dal Pogetto, sive dalle Campora, extra muros civitatis Florentie omnes et singulas reliqi<a>s sanctas, quas dictus dominus Iohannes magno

a copy of it. Ridolfi was Martino's intermediary, commissioned to obtain the book and consign it as quickly as possible to the bishop. Various hints suggest the close relations Ridolfi enjoyed with Martino: Ridolfi calls the friar his spiritual father and his illustrious *preceptor* twice, and remarks on his acquaintance with Martino's library (rather than the convent's), which he had often explored. This library was stocked with a great number of books, and Boccaccio's manuscripts, including his autographs, were among them. This means not only that Martino truly possessed those volumes, but that his library doors were open at least to his close acquaintances.

While we cannot know whether Ridolfi kept his promise to Iacopo Sozzini Tolomei, the quoted letter implies that the former was a member of the inner circle of Martino's friends and was allowed to browse in his manuscript collection. At the time of the letter, Ridolfi was so well acquainted with the precious treasure held under Martino's guardianship that he patently copied two other texts available in that library. In 1379, together with another Augustinian friar of Santo Spirito, Ridolfi copied what is now BML, Plut. 34.49.[32] Its main text is Boccaccio's *Buccolicum carmen* and it was transcribed by Friar Maurizio Massi directly from Boccaccio's autograph, MS Riccardiano 1232.[33] Massi did not sign the codex, but he is identified by Lorenzo Ridolfi as its copyist in his *ex libris* note on fol. 35[v]: "Iohannis Boccaccii de Certaldo Bucholicum Carmen explicit feliciter. Deo gratias amen. Unicus ex mille scripsit Mauritius ille Anno Domini m°ccc°lxxix die xxa augusti. Iste liber est Laurentii Anthonii de Rothulphis de Florentia". Ridolfi did not only own the manuscript; he also rubricated it, entered the names of the *collocutores* of the poems in

tempore et cum magno labore procuravit habere de diversis mundi partibus"; REGNICOLI, "I testamenti", p. 392.

[32] For a detailed description of this manuscript, see T. DE ROBERTIS, "Boccaccio ritratto fra gli agostiniani di Santo Spirito", in *Boccaccio autore e copista*, pp. 213–14.

[33] As mentioned at n. 22 above, this manuscript was still preserved in Santo Spirito's *parva libraria* in 1451. For a description, see T. DE ROBERTIS, "L'autografo del 'Buccolicum carmen'", in *Boccaccio autore e copista*, p. 211. For a general overview of Boccaccio's *Buccolicum carmen*, see A. PIACENTINI, "La poesia latina: il 'Buccolicum carmen' e i 'Carmina'", in *Boccaccio autore e copista*, pp. 157–76 with a summary of the previous scholarship.

the margins, and on fols 36ᵛ–38ʳ transcribed the so-called *epistola explanatoria*. This is Boccaccio's response to Martino da Signa's inquiry as to the real identities of the individuals hidden under fictional names in the *Buccolicum carmen*. Dated to 5 May 1374, Boccaccio's letter expounds the allegorical names at length, or at least the ones he remembered at that time.[34] Considering this response to be something that would also be of interest to others, Boccaccio wrote a new version of it, elaborating various sections. This second version dates from 10 October of the same year.[35] The text found in Plut. 34.49 represents the first version, the genuine letter received and preserved by Martino, its first addressee.

This evidence would be sufficient to prove the accessibility of Boccaccio's books in Martino's hands. But recently Teresa De Robertis has added a new proof. She recognized Ridolfi's hand in another witness, Oxford, New College Library, 262.[36] This is a copy of Boccaccio's geographical index *De montibus, silvis, fontibus, lacubus, fluminibus, stagnis seu paludibus et de nominibus maris*, one of his minor and less well known texts.[37] Copied in Florence in about 1380, the Oxford manuscript is our oldest witness of the said work.[38] Two scribes copied it, although only Ridolfi, responsi-

---

[34]   For the text of this letter, see G. Boccaccio, "Epistole e lettere", ed. by G. Auzzas, with a contribution by A. Campana, in *Tutte le opere*, vol. 5.1, 1992, pp. 712–23. For a general overview of this letter, see A. Piacentini, "La lettera di Boccaccio a Martino da Signa: alcune proposte interpretative", *Studi sul Boccaccio*, 43 (2015), pp. 147–76.

[35]   G. Billanovich, F. Čàda, "Testi bucolici nella biblioteca di Boccaccio", *Italia medioevale e umanistica*, 4 (1961), pp. 201–21, at 212–13.

[36]   For a detailed description of this manuscript, see T. De Robertis–V. Rovere, "Il 'De montibus' di Boccaccio nella biblioteca di Santo Spirito", *Italia medioevale e umanistica*, 59 (2018), pp. 277–303.

[37]   G. Boccaccio, "De montibus, silvis, fontibus, lacubus, fluminibus, stagnis seu paludibus et de diversis nominibus maris", ed. by M. Pastore Stocchi, in *Tutte le opere di Giovanni Boccaccio*, 8.2, pp. 1815–2122. For a general overview on this work, see C. M. Monti, "De montibus", in *Boccaccio autore e copista*, pp. 181–84, and M. Pastore Stocchi, *Tradizione medievale e gusto umanistico nel "De montibus" del Boccaccio*, Padua, 1963.

[38]   For preliminary remarks about the manuscript tradition of *De montibus*, see V. Rovere, "Il ruolo di Santo Spirito nella tradizione del 'De montibus': alcune ipotesi", in *Intorno a Boccaccio. Boccaccio e dintorni*, Atti del Seminario internazionale (Certaldo, 25 giugno 2014), ed. by G. Frosini, S. Zamponi, Florence, 2015, pp. 103–14. See also M. Papio, A. Lloret, "Notes for a crit-

ble for the main part, has been identified.[39] Ridolfi added also the paratexts, including the rubrics and the short titles in the upper margins, made a few adjustments to the text, and transcribed a metrical letter sent by Zanobi da Strada to Boccaccio found on fol. 57ʳ.[40] Interestingly, Ridolfi shaped the majuscule letters like those in the above-mentioned Plut. 34.49 with Boccaccio's *Buccolicum carmen*. In the latter manuscript he is known to have imitated the shape of Boccaccio's lettering from the autograph Riccardiano 1232. Majuscule letters in the New College manuscript are modelled in that same fashion. De Robertis proposes, accordingly, that also in this case Ridolfi worked directly from Boccaccio's autograph.[41]

The Oxford manuscript can be dated on palaeographical grounds to roughly 1380. This would mean that the *De montibus* was among the books left by Boccaccio to Martino da Signa.[42] The autograph of *De montibus* is now lost, and was already missing in 1451 when the libraries of Santo Spirito were inventoried.[43] Nonetheless, the manuscript tradition offers grounds to support the suggestion that

ical edition of the 'De montibus' and a few observations on 'Rupibus ex dextris'", *Studi sul Boccaccio*, 46 (2018), pp. 13–50, with a complete inventory of the manuscripts at pp. 49–50.

[39]   The unidentified copyist wrote fols 9ʳᵃ–10ʳᵇ, 12ᵛᵃ (from line 10)–16ᵛᵇ, 29ʳᵇ (from line 3)–30ʳᵇ, while Lorenzo Ridolfi copied fols 1ʳᵃ–7ʳᵇ; 10ᵛᵃ–12ᵛᵃ (until line 9), 17ʳᵃ–29ʳᵇ (lines 1–2), 30ᵛᵃ–56ʳᵇ and 57ʳ, constituting a major part of the volume.

[40]   Zanobi da Strada received his poetical crown in Pisa in 1355. Some months later he sent Boccaccio the poem *Quid faciam, que vita michi* asking his advice on the subject of poetry. This poem is preserved in the New College manuscript (262), fol. 57ʳ, BML, Redi 155, fol. 128ᵛ, and BAV, Vat. lat. 5223, fol. 69ʳ⁻ᵛ. The latter is also the only witness to Boccaccio's answer to Zanobi. On their exchange, see M. BAGLIO, "'Avidulus glorie': Zanobi da Strada tra Boccaccio e Petrarca", *Italia medioevale e umanistica*, 54 (2013), pp. 343–95; ID., "Zanobi da Strada", in *Autografi dei letterati italiani. Le origini e il Trecento*, ed. by G. BRUNETTI, M. FIORILLA, M. PETOLETTI, Rome, 2013, pp. 321–40; A. PIACENTINI, "Carmina", in *Boccaccio autore e copista*, pp. 223–29.

[41]   DE ROBERTIS, "Lorenzo Ridolfi", p. 280.

[42]   On the consequences of this identification as pertains to a new edition of Boccaccio's *De montibus*, see V. ROVERE, "Una copia del perduto autografo del 'De montibus' e la costituzione del testo critico", *Studi sul Boccaccio*, 49 (2021), pp. 101–43.

[43]   See n. 9 and n. 22 above.

this autograph had been available in Santo Spirito for some decades. Two manuscripts of *De montibus* are connected to the convent, both copied in the early fifteenth century. Almost twenty
years after Martino's death, a German Augustinian friar, Simon
de Grymmis, transcribed *in conventu Sancti Spiritus* a manuscript
now in Ravenna, Biblioteca Classense, 397. This is what its subscription records:

> Explicit liber De montibus, silvis, fontibus, lacubus, fluminibus,
> stagnis seu paludibus et ultimo de nominibus mari Iohannis Boc-
> caccii de Certaldo feliciter. Finitus est liber iste per me fratrem
> Symonem de Grymmis ordinis heremitarum sancti Augustini de
> provincia Saxonie et Thuringie, in studio florentino, in conventu
> Sancti Spiritus sub anno Domini MCCCCXI° in vigilia annucaa-
> cionis [sic] Dei genitricis Marie, pro illustrissimo ac magnifico
> domino domino [sic] Karolo Aryminensi principe, amacori [sic]
> et protectori ordinis sancti Augusti [sic] per conventum reverendi
> magistri Marci de Arymino ordinis supradicto, tunc predicatore
> existente Florentie.[44] (fol. 54rb)

The man who had commissioned this copy of Boccaccio's *De montibus* was Carlo Malatesta (1368–1429), lord of Rimini and, from
1417, lord of Cesena. In the quoted subscription, made six years
before that, he is called only *princeps* of Rimini. The fact that he
addressed his request to Santo Spirito confirms that forty years
after Boccaccio's death his copy of *De montibus* was still kept
there, and, importantly, that even outside Florence it was known
where his works could be found.

---

[44] "The book *De montibus, silvis, fontibus, lacubus, fluminibus, stagnis
seu paludibus et ultimo de nominibus mari* of Giovanni Boccaccio of Certaldo
ends happily. This book was finished by me, Brother Symon de Grimmis of
the Order of Hermits of Saint Augustine from the province of Saxony and
Thuringia in the Florentine school, in the convent of Santo Spirito in 1411 on
the eve of the Annunciation of Mary, Mother of God, for the illustrious and
excellent lord Carlo of Rimini, devotee and protector of the Order of Saint
Augustine through the convent of Master Marco of Rimini of the above-mentioned order, then preacher in Florence". For the manuscript, see *I manoscritti
datati della Classense e delle altre biblioteche della provincia di Ravenna*, ed. by
M. G. BALDINI with the contributions of T. De Robertis and M. Mazzotti,
Florence, 2004, p. 52; *Boccaccio in Romagna. Manoscritti, incunaboli e cinque-
centine nelle biblioteche romagnole*, ed. by P. ERRANI, C. GIULIANI, P. ZANFINI,
Bologna, 2013, pp. 46–47.

The second helpful manuscript is BAV, Barb. lat. 330, transcribed by a notary in Florence as is remarked in a colophon at fol. 54vb: "Liber Colucii Pyerii Cancellarii Florentini reddatur ei | Et scriptus per me Antonium ser Hectoris de Astancollibus de Tuderto in civitate Florentie".[45] Because the subscription mentions the Florentine Chancellor Coluccio Salutati (1332–1406), Hortis proposed that the volume had been Salutati's, an attribution subsequently disproved by Ullman, who observed that the manuscript lacks not only Salutati's marginal notes but also an identification number on the first folio as is typical of his books.[46] More recently, in 2013, Teresa De Robertis demonstrated that although it is datable to the first quarter of the fifteenth century, the manuscript postdates Salutati's death in 1406.[47] In other words, the first clause of the colophon derives from the source manuscript, which belonged to Salutati. The scribe scrupulously copied Salutati's *subscriptio*, adding his own immediately below.[48]

My textual criticism of the said three Florentine witnesses of *De montibus* suggests stemmatical proximity between them. While it is still unclear precisely how New College 262, copied by Lorenzo Ridolfi around 1380, Ravenna, 397, copied by the German friar around 1411, and Barb. lat. 330, transcribed from Coluccio's manuscript, are related to each other, textual affinities are several and obvious.[49] Their apparent stemmatical proximity and Florentine origin suggest that *De montibus* was held by Martino da Signa, that it went to Santo Spirito after his death, and that it was preserved there until at least the early fifteenth century.

---

[45]   "Book of the Florentine Chancellor Coluccio di Piero; to be returned to him | and written by me, Antonio of ser Ettore Astancolli from Todi in the city of Florence".

[46]   A. HORTIS, *Studj sulle opere latine del Boccaccio*, Trieste, 1879, p. 257; B. L. ULLMAN, *The Humanism of Coluccio Salutati*, Padua, 1963, pp. 209 and 219.

[47]   ROVERE, "Il ruolo di Santo Spirito", pp. 108–09, with a description of the manuscript at pp. 111–12.

[48]   This copyist and his father, ser Hector Astancollibus, are otherwise unknown. It may be important that Salutati was "cancelliere e notaio delle Riformagioni" in Todi from August 1367 to April 1368.

[49]   For their stemmatical proximity, see also PAPIO, LLORET, "Notes", pp. 28–33.

The involvement of Coluccio Salutati opens significant avenues for enquiry. Salutati was himself on terms of friendship with Boccaccio, as is witnessed by three known letters that he sent him.[50] The first was sent from Todi on 20 December 1367, the second from Rome on 8 April 1369, the last from Lucca on 21 January 1372, that is, in the last years of Boccaccio's life. These letters attest to a close friendship with Boccaccio, who is invariably referred to as one of Salutati's dearest friends and praised for his poetry.[51] After Boccaccio's death, Salutati, who remained close to the *circolo* of Santo Spirito, gathered a fine collection of Boccaccio's books.[52] In addition to his copy of the *De montibus*, now lost but witnessed by the subscription in the above-mentioned Vatican copy, Barb. lat. 330, Salutati owned at least *De mulieribus claris* and *Genealogia deorum gentilium*. The former is now Oxford, Bodleian Library, Canon. Misc. 58 (*SC* 19534), which, to judge by its handwriting, was made in Florence in, broadly, the late fourteenth century.[53] Tentatively, a more precise dating can be proposed on the evidence of the volume's illumination, done by Niccolò da Bologna or his *atelier*. A specimen of the same Bolognese workmanship is BAV, Ott. lat. 1883, Salutati's copy of Petrarch's *De*

---

[50]   The letters are preserved in Salutati's epistolary: C. Salutati, *Epistolario*, ed. by F. Novati, 4 vols, Rome, 1891–1911, vol. 4, pp. 48–49, 85–88, 156–57.

[51]   These three letters are respectively addressed "Facundissimo viro domino Iohanni Boccaccii de Certaldo egregio cultori Pyeridum sibique karissimo amico et optimo"; "Singularissimo cultori Pyeridum domino Iohanni Boccacio de Certaldo, amicorum optimo"; "Eliconio viro domino Iohanni Boccacio egregio cultori Pyeridum, amico karissimo". Boccaccio was mentioned as one of Salutati's best friends already in 1367. This relationship must have emerged c. 1359–1361, when Salutati was first introduced to the Florentine circle of intellectuals. For Salutati's intellectual contribution, see *Coluccio Salutati e l'invenzione dell'umanesimo*, ed. by T. De Robertis, G. Tanturli, S. Zamponi, Florence, 2008.

[52]   Salutati's friendship with Boccaccio is testified to by the lines he added to Boccaccio's epitaph, which he considered too humble (A. Piacentini, "L'addizione di Salutati all'autoepitaffio di Boccaccio", in *Coluccio Salutati*, pp. 68–70). The insertion briefly characterizes all Boccaccio's Latin works. The oldest extant witness of these twelve hexameters, BML, Gaddi 75, was made in the 1380s by Agnolo Torini Bencivenni, one of the executors of Boccaccio's will. For Salutati's Florentine network, see G. Tanturli, "Coluccio Salutati e i letterati del suo tempo", in *Coluccio Salutati*, pp. 41–47.

[53]   The most recent description is by F. Pasut, *ibid.*, pp. 296–98.

viris illustribus dating from 1380.[54] It is likely that he had these two volumes made at about the same time. If so, Salutati's copy of *De mulieribus* would have been made while Boccaccio's books were in the possession of Martino da Signa. It is worth noting that Salutati commissioned that Vatican copy of the *De viris illustribus* from Lombardo della Seta, one of Petrarch's heirs responsible for the primary dissemination of his texts. The impression one receives is that he was well aware of how to gain access to both Boccaccio's and Petrarch's originals. Salutati's copy of *Genealogia deorum gentilium* is now Chicago, University Library, 100, datable 1385 × 1387 or so. The dating relies on the identification of the so-called "fifth scribe", who was also responsible for the transcription of the above-mentioned manuscript of *De mulieribus claris* belonging to Salutati.[55]

Although only philological evidence may prove with confidence whether or not these two manuscripts descend from Boccaccio's autographs preserved in Santo Spirito, Salutati's connection with Martino and his circle has already been ascertained. Scholars have linked to the convent a series of three manuscripts owned by Salutati with Livio's *Ab Urbe condita*, and several other manuscripts with patristic works, especially Augustine's.[56] Likewise, Salutati's direct association with parties engaged with Boccaccio's books can be proved. Marco Petoletti recently found a letter sent by Salutati to the Florentine cardinal Angelo Acciaiuoli. This dates between May 1386 and June 1387 and offers a defence for Martino da Signa against some slanderous accusation.[57] This piece is to be added to the evidence that connects Salutati to Lorenzo Ridolfi. The latter was godfather to one of Salutati's sons, and one letter he sent to Salutati in 1382 is preserved in the previously mentioned manuscript, Panc. 147. On his side, Salutati first mentioned and then alluded to Ridolfi in two letters he sent to Pope Boniface IX and

[54] For the manuscript, see T. DE ROBERTIS, *ibid.*, pp. 292–93.

[55] The manuscript is described in detail by H. H. WILKINS, *The University of Chicago Manuscript of the 'Genealogia deorum gentilium' of Boccaccio*, Chicago, IL, 1927.

[56] A. MANFREDI, "Nella biblioteca di Coluccio Salutati", in *Coluccio Salutati*, pp. 219–25, at 222.

[57] The letter is preserved in Madrid, Biblioteca nacional, 17652, fols 168ᵛ–170ʳ, and will be soon published by M. Petoletti.

Cardinal Francesco Carbone in 1391, to obtain a good position for another of his sons, Piero.[58]

It should be noted that Ridolfi and Salutati were laymen, meaning that the works by Boccaccio held by Martino da Signa were accessible not only to religious. There is also more circumstantial evidence of lay consultation of Boccaccio's books in Santo Spirito. We may begin with Domenico Silvestri (1335–1411), a Florentine notary and poet close to Salutati, who had a key role in the transmission of some of the Latin works by Boccaccio, whose neighbour and friend he was.[59] Silvestri's autograph manuscript, Oxford, Bodleian Library, Bodley 558 (*SC* 2342) contains a corpus of texts he drew directly from Boccaccio's desk when the author was still alive. These are the so-called *Versus ad Affricam*, *Buccolicum carmen*, accompanied by the related *epistola explanatoria* to Martino da Signa,[60] and *Hac sub mole iacet*, the epitaph Boccaccio wrote for himself. But there is also other evidence for Silvestri's high esteem of Boccaccio's works. He was particularly enthusiastic about the already mentioned geographical index, *De montibus*. As denoted by its full title as cited above, islands were not included in the work. Silvestri resolved to supplement the work with his own catalogue thereof, entitled *De insulis*. This was conceived as a continuation of Boccaccio's work, with whose structure and selection criteria Silvestri complied, as explained in the preface.[61] He also composed a poem of eighteen hexameters, summarizing the main contents of Boccaccio's *Genealogia deorum gentilium*. This short summary, of which an autograph copy survives in Plut. 90 inf. 13, proved a success; it is now found in several copies of the *Genealogia*, including the *editio princeps*. To compose a continuation to *De montibus* and to summarize *Genealogia*, Silvestri had to

[58] Salutati, *Epistolario*, vol. 4.1, p. 258.

[59] On Silvestri's life and works, see A. Piacentini, "Domenico Silvestri", in *Autografi dei letterati italiani*, pp. 289–99, with references to previous scholarship.

[60] As in the already mentioned Plut. 34.49, Boccaccio's eclogues in this manuscript were copied directly from the autograph Riccardiano 1232, the earliest surviving draft of the work. For a general overview, see A. Piacentini, "Domenico Silvestri lettore del 'Buccolicum carmen' di Giovanni Boccaccio", *Studi sul Boccaccio*, 41 (2013), pp. 295–316.

[61] D. Silvestri, *De insulis et earum proprietatibus*, ed. by C. Pecoraro, Palermo, 1955.

be provided with copies of them, something he could easily find in Martino's library. Silvestri's recourse to Boccaccio's autographs after his death has recently been demonstrated. Angelo Piacentini has recognized Silvestri's hand in one of Boccaccio's most peculiar autographs, the so-called *Zibaldone magliabechiano*, a commonplace book. This is a paper codex of considerable length in which the poet for several years collected excerpts from different texts that had caught his interest.[62] In the margins names of several islands found in the main text are written down in Silvestri's hand. The connection with Silvestri's *De insulis* is obvious. Previous scholarship has also identified another annotator of Boccaccio's *Zibaldone*, namely Niccolò Niccoli, already mentioned above as the man who had Santo Spirito's new *armaria* made. While there is no positive proof that *Zibaldone* was passed to Martino and thereby to Santo Spirito, Niccoli's documented engagement in the convent hints that this had indeed been the case.

There were also other parties who potentially accessed Martino's library for Boccaccio's originals. Before 1383 the Florentine poet Cino Rinuccini (1350–1417) commissioned a copy of Boccaccio's *Genealogia*, now BAV, Ott. lat. 1156. Rinuccini took part in the literary and civil controversy that arose in response to Antonio Loschi's *Invectiva in Florentinos*. Rinuccini's brief *Invettiva contro i calunniatori di Dante, Petrarca e Boccaccio*, preserved in Plut. 90 sup. 63, attends, *inter alia*, to the debate on whether Latin or vernacular poetry should prevail. Some of his arguments are extracted from Boccaccio's *Genealogia*, whose fourteenth book is dedicated to that subject. Different kind of interests stand in the background of BNCF, Conventi Soppressi G.4.1111. The volume is a copy of the first version of the *De casibus virorum illustrium*, owned by Zenobi Guasconi (1325–1383). He was a Dominican friar of Santa Maria Novella in Florence, serving as its prior from 1362 to 1365. Because in this manuscript Guasconi is designated as a doctor, a title he obtained in 1369, that year is the *terminus a quo*. If made before 1375, the volume would have been contemporary with Boccaccio. If not, it represents another instance of the consultation of his works in Martino's library. Guasconi cer-

---

[62]   A. PIACENTINI, "Le annotazioni di Domenico Silvestri sullo Zibaldone Magliabechiano di Giovanni Boccaccio", *Aevum*, 91 (2017), pp. 571–84.

tainly knew Martino personally because the latter attended the former's doctoral examination in theology.[63] We may end with two manuscripts containing Boccaccio's works made and owned by the well-known Franciscan, Tedaldo della Casa (1330–1409), now Plut. 26 sin. 6 and sin. 7. The former bears the first version of Boccaccio's *De casibus* and was copied by Tedaldo in 1393.[64] The *De casibus* was probably copied directly from an autograph, as has been argued by Branca on account of Tedaldo's acquaintance with Martino da Signa and previously with Boccaccio.[65] Also, the other manuscript, which contains Boccaccio's *Genealogia*, seems to bear a direct relation with Boccaccio's autograph, a tentative proposition that philological analysis may be able to verify.

The evidence given above attests to networks linked, in various ways, to Boccaccio or to the first guardian of his library, Martino da Signa, or to both. This group included friars, other ecclesiastics and laymen from Florence and elsewhere. When wishing to obtain copies or otherwise consult Boccaccio's writings, this group knew how and where to do so. As requested by the author's testament, Martino da Signa guaranteed that access to his originals was granted to those who were interested.

[63]   S. GENTILI, "Zenobi, Guasconi", in *DBI*, 60 (2003), pp. 476–78.

[64]   Tedaldo's autograph note remarks that he sent this manuscript to Friar Tommaso da Signa: "Questo libro manda Frate Thedaldo della Chasa dell'Ordine de' Frati Minori di Sancta Croce da Firenze a Frate Tommaso da Signa custode d'Arbo de' Frati minori della Provincia di Schiavonia MCC-CLXXXXIIII a dì XII di marzo e mandalo a Iadra per mano di Paulo Berti e compagni di Guido di Messer Thomaso".

[65]   BRANCA, *Tradizione*, vol. 2, pp. 185–86.

Publishing in Laurentian Florence

Jacopo di Poggio Bracciolini's Edition
of Poggio's *Historiae Florentini populi*[*]

Outi MERISALO
(*Jyväskylä*)

Poggio Bracciolini's eldest son, Jacopo (1442–1478), was not only an author in Latin and the vernacular but also an accomplished scribe. Probably his most important project was the Latin edition (1472) and vernacular translation (1476) of his father's last, incomplete work, *Historiae Florentini populi*, an alternative history of Florence. This article will examine the publication in manuscript and print of the Latin and Italian texts.

Poggio Bracciolini (1380–1459), apostolic secretary from 1403 until 1418 and again from 1423 until 1453, is known not only for his role, from the late 1390s onwards, in developing the humanistic book script, *littera antiqua*, and the sensational, well-publicized manuscript discoveries during the Council of Constance between 1414 and 1418, but also for his extensive literary output comprising letters, moral dialogues such as *De avaritia* (1429) and works in dialogue form pertaining to contemporary history, such as *De varietate fortunae* (1447–1448), as well as a collection of novellas, *Facetiae* (1452). Furthermore, he made some translations from Greek (Diodorus Siculus as well as Xenophon's *Cyro-*

[*]   Part of the research for this article was carried out thanks to the Academy of Finland and University of Jyväskylä project Lamemoli no. 307635 (2017–2022). I have the pleasure of thanking David Speranzi (Florence), Ada Labriola (Florence), Iolanda Ventura (Bologna) and Susanna Niiranen (Jyväskylä/Lamemoli) for kind help in providing access to indispensable materials both manuscript and printed.

The Art of Publication from the Ninth to the Sixteenth Century, ed. by Samu Niskanen with the assistance of Valentina Rovere, IPM, 93 (Turnhout, 2023), pp. 331–346.
© BREPOLS ❧ PUBLISHERS   DOI 10.1484/M.IPM-EB.5.133088

paedia).[1] From early on a staunch Medicean, his career seemed to have been crowned by his appointment to the chancellorship of the Republic of Florence in 1453 at the age of 73. In 1456, however, the chancery was in such a state of chaos that Poggio was sidelined, embittering him greatly towards the Medici regime.[2]

Poggio's correspondence indicates that he was working on a lengthy text in the last years of his life.[3] In 1458 he wrote to his friend Domenico Capranica:

> Sed cum multa recenseantur, a quibus proficisci potuerit scribendi tarditas, una omissa res est, que precipua me occupatum tenuit diutius in scribendo, ut cum finis iam adesset, cupidus ac studiosus incubui ad absolvendum inceptum opus, quod, tanquam in tela accidit, tantummodo sum orsus. Textura adhuc caret; sed ea brevi, ut spero, perficietur. Sepius enim repetere iubemur que scribimus antequam edantur, ne qua detur detractoribus obloquendi occasio. Hec causa extitit que me ab reliquis distraheret curis.[4]

---

[1] The classic biography is E. WALSER, *Poggius Florentinus: Leben und Werke,* Leipzig, 1914. On his role in developing the new script, see now T. DE ROBERTIS, "Humanistic script: origins", in *The Oxford Handbook of Latin Palaeography,* ed. by F. T. Coulson, R. G. Babcock, Oxford, 2020, pp. 511–25. For the letters, see P. Bracciolini, *Lettere,* ed. by H. HARTH, 3 vols, Florence, 1984–1987; for the literary works mentioned, see P. Bracciolini, *Dialogus contra avaritiam,* ed. by G. GERMANO, Livorno, 1994; Id., *De varietate fortunae,* ed. by O. MERISALO, Helsinki, 1993 (Annales Academiae Scientiarum Fennicae, B 265); and Id., *Facéties: Confabulationes,* ed. and transl. by S. PITTALUGA, É. WOLFF, Paris, 2005. There is no modern edition of the Diodorus Siculus translation, see C. SIDERI, *Per la fortuna di Diodoro Siculo fra XV e XVI secolo: la traduzione latina di Poggio Bracciolini e i primi volgarizzamenti, con un saggio di edizione critica dei testi volgari,* unpublished PhD diss., Università Ca' Foscari, Venice, 2020, pp. 41–42, accessible at <http://dspace.unive.it/handle/10579/17835?show = full>, 29 November 2022. The Cyropaedia translation has not been printed.

[2] For Poggio and the Medici, see O. MERISALO, "The *Historiae Florentini populi* by Poggio Bracciolini. Genesis and fortune of an alternative History of Florence", in *Poggio Bracciolini and the Re(dis)covery of Antiquity. Textual and Material Traditions: Proceedings of the Symposium Held at Bryn Mawr College on April 8–9, 2016,* ed. by R. RICCI with assistance from E. L. PUMROY, Florence, 2020, pp. 25–40, at 25, with bibliography, n. 1.

[3] See Bracciolini, *Lettere,* ed. HARTH.

[4] "But while many things may be listed as having delayed my writing, one thing has been left unsaid. It has too long kept me particularly busy, as, the end approaching, I willingly and industriously set out to finish the work that I had begun and for which, as happens when weaving a web, I had

The only extensive text that seems to come into question here is Poggio's history of Florence, *Historiae Florentini populi*, which was published posthumously by his son Jacopo Bracciolini. The official, state-sponsored history of the city from Antiquity to the fifteenth century, also entitled *Historiae Florentini populi*, had been written by Poggio's friend Leonardo Bruni (1370–1444) between 1415 and 1442.[5] As indicated by the title *Historiae*, Poggio's work, while touching in brief upon Antiquity and the early Middle Ages, concentrates on the fourteenth and fifteenth centuries, from the wars against Archbishop Giovanni Visconti of Milan (*c.* 1290–1354) to the peace of Lodi (1454). It is not a straightforward continuation of Bruni's work but rather an alternative history of Florence.[6]

Jacopo di Poggio: Life and Works

The short life of Poggio's eldest son, Jacopo di Poggio, was heavily marked by his Republican convictions, a love-hate relationship with the Medici regime, and activity to promote his father's literary legacy. Exiled in 1466 for anti-Medicean activities, he was allowed to return to Florence on paying a fine of 2,000 florins. In the late 1460s and early 1470s he was definitely mixing in the highest echelons of Florentine society.[7] By 1477, however,

only put the threads in place. It is still lacking a well-defined structure, but I hope to complete it soon. Of course, we are told to revise our text several times before publication in order not to expose ourselves to slanderers. This reason has kept me from attending to other business." Letter to Domenico Capranica, *ep. fam.* 9.45.7–15; Bracciolini, *Lettere*, ed. HARTH, vol. 3, p. 507. For an analysis of this passage, see MERISALO, "Genesis and fortune", p. 26.

  5 See L. Bruni, *Historiae Florentini populi*, ed. and transl. by J. HANKINS, *History of the Florentine People*, 3 vols, Cambridge, MA, 2001–2007 (The I Tatti Renaissance Library, 3).

  6 For Poggio's friendship with, and somewhat complex attitude to, Bruni, see A. FIELD, *The Intellectual Struggle for Florence: Humanists and the Beginnings of the Medici Regime, 1420–1440*, Oxford, 2017, p. 293.

  7 A. DE LA MARE, "New research on humanistic scribes in Florence", in *Miniatura fiorentina del Rinascimento 1449–1525, Un primo censimento*, 2 vols, ed. by A. GARZELLI, Florence, 1985, vol. 1, pp. 395–574, at 448 (Inventari e cataloghi toscani, 18), identified him as Lorenzo's Secretary A, active between 1469 and 1471. Another possible identification of Secretary A is, however, with ser Luigi di Andrea Lotti of Barberino, Lorenzo's first chancellor, see V. ARRIGHI, "3.15 Le origini della cancelleria medicea: Luigi Lotti", *Consor-*

a progressive estrangement from the Medici, no doubt due to his
political views, led him to approach Lorenzo's political enemies.
In that year, he entered the service of Cardinal Raffaele Riario
(1461–1521), great-nephew of Pope Sixtus IV. One of the leaders
of the Pazzi conspiracy against Lorenzo and his brother Giuliano
on 26 April 1478, Jacopo was among the first to be hanged at the
Bargello.[8]

In addition to his scribal activities, Jacopo wrote some original texts in Latin, such as the dialogue *Contra detractores*,
dedicated to Lorenzo, probably at the end of the 1460s, and a
Life — of which only the *volgarizzamento* by Battista Fortini
has been preserved — of the *condottiero* Pippo Spano, a friend of
Poggio's.[9] Jacopo's edition of Poggio's *Historiae Florentini populi*
was the most important of his Latin-language works.[10] Imitating
Petrarch and Bruni, who had translated novellas from Boccaccio's *Decameron* into Latin, Jacopo also made a Latin version of
the novella of Quintius Fulvius and Gisippus (*Decameron* X 8).
On the other hand, Jacopo also specialized in translations from
Latin to Tuscan. Texts included Lives of the *Scriptores historiae*

---

terie politiche e mutamenti istituzionali in età laurenziana. Catalogo della mostra,
ed. by M. A. MORELLI TIMPANARO, R. MANNO TOLU, P. VITI, Florence, 1992,
pp. 98–100. I have the pleasure of thanking David Speranzi of the Biblioteca Nazionale Centrale of Florence for providing copies of this article; also
see D. SPERANZI, "Palatino Baldovinetti 62", in *I manoscritti datati della
Biblioteca Nazionale Centrale di Firenze*, III: *Fondi Banco Rari, Landau Finaly,
Landau Muzzioli, Nuove Accessioni, Palatino Capponi, Palatino Panciatichiano,
Tordi*, ed. by S. PELLE, A. M. RUSSO, D. SPERANZI, S. ZAMPONI, Florence,
2011, p. 100 (Manoscritti datati d'Italia, 21).

[8] For Jacopo's biography, see O. MERISALO, "Jacopo di Poggio Bracciolini,
traducteur des *Historiae Florentini populi* du Pogge", in *Passages. Déplacements
des hommes, circulation des textes et identités dans l'Occident médiéval*, ed. by
J. DUCOS, P. HENRIET, Toulouse, 2013 (Études médiévales ibériques. Méri-
diennes), pp. 57–64, and O. MERISALO, "Il concetto di *libertas* individuale da
Jacopo di Poggio Bracciolini", *Studi umanistici piceni*, 33 (2013), pp. 131–36,
with bibliography.

[9] See *ibid.*, p. 131 and n. 5, with bibliography. The dedication copy of the
dialogue is BML, 46.2 (fols 71–92).

[10] This is the title transmitted by both the dedication copy to Frederick,
BAV, Urb. lat. 491, and BNM, Lat. Z. 392 (= 1684). The Urbino manuscript
once gives the variant "Iacobi Poggii Florentini in historias Florentinas Poggii patris. prohemium" (fol. 1ʳ).

Augustae as well as Poggio's Latin translation of Xenophon's *Cyropaedia*, dedicated to Ferdinand I of Aragon, king of Naples, a connection inherited from Poggio and, again, no friend to the Medici. An even more important project was the *volgarizzamento* of his own edition of Poggio's History of Florence. In 1469–1471, Jacopo dedicated to Lorenzo a commentary on the chapter *Nel cor pien d'amarissima dolcezza* (*TF* Ia) of the first redaction of Petrarch's *Trionfo della fama*.[11]

Editing the *Historiae Florentini populi*: Jacopo's Edition of Poggio's Text

Judging by the preface to the dedicatee, Frederick of Montefeltro, duke of Urbino (1422–1482), another highly placed contact inherited from Poggio, Jacopo had finished his edition of Poggio's unfinished History in eight books by 1472.[12] Furthermore, Jacopo gives important information on the genesis of Poggio's treatise and his own role in editing the text:

> Poggius enim ingrauescente etate tamquam emeritis stipendiis, cum Roma, ubi magna cum laude uixerat, uenia a Pontifice impetrata in patriam reuertisset, ut memorie tante urbis consuleret,

---

[11]   MERISALO, "Il concetto di *libertas*", p. 132, with bibliography. The commentary circulated in both manuscript (e.g. BML, Ashburnham 965) and print: *GW* M34531 ("Poggius, Jacobus: Sopra il trionfo della fama di Francesco Petrarca, ital. [Rom: Apud S. Marcum (Vitus Puecher), vor 15.X.1476]", ISTC ip00851000; and *GW* M34528 ("Poggius, Jacobus: Sopra il trionfo della fama di Francesco Petrarca. Florenz: Francesco Bonaccorsi für Alexandro di Francesco Varrochi, 24.I.1485"), ISTC ip00852000.

[12]   In the preface, Frederick's successful siege of Volterra in 1472 is referred to: "Cumque hoc anno tua uirtute Volaterrani, antiquissima Etrurie ciuitas, montis asperitate et loci natura freti imperio nostro rebelles sub iugum uenerint", here quoted according to BNM, Lat. Z. 392 (= 1684), fol. 4[r]. ("And since this year, thanks to your valour, the Volterrans, a most ancient people of Etruria, who, trusting to the difficult mountain ground and the very nature of the site, had rebelled against us, were subjected to our power.")Frederick's letter of thanks has been preserved in BAV, Urb. lat. 1198 fol. 81[r–v]; Frederick refers to Jacopo as *amicus suus*; cf. also Jacopo's 1472 letter of presentation to Frederick added to his brother Battista's Life of Condottiero Niccolò Piccinini in BAV, Urb. lat. 916, fol. 58[v]: "Non nouus venio in amicitiam. sed paternam resumo. quae tibi egregia cum Poggio fuit". ("I am not establishing a new friendship [with you] but taking over my father's friendship — yours with Poggio was excellent.").

> inter priuata publicaque negocia commentaria rerum Florenti-
> narum, a primo bello cum Iohanne Mediolanensi Archiepiscopo
> usque ad pacem cum Alfonso per Nicolaum pontificem factam,
> morte preuentus reliquit. Mihi uero, ut primum per etatem licuit,
> ne nostre rei publice plurimorumque clarorum uirorum memo-
> ria deperiret, nihil fuit potius quam *omnia in octo digesta libros*
> summa cum diligentia in unum corpus redigere ac legenda posteris
> tradere.[13] (Emphasis mine.)

Jacopo's contribution is even more important according to his own translation of the preface:

> come prima et per l'eta et per molte occupationi m'e stato licito,
> achioche la memoria della cicta nostra et le opere di molti
> prestantissimi huomini per Ytalia non manchassi, a nessuna altra
> cosa o piu dato opera che a ridurla insieme, et *diuisola con somma
> diligentia in octo libri*, mandarla in luce et farne copia a ciascuno
> desideroso d'intendere.[14] (Emphasis mine.)

While the Latin text is somewhat vague as to the origin of the division of the text into eight books, the vernacular text attributes it to Jacopo. Interestingly enough, the vernacular version also explicitly refers to a very concrete operation of publishing (*mandarla in luce*) and distributing the text to those wishing to understand the subject (*farne copia a ciascuno desideroso d'inten-dere*). Considering the existence of Bruni's *Historiae*, the official state-sponsored history of Florence, it is safe to assume that

[13] "Poggio, getting on in years, retiring, as it were, from business, was given leave by the Pope to return from Rome to his native country. In order to enhance the memory of such an eminent city he wrote the first draft of a history of Florence from the first war with John, archbishop of Milan, until the peace made with Alfonso through the mediation of Pope Nicholas. He left this work incomplete at his death. My main occupation, as soon as my age would permit it, has been to preserve the memory of our state and the memory of many famous men. Thus, I have built up a text *out of one divided into eight books* and handed it over to posterity to read." BNM, Lat. Z. 392 (= 1684), fol. 3ᵛ. For a detailed analysis of this passage, see MERISALO, "Genesis and fortune", pp. 30–31.

[14] "as soon as [my] age and many occupations would permit me, in order to preserve the memory of our city and the deeds of many excellent men in Italy, I have concentrated on making a continuous narrative of [the text], and *after having divided it into eight books* with the greatest care, publishing it and giving a copy of it to whomever would wish to be informed"; BNCF, Palatino Baldovinetti 62, fol. 2ᵛ.

Poggio-Jacopo's treatise aims at presenting a fresh view on the latest period of the glorious and tormented history of the city-state. The public targeted will consist not only of Florentine readers but all those interested in expanding their knowledge of the subject.

That Jacopo carried out a thorough revision of Poggio's text, at least part of which might have remained at a very sketchy stage at the author's death, has been demonstrated elsewhere.[15] Jacopo's edition has been preserved in four manuscripts, of which two, BAV, Urb. lat. 491, and BNM, Lat. Z. 392 (= 1684) were written in the fifteenth century, and two others, BML, Plut. 65.40, and Naples, Biblioteca Nazionale di Napoli, V. G. 34, are from the sixteenth. Jacopo's *volgarizzamento*, variously entitled *Historie fiorentine/Istoria fiorentina* circulated in both manuscript and print in the fifteenth century. In addition, there is a very interesting fifteenth-century fragment with the first four of the books, BNCF, Palatino Capponiano 64 (see below, p. 339).[16]

Publishing the *Historiae Florentini populi* in Latin

a. Vespasiano da Bisticci

The celebrated publisher of luxury manuscripts, Vespasiano da Bisticci (1421–1498), author of *Vite* of important personalities encountered during his long professional life between 1440 and 1480, was responsible for the dedication copy of Jacopo's edition that was presented to Frederick of Montefeltro, Vat. Urb. lat. 491.[17] It was

---

[15] For a detailed analysis, see O. MERISALO, "*Terranovam natale meum solum*. Remarks on the textual history of Poggio Bracciolini's *Historiae Florentini populi*", *Renaessanceforum*, 3 (2007), < https://www.njrs.dk/3_2007/10_merisalo.pdf > (accessed 29 November 2022), and, more concisely, MERISALO, "Genesis and fortune", pp. 32–34.

[16] For a detailed analysis of this manuscript, see *ibid.*, pp. 33–34.

[17] For a detailed description of this manuscript, see *La biblioteca di un principe 'umanista'. Federico da Montefeltro e i suoi manoscritti*, ed. by M. G. CRITELLI,<https://spotlight.vatlib.it/it/humanist-library/catalog/Urb_lat_491> (accessed 29 November 2022), as well as A. LABRIOLA, "7. Poggio Bracciolini, Historia Florentina [*sic*]. Libri I–VIII", in *Federico Da Montefeltro and His Library*, ed. by M. SIMONETTA, J. J. G. ALEXANDER, C. MARTELLI, Milan, 2007, pp. 152–61. Frederick's arms on fol. iv^v, just as the emblem "F(redericus) C(omes)" on fol. 1^r, date the manuscript to the time before

written by Gundissalvus Fernandez de Heredia († 1511), apostolic protonotary, bishop of Barcelona (1478) and Tarragona (1490), who worked for Vespasiano da Bisticci between 1469 and 1482 producing volumes for Frederick of Montefeltro, Lorenzo and Pierfrancesco de' Medici, Alfonso di Ferdinando, duke of Calabria, as well as Matthias Corvinus, king of Hungary. The sumptuous programme of illumination and decoration was carried out by, among others, Pietro del Massaio, Francesco Rosselli, and the Master of the Hamilton Xenophon, active from 1460 until 1480, who was a member of the workshop of Francesco d'Antonio del Chierico until 1478.[18]

Even the second fifteenth-century manuscript, now BNM, Lat. Z. 392 (= 1684), is probably connected to Vespasiano's enterprise. This luxury manuscript on parchment was possibly decorated by Mariano del Buono and workshop, employed by Vespasiano between 1470 and 1480.[19] The script is an upright *littera antiqua*; the arms on fol. 1ʳ have yet to be identified (Pl. 5). The text conforms to that of Frederick's dedication copy. The manuscript was acquired by 1715 by G. B. Recanati (1687–1734), who used it for the first printed edition of the Latin text in that year.[20]

b. The Informal Circuit: Copying as an Exercise?

The publication history of Poggio-Jacopo's *Historiae* in manuscript ends with the Venice volume. There is, however, some dissemination of the Latin text in the sixteenth century. A volume, now BML, Plut. 65.40, on paper datable to the early years of the century, shows a series of more and less inexperienced hands seem-

August 1474 when he was created Duke of Urbino. Thanks to Ada Labriola for kindly providing a copy of her article (October 2020).

[18] *La biblioteca di un principe 'umanista'*, ed. by CRITELLI.

[19] MERISALO, "Genesis and fortune", p. 31, with bibliography.

[20] For this learned patrician, friend of Apostolo Zeno, among others, who bequeathed his important manuscript library to the Marciana in 1734 and edited the Latin version of Poggio-Jacopo's *Historiae Florentini populi* in 1715, see MERISALO, "Genesis and fortune", p. 31, with bibliography, and pp. 36–37, as well as *Archivio dei possessori, Biblioteca Nazionale Marciana*, < https://archiviopossessori.it/archivio/1130-recanati-giambattista >, (accessed 29 November 2022).

ingly without aesthetical ambitions either for the script or the volume's general appearance. The manuscript belonged to the learned Canon Antonio Petrei († 1570), a noted bibliophile and teacher, who bequeathed the volume to the private library of the Medici in 1568.[21] Unsurprisingly, it is the only volume containing Poggio-Jacopo's *Historiae* in the Medici collections. The text contains the full Urbino version. Copying out this long text might have been a school exercise. Another similar volume, slightly later, is Naples, Biblioteca Nazionale di Napoli, V. G. 34. It was written on Italian paper made between the 1510s and the 1530s, by several hands, mostly inexperienced, both Italian and Transalpine (at least one Germanic). The scripts are both Gothic *hybridae* and *all'antica* cursives, with all the marginal hands Italian.[22] The volume belonged to the Farnese library in the time of Cardinal Alessandro Farnese (1520–1589) and was found among the books in the *Guardarobba del S(ignor) Cardinale Farnese* at Palazzo della Cancelleria, Rome, inventoried at his death.[23] This volume might be another school exercise.

c. The Informal Circuit: Circulating in Draft

The first codicological unit (fols 1–88), datable to the end of the fifteenth and the beginning of the sixteenth century, of the paper manuscript that is now BNCF, Palatino Capponiano 64, contains the first four books of the treatise in a version attributable to

---

[21] MERISALO, "Genesis and fortune", pp. 31–32.

[22] For this manuscript, see *ibid.*, p. 32, and MERISALO, "Jacopo di Poggio Bracciolini (1442–1478), traducteur", p. 60 n. 18.

[23] See O. MERISALO, "I codici in scrittura latina di Alessandro Farnese (1520–1589) a Caprarola e al Palazzo della Cancelleria nel 1589", *Progressus*, 3/1 (2016), pp. 202–03 and bibliography, <https://www.rivistaprogressus.it/wp-content/uploads/outi-merisalo-codici-scrittura-latina-alessandro-farne-se-1520-1589-caprarola-al-palazzo-della-cancelleria-nel-1589.pdf> (accessed 29 November 2022). For the manuscript, see the list of books in Naples, Archivio di Stato, Farnese, 1853, fol. 104ʳ. A list of manuscripts in the Latin script from the 1589 inventory contained in the Naples volume on fols 99ᵛ–109ʳ was published by F. FOSSIER, *La bibliothèque Farnèse. Étude des manuscrits latins et en langue vernaculaire*, Rome, 1982 (Le Palais Farnese, III, 2), pp. 39–40, who introduced numbering of volumes not present in the original. I have the pleasure of thanking the staff of the State Archives of Naples for excellent working conditions in January 2020.

Poggio himself.[24] It must consequently be a copy of a now lost earlier draft by Poggio. The other texts in the volume are part of Bruni's translation of the *Corpus Demosthenicum* and part of a *volgarizzamento* of Petrarch's *De remediis utriusque fortunae*.[25]

Publishing *Historiae Florentini populi* in the Vernacular

a. In Manuscript

Jacopo not only edited the Latin-language treatise but also made a *volgarizzamento* of his own edition, variously entitled *Historie fiorentine/Istoria fiorentina*, most probably by August 1474. The translation had a limited circulation in manuscript at the end of the fifteenth century and a considerable success in print from 1476 onwards.

The manuscript tradition presents some interesting details as regards the overall publishing history of the treatise either in Latin or in the vernacular. The luxury manuscript, now BNCF, Palatino Baldovinetti 62 (for which see Pl. 6) was copied by Francesco di Niccolò di Berto de' Gentiluzzi, as stated by the colophon on fol. 151ʳ: "MCCCLXXIIII Fra<n>ciscus me scripsit".[26] In the midst of the Florentine vine-stem decoration of the left margin on fol. 1ʳ is Jacopo's portrait, probably by Francesco d'Antonio del Chierico, who frequently worked for Vespasiano da Bisticci's publishing house (see above, p. 337). The other texts are a chro-

---

[24] See MERISALO, "Genesis and fortune", pp. 32–34. The short preface describes the chronological limits and the structure of the work on fol. 1ʳ: "paulo na(m)q(ue) supra centesimum annum florentini bella p(o)p(u)li tum repulsa tum illata recensere institui quę sunt in otto libros digesta".

[25] The volume belonged to the extensive library of Canon and Marquis Giovan Vincenzio Capponi (1691–1748), which passed to Marquis Vincenzio Capponi, an important bibliophile in his own right. In 1854 Vincenzio Capponi's library entered the Grand Ducal Library, Biblioteca Palatina; see *ibid.*, p. 32 and bibliography.

[26] This scribe, active from 1460 until 1503, notary to the Signoria in 1475, was a specialist of vernacular manuscripts. He also copied BML, Plut. 43.15 for the Capponi, see DE LA MARE, "New research", pp. 425, 494. For a detailed description of this manuscript, see SPERANZI, "Palatino Baldovinetti 62", p. 100. The initial on fol. 4ʳ had been cut out by the eighteenth century, as is stated in the note on fol. ivᵛ. The Baldovinetti library entered the Biblioteca Palatina in 1852; *ibid.*

nicle on the Ciompi rebellion of 1378 by Alamanno Acciaioli and two 1446 letters of Neri di Gino Capponi.[27] The manuscript bears the Capponi arms.[28] The production of the volume was carefully supervised by Jacopo, who made a number of annotations in the margins. It also points to an interesting development in the publication history of the *volgarizzamento*, since the title of the first book on fol. 4[r] has been partly erased.

Incomincia el primo libro della hystoria//<f>iorentina composta per poggio bracciolini//[-----] eloquentissimo ag[---------] del[---- ----------]

In his description of the manuscript, David Speranzi read the erased text as follows: line 3, beg. "doctore", end "agli [...] del popolo fiorentino". Even the explicit on fol. 151[r] has been written on an erasure, the lower text on lines 5 and 6 reading "a excelsa et gloriosa signoria del popolo fiorentino".[29] It would seem therefore that Jacopo might have cherished the hope of dedicating the *volgarizzamento* to the Signoria of Florence, a hope squashed before the Baldovinetti manuscript was finished. All manuscripts and the printed version of the *volgarizzamento* bear the dedication to Frederick known from the Latin version. Since Frederick is not yet titled Duke but simply "s(ignore) di Urbino" (fol. 1[r]) and "s(ignore) di Urbino" as well as "conte d'Urbino" (fol. 151[r]), August 1474 is most probably the *terminus ante quem* of the *volgarizzamento*.[30]

BNCF, II.III.86, *Hystoria fiorentina*, is another Florentine luxury manuscript, probably written by no less a scribe than Niccolò di

---

[27]   *Ibid.*

[28]   Although the Capponi were not yet involved in anti-Medicean activities in the 1470s, they emerged as major opponents in the 1494 events that led to the exile of the Medici from Florence. For the Capponi and the Medici, see MERISALO, "Genesis and fortune", p. 35 n. 44.

[29]   See SPERANZI, "Palatino Baldovinetti 62", p. 100.

[30]   Frederick of Montefeltro was solemnly invested with the duchy of Urbino by Sixtus IV in August 1474; G. BENZONI, "Federico da Montefeltro, duca di Urbino", in *DBI*, 45 (1995), <https://www.treccani.it/enciclopedia/federico-da-montefeltro-duca-di-urbino_(Dizionario-Biografico)/>, (accessed 29 November 2022). It is of course possible, though rather unlikely, that Jacopo for some reason did not wish to update the title of the dedicatee. David Speranzi also noted that the remains of the apparently original binding point to Francesco di Amedeo, a Florentine *cartolaio* active *c.* 1475; SPERANZI, "Palatino Baldovinetti 62", p. 100.

Giampiero Fonzio.[31] It bears the Strozzi arms (Pl. 7).[32] The Strozzi connection runs deep in the publishing history of the *volgarizzamento*. This wealthy dynasty that had only recently, in 1466, been allowed to return to Florence, continued to be one of the most powerful opponents of the Medici.[33]

A third manuscript, now New Haven, CT, Yale University, Beinecke Library, 321, was most probably also copied for the Strozzi. It was written on paper in a very professional Humanist cursive hand that Albinia de la Mare identified as Niccolò Fonzio's, who frequently worked for the Florentine merchant Girolamo di Carlo Strozzi (1441/2–1481/2), making for him, for example, a copy of Bruni's *Historiae Florentini populi* in the translation of Donato Acciaiuoli, ordered by Marco di Carlo, Girolamo's younger brother, in 1474.[34] In fact, in the 1474–1475

---

[31] For the identification of the hand, see DE LA MARE, "New research", pp. 460–61 and 515-16. More recently, L. HELLINGA, "Poggio Bracciolini's *Historia Fiorentina* in manuscript and print", *La Bibliofilia*, 115 (2013), pp. 119–34, at 123–24 argued that both this volume and New Haven, Yale University, Beinecke Library, 321 (see below) would have been written by a Ser Antonio di Jacopo, an otherwise unknown scribe, mentioned in Girolamo Strozzi's accounts as having produced a copy of the *volgarizzamento* (see below p. 343). While the two hands resemble each other, the Nazionale one, characterized by de la Mare as Fonzio's cursive hand, is more inclined to the right, and also differs from the Beinecke one as regards the morphology of the *e*, the *g* and the ligature *ct*. While there is no conclusive evidence to contradict the Nazionale hand's identification as Fonzio's, the Beinecke hand might well be that of Ser Antonio di Jacopo. Further research is needed.

[32] The volume subsequently belonged to the library of the learned Florentine Jacopo Gaddi, was acquired by Emperor Francis Stephen I, Grand Duke of Tuscany in 1755. Francis Stephen donated it to the Biblioteca Magliabechiana, see MERISALO, "Genesis and fortune", p. 35 and n. 46.

[33] *Ibid.*, p. 35 and n. 45.

[34] See DE LA MARE, "New research", pp. 458 and n. 295; for the patron, p. 516, Appendix I, no. 40A. The manuscript was part of the Strozzi library until at least the nineteenth century; it then passed to Prince Piero Ginori-Conti (1865–1939) and was finally acquired by the Beinecke in 1964. For a detailed description, see B. S. SHAILOR, "Beinecke ms. 321", in Yale University, *Beinecke Rare Book and Manuscript Library. General Collection of Rare Books and Manuscripts. Medieval and Renaissance Manuscripts*, <https://pre1600ms.beinecke.library.yale.edu/docs/pre1600.ms321.htm> (accessed 29

accounts of Girolamo di Carlo Strozzi is found a payment for a copy of Jacopo's *volgarizzamento* of the *Historiae Florentini populi*.[35] It was finished by June 1475. The scribe is, however, identified in the accounts as Ser Antonio di Jacopo (see n. 31 above).[36]

b. In Print

It is probable that the Beinecke manuscript is indeed the model for the printed version of the *volgarizzamento*.[37] Girolamo di Carlo's accounts show that he would send books from Florence to Marco di Carlo Strozzi to be sold in London in the 1470s. In the end, the copy of Acciaiuoli's *volgarizzamento* was not sent to London but taken to Venice. There Girolamo spent eleven months between June 1475 and May 1476 not only doing business with Filippo and Lorenzo Strozzi & co. of Florence and Naples but also setting up an ambitious printing project of Bruni's and Poggio's histories in Acciaiuoli's and Jacopo's *volgarizzamenti*. He also ordered a new vernacular translation of Pliny the Elder by the renowned Florentine humanist Cristoforo Landino, most

---

November 2022). There is a digital copy at <https://collections.library.yale.edu/catalog/10269852> (accessed 29 November 2022).

[35] See F. EDLER DE ROOVER, "Per la storia dell'arte della stampa in Italia. Come furono stampati a Venezia tre dei primi libri in volgare", *La Bibliofilia*, 55 (1953), pp. 107–17, at 108. Girolamo began his career in Naples in the enterprise of Filippo and Lorenzo di Matteo Strozzi & co. before 1466, then proceeded to do business on his own or occasionally in collaboration with other merchants in Flanders and England, principally Southampton (in Italian *Antona*), also on behalf of Filippo and Lorenzo Strozzi and his younger brother Marco di Carlo who had settled in Southampton, then in London at the end of the 1460s. Girolamo was often in Venice in the 1460s and 1470s, sending merchandise from Italy to Marco di Carlo who reciprocated with merchandise from England, see *ibid.*, pp. 107–08. Girolamo Strozzi's accounts are now Florence, Archivio di Stato, Carte Strozziane V, 52 and 53.

[36] See EDLER DE ROOVER, "Per la storia", p. 108 and n. 3.

[37] HELLINGA, "Manuscript and print", pp. 125–29 gives a convincing comparative analysis of the manuscript and the print to bear out this conclusion. The use of the Beinecke manuscript as the model for the print had already been argued for by C. MEYERS, *The Transition from Pen to Press*, unpublished MA diss., Yale University, 1983, and endorsed by SHAILOR, "Beinecke ms. 321".

probably completed in February and printed in June 1476 by Nicolas Jenson, a famous printer of French origin, in Venice, and paid for by Girolamo and his associate Giambattista di Luigi Ridolfi.[38] Jacopo di Poggio was consulted on the choice of the translator.[39]

Acciaiuoli's translation of Bruni's *Historiae*, the *Historia fiorentina*,[40] was printed in Venice on 12 February 1476, whereas Jacopo's *volgarizzamento*, the *Istoria fiorentina*, came out on 8 March 1476.[41] Both were printed by "messer Iacopo de' Rossi di natione gallo",[42] i.e. Jacques Le Rouge alias Jacobus Rubeus, a productive printer of French origin active in Venice between 1473 and 1478, then in Pinerolo from 1479 until 1483; his types were still in use in Embrun in 1489/90 and there is a print attributed to him in 1505. Le Rouge printed classical and humanist authors but also Roman and canon law as well as, for example, breviaries. The two *volgarizzamenti*, in addition to the 1505 print, are his only vernacular texts.[43]

According to Girolamo di Carlo's accounts, both *volgarizzamenti* were printed in around six hundred copies, mostly on paper, and normally sold together. Considering the differences between the two histories, this is an interesting development and no doubt contributed to Poggio-Jacopo's dissemination also in pro-Medicean circles even after Jacopo's disgrace. A few copies on parchment have been preserved; they, of course, catered to the taste of more upmarket customers. The initial price for Bruni's twelve-book work was two florins and for Poggio's eight-book work, one florin. Copies were sent out to booksellers not only in Italy

[38] EDLER DE ROOVER, "Per la storia", pp. 108–10. The Pliny is *GW* M34342: "Plinius Secundus, Gaius: Historia naturalis, ital. Übers. Christophorus Landinus. Venedig: Nicolas Jenson, 1476. 2°"; ISTC ip00801000.

[39] EDLER DE ROOVER, "Per la storia", p. 109 and n. 3.

[40] *GW* 5612: "Brunus Aretinus, Leonardus: Historiae Florentini populi, ital. von Donatus Acciaiolus. Venedig: Jacobus Rubeus, 12.II.1476 2°"; ISTC ib01247000.

[41] *GW* M34604: "Poggius, Johannes Franciscus: Historia Florentina, ital. Übers. Jacobus Poggius. [Venedig]: Jacobus Rubeus, 8.III.1476 2°"; ISTC ip00873000.

[42] *GW* M34604; fol. <n.vii^r>.

[43] See ISTC, <https://data.cerl.org/istc/_search?query=Jacobus+Rubeus&from=0> (accessed 29 November 2022).

but also in London and Bruges, the likely targets being the large Florentine merchant communities in those places. Florence itself was rightly expected to provide a good market for both prints.[44] The Strozzi continued to sell the *volgarizzamenti* even beyond the death of Girolamo di Carlo in 1481/2, at least until 1483, though at a discount. It is not known when the 1476 run went out of print.[45] Of Jacopo's translation, more than 150 copies still survive in public holdings.[46]

Conclusion

The publishing history of Poggio's last work, the *Historiae Florentini populi* is interesting from a number of points of view. Reflecting Poggio's conflict with the Medici regime in the last few years of his life from 1456 until 1459, he set out to compose a non-official history of Florence that could be seen as a counterpart to Bruni's official, state-sponsored *Historiae Florentini populi*. Poggio did not complete his text, which was heavily edited and brought to conclusion by his son Jacopo, whose short life was marked by his Republican ideals that put him on a collision course with the Medici regime. Poggio-Jacopo's *Historiae*, dedicated to Poggio's friend Frederick of Montefeltro, count and later duke of Urbino, who was to be one of the backers of the Pazzi conspiracy of 1478, reflect Jacopo's political stance as regards both content and publishing history. A few Florentine luxury volumes, of which at least the dedication copy to Frederick, now BAV, Urb. lat. 491, was produced by Vespasiano da Bisticci's publishing house, catering for princes and kings, under the close supervision of Jacopo himself, represent the short-lived upscale circulation, or commercial circulation *tout court*, of the Latin work in the fifteenth century. The Poggio-Jacopo Latin text is only transmitted in the sixteenth century in two paper manuscripts written by a series of more and less inexperienced hands which suggest that the copies were made as writing exercises. Poggio's incomplete text is transmitted as a draft in a paper manuscript from *c.* 1500. The Latin text was

---

[44] EDLER DE ROOVER, "Per la storia", pp. 112–13.

[45] *Ibid.*, p. 113.

[46] ISTC, <https://data.cerl.org/istc/ip00873000> (accessed 29 November 2022).

first printed in 1715 by G. B. Recanati, whose work began a true Poggio renaissance, leading to the publication of other important treatises such as *De varietate fortunae* (1723). Jacopo's publishing project was not limited to the Latin text but also covered the dissemination of the work in his own vernacular translation. Jacopo again closely supervised one of the luxury manuscripts, now BNCF, Palatino Baldovinetti 62, and seems to have entertained the possibility of dedicating the translation not to Frederick but to the *Signoria* of Florence, thus conferring it a new municipal status vieing with that of the state-sponsored Bruni text. In the end, Frederick was not dislodged from the position of dedicatee. Jacopo was also in close contact with the international Florentine merchant Girolamo di Carlo Strozzi, a member of a dynasty with a long history of conflict with the Medici, who decided to print both Donato Acciaiuoli's vernacular translation of Bruni's *Historiae Florentini populi* and Jacopo's *volgarizzamento* of his own edition, *Istoria fiorentina*, in Venice in 1476. The two histories were also quite often sold together, which no doubt contributed to diminishing their differences in public perception and probably conferred some aura of officiality to Poggio-Jacopo's text, ensuring its success well beyond Jacopo's political disgrace in 1478.

History Rewritten

Francesco Guicciardini's *Storia d'Italia* and Fiammetta Frescobaldi[*]

Giovanna Murano
(*Florence*)

In the context of Renaissance Florence, rich in female writers, Fiammetta Frescobaldi (1523–1586), a Dominican nun, stands out by reason of the choice and variety of subjects that she decided to write about and which she introduced to the sisters of her convent. Fiammetta based the work to be discussed in this essay on the first edition of Francesco Guicciardini's *Storia d'Italia*, published by Lorenzo Torrentino at Florence in 1561. Two years later, in 1563, she completed her abbreviated rendition of that massive work. The focus here is on Fiammetta's editorial approach with reference to the question of how she released that work and for what audiences she intended it.

Fiammetta is an interesting case also with respect to the emergence of female authors publishing in print in Italy from the end of the fifteenth century onwards. The extensive corpus that has come to light in the past several decades demonstrates that in the fifteenth and sixteenth centuries writing practices in convents were widespread and varied. In most cases, however, pertinent texts remain unpublished. While several women, often connected

* The research presented here was carried out thanks to the financial support of the Franklin Research Grant of the American Philosophical Society (2020). I should like thank Prof. Elissa Weaver for sharing with me the discovery of Fiammetta Frescobaldi's new manuscript and for her help and support; and Prof. Samu Niskanen for the invitation to present this paper and for his comments on it.

The Art of Publication from the Ninth to the Sixteenth Century, ed. by Samu Niskanen with the assistance of Valentina Rovere, IPM, 93 (Turnhout, 2023), pp. 347–370.
© BREPOLS ❧ PUBLISHERS   DOI 10.1484/M.IPM-EB.5.133089

to literary circles, such as Antonia Tanini,[1]Vittoria Colonna, and Laura Battiferri Ammannati, published their works in print, these have often gone largely unobserved for centuries and are only now beginning to appear in modern editions. The art of printing had an influence on Fiammetta's design of her autograph manuscripts, as is evidenced by their choice of layout and script, the use of title pages, dedications and colophons, all aspects to be discussed below. These resonances seem to reflect her desire to have her work published in print. Unfortunately, her status as a woman and as a nun prevented her from realizing such ambitions, and her audience was limited to the narrow circle of nuns in the Florentine convent of San Jacopo di Ripoli.

Fiammetta Frescobaldi (1523–1586) and her Dominican Community

The manuscript BNCF, Conv. Soppr. B II 564 comes from the Dominican convent of S. Maria Novella in Florence and was taken to its current home in 1808 as a result of Napoleon's suppression of the religious houses.[2] At the end of the work, at fol. 162ᵛ, the text is briefly identified as an abbreviation of Guicciardini's *Storia d'Italia*:

> Il fine delle storie di m. Francesco Guicciardini gentilhuom fiorentino delle cose che ocorsono in Italia e parte di là da' monti dal 1492 insino al 1526 abreviate per più sadi[s]fatione de' lettori da una persona religiosa l'anno della nostra salute 1563, ridote in

---

[1] Antonia Tanini (1452–1501), the wife of Bernardo Pulci (brother of Luca and Luigi Pulci, both of whom were writers) published at least three *sacre rappresentazioni* in one of the earliest collections of Florentine plays (ISTC ir00029680), see E. B. WEAVER, *Convent Theatre in Early Modern Italy. Spiritual Fun and Learning for Women*, Cambridge, 2002, pp. 97–98.

[2] Paper, I+VI, 180 (179); coeval numeration that repeats 49 and 132 and omits 137; fols 163 and 176–79 blank; 205 × 143 (170 × 105); I–III⁸, IV¹²; V–XXII⁸, with alphabetical quire signature and catchwords. Original binding in cardboard covered with parchment and leather ties. Spine detached. Stamp of S. Maria Novella at fol. 1ʳ. In the lower margin of the same folio: "Ex commutatione duplicatorum voluminum posuit fr. Petrus Tacca. 1666." D. MORENI, *Bibliografia storico-ragionata della Toscana*, I, Florence, 1805, p. 399 still reports the volume as belonging to the library of Santa Maria Novella. Described in MANUS: <https://manus.iccu.sbn.it/opacSchedaScheda.php?ID=206198> where Fiammetta's handwriting goes unidentified.

otto libri e·ll'autore le à distinte in 16 come ne' suoi tomi stampati si vede.[3]

Elissa Weaver has identified the hand of the copyist with that
of Dominican nun Fiammetta Frescobaldi.[4] There is a precise
match between the script in our manuscript and Frescobaldi's
numerous known autographs, of which several are still preserved
by descendants.[5] While the abbreviator is not identified other
than "una persona religiosa", it is clear that she was Fiammetta.
Guicciardini's monumental work was an instant success after
its posthumous publication in 1561. In that year the work was
printed twice in Florence and two years later there appeared
two Venetian editions, by Giovanni Maria Bonelli and Francesco Sansovino; Fiammetta likewise finished her abbreviation
in 1563. Judging by the plural "suoi tomi stampati", she would
have worked from the second of the *Storia*'s 1561 Florentine editions, which was printed in two volumes; the *princeps* was a single tome.

Fiammetta was born Brigida, daughter of Lamberto Frescobaldi and Francesca Morelli, in Florence on 17 January 1523. She
took her vows in 1534 and spent her entire life in the convent of
San Jacopo di Ripoli in Florence. The names of the Pucci, Adimari

---

[3] "The end of the histories of m. Francesco Guicciardini Florentine gen-
tlemen, of the events that occurred in Italy and in part beyond the Alps
between 1492 and 1526, abridged for the greater satisfaction of readers by
a person of the cloth in the year of our Lord 1563, reduced to eight books
whereas the author organized them in sixteen as may be seen in his printed
volumes."

[4] On Fiammetta and her works, see E. Weaver, A. Cattaneo,
G. Murano, "Fiammetta Frescobaldi (1523–1586)", in *Autographa*. II.1
Donne, sante e madonne (da Matilde di Canossa ad Artemisia Gentileschi), by
G. Murano, Imola, 2018, pp. 173–81. Due to the inaccessibility of most of her
autographs, it is still fundamental to read G. Pierattini, "Suor Fiammetta
Frescobaldi cronista del monastero Domenicano di Sant'Jacopo a Ripoli in
Firenze (1523–1586)", *Memorie Domenicane*, 56 (1939, March–April), pp. 101–
16; 56 (1939, July–Oct.), pp. 233–40; 57 (1940, March–April), pp. 106–11;
57 (1940, Nov.–Dec.), pp. 260–69; 58 (1941, Jan.–Feb.), pp. 28–38; 58 (1941,
March–April), pp. 74–84; 58 (1941, Sept.–Oct.), pp. 226–34); 58 (1941, Nov.–
Dec.), pp. 258–68.

[5] For Fiammetta's manuscript production, see Weaver, Cattaneo,
Murano, "Fiammetta Frescobaldi (1523–1586)". Conv. Soppr. B II 564 was
identified as Fiammetta's after the publication of that study.

and Balducci, Panciatichi, Gaddi and Rucellai families recur in the convent's records. Fiammetta, therefore, lived in a community that managed to recruit from some of the most important Florentine families. Young women, educated, curious and informed, Fiammetta and her sisters were also well aware of what was happening outside the high walls of the convent, something they owed mostly to their relatives. At the age of twenty-five she suffered a form of paralysis of her legs and was no longer able to perform normal conventual duties. From then on, she dedicated herself to studying and writing for the enlightenment and entertainment of her conventual sisters, who had but little time to devote to study and of whom most could not read Latin. According to Giovanna Pierattini, it is likely that Fiammetta also taught writing to the younger nuns.[6] Frescobaldi was an extraordinarily prolific writer: between 1563 and her death in 1586, she produced no fewer than twenty-two volumes, each of over three hundred folios and all written in a perfect chancery cursive hand.

Pierattini, the first modern scholar to study our author, searched for "gli otto volumi [sic] in cui Suor Fiammetta aveva riassunto la famosa storia del Guicciardini", which were mentioned by Domenico Moreni in his *Bibliografia storico-ragionata della Toscana*.[7] Although unable find those volumes, Pierattini gave the following assessment of Fiammetta's authorial determination.

> Può sembrare strana la predilezione di questa suora per il grande storico fiorentino, ma Suor Fiammetta, benché abbia vissuto poco in famiglia, non può staccarsi dal carattere dei suoi avi e in lei, benché inferma e monaca, c'era ancora un po' dello spirito intraprendente dei Frescobaldi dei secoli precedenti.[8]

---

[6] PIERATTINI, "Suor Fiammetta Frescobaldi" (1939), p. 238.

[7] PIERATTINI, "Suor Fiammetta Frescobaldi" (1940), p. 109: "the eight volumes in which Sister Fiammetta had summarized Guicciardini's famous history".

[8] PIERATTINI, "Suor Fiammetta Frescobaldi" (1940), p. 109: "The predilection of this nun for the great Florentine historian may seem strange, but Sister Fiammetta, although she lived only a short time with her family, cannot detach herself from the character of her ancestors. Although infirm and a nun, inside her there was still a bit of the enterprising spirit of the Frescobaldi of previous centuries."

According to tradition, the Frescobaldis were originally from Germany and entered Italy in the course of the tenth century. Later they established themselves in Florence as merchants and bankers.[9] The family could boast illustrious names in literature. Dino, son of Lambertuccio and Monna Minga de' Cavicciuoli, and Matteo, son of Dino and Monna Giovanna, are known for their lyric poetry.[10] Lionardo di Niccolò (1324–*post* 1413) with Giorgio Guccio Gucci and Andrea di Francesco Rinuccini travelled to Egypt and the Holy Land in 1384–1385; a detailed record of their journey is preserved in multiple versions with the title *Viaggio in Egitto e in Terrasanta*.[11]

Fiammetta willingly accepted the Dominican rule and her inclusion in the ancient Florentine religious institution offered her a spiritual and cultural framework that allowed her to become one of the most prolific of Dominican women writers and, indeed, one of the major polygraphs of the sixteenth century. It should be mentioned that her circumstances were favourable to literary work. St Dominic of Caleruega began to build women's communities even before dedicating himself to the organization of his Order. Following his teachings, Dominican convents were provided with books from the time of their foundation, just as the order's male houses were. These provisions were not limited to materials necessary for the Divine Office, but also included the acquisition of spiritual and devotional books.[12] Over the centuries several *sorores*

---

[9] D. FRESCOBALDI, F. SOLINAS, *The Frescobaldi. A Florentine Family*, Florence, 2004, pp. 13–17.

[10] Dino Frescobaldi, *Canzoni e sonetti*, ed. by F. BRUGNOLO, Turin, 1984; on the work see also: G. BALDASSARI, "Considerazioni sul *corpus* di Dino Frescobaldi", *Studi romanzi*, 9 (2013), pp. 157–212; on Matteo di Dino, see A. DECARIA, "Storia e tradizione della lirica fiorentina tra Dante e Petrarca. Il caso di Matteo di Dino Frescobaldi", *Studi e problemi di critica testuale*, 89 (2014), pp. 47–97.

[11] There is a critical edition by G. BARTOLINI, in G. BARTOLINI, F. CARDINI, *Nel nome di Dio facemmo vela*, Rome–Bari, 1991, pp. 99–196. On this work and many others, see F. CARDINI, "Pellegrinaggio, spionaggio militare e crociata. A proposito del viaggio di Lionardo Frescobaldi in Egitto e in Terrasanta (1384–1385)", in *Ovidio Capitani. Quaranta anni per la storia medioevale*, 2 vols, Bologna, 2003, vol. 2, pp. 151–66.

[12] In the *corredo* of a nun of the convent of Santa Caterina da Siena in Florence, for instance, are mentioned, in addition to her bed, "un tavolino da scrivere" and also "un breviario, un diurno, un salmista, un libriccino della

wrote chronicles and other literary works and distinguished themselves in producing devotional art.[13] An important progenitor of this tradition was Sister Cecilia Romana. She had met St Dominic as a young girl, and many years later she wrote *Miracula beati Dominici*, which offers an extraordinary portrait of the founder of the Order. Unlike numerous other biographies of the saint, the *Miracula* narrates events Sister Cecilia had witnessed personally.[14]

The convent that welcomed Fiammetta had housed one of the first printing presses in Europe. During its eight years of activity, from 1477 to 1484, in which several nuns were engaged, San Jacopo produced about fifty titles, some in Latin, others in the vernacular.[15] Domenico da Pistoia and Fra Pietro di Salvatore da Pisa were involved in the enterprise. It is unclear precisely how much they were responsible for the selection of works to be prin-

---

Madonna, un processionario, et un salterino della Madonna, tutti dell'ordine di San Domenico; 4 libri vuolghari a beneplacito della fanciulla [...] 1 calamaio, temperatorio e sigillo"; see S. Barker, "Painting and Humanism in Early Modern Florentine Convents", in *Artiste nel chiostro. Produzione artistica nei monasteri femminili in età moderna*, ed. by S. Barker, Florence, 2016 (Memorie domenicane, new ser., 46), 105–40, at 107, n. 7.

[13]   On devotional art produced by late medieval religious women, see the classic study of J. F. Hamburger, *Nuns as Artists: The Visual Culture of a Medieval Convent*, Berkeley, CA, 1997, and, with particular relevance to Florence, *Artiste nel chiostro. Produzione artistica nei monasteri femminili*, ed. by Barker.

[14]   G. Murano, "*E disse che volea licenzia di predicare*. Onorio III, suor Cecilia Romana e la predicazione di San Domenico", in *Nuovi studi su Onorio III*, ed. by C. Grasso, Rome, 2017, pp. 73–104.

[15]   The activity of the printing house can be reconstructed thanks to its *diario*, which has been published several times, most recently (and to be used with a degree of caution), by M. Conway, *The Diario of the Printing Press of San Jacopo di Ripoli: 1476–1484. Commentary and Transcription*, Florence, 1999. See also M. A. and R. H. Rouse, *Cartolai, Illuminators, and Printers in Fifteenth-Century Italy: The Evidence of the Ripoli Press*, Los Angeles, CA, 1988; P. Scapecchi, "A new Ripoli incunable and its consequences for the history of the Ripoli press", in *Incunabula. Studies in Fifteenth-Century Printed Books presented to Lotte Hellinga*, ed. by M. Davies, London, 1999, pp. 169–73; E. Barbieri, "Per il Vangelo di san Giovanni e qualche altra edizione di San Jacopo a Ripoli", *Italia medioevale e umanistica*, 43 (2002), pp. 383–400; A. Thomas, "Dominican Marginalia: The Late Fifteenth-Century Printing Press of San Jacopo di Ripoli in Florence", in *At the Margins. Minority Groups in Premodern Italy*, ed. by S. J. Milner, Minneapolis, MN, 2005, pp. 192–216.

ted. Among the first volumes we find the Florentine *novella*, erroneously attributed to Leon Battista Alberti, *Ippolito Buondelmonti e Dianora de' Bardi*, a love story of two young people opposed by their hostile families (ISTC ia00214400); the poem in octave rhyme *Lamento di Negroponte* (ISTC il00029350); and the *Specchio di Narciso, ovvero Canzone d'amore* by Simone Serdini (ISTC is00468800). While devotional works prevailed, scholarly works were also produced, including Bartolomeo Fonzio's *Commentum in Persium* (1477), Donato Acciaiuoli's *Expositio Ethicorum Aristotelis* (1478) and, for Lorenzo de Alopa Veneto, who was made a partner in 1483, Marsilio Ficino's translation of Plato.[16] In addition to this brief period of printing activity, and perhaps of greater importance to the present discussion, the convent housed a scriptorium. In 1460, Sister Angelica Gaddi copied a *Specchio di Croce* (Florence, Biblioteca Riccardiana, MS. 2102);[17] in 1468, Sister Checha copied a *Vita di Santa Caterina* (MS. 1291 in the same library); in 1500 or so, Sister Angela Rucellai copied a collectar (BNCF, Conv. Soppr. D.7.344).[18] Together with Sister Lucrezia Panciatichi, Sister Angela also copied a gradual that is now Florence, Museo di San Marco, 630.[19]

The *libraria* of San Jacopo di Ripoli was certainly supplied with printed and manuscript books, but their number was not sufficient to satisfy Fiammetta's thirst for knowledge. As a rule, she mentions the sources she drew on at the beginning of her works. Thanks to her prologues we know that little by little, also with the financial help of her family, she enriched her personal book collection with works by Giovanni Battista Ramusio,[20] the histo-

---

[16]   P. O. Kristeller, "The first printed edition of Plato's works and the date of its publication (1484)", in *Science and History: Studies in Honor of Edward Rose* (Studia Copernicana, 16), Wroclaw, 1978, pp. 25–35; repr. in his *Studies in Renaissance Thought and Letters, III*, Rome, 1993 (Storia e Letteratura, 178), pp. 135–46.

[17]   M. Moreton, "Pious Voices: Nun-scribes and the Language of Colophons in Late Medieval and Renaissance Italy", *Essays in Medieval Studies*, 29 (2014), pp. 43–73, at 46, 52.

[18]   *Ibid.*, p. 46.

[19]   *Ibid.*, pp. 49–50.

[20]   G. B. Ramusio, *Primo volume, & seconda editione delle Nauigationi et viaggi* [...] Venice: nella stamperia haer. Lucantonio I Giunta, 1554; G. B. Ramusio, *Terzo volume delle navigationi et viaggi nel quale si contengono le navi-*

rian Giovanni Tarcagnota,[21] Gemma Frisio,[22] Alessandro Piccolomini,[23] and Giorgio Vasari, to whom I shall return below.

Fiammetta was a fine Latinist. She used her literary skills,
which were uncommon even in convents, to translate, for instance,
hagiographical texts. A case in point is her partial translation of
De vitis sanctorum by the German hagiographer Lorenz Sauer, a
copy of which she had received from her relatives as a gift.[24] In
that work her focus was on lesser known saints.[25] It may be mentioned that Sauer's work would later be used by the Bollandists
for the *Acta sanctorum*. What makes Fiammetta stand out is the
variety of her works and the subjects that she chose to study and
introduce to her conventual sisters. Her keen interest in the new
geography and cosmography of the age was most extraordinary,
such that she must be considered the first female geographer of the
modern era.[26] She was an author, translator and anthologist, and

gationi al mondo nuovo, alli antichi incognito, fatte da don Christoforo Colombo
genovese, che fu il primo a scoprirlo a i re catholici, detto hora le Indie occidentali,
Venice: haer. Lucantonio Giunta, 1556.

[21] G. Tarcagnota, *Historie del Mondo*, Venice: Tramezzino, 1562.

[22] Gemma Frisius, *De principiis astronomiae & cosmographiae. Deque usu*
globi ab eodem editi. De orbis divisione, & insulis, rebusque nuper inventis. Opus
nunc demum ab ipso auctore multis in locis auctum, ac sublatis omnibus erra-
tis integritati restitutum, Antwerpen: typis Joannes Grapheus in aed. Joannes
Steelsius, 1553.

[23] *De la sfera del mondo di m. Alessandro Piccolomini libri quattro, nova-*
mente da lui emendati, & di molte aggiunte in diversi luoghi largamente ampliati.
De le stelle fisse del medesimo auttore libro uno, con le loro favole, figure, nasci-
menti, & nascondimenti da lui novamente riveduto, & corretto, Venice: per Giovanni Varisco & C., 1561.

[24] Laurentius Surius, *De vitis sanctorum ab Aloysio Lipomano, episcopo*
Veronae, viro doctissimo, olim conscriptis: nunc primum a f. Laurentio Surio
Carthusiano emendatis & auctis, tomus primus [–tertius], Venice: apud Ludo-
vico Avanzi & C., 1573.

[25] The volume with the *Vite di XII santi Monachi che fiorirono nelle parti*
orientali was mentioned by Pierattini, "Suor Fiammetta Frescobaldi"
(1940), pp. 265–66: "Sono quelli [*the 12 saints*] dal tempo di Costantino imperatore fino al tempo di Eraclio. È una traduzione dal latino delle Vite di
Santi di Lipomano, terminata il 9 marzo del 1575 'mandato in luce questo
anno 1576'". Dedicated to the prioress, Sister Angela Malegonnelle, the manuscript is currently missing.

[26] E. Weaver, "Suor Fiammetta Frescobaldi, storica dell'Ordine dei Predicatori e del monastero fiorentino di San Jacopo di Ripoli", in *Il velo, la*

when faced with Francesco Guicciardini's monumental *Storia d'I-talia*, a modern edition of which takes up 1,960 pages,[27] she edited and abridged the text. The text found in Conv. Soppr. B II 564 is not a mere digest of Guicciardini's work. Not only did Fiammetta reduce the sixteen books of her source text to eight, but she also recast Guicciardini's highly complex rhetorical periods into shorter sentences, closer to spoken language. She intended to make the *Storia d'Italia* easier to receive and more pleasant to read and listen to. As explained in her authorial colophon quoted at the beginning of this paper, she abridged Guicciardini's work "for the greater satisfaction of readers". So that Fiammetta's contribution can be properly appreciated, Guicciardini and his monumental work must be introduced in brief.

The *Storia d'Italia* by Francesco Guicciardini

> Io ho deliberato di scrivere le cose accadute alla memoria nostra in Italia, dappoi che l'armi de' franzesi, chiamate da' nostri principi medesimi, cominciorono con grandissimo movimento a perturbarla: materia, per la varietà e grandezza loro, molto memorabile e piena di atrocissimi accidenti; avendo patito tanti anni Italia tutte quelle calamità con le quali sogliono i miseri mortali, ora per l'ira giusta d'Iddio, ora dalla empietà e sceleratezze degli altri uomini, essere vessati.[28]

---

penna e la parola. Le domenicane: storia, istituzioni e scritture, ed. by G. Festa, G. Zarri, Bologna, 2009, pp. 185–91; E. Weaver, "Fiammetta Frescobaldi (1523–1586) and her chronicle of the Florentine convent of San Jacopo di Ripoli", in *Ritratti. La dimensione individuale nella storia (secoli XV–XX). Studi in onore di Anne Jacobson Schutte*, ed. by R. Pierce and S. Seidel Menchi, Rome, 2009, pp. 177–91.

[27] See Francesco Guicciardini, *Storia d'Italia*, ed. by E. S. Seidel Menchi, Turin, 1971.

[28] Guicciardini, *Storia d'Italia*, I, 1, in *Opere*, ed. by E. Scarano, vols 2 and 3, Turin, 1981: "I have set out to write about those things that have occurred in Italy within our memory, since the time that French troops, summoned by our own princes, began to stir up great dissensions here: a most memorable subject, in view of its scope and variety, and full of the most terrible events, Italy, having suffered for so many years all those calamities with which miserable mortals are usually afflicted, sometimes because of the just anger of God, and sometimes because of the impiety and wickedness of other men."

Thus begins Guicciardini's *Storia d'Italia*. This opening sentence was subjected to extensive authorial revision, witnessed by at least eight manuscripts, which are autographs or include his notes and corrections, some preserved in the family archive, others in the Biblioteca Laurenziana.[29] Guicciardini reported events in Italy between 1494 and 1534, that is, from Charles VIII's descent on Italy until the death of Pope Clement VII, forty years beset by terrible events and atrocious wars, as was recalled by Agnolo Guicciardini, the author's nephew, in the dedicatory letter in the *editio princeps* to the Duke of Florence, Cosimo de' Medici.[30]

Francesco Guicciardini was a man of government, law and letters, and a protagonist of Florentine history.[31] After taking his leave of politics, he began writing his last work in the *otium* of his villa in Arcetri, on the hills above Florence. As his autographs prove, Guicciardini had difficulty in deciding the type of narrative voice he should use. He finally opted for the first person: "*Io* ho deliberato di scrivere" ('*I* have set out to write', emphasis mine).

The day before his death Guicciardini instructed that his writings should be burned, but his wife, Maria Salviati, in contravention of his last wish, rescued them from this fate.[32] Subsequent attempts by his nephew Lodovico to publish the work in the Netherlands were not successful. Two decades after Guicciardini's death, none of the thousands of pages he left had been

[29] V. BRAMANTI, "Il tormentato incipit della *Storia d'Italia* di Francesco Guicciardini", *Schede umanistiche*, 22 (2008), pp. 123–56. On the genesis of the work, see R. RIDOLFI, *Genesi della* Storia d'Italia *guicciardiniana*, Florence, 1939 (Collana guicciardiniana, 9); repr. in *Studi guicciardiniani*, Florence, 1978; and P. MORENO, *Come lavorava Guicciardini*, Rome, 2020.

[30] The said periodization contrasts with that announced by Fiammetta for her abbreviation, 1492–1526. She correctly derived the former year from the fact that the first book remarks the death of Lorenzo de' Medici. The latter terminus is that of book XVI, with which her source, Torrentino's edition, closes.

[31] For a convenient introduction to Guicciardini's life and works, see P. JODOGNE, G. BENZONI, in *DBI*, 61 (2004), at <https://www.treccani.it/enciclopedia/francesco-guicciardini_%28Dizionario-Biografico%29/>.

[32] R. RIDOLFI, *Fortune della* Storia d'Italia *prima della stampa*, Florence, 1978.

published.[33] In 1561, the *Storia d'Italia* was posthumously published in folio at Florence by Lorenzo Torrentino (or Laurens van
den Bleeck), a 'ducal printer' of Flemish origin. In the same
year, he published an octavo edition in two volumes.[34] The latter
was reprinted almost unchanged in the following year. Torrentino's editions embrace the first sixteen books, due to the fact
that the final four books were more incomplete than the previous ones. The 1561 print originates from collaboration between
Agnolo Guicciardini († 1581), the above-mentioned nephew of the
author,[35] and a public commission. The Benedictine monk and
philologist Vincenzio Borghini († 1580) and the powerful secretary of Duke Bartolomeo Concini[36] were involved in the enterprise. Borghini was a trusted man of Cosimo I de' Medici in
matters cultural. He was a scholar, among many other things,
of the Italian language and the author of the *Lettera intorno a'
manoscritti antichi*.[37] Unfortunately, the *editio princeps* does not
offer the complete work, witnessed by the Laurentian manuscript
Med. Pal. 166, but a text that had been subject to various editorial interventions (in particular by Concini), arbitrary mutila-

---

[33]   R. RIDOLFI, "Documenti sulle prime stampe della *Storia d'Italia*", *La
Bibliofilìa*, 61 (1959), pp. 39–52; repr. in *Studi guicciardiniani*, pp. 197–223.

[34]   *La historia di Italia di m. Francesco Guicciardini gentil'huomo fiorentino*,
Florence: appresso Lorenzo Torrentino, 1561. On the Italian editions of the
Storia d'Italia in the sixteenth century, see P. GUICCIARDINI, "Le prime edizioni e ristampe della *Storia d'Italia*: loro raggruppamento in famiglie tipogra-
fiche. Contributo alla bibliografia di Francesco Guicciardini", *La Bibliofilìa*,
49 (1947), pp. 76–91; V. BRAMANTI, "Gli 'ornamenti esteriori': in margine
alla *Storia d'Italia* di Francesco Guicciardini nelle stampe del XVI secolo",
Schede umanistiche, 20 (2006), pp. 59–91.

[35]   V. BRAMANTI, "Guicciardini, Agnolo", in *DBI*, 61 (2004), at https://
www.treccani.it/enciclopedia/agnolo-guicciardini.

[36]   P. MALANIMA, "Concini, Bartolomeo", in *DBI*, 27 (1982), at https://
www.treccani.it/enciclopedia/bartolomeo-concini_%28Dizionario-Biogra-
fico%29/.

[37]   VINCENZIO BORGHINI, *Lettera intorno a' manoscritti antichi*, a cura di
G. BELLONI, Rome, 1995 (Testi e documenti di Letteratura e di Lingue, 17).
On Borghini, see G. FOLENA, "Borghini, Vincenzio Maria" in *DBI*, 12 (1971),
at: https://www.treccani.it/enciclopedia/vincenzio-maria-borghini_%28Dizio-
nario-Biografico%29/.

tion, suppression, modification, and censorship.[38] The interventions did not go unnoticed, to which certain letters published by Roberto Ridolfi are vivid testimony in respect of the aforesaid Lodovico's reaction.[39]

Three years later, in 1564 (the dedication to Cosimo I de' Medici is dated 20 July), Gabriele Giolito published the last four books in Venice. The editor was again Agnolo Guicciardini.[40] A few months later, Seth Viotti of Parma likewise published the last four books.[41] The dedicatory letter, addressed in this case to Ottavio Farnese, duke of Parma and Piacenza, is dated 1 November 1564. The first printing of the twenty-book version of the *Storia d'Italia* was published by Giolito in Venice in 1567.[42] Because this edition, too, is mutilated of certain passages, deemed inappropriate, it cannot be regarded as complete. The full text was printed for the first time only in 1774. This so-called Fribourg edition was in fact printed in Florence. The editor was the canon Bonso Pio Bonsi.[43] The publisher relied on the same manuscript as was behind the Torrentino edition, the said

---

[38]   P. GUICCIARDINI, *La censura nella storia Guicciardiniana. Loci duo e Paralipomena. Quinto contributo alla bibliografia di Francesco Guicciardini*, Florence, 1954 (Collana guicciardiniana, 27).

[39]   RIDOLFI, "Sulle prime stampe".

[40]   *Dell'historia d'Italia di m. Franc.ᶜᵒ Guicciardini gentil'huomo fiorentino gli ultimi quattro libri non piu stampati*, Venice: appresso Gabriele Giolito De Ferrari, 1564. For a digital copy, see https://www.bdl.servizirl.it/vufind/Record/BDL-OGGETTO-2360.

[41]   *I quattro vltimi libri dell'historie d'Italia di m. Francesco Guicciardini gentil'huomo fiorentino. Nuovamente con somma diligenza ristampati, et ricorretti; con l'aggiunta de' sommarij a ciascadun libro, et di molte annotationi in margine delle cose più notabili; di m. Papirio Picedi. Con vna nuoua tauola copiosissima del medesimo, per maggiore commodità de' lettori*, Parma: appresso Seth Viotti, 1564.

[42]   *La Historia d'Italia di m. Francesco Guicciardini gentil'huomo fiorentino, doue si descrivono tutte le cose dal MCCCCLXXXXIIII per fino al MDXXXII. Riscontrate dal R. P. M. Remigio Fiorentino [...]. Con la vita del autore descritta dal medesimo*, Venice: appresso Gabriele Giolito De Ferrari, 1567; for a digital copy see <https://www.bdl.servizirl.it/vufind/Record/BDL-OGGETTO-2743>. On the edition and on the Dominican Remigio Nannini, see BRAMANTI, "Gli 'ornamenti esteriori'", pp. 71–84.

[43]   Francesco GUICCIARDINI, *Della storia d'Italia libri XX*, Freiburg: appresso Michele Kluch, 1774–1776 [*recte* Florence: Cambiagi], cf. P. GUICCIARDINI, *La storia guicciardiniana, edizioni e ristampe*, Florence, 1948

Med. Pal. 166. He restored the numerous passages that had been suppressed in the *princeps*, marking them with a manicula in the outer margin. At the foot of the pages, he recorded variant readings, for the most part arbitrarily, introduced by the previous editors.[44]

Those responsible for the text of the first sixteen books as published in the *princeps* had included no historians. This aspect did not go unnoticed by Giolito who inserted a "Tavola degli istorici co' quali s'è riscontrata la presente istoria" (or "Table of the historians to whom this history was compared") before Guicciardini's short prefatory statement in the first book. In the *tavola* are found such names as Leonardo Aretino, Giovio, Marcantonio Savellico, Pietro Bembo, Machiavelli and others.[45] The vicissitudes of the press did not prevent Guicciardini's *Storia d'Italia* from enjoying an extraordinary success, also highlighted by the numbers of editions and reprints: thirty up to 1645. The work has also been summarized,[46] annotated,[47] and, since its first appearance, translated into several languages.[48]

(Collana guicciardiniana, 21), p. 21. For a digital copy, see https://archive. org/details/bub_gb_S1wohqb2CRUC.

[44]   P. GUICCIARDINI, *La censura*, p. 13.

[45]   Available online: https://www.bdl.servizirl.it/bdl/bookreader/index. html?path=fe&cdOggetto=2743#page/74/mode/2up.

[46]   Cf. Manilio PLANTEDIO, *Compendio della storia di m. Francesco Guicciardini nuovamente ristampato. Al serenissimo principe d. Lorenzo di Toscana*, Florence: nella stamperia nuova di Amadore Massi e Lorenzo Landi, [1640].

[47]   *La historia d'Italia di m. Francesco Guicciardini gentil'huomo fiorentino. Nuovamente con somma diligenza ristampata, & da molti errori ricorretta. Con l'aggiunta de' sommarii à libro per libro: & con le annotazioni in margine delle cose più notabili, fatte dal reverendo padre Remigio fiorentino*, Venice: appresso Giovanni Maria I Bonelli, 1562; *La historia d'Italia di m. Francesco Guicciardini gentilhuomo fiorentino. Con le postille in margine delle cose notabili che si contengono in questo libro. Con la tavola per ordine d'alfabeto et con la vita dell'autore. Di nuovo riveduta & corretta per Francesco Sansovino*, Venice: appresso Francesco Sansovino, 1562.

[48]   In Latin (Basel: [excudebat Peter Perna et impensis Heinrich aus Basel Petri], 1567), in French (Paris: Bernard Turrisan, 1568), in German (Basel: [bey Samuel Apiarius inn verlegung Heinrich Petri und Peter Perna], 1574), in English (London: [Thoma Vautrollier], 1579) and in Dutch (Dordrecht: [Isaac Jansz Canin], 1599).

The Abbreviation and Rewriting of the *Storia d'Italia* by Fiammetta Frescobaldi

The first folio of Conv. Soppr. B II 564 bears the title *Delle storie di m. Francesco Guiciardini gentile huomo fiorentino libro primo*, written in the same hand as the main text. The opening sentence that then follows is not, however, found in the printed editions. It reads: "Correva gli anni del Signore 1490 quando la Italia per molti anni felicemente s'era riposata".[49] Guicciardini's first-person narrator has disappeared, as hinted by the opening words "Correva gli anni". One may be tempted to think that by the omission of "io", Fiammetta wished to ensure that readers would not consider her work an autobiographical piece. This was hardly the case, however. Since the time of Herodotus, the assertion of authorship, expressed either in the first or third person, frequently appeared at the beginning of historical works. Such a proemial practice could emphasize the eyewitness testimony of the author, which was considered more reliable than second-hand reports or written sources. Fiammetta may, then, have wished to avoid creating the impression that hers was first-hand testimony. It is also a possibility that the suppression of 'io' may been an operation inherent in the process of translation and transposition. In that case she would have decided to discard the first-person voice at the beginning only to offer her readers a brief introduction before entering *in medias res*.

Fiammetta also eliminated the first twenty-eight lines of text of the 1561 edition, as will be discussed in more detail below. Rather than simply deleting Guicciardini's opening, Fiammetta, as said, readjusted the narrative perspective; she disposed of his "io" and opted for a more impersonal voice. The need not only to abbreviate but also to intervene was due to Guicciardini's complex diction, which has been characterized as tentacular.[50] His prose is tangled, a sort of ball of yarn with which a cat has played undisturbed for a long time. His legal training was certainly a factor that made his expression more

---

[49] "It was in the year of the Lord 1490, when Italy had been happily at rest for many years."

[50] *La Storia d'Italia di Guicciardini e la sua fortuna*, ed. by C. BERRA, A. M. CABRINI, Milan, 2012, p. xi.

convoluted.[51] Fiammetta's rendition demonstrates exceptional ability to grasp the essential in the characters and events
in Guicciardini's accounts. Her omissions were directed, for
instance, at: orations; official letters and other such documents;
excessive details as to battles and small skirmishes; references to minor characters not central to the context of the event
narrated; unwieldy historical disquisitions; and topographical
descriptions. Considering the final item in our list, it is of interest that Fiammetta should have loved geography. According to
her obituary, when she talked to her conventual sisters about
distant places, her accounts were so vivid that they almost
felt she were speaking from first-hand experience. She did not,
however, regard detailed geographical descriptions as necessary
to an historical work, which in this case was one of monumental length. As a result, she eliminated them. Illustrative of her
approach is, once again, how she began her rendition. Guicciardini immediately enters the heart of the narrative by pointing
out to readers who the culprits of calamities in Italy from 1494
onwards were:

> [L]e cose accadute alla memoria nostra in Italia, dappoi che l'armi
> de' franzesi, chiamate da' nostri principi medesimi, cominciorono
> con grandissimo movimento a perturbarla.[52]

Fiammetta profoundly changed the setting. Having eliminated
the first twenty-eight lines found in the *princeps* of Torrentino, she
reminded her audience of how Italy had been before the arrival
of Charles VIII. This preamble was not entirely her own invention but takes its cue from the second paragraph of Guicciardini's
opening section, departing from it in form and style:

---

[51] For scholarship on Guicciardini, jurist and consultant, see O. CAVAL-
LAR, *Guicciardini giurista. I ricordi degli onorari*, Milan, 1988; ID., "Francesco
Guicciardini and the 'Pisan Crisis': Logic and Discourses", *Journal of Modern
History*, 65 (1993), pp. 245–85; ID., "Il tiranno, i 'dubia' del giudice, e i 'con-
silia' dei giuristi", *Archivio Storico Italiano*, 155 (1997), pp. 265–345; J. KIR-
SHNER, "Custom, Customary Law & Ius comune in Francesco Guicciardini",
in *Bologna nell'età di Carlo V e Guicciardini*, ed. by E. PASQUINI and P. PRODI,
Bologna, 2002, pp. 151–79.

[52] *Storia d'Italia*, I,1. "[A]bout those things that have occurred in Italy
within our memory, since the time that French troops, summoned by our own
princes, began to stir up great dissensions here."

Francesco Guicciardini	Fiammetta Frescobaldi
Perché, <u>ridotta tutta in somma pace & tranquillità</u>, <u>cultivata</u> non meno ne' luoghi piú montuosi & piú sterili, che nelle pianure, & regioni sue piú fertili: né sottoposta ad altro Imperio, che de' suoi medesimi, non solo era abbondantissima <u>d'habitatori, & di ricchezze</u>; ma illustrata sommamente dalla magnificentia di molti Príncipi, dallo splendore di molte nobilissime, & bellissime città, dalla sedia, & maestà della religione, <u>fioriva d'uomini prestantissimi nella amministrazione delle cose publiche</u>, & di ingegni molto nobili in tutte le scientie, & in qualunque arte preclara, & industriosa; né priva secondo l'uso di quella età di gloria militare & ornatissima di tante doti, meritamente appresso a tutte le nazioni nome, e fama chiarissima riteneva.	Correva gli anni del Signore 1490 quando la Italia per molti anni felicemente s'era riposata; abondava di richeze e d'huomini, di maniera che tutta era cultivata e abitata, e potentati che in quel tempo la governavano e reggevano erono insieme confederati e in pace. Ciaschuno godeva il suo stato sicure da le armi forestiere e questo si poteva lungamente mantenere non si dando molestia l'uno all'altro a ciò il molestato per difendersi non avessi cagione di chiamare in suo aiuto alcun principe esterno il che sarebbe la totale destrutione di tutti.[53]

According to Guicciardini, the primary cause of Italy's ruin was "l'armi de' franzesi", but according to Fiammetta "le armi forestiere". This adjustment was more than appropriate. Starting from 1494, Italy became a land of conquest not only for the French, but also for the Spaniards, the Swiss and the Landsknechts. Fiammetta also reversed the perspective that in Guicciardini's ingress is raw and immediate. In her view, the tragedy, the calamities to be recounted, could have been avoided if Italian states and the "potentates" who

---

[53] "It was in the year of the Lord 1490, when Italy had been happily at rest for many years: it abounded in riches and men so that all land was cultivated and inhabited and the potentates who governed and ruled it at that time were confederated and in peace with one another. Each one of them enjoyed his state safe from foreign weapons and could maintain it for a long time without harassing others, and to defend oneself, one who was harassed had no reason to call in any other prince for help, which would be the total destruction of all."

ruled them had continued to "be confederated and in peace" rather than starting to harass each other and invoking foreign help.

What remains of Guicciardini's history after Fiammetta's radical editorial intervention? First of all, she, naturally, retained the central narrative, reporting battles and wars, treaties, leagues and invariably intricate political manoeuvres and, above all, main protagonists. Fiammetta eliminated extraneous details and interludes and intervened at the level of syntax and punctuation. Thanks to her interventions the portraits of some of the protagonists are more vivid than in Guicciardini's original. As is well known, the latter did not spare his darts against the Church and clergy. Irrespective of her regular vows, Fiammetta did not censor this anti-clerical aspect to the work. Indeed, by improving the text she made some descriptions even more effective and incisive. What is more, she took Guicciardini's narration, already annalistic, towards a more rigid historical-temporal arrangement. To this end, she brought together different passages (sometimes from different books) in which Guicciardini narrated the same event or discussed the same character.

Fiammetta could depart from Guicciardini's text if she so wished. An illustrative case is what she writes about Savonarola. She dedicated a section to the preacher, without taking into account what the historian had written. Despite being a nun, and Dominican for that matter, what she offers is an impersonal portrait of Savonarola, neither one of a follower nor detractor.[54] The subject is weighty but, perhaps also because time had passed, the nun felt able to insert witty and sarcastic comments in her narration. Regarding the Florentines, for instance, she wrote, "riducendo colle sue predicationi et esortationi in gran parte il popol fiorentino al vivere cristiano, che ne avevon non poco bisognio".[55] She could also be critical of the pope:

---

[54] It may be remembered that during the years of its suppression by the Church, Savonarola's cult was maintained at San Jacopo, for which see S. T. STROCCHIA, "Savonarolan Witnesses: The Nuns of San Jacopo and the Piagnone Movement in Sixteenth-Century Florence", *Sixteenth Century Journal*, 38 (2007), pp. 393–418.

[55] Conv. Soppr. B II 564, fol. 16r: "By his preaching and exhortations, he brought back a large part of the Florentine people to Christian living — something of which they were in great need".

Non s'era mosso il papa né·lla prima, né·lla seconda volta perché fussi solito atendere a simil cose, ma per gratificare quegli ne lo richiedevono per essere il suo studio solo in pigliar piaceri e far grandi e figluoli.[56]

Finally, writing about the last days of Savonarola, she raised doubts concerning the authenticity of the testimonies during the trial:

E così fu incarcerato et vi stette insino a 24 di maggio co' compagni faccendolo disaminare a ciò si potessi formare il processo, il quale per essere di parole tronche non s'è per quello veduto chiaro se era innocente overo colpevole. Non mancò chi afirmassi che quello lo scrisse in qualche parte lo falsassi.[57]

To write on Savonarola, Fiammetta collected diverse information, also from oral sources. She read the proceedings of the trial but, she emphasized, these are of *parole tronche*, not immediately comprehensible. Because of such lack of clarity, she preferred not to pronounce whether the Ferrarese preacher was guilty or innocent. However, she did not wish to keep silent on the trial, or rather the trials.[58] The extract above shows that she was aware of deliberate flaws and biases in the evidence. In the absence of positive proof, she did not identify the party responsible for distorting the evidence, although this was known to all Florentines.

The Release and Intended Audience(s) of Conv. Soppr. B II 564

To appreciate the implications of Fiammetta's approach to Giucciardini's text, we must briefly consider the status of Conv. Soppr. B II 564 as a book. Fiammetta's manuscripts generally have a title page, a dedication, a colophon, and also a signature statement, a

---

[56] *Ibid.*, fol. 16ᵛ: "The pope had not moved either the first or the second time because he was used to doing things like that, but [rather] in order to gratify those who requested it, as his attitude was only to indulge in pleasures and make his sons great".

[57] *Ibid.*, fol. 16ᵛ: "And so he was imprisoned and remained so until 24 May together with his companions. He was examined so that the trial could be held, and since the trial proceedings consisted of truncated words, it was not clear whether he was innocent or guilty. There were those who claimed that the person who wrote it falsified part of it."

[58] *I processi di Girolamo Savonarola*, ed. by I. G. RAO, P. VITI, R. M. ZACCARIA, Florence, 2001.

commonplace in printed books of the age but rarely seen in manuscripts.[59] They are written in an elegant *cancelleresca*, or chancery cursive hand, and imitate printed books in format and style. In Conv. Soppr. B II 564 there appear the aforementioned colophon at the end of the *Storia d'Italia* and the signature statement at the conclusion of the volume.[60] The manuscript does not bear a title page or dedicatory letter, but it is evident from the collation that no folios have been excised. The abbreviation of Guicciardini's *Storia* was probably Fiammetta's first work, and it was only later in her career that she brought the design of her manuscripts closer to that of a printed book also in respect of title pages and dedicatory letters. The change, no doubt, had to do with Fiammetta's evolving authorial identity. In engaging with the *Storia d'Italia*, as we have seen here, she acted as an editor and abbreviator, occasionally assuming a more liberal approach. Her subsequent works are, in contrast, her own compositions or translations. Accordingly, the addition of a title page and dedicatory letter may be read as indications of her assertion of an authorial status. The title page of *Le vite di dieci Beati*, as laid out in the manuscript, may be cited here by way of illustration.[61]

> Le vite di dieci Beati
>
> Ritratte da' Libri delle vite de' Santi dal R. P. F. Lorenzo Surio
>
> Cartusiano: scritte latine d'autori provati et gravi
>
> Fatte vulgari per comodità delli studiosi
>
> Da suor Fiammetta Frescobaldi monaca del ordine
>
> di san Domenico, nel monasterio
>
> di Sa⟨n⟩ Iacopo di Ripoli l'anno del Signore
>
> M.D.LXXXV[62]

[59]   See, for example, WEAVER, CATTANEO, MURANO, *Fiammetta Frescobaldi*.

[60]   The abbreviation of the *Storia d'Italia* is followed by *Il modo solito usarsi nella coronatione de' Re di Francia molto devoto e bello* (fol. 164ʳ). It ends at fol. 175ᵛ: "Il fine delle obsequie de' Re di Francia cavate dalle Storie del Guazzo; scritte qui a consolatione di quelle persone che è impossibile che le posino vedere alla presentia e di quelle che non hanno copia di libri. Scritte l'anno del nostro signore 1564 del mese di febraio."

[61]   Marchesi Frescobaldi, MS XII, title page.

[62]   "*Lives of Ten Saints*. Retracted from *Books of Lives of Saints* of R. P. F. Lorenzo Surio, a Carthusian, Latin writings by reliable and serious authors, translated into the vernacular for the benefit of scholars by Sister Fiammetta

Dedications are one of the most interesting aspects of Frescobaldi's works. *Le cose prodigiose e calamitose del mondo* was written in 1584, two decades after the abbreviation of the *Storia d'Italia*.[63] A letter addressed to Sister Francesca da Filicaia follows a dedication to the nuns of San Jacopo. The opening deserves to be quoted here since, while writing to Francesca, Fiammetta refers to herself:

> Et cosa chiara e manifesta, sorella in Cristo amanti⟨ssi⟩[ma], che l'huomo rationale, e capace di ragione, si diletti di s⟨a⟩pere, però sia intento a ricercare da i libri e le cose passate et con esse misurare le presenti, e venire in qualche coniectura delle cose che debono seguire. Parlo di quelle che non dependon dalla assoluta volontà di Dio, ma delle conditionate, essendomi io sempre dilettata, come sapete, di legere e di investigare le cose de' passati tempi, dagli storici scritte e notate [...].[64]

The choice of the editorial layout that Fiammetta adopts here resonates with, and undoubtedly derives from, printed books. It is interesting to note how printed books feature in a short biography dedicated to her in the obituary of San Jacopo, quoted below.

> [...] era una suora molto spirituale si dilectava assai delle sacre lectione e era visitata volentieri dalle suore per i sua buon costumi e ragionamenti spirituali, perché era stata dotata da Idio di grande ingegno e acutissima memoria e sapeva parlare di tutte le cose e intendeva benissimo che pareva che fussi stata in tutti luoghi lontani e paese e era maraviglia e stupore delle persone che erano stati in quei luoghi che la sapessi raguagliare tutte le cose come stavano. E ancora essendo inferma e non si potendo exercitare nelli uffiti come l'altre, non à manchato di fare quanto à potuto a utilità del monastero perché à prochaciato di molti libri spirituali da sua parenti e ad altre persone e in particulare 12 libri

---

Frescobaldi, nun of the Order of Saint Dominic in the monastery of San Jacopo di Ripoli in the year of the Lord 1585."

[63] Marchesi Frescobaldi, MS VIII.

[64] WEAVER, CATTANEO, MURANO, *Fiammetta Frescobaldi*, pp. 173–74. "It is a clear and manifest thing, beloved Sister in Christ, that the man who is rational and capable of reasoning, delights in knowing, so that he searches in books for things from the past, and with these he measures those present and comes to assumptions about things that must ensue. I am speaking of those things that do not depend on the absolute will of God, but of things that are conditional, having always taken delight, as you know, in reading and investigating the things of the past, written down and observed by historians".

di Lorenzo Surio che sono i 12 mesi dell'anno e di molti altri per
non mi estendere no gli nomino e di poi à messo in volgare col suo
acutissimo et elegante ingegno, senza avere mai hauto precettore,
cento diciotto vite di santi groriosi. E dipoi di molte altre cose à
messo in iscritto a utilità delle suore [...].[65]

What is written in the obituary is confirmed by Fiammetta's prologues and dedication letters. In *Cose prodigiose e calamitose*, for
instance, she emphasized that her works and translations were
intended for conventual sisters, who

> son tanto ochupate che non resta loro tempo da cercare di tali
> cose in tanti libri i quali, per essere latini, non così da tutte con
> facilità sono intesi, però li ò adunati da varii autori per amor loro
> et fattogli vulgari se non come dovevo almeno come ò saputo, per
> mostrare in qualche parte lo obrigo che io tengo con loro.[66]

Fiammetta had a library that was well stocked with new publications, as mentioned above. Rather than follow an interest in nov-
els or poems, she consumed books about geographical discoveries

---

[65]   Florence, Archivio di Stato, Montalve, San Jacopo di Ripoli, 23: *Libro
di croniche segnato A.* (1508–1778), fols 137ᵛ–138ʳ. "She was a very spiritual
nun, she delighted much in the sacred readings and she was eagerly visited
by the nuns for her good manners and spiritual conversations because she
was endowed by God with great intellect and extraordinarily acute memory and could talk about all things and was so insightful that she seemed to
have been in all distant places and countries, and it was to the wonderment
and amazement for those who had been in those places that she knew how to
recount all things as they were. And despite being sick and unable to perform
her duties as the others, she did not fail to do what she could for the benefit
of the convent as she procured many spiritual books from her relatives and
other people and in particular twelve books by Lorenzo Surio, which are the
twelve months of the year, and many others, which I do not name in order not
to go on too long, and without having ever had a teacher, she then rendered
one hundred and eighteen lives of glorious saints into the vernacular with her
most acute and elegant wit. And afterwards she put many other things in
writing for the benefit of her sisters."
[66]   Cf. WEAVER, "Suor Fiammetta Frescobaldi, storica", p. 185: "They
are so busy that they do not have time to look for such things in such a
great number of books, which, being in Latin, are not so easily understood
by everyone. However, I have gathered these from various authors for their
sake and I have translated these into the vernacular, even if not as I should
but at least as I could, in order to show, in some part, the obedience I keep
with them."

and the New World. She preferred Lorenzo Surio's *Vitae* of saints to *cantari* and other liturgical poems as well as works of personal devotion. She was in possession of works, such as Vasari's, that allowed her to discover the beauty of art while she was confined in regular seclusion.

Deficient command of Latin, to which the afore-quoted prologue alludes, had already made vernacular translations a necessity for generations. Fiammetta's contributions in that area should accordingly be seen in the broader context of the monastic and mendicant translations of Holy Scripture, lives of saints, and devotional texts into the vernacular. But just as Latin texts had to be translated for the benefit of various religious and secular audiences, the idiom used by the literati in Renaissance Italy, the Tuscan dialect being the preferred form, was often far more intricate than that spoken commonly. Guicciardini's turn of phrase is characterized by a rich lexicon and complex syntax and is not easy to understand. Albeit written by a contemporary fellow Florentine, his prose is so different from everyday speech that editorial intervention was required for the benefit of Fiammetta's audiences. While Conv. Soppr. B II 564 does not have a dedicatory letter, a device found in her later works, its above-quoted colophon states her objectives in brief. She stressed that the *Storia* was abridged "per più sadi[s]fatione de' lettori". The choice of the word "sadisfatione" was deliberate. Guicciardini's work was not a novel, but a record of real experiences of the Italian people, expressed in a linguistic idiom that was convoluted, intricate and, most importantly, not the same as used by women and most of the men of the age. Fiammetta's audience was not made up of illiterate women, *donnicciuole*, but, as we have seen, it consisted of daughters and widows belonging to the most important Florentine families. Those who read, or listened to, her writings were her conventual sisters and their relations. Even if some could not read Latin, such upper-class audiences were familiar with books. To realize the objective stated in the colophon, Fiammetta had to do something more than just to offer a resumé; she had also to intervene at lexical and syntactical levels. In the process, words and phrases were replaced with less eloquent, less technical and less dense expressions and complex rhetorical periods were turned into shorter sentences. As a result, Guicciardini's burdensome historio-

graphical narrative was rendered into a thoroughly modern vernacular Italian.

In Renaissance Italy, the language used by social elites in
semi-formal contexts, such as those of cultured conversation, was
the so-called *lingua comune*.[67] This was the most suitable language
for a book to be read at the *mensa* of a nunnery. Yet, Fiammetta
did not imitate the Tuscan language and avoided Tuscanisms, in
contrast to several of her contemporaries.[68] Her mother tongue was
Florentine, which she used in a pleasant, often acute and always
very elegant style. She issued her works as high-quality manuscript volumes, which imitated the conventions of printed books.
As such, the physical aspect of her works gave an impression of
having been printed. Like many literati, both lay and religious,
Fiammetta would probably have wished to see her works published in print, but her condition as a woman and nun prevented
her from realizing such ambitions. So, she targeted her works at
the narrow circle of nuns in the Florentine convent of San Jacopo
di Ripoli. That mission was admirably accomplished according to
the above-quoted obituary, asserting that her works were read at
the mensa "con molto contento universale".

---

[67]   On the use of the *lingua comune* in Renaissance Italy, see B. RICHARD-
SON, "The Italian of Renaissance Élites in Italy and Europe", in *Multilin-
gualism in Italy Past and Present*, ed. by A. L. LEPSCHY, A. TOSI, Oxford,
2002, pp. 5–23, at 8–12; B. RICHARDSON, "The concept of a *Lingua comune*
in Renaissance Italy", in *Languages of Italy, Histories and Dictionaries*, ed. by
A. L. LEPSCHY, A. TOSI, Ravenna, 2007, pp. 11–28.

[68]   Cf. the prefatory letter in the Italian Bible translated probably by
Filippo Rustici of Lucca: "Imperochè havendo lasciati da parte tutti i mal
composti et importuni Toscanismi, ci siamo contentati senza obligarci a le
strette e superstitiose regole de la volgar lingua, di seguitare un parlare e
stile comune, e vario ancora tanto ne le voci quanto ne l'ortografia, da molti
e diversi però hoggi usitato et accettato, e ciò per satisfare a i varii gusti [...].
Imperochè non facciam poco conto, anzi riputiamo di grande importanza,
che nel tradur la Santa Scrittura si debba usare ogni semplicità e facilità di
parole e frase per darla bene ad intendere a le persone semplici, si come noi
ci siamo forzati di fare, senza far grand distintione tra l'alto o basso stile
e mediocre, e lasciando l'affetationi e toscanismi a quelli che si mettono a
ridurre i libri profani ne la volgar lingua Boccaccesca". *La Bibia che si chiama
Il vecchio Testamento, nuovamente tradutto in lingua volgare secondo la verità del
testo Hebreo*, [Geneva]: François Duron, 1562 (<https://www.e-rara.ch/gep_g/
ch16/content/zoom/10663023>). On this letter, see also RICHARDSON, "The
concept of a Lingua comune", p. 15.

Theories, Categories, Configurations

A Historian's Point of View on the Study
of Publishing in Manuscript

Jaakko Tahkokallio
(*Helsinki*)

Beginning an acquaintance with the still relatively meagre scholarship on manuscript publishing, one quickly becomes conscious of the ontological and epistemological insecurities faced by scholars in this field.[1] Was there such a thing as manuscript publishing? Is it possible to speak of such a thing? If so, what might that concept mean? It might, at first, be tempting to dismiss these recurring reflections as a kind of ritual dance that one is required to perform, to placate the spirits of *Positivismuskritik*, before commencing the actual enquiry — such things are not unheard of in the humanities. But on entering the fray oneself and beginning to write on the subject, one starts to feel a certain amount of respect towards this tradition of sceptical interrogation. While the concept of publishing is undoubtedly pre-modern and precedes the printing press, as is argued, for example, by Daniel Hobbins, one must admit that manuscript publishing is not as neat and self-evident a concept as print publishing is, or, at least, is commonly assumed to be.[2]

The roots of this difference, as I see it, lie in the fact that publishing in print brings together two moves that are both integral to our concept of publishing, even when we are discussing

[1] For a review of the scholarship, see J. Tahkokallio, *The Anglo-Norman Historical Canon. Publishing and Manuscript Culture*, Cambridge, 2019, pp. 3–9.

[2] D. Hobbins, *Authorship and Publicity before Print. Jean Gerson and the Transformation of Late Medieval Learning*, Philadelphia, PA, 2009, p. 153.

The Art of Publication from the Ninth to the Sixteenth Centuries, ed. by Samu Niskanen with the assistance of Valentina Rovere, IPM, 93 (Turnhout, 2023), pp. 371–382.
© BREPOLS ❧ PUBLISHERS   DOI 10.1484/M.IPM-EB.5.133090

manuscripts. Firstly, printing changes the status of the textual content, releasing it from its author's control. Secondly, printing makes this content available practically as physical objects, i.e. printed books. In the context of manuscripts propagated by hand, no single move creates similar results on these two fronts with comparable efficiency. Both the making public of textual content and the creating and disseminating of copies of it happened in the manuscript context as well, but always begging the question of where, precisely, the act of publishing begins and ends. This ambiguity is felt on both sides of the equation, both in regard to the aspect of the release of textual content (in what sense had the author released the text and for what kind of circulation?) and the physical aspect, i.e. making the text available in practice (at what point does publishing turn into dissemination?).

In this essay, I will not try to advance any final definition of manuscript publishing. I will instead begin by arguing that too rigorous attempts at defining the subject and clearing away the conceptual ambiguities are more likely to hinder than to benefit historical scholarship on this topic. I will then move on to the question of what kind of research is most likely to advance our understanding of this phenomenon which, all the ambiguities aside, nevertheless *is* a real historical phenomenon. How should we write the history of manuscript publishing?

I shall proceed in two steps. In the first part of this essay, I will relate the study of manuscript publishing to Louis Mink's ideas about different modes of scientific or scholarly comprehension. I seek to demonstrate that Mink's ideas, while not very widely known, are helpful in showing the way to the sort of terrain where the study of manuscript publishing — or indeed any historical phenomenon — is likely to succeed and bear fruit. In the second, and briefer, part of this paper, I will seek further guidance from the wider scholarly tradition of the history of the book and move from these theoretical ideas to more concrete, if always very hypothetical, suggestions on what kind of research could be fruitful in advancing the field.

*

Louis Mink (1921–1983) was an American philosopher, who contributed greatly to historical theory or, if preferred, the philosophy of history.[3] When Mink is referred to nowadays, it is most often in relation to the development of narrativism, a school of historical theory most famously and notoriously represented by Hayden White.[4] Indeed, Mink's ideas were of fundamental importance for the development of this tradition.[5] Their interest, however, extends beyond their significance for the development of historical theory. Historians' (as opposed to philosophers') engagement with the substance of Mink's ideas has been far from exhaustive and, in my view at least, his writings continue to offer fresh starting points also for practical considerations of historical approach and methodology.

One of Mink's brilliant analyses, and the one relevant here, concerns the nature of historical understanding. In two seminal essays, published in 1960 and 1970, Mink presented three different categories or modes of understanding, each of which he saw as typical (although not exclusive) to a specific scholarly field or tradition.[6] These categories were "theoretical", "categoreal" and "configurational", and they all need to be briefly outlined for the relationship of this separation of modes to historical methodology to make sense.

Mink's "theoretical" comprehension is the *modus operandi* of the natural sciences. Science seeks theories which consistently explain phenomena observed in the natural world. Its goal is to find the

---

[3] For Mink's life and career, see "Editors' introduction", in L. O. MINK, *Historical Understanding*, ed. by B. FAY, E. O. GOLOB, R. T. VANN, Ithaca, NY, 1987, pp. 1–34.

[4] For the mixed reception of Hayden White's ideas, see R. T. VANN, "The Reception of Hayden White", *History and theory* 37.2 (1998), pp. 143–61.

[5] On Mink's role in the development of narrativism, see J.-M. KUUK-KANEN, *Postnarrativist Philosophy of Historiography*, New York, NY, 2015, pp. 17–21.

[6] L. O. MINK, "Modes of comprehension and the unity of knowledge", in MINK, *Historical Understanding*, pp. 35–41 (first published in *Proceedings of the XIIth International Congress of Philosophy* V, Firenze, 1960, pp. 411–17) and L. O. MINK, "History and fiction as modes of comprehension", in MINK, *Historical Understanding*, pp. 42–60 (first published in *New Literary History*, 1 (1970), pp. 541–58). As regards debates on the nature of history, Mink executed here a clever reorientation. He departed from the prevailing fashion of thinking about the nature of history as a *Wissenschaft* in the light of the theory of knowledge, an approach which had, by Mink's time, proved rather barren. For the context, see KUUKKANEN, *Postnarrativist Philosophy*, pp. 14–21.

basic principles or governing laws according to which the universe functions. Theoretical comprehension studies one narrow aspect of reality at a time and explains it thoroughly and with great predictive power. For instance, a theoretical comprehension is achieved when we realize that the rusting of a nail and the burning of wood are, in the light of chemical theory, one and the same phenomenon, i.e. oxygenation. As a utopia of theoretical comprehension, Mink presents the ordered universe of Pierre-Simon La Place (1749–1827), in which — with the perfect knowledge of all the laws of nature and the positions and velocities of all its particles — the future of everything can be neatly calculated.[7]

Whereas theoretical understanding is concerned with the relationship of particulars to universals, "categoreal" understanding is interested in the relationships between various universals. This is the philosopher's domain. As Mink says, "Plato called divine the knowledge which would consist in the contemplative vision of a set of essences apprehended as a single intelligible system".[8] Such a division is not forged out of empirical facts like a theory, but it is, rather, imposed on reality on a linguistic level. Indeed, all that I have been writing about here, namely Louis Mink's division of understanding into theoretical, configurational and categoreal modes of comprehension, is a textbook example of categoreal understanding at work.[9]

Finally, we come to configurational comprehension. The quickest route to grasping its essence is to think of it as the opposite of theoretical comprehension. Theoretical comprehension looks at a thin slice of reality at a time. Pressure behaves according to Boyle's law, and whether the pressure is inside a volcano or a steam engine is of no consequence — it is simply pressure. Configurational comprehension, in contrast, seeks to understand complex phenomena in their particular context. In real life, where it is active all the time, configurational comprehension would seek to grasp the concrete situation of the particular volcano inside of which pressure is building, with due attention given, for example, to such human, social, economic, biological, and geophysical

---

[7] MINK, "History and fiction as modes of comprehension", p. 51.

[8] MINK, "Modes of comprehension and the unity of knowledge", p. 38.

[9] See MINK, "History and fiction as modes of comprehension", p. 54.

aspects of reality as would be related to the volcano. In the academic world, historical scholarship in its classic historicist guise, is the paradigmatic case of configurational comprehension. We look at a complex event or development — say, the Reformation or the French Revolution — and we want to *understand* how this process or event evolved and took place.

While configurational understanding is the traditional goal of historical scholarship, history is of course open to other sorts of attempts at comprehension as well. If we look into how the history of manuscript publishing has been studied we can see traces of all these three modes or approaches. Firstly, the theoretical. The search for governing laws or, more loosely, theoretical models, has not been the exclusive domain of the natural sciences. This idea has been seminal to the social sciences, and it has been applied to history as well.

In the historiography of manuscript publishing, one can distinguish a certain vein of scholarship seeking such models, i.e. mechanisms by which such publishing happened. Robert K. Root's article, "Publishing before print" (1913), named three such mechanisms, namely publication by presentation to a patron, publication sanctioned by religious authority, and commercial publication through presenting a text to urban, professional scribes.[10] Other scholars have elaborated on these mechanisms, and also proposed new ones, such as "organic publishing", a form of publishing by non-publishing.[11] Admittedly, these models have never been presented or intended as governing laws or even social-science theories of manuscript publishing, but they do nevertheless present attempts at coming to terms with manuscript publishing on the basis of theoretical models.

[10]   R. K. Root, "Publication before printing", *Publications of the Modern Language Association*, 28 (1913), pp. 417–31.

[11]   K. J. Holzknecht, "Literary patronage in the middle ages", unpublished PhD diss., University of Pennsylvania, 1923; H. S. Bennett, "The production and dissemination of vernacular manuscripts in the fifteenth century", *The Library*, 5th ser. 1 (1946), pp. 167–78; A. I. Doyle, "Publication by members of the religious orders", in *Book Production and Publishing in Britain 1375–1475*, ed. by J. Griffiths, D. Pearsall, Cambridge, 1989, pp. 109–23; A. N. J. Dunning, "Alexander Neckam's manuscripts and the Augustinian canons of Oxford and Cirencester", unpublished PhD diss., University of Toronto, 2016.

How fruitful have these, broadly speaking, theoretical attempts been? And how valuable is further work, seeking to test the validity of these models and to elaborate them further, likely to be? These suggested models have certainly been beneficial in outlining the landscape of manuscript publishing. At the same time, it is difficult to see how these different models could be very useful in guiding further research. Seeking to move on from them, one quickly runs into the typical problem of all historical theories, on which much was written by philosophers of history and scholars seeking such theories in the first half of the twentieth century. First there is a model or a theory, even a proposed historical law (say, that populist movements emerge in democracies at times of economic stress), followed by a series of corrections, caveats and emendations (but only if certain ideological developments are also taking place, and only if the state fails in particular ways, and not if certain things happen in international politics, and so on), which effectively turn what initially looked like a bold theoretical proposition into a mere common-sense observation on the likelihood of things. This is not to say that looking for models of manuscript publishing could not be a useful pursuit, but that it should probably take a clearly different route, embracing wholeheartedly the methods and aspirations of the social sciences and seeking a way forward by wide inter-cultural comparison. When we are seeking to advance our understanding of particular *historical* phenomena — and for better or worse, this is what historians do, and are expected to do, at least most of the time — we typically benefit most from approaches characteristic of theoretical modes of comprehension when they are left on the sidelines rather than brought to the centre of the analysis.

I would suggest that the same is true of categoreal comprehension. The theoretical attempts to define manuscript publishing try to pin down this elusive and protean phenomenon in reality. Categoreal attempts try to do the same in the realm of semantics. They are, in other words, epistemological attempts. In the historiography of manuscript publishing, something of a categoreal attempt is presented by Paul Meyvaert, in his seminal article on *Opus Caroli contra synodum*.[12] Meyvaert proposes that, for

---

[12] P. MEYVAERT, "Medieval notions of publication: the 'unpublished' *Opus Caroli regis contra synodum* and the Council of Frankfort (794)", *The Journal*

medieval authors, publishing was identical with the author's act of giving an exemplar of his or her work to another person or persons with the explicit permission to produce more copies of it. This is a neat and well-founded definition, and there is nothing wrong with it logically.

However, while the theoretical attempts send us down a route where we can easily get lost, thanks to the mismatch between the map and the terrain, this categorical attempt leads us almost straight into an impasse. For however logical it might be, there is very little historical research left to do after we subscribe to this definition, apart, perhaps, from identifying the moments at which an author handed over an exemplar with the permission to make copies of it. Whatever took place before and after that moment is not publishing and is the matter of some other research agenda. This is the philosopher cutting the Gordian knot of manuscript publishing.

As will have become clear, I think the most fruitful approach to the topic is not theoretical or categorical but configurational. In other words, we should study those concrete processes by which works were published in a manuscript context, with publishing by necessity remaining to some extent an open concept. We should probably simply be happy with the term "publishing" as a somewhat metaphorical concept; we have brought it in from a context in which it means the joint *releasing* and *disseminating* of content, and I think that both these elements should be part of the consideration of manuscript publishing as well. One might add that working with metaphorical concepts is far from exceptional in historical scholarship — rather, it is what is done all the time and is in fact integral to how historical understanding comes to be. Consider, for instance, terms such as the Renaissance, the Enlightenment, the Industrial Revolution or the Cold War.[13]

There is nothing new or very original in this suggestion. What I consider the most interesting studies of medieval publishing all do

of Medieval Latin, 12 (2002), pp. 78–89; see also HOBBINS, *Authorship and Publicity before Print*, pp. 153–54.

[13]   On the significance of metaphors in giving shape to historical knowledge, see F. R. ANKERSMIT, *Historical Representation. Cultural Memory in the Present*, Stanford, CA, 2002, pp. 13–20 and F. R. ANKERSMIT, *Meaning, Truth, and Reference in Historical Representation*, Ithaca, NY, 2012, pp. 73–76.

take this line. They are interested in some historical phenomenon of text release and distribution, although they each set their limits differently: Richard Sharpe's work on St Anselm, staying fairly close to the moment of release; Daniel Hobbins' moving back and forth between release and early distribution; Leah Tether's, focusing entirely on the distributive aspect.[14] These studies, in other words, are not theoretical enquiries into governing laws or categorical chases after semantic distinctions. What they all seek is, at least primarily, configurational understanding.

*

If we are happy with the idea of exploring the ways in which works were published in a manuscript context in this somewhat metaphorical light and, especially, with a flexible and porous border between publishing and dissemination, can anything else be said about where to go? Are all historical configurations of publishing equally interesting, or are there some alleys that look more promising than others? I suggest that the latter is true, and that it is the principle of configurational comprehension, i.e. seeing things in a wider context, that may serve as our guiding light.

To illustrate this, let us turn to something more concrete. As I see it, the opening for the study of medieval publishing has been created by importing the concept of publishing from the world of print and book history. Consequently, it is of interest to examine what has been achieved in this field. What kind of research into the history of the (printed) book has been most fruitful? The answers are subjective, of course, depending on how one defines the word "fruitful". But I think that one very meaningful way to think about the subject is to ask what kind of history of the book has had the biggest impact on our overall understanding of history — i.e. what has mattered *outside* the specialist field of the history of the book or historical bibliography?

I do not pretend to know the best answer to this question, but I would like to propose two undoubtedly *good* answers. These derive from debates on the Reformation and the cultural background of

---

[14]   R. SHARPE, "Anselm as author: publishing in the late eleventh century", *The Journal of Medieval Latin*, 19 (2009), pp. 1–87; HOBBINS, *Authorship and Publicity before Print*; L. TETHER, *Publishing the Grail in Medieval and Renaissance France*, Woodbridge, 2017.

the French Revolution. The overall contours of these debates are familiar outside the specialist domain of early-modern history, but I shall recap them very briefly. In the case of the Reformation, we may say that the debate started from a very big and somewhat mechanistic thesis, that the printing press made reformation happen or, more accurately, was its prerequisite.[15] Subsequent work on the history of the book and reformation has both challenged and elaborated this big thesis, but, most importantly, it has provided numerous new insights into how religious change, political change, books, reading and publishing interacted in early-modern Europe.[16] Whatever we think of the merits of particular arguments, it is by now inconceivable that any historian could consider the Reformation without some awareness of the role that the printing press, books, and publishing played in how it unfolded. Study of the history of the book — and of publishing — has here left a deep mark on the whole academic discipline of history and, to a degree, even in conceptions of history shared more widely in society.

The debate on the intellectual and social background of the French Revolution offers a similar case, connected more closely to specific scholars, of whom Roger Chartier and Robert Darnton are the best known. Indeed, the whole issue has even been called the Darnton debate.[17] In brief, this debate was started by Dar-

---

[15] See especially E. L. EISENSTEIN, *The Printing Press as an Agent of Change: Communications and Cultural Transformations in Early Modern Europe*, 2 vols, Cambridge, 1979; and, for elaboration of some of its topics, E. L. EISENSTEIN, *Divine Art, Infernal Machine. The Reception of Printing in the West from First Impressions to the Sense of an Ending*, Philadelphia, PA, 2011.

[16] For overviews of the topic, see the articles in *La Réforme et le livre. L'Europe de l'imprimerie (1517–v. 1570)*, ed. by J.-F. GILMONT, Paris, 1990, and M. U. EDWARDS, *Printing, Propaganda, and Martin Luther*, Berkeley, CA, 1994. Of more recent scholarship, see in particular L. RACAUT, *Hatred in Print: Catholic Propaganda and Protestant Identity During the French Wars of Religion*, Aldershot, 2002; A. PETTEGREE, *Reformation and the Culture of Persuasion*, Cambridge, 2005; E. MICHELSON, *The Pulpit and the Press in Reformation Italy*, Cambridge, MA, 2013. See also D. L. D'AVRAY, "Printing, mass communication, and religious reformation. The middle ages and after", in *The Uses of Script and Print*, ed. by J. C. CRICK, A. WALSHAM, Cambridge, 2004, pp. 50–70.

[17] For the debate, see the contributions in *The Darnton Debate. Books and Revolution in the Eighteenth Century*, ed. by H. T. MASON, Oxford, 1998. The

nton's work on the unique archival records of a Swiss publisher who produced forbidden, underground literature for the eighteenth-century French market. Darnton consequently argued that this literary underworld of the Enlightenment had a great significance in creating the ideological and social climate in which the French Revolution took place. Darnton's arguments have of course been challenged, defended and modified, but the important consequence is that this debate has greatly enhanced our understanding of the Enlightenment and the French Revolution — certainly two of the most thoroughly researched topics of modern historical scholarship.

Both the Reformation and Revolution debates are ones in which the history of ideas (or intellectual history) meets the material world of social and political history — i.e. those areas of history which in the larger picture of why history matters (to everyone, not only historians) occupy perhaps a more central place. My suggestion, in brief, is that it is in similar configurations of the immaterial and the material that the study of medieval manuscript publishing could best come into its own and make its importance felt. Something akin is certainly being done, and has already been done, with regard to medieval book history, for instance in the case of late-medieval heresies and the spread of texts, albeit this is not typically framed or thought about as "publishing".[18] Other topics of wider importance that could be examined through the concept of publishing might be, for instance, the Carolingian

central original works are R. DARNTON, *The Literary Underground of the Old Regime*, Cambridge, MA, 1982; R. DARNTON, *The Forbidden Best-Sellers of Pre-Revolutionary France*, New York, NY, 1995; R. CHARTIER, *Lectures et lecteurs dans la France d'Ancien Régime*, Paris, 1987, and R. CHARTIER, *Les Origines culturelles de la Révolution française*, Paris, 1990. See also the contributions in *Into Print. Limits and Legacies of the Enlightenment. Essays in Honor of Robert Darnton*, ed. by G. C. WALTON, University Park, PA, 2011, and those (including by Chartier and Darnton) in *The French Revolution. The Essential Readings*, ed. by R. SCHECHTER, Malden, MA, 2001.

[18] See, for example, the contributions in *Heresy and Literacy, 1000–1530*, ed. by P. BILLER, A. HUDSON, Cambridge, 1994; those in *Religious Controversy in Europe 1378–1536: Textual Transmission and Networks of Readership*, ed. by P. SOUKUP, M. VAN DUSSEN, Turnhout, 2013, and M. VAN DUSSEN, *From England to Bohemia: Heresy and Communication in the Later Middle Ages*, Cambridge, 2012.

reform, the Investiture context, the spread of Crusading ideals in the twelfth century, the reintroduction and development of rationalistic inquiry in theological scholarship, and the building of the Europe-wide catholic orthodoxy from the twelfth century onwards — a process which closely depended, I would suggest, on a pan-European book ecosystem which concurrently emerged around the schools and universities (the university of Paris most importantly of all).

Examples might be multiplied, but I think the point is clear. Wherever ideas, transmitted by texts, succeed in penetrating a social reality, there is publishing, and there is usually also change, friction and drama — in brief, history worth writing. To embrace these interesting configurations means steering away from conceptual and theoretical dogmatism and advocating a willingness to accept a certain ambiguity in how we define publishing in a manuscript context. We should remember that this ambiguity is not an intellectually unsatisfactory philosophical or logical ambiguity which leaves one adrift without a compass. Rather, it is just the kind of ambiguity which historical research is well suited to elucidate. The principle around which history as an academic pursuit took shape in the nineteenth century was the idea of historicism; that is, that to get to know what a thing is, we need to study its past — we need to write its history. Only by doing so can we give a *Gestalt* to a part of the past that is still at the periphery of our vision, not yet clearly defined, not yet clearly perceptible. That is what is now being done with manuscript publishing.

Abstracts

Jesse KESKIAHO, Publications and Confidential Exchanges: Carolingian Treatises on the Soul

This chapter examines what the publishing of theological texts meant in the Carolingian period, focusing on treatises on the nature and origin of the soul. Not everyone was supposed to publicly disseminate their theological writings, and successful publishing required connections to those in authority. The texts examined were written for different audiences and for different purposes, educational and controversial. Several of these treatises are connected to discussions in the 850s about the soul. Their analysis demonstrates how thinking about whether or in what sense they were published deepens our understanding of the nature of those discussions.

Lauri LEINONEN, Contextualizing the Publication of Dudo of Saint-Quentin's *Historia Normannorum*

This chapter discusses the publication of Dudo of Saint-Quentin's *Historia Normannorum*. The focus is the author's relationship with his commissioners, who were Dukes Richard I and Richard II of Normandy and Count Rolf of Ivry, and his dedicatee, Bishop Adalbero of Laon. Archbishop Robert of Rouen also played a significant role in the publication, as is evident from the numerous poems by which he is addressed at key junctures in the work. It is proposed that Dudo's choice of dedicatee reflected his objective of reaching his wider target audience, namely the classrooms of Normandy and France, and that this aspect is also evident in the work's contents. Building on the evidence of the manuscripts, the paper proposes that explanatory rubrics accompanying the verses in *Historia Normannorum* were directed towards that same end of gaining school readerships. The extant manuscripts, which include neither authorial nor primary copies, suggest that Dudo's publication plan proved successful only in part. The work was circulated in Norman monasteries and cathedrals and thus contributed to the establishment, shaping, and preservation of memories of the duchy's past, one of Dudo's other main objectives. Yet, the absence of pertinent evidence implies that the intended penetration into schools in France was not accomplished, at least for a significant while. The identification of *Historia Normannorum*'s publication context helps us more accurately to appreciate Dudo's authorial intention and voice.

Tuomas HEIKKILÄ, Publishing a Saint: The Textual Tradition of the Life and Miracles of St Symeon of Trier

Vita et miracula s. Symeonis Treverensis (*BHL* 7963–7964) is a hagiographic composite text written by various authors and released in several versions. Symeon died in the summer of 1035. The first version *vita* and *miracula* were composed within months, in order to be sent to the pope, who quickly canonized him. The author was Eberwinus, abbot of no fewer than three monasteries, who had known Symeon in person. For as long as Eberwinus lived, probably until *c.* 1040, he was undoubtedly in charge of polishing the text of the *vita* and adding new contents to the *miracula*. His successor as author, identified by a single manuscript, was Warnerus, schoolmaster of the collegiate church of St Symeon. Several additions to the *miracula* were made, the last one by an anonymous writer probably at St Symeon's in 1086. A very complex manuscript transmission ensued, characterized by several releases. This chapter maps relationships between all fifty-eight hitherto known extant witnesses. In addition to traditional textual criticism, the examination is based on computational analysis, with various algorithms applied. The result is a well-grounded hypothetical stemma, a point of reference for our historical enquiry into the publication and reception of St Symeon's *vita* and *miracula*. The textual history provides insights into how a saintly cult might be built in the high Middle Ages.

James WILLOUGHBY, The Chronicle of Ralph of Coggeshall: Publication and Censorship in Angevin England

The chronicle that was written by Ralph, abbot of the Cistercian abbey of Coggeshall in England, is one of the few contemporary chronicle sources for the reigns of Kings Richard (1189–1199)

and John (1199–1216), and is the unique source for some famous events in English history. There are several early manuscripts, including one, Cotton Vespasian D. x in the British Library, that contains numerous corrections, additions, and interfoliations of an authorial nature. This chapter identifies a group of interconnected manuscripts as having been made at Coggeshall and argues that they show Ralph to have been a keen compiler and publisher. He is himself identified here as the principal hand of the Cottonian manuscript of his chronicle, a hand that shows considerable deterioration over time. The question of Ralph's responsibility for the text is important since a large expurgation of annals relating to the central, painful years of John's reign would suggest something in the way of self-censorship, apparently carried out towards the end of Ralph's life. Evidence is presented for this lost material, which has historiographical significance. Various historical texts are communicated by the manuscripts produced during Ralph's abbacy or are otherwise attested as lost copies. These texts were received at Coggeshall, edited, and then transmitted as part of a dossier of historical material. It is owing entirely to the monks of Coggeshall — directed, it would seem, by Abbot Ralph — that they owe their survival.

Jakub Kujawiński, Nicholas Trevet OP (c. 1258–after 1334) as Publishing Friar. Part I. Commentaries on the Authors of Classical and Christian Antiquity

This chapter investigates the ways in which Nicholas Trevet's commentaries on Boethius's *Consolation of Philosophy*, Seneca the Elder's *Controversiae*, Seneca the Younger's *Tragedies*, Augustine's *City of God*, and Livy were published. Analysing authorial paratexts and the philological, codicological, and book-historical evidence of early manuscripts, extant and lost, it assesses pertinent actions by the author and his publishing circle, a group of associates who contributed to the release and primary circulation of his works. The dedicatory letter of Trevet's commentary on Boethius betrays two fair copies, made by him or under his oversight. Dedications of three of the said commentaries and the execution of certain illustrations in his expositions of the *Consolation* and the *Tragedies* likewise reflect his efforts to publish. The Dominican Order furnished Trevet with a setting to circulate his works, and his confreres are often mentioned as a target audience. The evidence of the primary circulation and reception suggests that the order actively assisted in publication. Trevet's teaching positions at Oxford also provided opportunities to obtain readerships. The clearest insight through our sources is, however, into publishing on the Continent, with the contribution of individuals within and without the order. Particularly important figures were Cardinal Niccolò da Prato OP and Pope John XXII. Besides commissioning two of the works studied, they supervised and financed the copying of Trevet's commentaries, perhaps combining them with the texts commented on, recommended them to potential readers, and made copies available.

Luca AZZETTA, Errors in Archetypes and Publication: Observations on the Tradition of Dante's Works

Several of Dante's works got into circulation only after his death, often derived from an original not prepared for publication and thus introducing errors and lacunae. This applies to *De vulgari eloquentia*, *Convivio*, and *Epistola a Cangrande*. This chapter first introduces the case of the two former works, both uncompleted treatises, and then focuses on *Epistola a Cangrande*. The analysis of the direct tradition, the reconstruction of the archetype, and insights provided by the indirect tradition up to the sixteenth century suggest that Dante wrote the *Epistola* towards the end of his sojourn at Verona, but that he never sent it to the addressee. Descending from an original not intended for publication, the archetype was a severely corrupt text, something that undermines the opinion that the letter was a forgery made in north-eastern Italy, as has been proposed in the past. In contrast, study of the manuscripts demonstrates that dissemination began at Florence after Dante's death, where the poet's sons brought their father's other writings, the *Epistola* among them.

Marco PETOLETTI, The Art of Publishing One's Own Work: Petrarch's *De vita solitaria*

Petrarch began writing his *De vita solitaria* for Bishop Philippe de Cabassole in Vaucluse in 1346. The process of composition took time: the work was sent to the dedicatee only in 1366. While that

she intervened at lexical and syntactical levels, rendering Guicciardini's highly complex rhetorical account in shorter sentences and a more accessible linguistic idiom. Her primary audience consisted of her conventual sisters, many of whom belonged to the most important Florentine families. She issued her works for their benefit as high-quality manuscript volumes, which imitated the conventions of printed books. As such, her works, released in a domestic setting, emulated publication in the wider world.

Jaakko Tahkokallio, Theories, Categories, Configurations: A Historian's Point of View on the Study of Publishing in Manuscript

Louis Mink (1921–1983) was an American philosopher who contributed greatly to historical theory. In two seminal essays, published in 1960 and 1970, Mink presented three different modes of understanding — theoretical, categoreal, and configurational — each of which he saw as typical of, although not exclusive to, a specific scholarly field or tradition. According to Mink, the theoretical mode is the classical approach of the natural sciences, with physics as a paradigmatic example; the categoreal mode is the home domain of philosophy; and history operates principally in the configurational mode. This methodological essay uses Mink's categories to analyze previous research into the history of manuscript publishing, arguing that all three have been applied to the topic. While all three approaches have contributed to our understanding of the phenomenon, it is argued that theoretical and categoreal approaches yield too specific results and cannot therefore open up very promising avenues for further research. The most fruitful access to the subject in that respect must be the configurational mode. Finally, drawing on parallels from the historiography of the printed book, this essay makes the case for not looking at the history of manuscript publishing in isolation from other historical phenomena. To cast new and interesting light on the past, such research needs to consider publishing in relation to social, political, and ideological developments, a suggestion which circles back to Mink's view of historical research as ultimately configurational scholarship.

Contributors

Luca Azzetta teaches Dantean philology at the University of Florence. He studies in particular the tradition of Dante's works, early commentaries on the *Commedia*, and fourteenth-century vernacular translations from the Florentine region. His most recent publications are a critical edition of Andrea Lancia's *Chiose alla Commedia* (Edizione Nazionale dei Commenti Danteschi, 2012); an annotated edition of Dante's *Epistle XIII* to Cangrande della Scala (Rome, 2016); *An Ancient and Honourable Citizen of Florence. The Bargello and Dante*, together with Sonia Chiodo and Teresa De Robertis (Florence, 2021); and *Il caso di Menghino Mezzani tra Dante e la Romagna*, together with Marco Petoletti (Ravenna, 2022).

Tuomas Heikkilä is Professor of Church History at the University of Helsinki. He has published extensively on medieval literary culture and manuscripts, stemmatology and the cult of saints. He has been the director of the Finnish Institute in Rome and is a member of the Academia Europaea.

Jesse Keskiaho is currently an Academy of Finland Research Fellow at the University of Helsinki, where he earned his doctorate in General History in 2013. He has held visiting scholarships at the Universities of Cambridge and Kent, the Institutum Romanum Finlandiae, the Institut für Mittelalterforschung at the Austrian Academy of Sciences in Vienna, and the Huygens Institute in Amsterdam. He currently researches early medieval ideas about the soul and has also worked on late antique and early medieval annotations in the manuscripts of some of the major works of Augustine of Hippo, and on early medieval ideas about dreams and visions.

Jakub Kujawiński, Assistant Professor of Medieval History at the Adam Mickiewicz University in Poznań and Visiting Researcher at the University of Helsinki, has published widely on medieval historiography, with a specific interest in the long-term reception of chronicles, glossed manuscripts, and the historical memory of Southern Italy. As a member of the project *Medieval Publishing from c. 1000 to 1500*, he studied authorial publication among mendicant friars, focusing on the output of the English Dominican Nicholas Trevet.

Lauri LEINONEN is a doctoral student in the project *Medieval Publishing from c.1000 to 1500* at the University of Helsinki. His dissertation enquires into how historical works were published in the Anglo-Norman realm in the eleventh century, with a special focus on pertinent social networks. He has worked extensively on the *Database of Medieval Publishing Networks* (*DMPN*), accessible at dmpn.helsinki.fi. Prior to his doctoral studies, he catalogued incunabula in the National Library of Finland and worked on the *Diplomatarium Fennicum* database of the National Archives of Finland.

Outi MERISALO, Professor of Romance Philology at the University of Jyväskylä, Secretary General of the Comité international de paléographie latine (CIPL, 2015–2025), has published extensively on Old French documents, Old and Middle French translations from Latin, Italian Renaissance texts and book history, Scandinavian book history from the sixteenth to the eighteenth century as well as medical manuscripts of the late Middle Ages.

Giovanna MURANO, a member of numerous projects and collaborations in Italy and abroad, is an expert in palaeography and codicology. Her main research foci are the history of medieval universities, their books, and autograph manuscripts of learned Italian writers. She has authored a number of studies in these domains, including the monograph *Opere diffuse per exemplar e pecia* (Turnhout, 2005). She is the General Editor of the series *Autographa*. Together with Elissa Weaver and Angelo Cattaneo, she has recently rediscovered Fiammetta Frescobaldi's works on astronomy, geography and history that survive in autograph manuscripts, one of which she studies in the present volume.

Samu NISKANEN is Professor of Medieval History at the University of Helsinki. His research is mainly concerned with intellectual life in the Middle Ages and medieval literature, its publication, transmission, and reception. His recent publications include *Letters of Anselm, Archbishop of Canterbury: The Bec Correspondence* (Oxford, 2019) and *Publication and the Papacy in Late Antiquity and the Middle Ages* (Cambridge, 2021). He has overseen the projects *Medieval Publishing from c.1000 to 1500* (European Research Council, 2017–2022) and *Authorial Publishing in Early Medieval Europe* (Academy of Finland, 2019–2023).

Marco PETOLETTI is full professor of Medieval Latin Literature at Università Cattolica in Milan. He is an editor of *Italia medioevale e umanistica* and a member of the Academic Board of the *Corpus Christianorum* and of the Scientific Committee of the *Edizione Nazionale delle opere di Francesco Petrarca*. He is chief librarian of the Archivio Capitolare di S. Ambrogio in Milan. He has studied the transmission of the Latin classics in the Middle Ages, Latin literature in the fourteenth century (authors such as Dante, Petrarch and Boccaccio), letter collections of the twelfth to the fourteenth centuries, medieval Latin epigraphy, and Carolingian literature. He has published extensively on these topics.

Jaakko TAHKOKALLIO is a Senior Researcher at the National Library of Finland, where he is currently running two research projects, *Books of the Medieval Parish Church* (European Research Council, 2021–2025) and *Tradition and Variation. Medieval Chant in the Diocese of Turku* (Academy of Finland, 2022–2026). His primary research interests concern Latin palaeography, the history of the book, and intellectual history, especially in Western and Northern Europe in the later Middle Ages.

Valentina ROVERE, a post-doctoral researcher on the project *Medieval Publishing from c.1000 to 1500* at the University of Helsinki, obtained her PhD in 2018 at the Università degli Studi di Roma Tre. She has studied Giovanni Boccaccio's Latin works, their publication, primary circulation, and reception. She is preparing a critical edition of Bocaccio's *De montibus* under the auspices of the *Ente Nazionale Giovanni Boccaccio*.

James WILLOUGHBY is a Research Fellow in Medieval History at New College, University of Oxford, who publishes on the making of books, libraries, and the transmission of texts in the Middle Ages. He is director of the project *Medieval Libraries of Great Britain* (MLGB3) and an editor for the British Academy series, Corpus of British Medieval Library Catalogues. He is co-Editor of *The Library: Transactions of the Bibliographical Society.*

INDICES

Manuscripts Cited

Manuscripts cited by shelf-marks and *sigla* in the main text and footnotes are included, while those referred to in *stemmata* and tables or under collective *sigla* for manuscript groups are excluded. The list is alphabetically arranged by holding institution, named according to the native language of each.

ADMONT, Stiftsbibliothek
24 (lost): 125

ANGERS, Bibliothèque municipale
276 (270): 31n

ANTWERPEN, Museum Plantin-Moretus/Prentenkabinet
17.2: 51n, 59n, 64n, 68, 72 and n, 73n

ASSISI, Biblioteca e Centro di documentazione francescana del Sacro Convento
Fondo Antico, ms. Assisi Com. 302: 209n, 224, 229n

AVIGNON, Bibliothèques (Ville d'Avignon)
1085: 185n, 186n, 188n, 189n, 195

BELLUNO, Biblioteca del Seminario
35: 290

BERGAMO, Biblioteca Civica Angelo Mai
MA 304: 284

BERLIN, Staatsbibliothek zu Berlin – Preussischer Kulturbesitz
Diez. C fol. 4: 209n, 211n, 220, 221, 229n
Hamilton 90: 316
Hamilton 101: 190n
Hamilton 203: 290

Lat. Fol. 437: 271
Lat. Fol. 570: 253n, 258n
Magdeb. 26 (lost): 125
Phill. 1854: 48n, 59n, 64n, 67 and n, 73n, 75n
Theol. Lat. Fol. 169: 99n, 108n, 123
Theol. Lat. Fol. 707: 108n, 115n, 117n, 124
Theol. Lat. Qu. 249: 175n

BERN, Burgerbibliothek
24: 99n, 104n, 115n, 120n, 123
390: 47n, 51 and n, 66n
584: 32n

BOLOGNA, Biblioteca Universitaria
732: 190n
1632: 232n

BONN, Universitäts- und Landesbibliothek
S 369: 104n, 115n, 123

BRUSSEL, Bibliothèque des Bollandistes
209: 115n, 120 and n, 124, 125n
445: 20, 101 and n, 104n, 105n, 124

BRUSSEL, Bibliothèque Royale de Belgique
207–08: 104n, 123
858–61: 108n, 115n, 123

DOUAI, Bibliothèque Marceline Desbordes-Valmore
880: 77

DUBLIN, Trinity College Library
508: 145n, 162, 163n
634: 145n

DURHAM, University Library
Cosin V.II.11: 190n

DÜSSELDORF, Universitäts- und
Landesbibliothek
C10b: 104n, 115n, 124

EINSIEDELN, Stiftsbibliothek
Codex 247 (379): 95n, 99n, 104n,
105n, 115n, 123
Codex 323 (1065): 99n, 124

ÉPINAL, Bibliothèque multimédia intercommunale Épinal
147: 90, 92n, 99n, 101, 104n, 108,
120n, 123

ERPERNBURG, Schlossbibliothek
7 (lost): 125

FIRENZE, Archivio di Stato
Carte Strozziane V, 52 and 53:
343n
Montalve, San Jacopo di Ripoli,
23: 367n

FIRENZE, Biblioteca Medicea Lauren-
ziana
Plut. 29.8: 270n
Plut. 34.49: 321–23, 328n
Plut. 40.2: 290
Plut. 40.16: 290
Plut. 40.19: 273n
Plut. 42.1: 316, 317
Plut. 43.15: 340n
Plut. 46.2: 334n
Plut. 52.9: 318n
Plut. 53.35: 299
Plut. 65.40: 337, 338

Plut. 76.56: 195n
Plut. 77.3: 206n
Plut. 82.20: 221, 231n
Plut. 22 dex. 9: 186n, 187 and n,
189n, 201, 208n
Plut. 23 dex. 11: 196n, 199n
Plut. 90 inf. 13: 328
Plut. 25 sin. 1: 186n, 188n, 189n,
201, 207
Plut. 25 sin. 6: 209n, 221, 222, 229n
Plut. 26 sin. 6 : 330
Plut. 26 sin. 7: 330
Plut. 33 sin. 7: 186n, 188n, 189n,
201
Plut. 89 sup. 87: 206n
Plut. 90 sup. 63: 329
Plut. 90 sup. 98[1]: 318n
Ash. 58: 108n, 124
Ash. 828: 290
Ash. 965: 335n
Conv. soppr. 509: 175n, 209n, 224,
230, 231
Edil. 163: 196n
Gadd. 75: 326n
Med. Pal. 166: 355, 359
Red. 155: 323n
Strozz. 160: 273n

FIRENZE, Biblioteca Nazionale Centrale
I.I.51: 316
II.III.86: 341, 342n, PLATE 7
B. R., 50: 329
Conv. Soppr. B II 564: 348, 349n,
355, 360, 363–65 and n, 368
Conv. Soppr. B.VII.1277: 248n
Conv. Soppr. D.7.344: 353
Conv. Soppr. G.4.1111: 329
Conv. Soppr. H.IX.1523: 175n
Conv. Soppr. J.IV.3: 192n
Magl. IX, 123: 312n
Pal. Baldovinetti 62: 336n, 340,
341, 346, PLATE 6
Pal. Capponiano 64: 337, 339
Filze Rinuccini, 19/a in I n.5: 284
Panc. 147: 319, 327

FIRENZE, Biblioteca Riccardiana
1010: 290
1043: 276
1044: 276
1232: 318n, 321, 323, 328n
1291: 353
1523: 200n
1540: 200n
2102: 353

FIRENZE, Museo di San Marco
630: 353

GLASGOW, University Library
Hunter 374: 190n

GRASSE, Bibliothèque Patrimonial
3: 216n

GRENOBLE, Bibliothèque Civique
580: 271

HEILIGENKREUZ, Stiftsbibliothek
12: 108, 115n, 117n, 120n, 123
130: 181n

KLOSTERNEUBURG, Stiftsbibliothek
708 (lost): 125

KOBLENZ, Landeshauptarchiv
Best. 701 nr. 129: 93n, 95n, 108n,
115n, 124

KÖLN, Historisches Archiv der Stadt Köln
W164: 108n, 115n, 123

KRAKÓW, Biblioteka Jagiellońska
Berol. Ms. Ital. fol. 174: 200n

LEIDEN, Universiteitsbibliotheek
VLF 47: 67n

LEIPZIG, Universitätsbibliothek
lat. 1253: 181n

LILIENFELD, Stiftsbibliothek
60 (lost): 125

LINCOLN, Cathedral Library
1: 160n
15: 161n
23: 160n
24: 160n
25: 160n
26: 160n
27: 160n

LISBOA, Biblioteca Nacional de Portugal
IL 134: 252–54 and n, 258n
IL 135: 252, 253n, 258n, 261 and n

LONDON, British Library
Add. 18359: 115n, 123
Add. 22793: 117, 124
Cotton Claudius A. xii: 66, 69n
Cotton Cleopatra B. i: 137 and n,
138, 146 and n
Cotton Cleopatra C. x: 158n
Cotton Nero D. viii: 47n, 59n,
64n, 67 and n, 70n, 71n, 73n
Cotton Vespasian D. x: 20, 134n,
137 and n, 138n, 142, 145–50 and
n, 152, 155–58 and n, 161, 162,
164 and n, 165, PLATE 1, PLATE 2,
PLATE 3, PLATE 4a, PLATE 4b
Egerton 943: 290
Harley 545: 145n
Harley 2800: 104n, 123
Harley 4093: 246n, 247n
Harley 4980: 30n
Harley 6563: 225n
Royal 13 A. xii: 145n, 162, 163n
Royal 13 B. xiv: 51n, 59n, 64n, 66
and n, 68–70 and n, 72–74 and n
Royal 13 B. xvi: 262n
Royal 13 D. v: 140, 141n
Royal 14 C. xiii: 246n, 250n
Royal 15 C. xii: 209n, 227–30 and n
Stowe 61: 145n

LONDON, College of Arms
Arundel 11: 137n, 145 and n, 146
and n, 154 and n, 157, 158n, 163n,
164
Arundel 24: 145n

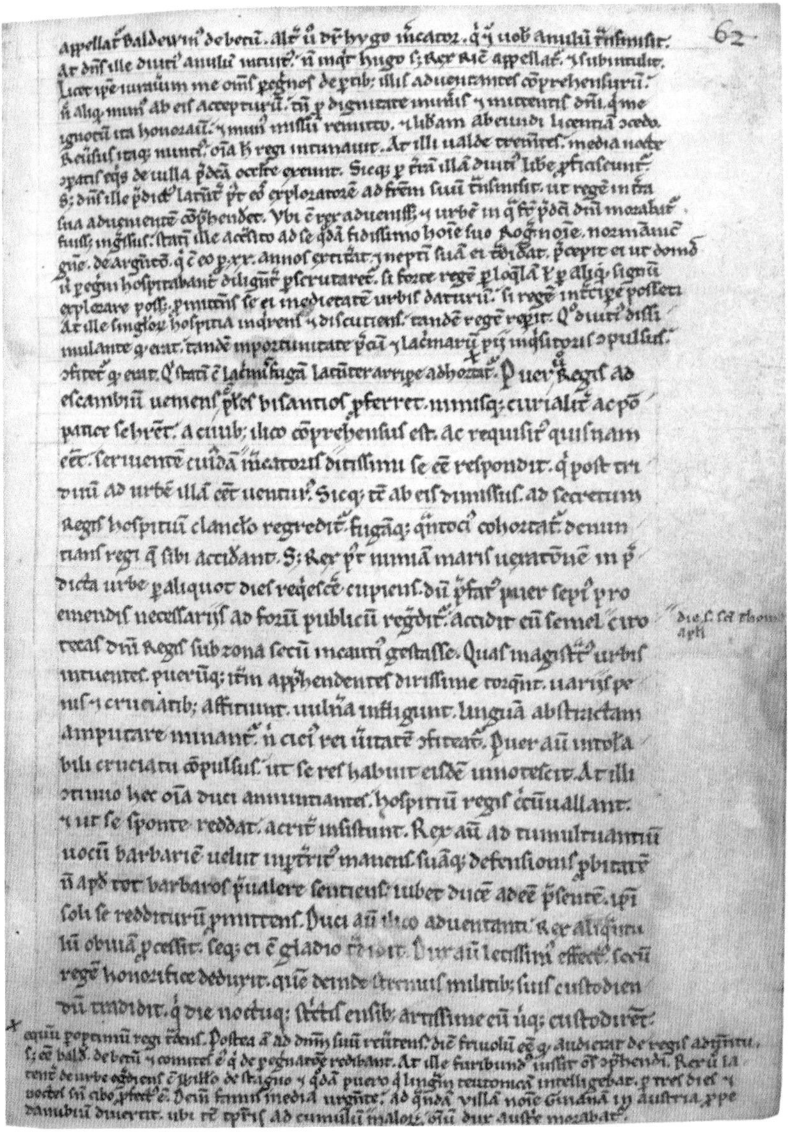

PLATE 1

Plate 1. Information from Anselm, a royal chaplain, added to the chronicle on an erasure, visible in the upper third of the page and continued in the lower margin. BL, Cotton MS Vespasian D. x, fol. 65r. (By kind permission of The British Library Board)

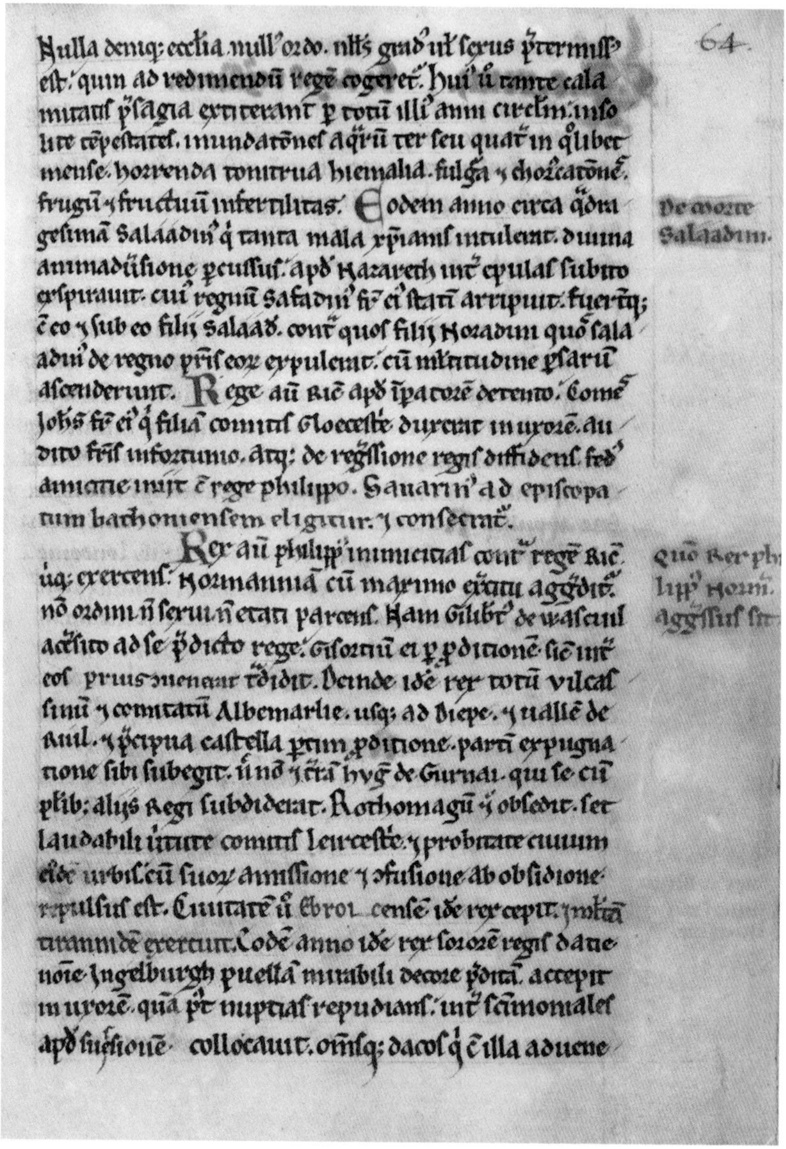

PLATE 2

64.

Plate 2. Suppressed and overwritten information, on two lines
in the centre of the image. BL, Cotton MS Vespasian D. x, fol.
67r. (By kind permission of The British Library Board)

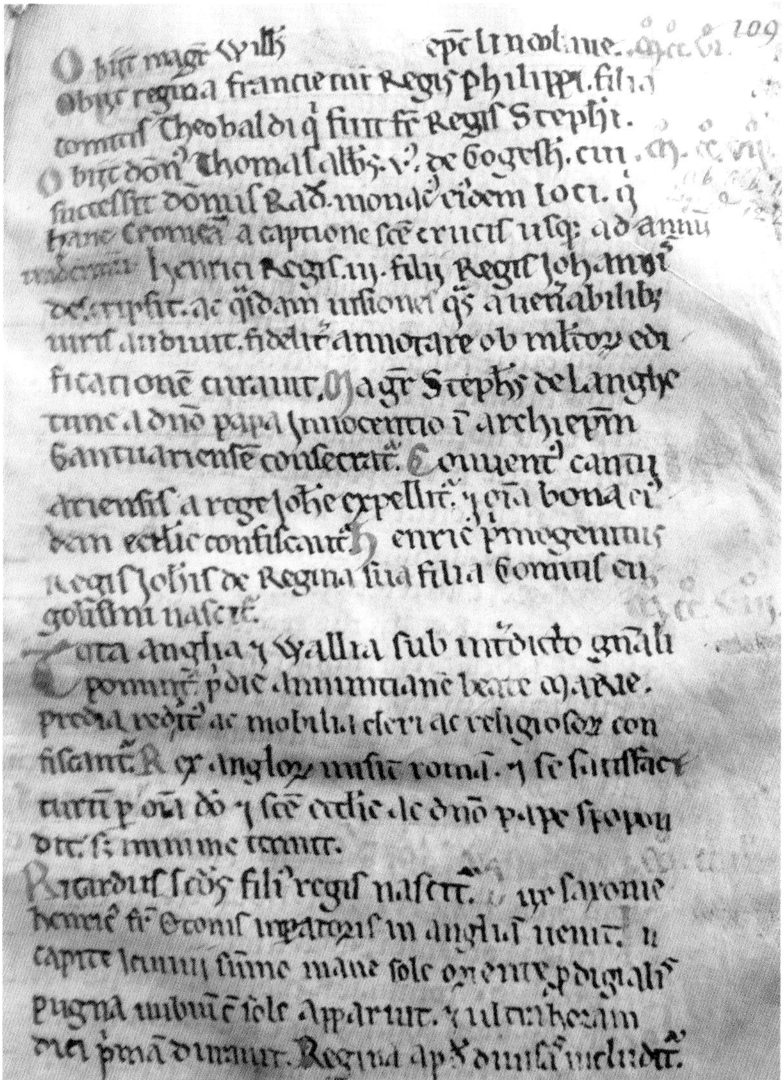

PLATE 3

Plate 3. An inserted leaf, supplying the annals for 1206 to 1212. BL, Cotton MS Vespasian D. x, fol. 112r. (By kind permission of The British Library Board)

PLATE 4

Plate 4a. The "Censor's" hand. BL, Cotton MS Vespasian
D. x, fol. 67r (detail)

Plate 4b. The "Censor's" hand. BL, Cotton MS Vespasian
D. x, fol. 112r (detail)

PLATE 5

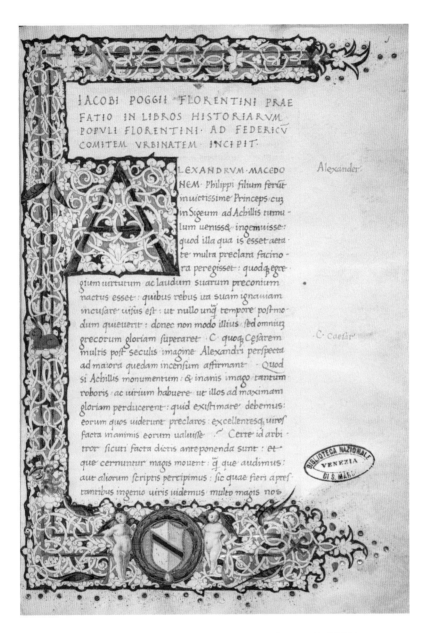

IACOBI POGGII FLORENTINI PRAE
FATIO IN LIBROS HISTORIARVM
POPVLI FLORENTINI· AD FEDERICV
COMITEM VRBINATEM· INCIPIT·

LEXANDRVM·MACEDO
NEM· Philippi filium ferũt
inuictissime Princeps·cuz
in Sigeum ad Achillis tumu-
lum ueniss& ingemuisse:
quod illa qua is esset aeta
te multa preclara facino-
ra peregisset: quodꝗ egre-
gium uirtutum ac laudum suarum preconium
nactus esset: quibus rebus ita suam ignauiam
incusare uisus est: ut nullo unꝗ tempore post mo-
dum quieuerit: donec non modo illius· sed omniuz
grecorum gloriam superaret· C· quoꝗ Ceʃarem
multis post seculis imagine· Alexandri perʃpecta
ad maiora quedam incensum affirmant· · Quod
si Achillis monumentum· & inanis imago tantum
roboris ac uirium habuere· ut illos ad maximam
gloriam perducerent: quid existimare· debemus:
eorum quos uiderunt preclaros· excellentesꝗ uiroʃ
facta inanimis eorum ualuisse· · Certe id arbi-
tror sicuti facta dictis anteponenda sunt: et
que cernuntur magis mouent: ꝗ que audimus:
aut aliorum scriptis percipimus: sic quae fieri a preʃ-
tantibus ingenio uiris uidemus multo magis nos

Alexander·

·C· Caesar·

Plate 5. BNM, Lat. Z. 392 (=1684), fol. 1r © BNM

PLATE 6

Plate 6. BNCF, Palatino Baldovinetti 62, fol. 1r,
with Capponi arms. Photo © MDI

PLATE 7

Plate 7. BNCF, II.III.86, fol. 1r. Photo D. Speranzi © BNCF

General Index

Personal and place names are included. Antique and medieval persons are indexed by forename or the name familiar in modern literature, and modern persons by surname. The turn of the fifteenth century is taken to be the rough line separating these two systems.

Eriugena, John Scottus: *see* John
    Scottus Eriugena
Essex:
    Augustinian priory of St Osyth:
    157, 158 and n, 159
Ettore Astancolli, notary: 325n
Eulalia: *see* Gundrada, Charlemagne's
    cousin
Eutropius: 68n
Exeter:
    cathedral: 150n
Eynsham:
    abbey: 139

Farnese, family: 339
    Alessandro, cardinal: 339
    Ottavio, duke of Parma and
    Piacenza: 358
Fenzi, Enrico: 272
Ferdinand I of Aragon, king of
    Aragon and Naples: 335
Ferreto de' Ferreti: 289
Ficino, Marsilio: *see* Marsilio Ficino
Filippo di ser Piero Doni, notary:
    314n
Filippo Strozzi: 343 and n, 345
Filippo Villani: 282
Flaminius, Roman consul: 261 and n
Flodoard of Reims: 33, 51n, 54n
Florence:
    San Jacopo di Ripoli: 348, 349,
    351–53, 363n, 365, 366 and n
    San Marco: 193n
    Santa Caterina da Siena: 351n
    Santa Croce: 187n, 201 and n, 222
    and n, 320n
    Santa Maria del Santo Sepolcro
    (delle Campora): 320 and n
    Santa Maria Novella: 225, 329, 348
    and n
    Santo Spirito: 312–14 and n, 317,
    318, 321, 323–29 and n
Florus of Lyon: 26 and n, 39, 44
Forese Donati: 280
Fortini, Battista: 334
Francesca da Filicaia, nun: 366
Francesca Morelli: 349

Franceschini, Ezio: 172 and n, 233n,
    237, 238n, 252n
Francesco di Amaretto Mannelli:
    316, 317
Francesco di Amedeo, Florentine *car-
    tolaio*: 341n
Francesco d'Antonio del Chierico,
    illuminator: 338, 340
Francesco de Belluno, friar: 251n
Francesco da Buti: 202n
Francesco Carbone, cardinal: 328
Francesco Casini of Siena: 296
Francesco di Lapo Bonamichi,
    notary: 315, 316
Francesco di Marano da Camerino:
    267n
Francesco di Niccolò di Berto de'
    Gentiluzzi: 340
Francesco Petrucci da Camerino: 267
    and n
Francesco Pipino, friar: 250n
Francesco Rosselli, illuminator: 338
Francescuolo da Brossano: 302 and n
Francis Stephen I, grand duke of
    Tuscany, emperor: 342n
Franzen, Christine: 150
Fraticelli, Pietro: 286
Freculph (Freculphus Lexoviensis):
    205n
Frederick I Barbarossa, emperor: 137
Frederick of Montefeltro, duke of
    Urbino: 334n, 335 and n, 337 and
    n, 338 and n, 341 and n, 345, 346
Freeman, Edward Augustus: 131 and
    n, 132, 144n, 166n
Frescobaldi, Fiammetta (Brigida di
    Lamberto Frescobaldi): 21, 347–69
Frescobaldi, Lamberto: 349
Frisio, Gemma: 354

Gaddi, family: 350
    Angelica: *see* Angelica Gaddi
    Jacopo: 342n
Galvano Fiamma, friar: 197, 198
Ganz, David: 27
Garin, Eugenio: 318
Gelli, Giovan Battista: 281